MOTOCOURSE™

THE WORLD'S LEADING GRAND PRIX & SUPERBIKE ANNUAL

icon
PUBLISHING LIMITED

CONTENTS

MOTOCOURSE 2014–2015

is published by:
Icon Publishing Limited
Regent Lodge
4 Hanley Road
Malvern
Worcestershire
WR14 4PQ
United Kingdom

Tel: +44 (0)1684 564511

Email: info@motocourse.com
Website: www.motocourse.com

Printed in Italy by
L.E.G.O. S.p.A
Viale dell'Industria, 2
I-36100 Vicenza
Email: info@legogroup.com
www.legogroup.com

ISBN: 978-1905334-98-8

DISTRIBUTORS

UNITED KINGDOM
Gardners Books
1 Whittle Drive, Eastbourne,
East Sussex BN23 6QH
Telephone: +44 (0)1323 521555
email: sales@gardners.com

Chaters Wholesale Ltd
25/26 Murrell Green Business Park,
Hook, Hampshire RG27 9GR
Telephone: +44 (0)1256 765443
Fax: +44 (0)1256 769900
email: books@chaters.co.uk

NORTH AMERICA
Motorbooks
Quayside Distribution Services
400 First Avenue North, Suite 300,
Minneapolis, MN 55401, USA
Telephone: (612) 344 8100
Fax: (612) 344 8691
email: customerservice@quartous.com
www.motorbooks.com

Dust jacket: Honda's Marc Marquez, who won 13 races in 2014 to take his second successive MotoGP World Championship.

Title page: Sylvain Guintoli won the Superbike World Championship on his Aprilia.
Photos: Gold & Goose

Acknowledgements

The Editor and staff of MOTOCOURSE wish to thank the following for their assistance in compiling the 2014–2015 edition: Nereo Balanzin, Majo Botella, Alex Briggs, Mufaddal Choonia, Peter Clifford, Rhys Edwards, William Favero, Milena Koerner, Isabelle Lariviere, Elisa Pavan, David Pato, Ignacio Sagnier, Julian Thomas, Mike Trimby, Michel Turco, Frine Vellila, Mike Webb, Ian Wheeler and Günther Wiesinger, among others too numerous to mention. A special thanks to Marlboro, Repsol and Honda hospitality staff; and to colleagues and friends for their comments and advice, always taken whence it comes.

Photographs published in MOTOCOURSE 2014–2015 have been contributed by:
Chief photographers: Gold & Goose.
Other photographs contributed by: AMA Pro Series, Gavan Caldwell, Clive Challinor, Dave Collister, Martin Heath, HRC, Milagro/Martino, Neil Spalding, Mark Walters, Yamaha Racing

publisher
STEVE SMALL
steve.small@iconpublishinglimited.com

commercial director
BRYN WILLIAMS
bryn.williams@iconpublishinglimited.com

editor
MICHAEL SCOTT

text editor
IAN PENBERTHY

results and statistics
PETER McLAREN

chief photographers
GOLD & GOOSE
David Goldman
Gareth Harford
Brian Nelson
David 'Chippy' Wood.

www.gngpix.com
tel +44 (0)20 8444 2448

bike and circuit illustrations
ADRIAN DEAN
f1artwork@blueyonder.co.uk

www.motocourse.com

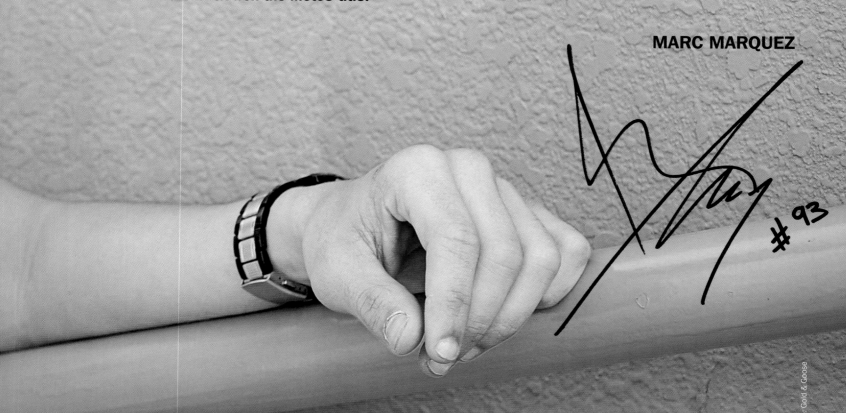

FOREWORD by MARC MARQUEZ

It may have looked different from the outside, but winning this second World Championship was not easy. I smiled and laughed a lot, but the pressure was there all year. Pressure from my rivals, and pressure from myself.

Every title is special. In 125 in 2010 it was more difficult, because I had to win it in the last race. Moto2 in 2012 had a bit of anger with it, because the year before I was out for five months injured. MotoGP in 2013 was, to be honest, a big surprise.

This 2014 championship is to thank Honda, who let me bring all my team back together this year, which made for a great atmosphere in the garage. It was all the more satisfying to win it at Honda's home circuit of Motegi.

I made some mistakes at the previous two races, maybe because of too much confidence, knowing I had a significant advantage. My early victories gave me the luxury of taking a few more risks than usual. After that, I really had to focus on the championship rather than just the race at Motegi. Then in the last three races, I could have some fun!

You always try to improve. Last year I was still learning everything about MotoGP. This year I have adapted much better to the Repsol Honda. We have developed a chassis more focused on my style and that helped me concentrate less on making the bike better and more on improving as a rider.

Racing is a team effort. I have to thank not only my pit crew, but also Honda – from the management that makes the big decisions to the engineers who design and develop every component of my beautiful RC213V.

And especially my family, who have supported my racing in every way from when I was a five-year-old with training wheels on my first bike. That support is clear from the fact that my younger brother Alex won the Moto3 title.

MARC MARQUEZ

93

Photo: Gold & Goose

IN SPITE OF IT ALL ...

Above: Golden boy. Marquez took 13 wins, a new record. Still just 21, and nobody really beat him once.

Top right: Double trouble. Alex Marquez got to test the MotoGP Honda as a reward for winning Moto3. For once, there was no brotherly bumping.

Main photo: Moto2 fields were healthy, the racing not so much.

Photos: Gold & Goose

CRITICISM of Dorna comes easily, especially to those who have known the company for a long time. A tub-thumping management style and a determination to rein in factory-team dominance are just two factors that generate censure. To some, the superiority of the factory machines is the main point of interest.

But if they wanted a show, they got one.

Some might put it down more to the riders than those up in the Ivory Control Tower. Still, something certainly worked out right in 2014.

Seldom does a dominant performance like that of Marquez coincide with a year of such exciting races, interest building as the season progressed. Seldom has the usually downbeat distinction of being best of the rest been so hard fought.

Much of this was down to the resurgent Rossi. For some years, everyone has been wondering what will happen to MotoGP when he goes away. With another two-year factory Yamaha contract inked mid-season, it's beginning to look as if he never will.

These are tough times for the factories. Emergence from economic gloom has been extended, but the situation was better in 2014 than 2013, evidenced by Yamaha finally regaining a title sponsor.

As ever, the biggest spender took the biggest prizes: it was a second successive triple crown for Honda, winning riders', constructors' and teams' championships. A big spend narrowly won them a vengeful Moto3 title as well, in a year when the smallest class yielded the biggest thrills.

Moto2 languished somewhat – here the deadening hand of Dorna's over-zealous cost control can be seen in action. Not so much, however, in the company's first year in charge of Superbikes, although two rounds, in South Africa and Russia, had to be cancelled. The series yielded a tense and entertaining season in spite of it all.

And in the USA, where a once highly productive Superbike series had dwindled to obscurity, a new initiative led by Wayne Rainey in league with Dorna turned gloom into cautious optimism.

The signs are good for more of the same in 2015.

MICHAEL SCOTT
Wimbledon, November, 2014

Above: Carmelo Ezpeleta (*right*), Grand Poobah of MotoGP and World Superbikes, with henchman Javier Alonso.

Above left: Aprilia won World Super-bikes, and decamped directly for MotoGP. Suzuki also return for 2015.
Photos: Gold & Goose

Top: Old god learned new tricks. Rossi was back. LOL.
Photo: Yamaha Racing

FIM WORLD CHAMPIONSHIP 2014
TOP TEN RIDERS
THE EDITOR'S CHOICE

Rider Portraits by Gold & Goose

1 MARC MARQUEZ

IT is slightly endearing that Marquez did make mistakes after the first ten flaw-less races – if 'endearing' is the right word. As with Rossi, the stripling super-star's veneer of cheerful charm overlays a brutal killer instinct. It was seldom shown more clearly than when he bamboozled briefly challenging team-mate Pedrosa in the final corners at Catalunya. His change of line was as cynical as it was successful.

The Repsol Honda rider, from a Catalunyan country town, embarked on a maiden MotoGP campaign in 2013 that went to the last race. He was still learning, while he was winning.

In 2014, Marquez was more experienced, and it was devastating to his rivals. Nobody beat him all year. Brno's set-up problems apart; when he didn't win, it was either because he could afford to be reckless or because he didn't have to. As when he secured the title with three races to spare at Motegi. It would have been much earlier, but for those crashes at Misano and Aragon.

It is in the nature of sport that its practitioners always improve. Seldom is it quite so obvious.

In his first season in MotoGP, Marquez broke all of Freddie Spencer's 'young-est-ever' records. In 2014, at the age of 21, he outranked Mike Hailwood as the youngest ever back-to-back champion. Spencer had a brilliant, but abbrevi-ated career; Hailwood's many years of achievement built a reputation that lives on today.

Which path will Marquez follow?

2 VALENTINO ROSSI

IT was not only changing his crew chief that turned Rossi's fortunes through 180 degrees. Replacing Jeremy Burgess with fresh broom Silvano Galbus-era was clearly only one aspect of a whole-life rethink, with only one major constant – the exuberant belief that he could still win races.

And so he could, twice – and at the same time back up those wins with enough points to outrank often-faster team-mate Lorenzo to take second overall.

The honour of being first loser was fiercely disputed. Rossi's strength grew through the year until the final decider.

His greatest achievement in 2014 was not the results, however. It was how he overcame the imposition of age and experience to learn all over again how to get the best out of the new generation of electronic-marvel motorcycles. As a rule, these are toys for a younger generation.

He had to learn not just the new tyres and so on, but also how to out-think the ECU, so as to bend it to his will rather than merely obey its instincts.

He seemed renewed in all sorts of areas, building the aura of confi-dence that was such a feature of his glory years. He has begun to seem perpetually renewable, and has given himself two more years for that purpose.

He'll be 36 in 2015, his 20th season. And still his cackling laugh is a regular feature on the rostrum.

3 JORGE LORENZO

WHEN things go perfectly for Jorge, he goes perfectly, too. The year showed that he has lost none of his speed or precision. But it also showed that when things don't go perfectly, he is prone to poor performance.

This ranged from two consecutive beginner's mistakes in the first two races to succumbing to fear in the wet at Assen, scene of his crash-and-comeback achievement of 2013.

How to reconcile this with the metronomic master of Motegi? Or his first win at Aragon, combining intelligent tactics with remorseless fast laps, keeping his head while all about were losing theirs?

The 27-year-old Mallorcan publicly blamed a lack of fitness after a winter of recuperation from surgery, but all problems stemmed from a hearty dislike of the new-generation Bridgestones, which played against his high-corner-speed style.

Long before he and the tyres had reached better agreement, his title chances had gone. Impressive then that he came so close to second overall, in an unusual best-of-the-rest year.

The double MotoGP champion will have something to prove in 2015; that the destabilisation of 2014 was only a temporary wobble.

4 DANI PEDROSA

ALAS, poor Dani. Though few could say "I knew him well", for he remains a private though nowadays slightly less austere character. The master of the matter-of-fact reply has a sense of humour perhaps best described as impish, although he keeps it quite well concealed.

His overwhelming attribute, however, is to be a magnet to misfortune. He escaped injury in 2014, unless you count the need for wrist surgery after the start of the European season. But things still went wrong.

The 29-year-old was put in his place too many times by his young team-mate, but at the same time he was showing his class. It was Dani who broke Marquez's run of wins at Brno, and in the first 15 races he was nine times on the podium.

At that stage, Pedrosa was still a strong candidate for second overall. Until misfortune struck at Phillip Island, in the form of Iannone, on a Ducati, from behind. Zero points.

A week later, Pedrosa was favourite for a third successive Sepang win. Instead, he fell off in the race. Twice.

It is a cliche that you make your own luck, and Dani's former paramount ability to start well deserted him. That spoiled his results and put him in a position for the Australian disaster.

He is still a superb MotoGP rider, though.

5 ANDREA DOVIZIOSO

FOR three years or possibly more, a Ducati has not been what you would choose, if you wanted to cover yourself with glory.

Dovizioso (28), never the most spectacular of riders, turned that idea upside down in 2014 with a series of fault-free races that built on the Desmosedici's strengths rather than succumbing to its weaknesses. He had to adapt, he explained, to "a very big limit", the so-far insoluble understeer that has plagued all the red bike's riders.

His consistency was remarkable. He finished every race except for the nightmare at Aragon, and apart from a typically well-judged second in the wet at Le Mans, made the podium in the dry in Texas. Nine of his finishes were in the top five, and fifth overall was a worthy reward.

Dovi makes up for fireworks with intelligence and a measured approach. That paid dividends not only for him, but also for Ducati's new race chief Dall'Igna. The Italian has raced factory Hondas and Yamahas in the premier class, and brought a wealth of experience that he, unlike predecessors including Rossi, was able to translate into performance.

The new regime at Ducati was enough to convince Dovizioso to stay put for the 2015 season. Now we wait to see just what sort of reward it will bring.

6 MAVERICK VINALES

THERE are certainly other applications of the name of the 'Top Gun' hero among those of Maverick Vinales's generation, but surely not one that is so apt.

Fresh from victory in a down-to-the-wire Moto3 championship, he jumped straight on to a portly, but more powerful Moto2 bike and won his second grand prix.

By the summer break, he'd added two more second places, and another at Indy directly afterwards. He was continuing to gain strength, and well-judged victories at Aragon and Phillip Island showed by how much.

His only bad mistake was in the crucial final race, where he scuppered his chances of seizing second overall at the last gasp with a headlong late-braking error that also took out his closest rival, Mika Kallio.

The 19-year-old from Salvador Dali's home town of Figueres in Catalunya would surely make stopwatches go limp, with a speed that comes partly from signal determination, of course from skill, but most profitably from his ability to adapt rapidly.

This will be put to the test in 2015, with a seemingly risky career step to join Suzuki in MotoGP. On the positive side, it's a full factory team. On the negative, Suzuki have a lot of catching up to do.

NOBODY could quite say that the elder Espargaro brother came in under the radar, because he had served notice in 2013 by rising head and shoulders above the other CRT riders.

In 2014, he was a revelation nonetheless. His Open Yamaha was all but a factory bike, although with the significant omission of the bespoke electronics that are such an important part of the M1 package.

It was clearly again head and shoulders above the other Open bikes, but he had two team-mates, one of them a former double world champion, and he was at least the same distance ahead of them.

Most especially, not only did he embarrass the lesser factory riders in qualifying, when he had the benefit of soft tyres, but also his pole position at Assen demonstrated clever tactics.

This hitherto underrated 25-year-old takes a big gamble in 2015, joining the Suzuki factory team. He was the first rider on track in tests the day after the final race at Valencia, and within five laps he was circulating faster than de Puniet had done in the race the day before. By the afternoon, he was going a second faster still.

Clearly he has the potential to bring a great deal of strength to the project.

8 TITO RABAT

FOR almost ten years, this Spanish racer has been a most unlikely candidate for this list. He's campaigned in 125cc and Moto2, and it was only in 2013 that he won his first race – and only one race.

For 2014, he was not just the most improved rider in any class, but world champion as well, after a campaign that delivered 11 pole positions, seven race wins and a record tally of points. He stood on the podium 14 times, scored points in every race and never finished lower than eighth.

The achievement proved that raw talent is not necessarily the most important element of success. Rabat (25) made up for it with relentless hard work, exemplified by a habit of running full non-stop race simulations in most free practice sessions, but also away from the track.

When he wasn't dirt-track training with the Marquez gang near home in Barcelona, he spent most of the year living in his motorhome at Almeria circuit, where he continued his relentless programme – running lap after lap after lap, at record speed, day after day.

Rabat is the first Moto2 champion who will stay to defend his title. The rest will have to knuckle down to it if he continues at the same pace.

9 JACK MILLER

MOTOCOURSE showed some prescience when we put Miller on this list in 2013, although he had yet to win a race.

We were not the only ones. Honda already had an eye on the Australian teenager, whose fighting spirit is redolent of several of his antipodean predecessors, especially the first 500 champion, Wayne Gardner.

Honda's interest couldn't stop him from switching to KTM for 2014, however; and when he got there, he did start winning, directly, building up an impressive title lead by mid-season.

Then the same fighting spirit served to undermine his progress. He crashed out of a strong early lead at Assen, an unforced error; then zero-pointed again at Aragon, because he was too eager to dispute a narrow dry line with Marquez, again early in the race.

With more patience, he would not have lost the points lead.

Miller (19) won six races and claimed eight pole positions. Title winner Marquez had only three of each.

In 2015, Miller follows another former Australian race winner, Garry McCoy, who was the last rider to move directly from the smallest to the biggest class. To Miller, a MotoGP bike is just another device with an engine and two wheels. Expect plenty of adventure.

10 ANDREA IANNONE

THE self-styled Maniac Joe's nickname is apt, but it doesn't do enough credit to the range of skills that the 25-year-old Italian showed during 2014.

These included fearlessness and impetuosity, but also a combination of speed and aggression that in one particular regard put him on the same level as the so-called Aliens. He refused to be cowed by Marquez.

At Brno and Valencia, he resisted the young master with conspicuous vigour. Marquez would push past; Iannone would push straight back again.

He crashed a lot (a total of 14 was only exceeded in the MotoGP class by the misfortunate Bradley Smith, 16), suffered some injury and earned opprobrium by at least two headlong attacks that took out other riders: Hayden at Le Mans and Pedrosa in Australia.

But he also qualified on the front row five times, and at Valencia he led the race for ten laps, before again succumbing to the Ducati's handling limits.

It is a racing truism that it is easier for a fast rider to learn how to stop crashing than a slow rider to learn how to go fast. If 2015's Ducati is the improvement that everyone expects, he will surely justify his place in the factory team.

DUMBING DOWN, BUT NOT OUT...

Cost cutting, Open-class bikes, new TV broadcasters, new rules and a long goodbye from Bridgestone. There was much to fascinate in the 2014 season, as MICHAEL SCOTT relates...

THE 2014 season was the first of two years of transition for MotoGP, in Dorna's long and winding road towards taming the factories and boosting the show. It is to CEO Carmelo Ezpeleta's credit that he has (eventually) got this far, without alienating the existing dominant duopoly of Honda and Yamaha. His new dumbed-down rules have instead attracted more factories to take part in MotoGP: both Suzuki and Aprilia will return for 2015; KTM in 2016. Can BMW be far behind?

All the same, there are many questions that were put on hold in 2014, and will be answered in 2015 and 2016, as electronic restrictions start to bite. Intended not only to level the playing field, but also to cut costs, they might have the opposite effect.

While the impetus to curb the runaway costs of ever more expensive electronics, which require many highly specialised man-hours, is understandable, the insistence that factories must pool their developments from the middle of 2015 cuts deeply into the very nature of competitive racing. There is also the vital matter of safety. Current developments by the factories have yielded unprecedented gains in performance and rider control. It is unlikely that the giants of racing will wish to share their hard-earned progress. Taking a backward step could undermine this platform dangerously.

The interim changes of 2014 were exemplified by the ending of the short-lived CRT era, when production power in prototype chassis gave independent teams the chance to compete – if only with one another. The humble non-GP racers had achieved their purpose, however, in demonstrating that Dorna was prepared to do almost anything to cut away at the factory control.

In came a different kind of dual-level MotoGP racing: Factory Option, and Open machines. The former were as before, although now compelled to use control Magneti Marelli CPU hardware, but free to apply their own software. This applies for 2015 as well, but in mid-September came a new diktat. Software development can continue only until 30th June. From that date, there can be no updating, except "minor bug fixes that might affect safety".

From the next day, 1st July, the factories will switch development to the 2016 'unified' software, and will be obliged to do so in an open and transparent fashion, pooling their knowledge and developments.

The other restriction from the start of 2014 was a further cut in fuel capacity: down by one litre to just 20. The engine allocation remained at five per rider for the year, but development was frozen from before the first race. Honda and Yamaha raced on under these restrictions.

Open MotoGP bikes had considerable concessions, by comparison, beyond 24 litres of fuel and access to tyres that were one grade softer. Each rider was allocated 12 engines, and most importantly development was not frozen. The only downside was the mandatory use of control software.

The bikes in the category were a motley crew, ranging from CRT hangovers to a for-sale production racer from Honda, built (reportedly at a substantial loss) to a price of 1.2 million euros. The RCV1000R lacked, among other things, pneumatic valve springs, and consequently was short of revs and horsepower, but nonetheless seemed to be entirely within the spirit of the regulations.

But the game was won by the Forward Racing team, who leased factory-level engines from Yamaha, then for convoluted reasons failed to come up with the chassis for which they were intended. Yamaha ended up supplying them with a complete motorcycle that not only comprehensively outperformed the Hondas, but also, in the hands of Aleix Espargaro, was able to challenge the Factory bikes, especially on softer tyres in qualifying.

The real trump card was played by Ducati Corse, now headed by ex-Aprilia race chief Gigi Dall'Igna. He took everyone by surprise before the season began by opting out of the Factory status that had seemed predetermined. Ducati needed considerable development, and frozen engine design didn't fit the plan. Accepting the control software was a small price to pay for the freedom of 12 engines, all of which could be different from one another.

Dorna and the Grand Prix Commission were stymied, until a series of hasty meetings came up with a compromise. Ducati, and indeed any constructor that had not won a dry race in the previous year (for example new arrivals like Suzuki), were given a special category: under the Factory label, but in a sort of no-man's land. They had all the concessions of the Open bikes, but were able to use their own software. Just in case they were too successful, a sliding scale was instituted: one dry race win in 2014 or 2015, two second places or three podium finishes would lead to a cut in fuel from 24 to 22 litres; three wins would also result in withdrawal of the soft tyre option.

MOTO2 TAME?

The cost cutting strategy does not apply only to the top class, and it continued to be effective in Moto2, thanks to that bluntest of instruments – a production engine, supplied by the organisers, along with the simplest of electronics. Over-tyred and underpowered, the class remained a poor relation and

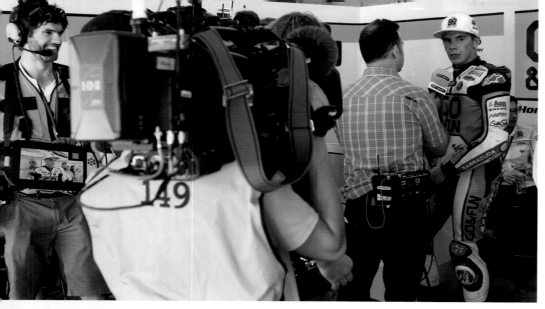

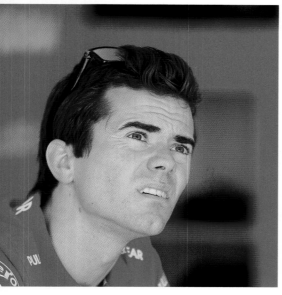

something of a graveyard for talent. There are many former world champions running around in the middle of the field. But it does remain cheap.

Attempts to control the costs in the Moto3 class, however, failed dismally.

KTM had already driven a wedge through the notion, being prepared to operate at a loss at GP level, to sidestep the pre-determined price of engines, etc. Now a vengeful Honda followed them through the widening gap, after their more sensibly priced production racer had been humiliatingly outclassed.

The NSF250R was replaced by the NSF250RW (for Works), and they meant it. Far from being just an upgrade of the previous model, it was a full grand prix racer, and it brought the name firmly back into the top echelon with the first race wins since July, 2012.

The rules were tightened all the same: six engines, to be supplied in three batches, enabling in-season development. But any notion of special unofficial factory-team specials was put to bed by a new system, whereby the motors were supplied to the organisers and distributed at random among the various teams. And from 2015, the rev limit drops from 14,000rpm to 13,500.

But there seems little that Dorna can do, if the factories choose to swallow the costs and go full-tilt, which is good news for the fans. Moto3 was reliably the most exciting race of the day, and the championship battle likewise.

At some levels, MotoGP had weathered the financial storm of the past decade; Yamaha finally found a sponsor to replace Fiat, in Movistar, while energy drinks expanded in numbers and in their spend – the financial problems of the departing GO&FUN notwithstanding.

Red Bull, Monster and Drive M7, to name just the three largest, had effectively replaced the departed tobacco sponsors that had been such a boon to GP racing. Not, however, to the same levels of free spending; also not to quite the same levels of controversy, though there was some of that as well.

But for all the apparently improved prosperity at the upper levels, there are still many riders, especially in the smaller classes, who earned their seats by bringing sponsorship; many who ride unpaid by their teams. Was it not ever thus?

TV OR NOT TV?

The flip side of cost saving is to try to increase income, and here Dorna scored a couple of direct hits. Although many people think the bulls-eye might have been the company's own foot.

The income was from the sale of TV rights, away from national broadcasters to more financially forthcoming pay-TV channels in Italy (Sky), Spain (Movistar) and Great Britain (BT Sport). These were lucrative deals that covered several core markets.

The cost was to viewing numbers, which in Britain for example plummeted from approaching two million on a good day for the BBC to sometimes fewer than 150,000 – a massive reduction, which must have come as a shock to the broadcaster and a body blow to the sponsors, whose main object is to get TV time.

Number reductions were similar in Italy and Spain, where Movistar played hard-ball, leaning on Dorna to block its own website's live broadcast to outraged subscribers in Spain, even though they had paid for this access. Dorna was soon obliged to relent.

In Britain, rather than pay, most viewers were prepared to wait to watch recorded highlights on free-to-air ITV the day after the race. BT Sport has a five-year contract and in its first year poured in plenty of resources. There was a platoon of presenters, commentators and interviewers at every event, at least one of whom could boast approaching 70,000 followers on Twitter – or half the viewing audience!

It remains to be seen what the network will do in the future, considering the paucity of attention paid to its broadcasts in 2014.

While in Britain, Dorna were also accused of take-the-money-and-run tactics when they declined to negotiate with Silverstone, instead moving the grand prix to the as-yet-unbuilt Circuit of Wales from 2015. It was soon announced that Donington Park would stand in for that first year, indeed for as long as necessary, until the new track does actually exist.

TYRE CHATTER

Bridgestone had a surprise in store for 2014. Having somewhat reluctantly shouldered the task of supplying control tyres at the end of 2008, and renewed the three-year contract from 2011, the company had doubtless tired of the stream of criticism endemic to the task. Invited to renew from 2015 to 2017, they politely declined.

So politely that they agreed to extend the current contract for 2015 only, buying time for Dorna to find a replacement.

Bridgestone's tenure has had its ups and downs. One-size-fits-all tyres are never going to suit every bike and every rider every weekend. Ducati suffered more than most from the woes of standardised rubber; in 2014, both Lorenzo and Rossi complained of variations in supposedly similar tyres.

There have been several spells when riders felt development could have been faster, particularly during

2012, when there was a spate of crashes on tyres that were reluctant to warm up.

And of course the debacle on the resurfaced Phillip Island in 2013, although Dunlop (and in World Super-bikes, Pirelli) suffered just as much as the Japanese company.

By and large, however, given the logistical constraints of having to ship large numbers of tyres (in a typical GP weekend, 400 slicks are used of a stock of almost 500) from Japan to Europe, requiring long-range predictive research, Bridgestone are beyond reasonable reproach and have continued to develop the black art.

The new-for-2014 asymmetric front tyre is an example, notwithstanding that it was badly undermined by the changing conditions in Australia, in a race scheduled to start two hours later than the locals would have recommended, in the interests of European TV viewers.

So who would take up the challenge now? In a reversal of previous policy, Michelin stepped in for 2016. The French company's reason for withdrawing at the end of 2008 had been a pronounced distaste for a non-competitive, single-supplier series.

Michelin's record in MotoGP is very strong, but not exemplary, and its previous long-standing superiority crumbled against the onslaught by Bridgestone.

Seven years away, in a time with many technical changes to the machines, gives them a lot to catch up on. They started by instituting limited testing during the season and decreeing a change in wheel diameter, from Bridgestone's 16.5 inches to 17.

Testing will intensify during 2015, with the retired Colin Edwards playing a major part, reprising a role he had with Michelin ten or more years ago.

Riders with experience of both tyres hope that the Michelins will offer better 'feel' than the hardwearing Bridgestone. Even so, teams and riders are nervous.

REVISING THE RULES

The first flurry of rule rewriting, on the very eve of the first race, created a special loophole for Ducati's Factory/Open hybrid, something of a camel created by committee via teleconference.

Thereafter the usual rule fiddling continued: a reduction in minimum weight from 160 to 158kg; in bike-change flag-to-flag races, the requirement to swap to different tyres was waived, to prevent riders from being obliged to exit the pits on slicks should their wet tyres have worn out. Oh, and the always surreal MotoGP Claiming Rule, never invoked, was officially abandoned.

The penalty points system remained much as before, with a back-of-the-grid start for four points, pit lane for seven and one race suspension for ten. The difference now was that the points would remain in force for 12 months; previously, all scores had been reset to zero at the end of the season. Nobody got anywhere near a penalty: the top scorers were (MotoGP) Iannone, with two points; Zarco and Simeon in Moto2 (two apiece); while several Moto3 riders were also on two, including Jack Miller.

Technically, the most significant rule revision concerned brakes, after increasing concerns that the mandatory 320mm carbon discs, carried over from the last-generation 800cc bikes, weren't powerful enough for the heavier and much faster one-litre bikes. Previously, larger 340mm discs had been optional at Montmelo, Motegi and Sepang. Late in May, in time for the Italian GP, they were made a free option for all circuits, and mandatory at Motegi.

New for 2014 were two-way dashboards, with upgraded transponders now able to receive signals not from the pits, but from Race Control. There were five of them: Red Flag, Black Flag (disqualification), Black-Yellow Flag (mechanical), Ride-Through, and Change Position.

In Moto2, the maximum age of 28 for wild-cards was dropped, opening the way for a 31-year-old woman racer at the Sachsenring: Nina Prinz was certainly the oldest beginner in modern GP racing.

Much more controversially, another special loophole was created by Dorna specifically to bring in under-aged Fabio Quartararo, who will turn 16 only after having missed the first three races. At Brno, a new clause to the rules was revealed: from then on, the minimum age in Moto3 would not apply to the winner of the Spanish national CEV championship.

Quartararo is the newest member of former 125 champion Emilio Alzamora's Monlau stable, joining among others the Marquez brothers, and though he was not named, by no coincidence, the young French rider had already won it in 2013, and did so again in 2014, this time with three races to spare. It smacked of special favour to the Spanish establishment.

Scott Redding's record of youngest ever GP winner is not in jeopardy, however; Quartararo will already be well beyond 15 years and 170 days at the first race.

OFFICIAL TIMEKEEPER

T + *Performance*

DOES SPEED MATTER?

You might think speed is everything in racing, but is it? MICHAEL SCOTT talks to racers past and present to find the answer...

Above: Spa Francorchamps, 1977. Sheene leads history's fastest race.

Top right: Steve Parrish then and now.

Above centre right: After a 1977 fatality, Sheene and Steve Baker tackle Salzburgring officials. The 500 race was boycotted.

Photos: Motocourse archive

Right: Christian Sarron and Randy Mamola ready to race at Spa.

Far right: Winner Phil Read (MV Agusta) leads team-mate Gianfranco Bonera and Suzuki's Sheene at Spa in 1975, setting a speed record Sheene would break two years later.

Photos: Gold & Goose

THE new Argentine circuit at Termas de Rio Hondo was received with great acclaim. Cleverly designed with bikes in mind, with computer-aided cambers and careful corner combinations, it pleased every rider.

There was one particular reason – speed. It joined the calendar as the second fastest circuit of the year. In fact, designer Dromo's computers had predicted an even faster lap time to move the average speed beyond Phillip Island. Human frailty, in the form of Marc Marquez, fell short. The best lap average was 177.1km/h, compared with Australia's 182.1. But it was faster than both Mugello (176.2) and Silverstone (175.9)

The numbers, however, do not impress anyone with a sense of history. Today's bikes may be much faster. Today's circuits and average speeds, however, are much slower.

The fastest ever GP was won by Barry Sheene at the old Spa Francorchamps in 1977, at an average of 217.370km/h (135.067mph). But Spa was just one of several tracks where riders spent long spells at blistering speeds, slipstreaming and hoping not to seize. Because in those days, crashing in such places could easily mean certain death.

Spa was cut in length, and the still daunting new track was last used for a GP in 1990. Something similar happened to the Hockenheimring in Germany (206.190km/h/128.121mph) and Austria's Salzburgring (196.226km/h/121.929mph) four years later.

So how important is speed in racing? What has been lost with the new generation of slower circuits? And what (apart from the obvious safety) has been gained?

I turned to riders both past and present for the answers. The old guys came up with by far the best stories. Being racers (and survivors), their accounts were often less about danger and fear, and more about the hunt for a technical edge.

Steve Parrish, a close fifth in that fastest ever race at Spa and later four times European truck champion, explains: "The fear and trepidation wasn't about dying, it was about not doing as well as you'd expected. I worked that out after I tried truck racing, because I got nearly as nervous, and clearly I was in nowhere near as much danger. I think most of the nerves actually come from wanting to achieve what you expect of yourself."

The Isle of Man TT was the scariest and most dangerous of

all, but it was dropped from the calendar in 1977. Top of the list thereafter was Spa – especially the old 14.1km circuit last used in 1978 (Yamaha rider Johnny Cecotto's pole time of 222.362km/h/138.169mph is GP racing's fastest ever lap). Austria's fearsome Salzburgring was a close second; Hockenheim was faster, but at least there riders weren't skimming the guard rail or brushing against rock faces. Several other now defunct tracks had at least one fifth- or even sixth-gear corner that set the heart racing and separated the men from the boys. They include the old Assen, Silverstone and Paul Ricard. Then there was turn one at Imola, the road track at Brno and even the old first corner at Le Mans. Randy Mamola recalls an awesome race there in 1979, his second podium as a rank rookie: "It was real fast – back one gear. I have a picture somewhere of me pinching Kenny Roberts on the ass going through that turn."

But Spa was The Place, and 1977 was The Race.

Grand Prix rookie Parrish was Sheene's team-mate on the Suzuki, and he was fifth after coming off worst in a battle with Steve Baker, Pat Hennen and Tepi Lansivuori, but less than 18 seconds behind Sheene after just short of 40 minutes of flat-out racing.

"I vividly remember that as probably the best race I ever had, as far as scaring the shit out of myself and enjoying every minute of it."

Christian Sarron also has vivid memories of the long circuit. His were at night – not at a GP, but in a 24-hour endurance race: "I never did grand prix at the old Spa, but I did a 24-hour, so I raced there even at night, on a 1000cc bike – Kawasaki, which was a fast bike. Not as fast as a 500, but still – down the hill into Malmedy, with the guard rail right by the track – you knew that if you made a mistake there you would probably die.

"At Spa, there were a lot of very-high-speed turns … some were full gas, some not quite. But fifth or six gear … If you wanted to make a good lap time, you had to take your chance there, because it made far more difference than trying to go fast in smaller corners, like La Source. Especially on the way up from the bottom of the track. You had some fast curves there and you carried your high speed for a long time, and gained a lot of seconds.

"It's difficult to find the limit. Are we really going to the real limit when we know that if you make a small mistake, it's finished? Some riders did crash in these corners by trying too hard."

Shortening the track reduced the number of lethal corners, but not the severity of those that remained. Most feared was Blanchimont, the almost flat-out pair of left-handers before the bus-stop chicane, where the guard rail hugged the edge of the track.

It was a matter of knowing where to leave a margin.

Mamola: "It was fifth gear, at least, and the guard rail was

Above: Flat out up the valley floor, then flat out back across the mountainside: Eddie Lawson leads the pack over the line at the end of practice at Austria's fearsome Salzburgring. Spencer (4), at the back here, would beat Lawson by three-hundredths of a second.

Photo: Gold & Goose

right there. Every time you went in there, you thought, 'I know I could go faster.' And when you did, you knew the danger. You didn't want nothing to happen there, but it was also one of those corners that made you a man, made you feel like you're doing something."

The new shorter Spa gave Sarron one career highlight – pole position by more than two seconds over Eddie Lawson in 1988: "That one lap is still in … more than just my memory. It is in my body. One of the biggest satisfactions in my whole career. I knew that by getting that real danger, I made a complete abstraction of it. And when you can do that and go faster, it gives a you a … rewarding feeling."

The race? It was a shortened half-wet nightmare; my report tells a sad story. Shadowing Lawson for second behind Gardner, "Sarron made yet another small mistake with big consequences. He touched a white line braking … and went down in the mud."

These fast corners, however, had a special allure for top riders. Wayne Rainey was in turns fascinated and appalled by Spa: "These were the kind of corners you'd look forward to all the time."

Look forward to? Yes, with a strange sort of fascination.

"Look at a track like Salzburgring, racing right up against the guardrail at 180 miles an hour. You're in sixth gear and you've got to change direction, and it's so heavy to steer because of the gyro effect. Everything seemed to be in slow motion, the

way the bike went. But as far as your brain went, that was in fast motion.

"Eau Rouge at Spa was really daunting in the dry, but in the wet it was unbelievable," the triple champion continued.

"You go down the bottom of that little valley there and up the other side, and there was guard rail on both sides of the track. You overcook it and … you hit something. But to get the lap time, you had to get an Isle of Man mind-set. You didn't think about what might happen…

"You go down through a left, then you flick it right, and when you did that in the wet you would lose both tyres. As you were losing it, you had to flick it back left, and now you were going uphill, so you had to be on the throttle. And as you get into the left, the bike goes light, over a blind crest.

"You'd be spinning and sliding sideways through there, and you had those little dips or divots from all the trucks using the road, and rain would be sitting in there in little puddles. That was a crazy corner. It was like you were balancing on disaster, especially in the rain. And it rained there every year that I raced."

The other corners mentioned by all were the almost flat-out left and subsequent fifth-gear right on the mountainside at the Salzburgring. On the right-hand side, guard rail; on the left, a rock face surmounted by banks of spectators, who have seen some grisly crashes there over the years, including one in 1977 that killed Swiss rider Hans Stadelmann and hurt a

number of others, and caused the 500-class factory riders to go on strike.

Niall Mackenzie, who claimed his first 500-class rostrum there in 1987, described it as "like threading a needle. The faster you go, the narrower it becomes. At the very fastest part, your shoulder and the guard rail are not that far apart. If things go wrong, it's going to be a bit of a mess, but you're not aware of that when you're riding around. It's the last thing that comes to your mind."

Parrish described it as the scariest corner of his career: "Making it even more interesting, there was a foot-wide rivulet running out of the rock face and across the slope of the track ... you either had to go really slow or you had to accept that when you crossed that, you would slide six or eight inches across the track and hopefully the bike would regain grip on the dry side. And it did, because I'm still alive. But some didn't."

Rainey also had an adventure there, on a 250 in 1984: "The bike would run leaner down the front straightaway because of the trees, then richer on the back straightaway over the hillside ... so we'd leaned it out a little bit. On a 250 up the back, you'd go left and right in sixth gear without knocking off at all. As I turned right, my bike locked up and high-sided me.

"I got the crap knocked out of me, and as I got up I heard these people laughing their asses off on the hillside above, just cracking up. They thought that was the funniest crash they'd

ever seen. That was the first time I'd ever been laughed at after high-siding at 150mph."

The fear was real, but as Rainey said, "When those thoughts occurred, you just didn't go there. But you knew that was all a part of it ... drafting three or four guys, changing direction flat out in sixth gear, the buffeting, the steel brakes of those days, those tyres, those bikes – it was a handful. Making sure your bike was the best it could be. At times trying to be more brave, go round the outside. It was real intense."

Mackenzie said, "I can't say I was ever aware of the speed. At that speed in close company, everything seems to slow down. With high gearing, the acceleration and everything is a lot slower. At tight tracks, you're accelerating fast and stopping fast, so you're more aware of that. It's a different experience."

When the speeds get high and the straights are long, slipstreaming becomes the key element. Certainly just that for Parrish on the old Spa: "You were flat out for so long, then you had to go back one gear for the Masta Kink, lined by two or three houses, then there was another long straight. By the end of the race, I'd worked out that if you led on to the straight, you got slipstreamed twice before you got to the kink, then once again afterwards. That was what Spa was about, particularly on an RG500. It wasn't slow, but it took a long while to get there. So you were constantly using slipstream. You didn't bother passing on a corner, just waited until you got the tow past."

Hockenheim, along with Paul Ricard, was another great slip-

Above: Freddie Spencer sweeps out of La Source past Jerry Burgess (with pit board) and Erv Kanemoto and down towards towards Eau Rouge in 1985. MOTOCOURSE described the shortened circuit as "still frighteningly dangerous, and there appear to be no moves afoot to improve safety on the very fast corners which have claimed lives in two- and four-wheel racing this year."

Photo: Gold & Goose/Takanao Tsubouchi

Insets, above left: The young Randy Mamola, and the seasoned broadcaster, with Niall Mackenzie.

Photos: Motocourse archive/Gold & Goose

Top: On the limit. Christian Sarron and Niall Mackenzie wrestle with danger at the Salzburgring's 'safety' chicane in 1987.

Photo: Motocourse archive

Above: Phillip Island became the undisputed fastest modern MotoGP track – after Assen was abbreviated – and a favourite with riders and fans.
Photo: Gold & Goose

Right: Smoothness and precision: Jorge Lorenzo asserts that nowadays "a rider must be fast in all corners, fast or slow. You must be complete."
Photo: Yamaha Racing

Centre and far right: Dani Pedrosa laments the loss of the old Assen. Here he battles with Stoner in 250s in 2005, the year before the circuit was truncated.
Photo: Gold & Goose

streaming track. Rainey: "At these tracks, the most important thing was to get the speed out of the bike. It was so important to get a drive. But these were two-strokes, and you needed to over-gear it. You'd gear the bike for a race in which you were expecting a draft. If you didn't gear the bike to deal with that, you were going to get stuffed. But if you were by yourself, then you were still going to get stuffed, because the bike wouldn't pull that gear.

"With that gearing with the two-stroke, you could backshift from sixth to fourth and you'd have no engine braking. So everything was on the front brake. Into that far corner, you'd brake to avoid hitting them and the draft would just suck you by. I remember seeing the trees and the road and the riders, and you were buffeting in the draft, and you'd put the brakes on and you just wouldn't stop."

Slipstreaming still happens, now and then, though not in the same me-first/you-first/me-first way of the long, long straights. Valentino Rossi: "Usually a long straight is good for the battle, because with the slipstream you can overtake. But is mainly smaller bikes, because with MotoGP the bikes are so fast, so the slipstream is important, but has less effect."

Mamola regrets its passing as a major element of tactics and skill: "At the Salzburgring, I lost the race to Eddie in '84. He was on the four-cylinder Yamaha and I was on the Honda three, and our speed wasn't strong enough, if I got out of the draft. I could attack, but I screwed up at the bottom corner and lost the draft going up the hill, and I couldn't deal with it. We've lost that scenario.

"We had bikes that could over-rev. The two-strokes. These

four-strokes can't do that. You see it more in Moto2: they pull out, but they can't go faster – because the gear ratios are all the same, the power's all the same, there's no advantage of putting on a different gear ratio or using your own knowledge.

"You see some of it at Mugello, but that's usually into the braking zone. The two-strokes were much more variable. You could pass and repass on the straight."

These speeds and dangerous fast corners were scary. How did riders prepare?

Christian: "You had to condition your mind before you get there. Once you get there, it's too late. You had to be prepared for the worst. It's as simple as that."

Conquering fear brought advantages, the Frenchman continued, "On fast tracks, even if you didn't have the best bike, if you were a little more brave ... you could be faster there. It's the same as racing in the wet [conditions in which Christian reliably excelled]. If you can dominate your fear, even on a fast bike in the wet ... it's the same procedure in your head. Condition yourself to go fast. Because it is also scary in the wet, to go close to the limit, especially in the fast turns."

For Mamola, fresh from the USA, the daunting tracks were just the way it was: "Kenny Roberts took me round, showed me some dangerous places. Back then, there was a lot of danger: in the winter Marlboro Series in Australia and New Zealand; the Wanganui street circuit ran through a cemetery! Also in the USA: the old Laguna Seca, Riverside, on the banking at Daytona. We were pushing 200mph, 25 to 30 years ago. When you think about that, with the brakes you have ... but you don't think about it, until now."

Danger was just a matter of fact. Parrish: "You decide whether or not you'll take the risk, I guess. I was only 23 or 24, and I didn't see many risks. I saw a piece of tarmac with a chequered flag at the end of it."

For Mackenzie, "fear in your 20s is not a problem. All you're thinking in your selfish rider's way is to get your bike working better than the last time you were there."

All the old-timers agreed on one thing: that something has been lost from racing. The combination of ingredients that a rider needs has a different balance. Sheer bravery is less important, believes Parrish, because safer and particularly slower modern tracks put more emphasis on riding technique.

"We talk about the knife-edge, and it is still pretty sharp, because you can easily paralyse yourself or get hit by a bike. But the chances are pretty slim now. We used to have to have skill, ability and bravery, and I think you can take a large percentage of bravery out of it now."

Not surprisingly, modern riders don't necessarily agree. Pedrosa: "I think the bravery they had was because they were racing with shit – the material of the leathers, the helmets, the bikes, the tyres and the brakes. And the race-tracks. That's where the bravery was.

"Now we have so much safety, but – it might look like you don't need that bravery because you don't ride against the wall or whatever. But still you have to go there, and when you ride at the limit, at the very limit, you need everything."

Lorenzo concurs: "Now a rider must be fast in all corners, fast or slow. You must be complete."

All agree, however, that something has been lost. Rossi: "Faster riders prefer the faster tracks. It is a dream to race especially at Spa. I love the circuit, but unfortunately it is too dangerous for MotoGP. For me, the safety of the riders is more important."

And for Pedrosa, who never had the chance to try the really fast tracks, the loss of the old Assen remains a wound: "Of course, a track like Spa and like Hockenheim – for the speed and the adrenalin, it is much higher. It is much more the spirit of racing.

"Assen is the track – everyone calls it the Cathedral. And it was. It was surreal – the corners, the layout. Then in 2006, they cut it completely, and for the guys in the grandstand they can see much more. For me, when they did this, I was in the Safety Commission and I was like, 'You guys are crazy.'" The

lost first section of Assen remains the Spanish multi-GP winner's favourite stretch of track, anywhere.

Safety remains paramount, and multi-race winner of the dangerous age Mamola is glad of it: "I'm proud that I raced at that time – not that I feel I'm a hero.

"Spa would be a frickin' awesome circuit now, but we'd have to move the guard rail a long way. Knowing what I know now, and with my son racing, I would choose safety over character. This is what I fought for, what we boycotted races for, what turned into IRTA and the Safety Commission, things that are still going on today."

FAST DATA

Fastest ever lap: 222.362km/h/138.169mph

Spa Francorchamps, Belgium

Johnny Cecotto (Yamaha), pole position, 1978

Fastest ever race: 217.370km/h/135.067mph

Spa Francorchamps, Belgium

Barry Sheene (Suzuki), 500cc GP, 1977

Top Three All-Time Circuit Speeds:

1 Spa Francorchamps, Belgium
   222.362km/h/138.169mph

2 Hockenheimring, Germany
   206.190km/h/128.121mph

3 Salzburgring, Austria
   196.226km/h/121.929mph

Top Three Modern Circuit Speeds:

1 Phillip Island, Australia
   182.173km/h/110.057mph

2 Termas de Rio Hondo, Argentina
   177.120km/h/110.057mph

3 Mugello, Italy
   176.208km/h/109.490mph

TECHNICAL ROUND-UP

THE BIKE THAT THINKS LIKE CASEY

In the constant search for greater performance, manufacturers are building bikes that can think for themselves. NEIL SPALDING looks at the intelligent machines...

Above: 2007 Ducati paints the track Bridgestone Black. Stoner's feel for the right amount of spin was phenomenal.

Above right: Under my thumb: Magneti Marelli's PlayStation switch.

Centre right: Dovizioso's every move is logged: Ducati's boffins scan the go-graphs at Brno.
Photos: Gold & Goose

Below right: And he saved it. The combination of Marquez's throttle control and Honda's pro-active electronics meant the rider was able to recover from this apparently terminal tumble.
Photo: Milagro/Martino

CASEY STONER was a phenomenon: a very fast rider who could deliver results on bikes that others simply couldn't come to terms with. Casey's style was to find out what corrections a given motorcycle needed to go fast and then work out how to deliver those corrections, on the track and in the races.

The Ducati 800 Desmosedici is the defining bike of his career. The initial design handled okay. It had a rearwards weight distribution, but the Bridgestone tyres had been developed to deal with that. Its steel-tube lattice frame was quite flexible, possibly a bit too flexible, but the throttle 'feel' was remote and the power delivery not linear.

Having won the championship in the first year of the 800 category, Ducati tried to deliver more power for the second year by using a variable-length inlet system. This gave more torque, but the power was even less linear than before. To be blunt, the desire for maximum acceleration had led to a brutal delivery of all that power.

The combination of the remote throttle and the rearward weight bias was so different from what he expected that Marco Melandri simply couldn't ride the bike. As a result, he was released from his contract early. But it is what Stoner was able to do, not what Marco couldn't do, that matters.

Consider a MotoGP bike coming out of a corner. Power has to be applied and delivered (in the most fuel-efficient manner) to maximise acceleration out of the corner, all while the bike is still leaned over. The bike has to turn and accelerate simultaneously, and it has to do both better than the bike next to it.

The Ducati seemingly has always been short of front wheel grip. You have only to look at any picture of the bike being used well. The rear end is sliding out, with the tyre spinning up to reduce the excess traction.

Stoner's greatest expertise was his ability to hold the bike

at just the right level of wheel-spin to achieve the maximum turning and acceleration. A difficult task on the spiky Ducati.

As engines are tuned to make more power, they tend to develop peaks and troughs in their torque curves; smoothing the curve is the holy grail of the intelligent racing motorcycle engine builder. This lets the rider balance traction and slip for the best lap time. The Ducati clearly didn't have a smooth torque curve, so to get the bike to do what he wanted, Stoner used the rear brake to smooth the power. He asked for power, and regardless of the bike's throttle design, he was very accurate in this; then he removed any excess torque by applying the rear brake on corner exit, with sufficient sensitivity to get the spin and acceleration he wanted without the damaging slide-inducing torque peaks.

At the time, senior Ducati engineers marvelled at the way Stoner moved around the bike and the way he used the rear brake. It is apparent now that all of their riders might have been more effective if the torque curve had been smoother in the first place.

Which brings us to the current Honda, a bike that thinks like Casey. To do what Casey was doing in smoothing the power delivery of the bike, but to do it automatically, you need the bike to possess the same sense of balance as a human rider. Stoner on the Ducati would constantly adjust his rear braking, factoring in tyre grip and torque delivery. As he brought the bike upright, it could take more power so he could brake less, but he still needed to smooth the transition: any sudden increase in torque would upset the whole balance.

Watching Marc Marquez perform his amazing riding feats in 2014 was a joy, but it is important to realise that we were watching a truly exceptional rider on a truly exceptional machine. This Honda had been in development for a long time. The basics were there in the second year of the 800cc cat-

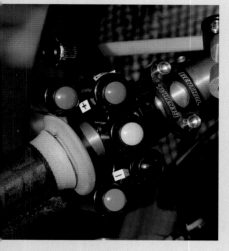

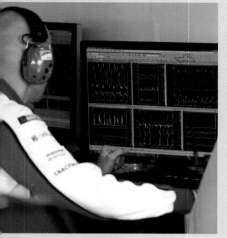

egory, but it took four years before the championship was won, by Casey Stoner. The current 1000 is a direct development from that bike and has continued to perform well.

MAINTAINING THE BALANCE

There was a time, not so long ago, when motorcycles were dead simple. Three cables and a couple of levers – throttle, front brake and clutch – gear and rear brake levers, were all you needed to control the bike. Hydraulics came during the 1970s, but since the Yamaha R6 came out with the first road-going ride-by-wire system in 2006, everything has been getting a lot more complex.

On the road, many bikes now have traction control and ABS, but they are still 'add-ons' to the basic systems of the bike; something has to have started to go wrong before they kick in to try to save the day. But there is another level that already is being developed, indeed perfected, for the top flight of MotoGP bikes – full electronic throttle control.

Modern MotoGP throttle systems are just that, complete throttle systems. You can still hear occasional wheelspin-taming ignition cuts from some bikes, but, the top factories in MotoGP have moved way beyond the idea of making too much power and then having to get rid of it quickly to a world where only the right amount of power is delivered in the first place. Since Yamaha's 2008 M1, built in response to Ducati's 800 championship win, the target has been to build systems that never let the tyre spin too much in the first place.

Electronic throttles control more than just power out of a corner. They also allow the bike to be controlled into and through the corner, by using varying levels of engine braking to load up the suspension and manage pitch.

Any race tyre has a point where it is at its most efficient, providing maximum drive out of a corner. That usually involves some movement, a small amount of spin. The trick is to get the bike to the point where it is developing that drive, but not letting it go too far.

Yamaha started the project with a system that calculated exactly where it was on track and that learned from each corner how much wheel-spin the bike was generating at certain throttle applications and lean angles. It would react to that information and on the next lap, the bike would work slightly differently. They called it 'Mu learning'.

Famously, Colin Edwards accidentally started a race in Motegi with a 'wet' map in dry conditions. By the end of the race, he was setting very fast laps, the system having 'learned' what additional grip was available.

The rules make MotoGP a fuel efficiency race, too, and any unnecessary wheel-spin is a waste of fuel, so the factories want to develop maximum drive without expending unnecessary energy. This is also safer and allows faster speeds: nevertheless, Honda and Marquez have done their best to provide fans with the spectacular spinning and sliding that they want to see.

In MotoGP, the whole exercise is made more difficult by the fuel limitations, intended as a means of keeping performance in check and also forcing the development of new fuel saving techniques. The electronics designers not only have to make the bike produce accurate power levels at a moment's notice, but also have to achieve this with a very high-power engine running very lean mixture. Both high power and lean running create engine characteristics that are difficult to control, and both need to be conquered if you are to deliver the precise changes in power with the required accuracy.

Honda have now taken Yamaha's Mu learning to a new level. Undoubtedly Marquez is a fantastic rider, but it would be foolish to think that Honda's electronics have not helped him in his rise to the top. It's the near crashes that are the most telling. In one during a test at Brno, the bike was nearly on its side, with the front wheel turned in to the corner and Marquez all but off the machine. He is attached only at the right handlebar, and his throttle input is the only thing that will save him; if his input is exactly right.

He did save it, and there is no question that he is very

skilled to have done so, but I believe he was helped by a bike that was capable of calculating exactly the position it was in and its lean angle, the likely load on the tyres, the angle of the steering and the yaw. You would need all of that information to apply exactly the right amount of throttle. Once that data had been calculated accurately, the ECU and its software would be able to limit the power applied to what was usable, and what would help bring the bike and its rider back up again. It would be useless to make too much power and then try to limit it, the old-fashioned traction-control way, as the crash would have happened by the time the intervention began.

To get a motorcycle to come back up from a high lean angle, you must either turn the front wheel in to the turn or apply power. Centrifugal force does the rest. To do this reliably, you need grip and exactly the right amount of power. Too much power and you crash; the same with not enough grip. The important thing was that Marc stayed attached to the bike and timed the throttle opening well. The precise amount of throttle, however, would be down to the bike's sensors, and the ECU.

Obviously the ECU and its programming are very important; but the thing that is different about a bike compared to any other road vehicle is its ability to lean and pitch while remaining on a two-dimensional surface. Cars don't lean, not much anyway, and aircraft have all three dimensions in which to move. Bikes are 'flying on the ground'; the tyre area available and the load being put through the tyres change dramatically with lean angle and power. Before you can use the programming and computational speed of the ECU, you need fast, accurate lean and pitch data, the basis for computing the bike's position and predicting the grip available. To confuse matters further, the different front and rear tyre sizes produce varying contact patches and rotational speeds for each tyre at different angles of lean, and that's before we get into the expansion and contraction of the contact patch as the bike's weight is pitched forwards or back.

All this data provides the option of setting the actual throttle limit, or as Honda have clearly done, of allowing the rider to use the now much smoother power delivery to slide the bike around, up to the point where it might get away from him.

If the rider applies too much throttle, the system's programmed limits come into play, but because the power delivery is much more linear, the rider can safely play below that point. Nevertheless, you can only hand over full control of the throttle to the ECU when you are sure the data is accurate all the time, as any incorrect data will result in the wrong power being delivered, with the strong likelihood of a crash.

Cast your mind back to Aragon in 2013, when Marquez accidentally cut Pedrosa's rear wheel speed sensor lead. Pedrosa applied throttle as he would normally do, and from what happened next (an instant crash), it is clear that rear wheel speed data is required for the ECU to calculate the maximum acceptable power. This isn't a bike that controls traction once a problem has started, it is a bike programmed to go to the limit, and over it only up to a point. The more accurate the sensors, the closer to the grip limit, or more accurately the 'drive' limit, the bike will be able to operate.

However, the electronics cannot make up for fundamental design decisions. The Honda is shorter and higher than the Yamaha, giving it advantages on some circuits and disadvantages on others. It was obvious at Misano, for example, that the circuit design favoured the longer and lower Yamahas. The Hondas were slowed there by the level of electronic intervention necessary to keep them stable.

What we have seen are several really gifted and fast riders on well-designed machines controlled electronically to be helpful to their pilots. The top Yamahas and Hondas don't require the rider to fight them to get the best lap times; they provide help. It is clear that the Yamaha needs to be treated in a very smooth fashion for the best performance, something Jorge Lorenzo seems able to do regularly. The Honda is more excitable, but clearly provides confidence, letting all of its riders know that they are very close to the limit, but giving them the opportunity to slide the bike if they wish. Both, however, are proof that accurate pitch, yaw and lean sensors are the holy grail of motorcycle throttle designers.

Above: The approach looks similar, but Lorenzo's Yamaha and Marquez's Honda respond quite differently at the limit, as their different lines demonstrate.

Top right: Control ECU: the capacious Magneti Marelli black box was mandatory, but Factory entries were allowed their own software.

Centre right: Torductor on Marquez's Honda. Acting like a real-time dynamometer measuring torque on the gearbox output shaft, it plays a vital role in smoothing engine response.

Bottom: Number-crunching on the grid. Team geeks play a crucial role.

Photos: Gold & Goose

CONTROL ECU AND SOFTWARE RESTRICTIONS

ALL the technologies mentioned so far are under attack from those running MotoGP. The nature of 'development by racing' is that factory teams end up with equipment that is far beyond the reach of privateers. That, in turn, is blamed for making the racing more processional and damaging the 'show'.

Motorcycle grand prix racing has always been defined by that factory technological superiority, but it is only in the last few years that the differences between factory bikes and privateers have grown so large.

Back in the 990 era, it was still possible to win races with a non-factory bike, but electronically the bikes were pretty much at the level of a young puppy dog slipping around on a polished kitchen floor. Now the top bikes are at the level of the humans who lean down to pick up the puppy.

The Dorna 'control' ECU, developed in 2013 on some of the CRT bikes, is Marelli's highest-spec 'off-the-shelf' unit, the AGO34. It has approximately twice the capacity of most of the ECUs used by the major factories. The manufacturers typically employed Marelli to build ECUs to their own specifications, the individual units being designed to be as light as possible and tailored very specifically to their specific requirements. The new control ECU, mandatory for all in 2014, is almost twice the size physically of the old works units and is endowed with more hardware capacity than even the factory bikes need.

The control software, compulsory for non-factory bikes in 2014, had a very slow development during 2013, but it improved towards the end of that season and received a major boost after the season finished, as it had to be good enough to support the works engines now available to the top Open MotoGP (as opposed to Factory Option) machines.

These 'customer use' engines can consume 24 litres in a race, so do not need the very complex fuel saving strategies of the 20-litre factory bikes. However, they do need the torque curve smoothing aspects designed into the electronic throttle system. Engines built with electronic throttle control in mind are much more aggressive, as a spiky torque curve can be 'controlled away'. The ride-by-wire system is designed to smooth the irregularities and make the power delivery feel more controllable for the rider.

Of the factory MotoGP bikes in 2014, only Honda had to change their ECU and develop new programming to suit: both Yamaha and Ducati already used Marelli equipment, so the basic operating system was similar. Rule changes were made in 2013 to allow wild-cards to return using any ECU, so theoretically Suzuki could have raced in 2014 with their current Mitsubishi ECU, but a Marelli solution was a requirement for a full-time return in 2015, and they made the switch for the 2014 test programme.

For 2015, the sensors will not change, and that does make a difference. Top-level sensors aren't cheap, and as we have seen they are leading-edge contributors to the efficiency of the whole throttle system. For 2016, everyone will have to use the Dorna 'inertial platform', and that is never going to be as accurate as the current sensors.

The rules have not been finalised yet, but 2016 already looks as though it will be a very interesting year.

HUMANS IN MOTION

A long, long time ago, we humans developed a sense of balance. Aided by very fine sensors in the inner ear, we learned to stand upright, balancing our weight perfectly, and furthermore to adjust our balance while moving around. Unless we stumble, drink too much alcohol or have a physical problem with our balance mechanisms, standing up, walking, running and even gymnastics are all considered perfectly normal actions.

Look around, though, and you start to realise just how unusual this walking upright lark is; humans are almost alone in being habitual bipeds. Several other mammals stand on two legs, but very few stand vertically for very long, and many of those that do have big tails to assist in balancing.

It has taken millions of years for these abilities to evolve. What makes them possible is not only the right bone and muscle structures, but also the mental capacity to maintain the right positions; to process the information from the sensors so that the brain can co-ordinate the response, getting the muscles to do the right thing to maintain the vertical stance.

To maintain balance, our brains rely on information from part of the inner ear called the vestibular organ. This area contains three semi-circular canals filled with fluid, which moves over 'hairs' on the canal walls to give important information on the attitude of the head. It also provides information on the direction in which the head is moving, and registers acceleration and deceleration. In another part of the inner ear, the otolith organs provide information on sudden movement or tilts of the head.

Surgeons have been working to create artificial replacements for all of these sensors. Dr Charles Della Santina founded and directs the John Hopkins Vestibular NeuroEngineering Laboratory in the USA. He is aiming to develop an implantable inner ear 'simulator' to restore the sensation of head movement and balance in patients with damage to the inner ear. According to the respected US magazine Popular Science, the prototypes, using gyros and accelerometers running outside the head, have been wired to the inner ears of chinchillas with dead inner ear hair cells. Development is now taking place with the target of shrinking the entire unit to allow it to be implanted in humans.

We live in a world where massive changes in consumer electronics have been seen in just the last decade: everyday items like iPhones and Wiimotes come equipped with fast and accurate position sensors and accelerometers, but there is a difference between components small enough and cheap enough to be used in what are really only toys and equipment that can be used for controlling 200mph vehicles with humans on board.

In Japan, Honda have been developing their little bipedal robot, Asimo, (Advanced Step in Innovative Mobility) since 2000. This has reached the point where it can now run, hop, kick a football and climb stairs, all as a human would. The sensors that allow Asimo to operate have now been redeveloped and toughened to work on Honda's MotoGP bikes with the purpose of telling the ECU where the bike is in space.

2014 MOTOGP · BIKE BY BIKE

DUCATI DESMOSEDICI

Above: Dovizioso's early-season Desmosedici – note angled sump and duplicated front engine mounts. Lower mount in use here, but upper alternative changes stiffness ratio.

Photos: Gold & Goose

Top right: Ducati fitted extra cooling ducts for the 320mm brake discs, and kept them when 340mm discs were allowed.

Right: New exhaust in mid-season retained the ECU-controlled flap valve for engine braking.

Far right: The external flywheel was changed frequently, clearly having an effect on controllability.

Photos: Neil Spalding

DUCATI started the year with a new bike: a major remodelling of the machine that had been developed over the previous year, shorter at the front and longer at the rear. It had a reshaped fuel tank that was similar in shape to the Honda's, showing that the motor was in pretty much the right place.

At the same time, Ducati were making it clear that they wanted to be able to develop their engine over the course of the year, and the new rules that required the design to be frozen at the start of the year were at best unhelpful. By the time the races started, Ducati were the beneficiaries of a revised set of rules that, as they had been unsuccessful in the dry since the start of 2013, allowed them to use 12 engines, and to redesign those engines as the year wore on. Even better, they could use 24 litres of fuel per race and employ the softer tyres intended for the Open-class bikes.

Over the first half of the season, the bike became progressively even shorter at the front and longer at the rear. For Sachsenring, a third new swing-arm arrived, noticeably stronger at the front and more slender at the axle. There was also a new linkage. New bodywork arrived, too, offering improved cooling, air intake efficiency and reduced drag.

Different engine set-ups were used, with different external flywheels being the most obvious. Mass dampers were also tried. The bike had quite a reputation for exhausting its riders, so anything that could help reduce the vibration was likely to be welcomed. Friction reduction in MotoGP has reached such a stage that exhaust 'flapper valves', which shut off most of the exhaust pipe on demand, became standard equipment on the Ducati to allow engine braking to be dialled in as required.

The final major update for the year was the 14.2, a version of the bike that was narrower in the middle, the better to allow the rider to shift his weight around, and which had a slightly relocated engine. This didn't make the advances that were expected, but Ducati was at the stage where such a signal would be heeded, and there was still time to adjust the main sections of the all-new bike due at Sepang in early February, 2015.

Above: New exhaust arrived for the fourth round. Longer primary pipes improved mid-range performance.

Right: Marquez used a top triple clamp cut away to allow more flex at his high lean angles.
Photos: Neil Spalding

Top: Honda's finest is an exercise in precise packaging.
Photo: Gold & Goose

HONDA RC213V

HONDA rolled out their masterpiece RC213V again for 2014, with only a few changes to its winning design. In 2013, their major issue had been a difficulty in using Bridgestone's alternate heat-resistant tyres, provided for circuits where the tyres were under additional stress. With an extra layer, they ended up slightly stiffer in construction and with limited edge grip.

Honda knew they had to find a solution and arrived at Sepang for the first test with three different chassis, all with identical geometries, but with different flexibilities. They were very lucky to discover that, just as they were sorting an answer to the problem, the tyres were becoming the standard fitment for 2014.

Marc Marquez could only try all the changes to the bike in practice before the first race at Qatar, thanks to a training accident that had stopped him from riding in the pre-season tests. His main job was to confirm a style of main frame. Pedrosa had already turned down all of the new offerings and had decided to campaign with an updated version of the 2013 design.

The bike retained its amazing throttle response and edgy nature. Both aspects are deliberate: the throttle provides power as smoothly and progressively as Honda can achieve; the edgy handling lets the rider know just how close the bike is to its limit. Both features have been developed over a number of years.

The Honda seemed noticeably immune to the braking problems suffered by most of the field. It could get away with 320mm discs, and on some occasions needed heat shrouds to keep the discs up to temperature, this on a bike that began the year as the fastest in the pack.

Knowing that 320mm discs were the largest allowed, Honda had developed a very robust engine able to take the enormous stresses of deliberate over-revving on down-shifts. The pneumatic-valve-spring system had variable pressure to ensure that there was no valve bounce at high over-rev, and the throttle system was designed to provide pre-programmed levels of engine braking to the rear wheel, when it was on the ground. This gave Honda a significant advantage on corner entry until the 340mm discs were allowed for all bikes from Mugello onwards.

Above: Unlike Pedrosa, Marquez used a fully electronic twist-grip. Note the very short brake lever.
Photo: Neil Spalding

Right: The Repsol bikes had the benefit of a 48-tooth clutch in 2014, for smoother starts.

Below: Bautista's RCV had different brakes and suspension, but otherwise was the same as the other works Hondas. Note the carbon 'modesty panels' hiding the precise orientation of the V4 motor.
Photos: Gold & Goose

YAMAHA YZR MI

Above: Bradley Smith's Yamaha shows off its web-style main beams. The slipper clutch is off for servicing.

Right, top row: Yamaha still uses conventional cables from the twist-grip to the throttle position sensor; new 340mm discs were so big the calipers had to be put on with the disc.

Second row: Rossi tried a 'short-front' fairing at Phillip Island to deal with crosswinds; small lever under the clutch has to be pressed to allow neutral to be selected.

Third row: The 'mechanics' dash gives a lot of information; Lorenzo preferred a late-2013 chassis.

Bottom row: Rossi preferred the chassis with more flex: note welded-in panel. The shorter exhausts arrived for Assen; Yamaha continued to mount the rear shock off the back of the crankcases.

Photos: Neil Spalding/Gold & Goose

YAMAHA didn't have the best start to the year. Their bikes live or die by the amount of edge grip available. Bridgestone changed the tyres, robbing Yamaha of valuable grip, and it took until round four at Jerez for Bridgestone to come up with revised versions of their medium-compound tyre, re-engineered to improve the edge grip levels. As soon as the new tyres were available, the Yamahas were on the pace again.

There were two new rules for 2014: the engine design freeze and the requirement that factory MotoGP bikes use only 20 litres of fuel in a race. That's not a lot of fuel for a 250bhp race engine running at race pace for around 120km. The previous 21 litres had been intended to restrict power, but in reality it only hurt performance a couple of times a year. Losing another litre, however, made it a real restriction.

The factories now are quite good at maintaining overall power output – this was the third time the fuel levels had been lowered – but the fuel restriction is felt most just as the throttle is opened. The initial throttle movement is critical on a race bike because that is the movement you have to make to get the bike to stand up again coming out of a corner, and you have to do it just as you are at maximum lean, balanced on the extreme side of the tyre. Any jerk at that point is very scary and is really felt by the rider.

For Yamaha, it was a perfect storm: they had lost valuable edge grip, and the one manoeuvre that needed good edge grip was the initial throttle opening, and that was going to be worse than before.

Yamaha had been fine-tuning their engine mapping all year, and by the time Bridgestone delivered the uprated-edge-grip tyres, the initial throttle situation had been improved dramatically. They brought new shorter Akrapovic exhausts to Assen, which became the standard fit for the factory team; they were louder, but critically also made low-rpm engine operation smoother.

Other changes had been made as well. Yamaha had continued to stiffen the chassis for 2014, but the changes to the tyre character called that into question. For Jerez, Rossi and Lorenzo were given the use of revised chassis that had been modified above the swing-arm pivot: a section of the beam had been removed and a plate welded into the resulting hole.

Rossi liked the change and used it to good effect; Lorenzo wasn't so sure and stuck with the old version. By Le Mans, the Spaniard was back on the late-2013 chassis, and he stayed on it for the rest of the year.

Yamaha's only other goodie for 2014 was a revised seamless-shift gearbox. The first version, introduced the year before at Misano, was seamless only from second to sixth; the new one added first by changing the gearbox pattern, just as Honda had done the year before, to N-1-2-3-4-5-6. The Yamaha box still wasn't as good as the Honda's, though, as it was only seamless on up-shifts, while the Honda's worked seamlessly in both directions. Yamaha worked at fine-tuning their throttle system, giving their riders better auto blip and slipper clutch operation, but they never had quite the same advantages as the Honda.

Undoubtedly this will be fixed for 2015, but 2014's engine design freeze prevented Yamaha from making the necessary modifications to the gearbox casings to fit the new mechanism.

Forward Yamaha

IT had been intended that Forward would only be supplied chassis, so that they could measure them to make their own copies, but once the riders had been out on them, they didn't want to give them up. Mark Taylor left FTR to design and build a chassis for Forward, noticeably less stiff than the original Yamaha item, but using the same geometry. This proved to be much better in slow corners, but not as stable in the fast ones.

Colin Edwards's post-Indianapolis replacement, Alex de Angelis, was intended to have used it all year, but as soon as it was announced that the team would be buying factory chassis in 2015, he stayed on the factory unit, too.

As an official Open MotoGP entrant, Forward employed the Dorna ECU and its inertial platform. In exchange, they were allowed the use of 24 litres of fuel, 12 engines and soft-compound tyres. The engines, provided by Yamaha, were to the same specification as those supplied to Tech 3. Rather than using 12 fresh engines, they had just five, which were returned to the factory in turn for regular rebuilds, cutting costs and giving Yamaha better information on how their engines were coping with the strain of competition with the control software.

The electronics were of a significantly lower spec than the engine had been designed for, with limited control functions and no way of changing the settings from corner to corner. It left the Forward riders with plenty of power, but not a lot of control going into, through and out of corners.

Honda RCV1000R

HONDA'S customer steel-valve-spring MotoGP bike, which they offered for sale, promised much. It handled well, at least once it was fitted with upgraded suspension, but it was fatally underpowered, and it soon became obvious that Honda had been trumped by Yamaha's decision to lease works engines and chassis.

Honda seem to have allowed the bike to rev a little higher than originally planned, requiring a more frequent maintenance schedule. Engines were only being used for two races before being withdrawn, most probably for a cylinder-head service, and then returned and resealed as 'new' engines.

The chassis was delivered with Öhlins suspension, but the 42mm-diameter forks were of a similar spec to those used in Moto2, and everyone promptly changed them to 48mm forks, like those fitted to the Factory MotoGP bikes.

It appeared that Honda wanted to keep the costs down, but no one else did.

Honda also transferred some top staff to the project. Casey Stoner's ex-crew chief, Cristian Gabarrini, was appointed to oversee development, and two of Stoner's old technicians joined him.

Avintia Kawasaki

KAWASAKI'S 2013 World Superbikes were given a new lease of life in MotoGP. With new engines prepared by race specialists Akira, combining World Superbike-spec bottom ends with in-house-developed pneumatic-valve-spring cylinder heads, the chassis didn't stay in their original spec for long.

As initially tested in Sepang, the bikes were still in their factory black paint. By the first race, Spanish fabricators Inmotec had extended the swing-arms to better suit the weight balance preferred by MotoGP's control Bridgestones. Over the course of the year, the main chassis were reinforced and modified, but they always retained their street origins; the swing-arms ended up being completely new.

It was an interesting project, and clearly done with some help from Kawasaki. However, the choice of an engine concept that seemed to ignore the advances Kawasaki's MotoGP operation had made at the end of their involvement in the championship kept them out of contention.

Ducati Open

AFTER deciding to stay in the Factory category (albeit with special privileges) with their official entries, Ducati opted to persevere also in Open MotoGP with Yonny Hernandez, and later with Hector Barbera, using the Dorna software and hardware.

Hernandez had a 2013 chassis for the whole year, his ex-Supermotard style clearly making up for some of that unit's rearwards weight bias.

Barbera received an early 2014 chassis, which was clearly superior to his previous Kawasaki-based Avintia bike, but also wasn't as good as the bikes that had received Dall'Igna's attentions for the whole year.

Far left: Major adjustments, minimal time – Forward Racing mechanics work on head angle settings mid-session after Espargaro had crashed.
Photo: Gold & Goose

Left: Ex-FTR designer Mark Taylor penned this new in-house frame for Forward, based on Yamaha geometry.
Photo: Neil Spalding

Below left: Honda's RCV1000R looked the part, handled well, but was too slow.

Below: Avintia's Kawasaki's started off the year as 2013 WSB bikes.

Bottom: Reddings RC1000V used Showa suspension and Nissin brakes, that meant he was on his own on set up.
Photos: Gold & Goose

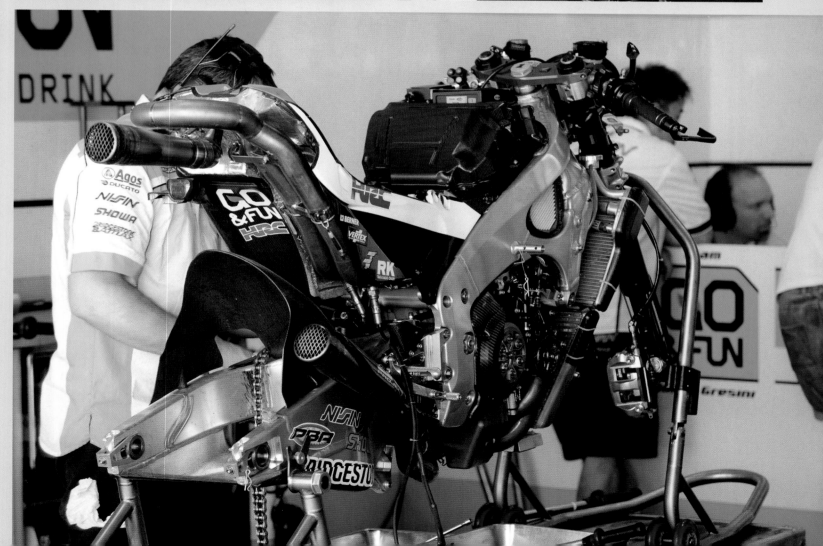

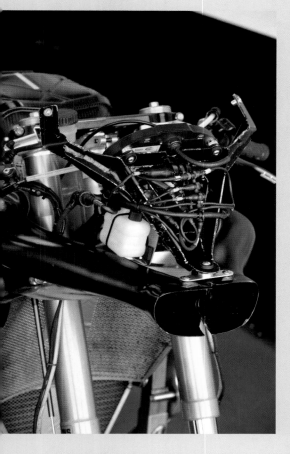

Left: PBM used a chassis from GPMS, with ART engines from Aprilia.

Photo: Gold & Goose

Below: It was a year of experiment for Aprilia. New air intakes appeared mid-season.

Photo: Neil Spalding

Left: I spy... Suzuki technician takes a good look at Pedrosa's Honda during pre-season tests at Sepang.

Photo: Gold & Goose

Below: The 2014 Suzuki gained a new exhaust and ECU. Several fairings and frames with differing rigidity were also tried out.

Photo: Neil Spalding

THE RETURN OF SUZUKI

SUZUKI had tested their new concept (to them) across-the-frame in-line four for almost two years before they decided to run a wild-card entry at Valencia.

The engine was similar in concept to the Yamaha, an in-line four-cylinder with a cross-plane, reverse-rotating crankshaft. But Suzuki had taken the idea a stage further, with the crank appearing to be set slightly higher and the cylinder leaned further forward, thus keeping a similar centre of gravity. This helped with ground clearance, something that's becoming an issue for Yamaha.

At the start of 2014, the decision was made to stop any further development of the Mitsubishi ECU, which Suzuki had used for a decade, and to switch to the Marelli control ECU. Suzuki want to use their own software, so they spent most of the year's testing fine-tuning this aspect.

APRILIA – PBM-ART, ART

APRILIA had two teams employing their engines: Paul Bird with his British GPMS-built chassis, and Ioda using their whole bike. It was a big change from 2013. PBM's bikes occasionally got into the points, but it was clear that the power of their superbike-tuned engines was way below that needed to compete against the MotoGP-engined bikes. The chassis looked the part, but they lacked the development time on track to work well.

Ioda, however, used the ART chassis. This was very different from those seen in the two years of the CRT bikes, which had been prototype versions of the street chassis. Now ART was trying something very different. The main beam was noticeably thinned, and the swing-arm was a much lighter structure. Compared to the all-conquering Japanese factories' chassis, it looked very spindly. Normally, race chassis designers seek to allow a little lateral flex, while limiting torsional twist and maintaining braking stability. The ART looked like it would allow a lot of flex, both laterally and torsionally. It will be interesting to see the further outcome of the experiment.

Left: The ART used this flimsy-looking, cut-away main-beam chassis and a lighter-construction swing-arm, both the results of intense efforts in 2013.

Photo: Gold & Goose

RULES RULE

A growing raft of endurance and economy rules aimed at cutting costs can have the opposite effect. But despite the unintended consequences, KEVIN CAMERON discovers that they can contribute to engineering advancement...

Above: MotoGP 2014-style – endurance race, economy run and budget battle.

Top right: Ducati have a special dispensation for extra engines, fuel and softer tyres.

Above right: Honda's Shuhei Nakamoto – dominant on track and in the committee room.

Right and far right: Race Director Mike Webb, Dorna CEO Carmelo Ezpeleta.

Below right: Strive as he might, Scott Redding couldn't make up for the production Honda's horsepower.

Photos: Gold & Goose

GRAND Prix racing, on two or four wheels, implies the use of prototype vehicles constructed with the single goal of winning races. There have been times when most of the fields have consisted of privately-entered, series-produced machines, such as in the late 1920s/early 1930s for cars, and the 1950s and 1970s for bikes, but even in those cases, the machines were built to win.

Now we are launched upon an era of growing rules complexity. As Formula One grew too rich for many teams' budgets, the idea of requiring engines to last longer became official. This deflected engine designers from the sole task of winning, to designing for what are effectively endurance races, run in segments, each of which is still called a grand prix.

When MotoGP proved too expensive for Aprilia (remember the Cosworth-designed Cube?), Team Roberts (their V5 eventually made 186hp), Suzuki, KTM (the lovely photos of the 14 completed 990cc engines) and Kawasaki, MotoGP adopted F1's endurance-racing idea and now requires Honda and Yamaha to use no more than five engines per season, per rider. Ducati, who have been in a five-year slump (mainly caused by a conflict between their design and the spec Bridgestone tyres), have been allowed to use more engines. And a special extra-soft rear tyre. And more fuel per race – 24 litres instead of the 20 litres allotted to Honda and Yamaha. This special assistance is Carmelo's 'dole'.

First things first. Doesn't it cost more to engineer a fast 900-mile engine than a fast 200-mile engine? Yes, it does, and the parts requiring the most redesign and testing are the pistons and valve train. Bearings, provided they are supplied with cooled, filtered, air-free oil, last forever. Transmissions are exempt from the five-engines rule. Pistons, being made from aluminium alloy, and subject to severe thermal and mechanical stress, fail by cracking and breaking.

The process by which tiny defects in the forgings become cracks, and cracks propagate, is strongly temperature dependent. When the engine endurance rule came into force, Yamaha software engineers wrote a detailed predictive pis-

ton temperature model, and an instrumented engine was used to validate the model (prove or correct it) at one of the pre-season Malaysia tests. With the model, they were able to reduce piston temperature in critical areas by up to 30 degrees C.

By the time major teams adopted pneumatic valve springs (2006–07), daily replacement of metal valve springs had become routine. The reason for daily replacement is that, even with the most expensive vacuum-remelted steel wire, the stress level at which springs must operate to deliver the necessary performance causes rapid loss of spring pressure and rapid development of cracking. Pneumatic springs obviated this Iron Age drama, and the new engine endurance rule enshrined this. That is, were anyone to design a new race engine using metal springs, those springs would have to last the specified 3.6 races. That, in turn, would require those springs to operate at a lower stress level so that they could survive for that mileage. The natural result would be reduced engine performance.

It has been estimated that Honda's RCV1000R production racer, hailed in 2013 as the answer for private MotoGP teams, is down 30hp from the factory bikes. The main difference is its metal valve springs, which cannot follow the high-lift, short-duration cam profiles that deliver broad, strong power. The RCV's profiles have to be softened to extend spring life.

Remember that the purpose of the engine endurance rule was to cut costs and thereby counter the dreaded grid shrinkage that led to the brief CRT or grid packing era. During those months, the term 'prototype' was stretched to include Superbike-kitted production engines in artisan chassis. Students of history will recall that in the first years of MotoGP, the prototype rule was used to exclude a Yamaha R-1-powered entry.

Did the engine endurance rule cut costs enough to keep teams on the grid who otherwise would have withdrawn? The rule became irrelevant to Ducati, who needed and were al-

lowed more engines. Perhaps the reader will remember the year when Ducati put fresh engines into its Superbikes after almost every practice because of chronically cracking cylinder liners and crankcases. Did that expense drive Ducati out of Superbike?

That leaves Honda and Yamaha. Does anyone seriously think either of them would have left the series had the rule not saved them oodles of cash? This leaves us with the feeling that the rule exists mainly because it is fashionable in the highest circles at present. Like so many other laws, its purpose may be just to show that somebody is doing something.

Perhaps building longer-lasting racing engines teaches R&D departments how to build more durable production bikes? Not likely – production engines are already costed down to the last centime, and very sophisticated engineering is used to make them no more durable than their duty cycle requires. The premium materials and processes employed in race engines are irrelevant to this and have no place in production – the two are distant, but not entirely separate worlds. I say not entirely because, in recent years, we have seen material and process upgrades in sportbike engines – for example, from cast to forged pistons.

So much for the conversion of prototype GP racing into an endurance contest. Now let us consider its conversion into an economy run – the 20 litres rule. Where did this come from? When we ask, we are told that MSMA insisted upon it (MSMA is Motor Sports Manufacturers' Association, currently consisting of Honda, Yamaha, and Ducati). That implies a democratic consensus that we mustn't question, but if we persist, insiders tell us that MSMA is *really* Honda.

When I spoke with MotoGP Technical Director Mike Webb in 2013, he told me that he was troubled by the 20 litres rule because complying with it is so expensive. He would have preferred other means of performance limitation, notably a simple rev limit. But Honda's MotoGP boss, Shuhei Nakamoto, has said that Honda will leave the series if a rev limit is imposed.

Some said a rev limit was unnecessary, since the mandated 81mm bore adopted with the return to 1000cc displacement effectively capped rpm because the implied 48.5mm stroke would subject pistons to 10,000g peak acceleration at 17,125rpm. That 10,000g is something F1 backed away from with rev limits in 2007 and 2009 – because it was so expensive to keep pistons alive at that extreme stress level. Yet calling the 81mm bore a rev limit begs the question, because the more R&D budget you can spend, the higher you can push the revs. To put things in perspective, the peak acceleration of a shell fired from a 5in gun is 20,000g, and the shell only has to last through one cycle – not thousands of cycles per minute. The idea of F1's rev limit is performance limitation – not creation of a filter through which only the biggest R&D spenders can pass.

Does MotoGP need performance limitation? Evidence that it does is accumulating. At COTA, MotoGP bikes reach speeds higher than F1 cars. Several brake and tyre durability crises have occurred, and it has been learned that official MotoGP maximum speeds are short of the truth. This is an accident of their measuring system, which times the machines over a 30m distance placed near the end of the fastest straight. The teams themselves, and Brembo in particular, need better information, and it is available to them as continuous GPS data. It shows that official speeds may be as much as 15–20km/h short of actual maxima. Does anyone think 225mph means better racing than, say, 200mph?

Some argue that high top speeds are minor compared with rising corner speeds, which have been cited by Valentino Rossi and others as requiring wider gravel traps and threatening graver consequences when tyre grip is lost. This has caused a few strange individuals to urge that, when Michelin take over from Bridgestone as MotoGP's spec tyre supplier, they be required to un-develop their product and make bad tyres.

Many times in recent years, we have heard that a rider's

Top and top right: Duopoly. Yamaha and Honda waged their private war as usual, and cost controls made it even more expensive.

Above: The engineering details of Rossi's Yamaha have little bearing on road bikes, but racing does improve the breed.

Above right: Brembo's carbon disc brakes are more in keeping with aircraft than motorcycles.

Photos: Gold & Goose

bike has unexpectedly clicked into super-economy mode, killing its acceleration and, in some cases, costing finish positions. That is not racing. Bikes have not yet quit running while duelling for the lead, but they have quit on the cool-off lap. This shows only that so far the series has been lucky. Fuel tank capacity is carefully measured; the on-board computer totals all the fuel injected and continuously computes the fuel remaining. If the race cannot be finished at the present rate of consumption, the system switches to alternative fuel and ignition maps that use less fuel – and deliver more sluggish performance.

The first fuel reduction in 2005 was accommodated via a fuel map that, where possible, switched from the usual best-power mixture to a chemically correct mixture. As fuel reduction continued, engineers sought to understand where on each circuit engines could be leaned out with the least effect on lap time – a large and costly analysis task that had to be backed up by physical testing.

Normal spark ignition systems can fire mixtures from 10:1 (rich) to 18:1 (lean). Lean down more and misfiring occurs. This is because all fuel-air mixtures are inhomogeneous, consisting of richer and leaner zones. As the mixture is leaned, the leanest of those zones pass beyond the ignitable range. Mr Nakamoto told me that Honda are using very-high-energy ignition to extend the ignitable range, enabling them to run leaner yet. Because the heat release of lean mixtures is lower, the mixture burns more slowly, so ignition timing must be advanced to compensate – more electronics.

Is this useful research, enabling construction of more economical production vehicles? Lean burn is already receiving millions in auto-maker R&D every year. We know what our industry will do first if governments impose fuel consumption limits; they will reduce engine revolutions per mile.

If turning MotoGP into an economy run does not have unique research value, what is its purpose? One possibility is that it's just 'greenwashing' – wrapping the series in the mantle of environmentalism. But we already know that 90 per cent of the fuel consumed in a MotoGP weekend is used to bring spectators to the track. There's another possibility; Honda, acting through MSMA, may find the 20 litres rule agreeable because it forces their competitors to blow money on meeting it – money that otherwise could make their bikes faster. It's an indirect budget attack that hurts.

Now we find a conflict. The stated purpose of the engine endurance rule is to save the teams money, but the 'economy run' rule has the opposite effect, forcing them to spend more. That is not the only example. Dual-clutch transmissions excited interest a few years ago, mainly driven by Porsche. In a DCT, one clutch controls the odd ratios and another controls the evens. As the machine accelerates in first, the even clutch is disengaged, allowing second gear to be pre-selected. When the shift is desired, the even clutch engages and the odd clutch lifts, transferring the drive to second gear. Conventional shift delay, caused by having to pass through a neutral between gears, does not exist, and the shift is 'soft', with minimum impact.

DCTs were banned in MotoGP, presumably to cut costs, but transmissions were not included in the engine endurance rule. This allowed Honda to develop its seamless-shift transmission, which accomplishes the same task as a DCT, but has all of its gear selection mechanism inside one of the two gearbox shafts. This requires that the parts be small, and

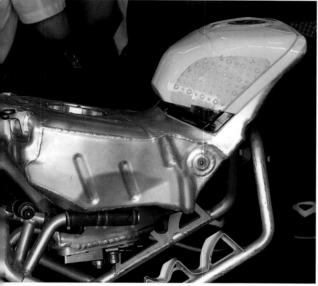

their relative delicacy leads to frequent replacement by specialised personnel under eyes-only conditions. A team can lease one for 400,000 euros per annum.

Another curious conflict exists in MotoGP between the 20 litres fuel allowance and the present fuel pressure limit of 10 bar (147psi). Direct cylinder fuel injection (DFI or GDI), which requires more pressure than this, is rapidly being adopted to improve the fuel economy of production automobiles. Why not encourage its use in MotoGP, therefore, as part of the emphasis on greater fuel economy?

A number of years ago, I was told by distinguished Yamaha engineer Masao Furusawa (now retired) that GDI could not operate at the high rpm of MotoGP, and certainly not at so low a fuel pressure. Yet now we find that use of GDI has been made mandatory in Formula One, along with a much higher fuel pressure limit of 500 bar (7,350psi). It must be noted that F1 now has a 15,000rpm rev limit, so GDI's rpm ceiling must have been raised. MotoGP engines still rev a bit higher than this, but not by much. Why turn MotoGP into a fuel economy run, yet deny it the use of a major fuel saving technology?

Regulations of this kind, operating at cross-purposes, are characteristic of a reactive style of rules making, with no consistent aims. Most sanctioning bodies work in this way, shoring up their rules with one emergency decree after another. Small wonder that so many are inconsistent. Such rules may be well intended, but the R&D to comply is very expensive, every such change giving further advantage to R&D-capable teams.

Formula One has operated in this way until recently, but today that series has solidly aligned itself with a major trend in the motor industry – to focus on producing fuel saving hybrid power trains rather than gambling on rapid, nationally subsidised conversion to all-electric propulsion. F1 has adopted the major auto industry trend of engine-downsizing-plus-turbocharging, dropping from 2.4 litres down to the 1.6-litre displacement that powers so many new cars. It requires the recovery of braking energy for storage in an onboard battery for re-use in assisting acceleration. An engine exhaust turbine not only supercharges the engine, but also, by spinning a motor generator, charges the battery. The battery, in turn, can spin the turbo to give instant boost.

Sixty years ago, Mercedes-Benz's race team manager, Alfred Neubauer, wrote that Formula One had become so specialised that its engineering was irrelevant to production cars. Why has F1 chosen to change that now? The obvious reasons are twofold: to make F1 attractive to manufacturers, who can use what is learned in racing to improve their production hybrids; and to benefit from 'greenwashing'.

If we seek a similar way to make MotoGP more relevant to the problems of production motorcycles, we find that relevance has never been lost, even if rules have often been inconsistent. Explosive development of racing two-stroke power during 1972–2001 gave us the advanced chassis, suspension and tyres we now enjoy. Electronic control strategies, coming to us from aerospace via F1 and MotoGP, are now giving motorcyclists heightened control and safety.

These things are not a choice; they are the future – think of what the motorcycle will be in ten years, or 20. Racing at its best embraces and develops technologies. MotoGP cannot become a glorified vintage series. Shortsighted or inconsistent rules may muddle the future for a time, but they can't stop the sun from coming up tomorrow.

Above: Control Bridgestones were introduced to stop the escalating costs of a tyre war.

Above left: Factory Honda fuel tank – just 20 litres in 2014.

Top: COTA track from the tower: MotoGP bikes achieve a higher top speed there than F1 cars.

Photos: Gold & Goose

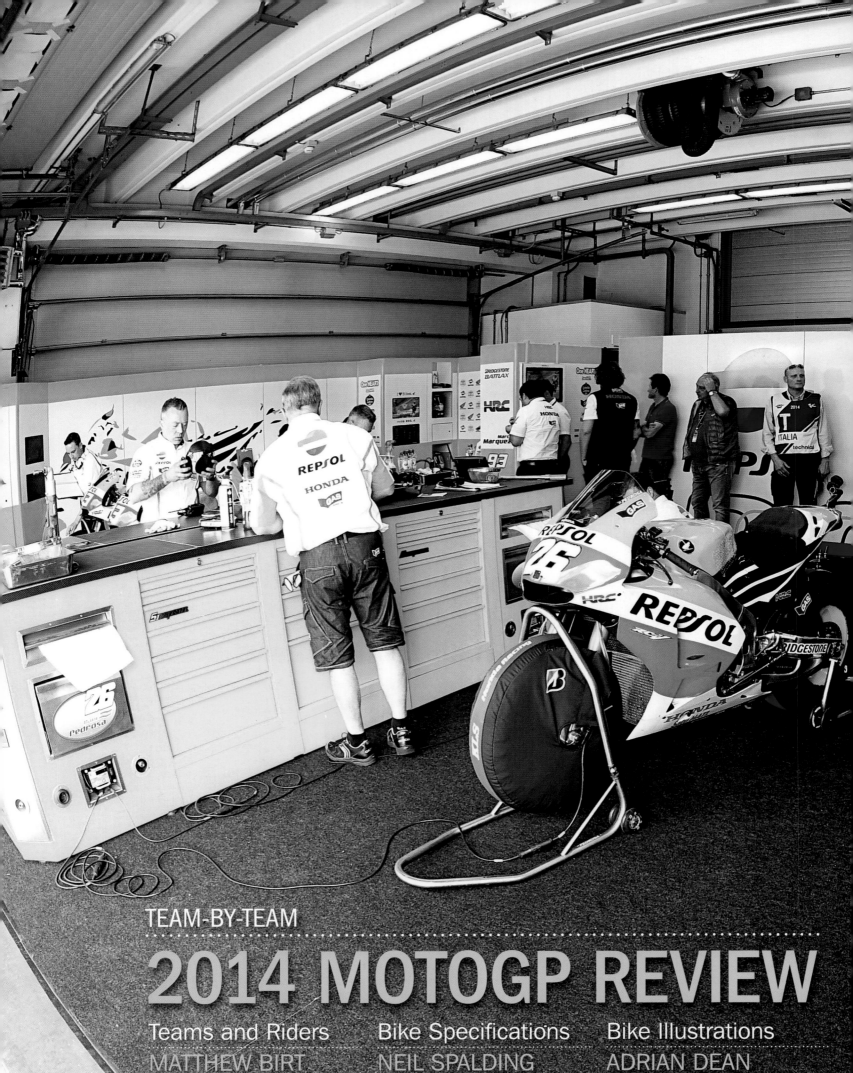

TEAM-BY-TEAM

2014 MOTOGP REVIEW

Teams and Riders · · · · · Bike Specifications · · · · · Bike Illustrations

MATTHEW BIRT · · · · · NEIL SPALDING · · · · · ADRIAN DEAN

REPSOL HONDA TEAM

TEAM STAFF

Shuhei NAKAMOTO: HRC Executive Vice-President
Livio SUPPO: Team Principal
Toshiyuki YAMAJI: Assistant Team Principal
Takeo YOKOYAMA: Technical Director
Teruaki MATSUBARA: HRC Engineer
Yukihide AKITSU: HRC Engineer
Tetsuhiro KUWATA: HRC Engineer
Takeshi MATSUMOTO: HRC Engineer
Roger VAN DER BORGHT: Co-ordinator
Katsura SHIBASAKI: Spare Parts Control
Rhys EDWARDS: Communication & Marketing Manager
Norihiko KATO: PR & Marketing
Vanessa GUERRA: PR & Marketing

MARC MARQUEZ PIT CREW

Santi HERNANDEZ: Race Engineer
Christophe LINAN: Chief Mechanic
Mechanics: Roberto CLERICI, Andrea BRUNETTI,
Jordi CASTELLA, Javier ORTIZ
Carlo LUZZI: Electronics Engineer
Gerold BUCHER: Data Engineer
Andy DAWSON: Ohlins engineer

DANI PEDROSA PIT CREW

Mike LEITNER: Chief Engineer
Christophe LEONCE: Chief Mechanic
Mechanics: Mark BARNETT (Engine Technician),
Emanuel BUCHNER, Masashi OGO, John EYRE
Jose Manuel ALLENDE: Data Analyst
Ramon AURIN: Data Engineer
Paul TREVATHAN: Ohlins Engineer
Chris HILLIAR: Alpinestars

DANI PEDROSA
Born: 29 September, 1985 – Sabadell, Spain
GP Starts: 229 (151 MotoGP, 32 250cc, 46 125cc)
GP Wins: 49 (26 MotoGP, 15 250cc, 8 125cc)
World Championships: 3 (2 250cc, 1 125cc)

MARC MARQUEZ
Born: 17 February, 1993 – Cervera, Spain
GP Starts: 114 (36 MotoGP, 32 Moto2, 46 125cc)
GP Wins: 43 (17 MotoGP, 16 Moto2, 10 125cc)
World Championships: 4 (2 MotoGP, 1 Moto2, 1 125cc)

Photos: Gold & Goose

WHEN Marc Marquez redefined expectations of rookie riders by restoring Honda to a position of MotoGP supremacy in 2013, he did so courtesy of a nail-biting final-round shootout in Valencia. In 2014, Honda and Marquez's domination was so emphatic that he successfully defended the title with three races to spare, becoming the first Honda rider to capture the crown at Honda's own track, the Twin Ring Motegi.

It could have been an earlier triumph had he not thrown caution to the wind in the latter stages of a season where, at one point, he had looked invincible.

The year had started in painful fashion, however, when he broke his right leg in a dirt-bike training acci-

dent in Spain, just days after dominating the opening winter test at Sepang. He missed subsequent tests back in Sepang and at Phillip Island, but then just as he had done in 2013, he began breaking records almost every time he left the pits.

He decimated the field in the first ten races, showing his repertoire of skills by winning close last-lap battles, dominating from start to finish, winning a flag-to-flag race in Assen and even taking victory from the pit lane in Germany.

For his first season in MotoGP, HRC had strongly resisted Marquez's attempts to bring with him the crew with whom he had formed a strong bond in the 125cc

HONDA RC213V - Repsol

Sponsors and Technical Suppliers: Repsol • One Heart • Estrella Galicia 0.0 • Gas • Red Bull • Bridgestone • GEOX Respira • NGK Spark Plugs • RK Chains • Shindengen Snap-on • Termignoni • Yuasa • Yutaka

Engine: 1000cc, 90-degree V4, 360-degree crank, pneumatic valve springs. *Power:* More than 260ps up to 17,000rpm

Ancillaries: HRC electronics, ride-by-wire throttle and fuel injection system with torducter; NGK sparking plugs *Lubrication:* Repsol *Fuel:* 20 litres

Transmission: Gear primary drive, multi-plate dry slipper clutch, six-speed seamless-shift cassette-style gearbox; RK chain

Suspension: Front, Ohlins TRSP25 48mm 'Through-Rod' forks • Rear, TRSP44 gas shock with linkage

Wheels: 16.5in Marchesini, front and rear *Tyres:* Bridgestone

Brakes: Front, Brembo carbon-carbon 320mm (340mm occasionally) • Rear, Yutaka steel 218mm

and Moto2 classes. HRC could hardly say no when the same request was made for 2014.

Crew chief Santi Hernandez and mechanic Carlos Linan were the two Marquez had been allowed to bring from Moto2 in 2013, and both continued. Carlo Luzzi was also retained as electronics engineer, but he was already in the squad when Marquez arrived and so highly rated that his place was non-negotiable.

Most of Marquez's 2013 crew were stalwarts of Casey Stoner, but Bruno Leoni, Giulio Nava and Filippo Brunetti were all replaced; only Andrea Brunetti and Roberto Clerici survived from the Stoner era.

In came Jordi Castella and Javi Ortiz, while Gerold Buchner took over as data engineer. Ex-125cc world champion Emilio Alzamora, Marquez's long-serving mentor and manager, oversaw the entire operation.

Marquez's first defeat was in Brno, where he slumped to fourth, his downfall largely due to a failing rear tyre rather than anything of his own making.

He returned to winning with a clinical late dismantling of arch-rival Lorenzo at Silverstone, before embarking on the worst barren run of his MotoGP career.

Marquez was in such a commanding position of authority in the rankings that he could afford the mistakes that ensued, and just as he'd torn up the record books, he started to tear up plenty of bodywork.

He crashed in pursuit of Valentino Rossi in Misano. Then he was leading at Motorland Aragon until a gamble to stay on slick tyres as rain battered the Spanish venue backfired spectacularly.

He clinched the title with a second place in Japan, but then flung himself into the Phillip Island undergrowth while controlling a 4.1s lead. He returned to winning ways in scorching heat in Sepang from a 13th pole position that became a new record in a season. That win also equalled Mick Doohan's record of 12 in a season, set in 1997, then he beat it with number 13

It came as no surprise, after Marquez had won the opening four races from pole position, that HRC was keen to retain him on a new two-year deal. HRC Vice-President Shuhei Nakamoto and Team Principal Livio Suppo were more than aware of his value, both on and off the track, and he was signed to a new contract just in advance of the fifth round at Le Mans.

Honda's title sponsors were also going nowhere. Backers of the official HRC squad since 1995, Repsol committed to a further three years, until the end of 2017, in a deal confirmed in mid-July.

Takeo Yokoyama continued in his role as technical director, with former RC211V and RC213V project leader Shinichi Kokubu charged with Honda's bid to end the KTM domination of the Moto3 class.

Yokoyama's latest RC213V dominated, with 14 wins and ten more podiums at the end of a season in which HRC took the triple crown of rider, team and constructor titles for the second year in succession.

But where would HRC be without Marquez's mercurial talent? Dani Pedrosa was back for a ninth season in an HRC hot seat, but 2014 was another year in which racing's biggest prize evaded his grasp.

Pedrosa's area of the Repsol garage was missing one key element: his mentor and manager, Alberto Puig, was no longer a permanent presence at his side. Although Puig continued as Pedrosa's manager, he had taken a prominent role in the new Shell Advance Asia Talent Cup, a Dorna initiative aimed at giving young talent in Asia and Australasia an opportunity to move into world championship competition.

Going it alone had little impact on Pedrosa's fortunes, however, and he won just once, in Brno. Six times he finished off the podium in the opening 15 races, before his fight to take second place in the rankings from Yamaha rivals Valentino Rossi and Jorge Lorenzo crumbled in Australia and Malaysia.

He was the innocent victim of a rash move by Iannone at Phillip Island. Then his quest for a third straight win in Sepang was ended by not one, but two crashes in the gruelling heat.

By that stage of the season, ill feeling and resentment had crept into the Pedrosa camp after he had controversially axed long-serving mechanics Mark Barnett and Christophe Leonce. Pedro Calvet, who spent 2014 with Cal Crutchlow at Ducati, and Denis Pazzaglini, who worked with Nicky Hayden in the Drive

M7 Aspar outfit, will replace the pair.

Pedrosa's decision didn't sit well with crew chief Mike Leitner. The Austrian had worked with him since 2004, and after Pedrosa had signed a new two-year deal to stay with HRC in early July, Leitner was offered a new contract for the same length of time. But in a move that shocked even Pedrosa, he decided to quit, informing HRC of his decision at Phillip Island.

Coming so late in the season, that left Pedrosa in a quandary to find a replacement. Former Gresini Honda and factory Ducati crew chief Juan Martinez was linked with the post, but Pedrosa confirmed that his data engineer, Ramon Aurin, previously Andrea Dovizioso's crew chief during the Italian's spell with Repsol Honda (2009–11), would be promoted.

Above right: Livio Suppo remained a powerful presence.

Above far right: Shuhei Nakamoto, HRC Executive Vice-President, ran the show.

Right: Marquez in full elbow-skimming flow.

Top: Dominant again, the team poses after a third one-two in Germany.

Top right: Dani Pedrosa managed just a single victory in a somewhat disappointing 2014 campaign.

Photos: Gold & Goose

MOVISTAR YAMAHA MOTOGP

TEAM STAFF

Kouichi TSUJI: MotoGP Group Leader
Lin JARVIS: Managing Director, Yamaha Motor Racing
Massimo MEREGALLI: Team Director
Kouji TSUYA: Yamaha M1 Project Leader
Wilco ZEELENBERG: Team Manager
William FAVERO: Communications Manager
Matteo VITELLO: Marketing Co-ordinator
Alen BOLLINI/Alberto GOMEZ: Press Officers
Mark CANELLA: Team Co-ordinator
Takehiro SUZUKI: Parts Co-ordinator

JORGE LORENZO PIT CREW

Ramon FORCADA: Crew Chief
Mechanics: Javier ULLATE, Jurij PELLEGRINI, Ian GIL-
PIN, Juan LLANSA HERNANDEZ

Takashi MORIYAMA: Yamaha Engineer
Davide MARELLI: Data Engineer

VALENTINO ROSSI PIT CREW

Sylvano GALBUSERA: Crew Chief
Mechanics: Alex BRIGGS, Bernard ANSIAU,
Brent STEVENS, Gary COLEMAN

Hiroya ATSUMI: Yamaha Engineer
Matteo FLAMIGNI: Data Technician

JORGE LORENZO
Born: 4 May, 1987 – Palma de Mallorca, Spain
GP Starts: 214 (120 MotoGP, 48 250cc, 46 125cc)
GP Wins: 54 (33 MotoGP, 17 250cc, 4 125cc)
World Championships: 4 (2 MotoGP, 2 250cc)

VALENTINO ROSSI
Born: 16 February, 1979 – Urbino, Italy
GP Starts: 312 (252 MotoGP/500cc, 30 250cc, 30 125cc)
GP Wins: 108 (82 MotoGP/500cc, 14 250cc, 12 125cc)
World Championships: 9 (6 MotoGP, 1 500cc, 1 250cc, 1 125cc)

THERE were two very distinct differences between the official factory Yamaha team that suffered nail-biting last-round defeat to rivals Honda in 2013 and the one that arrived to begin a renewed attack in 2014.

Firstly, Yamaha had secured a title sponsor for the first time since Fiat terminated its four-year association at the end of 2010, which coincided with Valentino Rossi's defection to Ducati. Spain's telecommunications giant Movistar had come on board in a five-year agreement, marking a welcome return to motorcycle racing for its parent company, Telefonica, which had a rich history of sponsorship with past projects associ-

ated with the likes of Dani Pedrosa, Casey Stoner, Sete Gibernau and Marco Melandri, to name just a few.

Just as BT had done in the UK, Movistar had created its own digital TV platform, but its deal with Dorna meant that the Spanish audience would have to pay to see all 18 races live. The deal with Yamaha was clearly engineered to push subscriptions, much in the same way that Sky in Italy had done with Rossi, by bank-rolling a big new Moto3 project under the nine-times champion's management, after taking over the Italian broadcast rights from Mediaset for 2014.

Rossi was also a principal figure in the second strik-

YAMAHA M1

Sponsors and Technical Suppliers: Movistar • Eneos • Semakin Di Depan • Monster • Yamalube • Eurasian Bank • FIAT • Suissegas • TW Steel • Akrapovic • Alpinestars • NH Hotels • Bridgestone • Magneti Marelli • Beta • BMC Air Filters • NGK Spark Plugs • DID • 2D • Exedy • Capit • Racing Boy

Engine: 1000cc, across-the-frame in-line 4; reverse-rotating cross-plane crankshaft, DOHC, 4 valves per cylinder, Pneumatic Valve Return System
    Power: Around 255bhp at approx. 16,500rpm

Ancillaries: Magneti Marelli electronics, NGK sparking plugs, full electronic ride-by-wire   *Lubrication:* Yamalube   *Fuel:* 20 litres

Transmission: Gear primary drive, multi-plate dry slipper clutch, six-speed seamless-shift cassette-style gearbox; DID chain

Suspension: Front, Ohlins TRSP25 48mm 'Through-Rod' forks • Rear, Ohlins TRSP44 shock with linkage   *Wheels:* 16.5in MFR, front and rear   *Tyres:* Bridgestone

Brakes: Front, Brembo carbon-carbon 320mm (340mm from Mugello onward) • Rear, Yamaha steel

KATSUYUKI NAKASUGA

Born: 9 August, 1981 – Shizuoka, Japan

GP Starts: 8 (5 MotoGP/500cc, 3 250cc)

ing change to Yamaha's garage. When his MotoGP career had begun in 2000, it did so with legendary Australian crew chief Jerry Burgess at his side. This had always been non-negotiable. As long as Rossi raced, Burgess would be his crew chief, and he followed him from Honda to Yamaha, to Ducati and back to Yamaha.

So when Rossi decided to fire Burgess at the final race of 2013 in Valencia, the paddock was aghast. Even worse, his ruthless plan had been leaked to the media before he had communicated it to Burgess, forcing Yamaha to host an awkward press conference.

Caught in the storm was Silvano Galbusera, who had the unenviable task of replacing Burgess. Previously an influential figure in Yamaha's World Superbike activity, he had no MotoGP experience, but had been handpicked by Rossi to inject some fresh motivation into the 35-year-old's 15th premier-class season.

Rossi's hyped return to Yamaha, after two years in the doldrums with Ducati, had been somewhat underwhelming, yet the 2014 season would vindicate his decision, as he delivered a series of inspired age-defying performances.

He was a podium threat in almost every race, and any fear that his new role as mentor to emerging young talents in his VR46 Academy, or Moto3 management role with Sky squad, would pose a possible distraction proved unfounded.

And any fear that Galbusera would find it difficult to mesh with a crew that was fiercely loyal to Burgess was also quickly dispelled.

Burgess had been sacrificed, but Alex Briggs, Brent Stevens, Bernard Ansiau and Gary Coleman all remained as mechanics, while Matteo Flamigni continued as data engineer. Hiroya Atsumi was also in place again as YMC engineer, serving as Rossi's direct line of communication between the garage and the factory in Japan.

Rossi's return to prominence won him the new two-year deal he'd craved, which was confirmed officially in early July.

Eventually he scored 13 top-three finishes, the highlights being a magnificent home victory in Misano and a sixth win at Phillip Island. He eventually beat Jorge Lorenzo for second position in the overall rankings after taking second the final race in Valencia.

Rossi certainly exceeded expectations, and Yamaha's management had no qualms in admitting that.

Masahiko Nakajima was again Yamaha Motor Racing president, but other projects were clearly occupying his time, as he became a less-public figure in the paddock. Yamaha's highest-profile presence on the front line in the paddock was MotoGP Group Leader Kouichi Tsuji, while Lin Jarvis was very much the public face of the operation in his role as Yamaha Motor Racing Managing Director.

Oncer again, responsibility for the YZR-M1 fell to

Project Leader Kouji Tsuya, with Massimo Meregalli Team Director and Wilco Zeelenberg Team Manager.

Zeelenberg, though, was predominantly entrenched on Lorenzo's side of the garage, despite the title.

If Rossi surpassed expectations, Lorenzo fell well short of delivering the widely anticipated big threat to Marc Marquez. With five wins in the last seven races of 2013, Lorenzo had missed out on a third premier-class crown by a mere four points, after he lost a dramatic last race in a winner-takes-all shootout with new nemesis Marquez.

Within the first two races of 2014, Lorenzo's challenge had all but evaporated. He crashed out of the lead on the first lap in Qatar and then committed one of the most embarrassing jump-starts witnessed at the Circuit of the Americas.

The Spaniard didn't win until round 14 at Motorland Aragon, and that came by virtue of Marquez and Pedrosa's brave and ultimately foolish decision to try to finish the flag-to-flag race using slick tyres on a sodden track.

He was back to his brilliant best with a masterful win at Twin Ring Motegi, and eventually he closed the season with nine successive podiums.

Like Rossi's, Lorenzo's crew had a different look to it in 2014. Ramon Forcada was Lorenzo's crew chief, as he had been since the Spaniard arrived in MotoGP in 2008, but it was under him that a reshuffle had been implemented.

Ian Gilpin and Jurij Pellegrini were back in the fold after both mechanics had impressed Yamaha when they worked with Ben Spies in the factory team in 2011 and '12.

As 2014 progressed, there were rumblings that Lorenzo was contemplating following the trend set by Rossi and wielding the axe on Forcada. This speculation had quickly followed Lorenzo's decision to commit his future to Yamaha in a new two-year contract announced in Indianapolis.

Forcada had been linked with a crew chief role for Maverick Vinales at Suzuki, and Lorenzo had spoken to Casey Stoner's ex-crew chief, Cristian Gabarrini, who was overseeing Honda's new production RCV1000R racer in 2014.

After much deliberation, a big team summit immediately after Silverstone's British Grand Prix, at the end of August, led to Forcada and Lorenzo continuing their relationship until the end of 2016.

Above: New crew chief Silvano Galbusera played a key role in the reinvention of Rossi.

Above right: Ramon Forcada remained at the head of Lorenzo's crew.

Photos: Gold & Goose

Top: Rossi leads Lorenzo at Phillip Island: Yamaha's one-two-three finish was the first such since 2008.

Right: Lorenzo was finally back to dry-weather winning form at Motegi.

Photos: Yamaha Racing

DUCATI TEAM

TEAM STAFF

Luigi DALL'IGNA: Ducati Corse General Manager
Paolo CIABATTI: Ducati Corse Sports Director
Fabiano STERLACCHINI: Track Technical Co-ordinator
Riccardo SAVIN: Track Technical Co-ordinator
Francesco RAPISARDA: Communications Director
Julian THOMAS: Press Manager
Paola BRAIATO: Administration, Logistics and Hospitality
Mauro GRASSILLI: Sponsorship Manager
Silvio SANGALLI: Crew Co-ordinator
Davide BARALDINI: Warehouse and Components

ANDREA DOVIZIOSO PIT CREW

Christian PUPULIN: Crew Chief
Alberto GIRIBUOLA: Track Engineer
Michele PERIGINI: Chief Mechanic
Mechanics: Enrico SAMPERI, Fabio ROVELLI,
Mark ELDER, Massimo TOGNACCI
Gabriele CONTI: Electronics Engineer

CAL CRUTCHLOW PIT CREW

Daniele ROMAGNOLI: Crew Chief
Massimo BARTOLINI: Chief Mechanic
Mechanics: Davide MANFREDI, Massimo MIRANO,
Pedro CALVET CARALT, Lorenzo CANESTRARI,
Luca ROMANO
Jose Manuel CASEAUX: Electronics Engineer

ANDREA DOVIZIOSO
Born: 23 March, 1986 – Forli, Italy
GP Starts: 222 (124 MotoGP, 49 250cc, 49 125cc)
GP Wins: 10 (1 MotoGP, 4 250cc, 5 125cc)
World Championships: 1 125cc

CAL CRUTCHLOW
Born: 29 October, 1985 – Coventry, England
GP Starts: 69 MotoGP,
World Championships: 1 World Supersport

Photos: Gold & Goose

DUCATI failed to bring an end to a losing streak in MotoGP that stretched back to the days of Casey Stoner in 2010, but signs of a sleeping giant rumbling from its slumber were evident from the beginning of a promising 2014.

Stability has not been a word closely associated with Ducati's recent turbulent history, and 2014 heralded another new era for the Bologna factory, with highly respected engineer Gigi Dall'Igna head-hunted from Aprilia. He succeeded Bernhard Gobmeier, who appeared to lack the air of authority that Audi had perhaps envisaged was needed to steer Ducati out of

its slump when he was installed as Filippo Preziosi's replacement in 2013.

Dall'Igna was the third Ducati Corse general manager in as many years, and he is renowned for being a no-nonsense character, though the true impact of his influence cannot be judged until 2015, when he rolls out a brand-new Desmosedici design.

But he was the man chosen by Ducati CEO Claudio Domenicali to try to halt Ducati's sharp decline, and he immediately made waves when he declared Ducati's intention to race in the new Open class. A limit of five engines and no in-season development

DUCATI Desmosedici GP14.1

Sponsors and Technical Suppliers: Philip Morris (Marlboro) • TIM (Telecom Italia) • Shell Advance • Riello UPS • Diadora • Akrapovic • Bridgestone • Bosch • Guabello Lampo • MAN • EMC² • Trenkwalder • Tudor • Capit • CM Composit • DID • FIAMM • Magneti Marelli • NGK • SKF • USAG • VAR • ZF

Engine: 1000cc, 90-degree V4; irregular-fire crank, DOHC, 4 valves per cylinder, Desmodromic valve gear, variable-length inlet tracts
    Power: Around 270bhp, revs up to 18,000rpm

Ancillaries: Magneti Marelli electronics, NGK sparking plugs, full electronic ride-by-wire   *Lubrication:* Shell Advance *Fuel:* 22 litres

Transmission: Cassette Xtrac seamless-shift gearbox

Suspension: Front, Ohlins TRSP25 48mm 'Through-Rod' forks • Rear, Ohlins TRSP44 shock with linkage

Wheels: 16.5in Marchesini, front and rear *Tyres:* Bridgestone *Brakes:* Front, Brembo carbon-carbon 320mm (340mm from Mugello onward) • Rear, steel 200mm

MICHELE PIRRO

Born: 5 July, 1986 – San Giovanni Rotondo, Italy

GP Starts: 81 (34 MotoGP, 18 Moto2, 29 125cc)

GP Wins: 1 Moto2

Right: Gigi Dall'Igna, poached from Aprilia, made for an effective new broom.

Far right: Davide Tardozzi also boosted the rejigged team management.

Below: Crutchlow, his father Dek (*left*) and joyful crew celebrate his Aragon podium.

Below right: Dovizioso's second year at Ducati was exemplary.

Photos: Gold & Goose

was too restrictive for Dall'Igna to attempt to engineer a Ducati revival, whereas the seven extra engines and unlimited engine development allowed in the Open class were considered essential to help the Desmosedici evolve and improve.

A late compromise saw Ducati slip into both Factory and Open classes. Without a win in the previous season, it could stay as a Factory entry and use its own sophisticated electronics, but benefit from the other Open-class concessions, like extra fuel, soft tyres and more engines.

Those concessions were subject to change based on results, but immediately it gave Dall'Igna room to manoeuvre. Upgrades like the GP14.2, which was first seen at Motorland Aragon, would not have been possible had Ducati stayed as a Factory entry with Honda and Yamaha.

Working directly below Dall'Igna was Sporting Director Paolo Ciabatti, while Davide Tardozzi, a man who had enjoyed incredible success with Ducati in World Superbikes, was drafted in as Team Supervisor. It was a similar role to the one carried out by Vittoriano Guareschi before he embarked on a short-lived management post in Valentino Rossi's new VR46 Moto3 squad.

Fabiano Sterlacchini and Riccardo Savin helped Dall'Igna immensely in their roles as Track Technical Co-ordinators, but Ducati's renaissance owed greatly to the experience and skill of Andrea Dovizioso. He immediately struck up a close relationship with Dall'Igna, and after struggling to claim just two top-six finishes in a torrid debut Desmosedici year in 2013, he was revitalised.

Dovizioso worked once again with crew chief Christian Pupulin, and a key element of the garage remained Gabriele Conti, a trusted electronics engineer

who had worked with Casey Stoner and Valentino Rossi during their time with Ducati.

Eleven top six finishes, which included brilliant podiums in Austin and Assen, vindicated Dall'Igna's decision to capitalise on the in-season development available, and Dovizioso was only beaten by elite quartet Marc Marquez, Rossi, Jorge Lorenzo and Dani Pedrosa in the final rankings.

Dovizioso also scored Ducati's first pole position in four years in Japan, and it was no surprise that Suzuki were keen to utilise his methodical approach and vast experience to lead its premier-class return in 2015.

Tangible signs of improvement and a loyalty to Dall'Igna convinced Dovizioso to sign a new two-year deal, however, which was made official during the World Ducati Week celebrations in Misano in July.

On the other side of the garage, Briton Cal Crutchlow was the latest high-profile rider to back himself to tame the fearsome reputation of the Desmosedici. His confidence was riding high after he'd been Britain's most successful rider since Barry Sheene, with four podiums and two pole positions in his final year with the Monster Yamaha Tech 3 squad.

He moved along with Italian crew chief Daniele Romagnoli, who had been with Crutchlow since he first entered MotoGP back in 2011.

It didn't take long for that confidence to be completely eroded, and by the end of the season Crutchlow had scored just three top six finishes. A heavy crash at the second race in Austin mangled his right hand so badly that he had to miss MotoGP's first visit to Argentina since 1999, while mechanical issues forced him out in Jerez, Catalunya and Sepang.

He crashed out in Mugello and Brno before enjoying a dramatic upturn in fortunes and speed in the final third of the campaign. He took a maiden Ducati

podium in the flag-to-flag race at Motorland Aragon and was on course for a sensational second place in Phillip Island when he crashed in the rapidly cooling conditions with just eight corners remaining.

By that stage of the season, Crutchlow was already heading for the exit door, after generating huge headlines in a typically frenetic silly season. He had inked a lucrative two-year deal with Ducati that included 2015. It was well known, though, that he had an early-release clause in his contract, and if invoked prior to 31st July, it allowed him the freedom to leave without incurring any penalties.

It all seemed academic, though, at World Ducati Week, when Crutchlow declared that he would honour the second year of his deal, despite rumours that he wanted out. At the same time, however, LCR Honda boss Lucio Cecchinello had secured a London-based title sponsor, and a whirlwind deal with Crutchlow was finalised. Within days of committing his future to Ducati at WDW, he was plotting 2015 on a factory-backed Honda RC213V, having invoked the escape clause.

Crutchlow had wanted to take Romagnoli with him to LCR, but it was a closed shop. The crew chief had a two-year contract with Ducati and he was slated to become Danilo Petrucci's crew chief at Pramac Ducati in 2015.

Crutchlow's crew will also be broken up for 2015, with something of a mass exodus from his side of the box. Electronics engineer Jose Manuel Caseaux landed a plum job as crew chief to Maverick Vinales at Suzuki, while mechanics Davide Manfredi and Massimo Mirano were also moving to work with the 2014 Moto2 Rookie of the Year on the new GSX-RR.

Pedro Calvet was signed to move to Repsol Honda with Dani Pedrosa.

MONSTER YAMAHA TECH 3

TEAM STAFF

Herve PONCHARAL: Team Manager
Gerard VALLEE: Team Co-ordinator
Laurence LASSERRE: Team Assistant
Eric REBMANN: Parts Manager
Eric LABORIE: Fuel/Tyres
Milena KOERNER: Press & Communications
Joeri RIEASSUW: Ohlins Suspension

POL ESPARGARO PIT CREW

Nicolas GOYON: Crew Chief
Mechanics: Julien LAJUNIE, Sebastien LETORT,
Xavier QUIEXALOS, Josian RUSTIQUE
Maxime REYSZ: Telemetry

BRADLEY SMITH PIT CREW

Guy COULON: Crew Chief
Mechanics: Laurent DUCLOYER, Jerome PONCHARAL,
Steve BLACKBURN
Andrew GRIFFITH: Telemetry

POL ESPARGARO
Born: 10 June, 1991 – Granollers, Spain
GP Starts: 140 (18 MotoGP, 51 Moto2, 71 125cc)
GP Wins: 10 Moto2; 5 125cc
World Championships: 1 Moto2

BRADLEY SMITH
Born: 28 November, 1990 – Oxford, England
GP Starts: 149 (36 MotoGP, 33 Moto2, 80 125cc)
GP Wins: 3 125cc

A PRE-SEASON flood, which caused widespread damage to its Bormes les Mimosas headquarters in the south of France, was the precursor to a year in which the Monster Yamaha Tech 3 team's impressive recent podium record dried up.

It seemed that for the first time since 2007, when it had raced Dunlop tyres, Herve Poncharal's team, in its 14th season as Yamaha's satellite squad, would fail to score a podium finish – until Bradley Smith grabbed third place in Philip Island.

After Colin Edwards, Ben Spies, Andrea Dovizioso and Cal Crutchlow had all been capable of putting the satellite YZR-M1 inside the top three, 2014 was very much a transition year for Poncharal's squad, which adopted the status of Yamaha 'junior team' more than ever before.

Poncharal has been keen to position his team as a feeder operation to Yamaha's official factory effort for some time. The prominent Frenchman, who continued in his role as President of the International Race Teams Association, is keen to nurture young talent in advance of a move to the factory operation.

The strategy has previous form: when Yamaha contracted Spies on a factory deal in 2010, but loaned

YAMAHA M1 – Tech 3

Sponsors and Technical Suppliers: Monster • DeWalt • Stanley • Antoniolupi • Facom • Bihr • Motul • Sakura • Capit Performance • Big Rock Holidays • Caffitaly LightTecht • Smeg • Roc de Calon • Rudy Project

Engine: 1000cc, across-the-frame in-line 4; reverse-rotating cross-plane crankshaft, DOHC, 4 valves per cylinder, Pneumatic Valve Return System
　　　Power: Around 255bhp at approx 16,200rpm

Ancillaries: Magneti Marelli electronics, NGK sparking plugs, full electronic ride-by-wire　*Lubrication:* Motul　*Fuel:* 20 litres

Transmission: Gear primary drive, multi-plate dry slipper clutch, six-speed constant-mesh floating-dog-ring cassette-style gearbox; DID chain

Suspension: Front, Ohlins TTxTR25 48mm forks • Rear, Ohlins TRSP44 shock with linkage

Wheels: 16.5in MFR, front and rear　*Tyres:* Bridgestone

Brakes: Front, Brembo carbon-carbon 320mm (340mm from Mugello) • Rear, Yamaha steel

him to Tech 3 for his rookie season to learn his craft before a promotion to the official factory team. The same policy was adopted in 2014 for highly-rated reigning Moto2 world champion Pol Espargaro. He had penned a two-year deal direct with Yamaha, but was installed as Bradley Smith's team-mate at Tech 3 for his rookie season.

Crutchlow's departure to Ducati's official factory squad had forced Poncharal to shuffle his crew, after the Briton had taken crew chief Daniele Romagnoli on his ill-fated switch to the Bologna brand.

Nicolas Goyon, Crutchlow's data engineer, who was also a pivotal figure in the Tech 3 Mistral 610 Moto2 project, was promoted to be Espargaro's crew chief. Taking his data role was Maxime Reysz, an internal promotion from the Tech 3 Moto2 project.

Espargaro was allowed to bring long-serving mechanic Xavier Queixalos with him, which meant no room for Briton Steve Blackburn, so he was integrated into Smith's crew.

Espargaro's first season mirrored that of many rookies finding their feet in the premier class, with the exception of record-breaking compatriot Marc Marquez. He recovered quickly from breaking his left collarbone on the final day of pre-season testing in Qatar to show blindingly fast speed on occasion. He often challenged his team-mate, but also made mistakes.

In the team's home race in Le Mans, he claimed a stunning second on the grid, and missed the podium in fourth by less than a second.

Espargaro never finished outside of the top 10, but never seriously threatened the podium again and Yamaha has demanded more consistency in future. He will remain a Tech 3 rider in 2015, having committed to stay for another season, though this was not in his career master-plan. He'd signed for Yamaha with the clear intention of impressing enough to replace Valentino Rossi in 2015 and join Jorge Lorenzo, but both of those riders signed new two-year contracts.

Locked out of the factory team for the foreseeable future, Espargaro declined to invoke a clause in his contract that would have permitted him to leave without penalty if Yamaha couldn't offer him a factory place for 2015.

British rider Smith was in his second season with Tech 3 and his crew remained the same, apart from the transfer of Blackburn. Tech 3 co-owner Guy Coulon continued as crew chief, with Andy Griffith a key figure as data engineer, and long-serving Tech 3 mechanics Laurent Ducloyer, Jerome Poncharal and Josian Rustique all staying put.

Under pressure to step up and fill the void left by Crutchlow, Smith started the season brilliantly. He was right in the podium hunt, after starting off the front row in the season-opener in Qatar, when he crashed out of contention late on. He was close to the rostrum again in Austin in fifth, but incredibly only two more top sixes followed as the season progressed – in Indianapolis and Motorland Aragon.

Indifferent results and the pressure of trying to secure a new deal for 2015 took its toll, culminating in an unforgettable weekend at Sachsenring, where a crash during the race took Smith's tally to five for the weekend!

While Smith struggled to recapture his early-season form, rumours gathered momentum that his prized YZR-M1 seat was up for grabs. It was no secret that Poncharal had spoken to rising Australian star Jack Miller and Jonas Folger, though he denied a bold claim by Moto3 title contender Alex Rins that he had rejected a formal Tech 3 offer.

After a summit between Yamaha, Tech 3 and Monster representatives in Indianapolis, it was decided to keep Smith, and his one-year extension was confirmed on the eve of the Brno round in the Czech Republic. Relieved of uncertainty, he resumed a steady progress, and in Australia he stayed on track to claim third, and wept with the emotion of finally grabbing that elusive podium place.

This season's struggles had little impact on the status of Tech 3 as the highest-profile non-factory outfit in MotoGP. That was highlighted at the beginning of the gruelling flyaway triple-header in October, when US energy drink supplier Monster Energy confirmed that it would remain as the team's naming rights sponsor. Monster has been the title backer of Poncharal's team since 2009, and its new agreement will see Tech 3 continue running the distinctive Monster 'M' claw for a further two years at least.

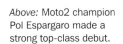

Above: Moto2 champion Pol Espargaro made a strong top-class debut.

Above right: Team principal Herve Poncharal.

Left: Hair today, gone tomorrow – Bradley Smith with renowned crew chief Guy Coulon.

Right: Smith's steadily growing strength was rewarded with a first-class podium at Phillip Island.

Photos: Gold & Goose

PRAMAC RACING

TEAM STAFF

Paolo CAMPINOTI: Team Principal

Francesco GUIDOTTI: Team Manager

Felix RODRIGUEZ: Team Co-ordinator

Lorenzo VENTURI: Press Officer

Francesco NAPOLI: Marketing and sponsorship

Alex GHINI: Hospitality and PR

Luciano BONCI: Warehouse and spare parts

ANDREA IANNONE PIT CREW

Marco RIGAMONTI: Track Engineer

Michele BUBBOLINI: Chief Mechanic

Mechanics: Cristian AIELLO, Edoardo CIFERRI

Simone FALCINI,

Guliano POLETTI: (tyres and fuel)

Tommaso PAGANO: Data Engineer

YONNY HERNANDEZ PIT CREW

Giacomo GUIDOTTI: Crew Chief

Nicola MANNA: Chief Mechanic

Mechanics: David GALLICO, Pedro RIVERA,

Francesco GALINDO

Dario MASSARIN: Data Engineer

ANDREA IANNONE

Born: 9 August, 1989 – Vasto, Italy

GP Starts: 161 (33 MotoGP, 51 Moto2, 77 125cc)

GP Wins: 12 (8 Moto2, 4 125cc)

YONNY HERNANDEZ

Born: 25 July, 1988 – Medellin, Colombia

GP Starts: 82 (51 MotoGP, 46 Moto2)

IN its 13th season in the MotoGP World Championship, the Italian Pramac Racing squad enjoyed something of a return to prominence after a long period in the doldrums.

The team, which had previously fielded the likes of Max Biaggi, Makoto Tamada, Alex Barros and Loris Capirossi, remained under the guidance of Team Principal Paolo Campinoti, who had maintained close ties with Ducati since Pramac's relationship with the Borgo Panigale factory had begun in 2005.

Francesco Guidotti, who had previously held key roles at Aprilia and KTM, was the public face of the project once again, as Team Manager.

Pramac began the 2014 campaign with the line-up that had finished the previous season: Andrea Iannone as the number one and Yonny Hernandez resigned after impressing in the last five races of 2013, when he had stood in for injured Texan Ben Spies.

Iannone was the team's flag bearer and again he worked with Marco Rigamonti as his track engineer, with Michele Bubbolini promoted from mechanic to chief mechanic for 2014.

Iannone had been derided after an underwhelming rookie season in MotoGP, during which he'd scored a best of eighth. Injury had a major impact on his performances, and when fit and healthy he excelled, showing the kind of raw speed that at times had made him an invincible force in the cut-throat Moto2 arena.

Ducati Desmosedici GP13 – Pramac

Sponsors and Technical Suppliers: Energy TI • Pramac • Shell Advance • Rifle • Beta • Regina • Bridgestone • Termorace • Speedfiber • Quantya
Birra Baladin • Bisetta Champagne • Maranello Cafe • Bwin • Diadora • Ma Fra • Cecchi • Blackzi • Flex

Engine: 1000cc, 90-degree L4; 360-degree crank, DOHC, 4 valves per cylinder, Desmodromic valve gear, variable-length inlet tracts
Power: Around 270bhp, revs up to 18,000rpm

Ancillaries: Magneti Marelli electronics, NGK sparking plugs, full electronic ride-by-wire *Lubrication:* Shell *Fuel:* 22 litres

Transmission: Xtrac seamless-shift cassette gearbox

Suspension: Front, Ohlins TRSP25 48mm forks • Rear, Ohlins TRSP44 shock with linkage

Wheels: 16.5in Marchesini, front and rear *Tyres:* Bridgestone *Brakes:* Front, Brembo carbon-carbon 320mm (340mm at Motegi) • Rear, steel 200mm

With rule concessions allowing Pramac to use softer Bridgestone tyres and 24 litres of fuel, Iannone claimed four front-row starts, which included second-place spots in Mugello and Misano.

Six times he finished inside the top six, with a best of fifth in Sachsenring and Brno, proving how much the Italian had improved on a Desmosedici GP14, already a step up from the unforgiving GP13 he'd toiled on the previous year.

Ducati was certainly more than aware of Iannone's potential, and his Desmosedici was a full factory version, identical to those of Andrea Dovizioso and Cal Crutchlow. And in a year of almost constant evolution from new Ducati technical guru Gigi Dall'Igna, whenever Dovizioso received an upgrade, Iannone did, too.

He was faster than tenth overall in the rankings suggested, and frequently at the start of several races he was a menace inside the top five. But a promising campaign fell away in the final phase of the season. He was in podium contention early on at Motorland Aragon when he lost control on slippery artificial grass in wet conditions and crashed heavily.

He was in a big group scrapping it out for fourth in Australia when he crashed after clipping the back of Dani Pedrosa's Repsol Honda. And he didn't even make the grid in Sepang after a left arm injury forced him to withdraw following a tangle with Marquez in Friday's second practice.

For the first half of the season, it looked certain that Iannone would remain a Pramac rider in 2015, but with full factory support and a factory contract again. But he spoke to Suzuki and to LCR Honda, and made it clear to Ducati that he wanted a move to the works team, as replacement for either Dovizioso or Crutchlow, both of whom had attracted interest from rival brands.

At the World Ducati Week extravaganza at Misano in mid-July, his aspirations for a factory Desmosedici ride seemed hopeless, but within days Crutchlow unexpectedly quit the 2015 factory team, and just as suddenly Ducati promoted Iannone into it.

His unexpected departure gave Pramac's management a major headache. Most of the other attractive options were already unavailable by the time he was no longer the team's future figurehead.

Stefan Bradl was one, and he certainly would have pleased Ducati's owners, Audi, given his German passport, but he was already on his way to Forward Racing. French Moto2 rider Johann Zarco and World Superbike star Loris Baz were also mentioned, and would have satisfied Dorna and the promoter of the Le Mans MotoGP race, who were eager to have a big-name French rider on the grid. Eugene Laverty, who had had a close relationship with Guidotti and Dall'Igna during his two-year spell in Aprilia's World Superbike squad, spoke at length with Pramac.

The seat was kept open for Scott Redding for a month while his future remained uncertain. It wasn't until early October that Pramac signed Italian Danilo Petrucci as Iannone's replacement.

With Ducati preparing to roll out a radical new GP15 machine for the new season, human and financial resources will limit the supply of the new concept to just Dovizioso and Iannone. Petrucci will race the GP14, used by the factory until Motorland Aragon, using the factory software.

Colombian Hernandez more than justified his selection as the second rider with a brilliantly consistent campaign on a year-old Desmosedici that most had written off as a no-hoper. It wasn't until the eighth round at Assen that Hernandez missed the points on the unruly GP13, and his best ever result came in the penultimate round in Malaysia, where he took a super seventh to claim a third top 10.

Giacomo Guidotti worked as his crew chief, while Nicola Manna, who was chief mechanic for Ben Spies, remained in the same role.

Hernandez was one of the few riders not on the market during the summer, having a two-year deal in place. He will ride a GP14.2 Desmosedici, which is the specification Dovizioso and Iannone raced after Misano in 2014, again with factory software.

Above: Andrea Iannone was fast and fearless, earning promotion to the factory squad for 2015.

Left: Team principal Paolo Campinoti (*right*) exchanges views with Forward Racing's Cuzari.

Top: Iannone celebrates a third front-row start in four races at Aragon.

Top left: Yonny Hernandez made friends with the wayward GP13 Ducati.

Photos: Gold & Goose

LCR HONDA MOTOGP

TEAM STAFF

Lucio CECCHINELLO: Team Owner and Manager
Martine FELLONI: Administration and Legal
Oscar HARO: Public Relations
Elisa PAVAN: Press Officer

STEFAN BRADL PIT CREW

Christophe BOURGIGNON: Chief Engineer
Mechanics: Joan CASAS, Xavier CASANOVAS,
Chris RICHARDSON
Brian HARDEN: Telemetry
Makoto NAGAYAMA/Yuki KIKUCHI: HRC Engineer
Ugo GELMI: Tyres
Masao AZUMA: Bridgestone Technician
Paul TREVATHAN: Ohlins Technician

STEFAN BRADL

Born: 29 November, 1989 – Augsberg, Germany
GP Starts: 139 (52 MotoGP, 33 Moto2, 54 125cc)
GP Wins: 7 (5 Moto2, 2 125cc)
World Championships: 1 Moto2

LUCIO CHECHINELLO'S LCR Honda squad's ninth season was one of under-achievement. Third-year rider Stefan Bradl had an HRC deal and virtually a full factory bike, but the 2011 Moto2 world champion couldn't capitalise on the golden opportunity.

The pit crew had been constant since 2008: Christophe Bourgignon as crew chief and Brian Harden on data recording; Xavier Casanovas, Joan Casas, Chris Richardson and Ugo Gelmi as mechanics, and Oscar Haro as team co-ordinator.

Bradl led the Qatar opener before crashing out, bagged a front-row start in Austin before claiming fourth, and was inside the top five in Argentina. After that, results slumped, testing Honda's patience to breaking point.

If Cecchinello were to keep Bradl, technical and financial input from HRC would be withdrawn. That left him hunting a major sponsor. Salvation came from London-based online trading and foreign-exchange company CWM FX, who sponsored the team at three races, and were confirmed as title sponsors for 2015.

By then, however, Bradl had agreed a switch to Forward Racing. Ironically, after signing up, twice he caused crashes that wiped out the rider he would replace, Aleix Espargaro.

Cecchinello approached Aleix Espargaro, but he was committed to Suzuki, while Iannone was tied by an option to Ducati. Then, with a British sponsor, he swooped on Cal Crutchlow.

After whirlwind negotiations, Crutchlow invoked an escape clause in his Ducati contract and was confirmed on a factory RC213V deal at the end of the summer hiatus. And for the first time, Cecchinello will realise a long-term ambition for a two-rider effort in 2015, although not even he could have envisaged the magnitude of the deal that unfolded.

Rising Australian Jack Miller shot to prominence in 2014 with a series of aggressive and daring Moto3 performances, which caught the attention of HRC Vice-President Shuhei Nakamoto.

Negotiations began around Le Mans, the move driven by HRC, with Cecchinello not part of the process at all. Miller wriggled out of a two-year 'pre-contract' Moto2 agreement with Marc VDS and vaulted straight from the smallest to the biggest class. Unprecedented in HRC history, he was given a three-year deal, during the first two years of which he will race for Cecchinello.

HRC also handpicked the majority of Miller's crew, to be led by the sought-after Cristian Gabarrini, who masterminded Stoner's two world title triumphs.

HONDA RCV213V – LCR

Sponsors and Technical Suppliers: Givi • Elf • Linear • Unibat • Rizoma • Red Bull • Parts Europe • Progrip • Planet Win 365 • PBR • Arrow
Beta • OZ Racing • Ohlins • RK • Bridgestone

Engine: 1000cc, 90-degree V4; 360-degree crank, pneumatic valve springs *Power:* More than 260ps

Ancillaries: HRC electronics, ride-by-wire throttle and fuel injection system, Denso sparking plugs *Fuel:* 20 litres

Transmission: Gear primary drive, multi-plate dry slipper clutch, six-speed seamless-shift constant-mesh cassette-style gearbox, RK chain

Suspension: Front, Ohlins TRSP25 48mm forks • Rear, Ohlins TRSP44 shock with linkage

Wheels: 16.5in OZ Racing, front and rear *Tyres:* Bridgestone

Brakes: Front, Nissin/Brembo carbon-carbon 320mm and 340mm • Rear, HRC steel 218mm

GO&FUN HONDA GRESINI

TEAM STAFF

Fausto GRESINI: Team Manager
Carlo MERLINI: Marketing Manager
Mattia RICCI: Marketing
Alberto CANI: Press and Media Relations
Elisa GIACON: Web and Social Media
Beppe FERRARIO: Guests Co-ordinator
Fulvia CASTELLI: Logistics

ALVARO BAUTISTA PIT CREW

Antonio JIMENEZ: Chief Mechanic
Mechanics: Federico VICINO, Alberto PRESUTTI
Gianpetro CANETTI
Elvio DEGANELLO: Telemetry

FAUSTO GRESINI started his 18th season with Honda in 2014, and few would have wagered that the long-standing and successful collaboration would cease at the conclusion of the campaign.

Gresini continued with his policy of fielding one factory RC213V and one bike for the grid-filling Open category. For the third season in succession, Spaniard Alvaro Bautista rode the team's prototype RC213V, and again he worked with crew chief Antonio Jimenez, with Elvio Deganello in charge of telemetry once more.

Bautista had established himself as a consistent top-six finisher in the second half of 2013, and optimism was high that the ex-125GP world champion would continue to edge closer to threatening the dominance of the official factory outfits.

ALVARO BAUTISTA

Born: 21 November, 1984 – Talavera de La Reina, Spain
GP Starts: 202 (86 MotoGP, 49 250cc, 67 125cc)
GP Wins: 16 (8 250cc, 8 125cc)
World Championships: 1 125cc

Instead he had a hellish season. A promising first race, in which he had started from second on the grid, ended with him crashing out of podium contention. He also crashed in the next two races, and he was so deflated after his early exit in Argentina that he was in tears in the garage.

Despite his tattered confidence, Bautista picked his morale off the floor to claim a surprise third in Le Mans, but after that his trust in the machine and his results slumped badly.

His difficulty stemmed from the team's exclusive use of Showa suspension and Nissin brakes. Both made financial contributions to Gresini's budget, and while nobody could fault their commitment, the kit was generally regarded as inferior to the Ohlins and Brembo equipment used by all the others.

Behind the scenes, however, Gresini, who also ran two-rider projects in Moto2 and Moto3, was having difficulties with finance. Italian energy drink backer GO&FUN was struggling to honour its existing deal, let alone commit further.

Weeks of negotiations failed to find a solution, and in September Gresini confirmed that his partnership with Honda would end.

He had agreed a four-year deal with new Aprilia boss Romano Albesiano to run the Italian manufacturer's official return to MotoGP, concomitantly put forward one year to 2015.

Collaboration with an existing team means that Aprilia will receive financial assistance from rights owners Dorna, and crucially will not have to shell out for expensive running costs like air freight and tyres.

Bautista was quickly confirmed as one rider; the second was not announced until the end of the season, by when former MotoGP race winner Marco Melandri had overcome his initial reluctance to spend a year on a development project before the roll-out of an all-new project for 2016.

HONDA RC213V – Gresini

Sponsors and Technical Suppliers: GO&FUN • Agos Ducato • Barracuda • Berner • Bike-Lift • Bridgestone • Castrol • Gaga Milano • Hop • Inox Centre • Nissin • OZ Palladio • Pascucci • PBR • Roland • SAGTubi • SC Project • Showa • Tenax • Thermal Technology • Vertex

Engine: 1000cc, 90-degree V4; 360-degree crank, pneumatic valve springs. *Power:* More than 260ps

Ancillaries: HRC electronics, ride-by-wire throttle and fuel injection system, NGK sparking plugs *Lubrication:* Castrol *Fuel:* 20 litres

Transmission: Gear primary drive, multi-plate dry slipper clutch, six-speed seamless-shift constant-mesh cassette-style gearbox, RK chain

Suspension: Front, Showa twin-tube 48mm forks • Rear, Showa twin-tube gas shock with linkage

Wheels: 16.5in OZ Racing, front and rear *Tyres:* Bridgestone

Brakes: Front, Nissin carbon-carbon 320mm and 340mm • Rear, HRC steel 218mm

FIM MOTOGP WORLD CHAMPIONSHIP

OPEN CLASS
TEAMS AND RIDERS

Left and above: Aleix Espargaro was the top non-factory rider again, thanks to a factory-spec Yamaha – and plenty of talent.

Photos: Gold & Goose

GO&FUN Honda Gresini

TEAM STAFF

Fausto GRESINI: Team Manager
Carlo MERLINI: Marketing Manager
Mattia RICCI: Marketing
Alberto CANI: Press and Media Relations
Elisa GIACON: Web and Social Media
Beppe FERRARIO: Guests Co-ordinator
Fulvia CASTELLI: Logistics

SCOTT REDDING PIT CREW

Diego GUBELLINI: Chief Mechanic
Mechanics: Ivan BRANDI, Marco ROSA GASTALDO,
Jerome GALLAND, Renzo PINI
Riccardo SANCASSANI: Telemetry

SCOTT REDDING

Born: 4 January, 1993 – Quedgeley, England

GP Starts: 117 (18 MotoGP, 66 Moto2, 33 125cc)
GP Wins: 4 (3 Moto2, 1 125cc)

FAUSTO GRESINI

SCOTT REDDING

ROOKIE Scott Redding was hired to race the RCV1000R, having graduated from Moto2, where he had narrowly missed becoming Britain's first grand prix world champion since late legend Barry Sheene.

Diego Gubellini was assigned as Redding's crew chief and Riccardo Sancassini took control of data, while veteran Gresini crew members Ivan Brandi, Marco Rosa Gastaldo and Renzo Pini remained.

Redding was allowed to bring one of his personnel from Moto2, and he moved across with Frenchman Jerome Galland, who was vastly experienced, having previously worked in Kawasaki's factory squad.

Redding's season was defined by the weak engine performance of the Honda RCV1000R, which was an additional handicap given his above-average height and weight.

The Briton was still eager to impress, however, to earn his big break on the prototype RC213V in 2015, which, contrary to popular belief, was not a definitive obligation that Gresini had to meet in his two-year deal with Redding. Contracts and clauses would all be academic, though, as the mid-season approached and murmurs about Gresini's budget issues started to gather momentum.

Redding had established himself as a consistent points scorer and the leading RCV1000R rider, and it seemed that a promotion to the factory RC213V was a formality, but the team's funding crisis left him in the lurch and scrambling for an alternative ride.

Forward Yamaha and Pramac Ducati both kept a seat open for a month in case he was back on the open market, but salvation came from an old ally.

In his four-year stint in Moto2 with the Belgium-based Marc VDS Racing squad, Redding had forged a close bond with mega-rich tycoon and team owner Marc van der Straten.

Marc VDS boss Michael Bartholemy, who is also Redding's personal representative, had long held an ambition to expand into the premier class, and the opportunity to lease a factory RC213V was too good to reject.

The issues were time and money. Bartholemy had fewer than 45 days to find the £5m needed to put a one-rider project together for Redding. With a major financial commitment from van der Straten in place, he sourced the rest through external sponsorship; a deal was agreed in Misano and made official at Twin Ring Motegi.

Redding would not be reunited with ex-crew chief Pete Benson, though, as he was working with Redding's replacement, Tito Rabat. The Spaniard will be the first in the short history of Moto2 to defend the intermediate-class title, and Benson will remain with Rabat.

Redding's main target was ex-Stoner chief engineer Cristian Gabarrini, with whom he had worked in 2014, the Italian being a prominent figure in the RCV1000R project. But Gabarrini was unavailable, and a shock move to tempt Valentino Rossi's legendary former crew chief, Jerry Burgess, out of retirement was politely knocked back by the pragmatic Aussie.

Redding eventually agreed a deal with Chris Pike, whose most recent assignment had been as Jonathan Rea's crew chief at Ten Kate Honda in the Superbike World Championship.

Honda RCV1000R Gresini

Engine: 1000cc 90-degree V4, 360-degree crank
Power: More than 230ps.

Ancillaries: Magneti Marelli control electronics and inertial platform, Dorna control software, NGK sparking plugs, full electronic ride-by-wire

Lubrication: Castrol *Fuel:* 22–23 litres

Transmission: Gear primary drive, multi-plate dry slipper clutch, six-speed constant-mesh cassette-style gearbox, RK chain

Suspension: Front, Showa twin-tube 48mm forks; Rear, Showa twin-tube gas shock with linkage

Wheels: 16.5in OZ Racing, front and rear
Tyres: Bridgestone

Brakes: Front, Nissin carbon-carbon 320mm and 340mm; Rear, HRC steel 218mm

HONDA RCV1000R

Photos: Gold & Goose

NGM FORWARD RACING

TEAM STAFF

Giovanni CUZARI: CEO

Marco CURIONI: Managing Director

Giulia DOGLIANI, Paolo MAFFIOLI: Team Co-ordination and Logistics

Laura BERETTA, Maria GUIDOTTI: PR and Press

Sergio VERBENA: Technical Co-ordinator

COLIN EDWARDS PIT CREW

Sergio VERBENA: Crew Chief

Mechanics: Florian FERRACI, Guglielmo ANDREINI, Jonny DONELLI

Manfred GEISSLER: Data Technician

ALEIX ESPARGARO PIT CREW

Matthew CASEY: Crew Chief

Mechanics: Antonio Perez HABA, Jaques ROCA, Danilo PIAZZA, Mirko FIUZZI

Bernard MARTIGNAC: Data Technician

Both Riders:
Sander DONKERS: Electronics and Strategies

Paolo PIAZZA: Mechanic and Spare Parts

GIOVANNI CUZARI

FORWARD YAMAHA M1

Engine: 1000cc across-the-frame in-line 4; reverse-rotating cross-plane crankshaft, DOHC, 4 valves per cylinder, pneumatic valve springs

Power: Around 255bhp up to approx. 16,200rpm

Ancillaries: Magneti Marelli control electronics and inertial platform, Dorna control software, NGK sparking plugs, full electronic ride-by-wire

Lubrication: Yamalube. *Fuel capacity:* 24 litres

Transmission: Gear primary drive, multi-plate dry slipper clutch, six-speed constant-mesh floating-dog-ring cassette-style gearbox, Regina chain, AFAM sprockets

Suspension: Front, Showa twin-tube 48mm forks; Rear, Ohlins TRSP 44 shock with linkage

Wheels: 16.5in MFR, front and rear

Tyres: Bridgestone

Brakes: Front, Nissin carbon-carbon 320mm and 340mm; Rear, Yamaha steel

COLIN EDWARDS
Born: 27 February, 1974 – Houston, Texas, USA

GP Starts: 196 MotoGP
World Championships: 2 World Superbike

ALEIX ESPARGARO
Born: 30 July, 1989 – Granollers, Spain

GP Starts: 160 (76 MotoGP, 17 Moto 2, 44 250cc, 23 125cc)

NO other team grasped the opportunity to acquire more affordable and more competitive machinery available in the new Open class than the Italian-based NGM Forward Racing squad. And they quickly became flag bearers of the new concept.

Yamaha had confirmed that it would lease a YZR-M1 engine package for the Open class in the summer of 2013. Initially it would also supply a chassis and swing-arm package on the strict stipulation that any team it collaborated with would eventually design, develop and race its own frame.

Only Forward Racing owner Giovanni Cuzari and Managing Director Marco Curioni were tempted by the Yamaha proposal, and it proved a master stroke.

The team had struggled through 2012 with popular American Colin Edwards on a Suter-BMW. Fortunes improved marginally in 2013 when using an FTR-Kawasaki project, but its deal with Yamaha catapulted Forward Racing from also-ran into a top-six challenging force.

Cuzari had managed to persuade Aleix Espargaro to break a signed deal with Aspar to join veteran Edwards (hoping to show that he was still competitive beyond his 40th birthday). Aspar's penalty clause was around 600,000 euros, which Espargaro's manager, Albert Valera, who also represents Jorge Lorenzo, had bartered down to 400,000.

Forward had contributed to the hefty fine, but for Cuzari and Curioni it was money well spent, as Espargaro emerged as one of the revelations of the season.

Even before testing began, accusations started flying that Yamaha had not adhered to the spirit of the Open class. While Forward's own chassis was delayed, Espargaro effectively rode a year-old factory bike, previously raced by Cal Crutchlow at Tech 3, but with key benefits, like softer tyres and more fuel.

Working with crew chief Matthew Casey, who had moved over from Aspar, Espargaro claimed eight starts from the second row, including five from fourth spot. One highlight was an outstanding pole in Assen, which he followed with a first Open bike podium in treacherous conditions at Motorland Aragon, courtesy of a perfectly timed strategy to switch to his wet bike.

So competitive was the package that Espargaro beat Smith and almost his younger brother Pol on the factory-supported Tech 3 YZR-M1s to take seventh overall in the championship.

Espargaro's time at Forward would be brief. Although common knowledge for months, his deal to spearhead Suzuki's factory return was only officially confirmed when the Japanese manufacturer unveiled its new GSX-RR at the Intermot motorcycle show in Cologne at the end of September.

Espargaro never actually raced Forward's own chassis, which eventually was ready by the Italian Grand Prix at Mugello in early June.

Forward had been fully committed to its own chassis, continuing the team's relationship with respected British specialists FTR. The collaboration quickly ended, but Mark Taylor, an influential figure at FTR who had subsequently left the company, designed a frame that was constructed by renowned British racing parts manufacturer Harris Performance.

Edwards had pushed hard for the frame, having

FORWARD YAMAHA M1

ALEX DE ANGELIS

Born: 26 February, 1984 – Rimini, Italy

GP Starts: 248 (47 MotoGP, 71 Moto 2, 65 250cc, 65 125cc)

GP Wins: 4 (3 Moto2, 1 250cc)

COLIN EDWARDS

struggled to adapt to the Yamaha version, but he only had a limited chance to demonstrate its potential before his glittering career was ended prematurely. He caught everybody, including his own team, by surprise at the second race in Texas, where he announced that he would be retiring at the end of the season.

Ninth in the first race was followed by only two more top-15 finishes, including a 13th at what turned out to be his farewell in Indianapolis, after plans for a last goodbye at Valencia fell through.

It was a sorry end to a distinguished career, but Edwards quickly began a new chapter as Yamaha's official test rider, with prime focus on evaluating Michelin tyres ahead of the French factory's return to MotoGP in 2016.

Alex de Angelis was released by the Tasca Racing Moto2 team to take over Edwards's seat. The San Marino rider began working with all of the Texan's crew, which once again was headed by crew chief Sergio Verbena, while ex-racer and former Suzuki data technician Manfred Geissler worked on the electronics systems.

The removal of Edwards did not drastically improve fortunes, though de Angelis did persevere with the Forward frame. He battled consistently for the points, points, but ninth at Phillip Island was his only top ten. Forward acted quickly to replace Espargaro well in advance of Suzuki's confirmation, signing Stefan Bradl during the summer break after his three-year tenure at LCR Honda came to an end.

The search for a second rider proved considerably more problematic. Cuzari had been keen on emerging Dutch talent Michael van der Mark, but he was off limits with a Ten Kate Honda World Superbike ride already agreed.

Then the team planned to test Swiss Moto2 rider Dominique Aegerter in a post-race session at Brno, but he agreed to stay in Moto2 on the morning of that race and the test was cancelled.

Experienced Moto2 rider Mika Kallio turned down an offer, later revealing that the fee offered had been less than he could make by staying in Moto2, as a title contender. French rider Loris Baz, who had initially expected to join Aspar Honda, eventually took the ride, after the Spanish squad unexpectedly decided that he was too tall.

At the Aragon GP, Cuzari confirmed that a new deal had been agreed with Yamaha for 2015. The Japanese manufacturer had originally intended to lend only the YZR-M1 chassis and swing-arm for 2015, but had revised its strategy to combat the arrival of Honda's upgraded Open RC213V-RS, and would support both riders with the same technical package given to Espargaro.

ALEIX ESPARGARO

CAME
SERGIO VERBENA

DRIVE M7 ASPAR

TEAM STAFF

Jorge MARTINEZ: Team Manager

Silvia PELUFO: Assistant Team Manager

Facundo GARCIA: Administration Manager

Gino BORSOI: Sporting Manager

Maria Jose BOTELLA: Media and Logistics

Ricardo PEDROS: Media Officer

Carmen PRYTZ, Leonor FONS: Administration

Agustin PEREZ: Maintenance

NICKY HAYDEN PIT CREW

Mauro NOCCIOLI: Crew Chief

Mechanics: Salvador FRANCO BORJA, Denis PAZZA-GLINI, Jordi CUNILL MALTAS, Oscar GRAU GALLEGO

Giulio NAVA: Data Engineer

HIROSHI AOYAMA PIT CREW

Andrea ORLANDI: Crew Chief

Mechanics: Miguel GRAU GALLEGO, Juan Manuel Alcaniz BOJ, Ignacio Cabeza LASALA, Salvador Moraleda GISBERT

Davide TAGLIATESTA: Data Engineer

JORGE 'ASPAR' MARTINEZ

Honda RCV10000R – Aspar

Engine: 1000cc 90-degree V4, 360-degree crank
Power: More than 230ps

Ancillaries: Magneti Marelli control electronics and inertial platform, Dorna control software, NGK sparking plugs, full electronic ride-by-wire

Lubrication: Castrol *Fuel:* 22–23 litres

Transmission: Gear primary drive, multi-plate dry slipper clutch, six-speed constant-mesh cassette-style gearbox, RK chain

Suspension: Front, Ohlins TRSP25 48mm forks; Rear, Ohlins TRSP44 shock with linkage

Wheels: 16.5in Marchesini, front, and rear
Tyres: Bridgestone

Brakes: Front, Nissin/Brembo carbon-carbon 320mm and 340mm; Rear, HRC steel 218mm

NICKY HAYDEN

Born: 30 July, 1981 – Owensboro, Kentucky, USA

GP Starts: 198 MotoGP
GP Wins: 3 MotoGP
World Championships: 1 MotoGP

HIROSHI AOYAMA

Born: 25 October, 1981 – Chiba, Japan

GP Starts: 168 (64 MotoGP, 104 250cc)
GP Wins: 9 250cc
World Championships: 1 250cc

FOR the Spanish-based Aspar outfit, 2014 was only its fifth season in MotoGP, but team owner Jorge Martinez had switched to a third different manufacturer since its premier-class debut in 2010.

Having already worked with Ducati and Aprilia, Aspar switched allegiance to Honda, after being sold on HRC Vice-President Shuhei Nakamoto's boast that the Japanese factory's new production Honda RCV1000R was only 0.3s a lap slower than its full-blown prototype RC213V.

Later Nakamoto would back-pedal, saying that he had been misunderstood in his analysis of the lap times, when it became blatantly obvious that the RCV1000R Open bike was undermined by a significant lack of horsepower.

Aspar, operating closely with Sporting Director Gino Borsoi, had only agreed a last-minute switch to the Honda production model, having initially been committed to remaining with Aprilia and using an upgraded version of the ART machine. But the late defection of key technical boss Gigi Dall'Igna to rivals Ducati left Aspar unconvinced that development of the ART would progress quickly enough without the Noale factory's engineering mastermind.

Malaysian energy drink brand Drive M7 was keen to expand its profile to a more global audience, so it came on board as new title sponsor. Aspar, meanwhile, signed 2006 world champion Nicky Hayden and the last 250GP title winner, Hiroshi Aoyama.

Popular American Hayden had rebuffed enticing World Superbike opportunities to renew his association with Honda, which had ended somewhat acrimoniously when he was fired at the end of 2008 to begin a five-year stint with Ducati.

He worked with crew chief Mauro Noccioli and especially closely with ex-Stoner and Marquez data engineer Giulio Nava to get the best from the more basic Open-class software introduced for 2014.

Like the majority in the paddock, Hayden had banked on Honda's famed obsession with speed and horsepower to galvanise his career. The optimism was quickly beaten out of him, however, as it hit home over the winter that at fast tracks, the RCV1000R was 10–15mph slower through the speed traps.

He started the season well with point-scoring finishes in the opening four rounds, including a season-best eighth in the Qatar curtain-raiser. But during round four in Jerez, a long-standing injury to his right wrist flared up and eventually he had to resort to surgery to save his career.

He withdrew after Friday practice at Mugello and had the surgery, before returning for Catalunya, Assen and Sachsenring. He continued to suffer pain and movement issues, however, and needed more extensive surgery during the summer break, which caused him to miss four races.

Honda World Superbike rider Jonathan Rea turned down the chance to replace Hayden, fearing that a MotoGP substitute ride would distract him from his main priority in SBK. A British rider did replace Hayden in Indianapolis, Brno, Silverstone and Misano, Leon Camier being given his first MotoGP ride at the age of 28. The ex-British Superbike champion did a sterling job on the RCV1000R, which, at over 6ft 3in, he dwarfed. Little did he know, but his physical size would play a pivotal role in one of the year's most puzzling and bizarre decisions.

Camier's best result was 15th in Brno, and he fin-

Honda RCV1000R

LEON CAMIER

Born: 4 August, 1986 – Ashford, England

GP Starts: 16 (4 MotoGP, 12 125cc)

ished in three of his four stand-in rides. He was on course for an excellent top-15 finish in his Indy debut until a faulty rear wheel speed sensor forced him to retire with the engine repeatedly losing power.

Aoyama was a model of consistency and the only rider to see the chequered flag in race. Working under the guidance of Italian crew chief Andrea Orlandi, he missed the points just once, in Assen, and scored four top-ten finishes, including a best of eighth in the chaotic Motorland Aragon and Phillip Island races.

His flawless finishing record didn't secure him a contract renewal, and his place eventually went to Irish rider Eugene Laverty, after a convoluted process that didn't reflect well on Aspar management. Aoyama instead was contracted as an official factory tester by Honda, to help the adaptation to Michelin tyres.

With Hayden locked in to a two-year deal, Aspar initially looked at bringing Alvaro Bautista back, before signing a deal with French factory Kawasaki World Superbike rider Loris Baz in early September. Inexplicably, Aspar reneged on the deal, with Baz more than forthcoming at expressing his shock at being hired and then fired, apparently for being too tall. Apparently Aspar had become spooked after realising how much performance had been sacrificed with Camier.

Laverty, who had also negotiated with Forward Yamaha and Pramac Ducati, agreed terms during the Misano weekend in mid-September, and his deal was formally announced shortly before the end-of-season flyaway triple-header.

Hayden and Laverty will ride the upgraded RC213V-RS, which essentially is the 2014 factory prototype version without a seamless-shift gearbox and the more sophisticated factory-spec electronic software.

HIROSHI AOYAMA

NICKY HAYDEN

LEON CAMIER

CARDION AB MOTORACING

TEAM STAFF

Karel ABRAHAM Sr: Team Manager

Jiri SMETANA: Communications

KAREL ABRAHAM PIT CREW

Lindo SPARRAGLIA: Logistics

Marco GRANA: Chief Mechanic

Mechanics: Yannis MAIGRET, Martin HAVLICEK, Martin NESVADBA, Pietro BERTI (tyres and transport)

Renato PENNACCHIO: Telemetry

KAREL ABRAHAM

Born: 2 January, 1990 – Brno, Czech Republic

GP Starts: 149 (57 MotoGP, 14 Moto2, 47 250cc, 31 125cc)
GP Wins: 1 Moto2

Honda RCV10000R – Abraham

Engine: 1000cc 90-degree V4 360-degree crank
Power: More than 230ps

Ancillaries: Magneti Marelli control electronics and inertial platform, Dorna control software, NGK sparking plugs, full electronic ride-by-wire

Lubrication: Castrol *Fuel:* 22–23 litres

Transmission: Gear primary drive, multi-plate dry slipper clutch, six-speed constant-mesh cassette-style gearbox, RK chain

Suspension: Front, Ohlins TRSP25 48mm forks; Rear, Ohlins TRSP44 shock with linkage

Wheels: Marchesini 16.5in, front and rear
Tyres: Bridgestone

Brakes: Front, Nissin/Brembo carbon-carbon 320mm and 340mm; Rear, HRC Steel 218mm

THE Cardion AB squad remained very much a family affair in 2014, with Karel Abraham and his father, Karel Abraham Senior, working in tandem in a one-rider effort for a fourth season in the MotoGP World Championship.

For the third season in succession, Abraham had opted to switch machinery, having previously raced with Ducati's Desmosedici and Aprilia's ART machine. In 2014, he relied again on the loyal support of leading Czech medical supplies company Cardion AB to fund the purchase of Honda's new RCV1000R production bike.

If Abraham Sr had demonstrated unwavering devotion and loyalty to his son's racing career, then Abraham Jr was as equally committed to his crew. For the ninth consecutive season, Italian Marco Grana was his crew chief, and several mechanics, among them Martin Havlicek and Pietro Berti, were also long-term fixtures in the Brno-based team.

Another long-server was mechanic Martin Nesvadba, who gained some notoriety in Germany when he stepped off the pit wall and into the path of Italian rider Mattia Pasini during a Moto2 practice session. Thankfully both escaped serious injury.

Injury had dominated 2012 and 2013 for Abraham, yet this season proved to be free from the physical problems that had so abruptly stalled his progress after an impressive rookie campaign with Ducati in 2011. A serious left shoulder fracture, suffered at Indianapolis in the summer of 2013, had required major reconstructive surgery and he had missed the final five races.

The recovering shoulder was still problematic during the pre-season testing campaign, but Abraham started the season well and scored points in the opening three rounds. It was a position he would become familiar with as the season progressed and his best result was 11th at Indianapolis, repeated at Misano, where he was also top Open finisher after Aleix Espargaro crashed out.

Throughout his grand prix career, Abraham has earned a reputation as a competent rider but prolific crasher, yet the first occasion in which he failed to finish in back-to-back races came in rounds 14 and 15 at Motorland Aragon and Twin Ring Motegi. Retirement in the former was due to machine failure rather than rider error when he was running in 12th, and he blamed brake problems for race crashes at Jerez then three more in Japan, Australia and Malaysia, switching to Nissin brakes for the final race.

Abraham will be back for a fifth straight season in MotoGP in 2015, after agreeing to continue its relationship with HRC by running one of the four new upgraded production Hondas, renamed RC213V-RS.

Honda RCV1000R

AVINTIA RACING

TEAM STAFF

Antonio MARTIN: CEO

Raul ROMERO: General Manager

Augustin ESCOBAR: Team Manager

Akikito ISHIDA: Technical Director

HECTOR BARBERA PIT CREW

Akikito ISHIDA: Chief Mechanic

Mechanics: Jonathan MORAL, Luis MARTINEZ, Jesus CONTRERA

Mario MARTINI: Data Engineer

MIKE DI MEGLIO PIT CREW

Jarno POLASTRI: Chief Mechanic

Mechanics: Jordi PRADES, Toni MIR, Jesus MORENO, Jose MA ROJAS

Miguel Angel ARIAS: Data Engineer

MIKE DI MEGLIO

Avintia Kawasaki

Engine: 1000cc in-line 4, DOHC, 4 valves per cylinder, pneumatic valve return system, gear-driven cams
Power: Around 240bhp, revs up to 16,000rpm

Ancillaries: Magneti Marelli control electronics and inertial platform, Dorna control software, full electronic ride-by-wire

Lubrication: Elf. *Fuel capacityl:* 23.8 litres

Transmission: Constant-mesh cassette-style gearbox

Suspension: Front, Showa forks; Rear, Showa shock with linkage

Wheels: Marchesini 16.5in front and rear
Tyres: Bridgestone

Brakes: Front, Brembo carbon-carbon 320mm; Rear, steel 200mm

HECTOR BARBERA

Born: 2 November, 1986 – Dos Aguas, Spain

GP Starts: 207 (85 MotoGP, 75 250cc, 47 125cc)
GP Wins: 10 (4 250cc, 6 125cc)

MIKE DI MEGLIO

Born: 17 January, 1988 – Toulouse, France

GP Starts: 184 (18 MotoGP, 59 Moto2, 16 250cc, 91 125cc)
GP Wins: 5 125cc
World Championships: 1 125cc

HECTOR BARBERA

THE Spanish-based Avintia Racing squad has found it hard to shake off the tag of perennial back-marker since joining MotoGP in 2012.

The 2014 season was no exception in what proved to be another difficult year toiling on its own uncompetitive Open-class project.

Raul Romero continued in his role as General Manager, though he remained the major driving force behind the team. He had created the venture in its previous guise, By Queroseno Racing, way back in 1994 for an attack on the Spanish domestic scene.

For the third season in succession, he persevered with a modified Kawasaki ZX-10R engine concept that was housed in the team's own frame.

Spanish rider Hector Barbera was in his second year with the team, but two point-scoring finishes in the first four races didn't prove to be a platform on which he could build for the remainder of the season.

Barbera was working with Akikoto Ishida, who served a dual role in the team. As well as being Barbera's chief mechanic, he was the team's Technical Director.

It became clear pretty soon that the Kawasaki ZX-10R engine project had run its course. The creation of the new Open class had opened the door for non-factory teams like Avintia to lease or buy more competitive machinery, of the likes of Honda and Yamaha, at more affordable prices.

Avintia missed the boat somewhat in 2014, but Romero would not make the same mistake for 2015. It became clear from mid-season that Ducati was interested in expanding its Desmosedici project, and Romero pounced on the opportunity.

Talks were hardly secretive, given that Romero and new Team Manager Augustin Escobar held discussions in the heart of the Indianapolis Motor Speed-

way media centre with Ducati Corse Sporting Director Paolo Ciabatti in early August.

One month later, at Ducati's home race in Misano, a two-year agreement was finalised between Avintia Racing CEO Antonio Martin and Ducati Corse General Manager Gigi Dall'Igna.

Avintia will be supplied with two 2014-spec GP14 machines for the 2015 season, and they will run the Open-class electronics software.

The agreement will be mutually beneficial for both parties. Avintia will have more competitive machinery, while Ducati can use the team as a guinea pig to study the Open class software in advance of unified electronics for all bikes, which will be mandatory in 2016. So eager was Dall'Igna that for the last five races of 2014, Barbera ditched the Kawasaki project and switched to Ducati (pictured right). He hadn't been in the Desmosedici hot seat for long when the bike erupted into a spectacular fireball during his very first session on board at Motorland Aragon.

The transfer to more competitive machinery initially didn't galvanise Barbera's season. However, at the tyre-led crash-fest in Australia, the Spaniard took a last-gasp fifth place for his best result of the year. He scored points on six occasions, with another top-ten at Sepang, and will remain with Avintia for a third season in 2015.

Avintia's poor results in the defunct CRT class had made the Kawasaki ZX-10R engine project a hard sell, and a team-mate for Barbera was not officially unveiled until early January.

Ex-125cc world champion Mike di Meglio tested the bike twice before Christmas as he sought to put his career back on track after a serious double pelvis fracture had ruled him out of the final eight Moto2 races of 2013. The Frenchman was signed for his

AVINTIA KAWASAKI

first assault on MotoGP and was assigned to crew chief Jarno Polastri. The most recognisable figure in his six-man crew was Jordi Prades, who had worked with Dani Pedrosa at Repsol Honda between 2006 and 2010.

The Toulouse rider had to labour for the entire season on the Kawasaki. His best result was 12th at Indianapolis, and he consistently finished inside the top 20, adding more points in Australia and Malaysia. Not even a broken bone in his right hand, suffered in a first-lap high-side at Misano, could side-line him.

His future, though, remained uncertain until the last race. Avintia had tested highly-rated Swiss Moto2 rider Dominique Aegerter in the official post-race session immediately after the Catalunya round near Barcelona in June. He impressed, but wanted to move to the premier class on more competitive machinery.

British rider Leon Camier was also in the frame, and Belgian rider Xavier Simeon was also offered the chance, though decided to stay in Moto2. At the last gasp, Di Meglio's contract was renewed for 2015.

PAUL BIRD MOTORSPORT

PAUL BIRD

MICHAEL LAVERTY

Born: 7 June, 1981 – Toombridge, N Ireland

GP Starts: 36 (36 MotoGP)

BROC PARKES

Born: 24 December, 1981 – Hunter Region, NSW, Australia

GP Starts: 19 (18 MotoGP, 1 125cc)

TEAM STAFF

Paul BIRD: Team Owner

Kelly ALLISON: Team Logistics and Co-ordination

Phil BORLEY: Technical Director

MICHAEL LAVERTY PIT CREW

Phil BORLEY: Crew Chief

Mechanics: Victor MORGADO, William MEYERS

BROC PARKES PIT CREW

Ryan RAINEY: Crew Chief

Mechanics: Dave PARKES, Tom HARRISON

Both Riders:

Andrew FARROW: Technician

Glen PREECE: Tyres and Transport

POULTRY magnate Paul Bird's private venture in the MotoGP world championship was in its third season, the multi-millionaire Briton fielding his own PBM chassis and Aprilia's ART motor for a second campaign in succession.

The upgraded Open-class projects from Honda and Yamaha only widened the gulf in performance to Bird's Cumbrian-based project, and it was at the resumption of action after the summer break in Indianapolis that he confirmed that 2014 would be his last in MotoGP.

PBM operated on a skeleton crew for much of the season, with Phil Borley doubling as Technical Director and crew chief for Michael Laverty, who was back for a second season with the team.

Having failed to tempt British Superbike champion Alex Lowes into a ride, Bird announced in mid-December that his second rider would be Andorran-based Broc Parkes. The Australian was vastly experienced and twice had been runner-up in the World

Supersport series. He had ridden for Bird in World Superbikes when he had run Kawasaki's official factory effort in 2009.

Parkes worked with crew chief Tom Larsen, who had previously been at BMW in World Superbikes with Troy Corser, and he scored a point on his debut in Qatar with 15th. His best result was 11th in Assen's flag-to-flag encounter, but he would score points in only two other races: 15th in Indianapolis and 14th in Sepang.

Laverty seemed permanently marooned just outside the points for most of the season, the Irishman finishing in 16th in no fewer than six races. He ended the season with a flourish, however, with 13th in Phillip Island and a best ever 12th in Sepang.

Bird's declaration in Indianapolis that he would shut the MotoGP arm of his big racing effort, which also included a two-rider assault, was not a bolt from the blue. To incentivise teams to be as competitive as possible, Dorna had implemented a policy that the

riders finishing in the bottom two places at the end of 2014 would lose subsidies like the freight allowance.

Parkes and Laverty were 23rd and 24th respectively, which meant Bird would lose all of his funding from Dorna and the International Race Teams Association. It was enough to end PBM's MotoGP adventure.

His initial plan was to move the entire MotoGP operation back to the burgeoning British Superbike championship, to run a four-rider super team with different manufacturers. At the end of the season, that ambitious plan had still to be finalised, with talk of him running a three-man BSB team, using the Kawasaki ZX-10R on which Shane Byrne had won a record fourth domestic title.

Parkes and Laverty were under consideration, though at season's end the Irish rider was also locked in talks with Aprilia for a MotoGP testing deal. He planned to find a ride in BSB that would allow him to test for Aprilia, who were dangling the carrot of two or three wild-card appearances in 2015.

PBM ART

Engine: 1000cc 65-degree V4, DOHC, 4 valves per cylinder, gear-driven cams

Power: Around 220bhp, revs up to 15,500rpm with variable-length inlet system

Ancillaries: Magneti Marelli control electronics and inertial platform, Dorna control software, full electronic ride-by-wire

Lubrication: Silkolene

Transmission: Constant-mesh cassette-style gearbox
Suspension: Front, Ohlins forks; Rear, Ohlins shock with linkage

Wheels: Marchesini 16.5in, front and rear

Tyres: Bridgestone

Brakes: Front, Brembo carbon-carbon 320mm; Rear, steel 200mm

PBM ART

OCTO IODARACING PROJECT

TEAM STAFF

Giampiero SACCHI; Team Principal

Monica RIVERO: Logistics

Michele BASSI: Hospitality

Luca BOLOGNA: Press

DANILO PETRUCCI PIT CREW

Giovanni SANDI: Chief Mechanic

Mechanics: Angelo ANGELI, Franco BRUGNARA,

Tiziano VERNIANI, Danilo PETRUCCI Sr

Adelio FRANCIA: Electronics

DANILO PETRUCCI
Born: 24 October, 1990 – Terni, Italy

GP Starts: 50 (50 MotoGP)

MICHEL FABRIZIO
Born: 17 September, 1984 – Rome, Italy

GP Starts: 30 (14 MotoGP, 16 125cc)

GIAMPIERO SACCHI

APRILIA ART 1000

Engine: 1000cc 65-degree V4, DOHC, 4 valves per cylinder, gear-driven cams

Power: Around 220bhp, revs up to 15,500rpm with variable-length inlet system

Ancillaries: Magneti Marelli control electronics and inertial platform, Dorna control software, full electronic ride-by-wire

Lubrication: Elf.   *Fuel capacity:* 23.8 litres

Transmission: Constant-mesh cassette-style gearbox

Suspension: Front, Ohlins forks; Rear, Ohlins shock with linkage

Wheels: Marchesini 16.5in, front and rear

Tyres: Bridgestone

Brakes: Front, Brembo carbon-carbon 320mm; Rear, steel 200mm

DANILO PETRUCCI

THOSE who thought MotoGP had finally ridden the storm of the global economic crisis received a stark reminder of its lingering impact from the Ioda Racing squad in 2014.

The Italian-based squad had been able to finance a two-rider effort in 2013 and fully intended to do so again in 2014. Danilo Petrucci was signed for a third successive season to ride an Aprilia ART machine in the new Open category, after the team had decided to relinquish the disappointing Suter-BMW project that the Italian had raced with Lukas Pesek during the previous season.

Pesek's place on the second ART package was to be taken by Leon Camier, who had been left without a ride in World Superbikes at the last minute when he was released from Paul Denning's Crescent Suzuki squad. Camier's name appeared on the provisional entry list with Ioda when it was released by the FIM on 14th January.

Even at that stage, though, there were murmurs that promised sponsorship had not materialised, and when the final starting line-up for MotoGP was unveiled on 28th February, it was no great shock that the Andorra-based Briton's name had been omitted.

The failure to honour the commitment to Camier did not sit well with respected General Manager Giampiero Sacchi. He has been an influential figure in unearthing talent, and his fingerprints are all over the early development of riders of the ilk of Valentino Rossi, Max Biaggi, Loris Capirossi, Jorge Lorenzo and the late Marco Simoncelli. A last-ditch attempt to seek funding to keep Camier on board came to nothing. The team was back to just one rider.

The budget shortfall facing the team was obvious. Ioda missed the first two pre-season tests at the

Sepang track in Malaysia, and Petrucci didn't even ride the updated Aprilia ART bike until just under two weeks before the season started in Qatar. A difficult start had become even more so.

Giovanni Sandi remained with the team under the title of Technical Manager, which effectively translated to crew chief. Having lost Gigi Dall'Igna to Ducati and then seen its number-one team, Aspar, defect to Honda in a turbulent ending to 2013, Aprilia remained committed to the Ioda project.

Electronics engineer Nicola Biliato and suspension technician Oscar Bolzonella were both Aprilia staff in the garage.

Despite the lack of any major pre-season preparation, Petrucci finished in the points in Qatar with 14th, and he would make five more visits to the top 15.

His best result was 11th in the flag-to-flag Motorland Aragon crash-fest, and his season was severely disrupted by a broken left wrist suffered pre-race at Jerez.

Camier seemed the obvious replacement, but he wanted the assurance of a future contract and was happy to continue deputising for injured French rider Sylvain Barrier in World Superbikes without that guarantee.

Pedercini World Superbike rider Luca Scassa was called up. The Italian had acquitted himself well when he rode the Aprilia ART as a replacement rider for injured Cardion AB rider Karel Abraham in the final five races of 2013. But within hours of Ioda officially announcing he'd replace Petrucci in Le Mans, Scassa broke his right femur while re-familiarising himself with the ART in a private test at Mugello. The team perforce missed the French round altogether.

A difficult season went from bad to worse when Petrucci failed a medical to race at Mugello. A frantic search for a replacement for the team's all-important home race led to experienced Michel Fabrizio being dragged from his sofa, having recently split from the Iron Brain Grillini Kawasaki Evo team in World Superbikes. He did not finish that race, but was 20th in Catalunya before Petrucci returned.

The season finished as it had started, with rumours that a lack of funding would scupper the project, and Petrucci left for Pramac Ducati. At the final race, however, de Angelis was signed up to continue the campaign.

APRILIA ART 1000

2014 TEAMS AND RIDERS

By PETER McLAREN

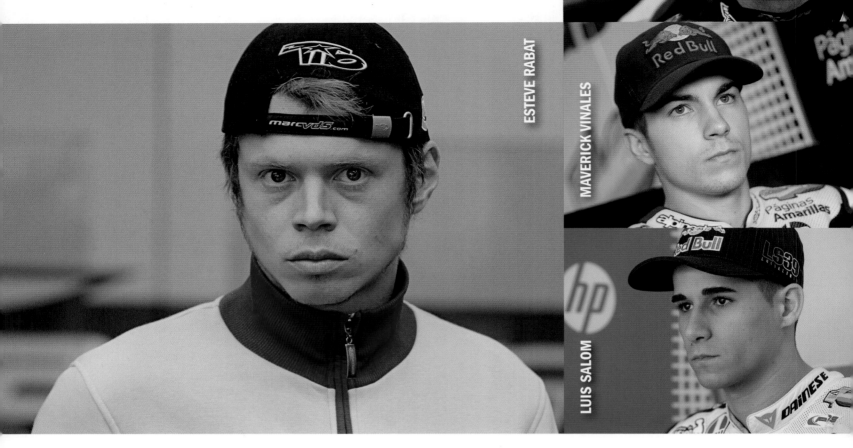

ESTEVE RABAT

MIKA KALLIO

MAVERICK VINALES

LUIS SALOM

PERSEVERANCE pays. That was the message from Esteve Rabat's popular Moto2 title victory. The rider had waited eight years to win a grand prix, then took ten wins in two seasons! In 2014, we were also treated to Moto2's first championship fight between team-mates, and Kalex became the undisputed class king.

It was the second year of a combined rider and bike minimum weight (215kg), but the key technical components – prototype chassis, control Honda 600cc engines and Dunlop tyres – remained unchanged from Moto2's first season in 2010.

Pol Espargaro had continued a perfect record of reigning Moto2 champions rising to MotoGP, while rival Scott Redding also moved to the premier class.

However, all but three of the remaining 2013 point scorers – Toni Elias (18th), Alex Marinelarena (27th) and Doni Tata Pradita (29th) – were back for more. The new line-up was led by Rabat and Mika Kallio, third and fourth respectively in 2013 and now team-mates at Marc VDS.

Fresh blood arrived in the form of 12 rookies, including reigning Moto3 champion Maverick Vinales and former title rival Luis Salom – team-mates at Pons – plus World Supersport champion Sam Lowes and American Superbike champion Josh Herrin.

The 34-rider start-of-year entry list was led by Spain (9), followed by Switzerland (4), Italy (4), Germany (3), Japan (2), Great Britain (2), France (2), Malaysia (2), Finland (1), Australia (1), Belgium (1), San Marino (1), Thailand (1) and the USA (1).

Wild-card surprise of the season came in the form of 50-year-old Jeremy McWilliams, who rolled back the years by giving the innovative Brough Superior its grand prix debut at Silverstone. Argentine Sebastian

Porto was another GP winner who made a welcome return in his home round, at a relatively youthful 35.

Despite the loss of Moriwaki, for the second time, permanent Moto2 constructors initially grew to seven with the arrival of Caterham Suter and Forward KLX, although the latter only lasted a handful of rounds.

MotoBI was officially reclassified as a TSR, continuing alongside Speed Up and Tech 3, but the ever-popular Kalex and Suter designs filled 24 of the grid places. That was four more than in 2013 as class variety continues to narrow.

KALEX

Marc VDS Racing Team – Esteve Rabat, Mika Kallio

Esteve Rabat (24, Spain) was signed to take over the seat vacated by Redding, with Pete Benson (Nicky Hayden's right-hand man during his title-winning 2006 MotoGP campaign) remaining as crew chief.

Somewhat erratic during his previous seven seasons, Rabat – who spends his spare time riding at Almeria or training with the Marquez brothers – had finally developed into a GP winner in 2013, when he was best of the rest behind Espargaro and Redding.

His decision to leave reigning champions Pons had raised eyebrows, but such expressions soon became nodding approval as the Rabat/Marc VDS fusion delivered a catch-me-if-you-can start to the season.

However cool-headed team-mate Mika Kallio (31, Finland) would turn up the heat in the summer. While Rabat enjoyed his best ever grand prix season, former MotoGP rider Kallio built on 2013's debut 600cc victory to deliver his finest form since the 2006 125cc World Championship.

One of the few Moto2 competitors over the age of 30, Kallio became the first Finn to reach 200 GP starts, putting his experience to good use in changeable track conditions as he sought to maintain pressure on the relatively unproven Rabat.

Rabat became the first Moto2 champion not to move to MotoGP, having signed to defend his title in 2015, when he will be joined at Marc VDS by Alex Marquez. Kallio will switch to Italtrans.

Pons HP 40 – Maverick Vinales, Luis Salom

With champion Pol Espargaro off to MotoGP and Rabat moving to Marc VDS, it was all change (except the nationality) for the 2014 Pons rider line-up.

Sito Pons entrusted his team's title defence to rookies Maverick Vinales (19, Spain) and Luis Salom (22, Spain). The pair had formed part of 2013's three-way Moto3 title showdown at Valencia, where Salom had fallen, and Vinales had snatched race and title glory from Alex Rins.

The momentum continued with Vinales as they moved to Moto2, and while an early victory proved deceptive in terms of a title challenge, he soon caught the attention of Suzuki's returning MotoGP team. The teenager would be victorious several more times in the closing stages of his only Moto2 season.

Salom also stood on the podium, although some dramatic moments in the gravel trap gave an insight into the pressure he was putting himself under. He had surgery for a fractured finger after Barcelona. He and Moto3 star Alex Rins will ride for Pons in 2015.

AGR Team – Jonas Folger, Axel Pons

Jonas Folger (19, Germany) left the lightweight grand prix class having been a winner on both 125 and

Photos: Gold & Goose

JONAS FOLGER · TAKAAKI NAKAGAMI · JULIAN SIMON · AXEL PONS · AZLAN SHAH · THITIPONG WAROKORN · LOUIS ROSSI · FRANCO MORBIDELLI · HAFIZH SYAHRIN · SANDRO CORTESE

Moto3 machinery, but having given the impression of unfulfilled potential.

He put his career back on track in 2014, handing the team its first Moto2 podiums, setting youngest-German records and becoming a target for MotoGP teams. A solid two-year contract with AGR means he will be back in 2015.

Axel Pons (22, Spain) left his father's team to ride alongside Folger. While he has a long way to go to silence his doubters, 2014 proved his best grand prix season to date.

IDEMITSU Honda Team Asia – Takaaki Nakagami, Azlan Shah
Four times a runner-up in 2013, Takaaki Nakagami (21, Japan) switched from Technomag-CIP to Tady Okada's IDEMITSU Honda Team Asia squad, reinforcing the view that he was destined for a MotoGP future with Honda.

Nakagami's arrival, plus the change from Moriwaki to Kalex, certainly ticked all the right boxes, and the Japanese duly collected another second place on his team debut in Qatar. However, an illegal air filter led to the result being erased. It seemed an innocuous setback, but the rest of the season proved otherwise.

Team-mate Azlan Shah (29, Malaysia) was starting his first full grand prix season, following six rides on Honda Team Asia's former Moriwaki machine at the tail end of 2013. Both will continue in 2015.

Italtrans Racing Team – Julian Simon, Franco Morbidelli
One of a handful of riders to have contested every Moto2 season, Julian Simon (26, Spain) began his second year on the Italtrans Kalex seeking to rebound

from a podium-less 2013 campaign. After Nakaga-mi's late transfer, rookie Franco Morbidelli (19, Italy) was hired for the second machine, and the teenager soon acquitted himself to earn a 2015 contract.

Dynavolt Intact GP – Sandro Cortese
Inaugural Moto3 world champion Sandro Cortese (24, Germany) had suffered a 'character building' rookie Moto2 season with the Dynavolt Intact team, ending up 20th in the standings. The 2014 season soon tested his mettle with a heel injury in Qatar qualifying, but the German would be rewarded with silverware later in the year.

Petronas Raceline Malaysia – Hafizh Syahrin
Best known for a belated home podium as a wild-card at Sepang in 2012 – following Anthony West's back-dated disqualification – Hafizh Syahrin (19, Malaysia) made four starts in 2013 prior to a full-time call-up with Petronas Raceline Malaysia.

SAG Team/APH PTT The Pizza SAG – Louis Rossi, Thitipong Warokorn
Louis Rossi (24, France) switched from Tech 3 to a SAG-run Kalex for his second Moto2 campaign.

After being parachuted into grand prix racing in place of countryman Ratthapark Wilairot at Gresini during 2013, points were the first target for Rossi's team-mate, Thitipong Warokorn (25, Thailand), during his full season debut with SAG.

NGM Forward Racing – Simone Corsi, Mattia Pa-sini, Florian Marino
A pre-Le Mans agreement led to NGM Forward securing official Kalex bikes for the remainder of the year.

Simone Corsi (26, Italy) had made a persuasive argument for Kalex to extend its numbers courtesy of early-season results on the Forward KLX. The Italian – a previous podium finisher with MotoBI, FTR and Speed Up machinery – then led the team's first race with official Kalex support. Corsi also found time to make a MotoGP debut in 2014, riding Forward's Open-class Yamaha in the post-Jerez test. However, his season was halted by a broken arm, prompting the call-up of WSS-star Florian Marino (21, France).

Team-mate Mattia Pasini (28, Italy) was just 21st in the championship by the time of the Kalex switch, and the former two-stroke ace would claim more TV time for incidents than achievements.

SUTER

Technomag carXpert – Dominique Aegerter, Robin Mulhauser
Fifth in the championship and the top Suter rider of 2013, Dominique Aegerter (23, Switzerland) began the season ominously when a technical failure ended a run of 33 successive point-scoring finishes, dating back to Qatar, 2012.

Fortunately for Aegerter – a Technomag Suter rider since the inaugural Moto2 season – it was not a sign of things to come. He would scale new heights in 2014, including a debut grand prix victory in a year when he also finished third in the Suzuka 8 Hours (alongside Yukio Kagayama and Noriyuki Haga) and make his MotoGP debut in a test for Avintia. He made headlines for a stunning save when clouted by the bouncing bike of Jordi Torres in Catalunya.

Rookie Robin Mulhauser (22, Switzerland) took over from Randy Krummenacher as second rider.

DOMINIQUE AEGERTER

THOMAS LUTHI

ANTHONY WEST

ALEX DE ANGELIS

ROBIN MULHAUSER

LORENZO BALDASSARRI

JORDI TORRES

RANDY KRUMMENACHER

GINO REA

NICOLAS TEROL

Photos: Gold & Goose

Technomag will merge with Interwetten in 2015 and field a Swiss line-up of Thomas Luthi, Aegerter and Mulhauser. However, in a sign of Suter's decline, the team will join the Kalex crowd – set to reach a massive 23 entries, largely at Suter's expense.

Mapfre Aspar Team Moto2 – Nicolas Terol, Jordi Torres, Dakota Mamola

Few could have foreseen the 2014 struggle awaiting Mapfre Aspar riders Nicolas Terol (25, Spain) and Jordi Torres (26, Spain). Both had won races for the team in the previous season and were expected to become stronger with experience. Instead of fighting for podiums, however, they faced a desperate challenge to get into the points.

Former 125c world champion Terol withdrew from Silverstone to seek treatment for mysterious muscle fatigue, being replaced by Dakota Mamola, son of four-time 500GP title runner-up Randy Mamola.

The only team other than Gresini racing in all three grand prix classes, Aspar will not contest Moto2 in 2015, when Terol will move to World Superbikes.

Interwetten Paddock Moto2 – Thomas Luthi

After seeing his 2013 title hopes wrecked by pre-season injuries, Thomas Luthi (27, Switzerland) began the new season fit, healthy and buoyed by three podiums from the final four rounds of the previous year.

In a season when younger countryman Aegerter's career took off, former 125cc world champion Luthi returned to the top step for the first time since 2012 and narrowly got the better of Aegerter overall.

Gresini Moto2/ Federal Oil Gresini Moto2 – Xavier Simeon, Lorenzo Baldassarri

Having taken his first grand prix podium on a Kalex in 2013, Xavier Simeon (24, Belgium) switched from SAG to Gresini. The Belgian's pre-season preparations were interrupted by a nasty mouth injury, however, which forced him to miss a test, but he was soon on the pace and would claim his best yet result.

Alongside Simeon was Lorenzo Baldassarri (17, Italy), promoted by Gresini from Moto3, where he felt his physical size had been a disadvantage.

Tasca Racing Moto2 – Alex de Angelis, Riccardo Rosso, Roberto Rolfo

After moving from the shrinking Forward Racing line-up, Alex de Angelis (30, San Marino) was having a low-key season at Tasca Racing until he was recalled by Forward to replace Colin Edwards in MotoGP.

Tasca responded by signing Italian rookie Riccardo Russo (22, Italy), with former grand prix rider – and 2014 WSS podium finisher – Roberto Rolfo (34, Italy) stepping in at Sepang and Valencia.

IodaRacing Project – Randy Krummenacher

Having switched from Technomag to Ioda, Randy Krummenacher (24, Switzerland) nonetheless remained with familiar Suter machinery for a second season.

AGT REA Racing – Gino Rea

Having kept his grand prix career alive by putting together a wild-card project for 2013, Gino Rea (24, Great Britain) was rewarded with a full-time seat courtesy of the new AGT REA Racing project. His pre-season preparations were hampered by a broken foot, however, and further injuries followed. It often took the intervention of poor weather for the former podium finisher to threaten the top ten.

SPEED UP

Speed Up – Sam Lowes

The most high-profile arrival from outside the GP paddock was reigning World Supersport champion Sam Lowes (23, Great Britain), who signed as the lone rider for Italian manufacturer Speed Up's official team.

The bike had only taken one podium in the previous season and, with no team-mate to directly compare data, it looked like a considerable gamble for Lowes, twin brother of reigning BSB champion Alex. Speed Up's use of a carbon fibre (rather than aluminium) swing-arm added further uncertainty.

There would be times when Lowes appeared to be lacking set-up direction from the team, and over-riding as a consequence, but the ever committed Englishman was soon labelled with the f-word: fast.

QMMF Racing Team – Anthony West, Roman Ramos, Nina Prinz

It was a difficult winter for Anthony West (32, Australia), whose results between 20th May, 2012 and 19th October, 2013 were erased from the books.

This move followed an appeal by the World Anti-Doping Agency for a harsher punishment than the one-month ban handed to West after he had tested positive for a prohibited stimulant, which the Australian had unwittingly consumed in an energy drink.

The outcome could have been much worse, with WADA pushing for a 24-month ban. Almost certainly, such a sentence would have ended West's racing career and doubtless had played on the former factory MotoGP rider's mind during 2013.

Thus the new season began with a huge weight lifted from West's shoulders, and he would go on to

RICARD CARDUS

ROMAN RAMOS

MATTIA PASINI

SIMONE CORSI

RATHAPARK WILAIROT

JOSH HERRIN

XAVIER SIMEON

TETSUTA NAGASHIMA

JOHANN ZARCO

pay back the loyalty of the QMMF team, which had stuck by him throughout, in the best possible way.

After occasional appearances in three previous Moto2 seasons, on MIR, MotoBI and FTR machinery, Roman Ramos (23, Spain) finally got his chance of a full season courtesy of the second QMMF seat. German woman racer Nina Prinz (31) made her GP debut on a third QMMF machine at the Sachsenring.

TECH 3

Tech 3 – Ricard Cardus, Marcel Schrotter

French race team/constructor Tech 3 was rocked preseason by serious injuries suffered by Alex Marinelarena. The 21-year-old was placed in a medically-induced coma after falling in a private test at Paul Ricard. He awoke one week later, but the slow healing process meant he would not return in 2014.

Ricky Cardus (26, Spain) took Marinelarena's seat; he had been cast on to the sidelines after scoring just seven points for Forward Racing in 2013. Riding his seventh different GP machine and eager to prove his doubters wrong, he exceeded expectations, making the most of his opportunity.

Having switched from a Kalex to Tech 3's Mistral 610, team-mate Marcel Schrotter (21, Germany) also enjoyed his best Moto2 season. Herve Poncharal rewarded both riders with new contracts for 2015.

FORWARD KLX

NGM Forward Racing – Mattia Pasini, Simone Corsi

Having split from Speed Up for a planned return to FTR, Forward Racing missed the first official pre-season test, before announcing that it would launch its own Forward KLX project, based on the 2013 Kalex.

Managing Director Marco Curioni explained: "We have applied the philosophy of the Open category in MotoGP to Moto2. We believe that the 2013 Kalex chassis still represents the best solution in Moto2, so we decided to buy it with the idea to modify it in the areas where we see room for improvement."

Mattia Pasini (29, Italy) proved the potential of the chassis by setting the best top speed on its debut in Qatar, while team-mate Simone Corsi (27, Italy) held fifth in the world championship after four events. But you won't see the chassis listed in the results after Jerez. Forward reached an agreement with Kalex to use its official 2014 chassis from Le Mans onwards.

CATERHAM SUTER

AirAsia Caterham Moto Racing – Johann Zarco, Josh Herrin, Rathapark Wilairot

The most high-profile new constructor in GP racing in 2014 was Caterham, headed by Malaysian entrepreneur Tony Fernandes, founder of Air Asia (the team's title sponsor), Tune Hotels and chairman of English football team Queens Park Rangers.

Former grand prix racer Johan Stigefelt was appointed team manager for the Moto2 project, based alongside Caterham's F1 team at Leafield in the UK, with Moto2 podium finisher Johann Zarco (23, France) and reigning American Superbike champion Josh Herrin (23, America) hired as its riders.

Rather than an off-the-shelf chassis, Caterham sought a technical partnership, resulting in a Caterham Suter design. However, the only real difference was in terms of aerodynamics, Caterham making use of wind tunnel and CFD knowledge from its F1 team.

Caterham endured a nightmare start to the season, as witnessed by the opening lap in Qatar, and while Zarco would present the new team with trophies, Herrin's misery continued. Former GP rider Ratthapark Wilairot (26, Thailand) returned from WSS to replace the injured American at Jerez, then took over for the final six rounds when Herrin was dropped.

Following the sale of Caterham's F1 team, it also became apparent that the Moto2 project would not continue in 2015, the team effectively morphing into a new Sepang International Circuit entry in Moto3.

TSR

Teluru Team JiR Webike – Tetsuta Nagashima

After four years using a TSR chassis badged as a MotoBI, JiR gave the Japanese chassis official naming rights in 2014. Initially, Kohta Nozane was set for the ride, but the sudden death of his father forced the young Japanese to rethink his career.

Tetsuta Nagashima (21, Japan) – who had made one start for JiR in 2013 – replaced Nozane from preseason testing onwards. The team's podiums during the early seasons of Moto2 remained a distant memory, however, with not a single point in 2014.

Nagashima's season was severely disrupted by shoulder and leg injuries sustained in a Silverstone practice clash with Azlan Shah. A series of riders were drafted in until Nagashima's return in the Valencia finale, among them former Moto2 racer and CEV Superbike star Kenny Noyes (35, United States). The team also trialled an NTS chassis ahead of a possible TSR split in 2015, when Randy Krummenacher will take over JiR riding duties

2014 TEAMS AND RIDERS

By PETER McLAREN

MOTO3 enhanced its reputation for thrilling racing in 2014, when a revived Honda challenge broke KTM's dominance and Alex Marquez became the first brother of a grand prix champion to win a title, after a showdown with Jack Miller.

The main technical specifications remained stable for year three of the 250cc four-stroke category. All competitors ran a control ECU and Dunlop tyres, and there was a 148kg combined minimum weight (rider and bike).

However, the latest chapter in Moto3's ongoing juggling act to allow engine and chassis competition, while seeking to limit technical favouritism, led to the introduction of random engine distribution. The new rule meant that rather than a manufacturer deciding which engines went to which of its teams, they were instead handed over to the Technical Director, who allocated them randomly. This underlined a rule that each manufacturer must supply all of its riders with the same engine specification.

Each manufacturer was also committed to charging a maximum of 68,000 euros per rider for a Moto3 engine package and had to supply up to 15 riders if requested. The loophole? There was no way of preventing manufacturers from building engines that exceeded the price limit and accepting the financial hit as a trade-off for track performance.

Title runner-up Alex Rins was the only rider from 2013's three-way championship showdown to remain in the class, champion Maverick Vinales and Luis Salom having been joined by Jonas Folger (fifth) in moving up to Moto2.

That put Rins and team-mate Alex Marquez as hypothetical 2014 favourites, albeit having made the change from KTM to Honda machinery. KTM signed Jack Miller to replace Salom as lead rider, and added Valentino Rossi's new VR46 team to its ranks.

Thirty-three riders lined up for round one at Qatar from the following nations: Italy (7), Spain (6), Australia (2), Czech Republic (2), France (2), Great Britain (2), Germany (2), Malaysia (2), Netherlands (2), and the one rider each from Portugal, South Africa, Belgium, Brazil, Finland and Venezuela. Nine were grand prix newcomers, including 2013 Red Bull MotoGP Rookies Cup graduates Karel Hanika, Enea Bastianini and Scott Deroue.

Left without a podium in the face of total KTM domination in 2013, Honda's response was a much more hands-on approach and an upgraded NSF250RW. The 'pure' Honda also became the only Honda-powered package, ending previous FTR, TSR and Suter chassis partnerships.

Meanwhile, KTM rebadged two of its entries as Husqvarnas, resulting in five official 2014 constructors, with Kalex KTM and Mahindra continuing.

The cost of a Moto3 engine package is to be reduced to 60,000 euros (excluding gearbox) for 2015, when a price limit will see a complete rolling chassis capped at 85,000 euros. Maximum rpm will also be cut from 14,000 to 13,500.

A more controversial rule change will allow the winner of the FIM CEV (Spanish) Moto3 Championship to compete in grands prix the following season, even if the rider has not reached the minimum age of 16.

The decision cleared the way for Fabio Quartararo, who will not turn 16 until 20th April, to race the full 2015 season. Quartararo rides for Emilio Alzamora's Estrella Galicia 0.0 Junior Team in CEV and will follow in the footsteps of Marquez and Rins by stepping up to the grand prix team.

KTM

Red Bull KTM Ajo – Jack Miller, Karel Hanika

From KTM's point of view, the only blot on its unbeaten 2013 season was seeing the riders' title snatched away from the official Red Bull Ajo team by the satellite Calvo squad. But at least it proved the evenness of machinery offered by the Austrian manufacturer, whose factory team returned with an all-new line-up for 2014.

Having wrung the maximum out of a Racing Team Germany-run FTR-Honda on the way to seventh the previous season, Jack Miller (19, Australia) was hired to replace Luis Salom as Ajo's title challenger. The charismatic teenager began the year without even a podium, but ended it within touching distance of the title, being left to ponder three non-scores as the championship slipped away by the smallest of margins.

Miller claimed the most race wins and had been confirmed as a 2015 Honda MotoGP rider by September. Look out for plenty of wheelies and 'goon riding' celebrations along the way.

Aside from the frustration of the final-round showdown, Miller was also handed penalty points by Race Direction at Mugello, and found himself at the centre of a contractual dispute with Marc VDS.

Paired with Miller was rookie Karel Hanika (18, Czech Republic), who followed in the footsteps of Danny Kent (2011) and Arthur Sissis (2012) in moving from the Red Bull Rookies Cup for a Moto3 debut with Aki Ajo's team. Hanika kept KTM's fairing builders busy as he found the GP limits.

He will continue in 2015, as part of a three-strong Ajo line-up alongside Miguel Oliveira and Brad Binder.

SKY Racing Team VR46 – Romano Fenati, Francesco Bagnaia

The big news for Moto3 was the debut of Valentino Rossi's new VR46 team, the legendary MotoGP star having called up figures from his own racing past, such as former Ducati team manager Vittoriano Guareschi and former Aprilia crew chief Rossano Brazzi, to assume key roles in the project.

Rossi's rider line-up was also unashamedly Italian, with Romano Fenati (18) and Francesco Bagnaia (17) entrusted with the team's Sky-backed KTMs.

Rossi wouldn't have to wait long for success as a team owner, as Fenati soon cast off a miserable 2013 to deliver the kind of form expected after his race-winning rookie campaign. Bagnaia had joined Fenati in moving from the underpowered FTR Honda at San Carlo Team Italia, where he had failed to score a point.

Inconsistent results and mechanical issues proved a headache for the VR46 team, and Guareschi made a surprise exit after Silverstone. Rossi's team was boosted, however, by the re-signing of Fenati for 2015, when Andrea Migno will ride the second entry and Pablo Nieto (son of Angel) takes over as team manager.

Junior Team GO&FUN Moto3 – Enea Bastianini, Niccolo Antonelli

After it was indicated that Isaac Vinales would join the retained Niccolo Antonelli (18, Italy) at Gresini's GO&FUN-backed Moto3 team, it was Enea Bastianini (16, Italy) who ultimately took the second seat.

Given Bastianini's age and absence of grand prix experience, many may have expected that he would have been the one testing Gresini's patience with an excessive number of falls. Instead, the Red Bull Rookies graduate was soon in contention for 'find of the season' as he increasingly held his own at the sharp

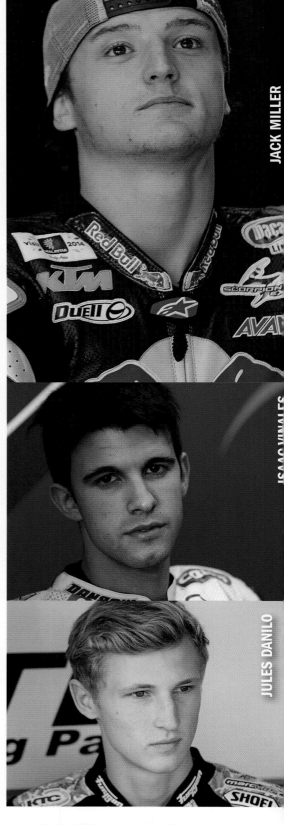

JACK MILLER

ISAAC VINALES

JULES DANILO

end of the field. Valentino Rossi would label him "the great surprise of this year among the Italian riders".

Meanwhile, Antonelli's third season was marred by mistakes, prompting statements such as "When the race starts, he rides the bike by himself" from team boss and former racer Fausto Gresini. Antonelli even fell during the summer break, fracturing his right collarbone and requiring surgery after a training accident, but he turned things around late in the year.

Gresini returns to Hondas in 2015, pairing Bastianini with Andrea Locatelli. Antonelli will move to Ongetta.

Calvo Team – Isaac Vinales, Jakub Kornfeil, Eric Granado

Having been announced as due to ride for Gresini in September, Isaac Vinales (20, Spain) was absent

FRANCESCO BAGNAIA

KAREL HANIKA

ROMANOO FENATI

NICCOLO ANTONELLI

ERIC GRANADO

JAKUB KORNFEIL

ENEA BASTIANINI

HAFIQ AZMI

ARTHUR SISSIS

ANDREA MIGNO

BRAD BINDER

ANDREA LOCATELLI

MATTEO FERRARI

MIGUEL OLIVEIRA

from the first draft of the 2014 entry list. Later it was confirmed that he would take the place of cousin and reigning champion Maverick Vinales at Team Calvo.

Isaac began to emerge from Maverick's shadow in 2014, which was his third world championship season. Alongside him was the experienced Jakub Kornfeil (20, Czech Republic), who had switched to Calvo from RW Racing. Eric Granado (17, Brazil) also arrived after a sponsorship clash scuppered his plan to ride for Aspar.

Vinales and Granado will be joined by Maria Herrera at Calvo in 2015, when the team will run the Husqvarna-branded KTMs.

SIC-AJO – Hafiq Azmi
Having raced the final four rounds of the 2013 season with Tasca Racing, Hafiq Azmi (17, Malaysia) was given

a full-season opportunity on an Ajo-run KTM backed by his local Sepang circuit.

MAHINDRA

Mahindra Racing – Miguel Oliveira, Arthur Sissis
It came as no surprise that Indian brand Mahindra, whose Suter-built MGP30 had been the revelation of the 2013 season, retained Miguel Oliveira (19, Portugal), who had been sixth in the championship that year, teaming him with Ajo outcast Arthur Sissis (18, Australia), who took over the seat vacated by Efren Vazquez.

As so often in motorsport, the final few tenths to the top proved the hardest, and Mahindra's upward momentum slowed in 2014, but it would still be their best season yet. Oliveira remained a contender, but Sissis –

who missed round one due to tonsillitis – rarely looked comfortable and was replaced by rookie Andrea Migno (17, Italy) after Brno.

Mahindra will cease to run an official Moto3 factory team in 2015, opting to concentrate on development of the bike for other teams, led by Aspar.

Ambrogio Racing – Brad Binder, Jules Danilo
This would be a breakthrough season for Brad Binder (18, South Africa), riding in his third full world championship campaign, but first on the MGP30 after Ambrogio's mid-2013 switch. Alongside Binder was Jules Danilo (18, Italy), who had made four GP starts the previous year.

While Brad Binder moves to Ajo, brother Daryn will join the team alongside Alessandro Tonucci in 2015.

Photos: Gold & Goose

San Carlo Team Italia – Matteo Ferrari, Andrea Locatelli
San Carlo Team Italia replaced the VR46-bound Fenati and Bagnaia with rival young Italian hopefuls Matteo Ferrari (17) and Andrea Locatelli (17) for what was the team's first season with Mahindra, having switched from FTR Honda.

CIP – Alessandro Tonucci, Bryan Schouten, Jasper Iwema
CIP parked its TSR-Hondas in favour of Mahindras, raced by an all-new rider line-up of Alessandro Tonucci (20, Italy) and Bryan Schouten (19, Netherlands). The experienced Tonucci arrived from Tasca Racing, while Schouten was given a full campaign after wild-card appearances over the previous three seasons.

Schouten and countryman Scott Deroue brought the sport to a wider audience when images of their German Grand Prix scuffle appeared in the mainstream media. Fellow Dutchman Jasper Iwema (24), who put an FTR KTM in the points as a home wild-card at Assen, made a GP return in place of Schouten for the closing rounds.

KALEX KTM

Mapfre Aspar Team Moto3 – Juanfran Guevara
The Kalex may be the machine of choice in Moto2, but its KTM-powered Moto3 entry would struggle to match the Honda, KTM and Mahindra motorcycles and is to disappear from grand prix in 2015.

The Mapfre Aspar Team reduced its Moto3 involvement to a single rider for 2014, with Juanfran Guevara (18, Spain). He had not scored a point in 2013 and was something of a surprise candidate after switching from CIP. Aspar will become the main Mahindra team in 2015, running Guevara, plus new signings Bagnaia and Jorge Martin, 2014 Rookies Cup champion.

Kiefer Racing – Gabriel Ramos, Luca Grunwald, Remy Gardner
Kiefer Racing relied on two new faces in the form of rookies Gabriel Ramos (19, Venezuela) and Luca Grunwald (19, Germany). When Grunwald was injured, the team called up Remy Gardner (16, Australia), son of 1987 500cc World Champion Wayne Gardner. Remy would also appear as a wild-card with Calvo for his home Phillip Island round and the following Malaysian Grand Prix. Kiefer will move to Honda machinery in 2015, signing Danny Kent and Hiroki Ono, while Gardner will become a full-time grand prix rider with the CIP Mahindra team.

Marc VDS Racing Team – Livio Loi, Jorge Navarro
After a late start to his rookie season, due to his age, Livio Loi (16, Belgium) was sacked halfway through his second year. A collapse in results after a brilliant ride in Argentina meant he didn't meet the top-15 target set by Marc VDS. Spanish Championship rider Jorge Navarro (18, Spain) took over for the rest of the year. Marc VDS will cease its Moto3 involvement in 2015.

RW Racing Grand Prix – Scott Deroue, Ana Carrasco
RW Racing was another with an all-new line-up, having made the difficult decision to replace Jasper Iwema with Scott Deroue (18, Netherlands), fresh from the Red Bull Rookies Cup. Points-scoring woman racer Ana Carrasco (17, Spain) effectively swapped teams with Jakub Kornfeil for her sophomore season, but would depart before the flyaways due to financial reasons. Deroue is due to remain at RW as it moves to a single Honda entry in 2015.

Interwetten Paddock Moto3 – Philipp Oettl
After gathering steam during the second half of his rookie year, Interwetten Paddock's Philipp Oettl (17, Switzerland) – like the other Kalex KTM riders – would find 2014 more of an uphill struggle.

HONDA

Estrella Galicia 0,0 – Alex Rins, Alex Marquez, Maria Herrera
Crushed by KTM in 2013, Japanese giant Honda took the gloves off its Moto3 effort, unleashing a heavily revised and far more 'factory' NSF250RW machine.

The Estrella Galicia 0,0 team – run by Emilio Alzamora's Monlau Competicion – switched back from KTM to spearhead HRC's attack, retaining both reigning title runner-up Alex Rins (18, Spain) and fellow race winner Alex Marquez (17, Spain).

Having lost 2013's crown by just 0.187 second, Rins should have been the man to beat. But he missed a pre-season test after undergoing surgery to remove a cyst from his right wrist, and it was Marquez, younger brother of MotoGP champion Marc, who soon held the upper hand.

While Marquez would claim title glory, Rins fractured a toe in Catalunya and suffered the embarrassment of an early victory celebration in Brno, before finally returning to the top step. Both considered future MotoGP stars – Rins claimed to have turned down an offer for 2015 – the pair will continue their rivalry at different teams in Moto2 in 2015. Taking over their Moto3 seats will be Navarro and Quartararo.

Maria Herrera, one of Estrella Galicia's CEV riders, raced as a wild-card in some of the Spanish rounds.

SaxoPrint-RTG – Efren Vazquez, John McPhee
Racing Team Germany may not have been able to retain Miller, but their top Honda efforts ensured continued support and the chance to benefit from the more potent 2014 machine.

Ex-Mahindra rider Efren Vazquez (27, Spain) took Miller's vacant seat, while John McPhee (19, Great Britain) kept his place for a second year. Vazquez would finally become a GP winner in 2014, his eighth season.

Ongetta-Rivacold/ Ongetta-AirAsia – Alexis Masbou, Zulfahmi Khairuddin
Ongetta-Rivacold's Alexis Masbou (26, France) would break an even longer losing streak than Vazquez's. He again rode in Rivacold colours, while former Red Bull KTM rider Zulfahmi Khairuddin (22, Malaysia) endured a tough season on an AirAsia-backed bike. He will be the star rider for the new Sepang International Circuit team, and back on a KTM, in 2015.

HUSQVARNA

Red Bull Husqvarna Ajo/Avant Tecno Husqvarna Ajo – Danny Kent, Niklas Ajo
KTM revived a tactic formally used by the Piaggio Group by badging two of its GP machines as Husqvarnas. KTM and Husqvarna had shared ownership, and the move allowed Husqvarna instant access to competitive machinery with all of the marketing benefits that go with it.

The downside was that, if the top Husqvarna rider finished ahead of the best KTM in a race, it would cost KTM points in the constructors' championship. With Honda and KTM having proved literally equally matched, that could have been pivotal. Ultimately, however, the situation didn't occur.

Aki Ajo ran both the official KTM and Husqvarna teams, underlining their close association, with son Niklas Ajo (19, Finland) joining class returnee Danny Kent (20, Great Britain) to form the Husky line-up.

The pair proved a little too closely matched in Argentina, Ajo having raised his game to podium contender early in his fourth season, only to suffer a broken ankle. Having arrived from a tough year of Moto2 at Tech 3, double 2012 Ajo KTM race winner Kent took longer to settle in, but ultimately beat Ajo to the rostrum.

Kent will switch to Honda machinery with Kiefer in 2015, when Ajo will join Carrasco and Gabriel Rodrigo in the debut grand prix season for Aleix Espargaro's BOE41 RBA (KTM) team.

Photos: Gold & Goose

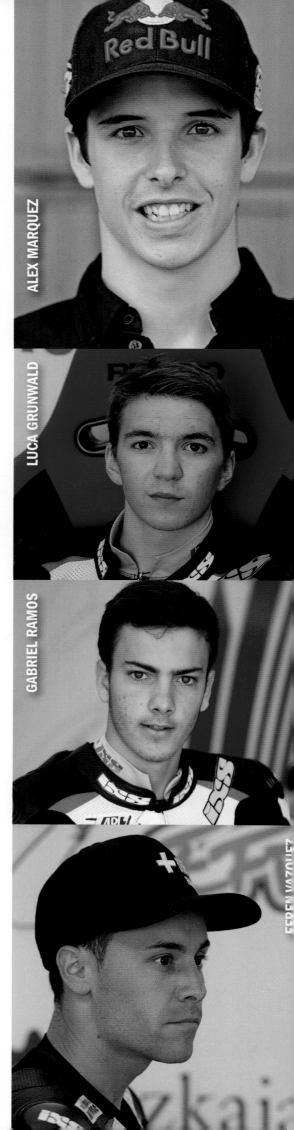

ALEX MARQUEZ

LUCA GRUNWALD

GABRIEL RAMOS

EFREN VAZQUEZ

THE CIRCUIT OF WALES

The Circuit of Wales is a £315m world-class motorsport and destination informed and inspired by nature and regeneration.

A business hub for high-technology excellence in the automotive and technology centres, the Circuit of Wales will provide:

- A state-of-the-art, purpose-built motorcycle Grand Prix circuit and facilities, attracting national and international motorsports

- A centre for low-carbon research and development, providing a base for leading educational institutions

- The home of advance manufacturing, precision engineering and automotive performance companies

- An elite indoor performance academy aimed at developing industry talent

- Leading educational, safety and training automotive infrastructure facilities

- A range of complementary Leisure & Retail offerings in the picturesque Rassau Valley

  aventa

For further information contact
www.circuitofwales.com

MOTOGP · MOTO2 · MOTO3

GRANDS PRIX 2014

Reports by MICHAEL SCOTT

Statistics compiled by PETER McLAREN

QATAR GRAND PRIX

LOSAIL CIRCUIT

Inset, left: "Good luck Cal – you'll need it!" Ducati's Paolo Ciabatti with his newest rider.

Inset, below: Dorna's Ezpeleta and Alonso were all smiles.
Photos: Gold & Goose

Inset, above: Nakagami's podium celebrations proved premature.

Inset, above centre: Aleix Espargaro impressed on his near-factory-level 'Open' Yamaha.

Main: Valentino Rossi gave his best, but could not defeat Marquez.
Photos: Gold & Goose

Above: Lorenzo leads – Lorenzo falls. The Yamaha rider is about to make "a learner's mistake".

Photo: Yamaha Racing

Top right: Alvaro Bautista qualified second, but was one of five to fall in the race.

Top far right: Bradley Smith also made the front row, but also bit the dust.

Above right: MotoGP rookie Redding emerged triumphant against former champion Hayden in the first production-racer Honda battle.

Centre near and far right: Class rookies – ex-125 champion Mike di Meglio was the sole French representative; GP newcomer Broc Parkes the only Australian.

Right: Ready to ride. Not even a broken leg could stand in the way of Marquez's first-race victory.

Photos: Gold & Goose

THE 2014 season could hardly have started better. After a maelstrom of confused new rules, rewritten twice before racing even started, and adjusted again (albeit only for clarification) on the day of the first race; after three days of practice and qualifying with some most unexpected consequences, the desert night was lit by fine close racing in all three classes.

The rules could take only a little credit. Of more significance was that non-factory riders in both categories had benefited from three nights of testing at Losail two weeks before. At a track with tricky grip and a complex technical challenge, this was a valuable head start.

In this way, both Bautista and Smith played strong roles in a leading group unexpectedly bereft of Lorenzo (a "learner's mistake" took him out on lap one); but otherwise the usual people filled out the rostrum. That one of them was Rossi was a touch of icing; that he had made Marquez ride like a devil to beat him all the more so. It restored faith not only in the fading icon of MotoGP, but also in racing itself. It also added to the Marquez legend: he hadn't ridden at all for the previous six weeks, missing the last two tests, after breaking his leg in a training crash.

All this was most timely, at a historic moment. The upshot of the shenanigans with the rules had been late factory agreement, long sought, to Ezpeleta's plan for control electronics for all in 2016. At this race, control software became mandatory for Open machines (control hardware for all), with most opting for the older-generation rather than the latest Ducati-style option tried at the later tests. Ducati themselves, having been returned to Factory status a week before, although retaining Open technical concessions, continued for this race with the latest control version.

The new Open bikes varied widely, ranging from the senior Espargaro's Yamaha, effectively a 2012 factory bike as used by Tech 3 in 2013, to the CRT survivors, a couple with Kawasaki power and the rest Aprilia. In between, the eagerly awaited Honda RCV1000R, the only bike built specifically for the new class, and suffering somewhat as a result.

Lap times are one measure, but these are slightly skewed not only by rider ability, but especially by the different tyres available, especially in practice. Top speeds on Losail's kilometre-long straight were more telling:

- *Fastest Factory Option* – Marquez, Honda: 348.3km/h (Race)
- *Slowest Factory Option* – Lorenzo, Yamaha: 340.0km/h (FP1)
- *Fastest Open* – Espargaro A., Yamaha: 338.1km/h (Race)
- *Fastest RCV1000R* – Aoyama: 330.8km/h (FP1)
- *Slowest Open* – Parkes, PBM-Aprilia: 321.4km/h FP1)

The last-named, aged 32, was a GP rookie (a 1999 125 wild-card ride aside) and understandably feeling his way on a low-grade bike. Mike di Meglio was up from Moto2, likewise 2013 title rivals Pol Espargaro and Scott Redding. The Spaniard was nursing a post-op collarbone injury from the final test, and suffered a crash and a breakdown; Redding would shine.

There were high-profile rookies also in Moto2 – Moto3 title winner Maverick Vinales and his rival, Luis Salom, now uneasy team-mates in the Pons HP 40 squad. The former made a blazing start less than half a second off the podium. Another first-timer made a big impression: World Supersport champion Sam Lowes was not a track virgin, but still impressed with a fine sixth in his first GP.

Tyres are always a major factor, all the more so with the varied allocation. Bridgestone brought a range of three compounds: Open bikes had access to the softer pair, Factory Option riders the harder. The choice overlapped. The four Open Honda riders all went for the soft rear, along with Petrucci, di Meglio and Laverty; the remaining four chose the middle tyre, as used by all but one of the Factory riders. The exception? Marquez chose the hard, and won.

They were especially a talking point for Lorenzo, whose lap-one crash was the culmination of an awful weekend. No grip, he complained, as he struggled through free practice – a repeat of his problems at the final tests at Sepang, where he had called the new-generation harder-construction tyres "dangerous". He repeated the assertion after both Espargaro Jr and Smith suffered big power-on high-side crashes in practice (Smith described his as "a typical 500 crash"). Some edge grip had been sacrificed in favour of better warm-

up and tyre life. A blow to him (and to a lesser extent Rossi), with his great reliance on mid-corner speed.

The biggest advantage of the soft tyre choice was expected in qualifying, but it was not so cut and dried. Espargaro Sr definitely took full benefit, heading every free session, only to fall twice in the more important 15 minutes of qualifying. But he and the Ducati riders had the same opinion. "It would be impossible to race the soft," said the Spaniard. "After only three laps, it is gone."

The other big change concerned fuel: Factory bikes gasping on 20 litres, one less than the previous season; the Open bikes awash with 20 per cent extra, on 24 litres. It was a particular concern to Yamaha: the previous year, Rossi had run out on the slow-down lap. They also complained of erratic engine braking, snatchy throttle response and lost speed. Rossi joked that on the straight, the engine felt as if "powered by air". At the pre-event conference, Marquez looked smug. "My bike is competitive on 20 litres," he said.

Rain in FP2 on Friday brought out red-cross flags, but the track stayed dry. Later that night, a heavy downpour revived memories of the race-postponing downpour of 2009; while a fresh track coating of sand required vacuum-cleaner lorries the next day.

There was a new tension in Moto3, with Honda striving to prevent another year of KTM domination. Honda's best rider, Jack Miller, had switched to the official Red Bull KTM team; but KTM's top remaining pair, Alexis Rins and Marquez, had crossed the floor along with their Estrella squad to ride the new Honda RS250FW, with its natty twin underseat exhausts. At the same time, Mahindra numbers had increased to eight.

Miller was the first rider out on track in 2014, with a trademark wheelie as he led the pack out on Thursday (uniquely this race spans four days); Hernandez was the first serious crasher, bringing out the first red flag in FP1 after a big fall left the track strewn with gravel and debris, and the rider with painful abrasions.

MOTOGP RACE – 22 laps

Marquez had to summon every ounce of talent to snitch pole at the last gasp from satellite riders Bautista and Smith. The other usual stars struggled, especially Lorenzo, a dismayed 11th after the first two sessions before moving up into Q2 with seventh at "maximum risk".

Much dismay came from Aleix Espargaro's older Open Yamaha, on control electronics, but using soft tyres. He led all three free sessions, but fell twice in qualifying.

Times were very close at this relatively long circuit: the top nine were inside half a second, Rossi less than a tenth beyond. (It was the first time since Jerez in 2007 that nine or more riders had been within half a second: back then, there were 12.)

Dovi led row two with a soft tyre, concerned about race pace on the hard: "We are better on corner entry now, but we still suffer understeer."

Lorenzo finally placed fifth, Pedrosa a smooth and steady sixth. Bradl led row three from Crutchlow (another to crash, and furthermore obliged to make it through from Q1) and the luckless Aleix Espargaro.

Then came Rossi, ahead of Iannone and Pol Espargaro, also through from Q1. Hayden was best of the rest, from Aoyama. Rookie Redding led row six.

Smith got away best from the front row, but not as well as Lorenzo from the second, and the factory man led – until the second-last of 16 corners, bamboozled by lower temperatures later in the evening and the new tyre construction. "The tyres were not ready yet. We are only human, we make mistakes," he explained.

By then, Bradl had pushed past Smith, about to lose second to Marquez. Iannone got ahead of Dovizioso also and was pushing Smith when he went down at the end of lap two. Rossi was next, then Pedrosa and Bautista.

Pedrosa lingered as Rossi and Bautista moved through to chase Marquez, while Bradl led for eight laps. Then he too lost the front, and it was Marquez in the lead.

Only briefly, for now Rossi seized the lead with a clean inside pass. The top five were covered by six-tenths: Rossi, Marquez, Pedrosa, Smith, Bautista. Marquez was hounding Rossi, teasingly faster on the straight.

Smith was at the back and losing ground as Marquez took to the front again on lap 14, but was closing on the tussling Pedrosa and Bautista as the leading pair drew slightly clear. Then Smith was gone with four laps left, another to lose the front. Bautista followed suit two laps later, soon after having passed Pedrosa again. He was the fifth victim.

The leaders were now alone, and their battle – a replay of the previous year – was absorbing. It came to a head on the penultimate lap. Rossi attacked at turn four, Marquez pushed aggressively past again at the next corner. They swapped again, Marquez once more emerging the victor. He started the last lap with enough of an advantage to win by a quarter of a second.

In 2013, Rossi had beaten him to second. Significantly, in 2014, the result went the other way. "It was important, because the injury meant I missed most of the pre-season," said Marquez, glowing with enjoyment. For Rossi, sporting as ever: "It looked like an old race from MotoGP from ten years ago, all together on the same pace, some mistakes, going wide and so on. Maybe Dorna had a great idea."

Relieved of Bautista's pressure, Pedrosa was satisfied with a well-judged third at a track he has never liked.

Eight seconds behind, the battle for fourth lasted until the end. Dovizioso held it for the first half, then Aleix Espargaro found his way through and stayed there, if only by half a second. For the Ducati rider, the better news was that bike improvements so far had halved 2013's gap to the leader.

New team-mate Crutchlow had stuck with the pair with some difficulty, after an early electronic glitch that had knocked him off the timing screens and made the bike increasingly difficult to ride. At the end, he coasted over the line, 26 seconds away, but narrowly safe in sixth.

The next pair were the best of the new Open Hondas, the order slightly surprising. Rookie Redding had been hounding Hayden until the American ran wide. Try as he might, he couldn't get back, and the Englishman took a fine debut seventh by three-hundredths.

Seven seconds down, Edwards was alone, with tenth going to the remounted Iannone. Aoyama and Hernandez battled to the end over 11th; the last points went to the still-recovering Abraham, Petrucci and lonely first-timer Parkes, who beat team-mate Laverty. He had suffered a ride-through penalty after a jumped start.

Pol Espargaro had played a strong role in the battle for fourth, but had retired with gearbox problems; Barbera also pulled out.

Phew, what a scorcher!

MOTO2 RACE – 20 laps

Things went wrong at the end of both qualifying and the race in Moto2, leaving Cortese with a fractured foot and Nakagami a broken heart, after he had been disqualified from second due to a minor, yet unforgivable, infringement of the technical rules.

Tito Rabat, in the colours of 2013 rival Redding, had dominated testing, and he snatched an ultra-close pole from Cortese in the closing minutes. Nakagami completed an all-Kalex front row.

The flag had fallen when both Cortese and Torres fell at turn two, the former being stretchered away. His bike had run back on to the track, where it lay in wait for a cruising Mika Kallio, who saw it too late. His bike was all but destroyed as it looped over its own smashed front wheel, the rider lucky to limp away.

Luthi led row two from the impressive Lowes; Kallio was at the far end.

Rabat started strongly, only to be pushed wide into the first corner by Nakagami. By the end of the lap, Kallio was second, then Luthi, soon to be passed again by Rabat.

Nakagami made a fair attempt at a breakaway, but Kallio chased him down again, and by lap six they had been joined by the avenging Rabat. Corsi was now fourth, but losing ground.

Crash survivor Kallio considered himself lucky to stay a close third as the other two battled it out. Nakagami led the first 12 laps over the line, and Rabat the remaining eight, but the stable numbers belied the high tension. In the end, Rabat just held the Japanese rider at bay by the narrowest of margins.

Both enjoyed the rostrum ceremony, but it turned sour for Nakagami when technical inspection revealed a non-standard air filter. This minor infringement was explained by a misunderstanding of the rules, and there had been no performance advantage. But race director Mike Webb conveyed the subsequent disqualification with the words, "Unfortunately, the situation is black and white." A bike either passes the tech inspection, or not. The team's appeal was turned down by the FIM.

This promoted all behind: Kallio second, Luthi third, after earlier dropping to sixth behind Aegerter, before his Swiss compatriot's Suter suffered a smoky demise and black flag – his first non-finish since crashing out in Catalunya in 2011, and first time out of the points in 34 races.

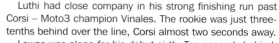

Left: Dancing with danger: early leader Bradl and Bautista are about to be swallowed up by Marquez and Rossi. Both would crash out.

Right: Supersport champion Sam Lowes qualified fifth and finished sixth in his first attempt at Moto2.

Below right: Alex Marquez: simultaneously tucked away and out of the saddle on the new Moto3 Honda.

Below: Moto2 winner Rabat looks back at Nakagami and Kallio.

Below left: Back on the rostrum: a good start for the revitalised Rossi.

Bottom: Miller (8) signals his first Moto3 victory. For the remainder, *(from left)* Marquez (12), Kornfeil (84), Oliveira (44), Vazquez (half-hidden) and Rins (out of frame), it was a matter of inches.

Bottom right: Efren Vazquez squeezed in for his first Moto3 podium.

Photos: Gold & Goose

Luthi had close company in his strong finishing run past Corsi – Moto3 champion Vinales. The rookie was just three-tenths behind over the line, Corsi almost two seconds away.

Lowes was alone for his debut sixth. Ten seconds behind, West had been leading a furious battle, only to lose by inches in the run to the line. Cortese took the place, then Torres and West; Rossi still close in tenth, and fending off another ex-Moto3 rookie, Folger, and Tech 3 substitute rider Ricky Cardus. Salom also took points in his first Moto2 race, and Malaysian Hafizh Syahrin his first championship point.

It was a disappointing debut for the new Caterham team, with both Josh Herrin and Johann Zarco crashing out on the first lap, in a four-bike tangle that also took out Simeon and de Angelis. Morbidelli, Pons and Schrotter also crashed; Rea and Terol were among a handful of retirements.

MOTO3 RACE – 18 laps

First blood to Honda, Rins snatching pole ahead of team-mate Marquez. But Miller's KTM was close and threatening, and the Austrian bikes controlled row two, Kornfeil heading Vinales and Kent, on his KTM-badged Husqvarna.

McPhee was a best ever seventh on the next Honda, heading free practice leader Fenati on the Rossi-backed KTM.

The opening race of the season was all action, from start to finish.

Marquez led the first 17 laps over the line, but under severe pressure from Miller. They drew two seconds clear while Rins, slow away and tenth at the end of lap one, battled to and fro in a large and fierce pursuit pack. He would frequently gain the lead of the group, only to be passed repeatedly on the straight by Vazquez's better-geared Honda.

Miller took to the front just before half-distance, and though Marquez grabbed it straight back, their tussle allowed the chasers to catch up for a thrilling last-lap showdown.

By then, Oliveira (Mahindra) was pushing hard and Rins was looking strong, but there were several other serious candidates for the win. Until Miller took control on the last lap, staying just far enough ahead to avoid an unseemly brawl for not only his first win, but also his first rostrum.

Rins got close as Marquez missed a gear, but the pursuers were shuffling at every corner, and all the way down the straight. Marquez retained second, 0.233 second down, with a photo-finish giving third to Vazquez from Oliveira; Rins was fifth. The top five finished within 0.369 second; Kornfeil was another two-tenths away.

Masbou reinforced the Honda's strong debut with a still-close seventh, Vinales almost alongside. Antonelli and Bagnaia completed the top ten, McPhee and Fenati within inches. Kent dropped back to hold 13th narrowly from rookie Hanika and Binder on the next-best Mahindra – team rider Arthur Sissis was out with acute tonsillitis.

COMMERCIALBANK
GRAND PRIX OF QATAR

20-23 MARCH, 2014

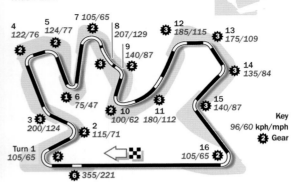

LOSAIL INTERNATIONAL CIRCUIT

22 laps
Length: 5.380 km. / 3,343 miles
Width: 12m

Key
96/60 kph/mph
Gear

MotoGP — RACE DISTANCE: 22 laps, 73.545 miles/118.360km · RACE WEATHER: Dry (air 20°C, humidity 60%, track 18°C)

Pos.	Rider	Nat.	No.	Entrant	Machine	Tyres	Race tyre choice	Laps	Time & speed
1	**Marc Marquez**	SPA	93	Repsol Honda Team	Honda RC213V	B	F: Hard/R: Hard	22	42m 40.561s
									103.4mph/
									166.4km/h
2	**Valentino Rossi**	ITA	46	Movistar Yamaha MotoGP	Yamaha YZR-M1	B	F: Hard/R: Medium	22	42m 40.820s
3	**Dani Pedrosa**	SPA	26	Repsol Honda Team	Honda RC213V	B	F: Hard/R: Medium	22	42m 43.931s
4	**Aleix Espargaro**	SPA	41	NGM Forward Racing	Forward Yamaha	B	F: Hard/R: Medium	22	42m 52.184s
5	**Andrea Dovizioso**	ITA	4	Ducati Team	Ducati Desmosedici	B	F: Hard/R: Medium	22	42m 52.720s
6	**Cal Crutchlow**	GBR	35	Ducati Team	Ducati Desmosedici	B	F: Hard/R: Medium	22	43m 09.087s
7	**Scott Redding**	GBR	45	GO&FUN Honda Gresini	Honda RCV1000R	B	F: Hard/R: Soft	22	43m 13.154s
8	**Nicky Hayden**	USA	69	Drive M7 Aspar	Honda RCV1000R	B	F: Hard/R: Soft	22	43m 13.189s
9	**Colin Edwards**	USA	5	NGM Forward Racing	Forward Yamaha	B	F: Hard/R: Medium	22	43m 20.108s
10	**Andrea Iannone**	ITA	29	Pramac Racing	Ducati Desmosedici	B	F: Hard/R: Medium	22	43m 23.921s
11	**Hiroshi Aoyama**	JPN	7	Drive M7 Aspar	Honda RCV1000R	B	F: Soft/R: Soft	22	43m 27.156s
12	**Yonny Hernandez**	COL	68	Energy T.I. Pramac Racing	Ducati Desmosedici	B	F: Soft/R: Medium	22	43m 27.249s
13	**Karel Abraham**	CZE	17	Cardion AB Motoracing	Honda RCV1000R	B	F: Hard/R: Soft	22	43m 31.142s
14	**Danilo Petrucci**	ITA	9	IodaRacing Project	ART	B	F: Hard/R: Soft	22	43m 43.688s
15	**Broc Parkes**	AUS	23	Paul Bird Motorsport	PBM-ART	B	F: Hard/R: Soft	22	43m 54.947s
16	Michael Laverty	GBR	70	Paul Bird Motorsport	PBM-ART	B	F: Hard/R: Soft	22	44m 13.154s
17	Mike di Meglio	FRA	63	Avintia Racing	Avintia	B	F: Hard/R: Soft	22	44m 16.646s
	Alvaro Bautista	SPA	19	GO&FUN Honda Gresini	Honda RC213V	B	F: Hard/R: Medium	20	DNF-crash
	Bradley Smith	GBR	38	Monster Yamaha Tech 3	Yamaha YZR-M1	B	F: Hard/R: Medium	18	DNF-crash
	Pol Espargaro	SPA	44	Monster Yamaha Tech 3	Yamaha YZR-M1	B	F: Hard/R: Medium	17	DNF-mechanical
	Stefan Bradl	GER	6	LCR Honda MotoGP	Honda RC213V	B	F: Hard/R: Medium	8	DNF-crash
	Hector Barbera	SPA	8	Avintia Racing	Avintia	B	F: Hard/R: Medium	4	DNF-mechanical
	Jorge Lorenzo	SPA	99	Movistar Yamaha MotoGP	Yamaha YZR-M1	B	F: Hard/R: Medium	0	DNF-crash

Fastest lap: Alvaro Bautista, on lap 4, 1m 55.575s, 104.1mph/167.5km/h.

Lap record: Casey Stoner, AUS (Ducati), 1m 55.153s, 104.5mph/168.1km/h (2008).

Event best maximum speed: Marc Marquez, 216.4mph/348.3km/h (race).

Qualifying

Weather: Dry

Air Temp: 21° **Track Temp:** 18°

Humidity: 50%

1	Marquez	1m 54.507s
2	Bautista	1m 54.564s
3	Smith	1m 54.601s
4	Dovizioso	1m 54.644s
5	Lorenzo	1m 54.661s
6	Pedrosa	1m 54.703s
7	Bradl	1m 54.871s
8	Crutchlow	1m 54.888s
9	A. Espargaro	1m 54.986s
10	Rossi	1m 55.096s
11	Iannone	1m 55.127s
12	P. Espargaro	1m 55.152s
13	Hayden	1m 55.894s
14	Edwards	1m 56.042s
15	Aoyama	1m 56.479s
16	Redding	1m 56.555s
17	Hernandez	1m 56.648s
18	Abraham	1m 56.715s
19	Barbera	1m 57.006s
20	Petrucci	1m 57.513s
21	Parkes	1m 57.574s
22	Di Meglio	1m 57.667s
23	Laverty	1m 58.254s

Fastest race laps

1	Bautista	1m 55.575s
2	Rossi	1m 55.621s
3	Marquez	1m 55.710s
4	Pedrosa	1m 55.843s
5	Smith	1m 55.871s
6	Bradl	1m 55.937s
7	Crutchlow	1m 56.064s
8	A. Espargaro	1m 56.192s
9	Iannone	1m 56.280s
10	Dovizioso	1m 56.285s
11	P. Espargaro	1m 56.345s
12	Redding	1m 56.416s
13	Hayden	1m 56.428s
14	Edwards	1m 57.119s
15	Abraham	1m 57.293s
16	Aoyama	1m 57.396s
17	Hernandez	1m 57.625s
18	Barbera	1m 57.822s
19	Di Meglio	1m 58.164s
20	Petrucci	1m 58.322s
21	Laverty	1m 58.396s
22	Parkes	1m 58.470s

Grid order	1	2	3	4	5	6	7	8	9	10	11	12	13	14	15	16	17	18	19	20	21	22	
93 MARQUEZ	6	6	6	6	6	6	6	6	46	46	46	46	46	93	93	93	93	93	93	93	93	93	1
19 BAUTISTA	93	93	93	93	93	19	93	46	93	93	93	93	93	46	46	46	46	46	46	46	46	46	2
38 SMITH	38	38	38	38	19	93	46	93	38	26	26	26	26	26	26	26	26	19	19	26	26		3
4 DOVIZIOSO	4	46	19	19	38	46	38	38	26	38	19	19	19	19	19	19	19	26	26	41	41	4	4
99 LORENZO	29	4	46	46	46	38	19	26	19	19	38	38	38	38	38	38	38	41	41	4	4		5
26 PEDROSA	46	19	4	26	26	26	26	19	4	41	41	41	41	41	41	41	41	4	4	35	35		6
6 BRADL	26	26	26	4	4	4	4	4	41	4	4	4	4	4	4	4	4	35	35	45	45		7
35 CRUTCHLOW	19	35	35	35	35	35	35	35	35	35	35	35	35	44	44	44	35	35	45	69	69	69	8
41 A. ESPARGARO	41	41	41	41	41	41	41	41	44	44	44	44	44	35	35	35	44	45	69	45	5	5	9
46 ROSSI	35	44	44	44	44	44	44	44	69	69	69	69	69	45	45	45	69	5	5	29	29		10
29 IANNONE	68	69	69	69	69	69	69	69	45	45	45	45	45	69	69	69	5	68	68	68	7		11
44 P. ESPARGARO	44	68	45	45	45	45	45	45	5	5	5	5	5	5	5	68	7	29	7	68			12
69 HAYDEN	69	45	68	68	68	5	5	5	68	68	68	7	7	7	7	7	17	17	17	17			13
5 EDWARDS	45	5	5	5	5	68	68	68	68	7	7	68	68	68	68	17	29	17	9	9			14
7 AOYAMA	5	7	7	7	7	7	7	7	7	17	17	17	17	17	17	9	9	23	23	15			15
45 REDDING	7	17	17	17	17	17	17	17	9	9	9	9	9	29	29	29	23	23	70	70			
68 HERNANDEZ	9	9	8	8	9	9	9	9	23	23	23	29	29	9	9	23	70	70	63	63			
17 ABRAHAM	17	8	9	9	63	23	23	23	63	29	29	23	23	23	23	63	63	63					
8 BARBERA	8	63	63	63	23	63	63	63	29	63	63	63	63	63	63	70							
9 PETRUCCI	63	23	23	23	29	29	29	29	70	70	70	70	70	70	70								
23 PARKES	23	70	70	29	70	70	70	70															
63 DI MEGLIO	70	29	29	70																			
70 LAVERTY																							

44 Pit stop   70 Ride-through penalty

Championship Points

1	Marquez	25
2	Rossi	20
3	Pedrosa	16
4	A. Espargaro	13
5	Dovizioso	11
6	Crutchlow	10
7	Redding	9
8	Hayden	8
9	Edwards	7
10	Iannone	6
11	Aoyama	5
12	Hernandez	4
13	Abraham	3
14	Petrucci	2
15	Parkes	1

Constructor Points

1	Honda	25
2	Yamaha	20
3	Forward Yamaha	13
4	Ducati	11
5	ART	2
6	PBM	1

Moto2

RACE DISTANCE: 20 laps, 66.860 miles/107.600km · RACE WEATHER: Dry (air 20°C, humidity 54%, track 19°C)

Pos.	Rider	Nat.	No.	Entrant	Machine	Laps	Time & Speed
1	**Esteve Rabat**	SPA	53	Marc VDS Racing Team	Kalex	20	40m 20.963s
							99.4mph
							160.0km/h
2	**Mika Kallio**	FIN	36	Marc VDS Racing Team	Kalex	20	40m 22.022s
3	**Thomas Luthi**	SWI	12	Interwetten Paddock Moto2	Suter	20	40m 24.704s
4	**Maverick Vinales**	SPA	40	Pons HP 40	Kalex	20	40m 25.006s
5	**Simone Corsi**	ITA	3	NGM Forward Racing	Forward KLX	20	40m 26.793s
6	**Sam Lowes**	GBR	22	Speed Up	Speed Up	20	40m 35.133s
7	**Sandro Cortese**	GER	11	Dynavolt Intact GP	Kalex	20	40m 45.906s
8	**Jordi Torres**	SPA	81	Mapfre Aspar Team Moto2	Suter	20	40m 46.159s
9	**Anthony West**	AUS	95	QMMF Racing Team	Speed Up	20	40m 46.285s
10	**Louis Rossi**	FRA	96	SAG Team	Kalex	20	40m 47.650s
11	**Jonas Folger**	GER	94	AGR Team	Kalex	20	40m 47.836s
12	**Ricard Cardus**	SPA	88	Tech 3	Tech 3	20	40m 47.877s
13	**Randy Krummenacher**	SWI	4	IodaRacing Project	Suter	20	40m 52.634s
14	**Luis Salom**	SPA	39	Pons HP 40	Kalex	20	41m 01.551s
15	**Hafizh Syahrin**	MAL	7	Petronas Raceline Malaysia	Kalex	20	41m 01.658s
16	Julian Simon	SPA	60	Italtrans Racing Team	Kalex	20	41m 02.773s
17	Mattia Pasini	ITA	54	NGM Forward Racing	Forward KLX	20	41m 04.993s
18	Azlan Shah	MAL	25	IDEMITSU Honda Team Asia	Kalex	20	41m 13.776s
19	Roman Ramos	SPA	97	QMMF Racing Team	Speed Up	20	41m 14.526s
20	Thitipong Warokorn	THA	10	APH PTT The Pizza SAG	Kalex	20	41m 31.958s
21	Tetsuta Nagashima	JPN	45	Teluru Team JiR Webike	TSR	20	41m 32.354s
22	Robin Mulhauser	SWI	70	Technomag carXpert	Suter	20	41m 32.774s
23	Johann Zarco	FRA	5	AirAsia Caterham	Caterham Suter	20	42m 13.311s
24	Xavier Simeon	BEL	19	Federal Oil Gresini Moto2	Suter	20	42m 13.409s
25	Franco Morbidelli	ITA	21	Italtrans Racing Team	Kalex	19	41m 07.253s
	Takaaki Nakagami	JPN	30	IDEMITSU Honda Team Asia	Kalex	20	DSQ
	Lorenzo Baldassarri	ITA	7	Gresini Moto2	Suter	19	DNF
	Dominique Aegerter	SWI	77	Technomag carXpert	Suter	15	DNF
	Nicolas Terol	SPA	18	Mapfre Aspar Team Moto2	Suter	15	DNF
	Marcel Schrotter	GER	23	Tech 3	Tech 3	11	DNF
	Axel Pons	SPA	49	AGR Team	Kalex	11	DNF
	Mashel Al Naimi	QAT	98	QMMF Racing Team	Speed Up	4	DNF
	Gino Rea	GBR	8	AGT REA Racing	Suter	2	DNF
	Alex de Angelis	RSM	15	Tasca Racing Moto2	Suter	0	DNF
	Josh Herrin	USA	2	AirAsia Caterham	Caterham Suter	0	DNF

Fastest lap: Maverick Vinales, on lap 9, 2m 0.168s, 100.1mph/161.1km/h (record).

Previous lap record: Marc Marquez, SPA (Suter), 2m 0.645s, 99.8mph/160.5km (2012).

Event best maximum speed: Mattia Pasini, 176.3mph/283.8km/h (race).

Qualifying

Weather: Dry
Air Temp: 22°   **Track Temp:** 21°
Humidity: 45%

1	Rabat	2m 00.081s
2	Cortese	2m 00.101s
3	Nakagami	2m 00.451s
4	Luthi	2m 00.459s
5	Lowes	2m 00.547s
6	Kallio	2m 00.621s
7	Simeon	2m 00.696s
8	De Angelis	2m 00.764s
9	Zarco	2m 00.806s
10	Corsi	2m 00.831s
11	Aegerter	2m 00.910s
12	Pasini	2m 00.914s
13	Schrotter	2m 01.004s
14	Vinales	2m 01.032s
15	Folger	2m 01.045s
16	Torres	2m 01.111s
17	Salom	2m 01.124s
18	Cardus	2m 01.185s
19	Simon	2m 01.190s
20	Rossi	2m 01.277s
21	Terol	2m 01.319s
22	Krummenacher	2m 01.334s
23	Baldassarri	2m 01.431s
24	Rea	2m 01.569s
25	Pons	2m 01.609s
26	West	2m 01.732s
27	Herrin	2m 02.258s
28	Shah	2m 02.355s
29	Morbidelli	2m 02.395s
30	Syahrin	2m 02.473s
31	Ramos	2m 02.676s
32	Warokorn	2m 03.329s
33	Al Naimi	2m 03.948s
34	Nagashima	2m 04.036s
35	Mulhauser	2m 04.147s

Fastest race laps

1	Vinales	2m 00.168s
2	Rabat	2m 00.175s
3	Nakagami	2m 00.253s
4	Kallio	2m 00.327s
5	Luthi	2m 00.388s
6	Lowes	2m 00.483s
7	Aegerter	2m 00.518s
8	Zarco	2m 00.545s
9	Corsi	2m 00.603s
10	Folger	2m 00.608s
11	Torres	2m 00.824s
12	Pasini	2m 00.903s
13	Schrotter	2m 00.926s
14	Simeon	2m 00.978s
15	Terol	2m 01.168s
16	Pons	2m 01.179s
17	Cardus	2m 01.180s
18	Rossi	2m 01.205s
19	Cortese	2m 01.274s
20	West	2m 01.315s
21	Baldassarri	2m 01.339s
22	Simon	2m 01.506s
23	Krummenacher	2m 01.648s
24	Salom	2m 01.712s
25	Shah	2m 01.891s
26	Ramos	2m 02.072s
27	Syahrin	2m 02.075s
28	Warokorn	2m 03.098s
29	Mulhauser	2m 03.224s
30	Nagashima	2m 03.333s
31	Morbidelli	2m 03.391s
32	Rea	2m 03.422s
33	Al Naimi	2m 11.410s

Championship Points

1	Rabat	25
2	Kallio	20
3	Luthi	16
4	Vinales	13
5	Corsi	11
6	Lowes	10
7	Cortese	9
8	Torres	8
9	West	7
10	Rossi	6
11	Folger	5
12	Cardus	4
13	Krummenacher	3
14	Salom	2
15	Syahrin	1

Constructor Points

1	Kalex	25
2	Suter	16
3	Forward KLX	11
4	Speed Up	10
5	Tech 3	4

Moto3

RACE DISTANCE: 18 laps, 60.174 miles/96.840km · RACE WEATHER: Dry (air 23°C, humidity 34%, track 22°C)

Pos.	Rider	Nat.	No.	Entrant	Machine	Laps	Time & Speed
1	**Jack Miller**	AUS	8	Red Bull KTM Ajo	KTM	18	38m 05.810s
							94.8mph
							152.5km/h
2	**Alex Marquez**	SPA	12	Estrella Galicia 0,0	Honda	18	38m 06.043s
3	**Efren Vazquez**	SPA	7	SaxoPrint-RTG	Honda	18	38m 06.090s
4	**Miguel Oliveira**	POR	44	Mahindra Racing	Mahindra	18	38m 06.105s
5	**Alex Rins**	SPA	42	Estrella Galicia 0,0	Honda	18	38m 06.179s
6	**Jakub Kornfeil**	CZE	84	Calvo Team	KTM	18	38m 06.396s
7	**Alexis Masbou**	FRA	10	Ongetta-Rivacold	Honda	18	38m 07.919s
8	**Isaac Vinales**	SPA	32	Calvo Team	KTM	18	38m 07.971s
9	**Niccolo Antonelli**	ITA	23	Junior Team GO&FUN Moto3	KTM	18	38m 13.963s
10	**Francesco Bagnaia**	ITA	21	SKY Racing Team VR46	KTM	18	38m 13.983s
11	**John McPhee**	GBR	17	SaxoPrint-RTG	Honda	18	38m 14.005s
12	**Romano Fenati**	ITA	5	SKY Racing Team VR46	KTM	18	38m 14.029s
13	**Danny Kent**	GBR	52	Red Bull Husqvarna Ajo	Husqvarna	18	38m 17.079s
14	**Karel Hanika**	CZE	98	Red Bull KTM Ajo	KTM	18	38m 17.102s
15	**Brad Binder**	RSA	41	Ambrogio Racing	Mahindra	18	38m 17.132s
16	Enea Bastianini	ITA	33	Junior Team GO&FUN Moto3	KTM	18	38m 27.969s
17	Livio Loi	BEL	11	Marc VDS Racing Team	Kalex KTM	18	38m 28.012s
18	Zulfahmi Khairuddin	MAL	63	Ongetta-AirAsia	Honda	18	38m 42.496s
19	Scott Deroue	NED	9	RW Racing GP	Kalex KTM	18	38m 42.501s
20	Philipp Oettl	GER	65	Interwetten Paddock Moto3	Kalex KTM	18	38m 42.565s
21	Alessandro Tonucci	ITA	19	CIP	Mahindra	18	38m 43.668s
22	Luca Grunwald	GER	43	Kiefer Racing	Kalex KTM	18	38m 43.686s
23	Andrea Locatelli	ITA	55	San Carlo Team Italia	Mahindra	18	38m 51.311s
24	Ana Carrasco	SPA	22	RW Racing GP	Kalex KTM	18	38m 51.460s
25	Bryan Schouten	NED	51	CIP	Mahindra	18	39m 14.504s
26	Niklas Ajo	FIN	31	Avant Tecno Husqvarna Ajo	Husqvarna	17	39m 47.308s
	Jules Danilo	FRA	95	Ambrogio Racing	Mahindra	17	DNF
	Matteo Ferrari	ITA	1	San Carlo Team Italia	Mahindra	14	DNF
	Juanfran Guevara	SPA	58	Mapfre Aspar Team Moto3	Kalex KTM	6	DNF
	Gabriel Ramos	VEN	4	Kiefer Racing	Kalex KTM	6	DNF
	Eric Granado	BRA	57	Calvo Team	KTM	2	DNF
	Hafiq Azmi	MAL	38	SIC-AJO	KTM	0	DNF

Fastest lap: Alexis Masbou, on lap 9, 2m 5.862s, 95.6mph/153.8km/h (record).

Previous lap record: Jonas Folger, GER Kalex KTM, 2m 6.839s, 94.8mph/152.6km/h (2013).

Event best maximum speed: Alex Marquez, 147.8mph/237.9km/h (free practice 1).

Qualifying

Weather: Dry
Air Temp: 23°   **Track Temp:** 23°
Humidity: 35%

1	Rins	2m 05.973s
2	Marquez	2m 06.125s
3	Miller	2m 06.365s
4	Kornfeil	2m 06.515s
5	Vinales	2m 06.843s
6	Kent	2m 06.864s
7	McPhee	2m 07.113s
8	Fenati	2m 07.126s
9	Antonelli	2m 07.205s
10	Bagnaia	2m 07.258s
11	Oliveira	2m 07.273s
12	Granado	2m 07.319s
13	Guevara	2m 07.354s
14	Masbou	2m 07.455s
15	Vazquez	2m 07.559s
16	Ajo	2m 07.564s
17	Binder	2m 07.844s
18	Deroue	2m 08.060s
19	Hanika	2m 08.109s
20	Loi	2m 08.177s
21	Bastianini	2m 08.255s
22	Oettl	2m 08.455s
23	Khairuddin	2m 08.696s
24	Grunwald	2m 08.980s
25	Carrasco	2m 09.084s
26	Ferrari	2m 09.183s
27	Schouten	2m 09.193s
28	Tonucci	2m 09.226s
29	Sissis	2m 09.357s
30	Azmi	2m 09.483s
31	Locatelli	2m 09.575s
32	Danilo	2m 10.300s
33	Ramos	2m 12.119s

Fastest race laps

1	Masbou	2m 05.862s
2	Fenati	2m 06.057s
3	Marquez	2m 06.068s
4	McPhee	2m 06.109s
5	Kornfeil	2m 06.146s
6	Vazquez	2m 06.161s
7	Miller	2m 06.165s
8	Rins	2m 06.196s
9	Vinales	2m 06.205s
10	Oliveira	2m 06.211s
11	Hanika	2m 06.293s
12	Binder	2m 06.328s
13	Guevara	2m 06.493s
14	Kent	2m 06.495s
15	Bagnaia	2m 06.520s
16	Antonelli	2m 06.615s
17	Bastianini	2m 07.002s
18	Ajo	2m 07.105s
19	Loi	2m 07.154s
20	Deroue	2m 07.475s
21	Oettl	2m 07.491s
22	Khairuddin	2m 07.658s
23	Locatelli	2m 07.700s
24	Grunwald	2m 07.826s
25	Tonucci	2m 07.841s
26	Carrasco	2m 07.895s
27	Danilo	2m 08.352s
28	Ferrari	2m 09.171s
29	Schouten	2m 09.563s
30	Granado	2m 11.312s
31	Ramos	2m 11.633s

Championship Points

1	Miller	25
2	Marquez	20
3	Vazquez	16
4	Oliveira	13
5	Rins	11
6	Kornfeil	10
7	Masbou	9
8	Vinales	8
9	Antonelli	7
10	Bagnaia	6
11	McPhee	5
12	Fenati	4
13	Kent	3
14	Hanika	2
15	Binder	1

Constructor Points

1	KTM	25
2	Honda	20
3	Mahindra	13
4	Husqvarna	3

GRAND PRIX OF THE AMERICAS

CIRCUIT OF THE AMERICAS

Main: Fly away Peter, fly away Paul: Marquez took early control of the race, pursued by Pedrosa.

Inset: The 'selfie' makes it to the MotoGP podium for the first time. Dovizioso *(right)* was an unexpected third party.

Photos: Gold & Goose

Above: Lorenzo made a flying start. Everyone else waited for the lights.

Right: The US contingent – it was a far cry from the glory days, with (left to right) Josh Herrin, Colin Edwards and Nicky Hayden consigned to the supporting cast.

Below right: One of the former US leading lights, Kevin Schwantz, beams as he is welcomed back to the party; fellow former champion Franco Uncini looks grim.

Far right: Dovizioso, pursued by the Monster Yamaha pair, rode with trademark precision, earning himself a podium place.

Photos: Gold & Goose

THERE were at least three significant returns at the second running of the Grand Prix of The Americas at the sweeping eponymous circuit at Austin, Texas.

One was by Kevin Schwantz. A year before, the Austin resident and all-time racing hero had been absent from a race and circuit with which he had been intimately involved from the outset. He had advised on design and had been the race's original promoter, a contract that had gone wrong and left him engaged in legal action against the circuit, which previously had banned his presence. In the interim, matters had been settled out of court, and Kevin was much in evidence, now as ambassador rather than outcast.

Another, of course, was Marquez. The Spaniard had set new youngest-ever records at the 2013 race: pole qualifier, then winner. That had been just the start of a youngest-ever year of triumph. He returned as champion and dominated utterly. The only rider who could have stopped him from winning was himself, and he almost succeeded, with a last-corner lapse of concentration that required yet another of his trademark heroic saves.

The third was Jorge Lorenzo, recast from Mr Perfect to Mr Blunder. A self-confessed amateurish error had cost him the Qatar GP. A second in succession cost him Austin. Distracted on the line after removing a tear-off because of a bug on his visor, he explained, he then jumped the start by a huge margin – well over two seconds. He managed to come through to

tenth after taking a ride-through penalty, his first points in a year when the defender had amassed a perfect 50.

There were others, including the return of Ducati to the rostrum – rather unexpectedly, and thanks to a ride of great maturity and intelligence as well, of course, as skill by Dovizioso; and the return of Rossi to the gloom box, as one of several to suffer severe front-tyre degradation.

And there was a departure, or at least the announcement thereof. Colin Edwards started the weekend at his home circuit by announcing that 2014 would be his last racing season, bringing to an end a long career encompassing two World Superbike championships and a GP tenure of 11 years, on a variety of motorcycles, from the unruly Aprilia Cube via satellite Honda and factory Yamaha to CRT and now Open category, but that never quite included a race win. The closest he had come was when he crashed on the last corner at Assen in 2006, handing a valuable win to that year's eventual champion, Nicky Hayden.

Retirement had been long deferred as Edwards's family grew (three children so far) and he established the Texas Tornado Boot Camp, where rider training is interspersed with recreational gunplay, including the chance to practise a drive-by shooting. "I've been in Europe since 1995, getting my arse kicked by young bastards like this," he said (gesturing at Marquez). The tipping point had come in pre-season testing with the new bikes and tyres: "I didn't see the im-

provement I wanted. I need to change my riding style, but hell, I'm 40 years old and trying to change my style wasn't working. As soon as you get into an intense moment, you go back to your instinct."

Much has been said about the new tyres, and how riders had to adapt their style to reduced mid-corner side-grip, sacrificed in the interest of better heat resistance. Came a surprise from Bridgestone, when the middle of their three options (shared by Open bikes as 'hard' and Factory as 'soft') was 2013's model. This aberration caused much muttering and discontent, and engendered suspicion that it had been done on Lorenzo's behalf, as the most persistent and vocal critic of the new tyres. "It was not my company that made the decision," he demurred; while the Japanese company cited "production difficulties" after unexpected heavy use of the same mid-range tyre at Qatar.

Unusually for an anti-clockwise circuit, COTA punishes the right side more than the left, thanks to the punishing triple-rights at the stadium section. The 3.426-mile lap presents a variety of disparate, ill-assorted challenges. The early slalom section (said to resemble Silverstone) requires precise steering and corner line – a bike set for fluent handling. Three first-gear corners, and especially the tight left-hooker after the longest straight of the season, demand a different configuration, favouring hard braking and acceleration. An extra complication was wavy bumps in the braking zones, following two F1 races.

Then there were the difficulties of wind, especially a problem for Moto3, and race-day rain, though happily this cleared without causing major disruption.

While a flu-stricken Dovizioso was covered with glory, new team-mate Crutchlow found yet more problems. At first, electronic, with a worrying and abrupt total engine failure on the first day, at speed on the main straight, luckily not when anyone was close behind. "This bike has too many systems," he complained, comparing it with the electronically simpler Yamaha. Worse followed: a major tyre problem in the race caused him to pit and put on a soft rear – only to crash, breaking bones in his right hand.

One possible explanation of the first glitch was damp: Ducati seemed worst hit by an intrusion of water into some flight cases en route from Qatar.

Extraordinarily for just the second race, contract talk filled the air. Lorenzo revealed that he had already started negotiations with Yamaha, again with a rumoured big-bucks bid from Honda to steal him away, and similar from Ducati. "It's

normal," he said. "A rider would be mad not to consider the alternatives."

Edwards's retirement announcement at the first 2014 visit to the USA threw focus on the lack of US riders in a series once dominated by them. Hayden managed to be top production Honda, but "no one's happy at coming 11th," while Edwards himself didn't finish after his engine quit in the late stages. There were no Americans in Moto3 and just one in Moto2, where AMA champion Josh Herrin continued his difficult start. Victim of a first-corner crash at Qatar, he suffered the same fate at COTA, remounting only to be eliminated in a second looping crash later in the race.

Where has all the talent gone? The blame fell partly on the downscaling of the AMA series. As Hayden said: "Five two-day weekends in a season doesn't give a rider much experience for international racing." Partly also on the other effects of the economic downturn, which had led to talented riders losing potential rides to others who could bring financial backing.

MOTOGP RACE – 18 laps

Merciless from the outset, Marquez dominated free practice, seldom less than a second ahead of the next fastest. He did it with a display of sustained on-the-limit riding – skittering over kerbs, using his rear tyre as a broad black crayon on the exits, saving at least one front-end crash with his elbow and knee, and finally reinforcing pole with two record-speed laps in succession.

Only in qualifying did Pedrosa close to within a tenth of his team-mate, until Marquez went faster still, to regain a three-tenths comfort zone.

Bradl was strong throughout to complete the front row. Lorenzo had a second worrying race, at first looking like he might not make the top ten. He had speeded up by day two, to within half a second, but he was not fastest Yamaha. That was qualifying hero Aleix Espargaro, through from Q1, with a soft-tyre flier that put him fourth, heading an all-Yamaha row two from Lorenzo and Rossi.

Crutchlow was top Ducati (also on a soft), heading row three from Smith and Iannone; Dovizioso led the fourth from Pol Espargaro and Bautista. Redding was best of the rest, missing the Q1 cut by less than a tenth.

Lorenzo blamed the distraction caused by removing a bug-spattered tear-off visor for tearing off on his own account. He slowed briefly, then took off again, moving out of danger and

hurrying towards the inevitable ride-through penalty without waiting for a flag, so that he rejoined in last place.

Marquez was again the only rider to choose the hard option tyre: Pedrosa explained, "I could have raced on either, but I wanted to have a difference with Marc."

The younger rider followed Lorenzo and led the first lap as the Yamaha pitted. He led every other lap, too, the two Hondas moving clear from the start. Dani shadowed impressively at first, but without ever looking threatening, until by half-distance the gap had stretched beyond two seconds. Marquez set a new record on lap three.

Iannone held third while a gang piled up behind Crutchlow, losing ground behind. After three laps, the order in his wake was Rossi, Bradl, Dovizioso, Smith, Espargaro and Bautista.

Crutchlow's problems started next time around: rear tyre chatter was so severe that he pitted for a change after nine laps. His efforts were doomed, however, and he crashed heavily after only three more laps, having hit a turn two bump. He suffered fractures to his right hand.

Now Rossi was ahead, and he stretched the pursuit as he sliced the one-second gap to Iannone to zero in just one lap. He stayed close until after one-third distance, though every attempt to overtake was repulsed. All the same, sooner or later he seemed set for the podium finish. Then, after one-third distance, he slowed visibly, the right side of his front tyre "destroyed", and his lap times with it.

Now the action behind intensified. Bradl led the way past Rossi, followed on lap 11 by Dovi, and then Pol Espargaro and Smith, one on either side. Bautista by now had slid off.

Iannone was suffering similar tyre trouble, and by lap 15 Bradl and Dovi were on him, and one lap later ahead. In the process, Dovi got ahead of the German, who remained inches behind.

More followed as Smith got the better of his team-mate, going on to pass Iannone and close on the two ahead. With less than two laps left, the Englishman attacked Bradl, and a furious to-and-fro through the early swerves ended with the German still ahead, but Dovizioso now having gained a valuable gap that he would maintain to the end.

Bradl and Smith were still close as they crossed the line; Espargaro was next, having also passed Iannone, with Rossi a distant eighth.

He was barely two seconds clear of Aleix Espargaro, his second-row start having been wasted when he flinched as Lorenzo came by. He'd been left trailing and also complaining of tyre issues.

Lorenzo had cut through to tenth, just another 1.5 seconds away.

His last victim had been Hayden, final victor in a three-way fight with Redding and Hernandez. Redding dropped back

Above: Bradl had to fight hard to save fourth from the attacking Smith.

Above right: Lorenzo found few reasons to be cheerful in Texas.

Right: Unanticipated front tyre wear hit several riders, including Redding and Rossi. Subsequently Bridgestone expanded the choice from two to three compounds.

Below: Dominique Aegerter leads Moto2 winner Maverick Vinales.

Below right: The reigning Moto3 champion rider celebrates winning his second Moto2 race.

Below far right: Miller (8) toughed it out to take a second Moto3 win from Vazquez (7), Fenati (5) and Marquez (hidden). The latter crashed out in the final corner.

Photos: Gold & Goose

and then crashed on the second-last lap, another to suffer front tyre problems. Aoyama had also passed Hernandez by the end in a strong late run.

Abraham was a lone 14th; Barbera took the last point from a feisty Laverty by a tenth. Petrucci and di Meglio trailed in; Edwards ran out of engine with four laps still to go; Parkes retired with power and chatter issues before the race had reached half-distance.

MOTO2 RACE – 19 laps

Rabat came through in the closing seconds to take his second pole of the year, displacing long-time leader Zarco, who had led free practice as well. Aegerter snatched the last front-row slot.

Simeon and Simon both displaced Moto3 champion Vinales from his own long-held front-row position. Another class rookie, Folger, led the third row from Corsi and Nakagami; Luthi was 13th and Cortese 15th after a spill in the final session.

Rain spattered the circuit as they waited on the grid, bringing out umbrellas on the hillsides and a red flag. Race delayed. Though the sky remained very threatening, the rain was gone at once, and a full-distance race started 12 minutes later.

It was soon over for five of the 34 in a first-corner tangle near the back, effectively eliminating 2013 winner Terol, as well as Salom, Lowes, Pons and Herrin, though all but Salom were able to rejoin. Herrin crashed again later, terminally; Terol retired.

Zarco was pushed wide at the same corner and finished lap one in sixth, behind Rabat. It was Aegerter ahead for two laps, repulsing an early attack from Simeon, although succumbing to the Belgian thereafter to follow closely as he led to lap 12.

By then, Vinales had slotted into third; Kallio was ahead of team-mate Rabat, and Nakagami had dropped out of the leading group into further trouble with the pursuit pack.

Zarco and fast-starter Simon were also out of contention. Battling to make up for his loss of position, the Frenchman had dived inside Simon at the end of the long straight, and promptly lost it, to take both down. They restarted at the back, but Zarco pitted to retire.

The crucial moment came on lap 13, when Simeon ran wide and dropped to fifth. Aegerter led briefly, but Vinales was ready to pounce. At the same time, Rabat – stricken with shifting problems that robbed him of first gear – was now finally ahead of Kallio, and both closed up.

They now engaged with Aegerter, and their battle gave Vinales the breathing space he needed to break clear. The reigning Moto3 champion won his second Moto2 race by a convincing four seconds.

Rabat moved clear for a safe second; Aegerter got the better of Kallio, who had been behind the returning Simeon when the Belgian crashed out. Corsi had been following and was barely a second adrift at the flag.

West again played a leading role in a fierce scrap for the next points, finally losing out to Luthi by half a second, but holding off de Angelis as well as Tech 3 team-mates Schrotter and replacement rider Cardus.

Nakagami faded to 11th; a long way back, Pasini narrowly held off Krummenacher, with Cortese a close spectator. Malaysian rookie Hafizh Syahrin took the last point; Lowes recovered impressively to 16th.

Folger also crashed out, as well as Rossi and Baldassarri.

MOTO3 RACE – 18 laps

The first race of the day also started with a first-corner tangle, when Locatelli fell, eliminating Sissis and slowing his team-mate, Oliveira, in a bad weekend for the Mahindras.

The KTM-Honda battle went on regardless, Miller's factory KTM heading all but the last free practice and qualifying on pole. His nemesis in FP3 was Vazquez's Honda, which qualified second ahead of Rins's official bike. Team-mate Marquez led row two from the KTMs of Antonelli and Kornfeil.

Miller led turn one from fast-starter Kornfeil, who had succumbed also to Vazquez by the end of the first lap.

The two leaders were almost 1.5 seconds clear after three laps, but now Marquez led the pursuit from Rins, and the former broke free to make it three up front.

Now Fenati was cutting through from eighth on lap one, and by half-distance his KTM was ahead of the fading Rins, and ready to make it four.

Miller was steadfast, resisting Vazquez's draft-past moves on the long straight by exploiting his favourite tactic: "I like to kill them on the brakes." All the same, it would clearly be a last-lap showdown, at the same place.

They all made it through with a last shuffle, Miller again regaining control, Marquez a couple of lengths adrift. He got on the paint while braking late for a final lunge through the second-last corner, and was down and out.

Miller stayed ahead from Fenati and Vazquez, all within two-tenths.

Rins had his hands full with Kornfeil to the finish; more than ten seconds away, Masbou held off Fenati's team-mate, Bagnaia, for sixth. Close behind, Kent did the same to McPhee and Hanika.

Vinales and Antonelli had been scrapping behind Kornfeil, but crashed out independently.

FIM WORLD CHAMPIONSHIP ROUND 2

RED BULL
GRAND PRIX OF
THE AMERICAS

11–13 APRIL, 2014

CIRCUIT OF THE AMERICAS
Circuit: 5.513km / 3.426 miles
21 laps
Width: 15m

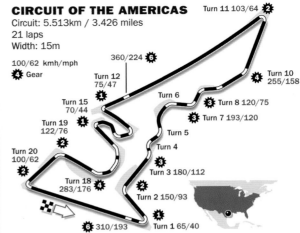

Turn 11 103/64
Turn 10 255/158
Turn 8 120/75
Turn 7 193/120
360/224
Turn 12 75/47
Turn 6
Turn 15 70/44
Turn 5
Turn 19 122/76
Turn 4
Turn 20 100/62
Turn 3 180/112
Turn 18 283/176
Turn 2 150/93
310/193
Turn 1 65/40
100/62 kmh/mph
Gear

MotoGP — RACE DISTANCE: 21 laps, 71.938 miles/115.773km · RACE WEATHER: Dry (air 26°C, humidity 71%, track 32°C)

Pos.	Rider	Nat.	No.	Entrant	Machine	Tyres	Race tyre choice	Laps	Time & speed
1	**Marc Marquez**	SPA	93	Repsol Honda Team	Honda RC213V	B	F: Hard/R: Hard	22	42m 40.561s 103.4mph/ 166.4km/h
2	**Valentino Rossi**	ITA	46	Movistar Yamaha MotoGP	Yamaha YZR-M1	B	F: Hard/R: Medium	22	42m 40.820s
3	**Dani Pedrosa**	SPA	26	Repsol Honda Team	Honda RC213V	B	F: Hard/R: Medium	22	42m 43.931s
4	**Aleix Espargaro**	SPA	41	NGM Forward Racing	Forward Yamaha	B	F: Hard/R: Medium	22	42m 52.184s
5	**Andrea Dovizioso**	ITA	4	Ducati Team	Ducati Desmosedici	B	F: Hard/R: Medium	22	42m 52.720s
6	**Cal Crutchlow**	GBR	35	Ducati Team	Ducati Desmosedici	B	F: Hard/R: Medium	22	43m 09.087s
7	**Scott Redding**	GBR	45	GO&FUN Honda Gresini	Honda RCV1000R	B	F: Hard/R: Soft	22	43m 13.154s
8	**Nicky Hayden**	USA	69	Drive M7 Aspar	Honda RCV1000R	B	F: Hard/R: Soft	22	43m 13.189s
9	**Colin Edwards**	USA	5	NGM Forward Racing	Forward Yamaha	B	F: Hard/R: Medium	22	43m 20.108s
10	**Andrea Iannone**	ITA	29	Pramac Racing	Ducati Desmosedici	B	F: Hard/R: Medium	22	43m 23.921s
11	**Hiroshi Aoyama**	JPN	7	Drive M7 Aspar	Honda RCV1000R	B	F: Soft/R: Soft	22	43m 27.156s
12	**Yonny Hernandez**	COL	68	Energy T.I. Pramac Racing	Ducati Desmosedici	B	F: Soft/R: Medium	22	43m 27.249s
13	**Karel Abraham**	CZE	17	Cardion AB Motoracing	Honda RCV1000R	B	F: Hard/R: Soft	22	43m 31.142s
14	**Danilo Petrucci**	ITA	9	IodaRacing Project	ART	B	F: Hard/R: Soft	22	43m 43.688s
15	**Broc Parkes**	AUS	23	Paul Bird Motorsport	PBM-ART	B	F: Hard/R: Medium	22	43m 54.947s
16	Michael Laverty	GBR	70	Paul Bird Motorsport	PBM-ART	B	F: Hard/R: Soft	22	44m 13.154s
17	Mike di Meglio	FRA	63	Avintia Racing	Avintia	B	F: Hard/R: Soft	22	44m 16.646s
	Alvaro Bautista	SPA	19	GO&FUN Honda Gresini	Honda RC213V	B	F: Hard/R: Medium	20	DNF-crash
	Bradley Smith	GBR	38	Monster Yamaha Tech 3	Yamaha YZR-M1	B	F: Hard/R: Medium	18	DNF-crash
	Pol Espargaro	SPA	44	Monster Yamaha Tech 3	Yamaha YZR-M1	B	F: Hard/R: Medium	17	DNF-mechanical
	Stefan Bradl	GER	6	LCR Honda MotoGP	Honda RC213V	B	F: Hard/R: Medium	8	DNF-crash
	Hector Barbera	SPA	8	Avintia Racing	Avintia	B	F: Hard/R: Medium	4	DNF-mechanical
	Jorge Lorenzo	SPA	99	Movistar Yamaha MotoGP	Yamaha YZR-M1	B	F: Hard/R: Medium	0	DNF-crash

Fastest lap: Alvaro Bautista, on lap 4, 1m 55.575s, 104.1mph/167.5km/h.

Lap record: Casey Stoner, AUS (Ducati), 1m 55.153s, 104.5mph/168.1km/h (2008).

Event best maximum speed: Marc Marquez, 216.4mph/348.3km/h (race).

Qualifying

Weather: Dry
Air Temp: 21° **Track Temp:** 50°
Humidity: 18%

1	Marquez	1m 54.507s
2	Bautista	1m 54.564s
3	Smith	1m 54.601s
4	Dovizioso	1m 54.644s
5	Lorenzo	1m 54.661s
6	Pedrosa	1m 54.703s
7	Bradl	1m 54.871s
8	Crutchlow	1m 54.888s
9	A. Espargaro	1m 54.986s
10	Rossi	1m 55.096s
11	Iannone	1m 55.127s
12	P. Espargaro	1m 55.152s
13	Hayden	1m 55.894s
14	Edwards	1m 56.042s
15	Aoyama	1m 56.479s
16	Redding	1m 56.555s
17	Hernandez	1m 56.648s
18	Abraham	1m 56.715s
19	Barbera	1m 57.006s
20	Petrucci	1m 57.513s
21	Parkes	1m 57.574s
22	Di Meglio	1m 57.667s
23	Laverty	1m 58.254s

Fastest race laps

1	Bautista	1m 55.575s
2	Rossi	1m 55.621s
3	Marquez	1m 55.710s
4	Pedrosa	1m 55.843s
5	Smith	1m 55.871s
6	Bradl	1m 55.937s
7	Crutchlow	1m 56.064s
8	A. Espargaro	1m 56.192s
9	Iannone	1m 56.280s
10	Dovizioso	1m 56.285s
11	P. Espargaro	1m 56.345s
12	Redding	1m 56.416s
13	Hayden	1m 56.428s
14	Edwards	1m 57.119s
15	Abraham	1m 57.293s
16	Aoyama	1m 57.396s
17	Hernandez	1m 57.625s
18	Barbera	1m 57.822s
19	Di Meglio	1m 58.164s
20	Petrucci	1m 58.322s
21	Laverty	1m 58.396s
22	Parkes	1m 58.470s

Grid order		1	2	3	4	5	6	7	8	9	10	11	12	13	14	15	16	17	18	19	20	21	
93	MARQUEZ	93	93	93	93	93	93	93	93	93	93	93	93	93	93	93	93	93	93	93	93	93	1
26	PEDROSA	99	26	26	26	26	26	26	26	26	26	26	26	26	26	26	26	26	26	26	26	26	2
6	BRADL	26	29	29	29	29	29	29	29	29	29	29	29	29	29	29	4	4	4	4	4	4	3
41	A. ESPARGARO	29	35	35	46	46	46	46	46	46	6	6	6	6	6	6	6	6	6	6	6	6	4
99	LORENZO	35	6	46	6	6	6	6	6	6	4	4	4	4	4	4	29	38	38	38	38	38	5
46	ROSSI	6	46	6	4	4	4	4	4	4	46	44	44	44	38	38	38	29	29	29	44	44	6
35	CRUTCHLOW	4	4	4	35	35	44	44	44	44	44	38	38	38	44	44	44	44	44	29	29	7
38	SMITH	46	38	38	38	38	19	19	19	19	38	46	46	46	46	46	46	46	46	46	46	46	8
29	IANNONE	38	44	44	44	44	38	38	38	38	41	41	41	41	41	41	41	41	41	41	41	41	9
4	DOVIZIOSO	44	19	19	19	19	35	35	35	35	68	68	68	68	68	69	99	99	99	99	99	99	10
44	P. ESPARGARO	19	41	41	41	41	41	41	41	41	69	69	69	69	99	68	69	69	69	69	69	69	11
19	BAUTISTA	41	68	45	45	45	68	68	68	68	45	45	45	45	99	68	68	68	7	7	7	7	12
45	REDDING	68	45	68	68	68	45	69	69	69	7	7	7	99	45	45	7	68	68	68	68	13
69	HAYDEN	45	69	69	69	69	69	45	45	45	99	99	99	7	7	7	45	45	45	17	17	14
68	HERNANDEZ	69	7	7	7	7	7	7	7	7	5	5	5	17	17	8	8	15
7	AOYAMA	7	5	5	5	5	5	5	5	8	17	17	17	17	17	17	70	70	70	70	
17	ABRAHAM	5	70	70	17	17	17	99	99	99	17	8	8	8	8	8	8	8	9	9	
8	BARBERA	70	63	17	8	8	8	17	8	8	70	70	70	70	70	70	9	9	63	63	
5	EDWARDS	63	17	63	70	70	70	8	17	17	9	9	9	9	9	9	63	63	
70	LAVERTY	23	8	8	63	63	99	70	70	70	63	63	63	63	63	63	63	
23	PARKES	9	9	9	9	9	63	9	9	9	35	35	35	
9	PETRUCCI	17	23	23	23	99	9	63	63	63	
63	DI MEGLIO	8	99	99	99	23	23	23	23	

23 Pit stop · 99 Ride-through penalty

Championship Points

1	Marquez	25
2	Rossi	20
3	Pedrosa	16
4	A. Espargaro	13
5	Dovizioso	11
6	Crutchlow	10
7	Redding	9
8	Hayden	8
9	Edwards	7
10	Iannone	6
11	Aoyama	5
12	Hernandez	4
13	Abraham	3
14	Petrucci	2
15	Parkes	1

Constructor Points

1	Honda	25
2	Yamaha	20
3	Forward Yamaha	13
4	Ducati	11
5	ART	2
6	PBM	1

Moto2

RACE DISTANCE: 20 laps, 66.860 miles/107.600km · RACE WEATHER: Dry (air 20°C, humidity 54%, track 19°C)

Pos.	Rider	Nat.	No.	Entrant	Machine	Laps	Time & Speed
1	**Esteve Rabat**	SPA	53	Marc VDS Racing Team	Kalex	20	40m 20.963s
							99.4mph
							160.0km/h
2	**Mika Kallio**	FIN	36	Marc VDS Racing Team	Kalex	20	40m 22.022s
3	**Thomas Luthi**	SWI	12	Interwetten Paddock Moto2	Suter	20	40m 24.704s
4	**Maverick Vinales**	SPA	40	Pons HP 40	Kalex	20	40m 25.006s
5	**Simone Corsi**	ITA	3	NGM Forward Racing	Forward KLX	20	40m 26.793s
6	**Sam Lowes**	GBR	22	Speed Up	Speed Up	20	40m 35.133s
7	**Sandro Cortese**	GER	11	Dynavolt Intact GP	Kalex	20	40m 45.906s
8	**Jordi Torres**	SPA	81	Mapfre Aspar Team Moto2	Suter	20	40m 46.159s
9	**Anthony West**	AUS	95	QMMF Racing Team	Speed Up	20	40m 46.285s
10	**Louis Rossi**	FRA	96	SAG Team	Kalex	20	40m 47.650s
11	**Jonas Folger**	GER	94	AGR Team	Kalex	20	40m 47.836s
12	**Ricard Cardus**	SPA	88	Tech 3	Tech 3	20	40m 47.877s
13	**Randy Krummenacher**	SWI	4	IodaRacing Project	Suter	20	40m 52.634s
14	**Luis Salom**	SPA	39	Pons HP 40	Kalex	20	41m 01.551s
15	**Hafizh Syahrin**	MAL	55	Petronas Raceline Malaysia	Kalex	20	41m 01.658s
16	Julian Simon	SPA	60	Italtrans Racing Team	Kalex	20	41m 02.773s
17	Mattia Pasini	ITA	54	NGM Forward Racing	Forward KLX	20	41m 04.993s
18	Azlan Shah	MAL	25	IDEMITSU Honda Team Asia	Kalex	20	41m 13.776s
19	Roman Ramos	SPA	97	QMMF Racing Team	Speed Up	20	41m 14.526s
20	Thitipong Warokorn	THA	10	APH PTT The Pizza SAG	Kalex	20	41m 31.958s
21	Tetsuta Nagashima	JPN	45	Teluru Team JiR Webike	TSR	20	41m 32.354s
22	Robin Mulhauser	SWI	70	Technomag carXpert	Suter	20	41m 32.774s
23	Johann Zarco	FRA	5	AirAsia Caterham	Caterham Suter	20	42m 13.311s
24	Xavier Simeon	BEL	19	Federal Oil Gresini Moto2	Suter	20	42m 13.409s
25	Franco Morbidelli	ITA	21	Italtrans Racing Team	Kalex	19	41m 07.253s
	Takaaki Nakagami	JPN	30	IDEMITSU Honda Team Asia	Kalex	20	DSQ
	Lorenzo Baldassarri	ITA	7	Gresini Moto2	Suter	19	DNF
	Dominique Aegerter	SWI	77	Technomag carXpert	Suter	15	DNF
	Nicolas Terol	SPA	18	Mapfre Aspar Team Moto2	Suter	15	DNF
	Marcel Schrotter	GER	23	Tech 3	Tech 3	11	DNF
	Axel Pons	SPA	49	AGR Team	Kalex	11	DNF
	Mashel Al Naimi	QAT	98	QMMF Racing Team	Speed Up	4	DNF
	Gino Rea	GBR	8	AGT REA Racing	Suter	2	DNF
	Alex de Angelis	RSM	15	Tasca Racing Moto2	Suter	0	DNF
	Josh Herrin	USA	2	AirAsia Caterham	Caterham Suter	0	DNF

Fastest lap: Maverick Vinales, on lap 9, 2m 0.168s, 100.1mph/161.1km/h (record).

Previous lap record: Marc Marquez, SPA (Suter), 2m 0.645s, 99.8mph/160.5km (2012).

Event best maximum speed: Mattia Pasini, 176.3mph/283.8km/h (race).

Qualifying

Weather: Dry · Air Temp: 22° · Track Temp: 21° · Humidity: 45%

1	Rabat	2m 00.081s
2	Cortese	2m 00.101s
3	Nakagami	2m 00.451s
4	Luthi	2m 00.459s
5	Lowes	2m 00.547s
6	Kallio	2m 00.621s
7	Simeon	2m 00.696s
8	De Angelis	2m 00.764s
9	Zarco	2m 00.806s
10	Corsi	2m 00.831s
11	Aegerter	2m 00.910s
12	Pasini	2m 00.914s
13	Schrotter	2m 01.004s
14	Vinales	2m 01.032s
15	Folger	2m 01.045s
16	Torres	2m 01.111s
17	Salom	2m 01.124s
18	Cardus	2m 01.185s
19	Simon	2m 01.190s
20	Rossi	2m 01.277s
21	Terol	2m 01.319s
22	Krummenacher	2m 01.334s
23	Baldassarri	2m 01.431s
24	Rea	2m 01.569s
25	Pons	2m 01.609s
26	West	2m 01.732s
27	Herrin	2m 02.258s
28	Shah	2m 02.355s
29	Morbidelli	2m 02.395s
30	Syahrin	2m 02.473s
31	Ramos	2m 02.676s
32	Warokorn	2m 03.329s
33	Al Naimi	2m 03.948s
34	Nagashima	2m 04.036s
35	Mulhauser	2m 04.147s

Fastest race laps

1	Vinales	2m 00.168s
2	Rabat	2m 00.175s
3	Nakagami	2m 00.253s
4	Kallio	2m 00.327s
5	Luthi	2m 00.388s
6	Lowes	2m 00.483s
7	Aegerter	2m 00.518s
8	Zarco	2m 00.545s
9	Corsi	2m 00.603s
10	Folger	2m 00.608s
11	Torres	2m 00.824s
12	Pasini	2m 00.903s
13	Schrotter	2m 00.926s
14	Simeon	2m 00.978s
15	Terol	2m 01.168s
16	Pons	2m 01.179s
17	Cardus	2m 01.180s
18	Rossi	2m 01.205s
19	Cortese	2m 01.274s
20	West	2m 01.315s
21	Baldassarri	2m 01.339s
22	Simon	2m 01.506s
23	Krummenacher	2m 01.648s
24	Salom	2m 01.712s
25	Shah	2m 01.891s
26	Ramos	2m 02.072s
27	Syahrin	2m 02.075s
28	Warokorn	2m 03.098s
29	Mulhauser	2m 03.224s
30	Nagashima	2m 03.333s
31	Morbidelli	2m 03.391s
32	Rea	2m 03.422s
33	Al Naimi	2m 11.410s

Championship Points

1	Rabat	25
2	Kallio	20
3	Luthi	16
4	Vinales	13
5	Corsi	11
6	Lowes	10
7	Cortese	9
8	Torres	8
9	West	7
10	Rossi	6
11	Folger	5
12	Cardus	4
13	Krummenacher	3
14	Salom	2
15	Syahrin	1

Constructor Points

1	Kalex	25
2	Suter	16
3	Forward KLX	11
4	Speed Up	10
5	Tech 3	4

Moto3

RACE DISTANCE: 18 laps, 60.174 miles/96.840km · RACE WEATHER: Dry (air 23°C, humidity 34%, track 22°C)

Pos.	Rider	Nat.	No.	Entrant	Machine	Laps	Time & Speed
1	**Jack Miller**	AUS	8	Red Bull KTM Ajo	KTM	18	38m 05.810s
							94.8mph
							152.5km/h
2	**Alex Marquez**	SPA	12	Estrella Galicia 0,0	Honda	18	38m 06.043s
3	**Efren Vazquez**	SPA	7	SaxoPrint-RTG	Honda	18	38m 06.090s
4	**Miguel Oliveira**	POR	44	Mahindra Racing	Mahindra	18	38m 06.105s
5	**Alex Rins**	SPA	42	Estrella Galicia 0,0	Honda	18	38m 06.179s
6	**Jakub Kornfeil**	CZE	84	Calvo Team	KTM	18	38m 06.396s
7	**Alexis Masbou**	FRA	10	Ongetta-Rivacold	Honda	18	38m 07.919s
8	**Isaac Vinales**	SPA	32	Calvo Team	KTM	18	38m 07.971s
9	**Niccolo Antonelli**	ITA	23	Junior Team GO&FUN Moto3	KTM	18	38m 13.963s
10	**Francesco Bagnaia**	ITA	21	SKY Racing Team VR46	KTM	18	38m 13.983s
11	**John McPhee**	GBR	17	SaxoPrint-RTG	Honda	18	38m 14.005s
12	**Romano Fenati**	ITA	5	SKY Racing Team VR46	KTM	18	38m 14.029s
13	**Danny Kent**	GBR	52	Red Bull Husqvarna Ajo	Husqvarna	18	38m 17.079s
14	**Karel Hanika**	CZE	98	Red Bull KTM Ajo	KTM	18	38m 17.102s
15	**Brad Binder**	RSA	41	Ambrogio Racing	Mahindra	18	38m 17.132s
16	Enea Bastianini	ITA	33	Junior Team GO&FUN Moto3	KTM	18	38m 27.969s
17	Livio Loi	BEL	11	Marc VDS Racing Team	Kalex KTM	18	38m 28.012s
18	Zulfahmi Khairuddin	MAL	63	Ongetta-AirAsia	Honda	18	38m 42.496s
19	Scott Deroue	NED	9	RW Racing GP	Kalex KTM	18	38m 42.501s
20	Philipp Oettl	GER	65	Interwetten Paddock Moto3	Kalex KTM	18	38m 42.565s
21	Alessandro Tonucci	ITA	19	CIP	Mahindra	18	38m 43.668s
22	Luca Grunwald	GER	43	Kiefer Racing	Kalex KTM	18	38m 43.686s
23	Andrea Locatelli	ITA	55	San Carlo Team Italia	Mahindra	18	38m 51.311s
24	Ana Carrasco	SPA	22	RW Racing GP	Kalex KTM	18	38m 51.460s
25	Bryan Schouten	NED	51	CIP	Mahindra	18	39m 14.504s
26	Niklas Ajo	FIN	31	Avant Tecno Husqvarna Ajo	Husqvarna	17	39m 47.308s
	Jules Danilo	FRA	95	Ambrogio Racing	Mahindra	17	DNF
	Matteo Ferrari	ITA	3	San Carlo Team Italia	Mahindra	14	DNF
	Juanfran Guevara	SPA	58	Mapfre Aspar Team Moto3	Kalex KTM	6	DNF
	Gabriel Ramos	VEN	4	Kiefer Racing	Kalex KTM	6	DNF
	Eric Granado	BRA	57	Calvo Team	KTM	2	DNF
	Hafiq Azmi	MAL	38	SIC-AJO	KTM	0	DNF

Fastest lap: Alexis Masbou, on lap 9, 2m 5.862s, 95.6mph/153.8km/h (record).

Previous lap record: Jonas Folger, GER Kalex KTM, 2m 6.839s, 94.8mph/152.6km/h (2013).

Event best maximum speed: Alex Marquez, 147.8mph/237.9km/h (free practice 1).

Qualifying:

Weather: Dry · Air Temp: 23° · Track Temp: 23° · Humidity: 35%

1	Rins	2m 05.973s
2	Marquez	2m 06.125s
3	Miller	2m 06.365s
4	Kornfeil	2m 06.515s
5	Vinales	2m 06.843s
6	Kent	2m 06.864s
7	McPhee	2m 07.113s
8	Fenati	2m 07.126s
9	Antonelli	2m 07.205s
10	Bagnaia	2m 07.258s
11	Oliveira	2m 07.273s
12	Granado	2m 07.319s
13	Guevara	2m 07.354s
14	Masbou	2m 07.455s
15	Vazquez	2m 07.559s
16	Ajo	2m 07.564s
17	Binder	2m 07.844s
18	Deroue	2m 08.060s
19	Hanika	2m 08.109s
20	Loi	2m 08.177s
21	Bastianini	2m 08.255s
22	Oettl	2m 08.455s
23	Khairuddin	2m 08.696s
24	Grunwald	2m 08.980s
25	Carrasco	2m 09.084s
26	Ferrari	2m 09.183s
27	Schouten	2m 09.193s
28	Tonucci	2m 09.226s
29	Sissis	2m 09.357s
30	Azmi	2m 09.483s
31	Locatelli	2m 09.575s
32	Danilo	2m 10.300s
33	Ramos	2m 12.119s

Fastest race laps

1	Masbou	2m 05.862s
2	Fenati	2m 06.057s
3	Marquez	2m 06.068s
4	McPhee	2m 06.109s
5	Kornfeil	2m 06.146s
6	Vazquez	2m 06.161s
7	Miller	2m 06.165s
8	Rins	2m 06.196s
9	Vinales	2m 06.205s
10	Oliveira	2m 06.211s
11	Hanika	2m 06.293s
12	Binder	2m 06.328s
13	Guevara	2m 06.493s
14	Kent	2m 06.495s
15	Bagnaia	2m 06.520s
16	Antonelli	2m 06.615s
17	Bastianini	2m 07.002s
18	Ajo	2m 07.105s
19	Loi	2m 07.154s
20	Deroue	2m 07.475s
21	Oettl	2m 07.491s
22	Khairuddin	2m 07.658s
23	Locatelli	2m 07.700s
24	Grunwald	2m 07.826s
25	Tonucci	2m 07.841s
26	Carrasco	2m 07.895s
27	Danilo	2m 08.352s
28	Ferrari	2m 09.171s
29	Schouten	2m 09.563s
30	Granado	2m 11.312s
31	Ramos	2m 11.633s

Championship Points

1	Miller	25
2	Marquez	20
3	Vazquez	16
4	Oliveira	13
5	Rins	11
6	Kornfeil	10
7	Masbou	9
8	Vinales	8
9	Antonelli	7
10	Bagnaia	6
11	McPhee	5
12	Fenati	4
13	Kent	3
14	Hanika	2
15	Binder	1

Constructor Points

1	KTM	25
2	Honda	20
3	Mahindra	13
4	Husqvarna	3

FIM WORLD CHAMPIONSHIP · ROUND 3

ARGENTINE GRAND PRIX

TERMAS DE RIO HONDO CIRCUIT

Insets: Nightlife in the quiet spa town was buzzing with bike fans from all over South America; the circuit was situated alongside the man-made Rio Hondo lake.

Main: Riders and fans loved the fast and challenging track, which had been completely redesigned for MotoGP by Italian circuit designer Jarno Zafelli.

Photos: Gold & Goose

Above: Under a cloudless sky and in front of packed stands, Lorenzo heads the field into the first corner. His lead would grow, but would not last.

Right: Mika Kallio celebrated his 200th GP start.

Centre right: Rolling back the years: Argentina's most successful GP racer, seven-time 250 winner Sebastian Porto, returned after seven years for a wild-card Moto2 ride.

Below right: Open class winner Hiro Aoyama, back from the doldrums in World Superbikes, fought hard for tenth on his Honda.

Far right: Early-laps scrapping: Ducati riders Iannone (29) and Dovizioso (4) hold temporary sway over Rossi, Bradl and winner Marquez.

Photos: Gold & Goose

THE return to Argentina after 15 years away evoked many memories. Some were good – a large and wildly enthusiastic crowd in party mood was reminiscent of the earliest and craziest times at Jerez and Brazil's Goiania. Others less so: a sketchy infrastructure (all the marshals were late, forcing a delay to first practice), facilities still under construction, and an event inconveniently distant and equally inconveniently timed were reminders of previous Latin American experiences. In 1987 in Buenos Aires, riders led by Sito Pons had to commandeer straw bales on race eve to put a chicane into the very fast and dangerous final corner. No run-off but the pit wall – a crash there not only would have put the rider in danger of his life, but also several pit crewmen.

It did something more important, however. It created fine new memories, and for the best of reasons: the circuit and the racing. Other shortcomings could be more easily overlooked, and the paddock made the rush trip back to Jerez by Thursday in a feel-good frame of mind.

Well most of them. Not so much Lorenzo. He did manage to make a complete race with no mistakes. He even led for a long spell. But he ended up a despondent third, thoroughly outpaced by triple-winner Marquez and then outraced by a lively Pedrosa. Hondas were firmly on top.

The venue was unique: a small town, miles from anywhere, built as a resort around extensive hot springs. Full of stray dogs, single-storey buildings, dust and race fans, it had a very old-school feeling. The fervour overflowed from a crowd officially numbered at 52,000 and drawn from all over Latin America. As early as Wednesday night, Rossi and Marquez, who happened to be eating at the same restaurant, were mobbed in the street when they tried to leave.

A dedicated traffic lane, however, helped race personnel to avoid huge queues; while the pit and nearby lake were patrolled by numerous armed guards. That was still not enough to prevent Aleix Espargaro from losing a backpack containing a tablet and wallet to a light-fingered intruder.

The circuit was alongside an extensive artificial lake fully 5km wide and long; the layout was deceptively simple. Italian designer Jarno Zafelli of Dromo had applied subtle logic as well as all the computer arts to give it 14 corners that made cunning use of fairly flat terrain to offer not only a high average speed, but also a variety of technical challenges, with blind brows, careful corner cambers and demanding corner sets. It was the best possible contrast to Tilke-designed circuits like Austin, where very slow corners are put in place purely in the interests of F1. Like old Assen, and to a large extent Phillip Island (thanks to Vincent legend Phil Irving's original input), this is a bike circuit.

The only lapse in Dromo's computer simulation was the predicted lap time: 1m 34.302s for MotoGP. Humanity in the form of Marquez fell short, at 1m 37.683s. The deficit took it out of contention for fastest track of the year, but at 177.1km/h pole average, it's second overall to Phillip Island (182.173 in 2013) and marginally ahead of Mugello (176.209).

Another lapse was the surface. Or what lay thereon: a fine dust with echoes of Qatar, which was both slippery and abrasive. Luckily Bridgestone at least had a little data from very limited tests in 2013. One response was to bring the only symmetrical rear slick of the season: although the circuit runs clockwise and numbers nine right-hand turns to five left-handers, two of the latter (turns six and eleven) are long and fast, putting maximum stress on that side.

Following the front tyre problems experienced by Rossi and several others at Austin, the Japanese tyre supplier also brought a choice of three, rather than two, front tyres with an extra allocation (up to ten from nine). This was supposed to be a one-off for the new track, but proved so popular that it was adopted at once for the rest of the season. This week-

end, rapid wear of rears on slippery day one prompted requests for an extra allocation for that end, too. This was firmly vetoed by HRC, however, taking advantage of the team's care in preserving sufficient numbers for when it mattered.

The dirt remained a weakness. Of course, as the track was used it became both cleaner and more rubbery: lap times dropped radically – by 5.121 seconds (almost five per cent) in MotoGP. But the grip was clearly defined on the racing line only. Where there should have been many more possible lines and overtaking opportunities, by race day it was rather a one-line track.

Paradoxically, this only added to the excitement. Moto3 is generally close, and this time it culminated in two different finish-line collisions, one of which robbed Jack Miller of a Marquez-matching third consecutive win. But the early laps of MotoGP quite outshone the smallest bikes, in a mauling to-and-fro tangle. This was much closer racing than the top class had become used to.

Ducati had good reason to be glad of their special blurred Factory-Option status, with 12 engines in the cupboard rather than Honda and Yamaha's five, after two proper blow-ups in practice. Dovizioso's was spectacular enough: a plume of smoke, but enough warning for him to run safely off the track, the bike still wreathed in its own destruction. Then it was the turn of Iannone. His Pramac bike locked up as he was wheeling into the U-turn at the end of the long straight, and he went flying, fortunately without injury.

Crutchlow missed the drama, nursing a right-hand little-finger injury that had required surgery; his place was taken by factory tester Michele Pirro.

The comeback to Argentina was matched by that of one of its citizens, and the country's most successful ever GP racer. Sebastian Porto had won seven 250 races between 1995 and 2006, when he retired. He started racing again in 2013, in his national series as well as some events in Spain, and now he made a GP return as a Moto2 wild-card, riding a Kalex. He qualified 33rd and finished a respectable 23rd.

MOTOGP RACE – 25 laps

Marquez laid down a blazing marker in first practice, in spectacular style, at maximum risk. Then went no faster, preserving his tyres as 13 other riders bettered his time on a rapidly improving surface. It was an example of how he had begun to add clever strategy to his raw talent. More would follow in the race.

When qualifying came, Marquez was on top, and when first Pedrosa and then the even-faster Lorenzo closed, he went out again to take three-quarters of a second out of them with apparent ease.

Soft-tyred Aleix Espargaro and similarly shod Dovizioso led row two from Rossi; Smith the third from Iannone and Bradl, who had suffered a thumping high-side mid-session, so atypical that he blamed traction control. Hayden was 12th on the top Open Honda, winning through to Q2.

As riders tripped over one another in the hectic early laps, sending rivals wide on to the low-grip dirt-track that lurked off-line, and changing places back and forth, Lorenzo made the most of a strong start to stage an early breakaway.

Rossi was second at the end of lap one, Dovi next time around; then Iannone took over in another strong early run. It was Marquez for the following lap, however, and he closed relentlessly on the Yamaha before settling back, content to follow Lorenzo and confident that he could pass whenever he chose.

The remainder had been piling up behind the difficult-to-pass Iannone.

Pedrosa was seventh after three laps, but was moving through. He was promoted to third when Rossi was pushed wide at the end of the straight as Bradl came flying past under brakes, barely in control. That put Rossi back to sixth, and he blamed the incident for costing him the podium.

He would recover, but not as strongly as Pedrosa, although both were ahead of Iannone on lap nine. By lap 12, it looked like another downbeat race for Dani, the leaders almost four

seconds ahead. But now he had gained confidence, and he started to take two- or three-tenths out of the lead every lap.

Three laps later, he was a second closer, and Marquez realised it was time to move. He firmly outbraked Lorenzo at the end of the straight and pulled away to take a fine clear third win in a row.

Lorenzo was the prey again, with Pedrosa setting fastest lap on the 22nd and closing rapidly. He was past on the penultimate lap into the last corner complex, and Lorenzo could do nothing but let him go. Later he opined, "This is probably the sweetest third place of my career, after two difficult races. We have to have patience and wait our moment."

Rossi, lapping at close to the leaders' pace, caught and passed the fading Iannone on lap ten, then closed quickly on Bradl, getting ahead on lap 13. He was just over 1.5 seconds behind his team-mate at the flag.

Bradl, badly knocked about and with front tyre problems, preferred to stay safe in a lone fifth, five seconds from an equally lonely Iannone.

Riders stayed close and brawling down the field, all enjoying the sweeping curves. Dovizioso had dropped away from Rossi, an oil-control problem costing him some power. He fell into the clutches of the Monster Yamahas. Smith had gained ascendancy over Pol Espargaro and then drew clear after putting the Ducati between them for six laps. Pol was eighth by the end.

The battle for tenth was long and absorbing, involving all four Open Hondas, each taking at least a brief turn ahead and all but one of them closing on Hernandez in the final stages. By the end, the Aspar team-mates were narrowly ahead of the Ducati, with Aoyama snatching tenth from Hayden over the line. Abraham was on Hernandez's tail; but Redding had lost touch in the closing laps, struggling with front grip under braking.

Aleix Espargaro had wasted another second-row start after slipping off on the first lap, remounting to ride through from last to salvage the final point. He finished ahead of a battle between Barbera and Crutchlow replacement Pirro.

Bautista crashed out on the first lap after tagging the younger Espargaro's back wheel, his third crash in as many races. He returned to the pit in tears. Petrucci crashed out independently, also on the first lap.

Looking back over the year, the Argentine GP was significant in many ways. Not least for the growing demonstration of maturity that 21-year-old Marquez was able to give in his second season. Guided by the increasingly impressive 1999 125 champion Emilio Alzamora, he had measured his weekend effectively, saving tyres for qualifying and patiently timing his attack on Lorenzo just right. One could even say that he had won the race Hailwood style, at the lowest possible speed – though the way he rides, it never looks like that.

MOTO2 RACE – 23 laps

If Dorna's attempts to create closer racing in the premier class were at last bearing fruit, the opposite happened in Moto2, where equality of horsepower could not be more strict. The third round of the season bore a strong resemblance to the worse days of MotoGP, with the front of the field spaced out and only a modicum of variation.

Rabat had not quite matched compatriot Marquez: three successive pole starts, but he had finished second at round two, beaten by Moto3 champion Vinales. The troublesome rookie scored zero at Rio Hondo, however, after crashing out, and Rabat's points lead became the biggest of any class.

His race looked somewhat sterile. He led into the first corner and stretched steadily ahead. "From the outside, it might have looked like an easy race," he said, "but on the bike, it was incredibly difficult. It is not easy to keep maximum concentration, and I knew that if I made a small mistake Simeon was ready to attack."

Both Folger and Zarco had showed well in free practice, but once Rabat found a combination of tyres and settings he liked, he ran a string of fast laps at the end of qualifying to edge Zarco to second; with Simeon coming through to third to complete the front row.

Vinales led the next from Folger and his own team-mate, Salom: three ex-Moto3 rivals, all class rookies, side by side; veterans Pasini, de Angelis and Corsi lined up behind. With 19 riders within one second, it was close stuff. Pasini didn't make the start, his engine failing on the warm-up lap.

Simeon slotted straight into second. He couldn't quite match the leader's pace, but he could stay there under pressure from Vinales and briefly also Folger.

Vinales ran off line and fell victim to the slippery surface on lap three, while under attack from Corsi. But now Salom had arrived, and his persistent attack on Corsi gave Simeon the chance to get some clean air.

Thus first and second were settled.

The battle for third raged to the end. Aegerter had tagged on by half-distance. Salom finally found a move that would stick to get ahead of Corsi for the last rostrum spot; so also did Aegerter on the final lap, taking fourth by barely a tenth as the Italian fought back.

De Angelis was alone in sixth; Kallio came through the next group for seventh.

Sam Lowes also came from behind to head the fight for eighth, from Cortese, Torres, Schrotter and West. Folger had been with this group, but was off the back and slowing drastically as they started the last lap, finally crossing the line at reduced speed, shrugging and looking down at his back wheel after losing four places and any chance of points on the final lap.

This had let the next trio through, newcomer Morbidelli impressively beating Terol and Nakagami. Zarco was a cautious and pointless 18th; Porto led his group over the line for 23rd, a steady ride gaining him two places in the closing laps.

MOTO3 RACE – 21 laps

Miller and fastest Honda rider Vazquez vied for supremacy throughout practice; the KTM man taking his second pole in a row by half a tenth. Kent's Husqvarna was alongside; row two all-KTM.

It should have been three in a row for Miller, who seemed to have played his cards right in a sustained and fearsome battle for the lead. He was in front when it mattered, into the penultimate right-hander.

At that point, Fenati's final inside lunge took him on to the slippery part and he almost lost the front, regaining control by bouncing off the Australian to snatch victory. He earned one penalty point, but 25 for the championship. "I had the race won," said Miller. "But sometimes it ends in tears."

Marquez was in the thick of it, second by a tenth; Miller recovered for third, half a second behind.

A remarkable 17th-birthday ride put Livio Loi a career-best fourth, right on Miller's back wheel. He'd caught, passed and outdistanced no less than Rins and Vazquez, still disputing fifth, but now four seconds adrift.

Vinales was seventh, then a battle for eighth ended in victory for team owner's son Niklas Ajo, after he had rammed team-mate Kent on the run to the line. Kent fell off, but was still touching the bike as it crossed the line.

It was another bad weekend for Mahindra, Oliveira being left on the line with clutch failure.

Top left: Pedrosa seized second from Lorenzo in a late charge.

Above, from top: Lorenzo was happy to be back on the podium; Simeon and Gresini likewise, in Moto2; Loi took a birthday best ever fourth in Moto3.

Above left: Hernandez heads the production Hondas. Hayden (69) and team-mate Aoyama will get past; Abraham (17) will not.

Left: Tito Rabat led Simeon away and would take a second win of the year.

Above right: "I had the race won." Fenati celebrates Moto3 victory; Miller contemplates his robust tactics.

Right: Fenati, Marquez, Miller and Loi: Moto3 was trademark close.

Photos: Gold & Goose

G.P. RED BULL DE LA REPUBLICA ARGENTINA
25-27 APRIL, 2014

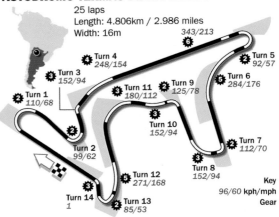

AUTÓDROMO TERMAS DE RÍO HONDO
25 laps
Length: 4.806km / 2.986 miles
Width: 16m

Turn 1 110/68
Turn 2 99/62
Turn 3 152/94
Turn 4 248/154
Turn 5 92/57
Turn 6 284/176
Turn 7 112/70
Turn 8 152/94
Turn 9 125/78
Turn 10 152/94
Turn 11 180/112
Turn 12 271/168
Turn 13 85/53
Turn 14 1
343/213

Key
96/60 kph/mph
Gear

MotoGP RACE DISTANCE: 25 laps, 74.658 miles/120.150km · RACE WEATHER: Dry (air 24°C, humidity 60%, track 21°C)

Pos.	Rider	Nat.	No.	Entrant	Machine	Tyres	Race tyre choice	Laps	Time & speed
1	Marc Marquez	SPA	93	Repsol Honda Team	Honda RC213V	B	F: Hard/R: Hard	25	41m 39.821s / 107.5mph/ 173.0km/h
2	Dani Pedrosa	SPA	26	Repsol Honda Team	Honda RC213V	B	F: Medium/R: Hard	25	41m 41.658s
3	Jorge Lorenzo	SPA	99	Movistar Yamaha MotoGP	Yamaha YZR-M1	B	F: Medium/R: Hard	25	41m 43.022s
4	Valentino Rossi	ITA	46	Movistar Yamaha MotoGP	Yamaha YZR-M1	B	F: Hard/R: Hard	25	41m 44.719s
5	Stefan Bradl	GER	6	LCR Honda MotoGP	Honda RC213V	B	F: Medium/R: Hard	25	41m 54.850s
6	Andrea Iannone	ITA	29	Pramac Racing	Ducati Desmosedici	B	F: Medium/R: Medium	25	41m 59.268s
7	Bradley Smith	GBR	38	Monster Yamaha Tech 3	Yamaha YZR-M1	B	F: Hard/R: Hard	25	42m 04.013s
8	Pol Espargaro	SPA	44	Monster Yamaha Tech 3	Yamaha YZR-M1	B	F: Medium/R: Hard	25	42m 08.939s
9	Andrea Dovizioso	ITA	4	Ducati Team	Ducati Desmosedici	B	F: Hard/R: Medium	25	42m 13.494s
10	Hiroshi Aoyama	JPN	7	Drive M7 Aspar	Honda RCV1000R	B	F: Medium/R: Medium	25	42m 23.100s
11	Nicky Hayden	USA	69	Drive M7 Aspar	Honda RCV1000R	B	F: Medium/R: Medium	25	42m 23.173s
12	Yonny Hernandez	COL	68	Energy T.I. Pramac Racing	Ducati Desmosedici	B	F: Medium/R: Medium	25	42m 24.640s
13	Karel Abraham	CZE	17	Cardion AB Motoracing	Honda RCV1000R	B	F: Medium/R: Medium	25	42m 24.999s
14	Scott Redding	GBR	45	GO&FUN Honda Gresini	Honda RCV1000R	B	F: Medium/R: Medium	25	42m 28.477s
15	Aleix Espargaro	SPA	41	NGM Forward Racing	Forward Yamaha	B	F: Hard/R: Medium	25	42m 32.071s
16	Hector Barbera	SPA	8	Avintia Racing	Avintia	B	F: Medium/R: Medium	25	42m 33.326s
17	Michele Pirro	ITA	51	Ducati Team	Ducati Desmosedici	B	F: Medium/R: Medium	25	42m 33.490s
18	Michael Laverty	GBR	70	Paul Bird Motorsport	PBM-ART	B	F: Medium/R: Medium	25	42m 36.391s
19	Mike di Meglio	FRA	63	Avintia Racing	Avintia	B	F: Medium/R: Medium	25	42m 42.961s
20	Colin Edwards	USA	5	NGM Forward Racing	Forward Yamaha	B	F: Hard/R: Medium	25	42m 45.581s
21	Broc Parkes	AUS	23	Paul Bird Motorsport	PBM-ART	B	F: Medium/R: Medium	25	42m 56.543s
	Alvaro Bautista	SPA	19	GO&FUN Honda Gresini	Honda RC213V	B	F: Medium/R: Hard	0	DNF-crash
	Danilo Petrucci	ITA	9	IodaRacing Project	ART	B	F: Medium/R: Medium	0	DNF-crash
	Cal Crutchlow	GBR	35	Ducati Team	Ducati Desmosedici	B	-	-	Absent-injured

Fastest lap: Dani Pedrosa, on lap 22, 1m 39.233s, 108.3mph/174.3km/h (record).
Previous lap record: New circuit.
Event best maximum speed: Stefan Bradl, 207.6mph/334.1km/h (race).

Qualifying
Weather: Dry
Air Temp: 25° **Track Temp:** 36°
Humidity: 46%

1	Marquez	1m 37.683s
2	Lorenzo	1m 38.425s
3	Pedrosa	1m 38.651s
4	A. Espargaro	1m 38.794s
5	Dovizioso	1m 38.856s
6	Rossi	1m 38.949s
7	Smith	1m 38.958s
8	Iannone	1m 39.237s
9	Bradl	1m 39.297s
10	Bautista	1m 39.429s
11	P. Espargaro	1m 39.822s
12	Hayden	1m 40.541s
13	Redding	1m 40.238s
14	Edwards	1m 40.476s
15	Abraham	1m 40.615s
16	Aoyama	1m 40.616s
17	Hernandez	1m 40.691s
18	Parkes	1m 40.981s
19	Pirro	1m 41.018s
20	Laverty	1m 41.103s
21	Barbera	1m 41.129s
22	Di Meglio	1m 41.267s
23	Petrucci	1m 41.686s

Fastest race laps

1	Pedrosa	1m 39.233s
2	Marquez	1m 39.264s
3	Rossi	1m 39.339s
4	Lorenzo	1m 39.603s
5	Smith	1m 40.049s
6	Bradl	1m 40.093s
7	Iannone	1m 40.160s
8	Dovizioso	1m 40.290s
9	P. Espargaro	1m 40.340s
10	A. Espargaro	1m 40.602s
11	Aoyama	1m 40.904s
12	Hayden	1m 41.020s
13	Hernandez	1m 41.171s
14	Pirro	1m 41.266s
15	Abraham	1m 41.296s
16	Redding	1m 41.296s
17	Barbera	1m 41.480s
18	Laverty	1m 41.506s
19	Edwards	1m 41.720s
20	Di Meglio	1m 41.776s
21	Parkes	1m 42.534s

Championship Points

1	Marquez	75
2	Pedrosa	56
3	Rossi	41
4	Dovizioso	34
5	Iannone	25
6	Bradl	24
7	Lorenzo	22
8	A. Espargaro	21
9	Smith	20
10	P. Espargaro	18
11	Hayden	18
12	Aoyama	15
13	Redding	11
14	Hernandez	11
15	Crutchlow	10
16	Abraham	8
17	Edwards	7
18	Petrucci	2
19	Barbera	1
20	Parkes	1

Constructor Points

1	Honda	75
2	Yamaha	47
3	Ducati	37
4	Forward Yamaha	21
5	ART	2
6	PBM	1
7	Avintia	1

Grid order

Rider	1	2	3	4	5	6	7	8	9	10	11	12	13	14	15	16	17	18	19	20	21	22	23	24	25	
93 MARQUEZ	99	99	99	99	99	99	99	99	99	99	99	99	99	99	99	99	93	93	93	93	93	93	93	93	93	1
99 LORENZO	46	4	29	93	93	93	93	93	93	93	93	93	93	93	93	93	99	99	99	99	99	99	26	26	26	2
26 PEDROSA	26	29	46	29	29	29	6	29	26	26	26	26	26	26	26	26	26	26	26	26	26	26	99	99	99	3
41 A. ESPARGARO	93	46	93	46	6	6	29	6	6	6	6	6	46	46	46	46	46	46	46	46	46	46	46	46	46	4
4 DOVIZIOSO	4	6	6	6	26	26	26	6	29	46	46	46	6	6	6	6	6	6	6	6	6	6	6	6	6	5
46 ROSSI	6	93	4	26	46	46	46	46	46	29	29	29	29	29	29	29	29	29	29	29	29	29	29	29	29	6
38 SMITH	29	26	26	4	4	4	4	4	4	4	38	38	38	38	38	38	38	38	38	38	38	38	38	38	38	7
29 IANNONE	44	44	44	44	44	38	44	38	38	38	38	4	4	4	4	4	4	44	44	44	44	44	44	44	44	8
6 BRADL	38	38	38	38	38	44	38	44	44	44	44	44	44	44	44	44	44	4	4	4	4	4	4	4	4	9
19 BAUTISTA	41	68	68	68	68	68	68	68	68	68	68	68	68	68	68	68	68	68	68	69	69	69	7			10
44 P. ESPARGARO	68	17	17	45	45	69	69	69	69	69	69	69	69	69	7	7	7	69	69	69	68	68	7	69		11
69 HAYDEN	45	69	69	69	69	17	17	7	7	7	7	7	7	69	69	69	7	7	7	7	7	17	68			12
45 REDDING	17	45	45	17	17	45	45	17	17	17	17	17	17	17	17	17	17	17	17	17	17	7	68	17		13
5 EDWARDS	69	51	51	7	7	7	7	45	45	45	45	45	45	45	45	45	45	45	45	45	45	45	45			14
17 ABRAHAM	51	7	7	63	63	63	51	51	51	51	8	8	8	8	8	8	8	8	8	8	41	41				15
7 AOYAMA	7	63	63	51	51	51	8	8	8	51	51	51	51	51	51	51	51	51	51	41	8	8				
68 HERNANDEZ	63	5	8	8	8	8	63	63	63	63	63	63	63	63	63	63	70	41	41	41	51	51	51			
23 PARKES	5	8	5	5	5	5	5	5	5	5	5	5	70	70	41	70	70	70	70	70	70	70				
51 PIRRO	23	23	23	70	70	70	70	70	70	70	70	70	5	63	63	63	63	63	63	63	63	63				
70 LAVERTY	70	70	70	23	23	23	23	23	23	23	41	41	41	41	41	41	5	5	5	5	5	5				
8 BARBERA	8	41	41	41	41	41	41	41	41	41	23	23	23	23	23	23	23	23	23	23	23	23				
63 DI MEGLIO																										
9 PETRUCCI																										

Moto2
RACE DISTANCE: 23 laps, 68.685 miles/110.538km · **RACE WEATHER:** Dry (air 23°C, humidity 60%, track 21°C)

Pos.	Rider	Nat.	No.	Entrant	Machine	Laps	Time & Speed
1	**Esteve Rabat**	SPA	53	Marc VDS Racing Team	Kalex	23	40m 06.114s 102.7mph/ 165.3,km/h
2	**Xavier Simeon**	BEL	19	Federal Oil Gresini Moto2	Suter	23	40m 08.208s
3	**Luis Salom**	SPA	39	Pons HP 40	Kalex	23	40m 09.816s
4	**Dominique Aegerter**	SWI	77	Technomag carXpert	Suter	23	40m 10.982s
5	**Simone Corsi**	ITA	3	NGM Forward Racing	Forward KLX	23	40m 11.124s
6	**Alex de Angelis**	RSM	15	Tasca Racing Moto2	Suter	23	40m 14.678s
7	**Mika Kallio**	FIN	36	Marc VDS Racing Team	Kalex	23	40m 19.271s
8	**Sam Lowes**	GBR	22	Speed Up	Speed Up	23	40m 25.870s
9	**Sandro Cortese**	GER	11	Dynavolt Intact GP	Kalex	23	40m 26.422s
10	**Jordi Torres**	SPA	81	Mapfre Aspar Team Moto2	Suter	23	40m 26.492s
11	**Marcel Schrotter**	GER	23	Tech 3	Tech 3	23	40m 27.084s
12	**Anthony West**	AUS	95	QMMF Racing Team	Speed Up	23	40m 27.613s
13	**Franco Morbidelli**	ITA	21	Italtrans Racing Team	Kalex	23	40m 32.913s
14	**Nicolas Terol**	SPA	18	Mapfre Aspar Team Moto2	Suter	23	40m 33.107s
15	**Takaaki Nakagami**	JPN	30	IDEMITSU Honda Team Asia	Kalex	23	40m 33.253s
16	Jonas Folger	GER	94	AGR Team	Kalex	23	40m 34.712s
17	Julian Simon	SPA	60	Italtrans Racing Team	Kalex	23	40m 39.547s
18	Johann Zarco	FRA	5	AirAsia Caterham	Caterham Suter	23	40m 42.583s
19	Thomas Luthi	SWI	12	Interwetten Paddock Moto2	Suter	23	40m 43.475s
20	Hafizh Syahrin	MAL	55	Petronas Raceline Malaysia	Kalex	23	40m 49.717s
21	Azlan Shah	MAL	25	IDEMITSU Honda Team Asia	Kalex	23	40m 53.833s
22	Roman Ramos	SPA	97	QMMF Racing Team	Speed Up	23	40m 54.400s
23	Sebastian Porto	ARG	99	Argentina TSR Motorsport	Kalex	23	40m 57.428s
24	Thitipong Warokorn	THA	10	APH PTT The Pizza SAG	Kalex	23	40m 59.900s
25	Louis Rossi	FRA	96	SAG Team	Kalex	23	40m 59.921s
26	Axel Pons	SPA	49	AGR Team	Kalex	23	41m 02.016s
27	Randy Krummenacher	SWI	4	IodaRacing Project	Suter	23	41m 02.926s
28	Lorenzo Baldassarri	ITA	7	Gresini Moto2	Suter	23	41m 06.713s
29	Robin Mulhauser	SWI	70	Technomag carXpert	Suter	23	41m 06.991s
30	Gino Rea	GBR	8	AGT REA Racing	Suter	23	41m 15.024s
31	Tetsuta Nagashima	JPN	45	Teluru Team JiR Webike	TSR	23	41m 15.092s
	Maverick Vinales	SPA	40	Pons HP 40	Kalex	3	DNF
	Ricard Cardus	SPA	88	Tech 3	Tech 3	2	DNF
	Mattia Pasini	ITA	54	NGM Forward Racing	Forward KLX	0	DNF

Fastest lap: Luis Salom, on lap 21, 1m 44.011s, 103.3mph/166.3km/h (record).

Previous lap record: New circuit.

Event best maximum speed: Julian Simon, 171.2mph/275.6km/h (race).

Qualifying
Weather: Dry
Air Temp: 26° **Track Temp:** 34°
Humidity: 45%

1	Rabat	1m 43.961s
2	Zarco	1m 43.971s
3	Simeon	1m 44.038s
4	Vinales	1m 44.168s
5	Folger	1m 44.174s
6	Salom	1m 44.322s
7	Pasini	1m 44.376s
8	De Angelis	1m 44.384s
9	Corsi	1m 44.440s
10	Nakagami	1m 44.444s
11	Torres	1m 44.496s
12	Schrotter	1m 44.648s
13	Cortese	1m 44.708s
14	Kallio	1m 44.715s
15	Morbidelli	1m 44.787s
16	Aegerter	1m 44.817s
17	Syahrin	1m 44.821s
18	Cardus	1m 44.838s
19	Simon	1m 44.946s
20	West	1m 45.077s
21	Baldassarri	1m 45.159s
22	Lowes	1m 45.161s
23	Krummenacher	1m 45.192s
24	Rossi	1m 45.199s
25	Terol	1m 45.223s
26	Pons	1m 45.235s
27	Luthi	1m 45.462s
28	Rea	1m 45.463s
29	Ramos	1m 45.883s
30	Nagashima	1m 45.964s
31	Shah	1m 46.045s
32	Porto	1m 46.127s
33	Warokorn	1m 46.296s
34	Mulhauser	1m 46.303s

Fastest race laps

1	Salom	1m 44.011s
2	Rabat	1m 44.076s
3	Aegerter	1m 44.097s
4	Corsi	1m 44.230s
5	De Angelis	1m 44.272s
6	Kallio	1m 44.276s
7	Simeon	1m 44.291s
8	Nakagami	1m 44.299s
9	West	1m 44.339s
10	Morbidelli	1m 44.370s
11	Torres	1m 44.373s
12	Cortese	1m 44.481s
13	Schrotter	1m 44.558s
14	Lowes	1m 44.616s
15	Folger	1m 44.762s
16	Luthi	1m 44.861s
17	Simon	1m 44.938s
18	Vinales	1m 45.009s
19	Terol	1m 45.047s
20	Baldassarri	1m 45.224s
21	Zarco	1m 45.282s
22	Syahrin	1m 45.346s
23	Shah	1m 45.530s
24	Warokorn	1m 45.618s
25	Porto	1m 45.619s
26	Ramos	1m 45.625s
27	Krummenacher	1m 45.738s
28	Pons	1m 45.870s
29	Rossi	1m 45.925s
30	Mulhauser	1m 45.933s
31	Rea	1m 46.065s
32	Nagashima	1m 46.250s
33	Cardus	1m 47.146s

Championship Points

1	Rabat	70
2	Kallio	42
3	Vinales	38
4	Corsi	33
5	Aegerter	29
6	Luthi	26
7	Simeon	20
8	West	20
9	Salom	18
10	Lowes	18
11	De Angelis	18
12	Cortese	18
13	Torres	14
14	Schrotter	12
15	Cardus	10
16	Rossi	6
17	Nakagami	6
18	Krummenacher	6
19	Folger	5
20	Pasini	4
21	Morbidelli	3
22	Terol	2
23	Syahrin	2

Constructor Points

1	Kalex	75
2	Suter	52
3	Forward KLX	33
4	Speed Up	27
5	Tech 3	16

Moto3
RACE DISTANCE: 21 laps, 62.713 miles/100.926km · **RACE WEATHER:** Dry (air 21°C, humidity 64%, track 21°C)

Pos.	Rider	Nat.	No.	Entrant	Machine	Laps	Time & Speed
1	**Romano Fenati**	ITA	5	SKY Racing Team VR46	KTM	21	38m 34.451s 97.5mph/ 156.9km/h
2	**Alex Marquez**	SPA	12	Estrella Galicia 0,0	Honda	21	38m 34.550s
3	**Jack Miller**	AUS	8	Red Bull KTM Ajo	KTM	21	38m 34.991s
4	**Livio Loi**	BEL	11	Marc VDS Racing Team	Kalex KTM	21	38m 35.075s
5	**Alex Rins**	SPA	42	Estrella Galicia 0,0	Honda	21	38m 39.981s
6	**Efren Vazquez**	SPA	7	SaxoPrint-RTG	Honda	21	38m 40.104s
7	**Isaac Vinales**	SPA	32	Calvo Team	KTM	21	38m 43.416s
8	**Niklas Ajo**	FIN	31	Avant Tecno Husqvarna Ajo	Husqvarna	21	38m 49.436s
9	**Danny Kent**	GBR	52	Red Bull Husqvarna Ajo	Husqvarna	21	38m 49.494s
10	**Enea Bastianini**	ITA	33	Junior Team GO&FUN Moto3	KTM	21	38m 51.761s
11	**Alexis Masbou**	FRA	10	Ongetta-Rivacold	Honda	21	38m 53.272s
12	**Juanfran Guevara**	SPA	58	Mapfre Aspar Team Moto3	Kalex KTM	21	38m 53.489s
13	**Alessandro Tonucci**	ITA	19	CIP	Mahindra	21	38m 53.648s
14	**Brad Binder**	RSA	41	Ambrogio Racing	Mahindra	21	39m 03.452s
15	**Zulfahmi Khairuddin**	MAL	63	Ongetta-AirAsia	Honda	21	39m 12.575s
16	Hafiq Azmi	MAL	38	SIC-AJO	KTM	21	39m 13.061s
17	Scott Deroue	NED	9	RW Racing GP	Kalex KTM	21	39m 13.120s
18	Bryan Schouten	NED	51	CIP	Mahindra	21	39m 13.258s
19	Eric Granado	BRA	57	Calvo Team	KTM	21	39m 23.168s
20	Jakub Kornfeil	CZE	84	Calvo Team	KTM	21	39m 33.376s
21	Philipp Oettl	GER	65	Interwetten Paddock Moto3	Kalex KTM	21	39m 34.033s
22	Arthur Sissis	AUS	61	Mahindra Racing	Mahindra	21	39m 34.480s
23	Ana Carrasco	SPA	22	RW Racing GP	Kalex KTM	21	39m 34.563s
24	Jules Danilo	FRA	95	Ambrogio Racing	Mahindra	21	39m 40.579s
25	Niccolo Antonelli	ITA	23	Junior Team GO&FUN Moto3	KTM	17	39m 44.629s
26	Gabriel Ramos	VEN	4	Kiefer Racing	Kalex KTM	17	39m 54.691s
	Matteo Ferrari	ITA	3	San Carlo Team Italia	Mahindra	19	DNF
	Karel Hanika	CZE	98	Red Bull KTM Ajo	KTM	18	DNF
	Luca Gunwald	GER	43	Kiefer Racing	Kalex KTM	9	DNF
	Francesco Bagnaia	ITA	21	SKY Racing Team VR46	KTM	8	DNF
	John McPhee	GBR	17	SaxoPrint-RTG	Honda	7	DNF
	Andrea Locatelli	ITA	55	San Carlo Team Italia	Mahindra	4	DNF
	Miguel Oliveira	POR	44	Mahindra Racing	Mahindra	0	DNS

Fastest lap: Alex Marquez, on lap 3, 1m 49.109s, 98.5mph/158.5km/h (record).

Previous lap record: New circuit.

Event best maximum speed: Livio Loi, 143.3mph/230.6km/h (race).

Qualifying:
Weather: Dry
Air Temp: 23° **Track Temp:** 35°
Humidity: 50%

1	Miller	1m 49.200s
2	Vazquez	1m 49.252s
3	Kent	1m 49.617s
4	Kornfeil	1m 49.785s
5	Fenati	1m 49.856s
6	Bagnaia	1m 49.875s
7	Ajo	1m 49.876s
8	Rins	1m 49.918s
9	Loi	1m 49.969s
10	Tonucci	1m 50.161s
11	Marquez	1m 50.185s
12	Guevara	1m 50.229s
13	McPhee	1m 50.237s
14	Oliveira	1m 50.324s
15	Antonelli	1m 50.370s
16	Hanika	1m 50.487s
17	Bastianini	1m 50.605s
18	Vinales	1m 50.672s
19	Binder	1m 50.702s
20	Masbou	1m 50.804s
21	Deroue	1m 50.831s
22	Locatelli	1m 51.118s
23	Ferrari	1m 51.278s
24	Schouten	1m 51.282s
25	Khairuddin	1m 51.287s
26	Grunwald	1m 51.453s
27	Granado	1m 51.677s
28	Carrasco	1m 51.827s
29	Sissis	1m 51.949s
30	Azmi	1m 52.133s
31	Oettl	1m 52.347s
32	Danilo	1m 52.581s
33	Ramos	1m 52.801s

Fastest race laps

1	Marquez	1m 49.109s
2	Vazquez	1m 49.298s
3	Miller	1m 49.345s
4	Rins	1m 49.359s
5	Fenati	1m 49.360s
6	Antonelli	1m 49.376s
7	Kent	1m 49.539s
8	Vinales	1m 49.563s
9	Loi	1m 49.593s
10	McPhee	1m 49.647s
11	Ajo	1m 49.831s
12	Bagnaia	1m 49.853s
13	Bastianini	1m 50.049s
14	Binder	1m 50.072s
15	Tonucci	1m 50.093s
16	Guevara	1m 50.114s
17	Masbou	1m 50.235s
18	Khairuddin	1m 50.455s
19	Grunwald	1m 50.557s
20	Kornfeil	1m 50.596s
21	Ferrari	1m 50.737s
22	Schouten	1m 50.755s
23	Danilo	1m 50.972s
24	Deroue	1m 50.990s
25	Granado	1m 51.039s
26	Azmi	1m 51.055s
27	Hanika	1m 51.309s
28	Oettl	1m 51.548s
29	Sissis	1m 51.951s
30	Ramos	1m 52.106s
31	Carrasco	1m 52.267s

Championship Points

1	Miller	66
2	Fenati	49
3	Vazquez	42
4	Marquez	40
5	Rins	35
6	Masbou	24
7	Kornfeil	21
8	Kent	18
9	Loi	17
10	Viñales	17
11	Bagnaia	15
12	Oliveira	14
13	McPhee	12
14	Ajo	10
15	Bastianini	9
16	Guevara	9
17	Hanika	8
18	Antonelli	7
19	Tonucci	3
20	Binder	3
21	Khairuddin	1

Constructor Points

1	KTM	75
2	Honda	56
3	Husqvarna	19
4	Kalex KTM	18
5	Mahindra	17

SPANISH GRAND PRIX

JEREZ CIRCUIT

Main photo: The Icon Has Landed. Marc Marquez greets Planet Earth.

Inset: Not falling, but waving – the winner gives the fans a last-lap thrill.

Photos: Gold & Goose

Above: : Bautista leads Dovizioso, Aleix Espargaro and Smith en route to his first finish of the year.

Top right: Surprise news for the scribblers: Bridgestone announce their departure.

Above right: A cheerful Vito Ippolito, entering his seventh season as FIM president and looking for a third term in 2014.

Above far right: Hand iced, eyes turned heavenward, Crutchlow's Ducati debut season continued to deteriorate.
Photos: Gold & Goose

Right: On the paint and pawing the air, the redux Rossi split the Repsol Honda pair.
Photo: Movistar Yamaha

"I AM sure," said the angelic young Spaniard with the disarming smile, "that sooner or later will come a race we are unable to win."

That wasn't this weekend, though, start of the European season, as Marquez continued to make history, his 100th start giving him 100 perfect points, to prove that the opening flyaway races are not *always* an unreliable indicator of form. Thanks to his usual on-the-brink pace, plus some exceedingly smart tactics in qualifying, Spain's new golden wonder fulfilled the expectations of most of the 117,001 (obviously scrupulously counted) race-day fans; most of the rest would have been happy to see Rossi finish second, though not quite as happy as if Pedrosa's belated hunt-down had resulted in him reversing the lesser podium places. He needed only "two or three more corners" to mount his attack. (Only the next day did he reveal that he had been suffering arm-pump so severe that he skipped the post-race tests for immediate surgery.)

Who knows what they thought of Lorenzo, merely best of the rest in his 200th grand prix, and only one place ahead of Dovi's Ducati. He had been humiliated in Jerez in 2013 by Marquez's last-corner barging attack; this time, he could only wish he could have been close enough for that to happen again.

The now-traditional start of the European season ran in benign conditions under clear blue skies. Yet it was still under a cloud of sorts. The meeting began with surprise news from Bridgestone. They were to quit as control tyre suppliers. Their second three-year contract would expire at the end of 2014, and the Japanese company had decided not to renew. However, they promised to supply tyres for 2015, to allow time for the changeover.

Beyond their obvious function, tyres are bike racing's scapegoats, taking the blame for all sorts of poor performance from riders, engineers and chassis designers. Doubtless Bridgestone had grown tired of the endless sniping – although some of it was justified, as in the slow development of tyres with better warm-up performance, after a spate of injurious early-lap or out-lap highside crashes in 2011. The spectre of imminent departure, however, caused many riders to discover a previously well-concealed affection for tyres that had made great strides in safety and durability, not to mention lap times, within a framework of 'one-size fits all'.

"For me, it is not good news," said Rossi, in a typical comment. "I think for any other manufacturer to be able to build tyres with the performance and safety will be very difficult." He even raised the spectre that the change might modify his plan to continue for another two seasons; Dovizioso affirmed that while 2016 would also see the introduction of stock electronics for all, "the different tyres will be the biggest point, much more than the new rules".

There were concerned faces also among engineers, who over the years had adapted chassis design around Bridgestones. Opined one Honda team man: "We'll have to build seven different chassis and try them all. Changing tyres will be very expensive."

There was worried speculation about who would take Bridgestone's place, but the deadline for applicants to submit tenders was just 22 days hence, suggesting that the matter had already been decided behind the scenes. In fact, rumours that Michelin were planning a return had first surfaced at only the second race; and all was confirmed three weeks later.

The French tyre manufacturer had entered GP racing in the 1970s and achieved a dominance that included 26 championships, but they had faltered as new rivals Bridgestone gained strength, and Stoner ended the streak in 2007. By the end of the following year, the axe had fallen with the introduction of control tyres for 2009. Michelin declined to tender, citing a preference for open competition. A clear change of heart had brought them back; they were already Moto2 control tyre suppliers for the important Spanish CEV championship.

Of more immediate impact, another change of heart – from Bridgestone. At Argentina's new track, they had added a third option to the front tyre range, the allocation upped from nine to ten. It proved so popular, and prompted also by their shortcomings in Texas, that it became normal practice from this race on.

The factory Yamaha riders had the choice of a slightly revised chassis – just one each. Rossi took to it at once, citing improved braking stability. The difference was small, he said, "but it is a good way to understand the way to work." He raced it to second. Lorenzo also had a run, then put it away until Monday's first post-race tests. "I prefer to keep both my bikes the same for the race," he said.

There wasn't much else new for the tests, although all but Ducati stayed on to take part, the Italian squad preferring to exercise alone at their official test track, Mugello, as this was more valuable for the forthcoming Italian GP. Suzuki were also absent, having elected instead to test at Argentina in private after the race there. Two days were washed out by heavy rain.

Crutchlow was back, still suffering, but hoping "the race will take my mind off it." He was to be sorely disappointed yet again, as his Ducati debut continued on a sour note – brake problems caused him to drop back and retire, very disgruntled, after four laps.

A sour note also at NGM Forward, whence came a rumour that, having announced he would retire at the end of the season, Colin Edwards had decided to cut a long story short and depart forthwith. The Texan flatly denied it, adding that he was looking forward to the oft-deferred arrival of the team's own chassis, having failed to come to terms with the Yamaha unit. "I just can't get this bike to turn," he said. Team chief Giovanni Cuzari said his words had been misunderstood, and the fact that Moto2 rider Corsi was to test the MotoGP bike on Monday was not significant. The new chassis would be on stream "in three or four races", he said; if disagreement with planned suppliers FTR could not be resolved, "we will build our own".

With Kallio taking Moto2 and Fenati a second straight win in Moto3, there was only one Spanish winner. It was the first time since the Australian GP in 2012 that there had not been two, and frequently three.

Above: Pedrosa mounted another spirited late attack, this time too late to defeat Rossi. You wouldn't have guessed that he was suffering severe arm-pump.

Top right: Kallio jubilant: he won; team-mate Rabat was off the podium.

Top far right: Kallio led away, Aegerter seized second, Luthi (12) headed the early Moto2 pursuit pack.

Above centre right: Aegerter ecstatic: the ever improving Swiss rider crossed the line second.

Above right: Class rookie Jonas Folger took his first Moto2 podium.

Photos: Gold & Goose

Right: Moto3 start, from the left: Antonelli, Vazquez, Miller, Vinales, Rins, Bastianini (half-hidden) and Marquez. Miller would prevail narrowly at the other end of the race.

Photo: Martin Heath

MOTOGP RACE – 27 laps

The weirdness of the flyaways gave way to the madness of Jerez – but one thing remained the same. Four races, four poles for Marquez, though with less dominance. Aleix Espargaro led first free practice; Pedrosa the combined free times. Bautista topped Q1 to join Q2, along with Hayden, for a second race in a row: factory riders Pirro (a Ducati wild-card), Iannone and Crutchlow missed out.

With the Yamaha's disadvantages less pronounced, Lorenzo seemed set for pole. But Marquez's crew had devised a new tactic, taking advantage of the short lap. Where most riders stop once during the 15-minute dash, he stopped twice. On his third soft tyre, he surpassed Lorenzo's target by better than four-tenths.

Furthermore he broke one of the longstanding 'best lap' times from 2008, last year of qualifying tyres, if only by less than a tenth. That had belonged to Lorenzo: similar records still stood at Le Mans, Catalunya, Sachsenring and Qatar. Marquez also set fastest race lap, this time short of Lorenzo's 2013 record.

Pedrosa was third; then Rossi led soft-tyre users Aleix Espargaro and Dovizioso.

Bradl led row three from Pol Espargaro and Smith; then came Bautista, Edwards and Hayden; Aoyama was best of the rest.

Marquez made a flying start, but Rossi bullied his way into the lead at far hairpin. "I knew his intention was to slow down the race to control the pace," said Marquez. "I realised I could go faster, so I tried to overtake him as soon as possible." Which was at the next hairpin at the other end of the lap. From then on, he pulled away steadily, by better than four seconds before half-distance. He had enough of a lead to wave his leg at the crowd on the final lap, and still win by 1.4 seconds.

Lorenzo had started badly with a wheelie off the line, but he finished the first lap third, ahead of Pedrosa, just behind Rossi. They stayed together until Lorenzo started to fade, almost a second adrift at half-distance; later he blamed "my physical condition".

It was not until lap 21 that Pedrosa, fighting front-tyre slides from lap one, was able to get past. Rossi was one second ahead, and the Honda closed by a few tenths every lap. Not quite enough, however. "I needed two or three more corners before I could attack," he said.

Whether he would have succeeded remained moot. Rossi was one of three riders on the hard front, which was paying dividends at race end.

Lorenzo was seven seconds down at the end, though still comfortably clear of a stirring five-bike battle for fifth.

Dovizioso held on more or less throughout, relying on strong braking and even stronger acceleration to hold the masses at bay. Aleix Espargaro got past briefly a couple of times towards the end, but lost out again at the next straight. Bautista, through from tenth on lap one, led the group for two laps, but when Dovi fought back on the last lap, the Spaniard narrowly succumbed, intent on his first finish of the year. Espargaro was another three-tenths down, and three-hundredths ahead of Smith, in turn just over half a second clear of team-mate Pol Espargaro, also on the hard front.

Bradl dropped back from this group suffering severe arm-pump (like Pedrosa, he too underwent surgery in the following days) and providing a tantalising target for Hayden, running the softest tyre option against Bridgestone's advice. He closed to within a fraction of a second with three laps left, then lost touch after running wide. "It would have been impossible to pass him anyway because of the factory bike's big jump out of the corners," he said.

He'd outpaced Redding early on, then Aoyama sped up to take 12th with seven laps to go.

Hernandez was a lone 14th. Some way behind, Colin Edwards had held 15th for most of the race before losing the last points-scoring position to Barbera on lap 22. Then the engine died on the final lap. It was, he said, as in Texas: "when the fuel gets hot, it stops feeding correctly." This left the PBM pair Laverty and Parkes to take distant and lonely 16th and 17th places.

Crutchlow pitted after four laps; fellow Ducatisti Iannone and Pirro both crashed out; likewise Abraham, also suffering brake problems.

MOTO2 RACE – 26 laps

For reasons that are hard to understand, Jerez brought out the worst in what is usually an exciting class, with a largely processional race and few battles of any import.

It brought out the best in Kallio, though, and turned the tables on his hitherto dominant team-mate, Tito Rabat, who had been on pole at all three flyaways, had won two of them and had been second at the other. In Jerez, he qualified sixth, and never got anywhere near the front.

Kallio took pole by a fair margin, a beaming Cortese second, now back to strength after his Qatar injuries, with Salom completing row one at the head of a close batch of times, third to 21st covered by a second. Luthi, Aegerter and Rabat lined up behind.

Kallio took off in the lead and would stay there throughout. "We went into the race with a clear plan: push hard to build a lead in the first five laps while the tyres were good and then manage the gap while conserving the tyres for the rest of the race. The plan worked perfectly. Even so, it was such a hard race, even if it didn't look that way. I had to stay on the limit the whole race," said Kallio.

The rider forcing the issue was Aegerter, who seized second from the second row of the grid and stayed there throughout, although blaming "little mistakes" in the early laps for losing touch with the leader. Try as he might, he couldn't get the gap to less than a second, and was 2.4 behind over the line, his best result in the class.

Best class rookie this time was Folger, third throughout, though living on his nerves in the closing stages, by which time Rabat was only a couple of seconds behind. The Spaniard had finished lap one eighth, but soon began gaining places, taking fourth off Salom after eight laps. He never got any further forward.

Then Salom suffered a late attack from fellow-rookie team-mate Vinales, succumbing with three laps to go.

Riders trailed along behind, with Simeon alone in seventh. Another three seconds behind him, Cortese had been engaged with Luthi, the younger former champion finally getting past on lap 21. By then, however, Zarco had gained comfort and pace, and was ahead of both for eighth by the end, for his first points of the year.

Then Luthi came under attack from Nakagami until the Japanese charger crashed out on the final lap.

There was a close battle for 11th, won by just over a tenth by redoubtable veteran West from Torres, Cardus, Simon, Krummenacher, Pons, de Angelis and Pasini; Krummenacher was the last rider to score points. The group redeemed Moto2's reputation for close racing: 11th to 18th covered by 2.7 seconds.

Corsi crashed out, as did Baldassari, Rossi and Schrotter – plus Sam Lowes, twice.

MOTO3 RACE – 23 laps

Moto3 made up for any lack of excitement elsewhere. Once again there was a big group up front, a trademark last-corner shoving match, and the first three over the line in much less than two-tenths. Once again, KTM won – the first win for Honda's revived effort remaining out of reach by a matter of feet.

Miller took his third pole in succession, by more than half a second over the close-packed pursuit. Antonelli was alongside, then Rins; Vinales led row two from Marquez and Bagnaia; Vazquez headed the third.

Miller led away, then Vazquez took over for the next three, then Fenati, briefly Vinales, then Fenati again in a spell to half-distance. It was all somewhat notional: Rins also took to the front a couple of times out on the lap, then for two laps over the line.

Fenati took the lion's share, however, and was still ahead as they braked for the last hairpin. Rins dived for the inside and took over – only to run wide, letting not only the Italian through, but also Vazquez.

Miller had been to and fro in the front group, saving his tyres for his own last-lap attack. He was foiled, however, when he was pushed wide and out of touch by Vinales. He got back ahead, to lead the next trio, just over a second adrift, from Calvo KTM team-mates Vinales and Kornfeil.

Marquez, narrowly unable to stay with the front group, ended up two seconds back, but comfortably clear of Bagnaia. Impressive rookie Bastianini took ninth, fending of Husqvarna team-mates Ajo and Kent; Masbou and McPhee were close behind. All had passed Oliveira, the Mahindra rider stricken with arm-pump problems.

GRAN PREMIO
bwin
DE ESPAÑA

2-4 MAY, 2014

CIRCUITO DE JEREZ

27 laps
Length: 4.423 km. / 2.748 miles
Width: 11m

Expo '92 100/62
Alex Criville 160/99
271/168
Peluqui 115/72
Turn 2 78/48
Ferrari 180/112
131/81
Michelin 155/96
Jorge Martinez Aspar
Turn 4 166/103
Angel Nieto 99/62
Turn 7 170/106
Sito Pons 131/81
Dry Sack 72/45
Jorge Lorenzo 72/45
275/171

Key
96/60 kph/mph
Gear

| MotoGP | RACE DISTANCE: 27 laps, 74.205 miles/119.421km · RACE WEATHER: Dry (air 28°C, humidity 25%, track 50°C) |

Pos.	Rider	Nat.	No.	Entrant	Machine	Tyres	Race tyre choice	Laps	Time & speed
1	**Marc Marquez**	SPA	93	Repsol Honda Team	Honda RC213V	B	F: Medium/R: Medium	27	45m 24.134s 98.1mph/ 157.8km/h
2	**Valentino Rossi**	ITA	46	Movistar Yamaha MotoGP	Yamaha YZR-M1	B	F: Hard/R: Medium	27	45m 25.565s
3	**Dani Pedrosa**	SPA	26	Repsol Honda Team	Honda RC213V	B	F: Medium/R: Medium	27	45m 25.663s
4	**Jorge Lorenzo**	SPA	99	Movistar Yamaha MotoGP	Yamaha YZR-M1	B	F: Medium/R: Medium	27	45m 32.675s
5	**Andrea Dovizioso**	ITA	4	Ducati Team	Ducati Desmosedici	B	F: Medium/R: Soft	27	45m 51.628s
6	**Alvaro Bautista**	SPA	19	GO&FUN Honda Gresini	Honda RC213V	B	F: Medium/R: Medium	27	45m 51.740s
7	**Aleix Espargaro**	SPA	41	NGM Forward Racing	Forward Yamaha	B	F: Medium/R: Soft	27	45m 52.051s
8	**Bradley Smith**	GBR	38	Monster Yamaha Tech 3	Yamaha YZR-M1	B	F: Medium/R: Medium	27	45m 52.081s
9	**Pol Espargaro**	SPA	44	Monster Yamaha Tech 3	Yamaha YZR-M1	B	F: Hard/R: Medium	27	45m 53.553s
10	**Stefan Bradl**	GER	6	LCR Honda MotoGP	Honda RC213V	B	F: Medium/R: Medium	27	45m 57.006s
11	**Nicky Hayden**	USA	69	Drive M7 Aspar	Honda RCV1000R	B	F: Medium/R: Extra-Soft	27	45m 59.624s
12	**Hiroshi Aoyama**	JPN	7	Drive M7 Aspar	Honda RCV1000R	B	F: Medium/R: Extra-Soft	27	46m 04.217s
13	**Scott Redding**	GBR	45	GO&FUN Honda Gresini	Honda RCV1000R	B	F: Hard/R: Extra-Soft	27	46m 07.964s
14	**Yonny Hernandez**	COL	68	Energy T.I. Pramac Racing	Ducati Desmosedici	B	F: Medium/R: Soft	27	46m 16.429s
15	**Hector Barbera**	SPA	8	Avintia Racing	Avintia	B	F: Medium/R: Extra-Soft	27	46m 19.007s
16	Michael Laverty	GBR	70	Paul Bird Motorsport	PBM-ART	B	F: Medium/R: Extra-Soft	27	46m 30.316s
17	Broc Parkes	AUS	23	Paul Bird Motorsport	PBM-ART	B	F: Medium/R: Extra-Soft	27	46m 47.554s
	Colin Edwards	USA	5	NGM Forward Racing	Forward Yamaha	B	F: Medium/R: Extra-Soft	26	DNF-mechanical
	Andrea Iannone	ITA	29	Pramac Racing	Ducati Desmosedici	B	F: Medium/R: Soft	22	DNF-crash
	Mike di Meglio	FRA	63	Avintia Racing	Avintia	B	F: Medium/R: Extra-Soft	21	DNF-mechanical
	Karel Abraham	CZE	17	Cardion AB Motoracing	Honda RCV1000R	B	F: Medium/R: Extra-Soft	10	DNF-crash
	Cal Crutchlow	GBR	35	Ducati Team	Ducati Desmosedici	B	F: Medium/R: Soft	4	DNF-mechanical
	Michele Pirro	ITA	51	Ducati Team	Ducati Desmosedici	B	F: Medium/R: Extra-Soft	2	DNF-crash
	Danilo Petrucci	ITA	9	IodaRacing Project	ART	B	–		DNS-injured

Fastest lap: Marc Marquez, on lap 5, 1m 39.841s, 99.0mph/159.4km/h.
Lap record: Jorge Lorenzo, SPA (Yamaha), 1m 39.565s, 99.4mph/159.9km/h (2013).
Event best maximum speed: Dani Pedrosa, 183.9mph/295.9km/h (free practice 4).

Qualifying

Weather: Dry
Air Temp: 28° **Humidity:** 29%
Track Temp: 50°

1	Marquez	1m 38.120s
2	Lorenzo	1m 38.541s
3	Pedrosa	1m 38.630s
4	Rossi	1m 38.857s
5	A. Espargaro	1m 39.007s
6	Dovizioso	1m 39.222s
7	Bradl	1m 39.243s
8	P. Espargaro	1m 39.293s
9	Smith	1m 39.390s
10	Bautista	1m 39.751s
11	Edwards	1m 39.814s
12	Hayden	1m 39.826s
13	Aoyama	1m 39.768s
14	Crutchlow	1m 39.849s
15	Iannone	1m 40.118s
16	Abraham	1m 40.126s
17	Pirro	1m 40.239s
18	Redding	1m 40.453s
19	Hernandez	1m 40.566s
20	Petrucci	1m 41.009s
21	Laverty	1m 41.124s
22	Di Meglio	1m 41.517s
23	Parkes	1m 41.702s
24	Barbera	1m 42.052s

Fastest race laps

1	Marquez	1m 39.841s
2	Pedrosa	1m 40.186s
3	Rossi	1m 40.195s
4	Lorenzo	1m 40.306s
5	Iannone	1m 40.783s
6	Crutchlow	1m 40.877s
7	Bradl	1m 40.879s
8	A. Espargaro	1m 40.937s
9	Smith	1m 41.057s
10	Dovizioso	1m 41.062s
11	Redding	1m 41.109s
12	Bautista	1m 41.153s
13	P. Espargaro	1m 41.409s
14	Hayden	1m 41.436s
15	Aoyama	1m 41.488s
16	Pirro	1m 41.803s
17	Edwards	1m 41.811s
18	Hernandez	1m 41.850s
19	Abraham	1m 42.024s
20	Barbera	1m 42.187s
21	Parkes	1m 42.578s
22	Laverty	1m 42.590s
23	Di Meglio	1m 42.957s

Championship Points

1	Marquez	100
2	Pedrosa	72
3	Rossi	61
4	Dovizioso	45
5	Lorenzo	35
6	Bradl	30
7	A. Espargaro	30
8	Smith	28
9	Iannone	25
10	P. Espargaro	25
11	Hayden	23
12	Aoyama	19
13	Redding	14
14	Hernandez	13
15	Bautista	10
16	Crutchlow	10
17	Abraham	8
18	Edwards	7
19	Petrucci	2
20	Barbera	2
21	Parkes	1

Constructor Points

1	Honda	100
2	Yamaha	67
3	Ducati	48
4	Forward Yamaha	30
5	ART	2
6	Avintia	2
7	PBM	1

Grid order	1	2	3	4	5	6	7	8	9	10	11	12	13	14	15	16	17	18	19	20	21	22	23	24	25	26	27	
93 MARQUEZ	93	93	93	93	93	93	93	93	93	93	93	93	93	93	93	93	93	93	93	93	93	93	93	93	93	93	93	1
99 LORENZO	46	46	46	46	46	46	46	46	46	46	46	46	46	46	46	46	46	46	46	46	46	46	46	46	46	46	46	2
26 PEDROSA	99	99	99	99	99	99	99	99	99	99	99	99	99	99	99	99	99	99	99	26	26	26	26	26	26	26	26	3
46 ROSSI	26	26	26	26	26	26	26	26	26	26	26	26	26	26	26	26	26	26	26	99	99	99	99	99	99	99	99	4
41 A. ESPARGARO	4	4	4	4	4	4	4	4	4	4	4	4	4	4	4	4	4	4	4	4	4	4	41	19	19	4		5
4 DOVIZIOSO	38	38	38	41	41	41	41	41	41	41	41	41	41	41	41	41	41	41	41	41	41	41	4	4	4	19		6
6 BRADL	6	41	41	38	38	38	38	38	38	38	38	38	38	38	19	19	19	19	19	19	19	19	19	41	41	41		7
44 P. ESPARGARO	41	29	29	29	29	6	6	6	6	6	6	19	19	19	38	38	38	38	38	38	38	38	38	38	38	38		8
38 SMITH	29	6	6	6	6	19	19	19	19	19	19	6	6	6	6	6	44	44	44	44	44	44	44	44	44	44		9
19 BAUTISTA	19	19	35	19	19	44	44	44	44	44	44	44	44	44	44	44	6	6	6	6	6	6	6	6	6	6		10
5 EDWARDS	44	35	19	44	44	69	69	69	69	69	69	69	69	69	69	69	69	69	69	69	69	69	69	69	69	69		11
69 HAYDEN	35	44	44	69	69	45	45	45	45	45	45	45	45	45	45	45	7		7	7	7	7	7					12
7 AOYAMA	69	69	69	45	45	68	7	7	7	7	7	7	7	7	7	7	45	7	45	45	45	45	45					13
35 CRUTCHLOW	68	45	45	35	68	7	7	68	68	68	68	68	68	68	68	68	68	68	68	68	68	68						14
29 IANNONE	45	68	68	68	7	5	5	5	5	5	5	5	5	5	5	5	5	8	8	8	8	8	8					15
17 ABRAHAM	5	51	7	7	5	8	8	8	8	8	8	8	8	8	8	8	8	5	5	5	5	5	70					
51 PIRRO	7	7	70	5	8	70	70	70	70	70	70	70	70	70	70	70	70	70	70	70	70	23						
45 REDDING	51	17	5	70	70	23	23	23	23	23	23	23	29	29	29	29	29	29	23	23	23	23						
68 HERNANDEZ	17	63	8	8	63	63	63	63	63	29	29	29	23	23	23	23	23	23										
70 LAVERTY	63	70	63	63	23	29	29	29	17	63	63	63	63	63	63	63	63											
63 DI MEGLIO	70	5	23	23	17	17	17	17	17	63																		
23 PARKES		8	8	17	17																							
8 BARBERA	23	23																										

35 Pit stop 63 Lapped rider

Moto2

RACE DISTANCE: 26 laps, 71.456 miles/114.998km · RACE WEATHER: Dry (air 27°C, humidity 26%, track 44°C)

Pos.	Rider	Nat.	No.	Entrant	Machine	Laps	Time & Speed
1	Mika Kallio	FIN	36	Marc VDS Racing Team	Kalex	26	44m 56.004s / 95.4mph / 153.5km/h
2	Dominique Aegerter	SWI	77	Technomag carXpert	Suter	26	44m 58.438s
3	Jonas Folger	GER	94	AGR Team	Kalex	26	44m 59.672s
4	Esteve Rabat	SPA	53	Marc VDS Racing Team	Kalex	26	45m 01.435s
5	Maverick Vinales	SPA	40	Pons HP 40	Kalex	26	45m 05.790s
6	Luis Salom	SPA	39	Pons HP 40	Kalex	26	45m 07.360s
7	Xavier Simeon	BEL	19	Federal Oil Gresini Moto2	Suter	26	45m 14.116s
8	Johann Zarco	FRA	5	AirAsia Caterham	Caterham Suter	26	45m 17.512s
9	Sandro Cortese	GER	11	Dynavolt Intact GP	Kalex	26	45m 17.612s
10	Thomas Luthi	SWI	12	Interwetten Paddock Moto2	Suter	26	45m 18.815s
11	Anthony West	AUS	95	QMMF Racing Team	Speed Up	26	45m 39.288s
12	Jordi Torres	SPA	81	Mapfre Aspar Team Moto2	Suter	26	45m 39.409s
13	Ricard Cardus	SPA	88	Tech 3	Tech 3	26	45m 39.910s
14	Julian Simon	SPA	60	Italtrans Racing Team	Kalex	26	45m 40.104s
15	Randy Krummenacher	SWI	4	IodaRacing Project	Suter	26	45m 40.438s
16	Axel Pons	SPA	49	AGR Team	Kalex	26	45m 40.712s
17	Alex de Angelis	RSM	15	Tasca Racing Moto2	Suter	26	45m 41.008s
18	Mattia Pasini	ITA	54	NGM Forward Racing	Forward KLX	26	45m 41.991s
19	Ratthapark Wilairot	THA	14	AirAsia Caterham	Caterham Suter	26	45m 43.444s
20	Franco Morbidelli	ITA	21	Italtrans Racing Team	Kalex	26	45m 53.180s
21	Hafizh Syahrin	MAL	55	Petronas Raceline Malaysia	Kalex	26	45m 58.632s
22	Tetsuta Nagashima	JPN	45	Teluru Team JiR Webike	TSR	26	45m 59.720s
23	Roman Ramos	SPA	97	QMMF Racing Team	Speed Up	26	46m 00.334s
24	Azlan Shah	MAL	25	IDEMITSU Honda Team Asia	Kalex	26	46m 01.427s
25	Edgar Pons	SPA	57	Pons HP 40	Kalex	26	46m 01.661s
26	Gino Rea	GBR	8	AGT REA Racing	Suter	26	46m 02.670s
27	Robin Mulhauser	SWI	70	Technomag carXpert	Suter	26	46m 09.624s
28	Thitipong Warokorn	THA	10	APH PTT The Pizza SAG	Kalex	26	46m 15.049s
	Takaaki Nakagami	JPN	30	IDEMITSU Honda Team Asia	Kalex	25	DNF
	Simone Corsi	ITA	3	NGM Forward Racing	Forward KLX	24	DNF
	Sam Lowes	GBR	22	Speed Up	Speed Up	18	DNF
	Marcel Schrotter	GER	23	Tech 3	Tech 3	11	DNF
	Louis Rossi	FRA	96	SAG Team	Kalex	8	DNF
	Lorenzo Baldassarri	ITA	7	Gresini Moto2	Suter	5	DNF

Fastest lap: Jonas Folger, on lap 2, 1m 42.876s, 96.1mph/154.7km/h (record).
Previous lap record: Esteve Rabat, SPA (Kalex), 1m 43.119s, 95.9mph/154.4km/h (2013).
Event best maximum speed: Sandro Cortese, 156.8mph/252.3km/h (free practice 3).

Qualifying
Weather: Dry
Air: 30° Track: 52°
Humidity: 28%

1	Kallio	1m 42.766s
2	Cortese	1m 43.060s
3	Salom	1m 43.174s
4	Luthi	1m 43.222s
5	Aegerter	1m 43.232s
6	Rabat	1m 43.234s
7	Folger	1m 43.235s
8	Vinales	1m 43.256s
9	Schrotter	1m 43.501s
10	Zarco	1m 43.513s
11	Corsi	1m 43.569s
12	Simeon	1m 43.615s
13	Nakagami	1m 43.625s
14	Cardus	1m 43.648s
15	Lowes	1m 43.664s
16	Simon	1m 43.716s
17	Wilairot	1m 43.775s
18	Pasini	1m 43.826s
19	De Angelis	1m 43.951s
20	Baldassarri	1m 43.978s
21	Rossi	1m 44.033s
22	Torres	1m 44.240s
23	Morbidelli	1m 44.395s
24	West	1m 44.438s
25	Krummenacher	1m 44.476s
26	Syahrin	1m 44.563s
27	Rea	1m 44.606s
28	Pons	1m 44.658s
29	Nagashima	1m 45.112s
30	Mulhauser	1m 45.358s
31	Shah	1m 45.511s
32	Warokorn	1m 45.606s
33	Ramos	1m 45.634s
34	Pons	1m 45.652s
	Terol	No Time

Fastest race laps

1	Folger	1m 42.876s
2	Kallio	1m 42.918s
3	Aegerter	1m 43.095s
4	Salom	1m 43.206s
5	Rabat	1m 43.207s
6	Vinales	1m 43.239s
7	Simeon	1m 43.552s
8	Nakagami	1m 43.647s
9	Cortese	1m 43.710s
10	Corsi	1m 43.792s
11	Luthi	1m 43.837s
12	Zarco	1m 43.893s
13	Lowes	1m 43.927s
14	West	1m 44.188s
15	Schrotter	1m 44.189s
16	Wilairot	1m 44.258s
17	Cardus	1m 44.264s
18	Simon	1m 44.308s
19	Pasini	1m 44.339s
20	Krummenacher	1m 44.402s
21	Baldassarri	1m 44.476s
22	Pons	1m 44.504s
23	Torres	1m 44.509s
24	De Angelis	1m 44.637s
25	Rossi	1m 44.742s
26	Morbidelli	1m 44.923s
27	Rea	1m 45.023s
28	Nagashima	1m 45.102s
29	Pons	1m 45.112s
30	Shah	1m 45.219s
31	Mulhauser	1m 45.261s
32	Ramos	1m 45.274s
33	Syahrin	1m 45.283s
34	Warokorn	1m 45.638s

Championship Points

1	Rabat	83
2	Kallio	67
3	Vinales	49
4	Aegerter	49
5	Corsi	33
6	Luthi	32
7	Simeon	29
8	Salom	28
9	Cortese	25
10	West	25
11	Folger	21
12	Lowes	18
13	De Angelis	18
14	Torres	18
15	Cardus	13
16	Schrotter	12
17	Zarco	8
18	Krummenacher	7
19	Rossi	6
20	Nakagami	6
21	Pasini	4
22	Morbidelli	3
23	Simon	2
24	Terol	2
25	Syahrin	2

Constructor Points

1	Kalex	100
2	Suter	72
3	Forward KLX	33
4	Speed Up	32
5	Tech 3	19
6	Caterham Suter	8

Moto3

RACE DISTANCE: 23 laps, 63.211 miles/101.729km · RACE WEATHER: Dry (air 23°C, humidity 39%, track 29°C)

Pos.	Rider	Nat.	No.	Entrant	Machine	Laps	Time & Speed
1	Romano Fenati	ITA	5	SKY Racing Team VR46	KTM	23	41m 28.584s / 91.4mph / 147.1km/h
2	Efren Vazquez	SPA	7	SaxoPrint-RTG	Honda	23	41m 28.728s
3	Alex Rins	SPA	42	Estrella Galicia 0,0	Honda	23	41m 28.731s
4	Jack Miller	AUS	8	Red Bull KTM Ajo	KTM	23	41m 29.808s
5	Isaac Vinales	SPA	32	Calvo Team	KTM	23	41m 29.828s
6	Jakub Kornfeil	CZE	84	Calvo Team	KTM	23	41m 30.441s
7	Alex Marquez	SPA	12	Estrella Galicia 0,0	Honda	23	41m 32.392s
8	Francesco Bagnaia	ITA	21	SKY Racing Team VR46	KTM	23	41m 35.215s
9	Enea Bastianini	ITA	33	Junior Team GO&FUN Moto3	KTM	23	41m 40.528s
10	Niklas Ajo	FIN	31	Avant Tecno Husqvarna Ajo	Husqvarna	23	41m 40.788s
11	Danny Kent	GBR	52	Red Bull Husqvarna Ajo	Husqvarna	23	41m 41.269s
12	Alexis Masbou	FRA	10	Ongetta-Rivacold	Honda	23	41m 41.423s
13	John McPhee	GBR	17	SaxoPrint-RTG	Honda	23	41m 41.454s
14	Miguel Oliveira	POR	44	Mahindra Racing	Mahindra	23	41m 43.377s
15	Philipp Oettl	GER	65	Interwetten Paddock Moto3	Kalex KTM	23	41m 43.491s
16	Juanfran Guevara	SPA	58	Mapfre Aspar Team Moto3	Kalex KTM	23	41m 44.170s
17	Maria Herrera	SPA	6	Junior Team Estrella Galicia 0,0	Honda	23	41m 44.337s
18	Alessandro Tonucci	ITA	19	CIP	Mahindra	23	41m 51.705s
19	Karel Hanika	CZE	98	Red Bull KTM Ajo	KTM	23	41m 52.325s
20	Zulfahmi Khairuddin	MAL	63	Ongetta-AirAsia	Honda	23	41m 59.744s
21	Marcos Ramirez	SPA	24	Calvo Team Laglisse	KTM	23	42m 00.021s
22	Bryan Schouten	NED	51	CIP	Mahindra	23	42m 05.445s
23	Ana Carrasco	SPA	22	RW Racing GP	Kalex KTM	23	42m 16.109s
24	Hafiq Azmi	MAL	38	SIC-AJO	KTM	23	42m 16.397s
25	Matteo Ferrari	ITA	3	San Carlo Team Italia	Mahindra	23	42m 16.699s
26	Luca Grunwald	GER	43	Kiefer Racing	Kalex KTM	23	42m 16.725s
27	Jules Danilo	FRA	95	Ambrogio Racing	Mahindra	23	42m 17.277s
28	Gabriel Ramos	VEN	4	Kiefer Racing	Kalex KTM	23	42m 51.074s
	Livio Loi	BEL	11	Marc VDS Racing Team	Kalex KTM	16	DNF
	Brad Binder	RSA	41	Ambrogio Racing	Mahindra	15	DNF
	Scott Deroue	NED	9	RW Racing GP	Kalex KTM	14	DNF
	Gabriel Rodrigo	ARG	91	RBA Racing Team	KTM	7	DNF
	Niccolo Antonelli	ITA	23	Junior Team GO&FUN Moto3	KTM	2	DNF
	Arthur Sissis	AUS	61	Mahindra Racing	Mahindra	2	DNF
	Eric Granado	BRA	57	Calvo Team	KTM	0	DNF

Fastest lap: Alex Rins, on lap 4, 1m 47.033s, 92.4mph/148.7km/h.
Lap record: Luis Salom, SPA (KTM), 1m 46.948s, 92.5mph/148.8km/h. (2013).
Event best maximum speed: Alex Marquez, 136.7mph/220.0km/h (race).

Qualifying:
Weather: Dry
Air: 28° Track: 43°
Humidity: 26%

1	Miller	1m 46.173s
2	Antonelli	1m 46.788s
3	Rins	1m 46.867s
4	Vinales	1m 46.867s
5	Marquez	1m 46.884s
6	Bagnaia	1m 47.012s
7	Vazquez	1m 47.049s
8	Ajo	1m 47.262s
9	McPhee	1m 47.329s
10	Fenati	1m 47.378s
11	Kornfeil	1m 47.431s
12	Oliveira	1m 47.432s
13	Kent	1m 47.459s
14	Oettl	1m 47.486s
15	Bastianini	1m 47.535s
16	Herrera	1m 47.556s
17	Guevara	1m 47.635s
18	Masbou	1m 47.688s
19	Rodrigo	1m 47.719s
20	Granado	1m 47.746s
21	Ramirez	1m 47.986s
22	Tonucci	1m 48.044s
23	Khairuddin	1m 48.073s
24	Loi	1m 48.091s
25	Sissis	1m 48.213s
26	Deroue	1m 48.243s
27	Schouten	1m 48.271s
28	Carrasco	1m 48.357s
29	Hanika	1m 48.365s
30	Binder	1m 48.371s
31	Ferrari	1m 48.383s
32	Azmi	1m 48.513s
33	Grunwald	1m 48.791s
34	Danilo	1m 48.897s
35	Ramos	1m 50.396s

Fastest race laps

1	Rins	1m 47.033s
2	Fenati	1m 47.238s
3	Marquez	1m 47.250s
4	Vinales	1m 47.276s
5	Miller	1m 47.315s
6	Kornfeil	1m 47.367s
7	Kent	1m 47.372s
8	Vazquez	1m 47.375s
9	Bagnaia	1m 47.388s
10	Ajo	1m 47.438s
11	Oliveira	1m 47.443s
12	Binder	1m 47.633s
13	Antonelli	1m 47.649s
14	Herrera	1m 47.712s
15	McPhee	1m 47.713s
16	Bastianini	1m 47.843s
17	Masbou	1m 47.895s
18	Oettl	1m 47.907s
19	Khairuddin	1m 47.916s
20	Guevara	1m 47.930s
21	Hanika	1m 47.936s
22	Loi	1m 47.976s
23	Tonucci	1m 48.053s
24	Rodrigo	1m 48.171s
25	Schouten	1m 48.297s
26	Deroue	1m 48.424s
27	Ferrari	1m 48.445s
28	Azmi	1m 48.482s
29	Ramirez	1m 48.526s
30	Carrasco	1m 48.806s
31	Grunwald	1m 48.961s
32	Danilo	1m 48.995s
33	Ramos	1m 50.152s
34	Sissis	1m 53.077s

Championship Points

1	Miller	79
2	Fenati	74
3	Vazquez	62
4	Rins	51
5	Marquez	49
6	Kornfeil	31
7	Vinales	28
8	Masbou	28
9	Bagnaia	23
10	Kent	23
11	Loi	17
12	Oliveira	16
13	Ajo	16
14	Bastianini	16
15	McPhee	15
16	Guevara	9
17	Hanika	8
18	Antonelli	7
19	Tonucci	3
20	Binder	3
21	Khairuddin	1
22	Oettl	1

Constructor Points

1	KTM	100
2	Honda	76
3	Husqvarna	25
4	Kalex KTM	19
5	Mahindra	19

FIM WORLD CHAMPIONSHIP · ROUND 5

FRENCH GRAND PRIX

LE MANS BUGATTI CIRCUIT

Above: Waiting for Marc: Rossi, Dovizioso, Bradl and Pol Espargaro scrap for the lead in the early laps.

Top right: Not so jolly green giant. Nicky Hayden's injury problems were aggravated when he was knocked down in the first corners.

Above centre right: Slow away, Aleix Espargaro soon joined a fierce four-way battle with the lesser prototypes.

Above near and far right: Legends from the Golden Age: Yamaha's Christian Sarron *(left)* and Honda's 'Fast Freddie' Spencer were both present.

Right: An on-form Pol Espargaro missed out on a first podium by less than a second.

Photos: Gold & Goose

LE MANS was in a good mood for the grand prix. The key was benign weather; cloudless skies and comfortable temperatures made the tyres work well and kept the crowds from triggering action by the ever-present CRS riot police. It is seldom like this here, where both the history and the exuberance of well-lubricated fans can be a bit overburdening, and the weather even more so.

And the racing was … depends on the class. Brilliant, as was the norm, for Moto3; less so in Moto2, as also was becoming the norm. And in MotoGP? Predictable enough. Another domineering triumph for the stripling superstar.

Marquez's weekend had started with the announcement that he had signed on for two more years with Honda. The financial side of it was kept secret with a slightly embarrassed smile; likewise any covert approaches from the other factories. Instead he extolled the comfort and security of two years' extended employment with the leader of the pack. "I am 21 years old. I'm not thinking about the money," he said, when asked if he had broken Rossi's record, a reported US \$12 million when he had signed for Ducati.

It was another triumph, flawed this time and all the more impressive for it. From his sixth consecutive pole, he was roughed up in the bump and grind of the first corners, then sent right off the track on the Garage Vert corner before the back straight after a hard pass by Lorenzo. He dropped back to tenth.

Rossi, on form, enjoyed a spell up front. Then Marquez arrived, and the older rider promptly made "my only mistake of the race", running wide under brakes to give the Honda an easy pass. But for that error, Rossi opined, he could have fought for the win. Two weeks later, he admitted something else. "After I went home and watched the TV from Le Mans, I am less confident. I thought Marc had come from fourth or fifth … not from tenth."

The race was less rewarding for others; Pedrosa was fresh from arm-pump surgery and off the rostrum for the first time in the season; former team-mate Hayden was at the other end of a not dissimilar problem with his right wrist. This much-abused joint, broken at Valencia at the end of 2011, had given trouble in 2013 when screws in the scaphoid bone had worked loose; post-season surgery had fixed that and cleared scar tissue: "I could ride all day at the Malaysia tests." But on Saturday night at Jerez, for no particular reason, the wrist had flared up again, painful and swollen. It was troublesome still at Le Mans, then he was knocked down on only the third corner by 'Maniac Joe' Iannone, slamming his hand down hard. He was out of this race and, as it transpired, the next as well.

Bradl, by the way, was recovering well from similar surgery at the same time as Pedrosa.

Hayden was leading calls for an extra tyre to be given to the two riders who make it through from Q1 to join the front half of the grid in Q2. By the time they get there, as he'd discovered at the previous two races, they don't have enough rears to make two runs. This time, however, he was relieved of the problem; instead it was Crutchlow (along with Aleix Espargaro) who won through, and who had a characteristically contrary take, after setting his time early in Q1, then sitting anxiously in the pit watching the monitors as Hayden and Hernandez came within mere hundredths of ousting him. "Being in Q1 is one of the worst experiences," he said. "I didn't want to use my second tyre, but by then you've given the other riders a target. But I think the rules are fair. If you don't get into the top ten, then that is your situation." Hayden's request would be denied.

Bridgestone's tyres had been given extra side grip for this track; another factor in remarkably few crashes, if yet more disquiet for the ultra-precise Lorenzo, by giving him another moving target.

The other technical news was for the next race, subsequently extended for all races: the option to use bigger brakes, diameter up from 320mm to 340. This followed increasing complaints that the brakes used on the 800s were hard pushed to cope with the faster, heavier 1000cc bikes. There was a history: the same concession had been made at Motegi in 2013, after problems with overheating at that par-

ticularly punishing venue. Brembo had gone all the way, Nissin stopped short at 330mm. The bigger brakes increased power slightly, but ran the same pad size: the value of the greater size being the ability to absorb and shed heat more effectively. One difficulty, however, was that they were too large to be slipped into place with the calipers in situ: these had to be detached from their quick-connection hydraulics and fitted to the wheels before they were returned along with the wheel to be plumbed back in, giving rise to minor, but real safety concerns.

The Sarron brothers, Christian and Dominique, were celebrated at Le Mans, and the pair rode a race-day lap, on the anniversary of the former's 250 championship. There have been others since – Arnaud Vincent and Mike di Meglio on 125s, Olivier Jacque on a 250 – but Christian, who later won a 500 GP in a spectacularly crash-strewn career, is the one they all remember.

The Bugatti circuit's stop-and-go nature does not make it popular among riders; but hopes of an imminent return to the fragrant and fascinating Paul Ricard on the Cote d'Azur – raised by the planned return of the Bol d'Or 24-hour race there in 2015 – were dashed, at least for the next seven years: the contract with promoter Claude Michy was renewed until 2021 during the weekend, and Ricard simply wasn't on the menu.

Finally, back to Marquez, who was still smashing records – the first rider to win the first five races since Agostini in 1972; perhaps more redolently, the youngest to win five in a row since Mike Hailwood in 1962. The history marched on.

MOTOGP RACE – 28 laps

As in Argentina, Honda's irresistible force spent the first session apparently trying to crash ("I like to begin by finding the limits.") and took a sixth consecutive pole, counting Valencia in 2013. It was a new absolute record, smashing Pedrosa's 2008 time set on qualifying tyres (these old times still stood at Montmelo and the Sachsenring, plus Qatar – though that would have to wait until 2015).

A somewhat renascent Lorenzo actually headed the sheets after FP3, but a surprise second went to Pol Espargaro, two-hundredths ahead of Dovizioso's Ducati, who thanked his soft tyres, and that the short corners made the red bike's reluctance to turn less of a drawback.

The remainder were close: Bradl led row two from Rossi and Lorenzo; then came Bautista, Aleix Espargaro, and only then Pedrosa.

The race started with the rare and always enjoyable sight of a Ducati in the lead, as Dovizioso seized control into the first corner, from Bradl and Espargaro. By the end of the lap, Rossi was ahead of the Spaniard, and by the end of the third, ahead of Bradl as well.

It had been an eventful first lap. Hayden had been knocked flying after completing just two corners; his assailant, Iannone, fell of himself a bit later, by which time Barbera had also gone down.

Also for the fast men. Marquez explained later: "On the first lap, I was too calm. Maybe I had too much confidence." Jostled out of the top six, he was passed into Garage Vert by Lorenzo: "He put on the brakes more than I expected, and I had to go wide." Right on to the paved run-off, dropping to tenth.

It was only a matter of time for Dovizioso: "It's an enjoyable feeling, but I knew it wouldn't last, because some riders are intelligent and don't push too hard in the early laps."

Soon he began dropping back, while the crowd roared approval as Rossi took the lead on lap four. In another five, he had a gap of almost a second, but by then Marquez had set a new record en route to fourth, and shortly would pass Bradl and Espargaro. Now second, he made light of the gap, then passed effectively unopposed on lap 13, to draw steadily clear. He was 3.4 seconds ahead as he started the last lap, and able to slow and celebrate over the line.

Above: Stop-and-go track for once suited Bautista's exclusively Nissin-braked and Showa-suspended Honda.

Top right: New boy Sam Lowes took a third top-ten finish.

Above right: NGM Forward team boss Giovanni Cuzari was happy with Corsi's Moto2 podium.

Above far right: Eventual Moto2 winner Kallio leads Corsi, Salom, Folger, Rabat, Vinales and the rest.

Right: Back to full fighting form, Miller took the Moto3 win from Rins, Vinales and Bagnaia, with Marquez, the displaced Vazquez and Bastianini scrapping for fifth.

Far right, above: Rookie Bastianini impressed again, here heading away from Fenati and Kornfeil for seventh.

Far right, below: A third win in five races for 'Jackass' Miller.

Below right: Isaac Vinales was all smiles after his first podium.

Photos: Gold & Goose

"When I caught him, I expected to have to battle harder. But he made a small mistake, and it was easy," he said, before adding, "Well … it looks easy, but it's very difficult."

Espargaro stayed in the hunt, but Bradl encountered familiar front grip issues and ran wide on lap 12, letting Bautista past to take up the chase. He had already dealt with Lorenzo and closed up, and with ten laps left he disposed of Espargaro to move clear for his first rostrum in more than a year.

Lorenzo's troubles weren't over, because Pedrosa was gaining speed. He'd been slumbering in ninth in the early stages, waiting for his front tyre to develop meaningful grip, and while that never happened to the full extent, he was able to pick up the pace after half-distance, cutting past his compatriot quite easily on lap 20.

Dani had more to come, but not quite enough, closing to within three-tenths of Espargaro, himself barely twice that behind Bautista, by the end.

Bradl was seventh, well out of touch with Lorenzo and well clear of a lively battle for eighth.

Smith had got the better of the fading Dovizioso by half-distance at the same time as slow-starting Aleix Espargaro had closed from behind, with Crutchlow see-sawing nearer and further in his wake: "Alone, I can go faster and catch up. Then when I am following, I can't brake as hard as the one in front and I lose them again."

Espargaro took to the head, but Dovizioso reasserted himself over the final laps, Espargaro and Smith right behind; Crutchlow was off the back again.

Redding's 12th put him top RCV1000R rider; he was alone for most of the race after taking the place off Hernandez. The latter held off Aoyama after a fight in the closing laps. Edwards had been part of it, but yet again his NGM Yamaha fell short on the final lap and he had to paddle it across the line, handing the last point to Abraham. He had plenty of fuel left, but as at Jerez, it wasn't getting to the engine. Laverty also crossed the line before the American got there; Parkes and di Meglio trailed in.

MOTO2 RACE – 26 laps

Rabat looked set to resume his control of pole until the closing minutes, when class rookie Jonas Folger beat the target by just over one-hundredth. In the same dying moments, fellow ex-Moto3 rider Salom nosed Kallio out of third to complete the front row. Luthi and Corsi were alongside the Finn on row two. With the top 19 within a second, positions were the usual lottery.

Vinales led row three from Cardus and Cortese, with the rest of the gang effectively inches behind. Doubtless the first corners would be exciting.

Again, however, and in comparison to the preceding Moto3 mayhem, the race failed to deliver. There was only a little variety and not much in the way of sustained combat, with Kallio's second straight win heading a top-six Kalex whitewash – and spicing up the points table by placing him within seven points of team-mate Rabat.

Kallio led away from the second row, ceding the lead to Corsi on lap three, but dogging the Italian's tracks for the next 15 laps. Salom was third, and they all held station, close, but without special excitement, until lap 18. Rabat was fourth, troubled a couple of times by Folger, who led him over the line ninth time around.

On the 19th, strategies came into play. Kallio slipped cleanly under Corsi and directly opened up a small, but secure lead.

Four laps later, Rabat pounced on Salom, who then found himself under strong attack from team-mate Vinales. The latter got ahead with three laps to go and pulled comfortably clear.

Now Salom was in the clutches of Folger, but he managed to hang on to fifth narrowly.

The top six were covered by four seconds; almost ten seconds behind, Luthi had been holding off Aegerter until he ran wide and lost touch, handing a lone seventh to his compatriot.

Lowes impressed once again, alone in a strong ninth; rookie Morbidelli was tenth; then came a battle for the lower points that again helped redeem the class's reputation. Twelfth to 17th was covered by 1.4 seconds; erstwhile leader West was pushed to 14th on the last lap by Cortese and Krummenacher; Syahrin took the last point for the third time in the season, with Nakagami and Torres out of luck.

Home hopes were dashed when a troubled Zarco qualified only 20th and retired early from the race; and Rossi crashed out near the end. Already out: Simeon on lap one, plus Cardus and Pasini together, then Nagashima, de Angelis, Warokorn and (once again) Pons.

Vinales set a new record on lap 18.

MOTO3 RACE – 24 laps

Sixteen within a second of pole, a career-first for Vazquez; Miller a tenth down, and then Vinales on a second KTM. Marquez's Honda headed the second row from Tonucci's Mahindra and Kornfeil.

Miller's third win in five races was a thriller, in determined style, in spite of a top-speed disadvantage. It came by less than a tenth, the first six over the line in less than a second. Miller looked to have been struggling with grip, with several out-of-saddle moments, but later he said, "That was just me, trying to get on the gas a bit earlier."

The Australian led away; Rins took over on lap five, in the closest company, with Vazquez's always surprisingly fast SaxoPrint Honda sweeping past time and again at the end of the straight, only to lose it on the brakes.

The last three laps saw almost constant overtaking, most often by Miller, mainly playing a late braking game against the faster Vazquez.

On the last lap, it happened again, then Miller firmly closed the door through the right into the S-Bleu at the end of the back straight, and Vazquez ran wide, going from a potential win to sixth at a stroke, and angrily, but unsuccessfully demanding a penalty for Miller after the race.

Rins was right there in second; Vinales was a couple of tenths behind in third. Then another two-tenths back was Bagnaia, who got the better of an unusually timid Marquez at the finish, and also the lap record. Vazquez was almost alongside, and rookie Bastianini a close seventh.

McPhee had been with the leaders to the finish in a close eighth; Masbou dropped back, but closed up again at the finish. Kornfeil came through for tenth.

Argentine winner Fenati dropped out of the lead pack with engine trouble.

MONSTER ENERGY
GRAND PRIX DE FRANCE

16–18 MAY, 2014

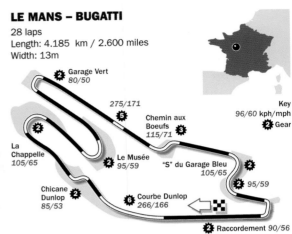

LE MANS – BUGATTI
28 laps
Length: 4.185 km / 2.600 miles
Width: 13m

Garage Vert 80/50
275/171
Chemin aux Boeufs 115/71
La Chappelle 105/65
Le Musée 95/59
"S" du Garage Bleu 105/65
95/59
Chicane Dunlop 85/53
Courbe Dunlop 266/166
Raccordement 90/56

Key
96/60 kph/mph
Gear

MotoGP — RACE DISTANCE: 28 laps, 72.812 miles/117.180km · RACE WEATHER: Dry (air 23°C, humidity 35%, track 42°C)

Pos.	Rider	Nat.	No.	Entrant	Machine	Tyres	Race tyre choice	Laps	Time & speed
1	Marc Marquez	SPA	93	Repsol Honda Team	Honda RC213V	B	F: Soft/R: Soft	28	44m 03.925s 99.1mph/ 159.5km/h
2	Valentino Rossi	ITA	46	Movistar Yamaha MotoGP	Yamaha YZR-M1	B	F: Soft/R: Soft	28	44m 05.411s
3	Alvaro Bautista	SPA	19	GO&FUN Honda Gresini	Honda RC213V	B	F: Soft/R: Soft	28	44m 07.069s
4	Pol Espargaro	SPA	44	Monster Yamaha Tech 3	Yamaha YZR-M1	B	F: Soft/R: Soft	28	44m 07.642s
5	Dani Pedrosa	SPA	26	Repsol Honda Team	Honda RC213V	B	F: Soft/R: Soft	28	44m 08.002s
6	Jorge Lorenzo	SPA	99	Movistar Yamaha MotoGP	Yamaha YZR-M1	B	F: Soft/R: Soft	28	44m 11.013s
7	Stefan Bradl	GER	6	LCR Honda MotoGP	Honda RC213V	B	F: Soft/R: Soft	28	44m 15.452s
8	Andrea Dovizioso	ITA	4	Ducati Team	Ducati Desmosedici	B	F: Soft/R: Soft	28	44m 26.028s
9	Aleix Espargaro	SPA	41	NGM Forward Racing	Forward Yamaha	B	F: Soft/R: Soft	28	44m 26.551s
10	Bradley Smith	GBR	38	Monster Yamaha Tech 3	Yamaha YZR-M1	B	F: Soft/R: Soft	28	44m 27.033s
11	Cal Crutchlow	GBR	35	Ducati Team	Ducati Desmosedici	B	F: Soft/R: Soft	28	44m 29.705s
12	Scott Redding	GBR	45	GO&FUN Honda Gresini	Honda RCV1000R	B	F: Soft/R: Extra-Soft	28	44m 43.448s
13	Yonny Hernandez	COL	68	Energy T.I. Pramac Racing	Ducati Desmosedici	B	F: Soft/R: Soft	28	44m 46.469s
14	Hiroshi Aoyama	JPN	7	Drive M7 Aspar	Honda RCV1000R	B	F: Soft/R: Extra-Soft	28	44m 46.661s
15	Karel Abraham	CZE	17	Cardion AB Motoracing	Honda RCV1000R	B	F: Medium/R: Extra-Soft	28	45m 00.569s
16	Michael Laverty	GBR	70	Paul Bird Motorsport	PBM-ART	B	F: Soft/R: Soft	28	45m 18.048s
17	Colin Edwards	USA	5	NGM Forward Racing	Forward Yamaha	B	F: Soft/R: Extra-Soft	28	45m 23.648s
18	Broc Parkes	AUS	23	Paul Bird Motorsport	PBM-ART	B	F: Soft/R: Soft	28	45m 34.859s
19	Mike di Meglio	FRA	63	Avintia Racing	Avintia	B	F: Soft/R: Extra-Soft	28	45m 38.446s
	Andrea Iannone	ITA	29	Pramac Racing	Ducati Desmosedici	B	F: Soft/R: Extra-Soft	1	DNF-crash
	Hector Barbera	SPA	8	Avintia Racing	Avintia	B	F: Soft/R: Extra-Soft	1	DNF-crash
	Nicky Hayden	USA	69	Drive M7 Aspar	Honda RCV1000R	B	F: Soft/R: Extra-Soft	0	DNF-crash
	Danilo Petrucci	ITA	9	IodaRacing Project	ART	B	–	–	Absent-injured

Fastest lap: Marc Marquez, on lap 8, 1m 33.548s, 100.0mph/161km/h (record).

Previous lap record: Dani Pedrosa, SPA (Honda), 1m 33.617s, 99.999mph/160.932km/h (2011).

Event best maximum speed: Dani Pedrosa, 195mph/313.8km/h (race).

Qualifying

Weather: Dry
Air Temp: 23° **Track Temp:** 43°
Humidity: 34%

1	Marquez	1m 32.042s
2	P. Espargaro	1m 32.734s
3	Dovizioso	1m 32.755s
4	Bradl	1m 32.846s
5	Rossi	1m 32.873s
6	Lorenzo	1m 32.899s
7	Bautista	1m 33.006s
8	A. Espargaro	1m 33.015s
9	Pedrosa	1m 33.023s
10	Smith	1m 33.058s
11	Iannone	1m 33.102s
12	Crutchlow	1m 33.315s
13	Hayden	1m 33.859s
14	Hernandez	1m 33.999s
15	Edwards	1m 34.203s
16	Redding	1m 34.233s
17	Aoyama	1m 34.457s
18	Abraham	1m 34.880s
19	Barbera	1m 35.499s
20	Parkes	1m 35.795s
21	Laverty	1m 35.932s
22	Di Meglio	1m 36.163s
23	Hernandez	1m 36.961s
24	Aoyama	1m 37.523s

Fastest race laps

1	Marquez	1m 33.548s
2	Pedrosa	1m 33.668s
3	Rossi	1m 33.878s
4	Bautista	1m 33.900s
5	P. Espargaro	1m 33.970s
6	Lorenzo	1m 33.977s
7	Bradl	1m 34.017s
8	Dovizioso	1m 34.172s
9	Smith	1m 34.246s
10	A. Espargaro	1m 34.426s
11	Crutchlow	1m 34.455s
12	Redding	1m 34.886s
13	Hernandez	1m 34.949s
14	Aoyama	1m 34.959s
15	Edwards	1m 35.128s
16	Abraham	1m 35.270s
17	Laverty	1m 36.087s
18	Parkes	1m 36.272s
19	Di Meglio	1m 36.759s

Championship Points

1	Marquez	125
2	Pedrosa	83
3	Rossi	81
4	Dovizioso	53
5	Lorenzo	45
6	Bradl	39
7	P. Espargaro	38
8	A. Espargaro	37
9	Smith	34
10	Bautista	26
11	Iannone	25
12	Hayden	23
13	Aoyama	21
14	Redding	18
15	Hernandez	16
16	Crutchlow	15
17	Abraham	9
18	Edwards	7
19	Petrucci	2
20	Barbera	2
21	Parkes	1

Constructor Points

1	Honda	125
2	Yamaha	87
3	Ducati	56
4	Forward Yamaha	37
5	ART	2
6	Avintia	2
7	PBM	1

Grid order

Grid order	1	2	3	4	5	6	7	8	9	10	11	12	13	14	15	16	17	18	19	20	21	22	23	24	25	26	27	28	
93 MARQUEZ	4	4	4	46	46	46	46	46	46	46	46	46	46	93	93	93	93	93	93	93	93	93	93	93	93	93	93	93	1
44 P. ESPARGARO	6	6	46	4	4	44	44	44	44	44	44	93	93	46	46	46	46	46	46	46	46	46	46	46	46	46	46	46	2
4 DOVIZIOSO	46	46	6	44	44	6	6	6	6	93	44	44	44	44	44	19	19	19	19	19	19	19	19	19	19	19	19	19	3
6 BRADL	44	44	44	6	6	4	93	93	93	6	6	19	19	19	19	19	44	44	44	44	44	44	44	44	44	44	44	44	4
46 ROSSI	38	38	38	38	99	99	4	99	99	19	19	6	6	6	6	99	99	99	26	26	26	26	26	26	26	26	26	26	5
99 LORENZO	29	19	99	99	93	93	99	19	19	99	99	99	99	99	26	26	26	26	99	99	99	99	99	99	99	99	99	99	6
19 BAUTISTA	19	99	93	93	38	19	19	4	26	26	26	26	26	26	6	6	6	6	6	6	6	6	6	6	6	6	6	6	7
41 A. ESPARGARO	99	26	19	19	19	38	38	26	4	4	4	38	38	38	38	41	41	41	41	41	41	41	4	4	4	4	4	4	8
26 PEDROSA	26	93	26	26	26	26	26	38	38	38	38	4	4	4	4	4	4	4	4	4	4	4	41	41	41	41	41	41	9
38 SMITH	93	35	35	35	41	41	41	41	41	41	41	41	41	41	41	38	38	38	38	38	38	38	38	38	38	38	38	38	10
29 IANNONE	35	41	41	41	35	35	35	35	35	35	35	35	35	35	35	35	35	35	35	35	35	35	35	35	35	35	35	35	11
35 CRUTCHLOW	41	68	68	68	68	68	68	68	45	45	45	45	45	45	45	45	45	45	45	45	45	45	45	45	45	45	45	45	12
69 HAYDEN	68	45	45	45	45	45	45	45	68	68	68	68	68	68	68	68	68	68	68	68	68	68	68	68	68	68	68	68	13
68 HERNANDEZ	45	7	7	7	7	7	7	7	7	7	7	7	7	7	7	7	7	7	7	7	7	7	7	7	7	7	7	7	14
5 EDWARDS	7	5	5	5	5	5	5	5	5	5	5	5	5	5	5	5	5	5	5	5	5	5	5	5	5	5	5	17	15
45 REDDING	5	17	17	17	17	17	17	17	17	17	17	17	17	17	17	17	17	17	17	17	17	17	17	17	17	17	17	70	
7 AOYAMA	70	63	63	70	70	70	70	70	70	70	70	70	70	70	70	70	70	70	70	70	70	70	70	70	70	70	70	5	
17 ABRAHAM	63	70	70	63	63	23	23	23	23	23	23	23	23	23	23	23	23	23	23	23	23	23	23	23	23	23	23	23	
8 BARBERA	17	23	23	23	23	63	63	63	63	63	63	63	63	63	63	63	63	63	63	63	63	63	63	63	63	63	63	63	
23 PARKES	23																												
70 LAVERTY	8																												
63 DI MEGLIO																													

Moto2

RACE DISTANCE: 26 laps, 67.611 miles/108.810km · RACE WEATHER: Dry (air 23°C, humidity 38%, track 40°C)

Pos.	Rider	Nat.	No.	Entrant	Machine	Laps	Time & Speed
1	Mika Kallio	FIN	36	Marc VDS Racing Team	Kalex	26	42m 41.696s 95.0mph/ 152.9km/h
2	Simone Corsi	ITA	3	NGM Forward Racing	Kalex	26	42m 42.711s
3	Esteve Rabat	SPA	53	Marc VDS Racing Team	Kalex	26	42m 42.999s
4	Maverick Vinales	SPA	40	Pons HP 40	Kalex	26	42m 43.883s
5	Luis Salom	SPA	39	Pons HP 40	Kalex	26	42m 45.315s
6	Jonas Folger	GER	94	AGR Team	Kalex	26	42m 45.614s
7	Dominique Aegerter	SWI	77	Technomag carXpert	Suter	26	42m 54.020s
8	Thomas Luthi	SWI	12	Interwetten Paddock Moto2	Suter	26	42m 57.248s
9	Sam Lowes	GBR	22	Speed Up	Speed Up	26	42m 59.323s
10	Franco Morbidelli	ITA	21	Italtrans Racing Team	Kalex	26	43m 10.400s
11	Marcel Schrotter	GER	23	Tech 3	Tech 3	26	43m 15.289s
12	Sandro Cortese	GER	11	Dynavolt Intact GP	Kalex	26	43m 17.854s
13	Randy Krummenacher	SWI	4	IodaRacing Project	Suter	26	43m 17.923s
14	Anthony West	AUS	95	QMMF Racing Team	Speed Up	26	43m 18.243s
15	Hafizh Syahrin	MAL	55	Petronas Raceline Malaysia	Kalex	26	43m 18.368s
16	Takaaki Nakagami	JPN	30	IDEMITSU Honda Team Asia	Kalex	26	43m 18.936s
17	Jordi Torres	SPA	81	Mapfre Aspar Team Moto2	Suter	26	43m 19.268s
18	Lucas Mahias	FRA	90	Promoto Sport	Transformers	26	43m 26.296s
19	Gino Rea	GBR	8	AGT REA Racing	Suter	26	43m 30.007s
20	Lorenzo Baldassarri	ITA	7	Gresini Moto2	Suter	26	43m 30.350s
21	Nicolas Terol	SPA	18	Mapfre Aspar Team Moto2	Suter	26	43m 30.582s
22	Josh Herrin	USA	2	AirAsia Caterham	Caterham Suter	26	43m 35.173s
23	Roman Ramos	SPA	97	QMMF Racing Team	Speed Up	26	43m 50.802s
24	Azlan Shah	MAL	25	IDEMITSU Honda Team Asia	Kalex	26	43m 51.022s
25	Robin Mulhauser	SWI	70	Technomag carXpert	Suter	26	43m 51.246s
26	Ricard Cardus	SPA	88	Tech 3	Tech 3	26	44m 03.051s
	Julian Simon	SPA	60	Italtrans Racing Team	Kalex	20	DNF
	Louis Rossi	FRA	96	SAG Team	Kalex	20	DNF
	Axel Pons	SPA	49	AGR Team	Kalex	13	DNF
	Thitipong Warokorn	THA	10	APH PTT The Pizza SAG	Kalex	9	DNF
	Alex de Angelis	RSM	15	Tasca Racing Moto2	Suter	6	DNF
	Tetsuta Nagashima	JPN	45	Teluru Team JiR Webike	TSR	5	DNF
	Johann Zarco	FRA	5	AirAsia Caterham	Caterham Suter	3	DNF
	Mattia Pasini	ITA	54	NGM Forward Racing	Kalex	2	DNF
	Xavier Simeon	BEL	19	Federal Oil Gresini Moto2	Suter	0	DNF

Fastest lap: Maverick Vinales, on lap 18, 1m 37.882s, 95.6mph/153.9km/h (record).
Previous lap record: Marc Marquez, SPA (Suter), 1m 38.533s, 95.010mph/152.903km/h (2011).
Event best maximum speed: Sandro Cortese, 161.6mph/260.1km/h (race).

Qualifying

Weather: Dry
Air Temp: 25° **Track Temp:** 45°
Humidity: 31%

1	Folger	1m 37.619s
2	Rabat	1m 37.623s
3	Salom	1m 37.731s
4	Kallio	1m 37.768s
5	Luthi	1m 37.773s
6	Corsi	1m 37.809s
7	Vinales	1m 37.884s
8	Cardus	1m 37.929s
9	Cortese	1m 37.963s
10	Lowes	1m 38.032s
11	Simeon	1m 38.112s
12	Simon	1m 38.153s
13	De Angelis	1m 38.202s
14	Morbidelli	1m 38.322s
15	Aegerter	1m 38.326s
16	Pasini	1m 38.432s
17	Schrotter	1m 38.449s
18	Rossi	1m 38.505s
19	Mahias	1m 38.616s
20	Zarco	1m 38.686s
21	Nakagami	1m 38.696s
22	Torres	1m 38.731s
23	Rea	1m 38.903s
24	Krummenacher	1m 38.980s
25	Pons	1m 38.988s
26	Syahrin	1m 39.126s
27	West	1m 39.255s
28	Terol	1m 39.298s
29	Baldassarri	1m 39.462s
30	Herrin	1m 39.621s
31	Nagashima	1m 39.639s
32	Warokorn	1m 39.724s
33	Ramos	1m 39.816s
34	Shah	1m 40.081s
35	Mulhauser	1m 40.755s

Fastest race laps

1	Vinales	1m 37.882s
2	Folger	1m 37.918s
3	Rabat	1m 38.007s
4	Lowes	1m 38.022s
5	Corsi	1m 38.037s
6	Salom	1m 38.048s
7	Kallio	1m 38.080s
8	Simon	1m 38.287s
9	Luthi	1m 38.327s
10	Aegerter	1m 38.345s
11	Cortese	1m 38.758s
12	Rossi	1m 38.771s
13	Nakagami	1m 38.837s
14	De Angelis	1m 38.855s
15	Morbidelli	1m 38.895s
16	Krummenacher	1m 38.897s
17	West	1m 38.912s
18	Schrotter	1m 38.986s
19	Mahias	1m 39.008s
20	Torres	1m 39.064s
21	Rea	1m 39.142s
22	Syahrin	1m 39.151s
23	Pons	1m 39.194s
24	Terol	1m 39.223s
25	Zarco	1m 39.268s
26	Pasini	1m 39.344s
27	Baldassarri	1m 39.457s
28	Herrin	1m 39.655s
29	Cardus	1m 39.675s
30	Nagashima	1m 39.872s
31	Shah	1m 40.015s
32	Warokorn	1m 40.075s
33	Mulhauser	1m 40.279s
34	Ramos	1m 40.375s

Championship Points

1	Rabat	99
2	Kallio	92
3	Vinales	62
4	Aegerter	58
5	Corsi	53
6	Luthi	40
7	Salom	39
8	Folger	31
9	Simeon	29
10	Cortese	29
11	West	27
12	Lowes	25
13	De Angelis	18
14	Torres	18
15	Schrotter	17
16	Cardus	13
17	Krummenacher	10
18	Morbidelli	9
19	Zarco	8
20	Rossi	6
21	Nakagami	6
22	Pasini	4
23	Syahrin	3
24	Simon	2
25	Terol	2

Constructor Points

1	Kalex	125
2	Suter	81
3	Speed Up	39
4	Forward KLX	33
5	Tech 3	24
6	Caterham Suter	8

Moto3

RACE DISTANCE: 24 laps, 62.411 miles/100.440km · RACE WEATHER: Dry (air 21°C, humidity 42%, track 34°C)

Pos.	Rider	Nat.	No.	Entrant	Machine	Laps	Time & Speed
1	Jack Miller	AUS	8	Red Bull KTM Ajo	KTM	24	41m 30.582s 90.2mph/ 145.1km/h
2	Alex Rins	SPA	42	Estrella Galicia 0,0	Honda	24	41m 30.677s
3	Isaac Vinales	SPA	32	Calvo Team	KTM	24	41m 30.812s
4	Francesco Bagnaia	ITA	21	SKY Racing Team VR46	KTM	24	41m 31.069s
5	Alex Marquez	SPA	12	Estrella Galicia 0,0	Honda	24	41m 31.513s
6	Efren Vazquez	SPA	7	SaxoPrint-RTG	Honda	24	41m 31.522s
7	Enea Bastianini	ITA	33	Junior Team GO&FUN Moto3	KTM	24	41m 31.608s
8	John McPhee	GBR	17	SaxoPrint-RTG	Honda	24	41m 31.803s
9	Alexis Masbou	FRA	10	Ongetta-Rivacold	Honda	24	41m 32.157s
10	Jakub Kornfeil	CZE	84	Calvo Team	KTM	24	41m 32.755s
11	Zulfahmi Khairuddin	MAL	63	Ongetta-AirAsia	Honda	24	41m 42.422s
12	Miguel Oliveira	POR	44	Mahindra Racing	Mahindra	24	41m 45.086s
13	Danny Kent	GBR	52	Red Bull Husqvarna Ajo	Husqvarna	24	41m 45.226s
14	Brad Binder	RSA	41	Ambrogio Racing	Mahindra	24	41m 45.552s
15	Philipp Oettl	GER	65	Interwetten Paddock Moto3	Kalex KTM	24	41m 52.808s
16	Hafiq Azmi	MAL	38	SIC-AJO	KTM	24	41m 53.523s
17	Arthur Sissis	AUS	61	Mahindra Racing	Mahindra	24	42m 04.866s
18	Luca Grunwald	GER	43	Kiefer Racing	Kalex KTM	24	42m 07.077s
19	Bryan Schouten	NED	51	CIP	Mahindra	24	42m 07.192s
20	Livio Loi	BEL	11	Marc VDS Racing Team	Kalex KTM	24	42m 07.881s
21	Matteo Ferrari	ITA	3	San Carlo Team Italia	Mahindra	24	42m 10.772s
22	Ana Carrasco	SPA	22	RW Racing GP	Kalex KTM	24	42m 22.821s
23	Michael Ruben Rinaldi	ITA	34	San Carlo Team Italia	Mahindra	24	42m 28.310s
24	Gabriel Ramos	VEN	4	Kiefer Racing	Kalex KTM	24	42m 30.281s
25	Scott Deroue	NED	9	RW Racing GP	Kalex KTM	23	42m 42.045s
	Niklas Ajo	FIN	31	Avant Tecno Husqvarna Ajo	Husqvarna	21	DNF
	Romano Fenati	ITA	5	SKY Racing Team VR46	KTM	19	DNF
	Alessandro Tonucci	ITA	19	CIP	Mahindra	7	DNF
	Niccolo Antonelli	ITA	23	Junior Team GO&FUN Moto3	KTM	6	DNF
	Karel Hanika	CZE	98	Red Bull KTM Ajo	KTM	3	DNF
	Jules Danilo	FRA	95	Ambrogio Racing	Mahindra	3	DNF
	Juanfran Guevara	SPA	58	Mapfre Aspar Team Moto3	Kalex KTM	0	DNF

Fastest lap: Francesco Bagnaia, on lap 13, 1m 42.636s, 91.2mph/146.7km/h (record).
Previous lap record: Maverick Vinales, SPA (KTM), 1m 43.916s, 90.0mph/144.9km/h (2013).
Event best maximum speed: Efren Vazquez, 139.1mph/223.9km/h (race).

Qualifying

Weather: Dry
Air Temp: 21° **Track Temp:** 35°
Humidity: 40%

1	Vazquez	1m 42.491s
2	Miller	1m 42.516s
3	Rins	1m 42.718s
4	Masbou	1m 42.752s
5	Ajo	1m 42.769s
6	Vinales	1m 42.815s
7	Marquez	1m 42.896s
8	McPhee	1m 42.936s
9	Khairuddin	1m 42.991s
10	Fenati	1m 43.068s
11	Hanika	1m 43.112s
12	Kent	1m 43.247s
13	Bastianini	1m 43.299s
14	Oliveira	1m 43.304s
15	Antonelli	1m 43.314s
16	Tonucci	1m 43.391s
17	Bagnaia	1m 43.487s
18	Guevara	1m 43.644s
19	Azmi	1m 43.786s
20	Kornfeil	1m 43.831s
21	Binder	1m 43.946s
22	Oettl	1m 43.983s
23	Deroue	1m 43.988s
24	Schouten	1m 44.194s
25	Loi	1m 44.237s
26	Grunwald	1m 44.324s
27	Sissis	1m 44.418s
28	Ferrari	1m 44.805s
29	Rinaldi	1m 45.067s
30	Carrasco	1m 45.067s
31	Granado	1m 45.094s
32	Danilo	1m 45.464s
33	Ramos	1m 46.099s
	Castillon	No Time

Fastest race laps

1	Bagnaia	1m 42.636s
2	Miller	1m 42.756s
3	Vazquez	1m 42.792s
4	Bastianini	1m 42.818s
5	Fenati	1m 42.836s
6	McPhee	1m 42.887s
7	Marquez	1m 42.935s
8	Masbou	1m 42.965s
9	Vinales	1m 42.988s
10	Rins	1m 42.995s
11	Kornfeil	1m 43.010s
12	Tonucci	1m 43.213s
13	Khairuddin	1m 43.295s
14	Antonelli	1m 43.335s
15	Oliveira	1m 43.355s
16	Ajo	1m 43.369s
17	Oettl	1m 43.395s
18	Hanika	1m 43.469s
19	Binder	1m 43.568s
20	Kent	1m 43.615s
21	Azmi	1m 43.709s
22	Sissis	1m 44.188s
23	Schouten	1m 44.318s
24	Loi	1m 44.348s
25	Grunwald	1m 44.353s
26	Ferrari	1m 44.451s
27	Carrasco	1m 44.743s
28	Deroue	1m 44.772s
29	Rinaldi	1m 44.851s
30	Ramos	1m 45.295s
31	Danilo	1m 46.071s

Championship Points

1	Miller	104
2	Fenati	74
3	Vazquez	72
4	Rins	71
5	Marquez	60
6	Viñales	44
7	Kornfeil	37
8	Bagnaia	36
9	Masbou	35
10	Kent	26
11	Bastianini	25
12	McPhee	23
13	Oliveira	20
14	Loi	17
15	Ajo	16
16	Guevara	9
17	Hanika	8
18	Antonelli	7
19	Khairuddin	6
20	Binder	5
21	Tonucci	3
22	Oettl	2

Constructor Points

1	KTM	125
2	Honda	96
3	Husqvarna	28
4	Mahindra	23
5	Kalex KTM	20

Marquez's finest win; Lorenzo's finest second place? The pair were at each other's throats for lap after lap.
Photo: Gold & Goose

OPTIMISTS marked Mugello as a turning point in the season. The winner was the same as usual. The difference was the margin. There was no last-lap celebration, as Marquez had to expend everything to keep Lorenzo at bay by a matter of feet.

What had changed?

A number of things. Where Marquez was concerned, Mugello was something of a bogey circuit. He'd fallen off four times there in 2013: one was a record-speed 220mph pearler in practice; another out of second place in the race. This time, his approach was quite different: he abandoned his usual reckless first-practice pace for a gradual approach. "I had some question marks about this track, my most difficult," he explained.

From Lorenzo's point of view, the change he spoke about was his improved level of physical fitness. In December, he'd gone under the knife: 11 screws and the titanium plate were removed from his left collarbone, injured at Assen and then the Sachsenring, plus he had more corrective intervention for his right thumb, an older injury. The inevitable interruption and delay to his training programme had been costly: "I thought it would be enough, but it was not," he said. Less overtly, he'd also switched back to his 2013 chassis, on which he had won his third Italian GP in succession 12 months before.

Then there's the track – a jewel in the crown for almost all riders. Sinuous fast ess-bends make up most of the lap, playing to the strengths of the Yamaha.

Marquez typically had a card up his sleeve, and it turned out to be an ace. Anticipating the slipstreaming chances on the long straight, he fitted a taller sixth gear on race morning. This meant he could pass Lorenzo at will before the first corner, and he did so several times, offering the Yamaha rider the chance to fight back immediately, thereby inadvertently revealing his potential. All Marquez had to do then was keep him behind for the final lap. He proved up to the task.

All the same, it proved beyond doubt that Lorenzo was back. With a similarly fast track coming up in two weeks, his appetite was clearly well whetted.

And, to the joy of almost 77,500 fans, Rossi was also back, in his landmark 300th GP start. Poor qualifying left him unable to join the leaders, but he could match their pace and would be with them on the rostrum without (as in past years) having to be invited as a special guest.

The same long straight was the reason for the allowance of big brakes: but in truth they weren't strictly necessary, and only the factory Ducati pair and Lorenzo used them. Although there is very hard braking into the first corner – from 361km/h to 123, according to Brembo, in a time of 6.1 seconds, over 323m, with the brakes reaching 700 degrees C – there is little more over the rest of the lap, and one problem was that the brakes cooled down too much. In any case, the feel was unfamiliar. Brembo also released a list of the latest brakers, culled from team data:

1 – Marc Marquez 2 – Valentino Rossi 3 – Cal Crutchlow
4 – Andrea Iannone 5 – Andrea Dovizioso

Aleix Espargaro used smaller brakes fitted with cooling scoops, which worked a treat – but for losing around 5km/h on the straight because of the extra drag. A Brembo insider suggested the next move might be shrouds for the big brakes, to keep them warm at tighter tracks.

Ducati's espousal of the 340mm discs may have had another trigger: new engine parts had made it "a rocket, especially in fifth and six gears" (Crutchlow), and "unbelievable on the straight" (Dovizioso); the former added, "It's supposed to be smoother, but it doesn't seem to have done that."

Thus five Ducatis (including wild-card Pirro) placed in the top seven speed-trap figures: Bautista's Honda drafted into second behind Iannone's Pramac bike, and Smith's Yamaha sixth, ahead of Pirro. In numbers, Iannone recorded 349.6km/h (217.2mph), the rest between 343 and 346;

more accurate data read-outs put the speeds more than 10km/h quicker than Dorna's speed trap.

Also new, and at last, was the long-awaited chassis for the NGM Yamaha, which turned one of the team's bikes into a genuine 'Open' machine. It belonged to Edwards, Espargaro preferring the 2012/13 factory unit reluctantly supplied by Yamaha, when it became clear that their proposed FTR chassis deal had run on to rocky ground. The source of the FTR-alike unit was not entirely clear, while both bikes were entered as usual as Forward Yamahas. With revised flex ratios, it was promising, but at the first attempt it made little difference to the veteran Texan's result.

Hayden's arm problems were exacerbated on the high-speed track: "worse than Le Mans, and it's hard to hold on, especially at the end of the front straightaway," he said on Friday evening, explaining that he was pulling out of the event for further keyhole surgery on the following Tuesday. The medical advice had come after only six laps in the morning and five more in the afternoon. Pedrosa was still not fully recovered from his surgery; while Crutchlow admitted that his Austin injury was "still broken – it's difficult to get my glove on, and I can't shake hands, but on the bike, I can use the brake okay." A comfort, no doubt, at well over 200mph.

Moto3 continued to become progressively better, with the Honda-KTM battle raging and Mahindra making a clear step up, Oliveira once again inches from the rostrum. Most visible were the wind-tunnel developments: a sort of winged chin-piece for the fairing belly-pan and a reshaped tail; at least as important was a major remapping of electronics.

The major excitement was on track, where a hatful of serious title contenders fought without let up over the full distance, the slipstreaming straight only one of several places where they would be four or five abreast. The game of dodgems went wrong on the last lap, however, following an over-ambitious move by Miller, the most daring of late brakers. Near the back of a ten-strong group, he passed three riders at once at the end of the back straight, only to run into Oliveira's back wheel at the apex. The consequence? Miller, Marquez and Bastianini went down in a heap, and the Australian was hit with two penalty points. He took responsibility, but was aggrieved at the punishment: it was a normal Moto3 last-lap incident, as Fenati had done to him in Argentina, among others such, though the consequences were worse.

That alone might have been enough, but Marquez narrowly escaped being badly run over, and with the memory of Marco Simoncelli (killed, like Shoya Tomizawa, in this manner) kept well in the forefront by his countrymen, this too was a factor.

The greater show of public sentiment came from the Italians, responding emotionally as Loris Capirossi rode another tribute lap on Marco's number 58 Honda; but there was official acknowledgment also, as he was made a 'MotoGP Legend' and inducted into the Hall of Fame. He joins fellow late legend-in-the-making Daijiro Kato on the list of names of great multi-champions.

MOTOGP RACE – 23 laps

Marquez's seventh successive pole was by a smaller margin. Rossi, for example, was barely half a second down – but only tenth. Soft-tyred Iannone was next, then Lorenzo, pushing Pedrosa to row two. Pol Espargaro was alongside, having walked away from a crash in the session; then Crutchlow.

Smith led the third row from Dovizioso and Bradl, who had crashed in the morning and again, heavily, in race-morning warm-up. Only then came Rossi, after a soft front tyre gamble had led to bad chatter.

The first real rain of the season ruined Friday afternoon's

Above: MotoGP bikes unleashed. Fast-starter Iannone heads Marquez, Dovizioso, Pol Espargaro and Rossi as they begin lap two. They are all chasing Lorenzo.

Top left: Bradley Smith qualified well (again), but fell (again) in the race.

Above centre left: A new bike for Edwards made little difference.

Above left: Scott Redding and his production Honda. He would have been top RSV again, but for Abraham's last-lap draft past.

Far left: 300 up for The Doctor.

Left: Loris Capirossi took the late Marco Simoncelli's Honda on a tribute lap; the rider was inducted into the Hall of Fame.

Below left: Press-ganged: Cal Crutchlow faces searching questions.
Photos: Gold & Goose

Top right: Pedrosa found Iannone a hard nut to crack.
Photo: Gold & Goose

Top right: Third-placed Rossi was on the Mugello rostrum by right rather than by special invitation. Lorenzo and winner Marquez wait in the wings as he milks the crowd.
Photo: Yamaha Racing

Above right: Folger leads Salom, but ultimately Rabat, running a harder tyre, would prevail.

Right: Salom enjoyed his return to the Moto2 podium.

Far right: Flying the flag: Moto3 winner Fenati, in special home-race colours, leads Rins, Masbou, Vinales (hidden), Bastianini and Miller.

Below right: Shuffle the pack. This time Vinales is in front.
Photos: Gold & Goose

FP2, leaving all a touch short of practice time, but at least with plenty of tyres left.

Iannone took off in the lead as the rest brawled behind him on the run to the first corner. Rossi was not the only one to use the pit-lane exit as they all fanned out in the opening sprint. Into the first turn, Lorenzo was second, then Marquez, Dovizioso, Pol Espargaro and Crutchlow; Rossi was seventh, having already gained three places.

Lorenzo forced roughly past Iannone into the right-left on the second drop off the hill – the one-time fiercest critic of rough riding showing that his change of policy late in 2013 was still in force. He would do so many more times.

Marquez followed a couple of laps later; Rossi was picking up places everywhere: fourth on lap two, and two laps later also past Iannone. By then, Marquez was more than a second ahead. Too far. All Rossi could do was match the leaders' pace, near enough to watch the battle ahead, but unable to get closer. The gap had grown to more than two seconds by the end: "I think I had a chance … but I gave it away in practice."

There was some early attrition: Smith crashed out on lap three; next time around, Crutchlow and Bradl had also gone, a lucky escape for each. Crutchlow's front tyre was inexplicably gaining heat and pressure, and losing grip. "Every time I opened the throttle in the corner, it would try to tuck." It happened terminally halfway through an ess-bend: he landed in the middle of the track and had a scary time struggling to his feet to run to safety. His bike, meanwhile, cut back across the track and slammed into Bradl, sending him flying for a second time that day and third in the weekend. Crutchlow hastened to apologise; Bradl simply pronounced himself "speechless".

At the front, Lorenzo was racking up the laps, with Marquez following closely.

He seemed to be biding his time, as in Argentina, but he said later, "I was on the limit, taking a lot of risks." But he

knew that when the tyres started sliding more and Lorenzo's corner-speed advantage was reduced, he could be stronger, for he had a trump card – a higher sixth gear. At the start of lap 18, he used it, appearing simply to motor past as he ducked out of the draft.

Game over? Not in Lorenzo's view. Into turn one, a strong braking attack put him ahead again, and for the next two laps, at least over the line. Out on the hillsides, the pair were back and forth: Marquez would push past, but Lorenzo would come straight back around the outside, cutting off the Honda's nose, over and over.

Marquez used his ace again as they started the final lap, and managed to keep just out of reach to the end of it. It was probably his finest win yet. And probably Lorenzo's finest second.

Rossi was third, but the rest were miles behind.

Pedrosa took until lap ten before he'd got through to pass Iannone, only for the superspeedy Ducati to keep passing him back. That went on until there were seven laps to go, when finally he was safe. Iannone was working wonders, but the bike had weaknesses, and he succumbed not only to Pol Espargaro with two laps to go, but also to Dovizioso's factory Ducati on the last lap, to finish seventh.

Bautista was a downbeat and lonely eighth, wondering why his uniquely Showa-suspended Honda could make the rostrum in France, but with no major changes was uncompetitive here.

Aleix Espargaro managed to outdistance his erstwhile rivals for ninth; the Ducatis of Hernandez and Pirro had the speed if not the handling to prevail over a production Honda trio: Abraham this time heading Redding and Aoyama in close order.

Edwards took the last point, untroubled by the PBM-ART bikes of Laverty and Parkes; di Meglio was two seconds behind. Both Barbera and Fabrizio (replacing Petrucci, though only from Saturday) retired.

MOTO2 RACE – 21 laps

Tito Rabat returned to pole for the first time in three races, claiming the position early in the session, then enduring a long spell of tension as other riders packed in threateningly close – the first 16 within one second. A sensational second: GP rookie and reigning World Supersport champion Sam Lowes had never seen Mugello before essaying some laps on a street bike earlier in the week; Cortese was alongside. Two more class rookies – Folger and Salom – sandwiched Aegerter on row two; Kallio was back in 11th, after winning the previous two races; Austin winner Vinales was 16th.

Rabat was back to his winning ways as well after the same three-race interval, though it didn't look that way for the first half of the race, with one of the several fast rookies leading for the first 13 laps. It was Folger, hotly pursued by fellow rookie Salom, the pair almost two seconds clear as half-distance approached.

The pursuit was led first by Aegerter, with Rabat pushed to fourth in the first turn; Lowes was eighth, behind Kallio, all still close.

Rabat was up to third by lap three. He alone of the front-runners had gone for the harder tyre, and in the end it paid dividends; while Folger admitted he'd pushed his soft tyre too hard in the early laps as he tried in vain to break away.

Salom and Rabat were past him on lap 14, and Rabat in front of his younger countryman one lap later.

Now he tried to escape and looked as though he'd done it with a record lap on the 19th, with Salom all but crashing as he lost the front in pursuit. But the former Moto3 star should not be underestimated, and he fought back to finish second, just a quarter of a second adrift.

Folger hung on to third, while Corsi defeated Aegerter and Kallio in a fierce battle for fourth; Zarco was right on the back of them at the end.

Lowes was eighth, having fended off a late attack from Maverick Vinales. Another GP new boy, Franco Morbidelli, led the next group for tenth.

MOTO3 RACE – 20 laps

Rins took pole, Miller a quarter of a second down at the head of a trio of KTMs. Kornfeil joined him on the front row; Fenati led the second, then came two more Hondas: Masbou and Marquez. Vazquez was on row three and destined for trouble.

Another great race: at half-distance, the lead group was still 15 strong, belting down the straight four or five abreast.

Leaders over the line included Miller, McPhee, Rins, Bastianini and Fenati, but it was never by more than an inch or two; invariably somebody else was ahead by the first corner.

Fenati led on to the last lap, from Marquez, Rins, Miller, Masbou, Bastianini and the rest. By then, Miguel Oliveira (Mahindra), who had qualified 19th, had picked his way through one place at a time to join in.

To and fro they swapped, then at the end of the back straight Miller went from eighth to fifth, with a feat of out-braking that took his opponents by surprise. As he arrived at the apex, Oliveira was just swinging in. Miller touched the Mahindra's back wheel, wobbling out to clip Marquez; Bastianini hit the wreckage and all went down.

Rins led out of the last corner, but knew his tactics were wrong. Fenati, Vinales and Oliveira were in his draft. Fenati had timed it perfectly, to win by a nose. Vinales and Rins could not be separated, but second went to the former because of a faster race lap; Oliveira was a tenth down, followed by Ajo, Masbou and Tonucci, all seven covered by less than six-tenths in the closest race finish in history.

Guevara led the next trio, now five seconds away, from Binder and Hanika. Vazquez claimed the record on lap three, but he had jumped the start. After taking his ride-through next time around and rejoining 34th, and last, he surged through for 12th and four points.

Miller's points lead shrank to just five. The contest just became closer still.

GRAN PREMIO D'ITALIA TIM

_30 MAY–1 JUNE, 2014

AUTODROMO INTERNAZIONALE DEL MUGELLO

23 laps
Length: 5.245 km / 3,259 miles
Width: 14m

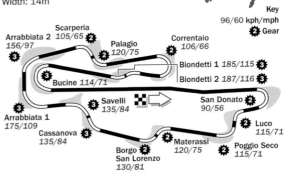

Key
96/60 kph/mph
2 Gear

Arrabbiata 2 156/97
Scarperia 105/65
Palagio 120/75
Correntaio 106/66
Biondetti 1 185/115
Biondetti 2 187/116
Bucine 114/71
Savelli 135/84
San Donato 90/56
Arrabbiata 1 175/109
Cassanova 135/84
Luco 115/71
Borgo San Lorenzo 130/81
Materassi 120/75
Poggio Seco 115/71

MotoGP

RACE DISTANCE: 23 laps, 74.959 miles/120.635km · RACE WEATHER: Dry (air 26°C, humidity 22%, track 45°C)

Pos.	Rider	Nat.	No.	Entrant	Machine	Tyres	Race tyre choice	Laps	Time & speed
1	**Marc Marquez**	SPA	93	Repsol Honda Team	Honda RC213V	B	F: Medium/R: Medium	23	41m 38.254s / 108.0mph/ 173.8km/h
2	**Jorge Lorenzo**	SPA	99	Movistar Yamaha MotoGP	Yamaha YZR-M1	B	F: Medium/R: Medium	23	41m 38.375s
3	**Valentino Rossi**	ITA	46	Movistar Yamaha MotoGP	Yamaha YZR-M1	B	F: Medium/R: Medium	23	41m 40.942s
4	**Dani Pedrosa**	SPA	26	Repsol Honda Team	Honda RC213V	B	F: Medium/R: Medium	23	41m 52.300s
5	**Pol Espargaro**	SPA	44	Monster Yamaha Tech 3	Yamaha YZR-M1	B	F: Medium/R: Medium	23	41m 53.857s
6	**Andrea Dovizioso**	ITA	4	Ducati Team	Ducati Desmosedici	B	F: Medium/R: Medium	23	41m 55.296s
7	**Andrea Iannone**	ITA	29	Pramac Racing	Ducati Desmosedici	B	F: Medium/R: Soft	23	41m 55.383s
8	**Alvaro Bautista**	SPA	19	GO&FUN Honda Gresini	Honda RC213V	B	F: Medium/R: Medium	23	42m 05.661s
9	**Aleix Espargaro**	SPA	41	NGM Forward Racing	Forward Yamaha	B	F: Medium/R: Medium	23	42m 20.140s
10	**Yonny Hernandez**	COL	68	Energy T.I. Pramac Racing	Ducati Desmosedici	B	F: Medium/R: Soft	23	42m 23.466s
11	**Michele Pirro**	ITA	51	Ducati Team	Ducati Desmosedici	B	F: Medium/R: Soft	23	42m 23.687s
12	**Karel Abraham**	CZE	17	Cardion AB Motoracing	Honda RCV1000R	B	F: Medium/R: Soft	23	42m 24.085s
13	**Scott Redding**	GBR	45	GO&FUN Honda Gresini	Honda RCV1000R	B	F: Medium/R: Soft	23	42m 24.093s
14	**Hiroshi Aoyama**	JPN	7	Drive M7 Aspar	Honda RCV1000R	B	F: Medium/R: Soft	23	42m 25.088s
15	**Colin Edwards**	USA	5	NGM Forward Racing	Forward Yamaha	B	F: Medium/R: Soft	23	42m 47.808s
16	Michael Laverty	GBR	70	Paul Bird Motorsport	PBM-ART	B	F: Medium/R: Soft	23	42m 56.043s
17	Broc Parkes	AUS	23	Paul Bird Motorsport	PBM-ART	B	F: Medium/R: Soft	23	43m 13.285s
18	Mike di Meglio	FRA	63	Avintia Racing	Avintia	B	F: Medium/R: Soft	23	43m 15.755s
	Hector Barbera	SPA	8	Avintia Racing	Avintia	B	F: Medium/R: Soft	7	DNF-mechanical
	Michel Fabrizio	ITA	84	Octo IodaRacing Team	ART	B	F: Medium/R: Soft	6	DNF-mechanical
	Cal Crutchlow	GBR	35	Ducati Team	Ducati Desmosedici	B	F: Medium/R: Medium	3	DNF-crash
	Stefan Bradl	GER	6	LCR Honda MotoGP	Honda RC213V	B	F: Medium/R: Medium	3	DNF-crash
	Bradley Smith	GBR	38	Monster Yamaha Tech 3	Yamaha YZR-M1	B	F: Medium/R: Medium	2	DNF-crash
	Nicky Hayden	USA	69	Drive M7 Aspar	Honda RCV1000R	B	–		DNS-injured

Fastest lap: Marc Marquez, on lap 5, 1m 47.892s, 108.7mph/175.0km/h.
Lap record: Marc Marquez, SPA (Honda), 1m 47.639s, 109.0mph/175.4km/h (2013).
Event best maximum speed (new MotoGP record): Andrea Iannone, 217.2mph/349.6km/h (free practice 3).

Qualifying

Weather: Dry
Air Temp: 23° **Track Temp:** 40°
Humidity: 35%

1	Marquez	1m 47.270s
2	Iannone	1m 47.450s
3	Lorenzo	1m 47.521s
4	Pedrosa	1m 47.584s
5	P. Espargaro	1m 47.612s
6	Crutchlow	1m 47.659s
7	Smith	1m 47.681s
8	Dovizioso	1m 47.754s
9	Bradl	1m 47.765s
10	Rossi	1m 47.791s
11	Bautista	1m 48.132s
12	A. Espargaro	1m 48.218s
13	Hernandez	1m 48.722s
14	Redding	1m 48.754s
15	Pirro	1m 48.794s
16	Abraham	1m 48.894s
17	Aoyama	1m 49.505s
18	Edwards	1m 49.780s
19	Barbera	1m 49.932s
20	Laverty	1m 50.505s
21	Di Meglio	1m 50.515s
22	Parkes	1m 50.875s
23	Fabrizio	1m 53.116s
	Hayden	No Time

Fastest race laps

1	Marquez	1m 47.892s
2	Lorenzo	1m 47.984s
3	Rossi	1m 48.084s
4	Iannone	1m 48.407s
5	Pedrosa	1m 48.461s
6	P. Espargaro	1m 48.569s
7	Dovizioso	1m 48.797s
8	Bautista	1m 48.846s
9	Hernandez	1m 49.126s
10	Bradl	1m 49.208s
11	Crutchlow	1m 49.233s
12	Smith	1m 49.481s
13	Redding	1m 49.642s
14	A. Espargaro	1m 49.689s
15	Pirro	1m 49.764s
16	Aoyama	1m 49.816s
17	Abraham	1m 49.865s
18	Edwards	1m 50.586s
19	Laverty	1m 51.019s
20	Barbera	1m 51.022s
21	Di Meglio	1m 51.064s
22	Parkes	1m 51.702s
23	Fabrizio	1m 53.332s

Championship Points

1	Marquez	150
2	Rossi	97
3	Pedrosa	96
4	Lorenzo	65
5	Dovizioso	63
6	P. Espargaro	49
7	A. Espargaro	44
8	Bradl	39
9	Bautista	34
10	Smith	34
11	Iannone	34
12	Hayden	23
13	Aoyama	23
14	Hernandez	22
15	Redding	21
16	Crutchlow	15
17	Abraham	13
18	Edwards	8
19	Pirro	5
20	Petrucci	2
21	Barbera	2
22	Parkes	1

Constructor Points

1	Honda	150
2	Yamaha	107
3	Ducati	66
4	Forward Yamaha	44
5	ART	2
6	Avintia	2
7	PBM	1

Grid order	1	2	3	4	5	6	7	8	9	10	11	12	13	14	15	16	17	18	19	20	21	22	23	
93 MARQUEZ	99	99	99	99	99	99	99	99	99	99	99	99	99	99	99	99	93	99	99	99	99	99	93	1
29 IANNONE	29	29	93	93	93	93	93	93	93	93	93	93	93	93	93	93	99	93	93	93	93	93	99	2
99 LORENZO	93	93	29	46	46	46	46	46	46	46	46	46	46	46	46	46	46	46	46	46	46	46	46	3
26 PEDROSA	4	46	46	29	29	29	29	29	26	26	26	29	26	26	26	26	26	26	26	26	26	26	26	4
44 P. ESPARGARO	44	4	4	44	44	44	44	26	26	29	29	26	29	29	29	29	44	44	29	44	44	44		5
35 CRUTCHLOW	46	44	44	4	4	4	26	44	44	44	44	44	44	44	44	44	29	29	44	29	29	4		6
38 SMITH	35	35	26	26	26	26	4	4	4	4	4	4	4	4	4	4	4	4	4	4	4	29		7
4 DOVIZIOSO	26	26	35	19	19	19	19	19	19	19	19	19	19	19	19	19	19	19	19	19	19	19		8
6 BRADL	38	38	19	68	45	41	41	41	41	41	41	41	41	41	41	41	41	41	41	41	41	41		9
46 ROSSI	19	68	6	41	41	45	45	45	68	68	68	68	68	68	45	68	68	68	68	68	68	68		10
19 BAUTISTA	68	19	68	45	68	68	68	68	68	45	45	45	45	68	45	51	51	51	51	51	51			11
41 A. ESPARGARO	6	6	41	51	51	51	51	51	51	51	51	51	51	51	51	45	45	45	45	17	17			12
68 HERNANDEZ	41	41	45	17	17	17	17	17	17	17	17	17	17	17	17	17	17	17	17	7	45			13
45 REDDING	45	45	51	7	7	7	7	7	7	7	7	7	7	7	7	7	7	7	7	7	7			14
51 PIRRO	51	51	17	5	5	5	5	5	5	5	5	5	5	5	5	5	5	5	5	5	5			15
17 ABRAHAM	7	7	7	63	63	63	70	70	70	70	70	70	70	70	70	70	70	70	70	70	70			
7 AOYAMA	17	17	5	23	70	70	63	63	63	63	63	63	23	23	23	23	23	23	23	23	23			
5 EDWARDS	5	5	63	70	8	8	23	23	23	23	23	23	63	63	63	63	63	63	63	63	63			
8 BARBERA	8	63	23	8	23	23	8																	
70 LAVERTY	63	23	70	84	84	84																		
63 DI MEGLIO	23	70	8																					
23 PARKES	70	8	84																					
84 FABRIZIO	84	84																						

84 Pit stop

Moto2 — RACE DISTANCE: 21 laps, 68.441 miles/110.145km · RACE WEATHER: Dry (air 24°C, humidity 27%, track 41°C)

Pos.	Rider	Nat.	No.	Entrant	Machine	Laps	Time & Speed
1	Esteve Rabat	SPA	53	Marc VDS Racing Team	Kalex	21	39m 45.660s 103.3mph/ 166.2km/h)
2	Luis Salom	SPA	39	Pons HP 40	Kalex	21	39m 45.908s
3	Jonas Folger	GER	94	AGR Team	Kalex	21	39m 49.260s
4	Simone Corsi	ITA	3	NGM Forward Racing	Kalex	21	39m 53.777s
5	Dominique Aegerter	SWI	77	Technomag carXpert	Suter	21	39m 53.784s
6	Mika Kallio	FIN	36	Marc VDS Racing Team	Kalex	21	39m 53.874s
7	Johann Zarco	FRA	5	AirAsia Caterham	Caterham Suter	21	39m 54.441s
8	Sam Lowes	GBR	22	Speed Up	Speed Up	21	39m 56.235s
9	Maverick Vinales	SPA	40	Pons HP 40	Kalex	21	39m 56.572s
10	Franco Morbidelli	ITA	21	Italtrans Racing Team	Kalex	21	40m 01.911s
11	Jordi Torres	SPA	81	Mapfre Aspar Team Moto2	Suter	21	40m 01.957s
12	Marcel Schrotter	GER	23	Tech 3	Tech 3	21	40m 02.302s
13	Sandro Cortese	GER	11	Dynavolt Intact GP	Kalex	21	40m 03.465s
14	Xavier Simeon	BEL	19	Federal Oil Gresini Moto2	Suter	21	40m 06.000s
15	Axel Pons	SPA	49	AGR Team	Kalex	21	40m 06.605s
16	Takaaki Nakagami	JPN	30	IDEMITSU Honda Team Asia	Kalex	21	40m 10.730s
17	Alex de Angelis	RSM	15	Tasca Racing Moto2	Suter	21	40m 24.133s
18	Anthony West	AUS	95	QMMF Racing Team	Speed Up	21	40m 24.163s
19	Ricard Cardus	SPA	88	Tech 3	Tech 3	21	40m 24.397s
20	Louis Rossi	FRA	96	SAG Team	Kalex	21	40m 24.772s
21	Gino Rea	GBR	8	AGT REA Racing	Suter	21	40m 26.084s
22	Julian Simon	SPA	60	Italtrans Racing Team	Kalex	21	40m 26.134s
23	Lorenzo Baldassarri	ITA	7	Gresini Moto2	Suter	21	40m 26.719s
24	Nicolas Terol	SPA	18	Mapfre Aspar Team Moto2	Suter	21	40m 28.637s
25	Hafizh Syahrin	MAL	55	Petronas Raceline Malaysia	Kalex	21	40m 28.671s
26	Randy Krummenacher	SWI	4	Octo IodaRacing Team	Suter	21	40m 35.914s
27	Azlan Shah	MAL	25	IDEMITSU Honda Team Asia	Kalex	21	40m 50.140s
28	Tetsuta Nagashima	JPN	45	Teluru Team JiR Webike	TSR	21	40m 50.205s
29	Roman Ramos	SPA	97	QMMF Racing Team	Speed Up	21	40m 50.478s
30	Robin Mulhauser	SWI	70	Technomag carXpert	Suter	21	40m 50.590s
31	Thitipong Warokorn	THA	10	APH PTT The Pizza SAG	Kalex	21	41m 08.523s
	Mattia Pasini	ITA	54	NGM Forward Racing	Kalex	8	DNF
	Thomas Luthi	SWI	12	Interwetten Paddock Moto2	Suter	4	DNF
	Josh Herrin	USA	2	AirAsia Caterham	Caterham Suter	0	DNF

Fastest lap: Esteve Rabat, on lap 19, 1m 52.587s, 104.2mph/167.7km/h (record).
Previous lap record: Thomas Luthi, SWI (Suter), 1m 52.815s, 104.000mph/167.371km/h (2012).
Event best maximum speed: Simone Corsi, 178.1mph/286.6km/h (race).

Qualifying
Weather: Dry
Air Temp: 23° Track Temp: 43°
Humidity: 35%

1	Rabat	1m 52.718s
2	Lowes	1m 52.901s
3	Cortese	1m 52.915s
4	Folger	1m 53.008s
5	Aegerter	1m 53.093s
6	Salom	1m 53.162s
7	Torres	1m 53.167s
8	Morbidelli	1m 53.258s
9	Luthi	1m 53.291s
10	Schrotter	1m 53.313s
11	Kallio	1m 53.331s
12	Zarco	1m 53.353s
13	Pasini	1m 53.505s
14	Pons	1m 53.589s
15	Nakagami	1m 53.610s
16	Vinales	1m 53.665s
17	Simeon	1m 53.827s
18	Terol	1m 53.834s
19	Cardus	1m 53.905s
20	Simon	1m 54.002s
21	Krummenacher	1m 54.152s
22	Corsi	1m 54.238s
23	Baldassarri	1m 54.265s
24	Rossi	1m 54.778s
25	Syahrin	1m 54.945s
26	Herrin	1m 54.954s
27	Nagashima	1m 54.958s
28	Rea	1m 55.066s
29	West	1m 55.093s
30	De Angelis	1m 55.268s
31	Mulhauser	1m 55.500s
32	Shah	1m 55.723s
33	Ramos	1m 56.240s
34	Warokorn	1m 56.495s

Fastest race laps
1	Rabat	1m 52.587s
2	Salom	1m 52.900s
3	Corsi	1m 53.039s
4	Kallio	1m 53.043s
5	Folger	1m 53.058s
6	Lowes	1m 53.080s
7	Zarco	1m 53.083s
8	Pasini	1m 53.170s
9	Aegerter	1m 53.196s
10	Morbidelli	1m 53.217s
11	Vinales	1m 53.423s
12	Torres	1m 53.432s
13	Cortese	1m 53.439s
14	Schrotter	1m 53.513s
15	Pons	1m 53.628s
16	Simeon	1m 53.685s
17	Nakagami	1m 53.725s
18	Luthi	1m 53.811s
19	Terol	1m 53.967s
20	Cardus	1m 54.239s
21	West	1m 54.250s
22	Baldassarri	1m 54.331s
23	Simon	1m 54.338s
24	Rossi	1m 54.348s
25	De Angelis	1m 54.375s
26	Rea	1m 54.601s
27	Syahrin	1m 54.638s
28	Krummenacher	1m 54.988s
29	Mulhauser	1m 55.474s
30	Nagashima	1m 55.481s
31	Shah	1m 55.580s
32	Ramos	1m 55.869s
33	Warokorn	1m 56.595s

Championship Points
1	Rabat	124
2	Kallio	102
3	Vinales	69
4	Aegerter	69
5	Corsi	66
6	Salom	59
7	Folger	47
8	Luthi	40
9	Lowes	33
10	Cortese	32
11	Simeon	31
12	West	27
13	Torres	23
14	Schrotter	21
15	De Angelis	18
16	Zarco	17
17	Morbidelli	15
18	Cardus	13
19	Krummenacher	10
20	Rossi	6
21	Nakagami	6
22	Pasini	4
23	Syahrin	3
24	Simon	2
25	Terol	2
26	Pons	1

Constructor Points
1	Kalex	150
2	Suter	92
3	Speed Up	47
4	Forward KLX	33
5	Tech 3	28
6	Caterham Suter	17

Moto3 — RACE DISTANCE: 20 laps, 65.182 miles/104.900km · RACE WEATHER: Dry (air 21°C, humidity 41%, track 33°C)

Pos.	Rider	Nat.	No.	Entrant	Machine	Laps	Time & Speed
1	Romano Fenati	ITA	5	SKY Racing Team VR46	KTM	20	39m 46.256s 98.3mph/ 158.2km/h)
2	Isaac Vinales	SPA	32	Calvo Team	KTM	20	39m 46.266s
3	Alex Rins	SPA	42	Estrella Galicia 0,0	Honda	20	39m 46.266s
4	Miguel Oliveira	POR	44	Mahindra Racing	Mahindra	20	39m 46.377s
5	Niklas Ajo	FIN	31	Avant Tecno Husqvarna Ajo	Husqvarna	20	39m 46.516s
6	Alexis Masbou	FRA	10	Ongetta-Rivacold	Honda	20	39m 46.615s
7	Alessandro Tonucci	ITA	19	CIP	Mahindra	20	39m 46.853s
8	Juanfran Guevara	SPA	58	Mapfre Aspar Team Moto3	Kalex KTM	20	39m 51.486s
9	Brad Binder	RSA	41	Ambrogio Racing	Mahindra	20	39m 51.609s
10	Karel Hanika	CZE	98	Red Bull KTM Ajo	KTM	20	39m 51.651s
11	Zulfahmi Khairuddin	MAL	63	Ongetta-AirAsia	Honda	20	40m 04.874s
12	Efren Vazquez	SPA	7	SaxoPrint-RTG	Honda	20	40m 11.594s
13	Philipp Oettl	GER	65	Interwetten Paddock Moto3	Kalex KTM	20	40m 11.967s
14	Matteo Ferrari	ITA	3	San Carlo Team Italia	Mahindra	20	40m 12.052s
15	Danny Kent	GBR	52	Red Bull Husqvarna Ajo	Husqvarna	20	40m 12.160s
16	Luca Grunwald	GER	43	Kiefer Racing	Kalex KTM	20	40m 12.261s
17	Arthur Sissis	AUS	61	Mahindra Racing	Mahindra	20	40m 13.355s
18	Andrea Locatelli	ITA	55	San Carlo Team Italia	Mahindra	20	40m 13.565s
19	Livio Loi	BEL	11	Marc VDS Racing Team	Kalex KTM	20	40m 24.706s
20	Ana Carrasco	SPA	22	RW Racing GP	Kalex KTM	20	40m 24.772s
21	Bryan Schouten	NED	51	CIP	Mahindra	20	40m 24.840s
22	Jules Danilo	FRA	95	Ambrogio Racing	Mahindra	20	40m 25.261s
23	Eric Granado	BRA	57	Calvo Team	KTM	20	40m 25.338s
24	Simone Mazzola	ITA	16	MT Racing Honda	FTR Honda	20	40m 26.787s
25	Anthony Groppi	ITA	69	Pos Corse	FTR Honda	20	40m 30.998s
26	Gabriel Ramos	VEN	4	Kiefer Racing	Kalex KTM	20	40m 55.381s
	Alex Marquez	SPA	12	Estrella Galicia 0,0	Honda	19	DNF
	Jack Miller	AUS	8	Red Bull KTM Ajo	KTM	19	DNF
	Enea Bastianini	ITA	33	Junior Team GO&FUN Moto3	KTM	19	DNF
	Scott Deroue	NED	9	RW Racing GP	Kalex KTM	19	DNF
	Jakub Kornfeil	CZE	84	Calvo Team	KTM	14	DNF
	Francesco Bagnaia	ITA	21	SKY Racing Team VR46	KTM	9	DNF
	John McPhee	GBR	17	SaxoPrint-RTG	Honda	6	DNF
	Niccolo Antonelli	ITA	23	Junior Team GO&FUN Moto3	KTM	4	DNF
	Hafiq Azmi	MAL	38	SIC-AJO	KTM	2	DNF

Fastest lap: Efren Vazquez, on lap 3, 1m 57.633s, 99.7mph/160.5km/h (record).
Previous lap record: Miguel Oliveira, POR (Mahindra), 1m 58.000s, 99.4mph/160.0km/h (2013).
Event best maximum speed: Juanfran Guevara, 150.1mph/241.6km/h (race).

Qualifying
Weather: Dry
Air Temp: 21° Track Temp: 36°
Humidity: 34%

1	Rins	1m 56.999s
2	Miller	1m 57.264s
3	Kornfeil	1m 57.326s
4	Fenati	1m 57.435s
5	Masbou	1m 57.580s
6	Marquez	1m 57.881s
7	Hanika	1m 57.937s
8	Guevara	1m 57.967s
9	Binder	1m 57.972s
10	Vazquez	1m 58.021s
11	McPhee	1m 58.054s
12	Vinales	1m 58.058s
13	Antonelli	1m 58.127s
14	Tonucci	1m 58.225s
15	Ajo	1m 58.265s
16	Bastianini	1m 58.276s
17	Bagnaia	1m 58.347s
18	Khairuddin	1m 58.677s
19	Oliveira	1m 58.696s
20	Azmi	1m 58.709s
21	Grunwald	1m 58.731s
22	Ferrari	1m 58.940s
23	Locatelli	1m 59.011s
24	Sissis	1m 59.078s
25	Oettl	1m 59.217s
26	Kent	1m 59.286s
27	Deroue	1m 59.394s
28	Loi	1m 59.413s
29	Granado	1m 59.530s
30	Groppi	1m 59.821s
31	Schouten	1m 59.875s
32	Mazzola	1m 59.896s
33	Carrasco	2m 00.078s
34	Danilo	2m 00.560s
35	Ramos	2m 00.865s

Fastest race laps
1	Vazquez	1m 57.633s
2	Bagnaia	1m 57.736s
3	Antonelli	1m 57.833s
4	Vinales	1m 57.840s
5	Tonucci	1m 57.890s
6	Guevara	1m 57.958s
7	Masbou	1m 58.090s
8	Marquez	1m 58.093s
9	Kornfeil	1m 58.100s
10	Oliveira	1m 58.107s
11	Miller	1m 58.121s
12	Bastianini	1m 58.141s
13	McPhee	1m 58.199s
14	Ajo	1m 58.208s
15	Rins	1m 58.223s
16	Fenati	1m 58.237s
17	Binder	1m 58.268s
18	Khairuddin	1m 58.325s
19	Hanika	1m 58.332s
20	Locatelli	1m 58.789s
21	Azmi	1m 58.812s
22	Sissis	1m 58.879s
23	Ferrari	1m 58.881s
24	Deroue	1m 58.894s
25	Grunwald	1m 58.900s
26	Oettl	1m 58.952s
27	Kent	1m 59.013s
28	Loi	1m 59.504s
29	Carrasco	1m 59.719s
30	Schouten	1m 59.766s
31	Granado	1m 59.866s
32	Mazzola	1m 59.957s
33	Danilo	2m 00.024s
34	Groppi	2m 00.346s
35	Ramos	2m 00.835s

Championship Points
1	Miller	104
2	Fenati	99
3	Rins	87
4	Vazquez	76
5	Viñales	64
6	Marquez	60
7	Masbou	45
8	Kornfeil	37
9	Bagnaia	36
10	Oliveira	33
11	Ajo	27
12	Kent	27
13	Bastianini	25
14	McPhee	23
15	Loi	17
16	Guevara	17
17	Hanika	14
18	Tonucci	12
19	Binder	12
20	Khairuddin	11
21	Antonelli	7
22	Oettl	5
23	Ferrari	2

Constructor Points
1	KTM	150
2	Honda	112
3	Husqvarna	39
4	Mahindra	36
5	Kalex KTM	28

Main: The Factory Four, joined by Bradl, lead away: Aleix Espargaro's yellow and black Open bike is prominent in pursuit.

Insets: Sibling supremacy: when the Brothers Marquez each won on the same day, they were the first in GP history.

Photos: Gold & Goose

FIM WORLD CHAMPIONSHIP · ROUND 7

CATALUNYA GRAND PRIX

CATALUNYA CIRCUIT

Above: Rossi fans give a standing ovation after he regained second from Pedrosa on a thrilling final lap.

Above right: Bigger Brembos for faster bikes. The main benefit was cooling, not power.

Right: TT legend John McGuinness was a spectator.

Below right: Scuffed leathers tell the tale of a major moment that Marquez couldn't save this time.

Below far right: That old Rossi magic still works, even in Marquez territory.

Photos: Gold & Goose

THE return, said some, of the Golden Age. Or, to be more precise, the start of a new one. Only time would tell, but this was certainly a pure gold race, and a feast for the fans – almost 93,000 of them on the Montmelo stands and hillsides, with at first a four-strong and then a three-strong battle for the lead that raged all race long. And it ended with the seventh win in a row for Marquez.

Sixty-five years almost to the day since the first GP in 1949, it was a weekend of broken records. With younger, but bigger brother Alex Marquez winning his second Moto3 race, it was the first time in history that two brothers had won two solo races at the same GP (in 1959, both Alfredo and Albino Milani had won at Monza, the former on a 500cc Gilera, but the latter on a sidecar). It may have been the first time, too, that three home-town (or at least home-province) riders had won all three races. And there were new lap records and new circuit best-lap records in both MotoGP and Moto3, the best lap set by a resurgent Pedrosa as he claimed his first pole in a year, the first strike in a landmark weekend for the older Repsol rider.

Marquez scored Honda's 100th four-stroke MotoGP win, compared to Yamaha's 79; the same company's victory in Moto3 was the first since the Italian GP in 2012.

Another record broken was Marquez's so-far crash-free season, when he slithered off harmlessly at the end of Q2, scotching his chances of an eighth pole in a row. He had played his personal strategy again by mounting three different tyre specs on his two bikes for the 15 minutes, something none of his rivals had done because of their fear of not performing their best with different bikes that never behave quite the same. This doesn't seem to affect Marquez. "We're at home, it was the last lap … I braked too late, but did not want to abort the lap. That was my biggest mistake," he said.

More talk about rider movement filled the preceding days. Both Lorenzo and Rossi had yet to sign: the latter spoke confidently about being close to agreeing two more years, though it seemed Yamaha were willing to renew for only one; Pedrosa – faced with a massive pay cut to stay at Honda – was thought to prefer that to a Suzuki offer; Dovizioso was another targeted by Suzuki, but he was under pressure to stay at Ducati, while satellite Ducati rider Iannone also admitted an approach from the Japanese returnees, but said his target was the factory Ducati team.

Where did that leave Crutchlow? A vexed question, as the rider revealed a bail-out clause in his two-year contract that would come into effect at the end of the following month, in two races' time. Neither he nor his employers had been having much fun together: he was struggling to adapt to the bike and vice versa, with the first six races offering one injurious crash and a parade of electronic and other glitches. It happened again at Montmelo: a technical disorientation that messed with his power program, giving him full boost where he didn't want it, and cutting back on the straight. He struggled on for a while, "then a load of warning lights came on and the bike stopped".

There was disappointment also for another brave Briton: Leon Camier had accepted the dare to make his premier-class debut on Hayden's Open Honda, should the American find that his fresh surgery made it too painful to ride. The former 125 rider was left sitting on his helmet, however, as Hayden pushed himself to continue, doubtless spurred by rumours that if he failed here he might be replaced for the rest of the season.

More details emerged of Edwards's new NGM chassis: aside from revised stiffness ratios, more space had been made for the fuel tank, which at 24 litres was three litres

larger than that fitted to the ex-factory chassis. Lack of space had led to overheating of the fuel at Cota, Jerez and Le Mans, such that it boiled in the closing laps and left the rider with petrol to spare, but none of it was getting to the engine. The chassis also had extra air ducts in the main spars. At least he finished this race still going strong, although without a significant change in his position. Team-mate Espargaro planned to test the chassis after the race. Meanwhile he was wrestling with problems in adapting the latest control software upgrade. "Before Le Mans, the bike was easier to ride. Now the traction control works well on maximum lean, but as soon as you lift the bike, you never know if the bike is going to spin," he said.

The factory Hondas joined the rest in switching to the larger 340mm front brake discs, while yet another rule change signalled eventual relief from the difficulty of wheel changes, albeit obliquely. The actual rewording deferred the requirement for homologated wheels from 2015 to 2016, for the MotoGP class only. The reason was a request from Michelin, due to rejoin as control tyre suppliers in 2016, who wanted to increase wheel size from the current 16.5 inches favoured by Bridgestone to 17 inches.

A red herring floated in the preceding week at the launch of the first biography of Marc Marquez was washed ashore by

the rider on the eve of the meeting. It had been suggested that he might emulate former 'youngest-ever' record holder Freddie Spencer in essaying a two-class title bid: Spencer won 250 and 500 titles in 1985. At the function, Dorna CEO Carmelo Ezpeleta insinuated that both the rules (banning the practice) and race schedules could be changed should Marquez wish it. "It would be funny, but also too difficult, almost impossible," he said. "In the past, it was completely different, but now we have meetings on data recording after every practice session. You need to work a lot in the garage. Also, you have the press conferences and everything. I don't have enough time."

MOTOGP RACE – 25 laps

Marquez's slip left the way open for Pedrosa's first pole, not only of the season, but also for a year. It was a tenth slower than his pole at the same track in 2013, thanks to hot and humid track conditions that meant the best times were laid down in the mornings, almost a second faster.

Lorenzo also outqualified Marquez for the first time in the season; Rossi was better than usual, in the middle of row two, between Bradl and Aleix Espargaro.

Dovizioso was top Ducati again, heading row three from Smith and Hernandez, ahead of team-mate Iannone (through from Q1). Crutchlow didn't make the cut; Bautista did, but crashed heavily in Q2.

Rain had threatened on Saturday and fallen heavily overnight, leaving damp patches for warm-up, with a forecast of more to come in the afternoon. Heavy clouds were gathering by the time the MotoGP grid formed, but it was a different confusion that saw the four leaders slow for a single lap after Pedrosa had held up his hand.

Lorenzo and Rossi led away, Marquez and Pedrosa immediately behind, followed by Bradl, Dovizioso, Iannone and the Espargaro brothers. On lap two, Abraham crashed out, and two laps later Bautista retired after suffering an electrical problem.

Only Bradl could follow the factory quartet, and only for a

Above: The deciding move. Pedrosa had passed Marquez twice, but now the leader changed his line. They touched. A near thing.

Top right: Rabat in control of Moto2 once more; Vinales in vain pursuit.

Above centre right: Zarco, Kallio and Luthi battle for third in Moto2. Zarco held them off.

Above near right: Assault with a deadly weapon. Fairing smashed, Aegerter battles to regain control after Torres's looping bike landed on top of him.

Above far right: With inches in it, the Moto3 battle behind Marquez: Ajo leads Vazquez and Binder.

Right: Alex Marquez was a runaway winner in a usually whisker-close class.

Photos: Gold & Goose

while; and they stretched away. Rossi took over on lap four; Lorenzo had drifted to fourth by lap seven, struggling to keep the pace and over a second adrift before half-distance.

At the start of lap 13, Marquez tried to pass Rossi, but almost hit him, taking to the paved run-off to avoid repeating his turn one qualifying crash. This gave Rossi a gap of almost one second, but it didn't last, and by lap 18 the front three were together, while Lorenzo was getting a little closer.

Now came the incident that everyone thought was prompted by rain on the track: both Honda riders raised their hands and slowed, shortly after Marquez had taken the lead off Rossi and Pedrosa had passed them both. It was dry in the pits, but mechanics started the spare bike engines and stripped off tyre warmers. But rain was not the issue, as Pedrosa would explain.

He had passed an unexpectedly slow Marquez, then noticed marshals by the track. Thinking that there must have been a yellow flag and fearing a penalty, his main aim had been to resume his previous position. Same for Marquez. That lap was some two seconds off the pace, but soon all four were back on full throttle.

This gave Lorenzo a chance to close right up again, but within two laps he had lost contact. Now Marquez was leading by nothing from Pedrosa and Rossi, who had a ringside seat for a heart-stopping last-lap battle.

Pedrosa took the lead at turn one; Marquez grabbed it straight back. At turn four, they swapped twice again. Then came turn 11. Marquez took a tight defensive line and slowed more than his rival expected. Their wheels just touched as Pedrosa swerved wide, both lucky not to crash; and Rossi lucky to inherit second place.

Had the move been deliberate and cynical, or just clever tactics? Marquez: "On the last lap, you always try to change your line to try to win, of course. You know the second rider will try to overtake you. On that corner in the other laps, I always went fast and wide, then came back, but on that lap, I braked and stayed a little bit in, stopped a little more and then I feel the touch."

Pedrosa, glowing with pleasure at having regained competitive strength, was not disposed to complain. He'd run in faster

to take advantage of Marquez's usual line, and had been bamboozled fair and square. But he'd shown real fighting spirit.

Lorenzo was fourth and disappointed, if not surprised, after struggling to find rear grip all weekend. "The bike was working well in braking, but in the last two corners we were very strong last year, and we weren't this year."

Bradl was a steadfast fifth, kept honest by the equally lonely Aleix Espargaro. His brother Pol eventually prevailed after a race-long battle with Dovizioso, joined towards the end for a spell by Iannone. Smith secured tenth after working his way past Hernandez.

A production Honda duel for 12th was resolved after the flag. Redding had held off Hayden by half a second for most of the race, but afterwards was penalised because he had "run off the track … and rejoined in such a way that he gained an advantage". He asserted he'd slowed on the next sector to compensate, but to no avail. A half-second penalty put him 13th.

Pirro had lost touch some time since, with Aoyama dropping away behind for the final point.

GP rookie Parkes was 16th in his best race so far, beating team-mate Laverty. Edwards, Barbera and Ioda-ART substitute Fabrizio followed along.

MOTO2 RACE – 23 laps

Barcelona resident Rabat had no rivals at his local track, as he proved from the very first session. In qualifying, he set six consecutive fastest laps on his first run, then went faster still to secure his fourth pole of the year. Kallio was second; then came another local hero, Vinales. Cortese, Folger and Pasini completed the second row, all on Kalex chassis, the best of them more than half a second down.

Rabat's fourth win gave him a 34-point lead over teammate Kallio, and he was starting to look unstoppable for a third consecutive Spanish title victory. At the same time, the race showed the promise of fast rookies Vinales, Salom and Folger, though the last two ran into misfortune.

Nobody was unluckier than Aegerter, who was battling for third when passed by an impetuous Jordi Torres on lap 17. A

couple of corners later, the Spaniard crashed, his bike flying high in the air right in the Swiss rider's path. It landed on his screen, but bounced off without doing more than breaking it; Aegerter ran on to the dirt, but recovered and rejoined, dropping to 16th, then climbing back into the points in 14th.

The race began with a three-way crash at turn one. Krummenacher and Morbidelli were able to rejoin, but Corsi was out. Further around on the same lap, Sam Lowes crashed out alone; Cortese likewise on lap two.

Kallio was the first leader, followed by Vinales, Rabat, Aegerter, Pasini, Salom and Folger.

The last named got no further than the start of lap three. Salom crashed awkwardly on the exit of turn one, sliding back across the track: Folger had to swerve into the gravel to avoid hitting him, and he too went down.

At the end of that messy lap, Rabat led again, tailed by Vinales. Only Kallio and Aegerter could follow, Luthi and Pasini slightly behind by lap four. Further back, Torres and Zarco chased; de Angelis and Cardus completed the early top ten.

Rabat took fastest lap, too fast for Vinales, and by lap 13 the gap between them was close to two seconds.

Torres was on the march, taking fourth off Kallio one lap later. He pushed past Aegerter and was setting out after Luthi when he crashed at the end of the back straight, taking Aegerter off in the process.

With three laps to go, Rabat was four seconds clear of Vinales and ten ahead of Luthi. But Zarco was on the charge, catching Luthi at the end to claim a maiden class podium. Then Kallio also passed Luthi, consigning him to fifth.

Pasini and Cardus came next, followed by a battling gang of five, over the line within just over half a second: Pons, Schrotter, West, Baldassarri and Simon. Nakagami, Aegerter and Frenchman Rossi took the final points.

De Angelis and Simeon had also crashed out by the end.

MOTO3 RACE – 22 laps

The margins of victory in the first six races were only twice more than a tenth, Qatar's 0.233 the biggest, Mugello's 0.010 the smallest. At Catalunya, Marquez Junior ran away from the lights to win by better than three seconds. The lap before it had been more than four. The usual hand-to-hand combat was for second.

It was Honda's first win in the fight back against KTM, and Marquez had earlier claimed Honda's fourth pole. A landmark, for his second career victory.

It was the opposite for team-mate Rins, who qualified third with hot rookie Enea Bastianini second, but fractured bones in his left foot in a heavy crash. Mechanics adjusted the position of the gear lever for the race – only for it to come adrift.

Miller was off the front row for the first time all year.

The first lap saw Antonelli slam heavily into the tyre wall, while Marquez grabbed a lead of six-tenths. Bastianini led the chase from Rins, Ajo, Binder, Vinales, Vazquez, Miller and Fenati. McPhee and Bagnaia would drop away as the race wore on, but not before the young Scotsman had set a new lap record.

They formed a typically wild group after Rins departed on lap four. No rider led for more than a few turns, but Miller seemed to be struggling to hold on.

On the final lap, Ajo was near the front of the gang, almost high-sided and ran off for an incredible save – both legs on the same side of the bike. Vinales lost his rostrum chance by running wide to avoid him.

At the same time, Miller was fighting back – but it was rookie Bastianini in second over the line, from Vazquez, Miller, Fenati, Binder and Vinales, less than a second covering second to seventh.

Ajo's acrobatics saved eighth; McPhee and Bagnaia swapped again for ninth on the last lap, when they'd been caught by the next gang, with Masbou narrowly ahead of Oliveira and Tonucci, plus Hanika. Kornfeil took the last point ahead of Khairuddin and Kent.

GP MONSTER ENERGY
DE CATALUNYA

13-15 JUNE, 2014

CIRCUIT DE CATALUNYA

25 laps
Length: 4.727km /
2.892 miles
Width: 12m

Turn 3 *145/90*
Seat *79/49*
Repsol *100/62*
Campsa *200/124*
Abolafio *175/109*
Turn 7 *110/68*
Europcar *147/91*
Banc Sabadell *102/63*
Elf *130/81*
Würth *105/65*
300/186
La Caixa *105/65*
Tourisme de Catalunya *158/98*

Key
96/60 kph/mph
Gear

MotoGP

RACE DISTANCE: 25 laps, 73.431 miles/118.175km · RACE WEATHER: Dry (air 22°C, humidity 61%, track 34°C)

Pos.	Rider	Nat.	No.	Entrant	Machine	Tyres	Race tyre choice	Laps	Time & speed
1	**Marc Marquez**	SPA	93	Repsol Honda Team	Honda RC213V	B	F: Medium/R: Medium	25	42m 56.914s
									102.5mph/
									165.0km/h
2	**Valentino Rossi**	ITA	46	Movistar Yamaha MotoGP	Yamaha YZR-M1	B	F: Medium/R: Medium	25	42m 57.426s
3	**Dani Pedrosa**	SPA	26	Repsol Honda Team	Honda RC213V	B	F: Medium/R: Medium	25	42m 58.748s
4	**Jorge Lorenzo**	SPA	99	Movistar Yamaha MotoGP	Yamaha YZR-M1	B	F: Medium/R: Medium	25	43m 01.454s
5	**Stefan Bradl**	GER	6	LCR Honda MotoGP	Honda RC213V	B	F: Hard/R: Medium	25	43m 08.062s
6	**Aleix Espargaro**	SPA	41	NGM Forward Racing	Forward Yamaha	B	F: Medium/R: Medium	25	43m 11.127s
7	**Pol Espargaro**	SPA	44	Monster Yamaha Tech 3	Yamaha YZR-M1	B	F: Medium/R: Medium	25	43m 13.041s
8	**Andrea Dovizioso**	ITA	4	Ducati Team	Ducati Desmosedici	B	F: Medium/R: Medium	25	43m 13.089s
9	**Andrea Iannone**	ITA	29	Pramac Racing	Ducati Desmosedici	B	F: Medium/R: Medium	25	43m 14.954s
10	**Bradley Smith**	GBR	38	Monster Yamaha Tech 3	Yamaha YZR-M1	B	F: Medium/R: Medium	25	43m 21.695s
11	**Yonny Hernandez**	COL	68	Energy T.I. Pramac Racing	Ducati Desmosedici	B	F: Medium/R: Soft	25	43m 34.067s
12	**Nicky Hayden**	USA	69	Drive M7 Aspar	Honda RCV1000R	B	F: Medium/R: Soft	25	43m 40.213s
13	**Scott Redding**	GBR	45	GO&FUN Honda Gresini	Honda RCV1000R	B	F: Medium/R: Soft	25	43m 40.321s
14	**Michele Pirro**	ITA	51	Ducati Team	Ducati Desmosedici	B	F: Medium/R: Medium	25	43m 52.071s
15	**Hiroshi Aoyama**	JPN	7	Drive M7 Aspar	Honda RCV1000R	B	F: Medium/R: Soft	25	43m 56.105s
16	Broc Parkes	AUS	23	Paul Bird Motorsport	PBM-ART	B	F: Medium/R: Soft	25	43m 57.820s
17	Michael Laverty	GBR	70	Paul Bird Motorsport	PBM-ART	B	F: Medium/R: Soft	25	43m 58.198s
18	Colin Edwards	USA	5	NGM Forward Racing	Forward Yamaha	B	F: Medium/R: Medium	25	44m 03.035s
19	Hector Barbera	SPA	8	Avintia Racing	Avintia	B	F: Medium/R: Soft	25	44m 22.109s
20	Michel Fabrizio	ITA	84	Octo IodaRacing Team	ART	B	F: Medium/R: Soft	25	44m 37.579s
	Mike di Meglio	FRA	63	Avintia Racing	Avintia	B	F: Medium/R: Soft	17	DNF-mechanical
	Cal Crutchlow	GBR	35	Ducati Team	Ducati Desmosedici	B	F: Medium/R: Soft	10	DNF-mechanical
	Alvaro Bautista	SPA	19	GO&FUN Honda Gresini	Honda RC213V	B	F: Medium/R: Soft	3	DNF-mechanical
	Karel Abraham	CZE	17	Cardion AB Motoracing	Honda RCV1000R	B	F: Medium/R: Soft	1	DNF-crash
	Danilo Petrucci	ITA	9	IodaRacing Project	ART	B	–	–	Absent-injured

Fastest lap: Marc Marquez, on lap 2, 1m 42.182s, 103.5mph/166.5km/h (record).

Previous lap record: Dani Pedrosa, SPA (Honda), 1m 42.358s, 103.304mph/166.251km/h (2008).

Event best maximum speed: Andrea Dovizioso, 215.0mph/346.0km/h (race).

Qualifying

Weather: Dry

Air Temp: 28°   **Track Temp:** 47°

Humidity: 42%

1	Pedrosa	1m 40.985s
2	Lorenzo	1m 41.100s
3	Marquez	1m 41.135s
4	Bradl	1m 41.220s
5	Rossi	1m 41.290s
6	A. Espargaro	1m 41.308s
7	Dovizioso	1m 41.337s
8	Smith	1m 41.491s
9	Hernandez	1m 41.671s
10	P. Espargaro	1m 41.677s
11	Iannone	1m 41.751s
12	Bautista	1m 42.024s
13	Crutchlow	1m 42.578s
14	Redding	1m 42.730s
15	Pirro	1m 42.955s
16	Hayden	1m 43.043s
17	Edwards	1m 43.226s
18	Abraham	1m 43.360s
19	Parkes	1m 43.530s
20	Aoyama	1m 43.564s
21	Laverty	1m 43.737s
22	Barbera	1m 44.115s
23	Di Meglio	1m 45.012s
24	Fabrizio	1m 46.214s

Fastest race laps

1	Marquez	1m 42.182s
2	Pedrosa	1m 42.364s
3	Lorenzo	1m 42.387s
4	Rossi	1m 42.408s
5	Bradl	1m 42.434s
6	A. Espargaro	1m 42.775s
7	Iannone	1m 42.873s
8	Hernandez	1m 42.942s
9	P. Espargaro	1m 42.975s
10	Dovizioso	1m 43.002s
11	Bautista	1m 43.216s
12	Smith	1m 43.416s
13	Redding	1m 43.779s
14	Crutchlow	1m 43.840s
15	Hayden	1m 44.003s
16	Aoyama	1m 44.289s
17	Parkes	1m 44.435s
18	Pirro	1m 44.504s
19	Edwards	1m 44.721s
20	Barbera	1m 44.850s
21	Laverty	1m 44.861s
22	Di Meglio	1m 45.163s
23	Fabrizio	1m 46.439s

Championship Points

1	Marquez	175
2	Rossi	117
3	Pedrosa	112
4	Lorenzo	78
5	Dovizioso	71
6	P. Espargaro	58
7	A. Espargaro	54
8	Bradl	50
9	Iannone	41
10	Smith	40
11	Bautista	34
12	Hayden	27
13	Hernandez	27
14	Redding	24
15	Aoyama	24
16	Crutchlow	15
17	Abraham	13
18	Edwards	8
19	Pirro	7
20	Petrucci	2
21	Barbera	2
22	Parkes	1

Constructor Points

1	Honda	175
2	Yamaha	127
3	Ducati	74
4	Forward Yamaha	54
5	ART	2
6	Avintia	2
7	PBM	1

Grid order	1	2	3	4	5	6	7	8	9	10	11	12	13	14	15	16	17	18	19	20	21	22	23	24	25	
26 PEDROSA	99	99	99	46	46	46	46	46	46	46	46	46	46	46	46	46	46	46	93	93	93	93	93	93	93	1
99 LORENZO	46	46	46	93	93	93	93	93	93	93	93	93	93	93	93	93	93	93	46	26	26	26	26	46		2
93 MARQUEZ	26	93	93	99	99	99	26	26	26	26	26	26	26	26	26	26	26	26	26	46	46	46	26			3
6 BRADL	93	26	26	26	26	26	99	99	99	99	99	99	99	99	99	99	99	99	99	99	99	99	99			4
46 ROSSI	6	6	6	6	6	6	6	6	6	6	6	6	6	6	6	6	6	6	6	6	6	6	6			5
41 A. ESPARGARO	4	4	4	41	41	41	41	41	41	41	41	41	41	41	41	41	41	41	41	41	41	41	41			6
4 DOVIZIOSO	44	44	41	4	44	44	44	44	44	44	44	44	44	44	44	44	44	4	44	44	4	44	44	44		7
38 SMITH	29	41	44	44	4	4	4	4	4	4	4	4	4	4	4	4	4	44	4	4	44	4	4	4		8
68 HERNANDEZ	41	29	29	29	29	29	29	29	29	29	29	29	29	29	29	29	29	29	29	29	29	29	29			9
44 P. ESPARGARO	35	68	68	68	68	68	68	68	68	68	68	68	68	38	38	38	38	38	38	38	38	38	38	38		10
29 IANNONE	68	35	19	35	35	38	38	38	38	38	38	38	38	68	68	68	68	68	68	68	68	68	68	68		11
19 BAUTISTA	38	19	35	38	38	35	35	35	45	45	45	45	45	45	45	45	45	45	45	45	45	45	45			12
35 CRUTCHLOW	19	38	38	45	45	45	45	35	69	69	69	69	69	69	69	69	69	69	69	69	69	69	69			13
45 REDDING	45	45	45	69	69	69	69	69	7	7	7	7	7	51	51	51	51	51	51	51	51	51	51			14
51 PIRRO	51	51	51	51	7	7	7	7	51	51	51	51	51	7	7	7	7	7	7	7	7	7	7			15
69 HAYDEN	69	69	69	7	51	51	51	51	51	23	23	23	23	23	23	23	23	23	23	23	23	23	23			
5 EDWARDS	23	23	7	23	23	23	23	23	5	5	5	5	5	70	70	70	70	70	70	70	70	70	70			
17 ABRAHAM	7	7	23	5	5	5	5	5	70	70	70	70	70	5	5	5	5	5	5	5	5	5	5			
23 PARKES	5	5	5	70	70	70	70	70	70	8	8	8	8	8	8	8	8	8	8	8	8	8	8			
7 AOYAMA	17	70	70	8	8	8	8	63	63	63	63	63	63	84	84	84	84	84	84	84	84	84				
70 LAVERTY	70	63	8	63	63	63	63	63	63	84	84	84	84	84	84	84										
8 BARBERA	63	8	63	84	84	84	84	84	84	35																
63 DI MEGLIO	8	84	84																							
84 FABRIZIO	84																									

35 Pit stop

Moto2

RACE DISTANCE: 23 laps, 67.556 miles/108.721km · RACE WEATHER: Dry (air 25°C, humidity 46%, track 45°C)

Pos.	Rider	Nat.	No.	Entrant	Machine	Laps	Time & Speed
1	**Esteve Rabat**	SPA	53	Marc VDS Racing Team	Kalex	23	41m 23.197s
							97.9mph/
							157.6km/h
2	**Maverick Vinales**	SPA	40	Paginas Amarillas HP 40	Kalex	23	41m 27.441s
3	**Johann Zarco**	FRA	5	AirAsia Caterham	Caterham Suter	23	41m 34.354s
4	**Mika Kallio**	FIN	36	Marc VDS Racing Team	Kalex	23	41m 34.498s
5	**Thomas Luthi**	SWI	12	Interwetten Paddock Moto2	Suter	23	41m 34.621s
6	**Mattia Pasini**	ITA	54	NGM Forward Racing	Kalex	23	41m 39.958s
7	**Ricard Cardus**	SPA	88	Tech 3	Tech 3	23	41m 44.472s
8	**Axel Pons**	SPA	49	AGR Team	Kalex	23	41m 55.990s
9	**Marcel Schrotter**	GER	23	Tech 3	Tech 3	23	41m 56.129s
10	**Anthony West**	AUS	95	QMMF Racing Team	Speed Up	23	41m 56.157s
11	**Lorenzo Baldassarri**	ITA	7	Gresini Moto2	Suter	23	41m 56.273s
12	**Julian Simon**	SPA	60	Italtrans Racing Team	Kalex	23	41m 56.566s
13	**Takaaki Nakagami**	JPN	30	IDEMITSU Honda Team Asia	Kalex	23	41m 59.387s
14	**Dominique Aegerter**	SWI	77	Technomag carXpert	Suter	23	42m 03.900s
15	**Louis Rossi**	FRA	96	SAG Team	Kalex	23	42m 04.101s
16	Josh Herrin	USA	2	AirAsia Caterham	Caterham Suter	23	42m 10.738s
17	Roman Ramos	SPA	97	QMMF Racing Team	Speed Up	23	42m 10.790s
18	Robin Mulhauser	SWI	70	Technomag carXpert	Suter	23	42m 10.841s
19	Azlan Shah	MAL	25	IDEMITSU Honda Team Asia	Kalex	23	42m 17.199s
20	Nicolas Terol	SPA	18	Mapfre Aspar Team Moto2	Suter	23	42m 22.254s
21	Franco Morbidelli	ITA	21	Italtrans Racing Team	Kalex	23	42m 31.024s
22	Gino Rea	GBR	8	AGT REA Racing	Suter	23	42m 35.050s
23	Tetsuta Nagashima	JPN	45	Teluru Team JiR Webike	TSR	23	42m 45.298s
24	Thitipong Warokorn	THA	10	APH PTT The Pizza SAG	Kalex	23	42m 48.896s
25	Randy Krummenacher	SWI	4	Octo IodaRacing Team	Suter	23	42m 50.175s
	Alex de Angelis	RSM	15	Tasca Racing Moto2	Suter	19	DNF
	Xavier Simeon	BEL	19	Federal Oil Gresini Moto2	Suter	17	DNF
	Jordi Torres	SPA	81	Mapfre Aspar Team Moto2	Suter	16	DNF
	Luis Salom	SPA	39	Paginas Amarillas HP 40	Kalex	2	DNF
	Jonas Folger	GER	94	AGR Team	Kalex	2	DNF
	Sandro Cortese	GER	11	Dynavolt Intact GP	Kalex	1	DNF
	Hafizh Syahrin	MAL	55	Petronas Raceline Malaysia	Kalex	1	DNF
	Sam Lowes	GBR	22	Speed Up	Speed Up	0	DNF
	Simone Corsi	ITA	3	NGM Forward Racing	Kalex	0	DNF

Fastest lap: Esteve Rabat, on lap 3, 1m 47.094s, 98.7mph/158.8km/h.
Lap record: Thomas Luthi, SWI (Suter), 1m 46.631s, 99.164mph/159.589km/h (2012).
Event best maximum speed: Sandro Cortese, 177.3mph/285.4km/h (free practice 3).

Qualifying
Weather: Dry
Air Temp: 29° **Track Temp:** 48°
Humidity: 44%

1	Rabat	1m 46.569s
2	Kallio	1m 47.140s
3	Vinales	1m 47.192s
4	Cortese	1m 47.267s
5	Folger	1m 47.444s
6	Pasini	1m 47.526s
7	Luthi	1m 47.594s
8	Zarco	1m 47.595s
9	Lowes	1m 47.600s
10	Aegerter	1m 47.604s
11	Salom	1m 47.665s
12	Morbidelli	1m 47.788s
13	De Angelis	1m 47.834s
14	Syahrin	1m 47.855s
15	Corsi	1m 47.907s
16	Torres	1m 47.926s
17	Schrotter	1m 47.932s
18	Simon	1m 47.932s
19	Krummenacher	1m 47.936s
20	Cardus	1m 48.026s
21	Simeon	1m 48.068s
22	Pons	1m 48.112s
23	Terol	1m 48.225s
24	Baldassarri	1m 48.230s
25	Nakagami	1m 48.296s
26	Rossi	1m 48.392s
27	West	1m 48.587s
28	Rea	1m 48.639s
29	Herrin	1m 48.737s
30	Mulhauser	1m 49.247s
31	Nagashima	1m 49.261s
32	Ramos	1m 49.487s
33	Shah	1m 49.771s
34	Warokorn	1m 50.234s

Fastest race laps

1	Rabat	1m 47.094s
2	Vinales	1m 47.238s
3	Kallio	1m 47.456s
4	Aegerter	1m 47.650s
5	Luthi	1m 47.663s
6	Torres	1m 47.678s
7	De Angelis	1m 47.812s
8	Zarco	1m 47.856s
9	Cardus	1m 47.879s
10	Simon	1m 48.086s
11	Baldassarri	1m 48.139s
12	West	1m 48.166s
13	Pasini	1m 48.184s
14	Simeon	1m 48.284s
15	Salom	1m 48.296s
16	Folger	1m 48.375s
17	Schrotter	1m 48.380s
18	Pons	1m 48.426s
19	Morbidelli	1m 48.453s
20	Nakagami	1m 48.614s
21	Rossi	1m 48.864s
22	Herrin	1m 49.023s
23	Ramos	1m 49.069s
24	Mulhauser	1m 49.075s
25	Shah	1m 49.126s
26	Nagashima	1m 49.270s
27	Terol	1m 49.333s
28	Krummenacher	1m 49.535s
29	Rea	1m 49.588s
30	Warokorn	1m 50.790s

Championship Points

1	Rabat	149
2	Kallio	115
3	Vinales	89
4	Aegerter	71
5	Corsi	66
6	Salom	59
7	Luthi	51
8	Folger	47
9	Zarco	33
10	Lowes	33
11	West	33
12	Cortese	32
13	Simeon	31
14	Schrotter	28
15	Torres	23
16	Cardus	22
17	De Angelis	18
18	Morbidelli	15
19	Pasini	14
20	Krummenacher	10
21	Pons	9
22	Nakagami	9
23	Rossi	7
24	Simon	6
25	Baldassarri	5
26	Syahrin	3
27	Terol	2

Constructor Points

1	Kalex	175
2	Suter	103
3	Speed Up	53
4	Tech 3	37
5	Caterham Suter	33
6	Forward KLX	33

Moto3

RACE DISTANCE: 22 laps, 64.619 miles/103.994km · RACE WEATHER: Dry (air 23°C, humidity 63%, track 34°C)

Pos.	Rider	Nat.	No.	Entrant	Machine	Laps	Time & Speed
1	**Alex Marquez**	SPA	12	Estrella Galicia 0,0	Honda	22	41m 11.656s
							94.1mph/
							151.4km/h
2	**Enea Bastianini**	ITA	33	Junior Team GO&FUN Moto3	KTM	22	41m 14.892s
3	**Efren Vazquez**	SPA	7	SaxoPrint-RTG	Honda	22	41m 15.168s
4	**Jack Miller**	AUS	8	Red Bull KTM Ajo	KTM	22	41m 15.420s
5	**Romano Fenati**	ITA	5	SKY Racing Team VR46	KTM	22	41m 15.518s
6	**Brad Binder**	RSA	41	Ambrogio Racing	Mahindra	22	41m 15.704s
7	**Isaac Vinales**	SPA	32	Calvo Team	KTM	22	41m 15.787s
8	**Niklas Ajo**	FIN	31	Avant Tecno Husqvarna Ajo	Husqvarna	22	41m 21.437s
9	**John McPhee**	GBR	17	SaxoPrint-RTG	Honda	22	41m 30.234s
10	**Francesco Bagnaia**	ITA	21	SKY Racing Team VR46	KTM	22	41m 30.253s
11	**Alexis Masbou**	FRA	10	Ongetta-Rivacold	Honda	22	41m 30.638s
12	**Miguel Oliveira**	POR	44	Mahindra Racing	Mahindra	22	41m 30.698s
13	**Alessandro Tonucci**	ITA	19	CIP	Mahindra	22	41m 30.984s
14	**Karel Hanika**	CZE	98	Red Bull KTM Ajo	KTM	22	41m 31.279s
15	**Jakub Kornfeil**	CZE	84	Calvo Team	KTM	22	41m 31.639s
16	Zulfahmi Khairuddin	MAL	63	Ongetta-AirAsia	Honda	22	41m 32.050s
17	Danny Kent	GBR	52	Red Bull Husqvarna Ajo	Husqvarna	22	41m 32.667s
18	Arthur Sissis	AUS	61	Mahindra Racing	Mahindra	22	41m 46.751s
19	Philipp Oettl	GER	65	Interwetten Paddock Moto3	Kalex KTM	22	41m 46.996s
20	Luca Grunwald	GER	43	Kiefer Racing	Kalex KTM	22	41m 47.245s
21	Matteo Ferrari	ITA	3	San Carlo Team Italia	Mahindra	22	41m 47.358s
22	Gabriel Rodrigo	ARG	91	RBA Racing Team	KTM	22	41m 47.888s
23	Eric Granado	BRA	57	Calvo Team	KTM	22	41m 47.956s
24	Bryan Schouten	NED	51	CIP	Mahindra	22	41m 50.191s
25	Livio Loi	BEL	11	Marc VDS Racing Team	Kalex KTM	22	41m 50.192s
26	Scott Deroue	NED	9	RW Racing GP	Kalex KTM	22	41m 50.262s
27	Jules Danilo	FRA	95	Ambrogio Racing	Mahindra	22	41m 54.249s
28	Juanfran Guevara	SPA	58	Mapfre Aspar Team Moto3	Kalex KTM	22	42m 07.806s
29	Andrea Locatelli	ITA	55	San Carlo Team Italia	Mahindra	22	42m 07.866s
30	Ana Carrasco	SPA	22	RW Racing GP	Kalex KTM	22	42m 12.808s
31	Gabriel Ramos	VEN	4	Kiefer Racing	Kalex KTM	22	42m 12.905s
	Alex Rins	SPA	42	Estrella Galicia 0,0	Honda	4	DNF
	Hafiq Azmi	MAL	38	SIC-AJO	KTM	1	DNF
	Maria Herrera	SPA	6	Junior Team Estrella Galicia 0,0	Honda	1	DNF
	Niccolo Antonelli	ITA	23	Junior Team GO&FUN Moto3	KTM	0	DNF

Fastest lap: John McPhee, on lap 5, 1m 51.299s, 94.9mph/152.8km/h (record).
Previous lap record: Maverick Vinales, SPA (KTM), 1m 51.475s, 94.8mph/152.6km/h (2013).
Event best maximum speed: Efren Vazquez, 149.6mph/240.8km/h (free practice 3).

Qualifying:
Weather: Dry
Air Temp: 32° **Track Temp:** 49°
Humidity: 29%

1	Marquez	1m 50.232s
2	Bastianini	1m 50.850s
3	Rins	1m 50.912s
4	Binder	1m 51.024s
5	Ajo	1m 51.308s
6	Vinales	1m 51.360s
7	Oliveira	1m 51.456s
8	Vazquez	1m 51.471s
9	Miller	1m 51.481s
10	McPhee	1m 51.499s
11	Kornfeil	1m 51.667s
12	Antonelli	1m 51.693s
13	Guevara	1m 51.693s
14	Tonucci	1m 51.704s
15	Hanika	1m 51.812s
16	Fenati	1m 51.848s
17	Masbou	1m 52.131s
18	Khairuddin	1m 52.227s
19	Kent	1m 52.251s
20	Bagnaia	1m 52.363s
21	Azmi	1m 52.439s
22	Ferrari	1m 52.463s
23	Loi	1m 52.614s
24	Herrera	1m 52.712s
25	Grunwald	1m 52.909s
26	Granado	1m 52.911s
27	Sissis	1m 52.934s
28	Deroue	1m 53.130s
29	Schouten	1m 53.263s
30	Oettl	1m 53.266s
31	Locatelli	1m 53.504s
32	Danilo	1m 53.912s
33	Ramos	1m 53.915s
34	Rodrigo	1m 54.070s
35	Carrasco	1m 54.369s

Fastest race laps

1	McPhee	1m 51.299s
2	Binder	1m 51.301s
3	Fenati	1m 51.362s
4	Ajo	1m 51.383s
5	Vinales	1m 51.408s
6	Marquez	1m 51.452s
7	Bastianini	1m 51.462s
8	Rins	1m 51.507s
9	Bagnaia	1m 51.575s
10	Vazquez	1m 51.594s
11	Miller	1m 51.615s
12	Guevara	1m 51.948s
13	Kornfeil	1m 52.059s
14	Hanika	1m 52.101s
15	Kent	1m 52.110s
16	Masbou	1m 52.183s
17	Khairuddin	1m 52.208s
18	Tonucci	1m 52.221s
19	Oliveira	1m 52.260s
20	Grunwald	1m 52.559s
21	Loi	1m 52.593s
22	Oettl	1m 52.599s
23	Ferrari	1m 52.774s
24	Deroue	1m 52.830s
25	Rodrigo	1m 52.839s
26	Granado	1m 52.862s
27	Sissis	1m 52.956s
28	Schouten	1m 53.209s
29	Danilo	1m 53.310s
30	Carrasco	1m 53.791s
31	Ramos	1m 53.860s
32	Locatelli	1m 53.876s

Championship Points

1	Miller	117
2	Fenati	110
3	Vazquez	92
4	Rins	87
5	Marquez	85
6	Vinales	73
7	Masbou	50
8	Bastianini	45
9	Bagnaia	42
10	Kornfeil	38
11	Oliveira	37
12	Ajo	35
13	McPhee	30
14	Kent	27
15	Binder	22
16	Loi	17
17	Guevara	17
18	Hanika	16
19	Tonucci	15
20	Khairuddin	11
21	Antonelli	7
22	Oettl	5
23	Ferrari	2

Constructor Points

1	KTM	170
2	Honda	137
3	Husqvarna	47
4	Mahindra	46
5	Kalex KTM	28

FIM WORLD CHAMPIONSHIP · ROUND 8

DUTCH TT

ASSEN CIRCUIT

Above: Swimming to victory: Marquez's latest success came in his first real wet-dry race.

Main: Marquez leads the early stages of a mixed-up race from Dovizioso and Aleix Espargaro.

Photos: Gold & Goose

Above: A tentative start: Dovizioso leads the Hondas and Aleix Espargaro early on lap one.

Top right: Broc Parkes, tailed by Smith, started on slicks from the pit lane, and brought the ill-favoured PBM ART home a creditable 11th.

Above centre right: Moto2 rainmaster Anthony West scratched an 11-year itch, to claim a career second win in similar circumstances to his first.

Above far right: Dovizioso got everything right, challenging Marquez and claiming second, Ducati's second podium of the season.

Right: The returned Petrucci, battling with Pol Espargaro and Barbera, took the final point on a good day for the underdogs.

Below right: Canny timing won Aleix Espargaro a first pole position for an Open bike.

Photos: Gold & Goose

THE emasculation of Assen took place almost ten years ago, at the end of 2005. An act of corporate vandalism replaced the first loop with a tight stadium section and removed the fascinating flat-out zig-zag of the back straight, among other subtleties.

This was the ninth time at the new version. Long enough, you might think, for memories to fade.

Far from it. Without any prompting, older riders talked frequently and fondly of the old track; new riders spoke wistfully of only having the chance to ride it on the PlayStation. It was all about character.

But the northernmost GP would oblige; one aspect of Assen cannot be changed – the weather. A particular kind of weather, where rain showers are often very local and quite short-lived, although sometimes heavy. In between, the surface dries quickly.

After a balmy start on Thursday, that aspect of 'the old Assen' reasserted itself on qualifying Friday and more so on race Saturday, with changes of weather perfectly timed to disrupt even the most carefully laid plans.

In this manner, Marquez won his first ever flag-to-flag bike-change race in genuine wet/dry conditions (Australia's ersatz 2013 race doesn't count), and while Pedrosa managed a stalwart third, his main rivals fell foul in several ways.

Rossi was caught out when rain fell early in the final qualifying session – he'd delayed his fast lap too long. Then he was doubly bamboozled for the race: he gambled on starting on slicks, then changed his mind on the sighting lap when the rain proved more persistent. That dictated a start from the pit lane, which effectively ruined any hopes of repeating 2013's victory or even gaining a podium.

Lorenzo suffered a fate both harder and easier to understand: he succumbed to fear and dropped to 13th, his worst ever MotoGP finish. "I was not able to be brave," he explained afterwards, ashen-faced. Memories of his wet crash at Assen in 2013 were vivid over the treacherous damp patches. He apologised to his team and the fans. Everyone tried very hard not to see it as a turning point, for, as he also explained, "I am not fighting for the World Championship."

GP novice Broc Parkes had his best race yet, if by mistake. The Australian blamed contact with another rider for having crashed out on the warm-up lap, which left him with little option but to jump on his other PBM Aprilia, set up for the dry. He also started from the pit lane, one of only two riders on

slicks. He tiptoed around and, when the rain increased after a few laps, contemplated coming in, "but then it started to dry." As others dived into the pits, he was already working up a good rhythm and track understanding, and when they returned he found himself in sixth, engaged in battle with the likes of Crutchlow and Bautista. He gave a good account of himself on his ill-favoured bike, finally dropping to 11th. The other slick-shod starter was Hernandez, who pitted after one lap to swap bikes, and again later in the race when it dried. What would Rossi have done if he had stuck with his slicks from the start?

Dovizioso, canny and ever reliable as well as steadily fast, played his hand to perfection, to claim Ducati's best finish since Rossi's second at Misano in 2012 and his second rostrum of the year. Since it was not a dry race, it did not threaten their extra fuel allocation.

Team-mate Crutchlow so far had been a long way short of contributing to the improvement and now articulated some details of the conundrum that had caused it, along with much puzzlement to rider and crew alike. Data showed that riding on the limit, "if I leaned the bike over any more, I'd be on the ground. I have four or five degrees less lean angle than Dovizioso or Iannone, on every corner. Last year at Yamaha, I used one degree less lean angle than Lorenzo and one degree more than Valentino." At least there was one wry celebration – his first finish, albeit only ninth, in six weeks. The Englishman also did his best to rebut rumours that he planned to exercise his unusual end-of-July opt-out clause to seek something different for 2015. "My priority is to stay with Ducati."

There was no other news on movements, though in the following weeks Pedrosa and Rossi both signed up to stay where they were for two years apiece.

Yamaha had a stubby new exhaust that had appeared at the post-Barcelona tests, but there were only three sets. Lorenzo took two of them. Rossi used one on Thursday, but opted to stay with the older system, in the interests of keeping both his bikes the same. The bottom-end performance was better, he said, "but you also lose something at the top."

Assen having fewer braking demands than many circuits, the bigger brakes were back in the box, and the factory Hondas even had shrouds to sustain heat.

Australian veteran Anthony West's Moto2 win was his career second, the previous one in similar circumstances at the

same track. His victory brought joy and amusement, and not only to the rider.

Race Direction were handing out the penalty points again, in an attempt to address the dangerous practice of riders cruising on-track during qualifying, hoping to pick up a tow. This was particularly prevalent in Moto3, where a slipstream could make a huge difference, and in qualifying Miller was put off the track on a fast lap when he came upon a gang of four: Ajo, plus rookies Azmi, Danilo and Hanika. He re-gained the tarmac with much shaking of his fist; all four were awarded a single penalty point; some satisfaction perhaps for Miller, who had earned two for his headstrong last-lap crash at Mugello.

MOTOGP RACE – 26 laps

Qualifying was a lottery, and Aleix Espargaro the winner; it was the first time for a soft-tyred Open bike. Frequently fast-est in free practice, he'd hung back from the first jostling group pit exit, when rain was starting to fall, to gain a clear track for his first flying lap. The advantage was a massive 1.4 seconds.

Anyone who hadn't set a fast second lap was in danger-ous territory as the rain arrived. Marquez and Pedrosa had the timing right to complete the front row; Iannone and Crutchlow (on soft tyres) were fourth and fifth, the latter through from Q1; Lorenzo was ninth and too-late Rossi 12th.

Petrucci was back on the Ioda ART and placed a respecta-ble 17th – since Q1 was dry, his time and indeed all of those from 13th downwards were much faster than the elite Q2.

With patchy rain falling and extra time for another sight-ing lap if desired, the start (already late) was delayed again, and procedure restarted with more sighting laps. Bradl had fallen in the first outing, but there was time for hasty repairs, and the race finally got under way in the worst kind of mixed conditions 20 minutes later than planned.

Rossi and Parkes started from the pit lane as Dovizioso led away, Marquez taking over before the end of lap one. The pair quickly drew clear of Espargaro, Pedrosa and the rest as the rain grew heavier, then stopped.

For most, it would be a race of two halves, the majority pitting to change to a dry bike after six laps – leading to some havoc in the pit lane and at least one near collision, between Abraham and Pol Espargaro. Towards the end, pit crews were warming up wet bikes again as the sprinkling recommenced, bringing out the flags once more around half-distance – but it was never heavy enough to force yet another change.

Rossi was 19th at the end of lap one and had gained six places by the time the pit stops began.

The front two had carried on pulling clear, while Lorenzo dropped to seventh, with Crutchlow ahead, somewhat ben-efiting from the wet and engaged with Iannone.

Part two, with all on slicks, saw more variety, including up front – Marquez had a big moment on his out-lap, taking to the run-off area and giving the lead back to the shadowing Dovizioso, who gained four seconds in the process. There-after, it was a matter of hunting him down, and Marquez caught and passed him on lap 16, pulling away to win by better than six seconds. As he crossed the line, he lay flat on the tank, legs out behind, miming the actions of a breast-stroke swimmer. The showman emerges.

Dovi was not challenged for second, thanks, he said, to "a good start, the right choice of tyres and a perfect race strategy. Both Marc and I were able to interpret the track quicker than the others, and we pulled out a good gap straight away."

Some way behind, Pedrosa and Espargaro were engaged in a most entertaining scrap, with countless changes of posi-tion. As the latter put it, "He killed me on the straights, and I killed him on the brakes." In this way, Aleix led the factory Honda over the line more often than not. It was resolved with eight laps to go, when Pedrosa finally managed to make

a pass stick and then escape to take a second third place in a row.

Rossi got back out in tenth after the tyre change, a couple of seconds adrift of Iannone, himself trailing a group of three disputing fifth, with Bautista heading Crutchlow and Parkes, who was making a good fist of staying in touch.

The Yamaha was soon with them, and ahead by lap 15. Only Iannone was able to follow, but he was out of touch by the end. Bautista fell back to be caught, but not passed by Smith. Crutchlow, suffering familiar understeer, was ninth.

Bradl was a lone tenth, after finally getting ahead of Parkes on lap 23. Pol Espargaro was 12th when he crashed out after half-distance.

Redding was top production Honda, ahead of a dismal Lorenzo; the last points went to Abraham and Petrucci. Both Drive M7 Hondas were out of the points, with Aoyama 16th and Hayden 17th, having dropped back with a recalcitrant dry bike after a good run in the wet.

Marquez was the first to win the opening eight rounds since Agostini in 1970, with a 72-point lead giving him almost a three-race advantage over the now-equal Pedrosa and Rossi.

MOTO2 RACE – 24 laps

Chaos, with heavy rain and even hail coming and going as they lined up, played into the hands of Rabat, who had crashed on the sighting lap at the unexpectedly sodden Stek-kenwal. He got back to the pits and was reprieved less than two minutes later when the start was delayed by 20 minutes.

It played also for Anthony West, master of dire conditions and steadfast to the last. His hard-earned win was a replay of a similar victory at Assen 11 years earlier, bringing his career total to two.

And it played against Aegerter, whose slick rear tyre gamble was a disaster.

Rabat was on pole number six, but only narrowly from Aegerter, hungry for his own first win. Prior experience helped rookie star Lowes to a second front row, edging Kallio, who headed the second from Nakagami and Corsi; the first 15 were within a second, with Vinales eighth and Salom 15th.

It was properly wet at the eventual start. Lowes took off, hotly pursued by Corsi, the pair drawing ahead, though both doomed. Corsi took over on lap two, but they were still together when Lowes lost the front and slipped out on lap nine, remounting only to fall again two corners later.

Left: Fear struck Lorenzo, cruising home crestfallen in a downbeat 13th.

Far left: West leads Vinales and Kallio on his way to his second victory in the Dutch TT.

Below left: The Moto2 race was delayed by the changing conditions – there was even hail.

Bottom left: Early Moto2 race leaders Lowes and Corsi. Both joined a long crash list.

Below: Honda's first 1-2 in Moto3, and a podium for Mahindra.

Bottom: Exchanging paint in the only dry race of the day: Oliveira squeezes his Mahindra ahead of McPhee's Honda and Ajo's Husqvarna.

Photos: Gold & Goose

By lap 11, Corsi was better than 11 seconds clear of a pack now led by West, through to second from seventh on lap one. By lap 12, Corsi wasn't there any more, also having fallen victim to the increasingly difficult conditions.

Now West led narrowly from Simon, Vinales, Luthi, de Angelis and Kallio, with Salom closing.

There would be no rest for the Australian, focused intently on "pushing and keeping it clean". In his wake, Vinales took up the pursuit as Simon dropped to the back of the group; team-mate Salom joined in, taking second on lap 18, only to slip off two laps later.

By then, Kallio was the last of the group still in touch, while the Spanish team-mates' battle had given West a little breathing space. That had gone again by the start of the last lap, but he was rock solid to stay just out of Vinales's reach, while Kallio had decided that a safe third was good enough. Even so, he was only three-quarters of a second behind.

Zarco had been climbing in the latter stages and took fourth off the slowing de Angelis with five laps to spare; Luthi had dropped back right out of touch; likewise Simon, who was seventh.

Rabat was next after playing it safe, well clear by the end of erstwhile rival Baldassarri; Hafizh Syahrin led the next group for tenth; from Rea and Schrotter, the remounted Corsi made it back up to 13th; Salom to 15th, behind Nakagami. Folger was 23rd, after a ride-through penalty for speeding in the pit lane; Aegerter was 21st, a lap down, after starting on slicks.

Riders were in and out of the pits, and with more rain falling just after the start; the crash list was long: Morbidelli and Nagashima both on the second sighting lap; Pasini the first of nine fallers and Cortese the last. Lowes was not the only one to remount and fall again: Pons crashed twice, and Nagashima again in the race.

MOTO3 RACE – 22 laps

This was the only dry race, and thus fairly straightforward, especially after two leading lights left early. Title rivals Miller and Fenati both failed to score, leaving the Australian – starting from pole number four – still seven points ahead, but both now under serious threat from the Honda gang: especially double winner Marquez, plus Rins and Vazquez.

Miller took off in the lead, intent on emulating Marquez's Barcelona breakaway and had a little gap in hand after one lap. Then, into the first corner, "I didn't brake late or anything, but I went over the bump and it was a little slicker than I expected." He was down and out.

That left Marquez in the lead, and looking like repeating his feat: he was 1.2 seconds clear at the end of lap two. Rins led the pursuit, from Hanika and Ajo, both destined to crash out, the latter spectacularly and injuriously, badly breaking his ankle.

Fenati meanwhile had been pushed on to the grass at the chicane on the first lap, dropping to the back. He had climbed to 11th by lap 13, when he crashed, remounting for a pointless 18th.

Up front, Rins caught and passed Marquez, only because the leader had made a slip while braking for the first corner, taking to the paved run-off. He regained the lead at once, and soon was alone again, moving clear to win a second race in a row by almost three seconds.

At the same time, Oliveira had started well from 13th to get up to eighth by lap two. He picked his way steadily through a typically battling gang and was third by lap six, moving clear to close on Rins. He caught and passed him with six laps left, but Rins stalked to the end and pounced successfully under braking for the final chicane. It was a first Honda one-two; and Mahindra's first rostrum since Malaysia in 2013.

Masbou won the brawl for fourth, from Antonelli, Vazquez, Vinales, Kent, Binder and McPhee – fourth to tenth covered by less than four-tenths.

TT ASSEN
26 laps
Length: 4.542km / 2.822 miles
Width: 10-14m

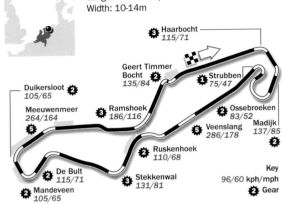

Haarbocht 115/71
Geert Timmer Bocht 135/84
Strubben 75/47
Duikersloot 105/65
Meeuwenmeer 264/164
Ramshoek 186/116
Ossebroeken 83/52
Veenslang 286/178
Madijk 137/85
Ruskenhoek 110/68
De Bult 115/71
Stekkenwal 131/81
Mandeveen 105/65

Key
96/60 kph/mph
Gear

WET RACE

**IVECO DAILY
TT ASSEN**

26-28 JUNE, 2014

MotoGP

RACE DISTANCE: 26 laps, 73.379 miles/118.092km · RACE WEATHER: Wet-Dry (air 19°C, humidity 69%, track 25°C)

Pos.	Rider	Nat.	No.	Entrant	Machine	Tyres	Race tyre choice	Laps	Time & speed
1	Marc Marquez	SPA	93	Repsol Honda Team	Honda RC213V	B	F: Soft Wet/R: Soft Wet	26	43m 29.954s / 101.2mph/ 162.8km/h
2	Andrea Dovizioso	ITA	4	Ducati Team	Ducati Desmosedici	B	F: Soft Wet/R: Soft Wet	26	43m 36.668s
3	Dani Pedrosa	SPA	26	Repsol Honda Team	Honda RC213V	B	F: Soft Wet/R: Soft Wet	26	43m 40.745s
4	Aleix Espargaro	SPA	41	NGM Forward Racing	Forward Yamaha	B	F: Soft Wet/R: Soft Wet	26	43m 49.153s
5	Valentino Rossi	ITA	46	Movistar Yamaha MotoGP	Yamaha YZR-M1	B	F: Soft Wet/R: Soft Wet	26	43m 55.767s
6	Andrea Iannone	ITA	29	Pramac Racing	Ducati Desmosedici	B	F: Soft Wet/R: Soft Wet	26	43m 58.957s
7	Alvaro Bautista	SPA	19	GO&FUN Honda Gresini	Honda RC213V	B	F: Soft Wet/R: Soft Wet	26	44m 00.836s
8	Bradley Smith	GBR	38	Monster Yamaha Tech 3	Yamaha YZR-M1	B	F: Soft Wet/R: Soft Wet	26	44m 00.939s
9	Cal Crutchlow	GBR	35	Ducati Team	Ducati Desmosedici	B	F: Soft Wet/R: Soft Wet	26	44m 13.985s
10	Stefan Bradl	GER	6	LCR Honda MotoGP	Honda RC213V	B	F: Soft Wet/R: Soft Wet	26	44m 18.616s
11	Broc Parkes	AUS	23	Paul Bird Motorsport	PBM-ART	B	F: Soft Slk/R: Soft Slk	26	44m 21.817s
12	Scott Redding	GBR	45	GO&FUN Honda Gresini	Honda RCV1000R	B	F: Soft Wet/R: Soft Wet	26	44m 30.283s
13	Jorge Lorenzo	SPA	99	Movistar Yamaha MotoGP	Yamaha YZR-M1	B	F: Soft Wet/R: Soft Wet	26	44m 34.595s
14	Karel Abraham	CZE	17	Cardion AB Motoracing	Honda RCV1000R	B	F: Soft Wet/R: Soft Wet	26	44m 35.934s
15	Danilo Petrucci	ITA	9	Octo IodaRacing Team	ART	B	F: Soft Wet/R: Soft Wet	26	44m 47.565s
16	Hiroshi Aoyama	JPN	7	Drive M7 Aspar	Honda RCV1000R	B	F: Soft Wet/R: Soft Wet	26	44m 49.707s
17	Nicky Hayden	USA	69	Drive M7 Aspar	Honda RCV1000R	B	F: Soft Wet/R: Soft Wet	26	44m 57.584s
18	Hector Barbera	SPA	8	Avintia Racing	Avintia	B	F: Soft Wet/R: Soft Wet	26	44m 58.096s
19	Yonny Hernandez	COL	68	Energy T.I. Pramac Racing	Ducati Desmosedici	B	F: Soft Slk/R: Soft Slk	25	43m 41.754s
20	Mike di Meglio	FRA	63	Avintia Racing	Avintia	B	F: Soft Wet/R: Soft Wet	25	43m 58.159s
21	Michael Laverty	GBR	70	Paul Bird Motorsport	PBM-ART	B	F: Soft Wet/R: Soft Wet	25	44m 49.966s
22	Colin Edwards	USA	5	NGM Forward Racing	Forward Yamaha	B	F: Soft Wet/R: Soft Wet	23	43m 33.704s
	Pol Espargaro	SPA	44	Monster Yamaha Tech 3	Yamaha YZR-M1	B	F: Soft Wet/R: Soft Wet	18	DNF-crash

* At start of race.

Fastest lap: Marc Marquez, on lap 19, 1m 34.575s, 107.4mph/172.8km/h.
Lap record: Dani Pedrosa, SPA (Honda), 1m 34.548s, 107.460mph/172.940km/h (2012).
Event best maximum speed: Marc Marquez, 194.7mph/313.4km/h (free practice 4).

Qualifying

Weather: Wet
Air Temp: 20° **Track Temp:** 26°
Humidity: 64%

1	A. Espargaro	1m 38.789s
2	Marquez	1m 40.194s
3	Pedrosa	1m 40.732s
4	Iannone	1m 40.786s
5	Crutchlow	1m 40.796s
6	Smith	1m 40.818s
7	Dovizioso	1m 41.140s
8	Bradl	1m 41.982s
9	Lorenzo	1m 42.259s
10	Bautista	1m 42.884s
11	P. Espargaro	1m 43.085s
12	Rossi	1m 43.625s
13	Abraham	1m 34.907s
14	Aoyama	1m 34.930s
15	Hernandez	1m 35.056s
16	Redding	1m 35.059s
17	Petrucci	1m 35.346s
18	Edwards	1m 35.484s
19	Parkes	1m 35.513s
20	Barbera	1m 35.631s
21	Laverty	1m 35.731s
22	Hayden	1m 35.792s
23	Di Meglio	1m 35.980s

Fastest race laps

1	Marquez	1m 34.575s
2	Pedrosa	1m 34.692s
3	Smith	1m 34.870s
4	Rossi	1m 35.001s
5	Dovizioso	1m 35.047s
6	Lorenzo	1m 35.288s
7	Iannone	1m 35.349s
8	Bautista	1m 35.379s
9	A. Espargaro	1m 35.513s
10	Bradl	1m 35.971s
11	Crutchlow	1m 36.291s
12	Abraham	1m 36.364s
13	Redding	1m 36.589s
14	P. Espargaro	1m 36.611s
15	Hernandez	1m 36.617s
16	Laverty	1m 36.716s
17	Aoyama	1m 36.847s
18	Barbera	1m 36.896s
19	Parkes	1m 36.955s
20	Petrucci	1m 37.390s
21	Hayden	1m 37.400s
22	Di Meglio	1m 37.505s
23	Edwards	1m 38.534s

Championship Points

1	Marquez	200
2	Rossi	128
3	Pedrosa	128
4	Dovizioso	91
5	Lorenzo	81
6	A. Espargaro	67
7	P. Espargaro	58
8	Bradl	56
9	Iannone	51
10	Smith	48
11	Bautista	43
12	Redding	28
13	Hayden	27
14	Hernandez	27
15	Aoyama	24
16	Crutchlow	22
17	Abraham	15
18	Edwards	8
19	Pirro	7
20	Parkes	6
21	Petrucci	3
22	Barbera	2

Constructor Points

1	Honda	200
2	Yamaha	138
3	Ducati	94
4	Forward Yamaha	67
5	PBM	6
6	ART	3

Grid order	1	2	3	4	5	6	7	8	9	10	11	12	13	14	15	16	17	18	19	20	21	22	23	24	25	26	
41 A. ESPARGARO	93	93	93	93	93	93	7	4	4	4	4	4	4	4	4	93	93	93	93	93	93	93	93	93	93	93	1
93 MARQUEZ	4	4	4	4	4	4	93	93	93	93	93	93	93	93	93	4	4	4	4	4	4	4	4	4	4	4	2
26 PEDROSA	41	41	41	41	41	41	99	41	41	41	41	41	41	41	41	41	41	26	26	26	26	26	26	26	26	26	3
29 IANNONE	26	26	26	26	26	26	69	26	26	26	26	26	26	26	41	41	41	41	41	41	41	41	41	41	41	41	4
35 CRUTCHLOW	29	29	29	29	35	99	38	7	19	19	19	29	29	46	46	46	46	46	46	46	46	46	46	46	46	46	5
38 SMITH	99	99	35	35	29	7	6	23	23	35	35	19	35	46	19	29	29	29	29	29	29	29	29	29	29	29	6
4 DOVIZIOSO	35	35	99	99	99	69	19	35	29	23	23	35	19	35	35	19	19	19	19	19	19	19	19	19	19	19	7
6 BRADL	38	7	7	7	19	38	17	35	29	29	29	23	46	19	19	35	35	35	38	38	38	38	38	38	38	38	8
99 LORENZO	7	38	38	19	7	6	26	29	46	46	46	46	23	23	23	38	38	38	35	35	35	35	35	35	35	35	9
19 BAUTISTA	6	19	19	38	69	35	41	46	6	38	38	38	38	38	38	23	23	23	23	23	23	6	6	6	6	6	10
44 P. ESPARGARO	19	6	6	69	38	29	9	6	38	6	6	6	6	6	6	6	6	6	6	6	6	23	23	23	23		11
46 ROSSI	69	69	69	6	6	19	44	38	99	44	44	44	44	44	45	45	45	45	45	45	45	45	45	45			12
17 ABRAHAM	5	5	46	46	46	46	8	99	44	45	45	45	45	17	17	17	17	17	17	17	99	99	99				13
7 AOYAMA	44	46	5	17	17	17	19	69	9	99	9	9	17	17	9	9	99	99	99	99	17	17	17				14
68 HERNANDEZ	8	44	17	44	44	44	23	17	9	9	17	17	9	9	99	99	9	9	9	9	9	9	9				15
45 REDDING	17	17	44	9	9	9	35	17	69	17	99	7	7	7	99	7	7	7	7	7	7	7	7				
9 PETRUCCI	45	9	8	5	8	9	29	9	17	69	7	99	99	99	7	8	8	69	69	69	69	69	69				
5 EDWARDS	70	45	45	9	5	63	46	45	7	7	69	69	69	8	69	69	8	8	8	8	8	8	8				
23 PARKES	46	70	63	63	63	5	45	5	5	5	5	8	8	44	68	68	68	68	68	68	68	68					
8 BARBERA	63	63	70	45	70	23	5	8	68	68	68	68	68	63	63	63	63	63	63	63	63						
70 LAVERTY	9	9	9	70	45	70	63	63	63	63	63	63	63	44	44	70	70	70	70	70	70						
69 HAYDEN	68	23	68	68	23	45	70	68	68	68	5	70	70	70	70	5	5	5	5	5							
63 DI MEGLIO	23	68	23	23	68	68	68	70	70	70	70	5	5	5	5	5	5										

93 Pit stop   68 Lapped rider

Moto2

RACE DISTANCE: 24 laps, 67.734 miles/109.008km · **RACE WEATHER:** Wet (air 18°C, humidity 72%, track 25°C)

Pos.	Rider	Nat.	No.	Entrant	Machine	Laps	Time & Speed
1	**Anthony West**	AUS	95	QMMF Racing Team	Speed Up	24	46m 02.089s 88.2mph/ 142.0km/h
2	**Maverick Vinales**	SPA	40	Paginas Amarillas HP 40	Kalex	24	46m 02.407s
3	**Mika Kallio**	FIN	36	Marc VDS Racing Team	Kalex	24	46m 02.832s
4	**Johann Zarco**	FRA	5	AirAsia Caterham	Caterham Suter	24	46m 09.389s
5	**Alex de Angelis**	RSM	15	Tasca Racing Moto2	Suter	24	46m 13.342s
6	**Thomas Luthi**	SWI	12	Interwetten Paddock Moto2	Suter	24	46m 17.021s
7	**Julian Simon**	SPA	60	Italtrans Racing Team	Kalex	24	46m 19.747s
8	**Esteve Rabat**	SPA	53	Marc VDS Racing Team	Kalex	24	46m 22.266s
9	**Lorenzo Baldassarri**	ITA	7	Gresini Moto2	Suter	24	46m 27.349s
10	**Hafizh Syahrin**	MAL	55	Petronas Raceline Malaysia	Kalex	24	46m 52.850s
11	**Gino Rea**	GBR	8	AGT REA Racing	Suter	24	46m 53.615s
12	**Marcel Schrotter**	GER	23	Tech 3	Tech 3	24	46m 53.781s
13	**Simone Corsi**	ITA	3	NGM Forward Racing	Kalex	24	46m 59.197s
14	**Takaaki Nakagami**	JPN	30	IDEMITSU Honda Team Asia	Kalex	24	47m 08.702s
15	**Luis Salom**	SPA	39	Paginas Amarillas HP 40	Kalex	24	47m 17.589s
16	Ricard Cardus	SPA	88	Tech 3	Tech 3	24	47m 19.328s
17	Mattia Pasini	ITA	54	NGM Forward Racing	Kalex	24	47m 19.617s
18	Josh Herrin	USA	2	AirAsia Caterham	Caterham Suter	24	47m 44.267s
19	Roman Ramos	SPA	97	QMMF Racing Team	Speed Up	24	47m 50.213s
20	Tetsuta Nagashima	JPN	45	Teluru Team JiR Webike	TSR	23	46m 37.465s
21	Dominique Aegerter	SWI	77	Technomag carXpert	Suter	23	47m 28.629s
22	Nicolas Terol	SPA	18	Mapfre Aspar Team Moto2	Suter	23	47m 46.538s
23	Jonas Folger	GER	94	AGR Team	Kalex	22	46m 07.981s
24	Franco Morbidelli	ITA	21	Italtrans Racing Team	Kalex	22	47m 05.045s
25	Xavier Simeon	BEL	19	Federal Oil Gresini Moto2	Suter	22	47m 05.225s
26	Jordi Torres	SPA	81	Mapfre Aspar Team Moto2	Suter	22	47m 31.147s
27	Robin Mulhauser	SWI	70	Technomag carXpert	Suter	22	47m 47.427s
28	Louis Rossi	FRA	96	SAG Team	Kalex	21	46m 37.413s
29	Thitipong Warokorn	THA	10	APH PTT The Pizza SAG	Kalex	20	47m 22.548s
	Sandro Cortese	GER	11	Dynavolt Intact GP	Kalex	18	DNF
	Randy Krummenacher	SWI	4	Octo IodaRacing Team	Suter	12	DNF
	Sam Lowes	GBR	22	Speed Up	Speed Up	8	DNF
	Axel Pons	SPA	49	AGR Team	Kalex	7	DNF
	Azlan Shah	MAL	25	IDEMITSU Honda Team Asia	Kalex	3	DNF

Fastest lap: Dominique Aegerter, on lap 23, 1m 43.463s, 98.2mph/158.0km/h.

Lap record: Marc Marquez, SPA (Suter), 1m 38.391s, 103.263mph/166.185km/h (2012)

Event best maximum speed: Nicolas Terol, 161.5mph/259.9km/h (free practice 1).

Qualifying

Weather: Dry

Air Temp: 20° **Track Temp:** 25°

Humidity: 61%

1	Rabat	1m 37.311s
2	Aegerter	1m 37.462s
3	Lowes	1m 37.674s
4	Kallio	1m 37.699s
5	Nakagami	1m 37.876s
6	Corsi	1m 37.893s
7	Zarco	1m 37.921s
8	Vinales	1m 37.960s
9	Cardus	1m 38.027s
10	Simeon	1m 38.043s
11	Simon	1m 38.129s
12	Pasini	1m 38.147s
13	Morbidelli	1m 38.295s
14	Cortese	1m 38.306s
15	Salom	1m 38.309s
16	Schrotter	1m 38.358s
17	Luthi	1m 38.385s
18	Pons	1m 38.407s
19	De Angelis	1m 38.441s
20	Torres	1m 38.464s
21	Folger	1m 38.546s
22	Rossi	1m 38.681s
23	West	1m 38.851s
24	Terol	1m 38.863s
25	Baldassarri	1m 38.963s
26	Krummenacher	1m 38.992s
27	Herrin	1m 39.091s
28	Syahrin	1m 39.138s
29	Shah	1m 39.368s
30	Nagashima	1m 39.419s
31	Mulhauser	1m 39.747s
32	Ramos	1m 39.766s
33	Rea	1m 39.769s
34	Warokorn	1m 40.652s

Fastest race laps

1	Aegerter	1m 43.463s
2	Cortese	1m 46.034s
3	Folger	1m 47.472s
4	Cardus	1m 47.520s
5	Zarco	1m 47.944s
6	Kallio	1m 48.077s
7	Vinales	1m 48.185s
8	West	1m 48.425s
9	Schrotter	1m 48.856s
10	De Angelis	1m 48.980s
11	Terol	1m 49.559s
12	Syahrin	1m 49.880s
13	Rabat	1m 49.881s
14	Luthi	1m 49.985s
15	Morbidelli	1m 50.264s
16	Simon	1m 50.449s
17	Pasini	1m 50.678s
18	Torres	1m 50.996s
19	Salom	1m 51.159s
20	Rea	1m 51.272s
21	Baldassarri	1m 51.427s
22	Nakagami	1m 51.716s
23	Corsi	1m 51.928s
24	Simeon	1m 52.151s
25	Ramos	1m 52.300s
26	Rossi	1m 52.438s
27	Nagashima	1m 52.976s
28	Herrin	1m 53.165s
29	Mulhauser	1m 53.929s
30	Lowes	1m 56.181s
31	Warokorn	1m 56.202s
32	Krummenacher	1m 56.458s
33	Pons	1m 57.779s
34	Shah	2m 02.630s

Championship Points

1	Rabat	157
2	Kallio	131
3	Vinales	109
4	Aegerter	71
5	Corsi	69
6	Luthi	61
7	Salom	60
8	West	58
9	Folger	47
10	Zarco	46
11	Lowes	33
12	Cortese	32
13	Schrotter	32
14	Simeon	31
15	De Angelis	29
16	Torres	23
17	Cardus	22
18	Simon	15
19	Morbidelli	15
20	Pasini	14
21	Baldassarri	12
22	Nakagami	11
23	Krummenacher	10
24	Pons	9
25	Syahrin	9
26	Rossi	7
27	Rea	5
28	Terol	2

Constructor Points

1	Kalex	195
2	Suter	114
3	Speed Up	78
4	Caterham Suter	46
5	Tech 3	41
6	Forward KLX	33

Moto3

RACE DISTANCE: 22 laps, 62.090 miles/99.924km · **RACE WEATHER:** Dry (air 19°C, humidity 70%, track 25°C)

Pos.	Rider	Nat.	No.	Entrant	Machine	Laps	Time & Speed
1	**Alex Marquez**	SPA	12	Estrella Galicia 0,0	Honda	22	38m 07.648s 97.7mph/ 157.2km/h)
2	**Alex Rins**	SPA	42	Estrella Galicia 0,0	Honda	22	38m 10.608s
3	**Miguel Oliveira**	POR	44	Mahindra Racing	Mahindra	22	38m 11.292s
4	**Alexis Masbou**	FRA	10	Ongetta-Rivacold	Honda	22	38m 23.998s
5	**Niccolo Antonelli**	ITA	23	Junior Team GO&FUN Moto3	KTM	22	38m 24.114s
6	**Efren Vazquez**	SPA	7	SaxoPrint-RTG	Honda	22	38m 24.135s
7	**Isaac Vinales**	SPA	32	Calvo Team	KTM	22	38m 24.179s
8	**Danny Kent**	GBR	52	Red Bull Husqvarna Ajo	Husqvarna	22	38m 24.207s
9	**Brad Binder**	RSA	41	Ambrogio Racing	Mahindra	22	38m 24.291s
10	**John McPhee**	GBR	17	SaxoPrint-RTG	Honda	22	38m 24.334s
11	**Jakub Kornfeil**	CZE	84	Calvo Team	KTM	22	38m 30.880s
12	**Jasper Iwema**	NED	13	KRP Abbink Racing	FTR KTM	22	38m 32.472s
13	**Matteo Ferrari**	ITA	3	San Carlo Team Italia	Mahindra	22	38m 33.341s
14	**Zulfahmi Khairuddin**	MAL	63	Ongetta-AirAsia	Honda	22	38m 33.358s
15	**Philipp Oettl**	GER	65	Interwetten Paddock Moto3	Kalex KTM	22	38m 33.422s
16	Bryan Schouten	NED	51	CIP	Mahindra	22	38m 33.569s
17	Andrea Locatelli	ITA	55	San Carlo Team Italia	Mahindra	22	38m 33.958s
18	Romano Fenati	ITA	5	SKY Racing Team VR46	KTM	22	38m 36.986s
19	Eric Granado	BRA	57	Calvo Team	KTM	22	38m 40.233s
20	Scott Deroue	NED	9	RW Racing GP	Kalex KTM	22	38m 46.414s
21	Arthur Sissis	AUS	61	Mahindra Racing	Mahindra	22	38m 54.578s
22	Jules Danilo	FRA	95	Ambrogio Racing	Mahindra	22	38m 54.765s
23	Thomas van Leeuwen	NED	71	71Workx.com Racing Team	Kalex KTM	22	38m 56.710s
24	Ana Carrasco	SPA	22	RW Racing GP	Kalex KTM	22	38m 59.917s
25	Livio Loi	BEL	11	Marc VDS Racing Team	Kalex KTM	22	39m 00.007s
26	Alessandro Tonucci	ITA	19	CIP	Mahindra	22	39m 18.252s
27	Gabriel Ramos	VEN	4	Kiefer Racing	Kalex KTM	22	39m 27.051s
28	Luca Grunwald	GER	43	Kiefer Racing	Kalex KTM	22	39m 56.367s
29	Hafiq Azmi	MAL	38	SIC-AJO	KTM	21	38m 15.759s
	Juanfran Guevara	SPA	58	Mapfre Aspar Team Moto3	Kalex KTM	21	DNF
	Karel Hanika	CZE	98	Red Bull KTM Ajo	KTM	17	DNF
	Niklas Ajo	FIN	31	Avant Tecno Husqvarna Ajo	Husqvarna	6	DNF
	Jack Miller	AUS	8	Red Bull KTM Ajo	KTM	1	DNF
	Enea Bastianini	ITA	33	Junior Team GO&FUN Moto3	KTM	0	DNS

Fastest lap: Romano Fenati, on lap 12, 1m 42.914s, 98.7mph/158.8km/h (record).

Previous lap record: Miguel Oliveira, POR (Mahindra), 1m 43.414s, 98.2mph/158.1km/h (2013).

Event best maximum speed: Jasper Iwema, 137.3mph/221.0km/h (free practice 1).

Qualifying

Weather: Dry

Air Temp: 18° **Track Temp:** 22°

Humidity: 72%

1	Miller	1m 42.240s
2	Marquez	1m 42.356s
3	Ajo	1m 42.430s
4	Masbou	1m 42.458s
5	Antonelli	1m 42.515s
6	Rins	1m 42.564s
7	Vinales	1m 42.579s
8	Hanika	1m 42.582s
9	Fenati	1m 42.594s
10	McPhee	1m 42.730s
11	Kent	1m 42.820s
12	Bastianini	1m 42.822s
13	Oliveira	1m 42.872s
14	Kornfeil	1m 42.914s
15	Vazquez	1m 42.948s
16	Binder	1m 43.058s
17	Iwema	1m 43.108s
18	Sissis	1m 43.176s
19	Bagnaia	1m 43.339s
20	Guevara	1m 43.393s
21	Deroue	1m 43.397s
22	Locatelli	1m 43.468s
23	Azmi	1m 43.552s
24	Ferrari	1m 43.629s
25	Oettl	1m 43.680s
26	Granado	1m 43.691s
27	Khairuddin	1m 43.794s
28	Tonucci	1m 43.810s
29	Schouten	1m 43.827s
30	Loi	1m 43.851s
31	Grunwald	1m 43.982s
32	Danilo	1m 44.514s
33	Carrasco	1m 45.077s
34	Van Leeuwen	1m 45.138s
35	Ramos	1m 45.943s

Fastest race laps

1	Fenati	1m 42.914s
2	Oliveira	1m 43.256s
3	Marquez	1m 43.306s
4	Vazquez	1m 43.334s
5	Vinales	1m 43.371s
6	Binder	1m 43.404s
7	Rins	1m 43.406s
8	McPhee	1m 43.425s
9	Hanika	1m 43.454s
10	Kent	1m 43.530s
11	Kornfeil	1m 43.566s
12	Iwema	1m 43.609s
13	Masbou	1m 43.641s
14	Antonelli	1m 43.656s
15	Tonucci	1m 43.693s
16	Azmi	1m 43.694s
17	Guevara	1m 43.808s
18	Ajo	1m 43.840s
19	Ferrari	1m 43.857s
20	Khairuddin	1m 43.884s
21	Schouten	1m 43.889s
22	Grunwald	1m 43.932s
23	Oettl	1m 44.018s
24	Locatelli	1m 44.029s
25	Granado	1m 44.381s
26	Deroue	1m 44.516s
27	Van Leeuwen	1m 44.537s
28	Danilo	1m 44.792s
29	Sissis	1m 44.933s
30	Carrasco	1m 45.321s
31	Loi	1m 45.382s
32	Ramos	1m 45.945s

Championship Points

1	Miller	117
2	Fenati	110
3	Marquez	110
4	Rins	107
5	Vazquez	102
6	Viñales	82
7	Masbou	63
8	Oliveira	53
9	Bastianini	45
10	Kornfeil	43
11	Bagnaia	42
12	McPhee	36
13	Ajo	35
14	Kent	35
15	Binder	29
16	Antonelli	18
17	Loi	17
18	Guevara	17
19	Hanika	16
20	Tonucci	15
21	Khairuddin	13
22	Oettl	6
23	Ferrari	5
24	Iwema	4

Constructor Points

1	KTM	181
2	Honda	162
3	Mahindra	62
4	Husqvarna	55
5	Kalex KTM	29
6	FTR KTM	4

FIM WORLD CHAMPIONSHIP · ROUND 9

GERMAN GRAND PRIX

SACHSENRING

Inset, left: The chase is on, as the fast men blast out of the pit lane.

Inset, below left: The LCR crew work furiously on Bradl's Honda on the grid. They would not have enough time to finish the job.
Photos: Gold & Goose

Inset, below right: Nine and counting for Marquez. He would run out of fingers at the same time as his winning streak was broken.
Photo: Martin Heath

Main: Bradl leads the tail-enders from the depleted starting grid.
Photo: Gold & Goose

Above: When push comes to shove: the MotoGP heavyweights jostle for track position.
Photo: Martin Heath

Centre, from left: Moto2 wild-card Nina Prinz made a debut at 31; Cal Crutchlow's Ducati experience would last just one season; Jorge Lorenzo remained enigmatic about his future.

Below right: Alvaro Bautista's erratic season continued, his job under threat from Scott Redding.
Photos: Gold & Goose

Below far right: The Ducatis of Dovizioso and Crutchlow do battle with Aleix Espargaro.
Photo: Martin Heath

"I T was like a motocross start, everyone with elbows. It was quite nice ... but a bit dangerous for every-body, when we pushed the brakes and don't stop because they are too cold." Marquez smiled his 'Joker' smile. As well he might. Even freakier circumstances than Assen had caused a new type of chaos, but with the same result. His ninth clear win. That it came after a heavy crash on day one made it all the more remarkable.

Early in FP1. Marquez had inadvertently tipped the lever up one gear in turn two and landed on his head after a loop-ing high-sider. It looked bad from the sidelines, but it barely dented his momentum.

Just as a fortnight before, race-day rain played havoc at the Sachsenring. The major outcome was unprecedented – more than half the MotoGP grid, including all of the front five rows bar one, started from the pit lane.

This opportunity is available for any rider. At the end of the warm-up lap, you dive into the pits, change bikes, then line up at end of the pit lane, waiting for the green light when the last rider on the grid has passed the track exit. But in nine-and-a-half years since flag-to-flag rules were introduced for rain-hit races, there had never been anything like this, and no system was in place to cope. Instead of respecting qualifying positions, the line up (riders managed five abreast in the narrow pit lane) was on a first-come, first-served basis. Pedrosa had taken the trouble to qualify second; now he found five riders in front of him.

This unfairness didn't seem to bother Race Director Mike Webb: "If a rider chooses to start from pit lane, he has aban-doned his grid position." The obvious danger did: "We got away with it, but we are working hard to avoid it happening like that again."

Unfairness aside, there was the question of the cold car-bon brakes and the cold slick tyres. Lorenzo had to swerve on to the track out of the pit lane to avoid running into the back of the gaggle in front of him, immediately ceding two places to compensate. Then the fast men had the task of overhauling and overtaking the back-markers, which in itself

can be perilous. The whole thing was spiced with risk and danger; highly enjoyable for the fans, and for the rider who came out best.

It was a fine demonstration of unintended consequences in action, an eventuality undreamt of when the flag-to-flag rules were introduced in 2005. But while it was a freakish occurrence, new rules revising the revised new rules would soon be forthcoming.

It was certainly an exciting way to close off the first half of the season, and an all-action feast for the usual capacity crowd of almost 90,000, many of whom had endured violent storms in their campsites during the preceding days, and most of whom would be further compensated by Germany's football World Cup victory in Brazil, relayed to the faithful on the giant track-side screens later that night.

With Rossi and Pedrosa now settled for the next two years, there was still lots of rumour-ridden contract talk: more key elements would fall into place shortly, with announce-ments at the World Ducati Week in Italy that Dovizioso and Crutchlow would be staying put in 2015, and a third fac-tory bike would be found for Iannone. Soon afterwards, all change: Crutchlow was leaving to replace Bradl at LCR Hon-da, and Iannone joining the factory team.

Bradl compounded his problems with a nightmare week-end, but was not the only satellite rider under threat. Bautis-ta was expected to have to give way to Redding for 2015.

Of the top guys, only Lorenzo remained in limbo. Eccen-tric as ever, he described how while Yamaha wanted him to match Rossi's two-year commitment, his bad results in 2014 suggested "it would be better for both of us" to go one year at a time. With a big-money Ducati deal still in the offing at the time, perhaps there was another reason to want to stay light on his feet.

There was contract talk of a different kind in Moto3, where the Marc VDS team issued a statement insisting that they had Jack Miller signed up for Moto2 for 2015 and 2016; the increasingly high-profile rider insisted, however, that there was no contract, "Nothing binding, anyway."

The Sachsenring is the shortest and most compact track of the year, with the first section "more like a go-kart track" (Marquez again); it terminates in a punishing run of eight successive left-handers, followed at last by an over-the-brow fast right that plunges into the Waterfall straight – the scene of many fast, cold-tyre crashes. A pre-event test session, delayed and abbreviated by the weather, put Bradl, Smith and Iannone around a changed layout, with temporary kerbing making the right-hander tighter and slower. It was a non-starter, however, simply (as Smith described it) requiring an even greater angle of lean, which made the existing problem even worse.

Bridgestone had planned to bring an asymmetric front for the same tests, but freighting problems meant that none had arrived. At this track in 2013, the company had ruled out this solution, because in past dual-compound-front tests riders hadn't liked the queasy feel. A different construction method had been used this time, a spokesman explained: "We are confident it will work better, but it needs to be tested before we can decide whether to introduce it." An alternate test venue was found two races later, after Brno.

Enough of Marquez's youngest-ever records: German woman racer Nina Prinz set an oldest-yet record in Moto2, making her debut as a wild-card at the age of 31 and generally keeping out of trouble. She explained that it had come a year later than she had wanted, "but last year there was an [upper] age limit, and this year not."

Mahindra gained a prestigious new customer, announcing on Sunday that the Aspar team would be switching to the Swiss-built Indian-owned bikes for the 2015 season.

The sidecars were present again, but the event was marred by a fatal accident in practice: German veteran Kurt Hock was critically injured and his passenger, Enrico Becker, mortally so after suspected brake failure at the bottom of

the Waterfall straight. The race went ahead, however, at the request of both team and family.

It was an uncomfortable reminder of the dangers of racing; another came on race day, with the memory that it was 45 years ago to the day that doomed British star Bill Ivy had lost his life on the original Sachsenring road circuit.

MOTOGP RACE – 30 laps

Marquez bounced back from his early crash, returning to pole after two races with a new record, having broken another of the few remaining 2008 qualifying tyre 'circuit best' laps, this one held by Stoner on a Ducati.

He led an all-Honda front row; multiple Sachsenring winner Pedrosa was alongside, then Bradl, with a first home front row for a German. Aleix Espargaro headed an all-Yamaha row two from a calm and confident Lorenzo, and Rossi.

Iannone was top Ducati and led row three, from Pol Espargaro and team-mate Smith, who had crashed four times in practice and would again in the race.

It had been dry throughout Sunday, but then with 20 minutes to MotoGP, heavy rain swept across the hillside, drenching the track, throwing tactics into turmoil and posing a tricky tyre conundrum.

The rain ceased, and while the track dried quickly, parts were still very wet. Most stuck with their wet bikes. Bradl took a different gamble, fitting slicks to his 'wet' bike on the grid. The problem was time, and the team ran out of it before adjusting the front forks to the correct setting. Thus he had a sort of hybrid, on slicks with carbon brakes, but soft suspension. Even so, perhaps conditions might play his way.

Or not. The other way turned out better. At the end of the warm-up lap, the rest of the front five rows dived into the pits to change to dry bikes. Positions on this impromptu new

Above: Hondas on tiptoe: Marquez fends off Pedrosa once more on the treacherous track.

Top right: Breakthrough for Aegerter, with a long-awaited first win from a first pole.

Above right: Corsi chases Rabat in the battle for third. The order would be reversed at the flag.

Right: Old pals act: Brad Binder was delighted with his first podium, beaten by Miller's "perfect last lap". Masbou was happy to be top Honda, even if he didn't show it.

Below right: Binder's Mahindra leads Marquez's Honda and Kent's Husqvarna.

Photos: Gold & Goose

grid went to whoever got there first, or pushed in hardest, with five bikes across at the front facing a narrowing pit lane: Dovizioso, Rossi, Aleix Espargaro, Iannone and Marquez up front. There would be further shuffling before the first apex.

Bradl, of course, led away, opening up on the back-rows gaggle; Laverty had the unusual experience of holding second on lap one, soon lost to a charging Petrucci. Soon afterwards, Laverty crashed out. Aoyama, Abraham (both also having started on slicks), Edwards, di Meglio, Barbera and second PBM rider Parkes filled the rest of the front positions, for a while.

Marquez came out of the unceremonious pit-lane send-off best, after repassing chief elbower Rossi into turn one as the Italian ran wide, caught out by cold brakes. As was Lorenzo, who had to swerve on to the track early to avoid hitting riders ahead; he held up his hand to drop two places in recompense.

Pedrosa was right with Marquez by the end of the lap; Rossi was next, having repassed Aleix Espargaro; Lorenzo was another place down, behind Smith.

It was still tiptoe-wet at the bottom of the hill, with riders wobbling through that section more or less tentatively, and it was pretty confusing for a while, mid-field. Petrucci in particular demonstrated great daring through the slow-drying last corners.

Bradl was in dire straits. His advantage over Marquez had been cut to less than eight seconds in the first lap alone, and his run up front lasted only six of the 30 laps. From there, he would keep on dropping back, ending up out of the points in 16th, after being passed by Petrucci in the closing stages. A small tactical error had been compounded by events. "I am speechless," he said, once again.

The factory Hondas were firmly in control, Marquez circulating steadily, Pedrosa matching him by tenths, but never quite close enough. With ten of the short laps to go, the gap was over a second for the first time. Marquez claimed fastest lap to underline win number nine.

Rossi succumbed to Lorenzo on lap nine and lost touch when he took one more lap to get by Bradl. The Spaniard

was back to his metronomic best for his first podium in three races; Rossi was fourth.

Iannone was next and top Duke: like all Open riders, he had used the softest rear tyre, the first time it had been employed successfully in a race.

Aleix was chasing manfully throughout; there was much action behind for seventh as slow starters on fast bikes came through to join an already lively fight between the factory Ducati riders.

Dovizioso had inadvertently left his pit-lane limiter on after the start and lost places; then he came under attack from a feisty Crutchlow, delighted at last to find himself on the pace. At the same time, Bautista and Pol Espargaro had finally got up to speed and through the Open bikes; both caught the red bikes in the last two laps. Pol took seventh ahead of Dovi, and Bautista ninth from Crutchlow, who had battled with front grip problems in the later stages.

Redding had been engaged with this group and finished a lone 11th, comfortably top production Honda; the next two – Aoyama and Abraham – disputed 12th in that order to the end. Hayden's RCV was next, having picked up speed and positions in the closing laps. Lack of confidence and "so much prudence" had dropped him to last in the early laps.

Petrucci took the last point, a second ahead of the downcast Bradl, now in danger of losing 16th to Hernandez.

Smith had a fifth crash of the weekend, but remounted for an eventual 19th.

MOTO2 RACE – 29 laps

The peculiar little track produced a slightly peculiar, if not entirely unexpected, result as Aegerter finally took the step from promising to delivering. He won his first grand prix from his first pole position, in fighting style. The Swiss rider, in his eighth full season, had been knocking on the door for most of 2014, but until now had never quite been able to reach the handle.

Kallio had looked dominant in qualifying; and even after Aegerter deposed him from pole, it appeared that it was only

eni MOTORRAD GRAND PRIX DEUTSCHLAND

Sachsenring 2014

because he'd been following Rabat. "I can do that time on my own," he insisted.

Kallio and Rabat completed row one; 2013's surprise Sachsenring winner, Jordi Torres, led the second from impressive rookie Morbidelli and old campaigner Corsi.

Some fast men were out of sorts: Vinales down in 13th and team-mate Salom 24th.

The qualifying pattern was repeated in the race. Aegerter led lap one, Kallio took over and Torres briefly assumed second next time around, but by lap four Corsi was ahead of the Spaniard, and the first two were already pulling clear.

They went on like this for the rest of the race: Aegerter poised on Kallio's back wheel, seldom more than half a second adrift. The showdown started with three laps to go, when the Suter rider finally pounced to lead over the line for the first time. Kallio counterattacked at once – too soon, he later admitted. His attempted escape on the penultimate lap came to naught as Aegerter closed again, and he pounced for a second and final time into turn 12 after getting a flying drive on to the Waterfall back straight.

There was just 0.091 second in it over the line.

Corsi had led a four-bike battle for second, but Rabat took over again with ten laps to go. It looked as though he might escape, but the Italian pegged him back to retake the last rostrum place on the final lap.

Close behind, Vinales had come through impressively all race and finally had prevailed over outstandingly persistent rookie Morbidelli.

De Angelis crashed out after losing ground in the next pack. By the end, Krummenacher had snatched seventh from Pasini and Luthi. Simeon and Cardus battled over tenth to the finish, the former taking the place by just over a tenth.

Herrin retired; Caterham team-mate Zarco walked away from a dramatic crash that turned his bike into a fireball.

Rabat's early domination had been broken, but his midway title lead was still strong: 170 to team-mate Kallio's 151.

MOTO3 RACE – 17 laps

Moto3 qualifying got the worst of fickle weather, with a shower at the mid-point. Among those yet to secure a decent position were title contenders Vazquez (17th) and Fenati (25th), along with Oliveira (19th). Miller, dominant throughout, had already secured his fifth pole, with the Hondas of Masbou and Marquez alongside.

Hanika led row two from the on-form Kent and Binder's customer Mahindra; being Moto3 and being the Sachsenring, the margins were very narrow, and they would continue to be so in the race.

Miller led away while Rins crashed out on the second corner after a collision.

Marquez headed the pursuit, Masbou in his tracks. Together with Kent and Binder, they made a breakaway quartet.

Places changed frequently, except for first. That belonged to Jack, if only by inches at times. Before half-distance, however, Binder was second, and over the last four laps the pair drew away. Several lunges by Binder came to naught, and what he described as "Jack's perfect last lap" secured a fourth victory of the year for the rising Australian.

Close behind, Masbou prevailed in the final scramble, from Marquez and Kent.

Vazquez made his way through to sixth, from team-mate McPhee; but Fenati suffered a second race crash and worryingly was unable to get to his feet for a while.

Sixth to 13th was covered by just over a second, Vinales recovering from fever to head Ferrari, Guevara, Kornfeil, Oettl and Sissis, the Australian's first points of the year.

Lead Mahindra rider Oliveira had forged through from 19th to sixth at the front of the chase pack, only to be knocked off by the crashing Hanika.

There was some relief in the title chase for Miller, with his closest rivals not scoring well, and Fenati and Rins not at all.

OFFICIAL TIMEKEEPER TISSOT

SACHSENRING GP CIRCUIT

30 laps
Length: 3.671 km / 3,259 miles
Width: 12m

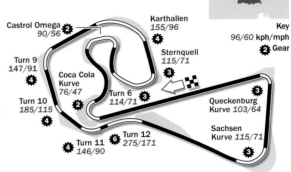

Key
96/60 kph/mph
2 Gear

Castrol Omega 90/56
Karthallen 155/96
Sternquell 115/71
Turn 9 147/91
Coca Cola Kurve 76/47
Turn 6 114/71
Queckenburg Kurve 103/64
Turn 10 185/115
Turn 11 146/90
Turn 12 275/171
Sachsen Kurve 115/71

eni MOTORRAD
GRAND PRIX DEUTSCHLAND

11-13 JULY, 2014

MotoGP

RACE DISTANCE: 30 laps, 68.432 miles/110.130km · RACE WEATHER: Wet-Dry (air 21°C, humidity 66%, track 27°C)

Pos.	Rider	Nat.	No.	Entrant	Machine	Tyres	Race tyre choice	Laps	Time & speed
1	**Marc Marquez**	SPA	93	Repsol Honda Team	Honda RC213V	B	F: Medium/R: Medium	30	41m 47.664s 98.2mph/ 158.1km/h
2	**Dani Pedrosa**	SPA	26	Repsol Honda Team	Honda RC213V	B	F: Medium/R: Medium	30	41m 49.130s
3	**Jorge Lorenzo**	SPA	99	Movistar Yamaha MotoGP	Yamaha YZR-M1	B	F: Medium/R: Medium	30	41m 57.981s
4	**Valentino Rossi**	ITA	46	Movistar Yamaha MotoGP	Yamaha YZR-M1	B	F: Medium/R: Medium	30	42m 06.858s
5	**Andrea Iannone**	ITA	29	Pramac Racing	Ducati Desmosedici	B	F: Soft/R: Soft	30	42m 11.173s
6	**Aleix Espargaro**	SPA	41	NGM Forward Racing	Forward Yamaha	B	F: Soft/R: Soft	30	42m 15.473s
7	**Pol Espargaro**	SPA	44	Monster Yamaha Tech 3	Yamaha YZR-M1	B	F: Medium/R: Medium	30	42m 20.917s
8	**Andrea Dovizioso**	ITA	4	Ducati Team	Ducati Desmosedici	B	F: Soft/R: Soft	30	42m 21.532s
9	**Alvaro Bautista**	SPA	19	GO&FUN Honda Gresini	Honda RC213V	B	F: Medium/R: Medium	30	42m 21.895s
10	**Cal Crutchlow**	GBR	35	Ducati Team	Ducati Desmosedici	B	F: Soft/R: Soft	30	42m 22.340s
11	**Scott Redding**	GBR	45	GO&FUN Honda Gresini	Honda RCV1000R	B	F: Hard/R: Soft	30	42m 25.408s
12	**Hiroshi Aoyama**	JPN	7	Drive M7 Aspar	Honda RCV1000R	B	F: Soft/R: Soft	30	42m 32.682s
13	**Karel Abraham**	CZE	17	Cardion AB Motoracing	Honda RCV1000R	B	F: Soft/R: Soft	30	42m 32.841s
14	**Nicky Hayden**	USA	69	Drive M7 Aspar	Honda RCV1000R	B	F: Medium/R: Soft	30	42m 34.340s
15	**Danilo Petrucci**	ITA	9	Octo IodaRacing Team	ART	B	F: Medium/R: Soft	30	42m 40.433s
16	Stefan Bradl	GER	6	LCR Honda MotoGP	Honda RC213V	B	F: Soft/R: Medium	30	42m 41.553s
17	Yonny Hernandez	COL	68	Energy T.I. Pramac Racing	Ducati Desmosedici	B	F: Soft/R: Soft	30	42m 42.140s
18	Hector Barbera	SPA	8	Avintia Racing	Avintia	B	F: Soft/R: Soft	30	42m 43.879s
19	Bradley Smith	GBR	38	Monster Yamaha Tech 3	Yamaha YZR-M1	B	F: Medium/R: Medium	30	42m 43.957s
20	Colin Edwards	USA	5	NGM Forward Racing	Forward Yamaha	B	F: Soft/R: Soft	30	42m 51.747s
21	Broc Parkes	AUS	23	Paul Bird Motorsport	PBM-ART	B	F: Medium/R: Soft	30	42m 58.592s
22	Mike di Meglio	FRA	63	Avintia Racing	Avintia	B	F: Soft/R: Soft	30	43m 07.639s
	Michael Laverty	GBR	70	Paul Bird Motorsport	PBM-ART	B	F: Medium/R: Soft	17	DNF-crash

Fastest lap: Marc Marquez, on lap 21, 1m 22.037s, 100.0mph/161.0km/h.

Lap record: Dani Pedrosa, SPA (Honda), 1m 21.846s, 100.332mph/161.469km/h (2011).

Event best maximum speed: Dani Pedrosa, 183.7mph/295.6km/h (race).

Qualifying

Weather: Dry
Air Temp: 19° **Track Temp:** 28°
Humidity: 70%

1	Marquez	1m 20.937s
2	Pedrosa	1m 21.233s
3	Bradl	1m 21.340s
4	A. Espargaro	1m 21.376s
5	Lorenzo	1m 21.508s
6	Rossi	1m 21.651s
7	Iannone	1m 21.679s
8	P. Espargaro	1m 21.771s
9	Smith	1m 21.794s
10	Bautista	1m 21.906s
11	Dovizioso	1m 22.120s
12	Hayden	1m 22.647s
13	Hernandez	1m 22.411s
14	Redding	1m 22.436s
15	Crutchlow	1m 22.529s
16	Aoyama	1m 22.659s
17	Abraham	1m 22.778s
18	Laverty	1m 22.845s
19	Edwards	1m 22.888s
20	Barbera	1m 23.029s
21	Di Meglio	1m 23.423s
22	Parkes	1m 23.428s
23	Petrucci	1m 23.484s

Fastest race laps

1	Marquez	1m 22.037s
2	Pedrosa	1m 22.162s
3	Lorenzo	1m 22.284s
4	Rossi	1m 22.513s
5	P. Espargaro	1m 22.670s
6	A. Espargaro	1m 22.688s
7	Iannone	1m 22.718s
8	Smith	1m 22.803s
9	Bautista	1m 22.869s
10	Crutchlow	1m 23.038s
11	Dovizioso	1m 23.070s
12	Redding	1m 23.153s
13	Hayden	1m 23.335s
14	Laverty	1m 23.347s
15	Abraham	1m 23.446s
16	Edwards	1m 23.538s
17	Barbera	1m 23.659s
18	Aoyama	1m 23.665s
19	Hernandez	1m 23.683s
20	Petrucci	1m 24.012s
21	Parkes	1m 24.243s
22	Bradl	1m 24.318s
23	Di Meglio	1m 24.731s

Championship Points

1	Marquez	225
2	Pedrosa	148
3	Rossi	141
4	Dovizioso	99
5	Lorenzo	97
6	A. Espargaro	77
7	P. Espargaro	67
8	Iannone	62
9	Bradl	56
10	Bautista	50
11	Smith	48
12	Redding	33
13	Hayden	29
14	Crutchlow	28
15	Aoyama	28
16	Hernandez	27
17	Abraham	18
18	Edwards	8
19	Pirro	7
20	Parkes	6
21	Petrucci	4
22	Barbera	2

Constructor Points

1	Honda	225
2	Yamaha	154
3	Ducati	105
4	Forward Yamaha	77
5	PBM	6
6	ART	4
7	Avintia	2

Grid Order	1	2	3	4	5	6	7	8	9	10	11	12	13	14	15	16	17	18	19	20	21	22	23	24	25	26	27	28	29	30	
93 MARQUEZ	6	6	6	6	6	93	93	93	93	93	93	93	93	93	93	93	93	93	93	93	93	93	93	93	93	93	93	93	93	93	1
26 PEDROSA	70	9	9	93	93	6	26	26	26	26	26	26	26	26	26	26	26	26	26	26	26	26	26	26	26	26	26	26	26	26	2
6 BRADL	9	70	93	26	26	26	6	6	6	99	99	99	99	99	99	99	99	99	99	99	99	99	99	99	99	99	99	99	99	99	3
41 A. ESPARGARO	7	17	70	9	9	9	46	46	99	6	46	46	46	46	46	46	46	46	46	46	46	46	46	46	46	46	46	46	46	46	4
99 LORENZO	17	7	26	7	7	7	9	99	46	46	29	29	29	29	29	29	29	29	29	29	29	29	29	29	29	29	29	29	29	29	5
46 ROSSI	5	5	7	70	46	46	99	29	29	29	6	6	6	41	41	41	41	41	41	41	41	41	41	41	41	41	41	41	41	41	6
29 IANNONE	63	93	17	17	70	99	7	9	7	41	41	41	41	6	4	4	4	4	4	4	4	4	4	35	35	35	44	44	44	44	7
44 P. ESPARGARO	8	63	63	46	17	29	29	7	41	7	4	4	4	35	35	35	35	35	35	35	35	4	4	44	35	35	4	4			8
38 SMITH	23	8	5	29	99	17	41	41	9	7	35	35	35	6	45	45	45	45	45	44	44	44	44	4	4	4	35	19			9
19 BAUTISTA	93	26	46	63	29	41	17	35	35	35	7	45	45	45	6	6	44	44	44	45	45	19	19	19	19	19	19	35			10
4 DOVIZIOSO	26	23	8	41	41	4	4	4	4	45	45	45	7	7	7	19	19	19	19	45	45	45	45	45	45	45	45	45			11
69 HAYDEN	41	46	38	99	4	35	35	17	45	9	17	9	17	44	44	44	7	7	7	7	7	7	7	7	7	7	7	7			12
68 HERNANDEZ	46	41	41	5	35	70	45	45	17	17	9	17	9	17	19	7	17	17	17	17	17	17	17	17	17	17	17	17			13
45 REDDING	38	38	23	4	45	45	70	70	70	19	19	44	44	19	17	17	17	17	6	6	6	6	69	69	69	69	69	69			14
35 CRUTCHLOW	29	99	29	35	63	63	19	19	19	44	44	19	19	9	9	9	9	6	69	69	69	69	6	9	9	9	9	9			15
7 AOYAMA	99	29	99	45	5	19	44	44	44	44	70	70	70	70	70	70	69	69	9	9	9	9	9	6	6	6	6	6			
17 ABRAHAM	35	4	4	8	19	44	63	63	63	69	69	69	69	69	69	69	68	68	68	68	68	68	68	68	68	68	68	68			
70 LAVERTY	45	45	45	23	8	69	68	68	68	68	68	68	68	68	68	68	5	5	5	5	5	5	5	5	5	5					
5 EDWARDS	4	35	35	44	44	68	69	69	69	5	5	5	5	5	5	23	5	5	38	38	38	38	38	38	38	38					
8 BARBERA	68	68	68	19	68	8	8	8	8	63	63	63	63	63	63	5	38	38	5	5	5	5	5	5							
63 DI MEGLIO	44	44	44	68	23	23	23	23	23	23	23	23	23	5	63	63	63	63	23	23	23	23	23	23	23	23	23	23			
23 PARKES	19	19	19	69	69	5	5	5	5	38	38	38	38	38	38	38	38	63	63	63	63	63	63	63	63	63	63	63			
9 PETRUCCI	69	69	69	38	38	38	38	38	38	38	38	38	38	38	38	38															

Moto2

RACE DISTANCE: 29 laps, 66.151 miles/106.459km · RACE WEATHER: Dry (air 22°C, humidity 43%, track 32°C)

Pos.Rider	Nat.	No.	Entrant	Machine	Laps	Time & Speed
1 Dominique Aegerter	SWI	77	Technomag carXpert	Suter	29	41m 12.461s 96.3mph/ 155.0km/h
2 Mika Kallio	FIN	36	Marc VDS Racing Team	Kalex	29	41m 12.552s
3 Simone Corsi	ITA	3	NGM Forward Racing	Kalex	29	41m 22.975s
4 Esteve Rabat	SPA	53	Marc VDS Racing Team	Kalex	29	41m 23.127s
5 Maverick Vinales	SPA	40	Paginas Amarillas HP 40	Kalex	29	41m 23.879s
6 Franco Morbidelli	ITA	21	Italtrans Racing Team	Kalex	29	41m 26.561s
7 Randy Krummenacher	SWI	4	Octo IodaRacing Team	Suter	29	41m 34.344s
8 Mattia Pasini	ITA	54	NGM Forward Racing	Kalex	29	41m 34.437s
9 Thomas Luthi	SWI	12	Interwetten Paddock Moto2	Suter	29	41m 34.510s
10 Xavier Simeon	BEL	19	Federal Oil Gresini Moto2	Suter	29	41m 38.971s
11 Ricard Cardus	SPA	88	Tech 3	Tech 3	29	41m 39.127s
12 Marcel Schrotter	GER	23	Tech 3	Tech 3	29	41m 45.505s
13 Louis Rossi	FRA	96	SAG Team	Kalex	29	41m 45.881s
14 Luis Salom	SPA	39	Paginas Amarillas HP 40	Kalex	29	41m 49.654s
15 Axel Pons	SPA	49	AGR Team	Kalex	29	41m 50.288s
16 Julian Simon	SPA	60	Italtrans Racing Team	Kalex	29	41m 50.572s
17 Anthony West	AUS	95	QMMF Racing Team	Speed Up	29	41m 52.433s
18 Hafizh Syahrin	MAL	55	Petronas Raceline Malaysia	Kalex	29	41m 55.065s
19 Nicolas Terol	SPA	18	Mapfre Aspar Team Moto2	Suter	29	41m 56.107s
20 Sam Lowes	GBR	22	Speed Up	Speed Up	29	41m 58.493s
21 Takaaki Nakagami	JPN	30	IDEMITSU Honda Team Asia	Kalex	29	42m 00.936s
22 Tetsuta Nagashima	JPN	45	Teluru Team JiR Webike	TSR	29	42m 05.293s
23 Roman Ramos	SPA	97	QMMF Racing Team	Speed Up	29	42m 15.738s
24 Robin Mulhauser	SWI	70	Technomag carXpert	Suter	29	42m 15.895s
25 Gino Rea	GBR	8	AGT REA Racing	Suter	29	42m 27.781s
26 Thitipong Warokorn	THA	10	APH PTT The Pizza SAG	Kalex	28	41m 23.540s
27 Nina Prinz	GER	33	QMMF Racing Team	Speed Up	28	41m 24.674s
28 Azlan Shah	MAL	25	IDEMITSU Honda Team Asia	Kalex	27	41m 16.004s
Alex de Angelis	RSM	15	Tasca Racing Moto2	Suter	22	DNF
Sandro Cortese	GER	11	Dynavolt Intact GP	Kalex	22	DNF
Johann Zarco	FRA	5	AirAsia Caterham	Caterham Suter	14	DNF
Josh Herrin	USA	2	AirAsia Caterham	Caterham Suter	12	DNF
Jonas Folger	GER	94	AGR Team	Kalex	8	DNF
Lorenzo Baldassarri	ITA	7	Gresini Moto2	Suter	6	DNF
Jordi Torres	SPA	81	Mapfre Aspar Team Moto2	Suter	4	DNF

Fastest lap: Mika Kallio, on lap 14, 1m 24.902s, 96.7mph/155.6km/h.
Lap record: Julian Simon, SPA (Kalex), 1m 24.809s, 96.8mph/155.8km/h (2013).
Event best maximum speed: Mika Kallio, 157.8mph/254.0km/h (free practice 3).

Qualifying
Weather: Dry
Air Temp: 19° Track Temp: 32°
Humidity: 67%

1	Aegerter	1m 24.761s
2	Kallio	1m 24.885s
3	Rabat	1m 25.032s
4	Torres	1m 25.108s
5	Morbidelli	1m 25.118s
6	Corsi	1m 25.132s
7	Zarco	1m 25.142s
8	Luthi	1m 25.188s
9	De Angelis	1m 25.240s
10	Krummenacher	1m 25.272s
11	Simeon	1m 25.484s
12	Baldassarri	1m 25.512s
13	Vinales	1m 25.517s
14	Schrotter	1m 25.545s
15	Simon	1m 25.592s
16	Cardus	1m 25.620s
17	Syahrin	1m 25.675s
18	Pasini	1m 25.704s
19	Terol	1m 25.707s
20	Folger	1m 25.715s
21	Cortese	1m 25.730s
22	Rossi	1m 25.743s
23	Pons	1m 25.754s
24	Salom	1m 25.867s
25	West	1m 25.904s
26	Lowes	1m 25.994s
27	Rea	1m 26.087s
28	Nakagami	1m 26.109s
29	Shah	1m 26.153s
30	Herrin	1m 26.602s
31	Ramos	1m 26.636s
32	Nagashima	1m 26.689s
33	Mulhauser	1m 26.763s
34	Warokorn	1m 28.281s
35	Prinz	1m 28.739s

Fastest race laps

1	Kallio	1m 24.902s
2	Aegerter	1m 24.907s
3	Vinales	1m 24.985s
4	Rabat	1m 25.070s
5	Corsi	1m 25.180s
6	Morbidelli	1m 25.240s
7	Cortese	1m 25.410s
8	Pasini	1m 25.428s
9	Zarco	1m 25.462s
10	Krummenacher	1m 25.492s
11	Baldassarri	1m 25.562s
12	De Angelis	1m 25.562s
13	Luthi	1m 25.583s
14	Cardus	1m 25.649s
15	Torres	1m 25.695s
16	Salom	1m 25.716s
17	Simeon	1m 25.721s
18	Rossi	1m 25.732s
19	Simon	1m 25.738s
20	West	1m 25.795s
21	Schrotter	1m 25.927s
22	Pons	1m 25.931s
23	Folger	1m 26.078s
24	Lowes	1m 26.110s
25	Nakagami	1m 26.129s
26	Terol	1m 26.180s
27	Syahrin	1m 26.196s
28	Nagashima	1m 26.311s
29	Rea	1m 26.507s
30	Mulhauser	1m 26.756s
31	Ramos	1m 26.851s
32	Herrin	1m 27.211s
33	Shah	1m 27.233s
34	Warokorn	1m 27.583s
35	Prinz	1m 28.049s

Championship Points

1	Rabat	170
2	Kallio	151
3	Vinales	120
4	Aegerter	96
5	Corsi	85
6	Luthi	68
7	Salom	62
8	West	58
9	Folger	47
10	Zarco	46
11	Simeon	37
12	Schrotter	36
13	Lowes	33
14	Cortese	32
15	De Angelis	29
16	Cardus	27
17	Morbidelli	25
18	Torres	23
19	Pasini	22
20	Krummenacher	19
21	Simon	15
22	Baldassarri	12
23	Nakagami	11
24	Pons	10
25	Rossi	10
26	Syahrin	9
27	Rea	5
28	Terol	2

Constructor Points

1	Kalex	215
2	Suter	139
3	Speed Up	78
4	Caterham Suter	46
5	Tech 3	46
6	Forward KLX	33

Moto3

RACE DISTANCE: 27 laps, 61.588 miles/99.117km · RACE WEATHER: Dry (air 21°C, humidity 45%, track 31°C)

Pos. Rider	Nat.	No.	Entrant	Machine	Laps	Time & Speed
1 Jack Miller	AUS	8	Red Bull KTM Ajo	KTM	27	39m 26.927s 93.6mph/ 150.7km/h
2 Brad Binder	RSA	41	Ambrogio Racing	Mahindra	27	39m 27.107s
3 Alexis Masbou	FRA	10	Ongetta-Rivacold	Honda	27	39m 28.046s
4 Alex Marquez	SPA	12	Estrella Galicia 0,0	Honda	27	39m 28.107s
5 Danny Kent	GBR	52	Red Bull Husqvarna Ajo	Husqvarna	27	39m 28.217s
6 Efren Vazquez	SPA	7	SaxoPrint-RTG	Honda	27	39m 53.158s
7 John McPhee	GBR	17	SaxoPrint-RTG	Honda	27	39m 53.263s
8 Isaac Vinales	SPA	32	Calvo Team	KTM	27	39m 53.401s
9 Matteo Ferrari	ITA	3	San Carlo Team Italia	Mahindra	27	39m 53.510s
10 Juanfran Guevara	SPA	58	Mapfre Aspar Team Moto3	Kalex KTM	27	39m 53.662s
11 Jakub Kornfeil	CZE	84	Calvo Team	KTM	27	39m 53.800s
12 Philipp Oettl	GER	65	Interwetten Paddock Moto3	Kalex KTM	27	39m 53.936s
13 Arthur Sissis	AUS	61	Mahindra Racing	Mahindra	27	39m 54.232s
14 Eric Granado	BRA	57	Calvo Team	KTM	27	39m 57.011s
15 Enea Bastianini	ITA	33	Junior Team GO&FUN Moto3	KTM	27	40m 12.052s
16 Alessandro Tonucci	ITA	19	CIP	Mahindra	27	40m 12.466s
17 Jules Danilo	FRA	95	Ambrogio Racing	Mahindra	27	40m 12.952s
18 Hafiq Azmi	MAL	38	SIC-AJO	KTM	27	40m 13.037s
19 Luca Grunwald	GER	43	Kiefer Racing	Kalex KTM	27	40m 23.714s
20 Ana Carrasco	SPA	22	RW Racing GP	Kalex KTM	27	40m 24.076s
21 Maximilian Kappler	GER	97	SaxoPrint RTG	FTR	27	40m 36.239s
22 Gabriel Rodrigo	ARG	91	Avant Tecno Husqvarna Ajo	Husqvarna	26	39m 41.056s
23 Kevin Hanus	GER	86	Fai Rent-A-Jet	Honda	26	39m 44.682s
Niccolo Antonelli	ITA	23	Junior Team GO&FUN Moto3	KTM	24	DNF
Miguel Oliveira	POR	44	Mahindra Racing	Mahindra	19	DNF
Karel Hanika	CZE	98	Red Bull KTM Ajo	KTM	19	DNF
Andrea Locatelli	ITA	55	San Carlo Team Italia	Mahindra	15	DNF
Livio Loi	BEL	11	Marc VDS Racing Team	KTM	13	DNF
Gabriel Ramos	VEN	4	Kiefer Racing	Kalex KTM	12	DNF
Romano Fenati	ITA	5	SKY Racing Team VR46	KTM	3	DNF
Zulfahmi Khairuddin	MAL	63	Ongetta-AirAsia	Honda	3	DNF
Scott Deroue	NED	9	RW Racing GP	Kalex KTM	1	DNF
Bryan Schouten	NED	51	CIP	Mahindra	1	DNF
Alex Rins	SPA	42	Estrella Galicia 0,0	Honda	0	DNF

Fastest lap: Brad Binder, on lap 8, 1m 26.877s, 94.5mph/152.1km/h(record).
Previous lap record: Luis Salom, SPA (KTM), 1m 27.183s, 94.1mph/151.5km/h (2013).
Event best maximum speed: Efren Vazquez, 133.5mph/214.8km/h (race).

Qualifying
Weather: Dry
Air Temp: 15° Track Temp: 23°
Humidity: 88%

1	Miller	1m 26.997s
2	Masbou	1m 27.106s
3	Marquez	1m 27.143s
4	Hanika	1m 27.357s
5	Kent	1m 27.357s
6	Binder	1m 27.453s
7	Rins	1m 27.585s
8	Granado	1m 27.603s
9	Guevara	1m 27.673s
10	Bastianini	1m 27.752s
11	Oettl	1m 27.770s
12	Antonelli	1m 27.853s
13	Khairuddin	1m 27.885s
14	Ferrari	1m 27.926s
15	Tonucci	1m 27.955s
16	Vinales	1m 27.970s
17	Vazquez	1m 27.981s
18	Kornfeil	1m 28.013s
19	Oliveira	1m 28.054s
20	Locatelli	1m 28.113s
21	Gunwald	1m 28.224s
22	Sissis	1m 28.370s
23	Azmi	1m 28.414s
24	Schouten	1m 28.439s
25	Fenati	1m 28.463s
26	Bagnaia	1m 28.531s
27	Rodrigo	1m 28.569s
28	McPhee	1m 28.770s
29	Loi	1m 29.099s
30	Kappler	1m 29.100s
31	Danilo	1m 29.192s
32	Carrasco	1m 29.264s
33	Deroue	1m 29.398s
34	Hanus	1m 30.571s
35	Ramos	1m 30.873s

Fastest race laps

1	Binder	1m 26.877s
2	Kent	1m 27.104s
3	Miller	1m 27.178s
4	Marquez	1m 27.186s
5	Masbou	1m 27.235s
6	Oliveira	1m 27.441s
7	Fenati	1m 27.503s
8	McPhee	1m 27.626s
9	Kornfeil	1m 27.838s
10	Vazquez	1m 27.872s
11	Hanika	1m 27.884s
12	Oettl	1m 27.888s
13	Guevara	1m 27.911s
14	Vinales	1m 27.931s
15	Antonelli	1m 27.960s
16	Bastianini	1m 27.973s
17	Sissis	1m 28.006s
18	Ferrari	1m 28.027s
19	Granado	1m 28.041s
20	Locatelli	1m 28.141s
21	Tonucci	1m 28.304s
22	Khairuddin	1m 28.477s
23	Grunwald	1m 28.650s
24	Danilo	1m 28.674s
25	Kappler	1m 28.740s
26	Azmi	1m 28.801s
27	Ramos	1m 28.817s
28	Carrasco	1m 28.979s
29	Rodrigo	1m 29.091s
30	Loi	1m 29.784s
31	Hanus	1m 30.700s

Championship Points

1	Miller	142
2	Marquez	123
3	Vazquez	112
4	Fenati	110
5	Rins	107
6	Vinales	90
7	Masbou	79
8	Oliveira	53
9	Binder	49
10	Kornfeil	48
11	Bastianini	46
12	Kent	46
13	McPhee	45
14	Bagnaia	42
15	Ajo	35
16	Guevara	23
17	Antonelli	18
18	Loi	17
19	Hanika	16
20	Tonucci	15
21	Khairuddin	13
22	Ferrari	12
23	Oettl	10
24	Iwema	4
25	Sissis	3
26	Granado	2

Constructor Points

1	KTM	206
2	Honda	178
3	Mahindra	82
4	Husqvarna	66
5	Kalex KTM	35
6	FTR KTM	4

Main: Marquez bided his time, then ran away.

Inset below: Ten out of ten for the defending champion.

Inset bottom: Rossi, Dovizioso, Marquez and Lorenzo head out on to the infield in front of the near empty grandstand.

Photos: Gold & Goose

FIM WORLD CHAMPIONSHIP · ROUND 10

INDIANAPOLIS GRAND PRIX

INDIANAPOLIS MOTOR SPEEDWAY

Above: The family that races together stays together. The full Hayden clan were at the Speedway to promote Earl's autobiography.

Above right: Camouflaged Colin: Edwards announced his retirement, but hoped to make a year-end farewell appearance at Valencia.

Top: Room for one more? Marquez makes his own space in a thrilling battle for the lead.

Centre, from top: Wayne Rainey with Yamaha's Bob Starr; Dovizioso is congratulated by Ducati's Dall'Igna after qualifying second; Leon Camier impressed on Hayden's Honda.

Right: Crutchlow needed all his Ducati's horsepower to defeat Redding's production Honda.

Photos: Gold & Goose

DWARFED by the banked speedway, the Indianapolis infield has always been a poor relation. For the 2014 season, however, much had been bestowed, at considerable expense, on the MotoGP circuit, following consultations with Dorna and the riders' Safety Commission. The IMS could bask in the riders' gratitude; while the changes demonstrated an impressive commitment to MotoGP, considering that this was the final year of the circuit's current contract.

In truth, the alterations changed the track from unpopular to merely uninspiring, or perhaps a little on the right side of that. But the most complained-about aspect had been eliminated. A mix of three (or four, depending on how you counted them) different surfaces and lots of bumps had been replaced by a full resurface of the infield section.

At the same time, three corner sets had been reprofiled to make them more flowing, subtracting 46 metres. The first and last corner complexes, plus turns seven and eight had been eased. The aim was to create more overtaking opportunities, though that was debatable. It certainly raised the average speed, by a whopping 4.9km/h, the lap time almost eight seconds quicker, and the run on to the long main straight starting at least one gear higher.

The riders preferred it. Except, it seems, for two, both in the Repsol Honda pit. The loss of two first-gear corners robbed the factory Honda riders of one of their strengths – class-leading acceleration out of stop-and-go corners. The changes, opined Pedrosa, meant the track "was less enjoyable". The results, with two Yamahas on the podium ahead of him, proved the point.

Not that it stopped Marquez from winning. He held up

ten fingers to the cameras. Significantly, perhaps, now he had run out.

The return from the holidays saw riders recharged in a variety of ways, be it by renewal of contract, by surgical intervention, or merely by rest and recreation. All three applied in the somewhat extraordinary case of Cal Crutchlow. Having started the holiday first by announcing that he would remain with Ducati for 2015, then going under the knife to relieve problems in both forearms, he ended it with a *volte face* that took everyone by surprise. He would leave Ducati in 2015, to replace Bradl at LCR, on a satellite factory Honda.

Clearly this suited all concerned: a chance for the rider to recover his pole-setting, rostrum-sitting form of 2013 after a half-season of compound misfortune and underperformance; a chance for Ducati to move the increasingly impressive and loudly demanding Iannone to join Dovi in an all-Italian factory squad.

Lorenzo's renewal was also belatedly announced shortly before the race: one-plus-one years; also that the displaced Bradl would replace Aleix Espargaro (close to agreement with Suzuki) on the NGM Forward Open Yamaha. Suzuki had also enlisted Maverick Vinales, while Aprilia were moving towards early re-entry in 2015, with Bautista's name on the list, alongside Marco Melandri's.

One door opens, another closes – for Colin Edwards, whose weekend was bathed in confusion as to whether this was the popular veteran's last GP on home soil, or his last GP full stop. Hopes of a farewell appearance at Silverstone would be dashed, and likewise, later in the year, those of another at Valencia. His replacement would turn out to be Alex de Angelis, snatched from Moto2.

Also back from the doctor was home star Nicky Hayden, but his surgery had been somewhat drastic: three bones had been removed from his increasingly troublesome right wrist. This had been progressively damaged through his career, the most significant injury having occurred when he was knocked off by Bautista at Valencia in 2011, breaking the crucial scaphoid bone. Ever since it had been playing up badly, increasingly so in 2014; this was his second operation of the season. Nicky was in town not only to see the fans, but also to join his whole family in launching his father Earl's autobiography, *The First Family of Racing*. Three weeks after the operation, medical reports were encouraging. "I'm already in a lot less pain. Now we have to wait and see how much strength and range of motion I can get back. I'll definitely be back this season," he promised optimistically.

Meanwhile, his Drive M7 Honda RCV seat was to be filled by Briton Leon Camier, who had already been on standby at the Catalunyan GP. Left without a ride when his contract with the Ioda team had fallen through, the former 125cc GP and later World Superbike rider seized the chance firmly. He rapidly came to terms with the bike, praising the Aspar team for their professionalism in helping with the task, and qualified an impressive 16th, though he would be visited by electronic gremlins in the race.

There was the usual visit to the Indianapolis State Fairground on Friday evening to watch the Indy Mile dirt-track race, where Marquez was declared Grand Marshal; there were the usual Harley-Davidson cup races, too, the first won by visiting ex-GP winner Jeremy McWilliams, aged 50. He would soon return.

There was a new face in Moto3, as Belgian teenager Livio Loi's tenancy at the Marc VDS team was finally terminated after persistent underperformance. In came Spaniard Jorge Navarro, who qualified an impressive sixth, though eventually he dropped out of the top ten to 14th in the race.

A perennial topic at all American races is the dearth of US talent. The years of almost complete domination in the 1980s and early 1990s are now a distant memory, while with Hayden off sick and Edwards out, the following week's MotoGP race at Brno would be the first without a single US rider since that time.

AMA Superbike champion Josh Herrin's difficulties in Moto2 were indicative of how the level of the national championship had slumped, especially since the Daytona Motorsports Group had taken over from the AMA in 2008. In 2014, there were just seven rounds on the calendar, with no factory teams taking part, and a corresponding lack of interest from sponsors and fans.

Wayne Rainey's presence at Indianapolis gave substance to strong rumours that he was heading a Dorna-backed rescue bid to regain control and rebuild what was once a fertile ground for talent. An announcement would be made later in the year.

MOTOGP RACE – 27 laps

It was back to business as usual for Marquez, with an assured eighth pole in ten races. Dovizioso slotted the Ducati in the Honda's wake on a fast lap to qualify second; his second front row of the year. Partly this was because the Ducati seemed to like the circuit, "at least on new tyres"; even more, it was thanks to Marquez, "following his crazy lines."

Lorenzo was third, back on the front row, with erstwhile second-fastest Pedrosa consigned to eighth in the late scramble, first to tenth within one second.

The brothers Espargaro sandwiched Rossi on an all-Yamaha second row; then came Iannone, Pedrosa, and Smith. Bradl went from first in free practice to tenth on the grid, alongside a best-yet Redding, who had got through to Q2 for the first time. Crutchlow also made it, but stayed 12th; Hernandez was best of the rest, ahead of Bautista's factory Honda. The Spaniard had survived a spectacular and frightening high-side in FP3, caused by a lack of rear grip that he was still unable to solve.

The opening six laps were more like Moto3 than MotoGP, much entertainment for the crowd of almost 80,000, dwarfed by the empty 250,000-capacity grandstands of the banked oval Brickyard. There followed a race of attrition, especially among the lesser lights, with only 15 finishers.

Dovi got away first, with Rossi jumping through to take over before the end of the first lap. Iannone had blazed away from row three to third; Marquez and Pedrosa were next,

then Lorenzo shuffled down to sixth, though he was past Pedrosa directly.

Dovizioso's Ducati was clearly faster on the straight, and this time he had chosen the softest tyre; he was peering past Rossi at other points as well, before taking the lead on lap five. Then he and Rossi touched as the multi-champion fought back, and both Marquez and Lorenzo got ahead briefly, only for Rossi to grasp the lead again.

He stayed there until lap ten, but now a pattern was establishing, with Dovizioso and Iannone dropping back somewhat, the latter soon to retire by the trackside, out of power.

They were still all close, though, with frequent skirmishes slowing the pace.

Marquez's crucial move came as they started lap 11. Lorenzo attacked into the first sweeping left-hand corner and seemed to have taken second off the Honda rider. Not so easy. Into the next tight right, Marquez made a gap for himself at the apex, displacing also Rossi. It was not the first time he had been in front, but it was decisive.

Cautious at first with front tyre worries, now he let loose as the rear started sliding instead. It was only by tenths, but his lead grew with inexorable inevitability. By lap 17, when he set fastest lap, his margin was 1.7 seconds, and he would maintain it to the end.

Lorenzo all but matched him, but it had taken him another five laps to get past Rossi: "It was too long. By then, Marc was too far." Rossi finished five seconds down.

Dovi had succumbed first to Pedrosa, still short of set-up, then to Pol Espargaro as his rear tyre faded. By the end, he fell victim also to Smith, who was having a quietly steady race after a crash in qualifying had ripped open the little finger of his left hand once again.

He'd been relieved of pressure, after tailing a lively battle between Aleix Espargaro and Bradl. Increasingly frustrated by the Spaniard's braking and corner speed on the slower Yamaha, Bradl had launched an attack that ended instead in a collision. He fell, while Espargaro's bike was too damaged to continue.

Some way back, there was an entertaining British battle for eighth, between Crutchlow's factory Ducati and Redding's Open Honda. The latter got ahead time and again through the turns, but Crutchlow had the speed to pass him back down the straight, including the final occasion.

Two more production Hondas came next: Aoyama dropped well back from this pair; then Abraham, who narrowly won an almost race-long dice with di Meglio.

Edwards made the points in (probably) his last grand prix, starting strongly before dropping back to fend off Laverty's PBM. A long way back, Parkes nursed the second PBM home 15th and last.

Attrition had begun on the very first lap, when Bautista and Hernandez had crashed out together, while Barbera and Petrucci had retired.

Indy and MotoGP first-timer Camier was a minor hero, racing in the points in spite of a failed sensor that eventually forced him to retire.

MOTO2 RACE – 16 laps

Kallio's second pole of the season came after a slow start, and at the expense of team-mate Rabat by a handy two-tenths of a second. "I didn't expect it at a track where I've never had good results … but this year I've been much more competitive," he said prophetically.

German GP winner Aegerter was third; Zarco, Corsi and Vinales filled the second row; with Nakagami showing a return to form as he headed the third. In 2013, he had led much of the race here.

There were two attempts at the race, originally scheduled for 25 laps, but slashed to just 16 after a four-bike crash on lap three left Mattia Pasini briefly unconscious by the track, bringing out the red flags. Krummenacher was unhurt, but unable to restart; West and Azlan Shah got away with it.

The first attempt had been indicative of the final result, as Kallio sprinted away by two seconds after two laps, from Aegerter, Rabat and Vinales, with Corsi chasing hard.

Proceedings were delayed by just over half an hour, with most taking the chance of switching to softer tyres for the shorter distance. Not Kallio, however, who decided to keep things just as they were.

This made it harder for him to break away from the second start, but all the same he was better than a second clear after one lap, and he managed to hang on to that lead for his third win of the season.

It was a dour race compared with the other two classes. Rabat was second, but pressed hard by Vinales and Aegerter. They both passed him in one swoop with four laps left, finishing in that order.

Corsi had been close, but had dropped to a lone fifth by the end.

A long way back, there was the sort of mass battle expected of the class, with sixth to 11th covered by less than 1.5 seconds over the line.

Cortese narrowly headed the gang from Malaysian hot-shot Hafizh Syahrin's similar Kalex; de Angelis (Suter) was right behind, with West (Speed Up) breathing down his neck while fending off Zarco (Suter) and Nakagami (Kalex).

Torres, Rossi, Schrotter and Cardus took the rest of the points, with Pons out of luck by two-tenths.

Herrin had a second home-race nightmare, one of three brought down in the first corners, along with Luthi and Simon. Herrin rejoined to finish three laps down. Simeon, who

Above: Marquez's Indy Special helmet.

Above left: Thumbs up as Redding and crew celebrate winning the Open class.

Top: Kallio takes command, ahead of Aegerter, Rabat (hidden), Vinales et al, as the Moto2 field scream around the newly resurfaced infield.

Above centre right: Masbou (10) and Oliveira (44) impressed as they cut through the pack. Marc VDS new boy Navarro (99) follows.

Above right: Bradley Smith overcame a painful practice crash for sixth.

Right: Efren Vazquez celebrates his first win after 116 attempts.

Far right: Moto3 at its best: Vazquez heads Fenati, Miller, Masbou and the rest over the line.

Photos: Gold & Goose

had triggered that crash, later crashed out alone; Salom and Morbidelli also crashed out together.

If the race was uninspiring, the result added tension to the championship, with Kallio now just seven points down on early runaway leader Rabat.

MOTO3 RACE – 23 laps

Miller took his third Moto3 pole in a row and his sixth of the year in confident style, but only narrowly ahead of Vazquez's reliably fast Honda; Marquez was alongside. Fenati led an all-KTM row two from an on-form Guevara and new Marc VDS rookie Navarro.

It was another cracking Moto3 race, the ten-strong lead group still almost as close at the end as in the early laps, and victory a matter of luck as well as skill and timing.

And, in the case of first-time winner Efren Vazquez (at his 116th attempt!), of speed. The Spaniard's Honda had posted the best top speed figures all year, and it was just such a surge that took him past almost-winner Fenati's KTM.

The win was by less than six-hundredths; Miller was hardly further behind, likewise veteran Masbou from the Estrella Honda pair of Rins and Marquez and the rest. First to sixth was covered by one second; first to tenth by 2.6.

All the top six had led at least once, and the final tactics, after 95km of racing in the closest company, were desperate. Every passing move left the executor vulnerable; they shuffled on almost every corner.

Miller led away, but any hopes he had of breaking free were scotched with slipstreaming down the long straight, and the order changed over and over.

One particular hero was fourth-placed Masbou, who had tangled with Ajo on the first lap and rejoined last. Most of practice had been dampish, and he'd crashed in qualifying, but his guessed-at settings gave him a bike that was "faster than the others", and he surged rapidly through, picking up Oliveira's Mahindra on the way, and even taking the lead for two laps, with four left to go.

Oliveira (through from 18th on the grid) was a close seventh, having fended off Guevara, Binder and Kornfeil.

Miller's points lead stretched; Vazquez took over second from Marquez.

OFFICIAL TIMEKEEPER

RED BULL
INDIANAPOLIS
GRAND PRIX

8–10 AUGUST, 2014

INDIANAPOLIS MOTOR SPEEDWAY

27 laps
Length: 4.216 km / 2.620 miles
Width: 16m

Key
96/60 kph/mph
Gear ⚙

Turn 6 110/68
Turn 5 185/115
Turn 12 160/99
Turn 10 90/56
Hulman Boulevard
Turn 8
Turn 7 90/56
Turn 3
Turn 13 115/71
Turn 9 130/81
Turn 11 105/65
Turn 2 75/47
Turn 4 55/34
Turn 14 160/99
Turn 15 105/65
Turn 1 140/87
Turn 16 80/50
305/190

MotoGP
RACE DISTANCE: 27 laps, 69.960 miles/112.590km · RACE WEATHER: Dry (air 29°C, humidity 61%, track 46°C)

Pos.	Rider	Nat.	No.	Entrant	Machine	Tyres	Race tyre choice	Laps	Time & speed
1	**Marc Marquez**	SPA	93	Repsol Honda Team	Honda RC213V	B	F: Medium/R: Hard	27	42m 07.041s 99.6mph/ 160.3km/h
2	**Jorge Lorenzo**	SPA	99	Movistar Yamaha MotoGP	Yamaha YZR-M1	B	F: Medium/R: Hard	27	42m 08.844s
3	**Valentino Rossi**	ITA	46	Movistar Yamaha MotoGP	Yamaha YZR-M1	B	F: Medium/R: Hard	27	42m 13.599s
4	**Dani Pedrosa**	SPA	26	Repsol Honda Team	Honda RC213V	B	F: Hard/R: Hard	27	42m 17.057s
5	**Pol Espargaro**	SPA	44	Monster Yamaha Tech 3	Yamaha YZR-M1	B	F: Medium/R: Hard	27	42m 24.848s
6	**Bradley Smith**	GBR	38	Monster Yamaha Tech 3	Yamaha YZR-M1	B	F: Medium/R: Hard	27	42m 26.645s
7	**Andrea Dovizioso**	ITA	4	Ducati Team	Ducati Desmosedici	B	F: Medium/R: Medium	27	42m 27.800s
8	**Cal Crutchlow**	GBR	35	Ducati Team	Ducati Desmosedici	B	F: Medium/R: Medium	27	42m 46.837s
9	**Scott Redding**	GBR	45	GO&FUN Honda Gresini	Honda RCV1000R	B	F: Medium/R: Medium	27	42m 47.548s
10	**Hiroshi Aoyama**	JPN	7	Drive M7 Aspar	Honda RCV1000R	B	F: Medium/R: Medium	27	43m 02.801s
11	**Karel Abraham**	CZE	17	Cardion AB Motoracing	Honda RCV1000R	B	F: Medium/R: Medium	27	43m 12.171s
12	**Mike di Meglio**	FRA	63	Avintia Racing	Avintia	B	F: Medium/R: Medium	27	43m 12.387s
13	**Colin Edwards**	USA	5	NGM Forward Racing	Forward Yamaha	B	F: Medium/R: Medium	27	43m 15.960s
14	**Michael Laverty**	GBR	70	Paul Bird Motorsport	PBM-ART	B	F: Medium/R: Medium	27	43m 16.244s
15	**Broc Parkes**	AUS	23	Paul Bird Motorsport	PBM-ART	B	F: Medium/R: Medium	27	43m 37.654s
	Leon Camier	GBR	2	Drive M7 Aspar	Honda RCV1000R	B	F: Medium/R: Medium	19	DNF-mechanical
	Andrea Iannone	ITA	29	Pramac Racing	Ducati Desmosedici	B	F: Medium/R: Medium	14	DNF-mechanical
	Aleix Espargaro	SPA	41	NGM Forward Racing	Forward Yamaha	B	F: Medium/R: Medium	12	DNF-crash
	Stefan Bradl	GER	6	LCR Honda MotoGP	Honda RC213V	B	F: Medium/R: Hard	12	DNF-crash
	Danilo Petrucci	ITA	9	Octo IodaRacing Team	ART	B	F: Hard/R: Medium	6	DNF-mechanical
	Hector Barbera	SPA	8	Avintia Racing	Avintia	B	F: Medium/R: Medium	5	DNF-mechanical
	Yonny Hernandez	COL	68	Energy T.I. Pramac Racing	Ducati Desmosedici	B	F: Medium/R: Medium	0	DNF-crash
	Alvaro Bautista	SPA	19	GO&FUN Honda Gresini	Honda RC213V	B	F: Medium/R: Hard	0	DNF-crash
	Nicky Hayden	USA	69	Drive M7 Aspar	Honda RCV1000R	B	–	–	Absent-injured

Fastest lap: Marc Marquez, on lap 17, 1m 32.831s, 100.5mph/161.7km/h (record).
Previous lap record: New circuit layout.
Event best maximum speed: Dani Pedrosa, 216.9mph/349.0km/h (free practice 4).

Qualifying
Weather: Dry
Air Temp: 27° **Humidity:** 60%
Track Temp: 35°

1	Marquez	1m 31.619s
2	Dovizioso	1m 31.844s
3	Lorenzo	1m 31.869s
4	A. Espargaro	1m 32.113s
5	Rossi	1m 32.160s
6	P. Espargaro	1m 32.243s
7	Iannone	1m 32.254s
8	Pedrosa	1m 32.331s
9	Smith	1m 32.343s
10	Bradl	1m 32.514s
11	Redding	1m 32.714s
12	Crutchlow	1m 32.794s
13	Hernandez	1m 33.166s
14	Bautista	1m 33.294s
15	Edwards	1m 33.625s
16	Camier	1m 33.747s
17	Petrucci	1m 33.837s
18	Aoyama	1m 33.948s
19	Di Meglio	1m 34.244s
20	Barbera	1m 34.332s
21	Abraham	1m 34.369s
22	Parkes	1m 34.764s
23	Laverty	1m 34.814s

Fastest race laps

1	Marquez	1m 32.831s
2	Lorenzo	1m 32.939s
3	Rossi	1m 33.191s
4	Dovizioso	1m 33.376s
5	Pedrosa	1m 33.456s
6	Smith	1m 33.581s
7	Iannone	1m 33.631s
8	P. Espargaro	1m 33.666s
9	A. Espargaro	1m 33.878s
10	Bradl	1m 33.886s
11	Redding	1m 34.099s
12	Crutchlow	1m 34.165s
13	Aoyama	1m 34.536s
14	Abraham	1m 34.956s
15	Edwards	1m 34.971s
16	Camier	1m 35.238s
17	Di Meglio	1m 35.257s
18	Laverty	1m 35.402s
19	Barbera	1m 35.647s
20	Parkes	1m 35.891s
21	Petrucci	1m 36.105s

Championship Points

1	Marquez	250
2	Pedrosa	161
3	Rossi	157
4	Lorenzo	117
5	Dovizioso	108
6	P. Espargaro	78
7	A. Espargaro	77
8	Iannone	62
9	Smith	58
10	Bradl	56
11	Bautista	50
12	Redding	40
13	Crutchlow	36
14	Aoyama	34
15	Hayden	29
16	Hernandez	27
17	Abraham	23
18	Edwards	11
19	Pirro	7
20	Parkes	7
21	Di Meglio	4
22	Petrucci	4
23	Laverty	2
24	Barbera	2

Constructor Points

1	Honda	250
2	Yamaha	174
3	Ducati	114
4	Forward Yamaha	80
5	PBM	8
6	Avintia	6
7	ART	4

Grid order	1	2	3	4	5	6	7	8	9	10	11	12	13	14	15	16	17	18	19	20	21	22	23	24	25	26	27	
93 MARQUEZ	46	46	46	46	46	46	46	46	46	46	93	93	93	93	93	93	93	93	93	93	93	93	93	93	93	93	93	1
4 DOVIZIOSO	4	4	4	4	93	93	93	93	93	46	46	46	99	99	99	99	99	99	99	99	99	99	99	99	99	99	99	2
99 LORENZO	29	93	93	93	99	99	99	99	99	99	99	99	46	46	46	46	46	46	46	46	46	46	46	46	46	46	46	3
41 A. ESPARGARO	93	29	99	99	99	4	4	4	4	4	4	4	26	26	26	26	26	26	26	26	26	26	26	26	26	26	26	4
46 ROSSI	26	99	29	29	29	29	29	29	29	26	26	26	26	4	4	4	4	4	44	44	44	44	44	44	44		5
44 P. ESPARGARO	99	26	26	26	26	26	26	26	26	29	29	44	44	44	44	44	44	44	4	4	4	4	4	38	38		6
29 IANNONE	44	44	44	44	44	44	44	44	44	44	44	29	29	29	38	38	38	38	38	38	38	38	38	4	4		7
26 PEDROSA	41	6	41	41	41	41	41	41	41	41	41	41	38	38	35	35	35	35	45	35	35	35	35	35	35		8
38 SMITH	6	41	6	6	6	6	6	6	6	6	6	6	35	35	45	45	45	35	35	45	45	45	45	45	45		9
6 BRADL	38	38	38	38	38	38	38	38	38	38	38	38	45	45	7	7	7	7	7	7	7	7	7	7	7		10
45 REDDING	35	35	45	45	35	35	35	35	35	35	35	7	7	17	17	17	63	63	63	63	17	17	17	17	17		11
35 CRUTCHLOW	45	45	45	35	45	45	45	45	45	45	45	5	17	63	63	63	17	17	17	17	63	63	63	63	63		12
68 HERNANDEZ	7	7	7	7	7	7	7	7	7	7	7	17	5	5	5	5	5	5	5	5	5	5	5	5			13
19 BAUTISTA	5	5	5	5	5	5	5	5	5	5	5	63	63	70	70	70	70	70	70	70	70	70	70	70			14
5 EDWARDS	2	63	2	2	17	17	17	17	17	17	17	70	70	23	23	23	23	23	23	23	23	23	23	23			15
2 CAMIER	63	2	17	17	63	63	63	63	63	63	63	23	23	2	2	2	2	2									
9 PETRUCCI	8	17	63	63	2	2	2	2	70	70	70	70	2	2													
7 AOYAMA	70	8	8	8	8	70	70	70	23	23	23	23															
63 DI MEGLIO	17	9	9	70	70	23	23	23	2	2	2	2															
8 BARBERA	9	70	70	9	9	9																					
17 ABRAHAM	23	23	23	23	23																						
23 PARKES																											
70 LAVERTY																											

2 Pit stop   2 Lapped rider

Moto2

RACE DISTANCE: 16 laps, 41.458 miles/66.720km · **RACE WEATHER:** Dry (air 29°C, humidity 62%, track 43°C)

Pos.	Rider	Nat.	No.	Entrant	Machine	Laps	Time & Speed
1	**Mika Kallio**	FIN	36	Marc VDS Racing Team	Kalex	16	26m 07.410s 95.2mph/ 153.2km/h
2	**Maverick Vinales**	SPA	40	Paginas Amarillas HP 40	Kalex	16	26m 08.790s
3	**Dominique Aegerter**	SWI	77	Technomag carXpert	Suter	16	26m 09.106s
4	**Esteve Rabat**	SPA	53	Marc VDS Racing Team	Kalex	16	26m 09.969s
5	**Simone Corsi**	ITA	3	NGM Forward Racing	Kalex	16	26m 14.058s
6	**Sandro Cortese**	GER	11	Dynavolt Intact GP	Kalex	16	26m 26.049s
7	**Hafizh Syahrin**	MAL	55	Petronas Raceline Malaysia	Kalex	16	26m 26.084s
8	**Alex de Angelis**	RSM	15	Tasca Racing Moto2	Suter	16	26m 26.402s
9	**Anthony West**	AUS	95	QMMF Racing Team	Speed Up	16	26m 26.897s
10	**Johann Zarco**	FRA	5	AirAsia Caterham	Caterham Suter	16	26m 27.332s
11	**Takaaki Nakagami**	JPN	30	IDEMITSU Honda Team Asia	Kalex	16	26m 27.423s
12	**Jordi Torres**	SPA	81	Mapfre Aspar Team Moto2	Suter	16	26m 28.373s
13	**Louis Rossi**	FRA	96	SAG Team	Kalex	16	26m 30.082s
14	**Marcel Schrotter**	GER	23	Tech 3	Tech 3	16	26m 31.246s
15	**Ricard Cardus**	SPA	88	Tech 3	Tech 3	16	26m 32.735s
16	Axel Pons	SPA	49	AGR Team	Kalex	16	26m 32.924s
17	Lorenzo Baldassarri	ITA	7	Gresini Moto2	Suter	16	26m 36.390s
18	Jonas Folger	GER	94	AGR Team	Kalex	16	26m 40.372s
19	Roman Ramos	SPA	97	QMMF Racing Team	Speed Up	16	26m 43.974s
20	Azlan Shah	MAL	25	IDEMITSU Honda Team Asia	Kalex	16	26m 44.317s
21	Nicolas Terol	SPA	18	Mapfre Aspar Team Moto2	Suter	16	26m 46.034s
22	Robin Mulhauser	SWI	70	Technomag carXpert	Suter	16	26m 47.079s
23	Tetsuta Nagashima	JPN	45	Teluru Team JiR Webike	TSR	16	26m 47.133s
24	Sam Lowes	GBR	22	Speed Up	Speed Up	16	26m 51.909s
25	Gino Rea	GBR	8	AGT REA Racing	Suter	16	27m 15.200s
26	Luis Salom	SPA	39	Paginas Amarillas HP 40	Kalex	16	27m 36.420s
27	Thitipong Warokorn	THA	10	APH PTT The Pizza SAG	Kalex	16	27m 41.654s
28	Josh Herrin	USA	2	AirAsia Caterham	Caterham Suter	13	27m 10.554s
	Franco Morbidelli	ITA	21	Italtrans Racing Team	Kalex	4	DNF
	Xavier Simeon	BEL	19	Federal Oil Gresini Moto2	Suter	3	DNF
	Thomas Luthi	SWI	12	Interwetten Paddock Moto2	Suter	0	DNF
	Julian Simon	SPA	60	Italtrans Racing Team	Kalex	0	DNF
	Mattia Pasini	ITA	54	NGM Forward Racing	Kalex	0	DNS
	Randy Krummenacher	SWI	4	Octo IodaRacing Team	Suter	0	DNS

Fastest lap: Mika Kallio, on lap 13, 1m 37.275s, 95.9mph/154.3km/h (record).

Previous lap record: New circuit layout.

Event best maximum speed: Mika Kallio, 179.2mph/288.4km/h (warm up).

Qualifying

Weather: Dry

Air: 27° **Track:** 36°

Humidity: 59%

1	Kallio	1m 36.883s
2	Rabat	1m 37.056s
3	Aegerter	1m 37.209s
4	Zarco	1m 37.452s
5	Corsi	1m 37.456s
6	Vinales	1m 37.513s
7	Nakagami	1m 37.524s
8	Cortese	1m 37.558s
9	Luthi	1m 37.582s
10	Lowes	1m 37.664s
11	Salom	1m 37.758s
12	Torres	1m 37.891s
13	Morbidelli	1m 37.913s
14	Simon	1m 37.949s
15	Pasini	1m 37.970s
16	Simeon	1m 37.981s
17	Pons	1m 37.996s
18	Krummenacher	1m 38.010s
19	Folger	1m 38.062s
20	Syahrin	1m 38.083s
21	De Angelis	1m 38.086s
22	West	1m 38.106s
23	Herrin	1m 38.123s
24	Schrotter	1m 38.130s
25	Rea	1m 38.171s
26	Cardus	1m 38.202s
27	Rossi	1m 38.369s
28	Shah	1m 38.411s
29	Terol	1m 38.505s
30	Nagashima	1m 38.638s
31	Mulhauser	1m 38.680s
32	Baldassarri	1m 39.084s
33	Warokorn	1m 39.129s
34	Ramos	1m 39.406s

Fastest race laps

1	Kallio	1m 37.275s
2	Aegerter	1m 37.306s
3	Rabat	1m 37.317s
4	Vinales	1m 37.327s
5	Corsi	1m 37.397s
6	Salom	1m 37.982s
7	Syahrin	1m 38.046s
8	Cortese	1m 38.103s
9	West	1m 38.133s
10	Zarco	1m 38.171s
11	Lowes	1m 38.176s
12	Morbidelli	1m 38.218s
13	De Angelis	1m 38.232s
14	Folger	1m 38.290s
15	Nakagami	1m 38.298s
16	Torres	1m 38.358s
17	Simeon	1m 38.359s
18	Rossi	1m 38.367s
19	Cardus	1m 38.419s
20	Baldassarri	1m 38.482s
21	Schrotter	1m 38.498s
22	Pons	1m 38.543s
23	Terol	1m 38.688s
24	Shah	1m 38.866s
25	Ramos	1m 38.962s
26	Nagashima	1m 39.048s
27	Mulhauser	1m 39.112s
28	Warokorn	1m 39.187s
29	Rea	1m 39.323s
30	Herrin	1m 39.961s

Championship Points

1	Rabat	183
2	Kallio	176
3	Vinales	140
4	Aegerter	112
5	Corsi	96
6	Luthi	68
7	West	65
8	Salom	62
9	Zarco	52
10	Folger	47
11	Cortese	42
12	Schrotter	38
13	Simeon	37
14	De Angelis	37
15	Lowes	33
16	Cardus	28
17	Torres	27
18	Morbidelli	25
19	Pasini	22
20	Krummenacher	19
21	Syahrin	18
22	Nakagami	16
23	Simon	15
24	Rossi	13
25	Baldassarri	12
26	Pons	10
27	Rea	5
28	Terol	2

Constructor Points

1	Kalex	240
2	Suter	155
3	Speed Up	85
4	Caterham Suter	52
5	Tech 3	48
6	Forward KLX	33

Moto3

RACE DISTANCE: 23 laps, 59.596 miles/95.910km · **RACE WEATHER:** Dry (air 26°C, humidity 71%, track 33°C)

Pos.	Rider	Nat.	No.	Entrant	Machine	Laps	Time & Speed
1	**Efren Vazquez**	SPA	7	SaxoPrint-RTG	Honda	23	39m 12.977s 91.2mph/ 146.7km/h
2	**Romano Fenati**	ITA	5	SKY Racing Team VR46	KTM	23	39m 13.042s
3	**Jack Miller**	AUS	8	Red Bull KTM Ajo	KTM	23	39m 13.196s
4	**Alexis Masbou**	FRA	10	Ongetta-Rivacold	Honda	23	39m 13.349s
5	**Alex Rins**	SPA	42	Estrella Galicia 0,0	Honda	23	39m 13.696s
6	**Alex Marquez**	SPA	12	Estrella Galicia 0,0	Honda	23	39m 13.990s
7	**Miguel Oliveira**	POR	44	Mahindra Racing	Mahindra	23	39m 14.287s
8	**Juanfran Guevara**	SPA	58	Mapfre Aspar Team Moto3	Kalex KTM	23	39m 14.872s
9	**Brad Binder**	RSA	41	Ambrogio Racing	Mahindra	23	39m 15.014s
10	**Jakub Kornfeil**	CZE	84	Calvo Team	KTM	23	39m 15.238s
11	**Enea Bastianini**	ITA	33	Junior Team GO&FUN Moto3	KTM	23	39m 16.409s
12	**Danny Kent**	GBR	52	Red Bull Husqvarna Ajo	Husqvarna	23	39m 17.416s
13	**Karel Hanika**	CZE	98	Red Bull KTM Ajo	KTM	23	39m 22.575s
14	**Jorge Navarro**	SPA	99	Marc VDS Racing Team	Kalex KTM	23	39m 22.657s
15	**Zulfahmi Khairuddin**	MAL	63	Ongetta-AirAsia	Honda	23	39m 29.376s
16	Jules Danilo	FRA	95	Ambrogio Racing	Mahindra	23	39m 29.408s
17	Isaac Vinales	SPA	32	Calvo Team	KTM	23	39m 29.582s
18	Niccolo Antonelli	ITA	23	Junior Team GO&FUN Moto3	KTM	23	39m 29.638s
19	Luca Grunwald	GER	43	Kiefer Racing	Kalex KTM	23	39m 33.768s
20	Philipp Oettl	GER	65	Interwetten Paddock Moto3	Kalex KTM	23	39m 34.000s
21	Arthur Sissis	AUS	61	Mahindra Racing	Mahindra	23	39m 36.823s
22	Eric Granado	BRA	57	Calvo Team	KTM	23	39m 37.077s
23	Scott Deroue	NED	9	RW Racing GP	Kalex KTM	23	39m 49.502s
24	Hafiq Azmi	MAL	38	SIC-AJO	KTM	23	39m 58.821s
25	Andrea Locatelli	ITA	55	San Carlo Team Italia	Mahindra	23	40m 03.205s
26	Ana Carrasco	SPA	22	RW Racing GP	Kalex KTM	23	40m 05.783s
27	Bryan Schouten	NED	51	CIP	Mahindra	23	40m 13.616s
	Francesco Bagnaia	ITA	21	SKY Racing Team VR46	KTM	13	DNF
	Alessandro Tonucci	ITA	19	CIP	Mahindra	13	DNF
	Niklas Ajo	FIN	31	Avant Tecno Husqvarna Ajo	Husqvarna	9	DNF
	Gabriel Ramos	VEN	4	Kiefer Racing	Kalex KTM	2	DNF
	Matteo Ferrari	ITA	3	San Carlo Team Italia	Mahindra	2	DNF
	John McPhee	GBR	17	SaxoPrint-RTG	Honda	0	DNF

Fastest lap: Alex Rins, on lap 3, 1m 40.800s, 92.5mph/148.9km/h (record).

Previous lap record: New circuit layout.

Event best maximum speed: Efren Vazquez, 152.5mph/245.4km/h (free practice 3).

Qualifying:

Weather: Dry

Air: 26° **Track:** 37°

Humidity: 61%

1	Miller	1m 40.727s
2	Vazquez	1m 40.807s
3	Marquez	1m 40.808s
4	Fenati	1m 40.829s
5	Guevara	1m 41.007s
6	Navarro	1m 41.248s
7	McPhee	1m 41.284s
8	Bagnaia	1m 41.293s
9	Tonucci	1m 41.296s
10	Hanika	1m 41.311s
11	Masbou	1m 41.342s
12	Rins	1m 41.387s
13	Ajo	1m 41.419s
14	Kornfeil	1m 41.443s
15	Khairuddin	1m 41.468s
16	Bastianini	1m 41.691s
17	Kent	1m 41.710s
18	Oliveira	1m 41.773s
19	Binder	1m 41.803s
20	Antonelli	1m 41.814s
21	Grunwald	1m 41.974s
22	Vinales	1m 42.047s
23	Sissis	1m 42.117s
24	Schouten	1m 42.120s
25	Granado	1m 42.335s
26	Danilo	1m 42.410s
27	Oettl	1m 42.483s
28	Ferrari	1m 42.574s
29	Locatelli	1m 42.927s
30	Deroue	1m 42.989s
31	Azmi	1m 43.026s
32	Ramos	1m 43.536s
33	Carrasco	1m 43.926s

Fastest race laps

1	Rins	1m 40.800s
2	Binder	1m 40.883s
3	Fenati	1m 40.908s
4	Vazquez	1m 40.923s
5	Masbou	1m 40.923s
6	Marquez	1m 40.995s
7	Guevara	1m 41.145s
8	Miller	1m 41.222s
9	Oliveira	1m 41.301s
10	Vinales	1m 41.309s
11	Bastianini	1m 41.323s
12	Kornfeil	1m 41.349s
13	Khairuddin	1m 41.410s
14	Navarro	1m 41.419s
15	Hanika	1m 41.428s
16	Danilo	1m 41.521s
17	Bagnaia	1m 41.522s
18	Antonelli	1m 41.525s
19	Ajo	1m 41.568s
20	Kent	1m 41.710s
21	Tonucci	1m 41.793s
22	Schouten	1m 41.797s
23	Oettl	1m 41.860s
24	Grunwald	1m 41.861s
25	Deroue	1m 42.053s
26	Sissis	1m 42.091s
27	Granado	1m 42.302s
28	Azmi	1m 42.876s
29	Ramos	1m 43.005s
30	Ferrari	1m 43.234s
31	Carrasco	1m 43.436s
32	Locatelli	1m 43.595s

Championship Points

1	Miller	158
2	Vazquez	137
3	Marquez	133
4	Fenati	130
5	Rins	118
6	Masbou	92
7	Vinales	90
8	Oliveira	62
9	Binder	56
10	Kornfeil	54
11	Bastianini	51
12	Kent	50
13	McPhee	45
14	Bagnaia	42
15	Ajo	35
16	Guevara	31
17	Hanika	19
18	Antonelli	18
19	Loi	17
20	Tonucci	15
21	Khairuddin	14
22	Ferrari	12
23	Oettl	10
24	Iwema	4
25	Sissis	3
26	Granado	2
27	Navarro	2

Constructor Points

1	KTM	226
2	Honda	203
3	Mahindra	91
4	Husqvarna	70
5	Kalex KTM	43
6	FTR KTM	4

Main: A Repsol Honda leads again ... but it's the other one. Pedrosa escaped a late challenge from Lorenzo.

Insets: Around 140,000 fans provided a noisy and colourful backdrop, in spite of unfriendly weather.
Photos: Gold & Goose

FIM WORLD CHAMPIONSHIP · ROUND 11

CZECH REPUBLIC GRAND PRIX

BRNO CIRCUIT

Above: A vain pursuit – Marquez chases Rossi for the last position on the podium.

Above right, from top: Alex de Angelis returned from the Moto2 midfield to take the place of Edwards on the NGM Forward Yamaha; thumbs up for Bradley Smith and Herve Poncharal after their Tech 3 contract renewal; Scott Redding's factory-bike future was up for grabs.

Centre right: Dovizioso and Iannone put their Ducatis on the front row.

Below right: Inscrutability in action: Yamaha's Kouichi Tsuji, HRC's Shuhei Nakamoto and Ducati's Gigi Dall'Igna preserve their secrets in a first such press conference.

Photos: Gold & Goose

MARQUEZ was accused, before the race, of "playing with his rivals" at Indy. Not so, he insisted: "You don't play." He went on to prove it. Brno marked not only the first time in 2014 that he didn't win the race, but also the first time in MotoGP that he had reached the end of a race and not climbed on to the podium.

If this was not what the almost 140,000-strong crowd had been expecting, they should have stayed on for the Monday test. Set-up and traction difficulties had spoiled his race, he explained later, in a sportingly gleeful mood, adding, "I won't have to answer the question, 'Can you win every race?' anymore." The problems were solved for the test. Marquez was fastest, with a new ultimate track record to boot.

The resumption of European racing was marked by a first ever all-party press conference – the parties being MotoGP's three manufacturers (Aprilia sporting director Romano Albesiano was at Brno preparing for the rescheduled early return, but wasn't invited). HRC's Shuhei Nakamoto, Ducati's Gigi Dall'Igna and Yamaha's Kouichi Tsuji variously found ways to sidestep most questions; Nakamoto displayed particular skill with a combination of pretended language difficulties, humour and plain obfuscation.

He did admit that he was "disappointed" that the 2014 RCV1000R production racer had been so thoroughly outclassed by Yamaha's Open bike, as ridden with distinction by the elder Espargaro; and he revealed that 2015's version would be upgraded with the 2014 factory RC213V engine, including pneumatic valve springs, although not the seamless-shift gearbox. Asked if he had considered upgrading the 2014 bike, he retreated into feigned confusion: later a senior HRC functionary explained that it would have been too expensive. Understandable, given that they already sold each bike at a loss. The real culprit, apparently, was loose framing of the regulations. Honda (and most others) understood that Open bikes had to be available for sale – until Yamaha proved that there was no barrier to leasing rather than selling engines, and ultimately a whole factory bike.

A greater revelation was that all three were on the brink of first tests of 2016's Michelin tyres: Honda in Japan within two weeks, the other two in Europe a little later. There was much disquiet about the inevitable expense, and not only because of the change from 16.5in wheels to 17in. Ever since 2009, chassis and suspension development had been tailored around the heavier and stiffer-carcase Japanese tyres. Now effectively it would have to start again.

Out where the racing was happening, there was a worrying moment for Rossi, and not only him. It was in FP4 on Saturday when he had his second crash of the year. The reason for the fall was an innocent error, or possibly something on the track; the consequences stopped rather miraculously short of disastrous.

Firstly, for the rider: Rossi landed up in the gravel trap; seconds later, Bautista had a carbon-copy spill, and his looping bike missed Rossi by a matter of metres. Considering the possible outcome, merely spraining and gashing the little finger of his left hand was merciful. Particularly when the feared fracture failed to appear on X-rays. "A finger fracture can be very painful," said Rossi, after returning for qualifying, "because of the vibration on the handlebar."

Secondly, for assorted marshals and a Dorna VIP guest car on the adjacent service road. While Bautista's Honda bounced off the barrier safely, the Yamaha cleared it completely, happily missing anyone standing there, and only very narrowly failing to land on top of the courtesy car.

Dall'Igna had revealed that the 2015 Ducati, all new, would only be ready for testing in the New Year, the rest stayed on to test on Monday, with the usual current-season upgrades and following-year prototypes. Also for the delayed trial of Bridgestone's new asymmetric front tyre. Although Brno is not a track that requires such a solution, the tests went well enough for them to put it on the list for Phillip Island and Valencia.

Lorenzo couldn't wait, raiding Yamaha's untested upgrades during qualifying on the grounds that "if there was something good, I didn't want to regret it on Monday." There wasn't, and it left him with a scramble to qualify sixth.

Late contract news: Bradley Smith could at last put away the tenterhooks from which he had been hanging for most of the season after his contract with the Monster Tech 3 Yamaha team was finally renewed; but there was doom and gloom at the GO&FUN team, where sponsorship woes had caused owner Fausto Gresini to waver on renewing his Honda contract, and HRC likewise, though they extended the deadline until the British GP at Silverstone. Gresini had been not only

a highly successful team operator, with 250 and Moto2 title wins, but also a long-time close ally of HRC, so this would be a major upheaval. His alternative was to run the Aprilia factory team.

It was bad news for Scott Redding, too, whose prowess as top RCV1000R rider had seemed to make him a shoo-in for Bautista's satellite RC213V for 2015. Fortunately, the Aspar Drive M7 team loomed as an attractive alternative.

De Angelis took Edwards's place on the NGM Forward Yamaha, using the team's own chassis. His results, qualified 20th and out of the points, were not much different from the abruptly departed American's.

Given that other than tyres, the chassis and suspension are the only true racing components on a Moto2 bike, the lack of variety among the five remaining independent chassis suppliers was disappointing to the technically adventurous. Welcome back occasional wild-card the Transfiormer, with wishbone front suspension following the principles of Claude Fior, who did the same thing in the 500 class in the 1980s. In his fourth GP, French rider Lucas Mahias qualified a creditable 23rd, but had his race spoiled when he and Baldassari tangled on the first lap. He rejoined, but to little avail, finishing last.

While Jack Miller remained talk of the town, his best racing friend and house-mate Arthur Sissis came to the end of a disappointing first half-season alongside Oliveira at Mahindra. The former Red Bull rostrum finisher planned to return to his roots in speedway; his place would be taken by Italian rookie Andrea Migno.

The weekend opened with big news about the British Grand Prix: Dorna had signed to move to the (as yet unbuilt) Circuit of Wales from 2015 to 2024! The majority reaction was incredulity, but Dorna's Ezpeleta said firmly, "If the circuit is not ready next year, we will find somewhere else." Donington, perhaps…

MOTOGP RACE – 22 laps

There was almost an upset in qualifying. Marquez was set for pole, but Iannone's satellite Ducati was following him and went slightly quicker to top the sheets. "I thought 'F**k, he will be on pole,'" said Marquez, the first time he had used such language in public.

He did another lap, took pole number nine. Dovizioso, riding alone, slotted between the two: two Ducatis up front!

It was all so close: the top ten covered by barely more than half a second – on a long, two-minute lap.

Smith celebrated his contract renewal as top Yamaha, heading row two from Pedrosa and Lorenzo. The battered Rossi led the next from Bradl (through from Q1) and Pol Espargaro; Aleix headed row four from Crutchlow and Hernandez, also from Q1. Wild-card Pirro's Ducati was best of the rest, from Bautista's factory Honda, only just over a tenth faster than Redding's production bike. Camier continued to progress, one row behind.

The race escaped the threat of rain after a cool start to the day.

Iannone seized the lead off the line with Dovi following, and the positions reversed at the beginning of the second lap. But now Lorenzo had emerged from an all-action brawl just behind, and he took off by almost a second as Pedrosa also found his way past the Ducatis.

The Honda closed remorselessly, took over on lap six, and pulled gradually clear. Pedrosa had set a new lap record during the pursuit; and at best was 1.8 seconds ahead.

By the end, he was struggling with slides and chatter, and Lorenzo was closing fast enough to say later, "With one more lap, I could try to beat him." But Pedrosa's return to form included racecraft. "I knew he was coming, but I could count down the laps."

All eyes were on Marquez after the start, but it took him until lap five to clear the Ducatis, with Iannone proving particularly troublesome (they collided during one of several skirmishes). By then, he was more than a second off the leaders, and Rossi was with him.

Over the next laps he drew clear, but closed only marginally on Lorenzo. Then Rossi caught up again. The dream of win number 11 was clearly over; on lap 13, he was behind Rossi, staying close for a couple of laps, before "I decided to relax and think of the championship. You get the same points for fourth whether you are one second behind or 20 seconds." The problem was rear grip. "Compared with Dani, I was losing a tenth in every acceleration."

Rossi's seventh rostrum was a reward for battling on. "In warm-up, I tried to ride without painkillers, but it was very difficult. For the race, we found a better setting – for the finger and for the bike," he said.

The Ducatis fought over fifth to the end. Dovizioso did manage to get ahead of Iannone again before the end, but said afterwards, "From the start, my engine wasn't pushing." Even so, he wasn't sure he could have prevailed: "I was better in braking, but Iannone was really fast in corner speed … if he had been following me rather than leading, he probably could have gone faster." They finished still close,

and less than 20 seconds off the lead – improving on their benchmark.

Bradl led the pursuit from Pol Espargaro until the latter crashed out again on lap seven, leaving the German to an unchallenged seventh. Behind him, Aleix Espargaro gradually escaped from Smith, suffering a mysterious lack of pace – blamed on a poor rear tyre. "My traction control had to work considerably harder," he said.

But he had enough to stay clear of Bautista in tenth.

Wild-card Pirro held 11th for most of the race, under pressure from Redding, until the determined Englishman took advantage of the expected Ducati fade to get clear over the last three laps, another impressive ride.

Pirro had his hands full over the last laps with Aoyama, crossing the line just over a tenth ahead.

Two more production Hondas took the final points; only in the last two laps did local hero and trackside resident Abraham manage to get back in front of Hayden replacement Camier.

De Angelis finally won a long tussle, but only after Petrucci retired with two laps to go. By then, the Avintia bikes of Barbera and di Meglio had lost touch; Broc Parkes was another ten seconds behind, last finisher.

Crutchlow endured another nightmare, running off on lap two and almost dislocating his shoulder as he wrestled the bike across the gravel before tumbling off. He remounted, but with no prospect of points and in serious pain, he soon retired. Hernandez also retired; Laverty crashed out early on.

MOTO2 RACE – 20 laps

Rabat turned the tables on troublesome team-mate Kallio in qualifying, securing his seventh pole of the year by two-tenths from Luthi, with Cortese alongside, the former Moto3 champion's fourth time on the front row in 2014.

Kallio was on the far end of row two after crashing on his fast lap. GP rookie Lowes led the row from veteran Corsi;

Aegerter headed the third from Schrotter and Folger; Maverick Vinales was 17th.

The lap chart told a static story of another undeniably dull Moto2 race, potentially but not actually enlivened with six laps remaining by spots of rain that brought out the flags, although they didn't wet the track.

Rabat led away, with Lowes in hot pursuit for the first four laps, until he slid off and out. The leader broke the lap record fifth time around, and was never troubled again. He took his fifth win of the year by better than three seconds.

Title rival Kallio pushed through impressively on the first lap to finish it third, then was promoted to second when Lowes fell; he too was alone for most of the race. Likewise third-placed Cortese, who held station throughout.

There was tension in the fight for fourth, but only one overtake. That came when Vinales took sixth off Simon just after one-third distance.

They were trailing Luthi and Aegerter, fourth to seventh covered by just over two seconds as they spread out towards the end.

Rookie Morbidelli injected a bit of excitement as he came through to take eighth ahead of a hard-pressing Zarco and Schrotter; Pons led a big gang for 11th, from an off-form Corsi, Syahrin, Simeon and Folger, with Rossi, Pasini, Torres, Nakagami and Cardus narrowly missing out on the points.

Salom was among a number of fallers, out of 11th place, and the most histrionic as he beat the ground where he landed in the gravel trap.

His fifth win eased Rabat away again in the title battle, now with a 14-point cushion ahead of his team-mate.

MOTO3 RACE – 19 laps

The Hondas seemed strongest in practice, but qualifying was spoiled by spatters of rain, then interrupted by a red flag after the air-fence was punctured by a flying bike; the final results were a little skewed.

Left: Rising star Iannone led away, Dovizioso ready to pounce, but the Ducatis couldn't hold off the Hondas and Yamahas.

Far left: Pedrosa's win was his first since Malaysia in 2013.

Below left: Sandro Cortese made the Moto2 podium.

Bottom left: Veteran Alex Masbou leads Marquez, Binder and the rest en route to his first win.

Below: Moto3 mixes the pack: a surprise podium line-up of Bastianini, Masbou and Kent.

Photos: Gold & Goose

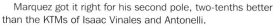

Marquez got it right for his second pole, two-tenths better than the KTMs of Isaac Vinales and Antonelli.

Rins led row two from Oliveira's Mahindra, with title leader Miller sixth and angry after repeatedly being held up by dawdling riders. He was lucky to escape further penalty points after aiming a punch at Bagnaia.

It was another thriller, with a lead group of 17 still 16-strong at the end, crossing the line within 1.9 seconds, the hindmost out of the points.

Almost any of them could have won, and Rins thought he had done so, by inches. He crossed the line, stood up in the seat and punched the air. Sadly, it was one lap too early, so he hastily sat down again and took up the pursuit, eventually finishing a shamefaced ninth.

The victory, his first in 133 races, went to French Honda rider Masbou, by less than two-tenths from rookie Bastianini, with Danny Kent third.

Experience counted for something, daring for something, and luck for a great deal more. It is usual in Moto3 for the lead to change hands several times every lap, but seldom with quite so many candidates.

As title leader, Miller explained, however, "When you get into these big groups, you can't get away and it slows the whole pace down, so the group just gets bigger and bigger."

Miller had stayed cool in the pack until the closing laps, and only then did he come through to lead at sundry points on the track, though never over the line.

The rider who did that more than anybody was Marquez, eight times, and at the end he headed Miller by two-hundredths for fourth.

Binder led on track now and then in an impressive push, but also never over the line, and he was inches behind; then came official Mahindra rider Oliveira, seventh, inches ahead of Vazquez and the recovered Rins.

With Vinales tenth, three-times race winner Fenati was something of a loser in 11th; Ajo, Antonelli, Kornfeil and Hanika took the rest of the points.

bwin
GRAND PRIX
CESKE REPUBLIKY
15–17 AUGUST, 2014

AUTODROM BRNO
22 laps
Length: 5.403 km / 3.357 miles
Width: 15m

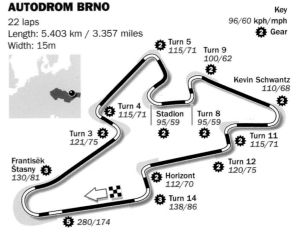

Key
96/60 kph/mph
2 Gear

Turn 5 115/71
Turn 9 100/62
Kevin Schwantz 110/68
Turn 4 115/71
Stadion 95/59
Turn 8 95/59
Turn 11 115/71
Turn 3 121/75
Turn 12 120/75
František Štasny 130/81
Horizont 112/70
Turn 14 138/86
280/174

MotoGP

RACE DISTANCE: 22 laps, 73.860 miles/118.866km · RACE WEATHER: Dry (air 17°C, humidity 71%, track 23°C)

Pos.	Rider	Nat.	No.	Entrant	Machine	Tyres	Race tyre choice	Laps	Time & speed
1	**Dani Pedrosa**	SPA	26	Repsol Honda Team	Honda RC213V	B	F: Medium/R: Medium	22	42m 47.800s
									103.5mph/
									166.6km/h
2	**Jorge Lorenzo**	SPA	99	Movistar Yamaha MotoGP	Yamaha YZR-M1	B	F: Soft/R: Medium	22	42m 48.210s
3	**Valentino Rossi**	ITA	46	Movistar Yamaha MotoGP	Yamaha YZR-M1	B	F: Medium/R: Medium	22	42m 53.059s
4	**Marc Marquez**	SPA	93	Repsol Honda Team	Honda RC213V	B	F: Medium/R: Medium	22	42m 58.254s
5	**Andrea Iannone**	ITA	29	Pramac Racing	Ducati Desmosedici	B	F: Medium/R: Soft	22	43m 05.439s
6	**Andrea Dovizioso**	ITA	4	Ducati Team	Ducati Desmosedici	B	F: Medium/R: Soft	22	43m 05.634s
7	**Stefan Bradl**	GER	6	LCR Honda MotoGP	Honda RC213V	B	F: Medium/R: Medium	22	43m 11.619s
8	**Aleix Espargaro**	SPA	41	NGM Forward Racing	Forward Yamaha	B	F: Medium/R: Soft	22	43m 17.421s
9	**Bradley Smith**	GBR	38	Monster Yamaha Tech 3	Yamaha YZR-M1	B	F: Soft/R: Medium	22	43m 18.164s
10	**Alvaro Bautista**	SPA	19	GO&FUN Honda Gresini	Honda RC213V	B	F: Medium/R: Medium	22	43m 25.439s
11	**Scott Redding**	GBR	45	GO&FUN Honda Gresini	Honda RCV1000R	B	F: Medium/R: Soft	22	43m 43.404s
12	**Michele Pirro**	ITA	51	Ducati Team	Ducati Desmosedici	B	F: Medium/R: Soft	22	43m 44.527s
13	**Hiroshi Aoyama**	JPN	7	Drive M7 Aspar	Honda RCV1000R	B	F: Medium/R: Soft	22	43m 44.708s
14	**Karel Abraham**	CZE	17	Cardion AB Motoracing	Honda RCV1000R	B	F: Medium/R: Soft	22	43m 51.935s
15	**Leon Camier**	GBR	2	Drive M7 Aspar	Honda RCV1000R	B	F: Medium/R: Soft	22	43m 52.702s
16	Alex de Angelis	RSM	15	NGM Forward Racing	Forward Yamaha	B	F: Soft/R: Soft	22	44m 08.466s
17	Hector Barbera	SPA	8	Avintia Racing	Avintia	B	F: Medium/R: Soft	22	44m 12.082s
18	Mike di Meglio	FRA	63	Avintia Racing	Avintia	B	F: Medium/R: Soft	22	44m 15.236s
19	Broc Parkes	AUS	23	Paul Bird Motorsport	PBM-ART	B	F: Soft/R: Medium	22	44m 26.667s
	Danilo Petrucci	ITA	9	Octo IodaRacing Team	ART	B	F: Medium/R: Soft	20	DNF-mechanical
	Cal Crutchlow	GBR	35	Ducati Team	Ducati Desmosedici	B	F: Medium/R: Soft	7	DNF-crash
	Pol Espargaro	SPA	44	Monster Yamaha Tech 3	Yamaha YZR-M1	B	F: Medium/R: Medium	6	DNF-crash
	Michael Laverty	GBR	70	Paul Bird Motorsport	PBM-ART	B	F: Soft/R: Soft	6	DNF-crash
	Yonny Hernandez	COL	68	Energy T.I. Pramac Racing	Ducati Desmosedici	B	F: Medium/R: Soft	5	DNF-mechanical
	Nicky Hayden	USA	69	Drive M7 Aspar	Honda RCV1000R	B	–		Absent-injured

Fastest lap: Dani Pedrosa, on lap 4, 1m 56.027s, 104.1mph/167.6km/h (record).
Previous lap record: Marc Marquez, SPA (Honda), 1m 56.135s, 104.0mph/167.4km/h (2013).
Event best maximum speed: Dani Pedrosa, 194.2mph/312.5km/h (free practice 1).

Qualifying

Weather: Dry
Air Temp: 21° **Track Temp:** 38°
Humidity: 51%

1	Marquez	1m 55.585s
2	Dovizioso	1m 55.714s
3	Iannone	1m 55.726s
4	Smith	1m 55.730s
5	Pedrosa	1m 55.812s
6	Lorenzo	1m 55.815s
7	Rossi	1m 55.821s
8	Bradl	1m 55.871s
9	P. Espargaro	1m 55.899s
10	A. Espargaro	1m 56.090s
11	Crutchlow	1m 56.129s
12	Hernandez	1m 56.622s
13	Pirro	1m 57.093s
14	Bautista	1m 57.428s
15	Redding	1m 57.557s
16	Aoyama	1m 57.984s
17	Abraham	1m 58.100s
18	Camier	1m 58.635s
19	Petrucci	1m 58.863s
20	De Angelis	1m 58.948s
21	Barbera	1m 58.968s
22	Laverty	1m 58.968s
23	Parkes	1m 59.581s
	Di Meglio	No Time

Fastest race laps

1	Pedrosa	1m 56.027s
2	Lorenzo	1m 56.066s
3	Marquez	1m 56.163s
4	Rossi	1m 56.280s
5	Iannone	1m 56.396s
6	Dovizioso	1m 56.684s
7	Bradl	1m 56.910s
8	P. Espargaro	1m 57.239s
9	Smith	1m 57.267s
10	A. Espargaro	1m 57.319s
11	Bautista	1m 57.711s
12	Hernandez	1m 58.096s
13	Crutchlow	1m 58.123s
14	Redding	1m 58.305s
15	Aoyama	1m 58.449s
16	Pirro	1m 58.452s
17	Camier	1m 58.576s
18	Abraham	1m 58.796s
19	De Angelis	1m 59.103s
20	Petrucci	1m 59.437s
21	Laverty	1m 59.487s
22	Barbera	1m 59.517s
23	Di Meglio	1m 59.553s
24	Parkes	1m 59.945s

Championship Points

1	Marquez	263
2	Pedrosa	186
3	Rossi	173
4	Lorenzo	137
5	Dovizioso	118
6	A. Espargaro	85
7	P. Espargaro	78
8	Iannone	73
9	Bradl	65
10	Smith	65
11	Bautista	56
12	Redding	45
13	Aoyama	37
14	Crutchlow	36
15	Hayden	29
16	Hernandez	27
17	Abraham	25
18	Edwards	11
19	Pirro	11
20	Parkes	7
21	Di Meglio	4
22	Petrucci	4
23	Laverty	2
24	Barbera	2
25	Camier	1

Constructor Points

1	Honda	275
2	Yamaha	194
3	Ducati	125
4	Forward Yamaha	88
5	PBM	8
6	Avintia	6
7	ART	4

Grid order / Lap chart

Grid order		1	2	3	4	5	6	7	8	9	10	11	12	13	14	15	16	17	18	19	20	21	22	
93	MARQUEZ	29	99	99	99	99	26	26	26	26	26	26	26	26	26	26	26	26	26	26	26	26	26	1
4	DOVIZIOSO	4	29	26	26	26	99	99	99	99	99	99	99	99	99	99	99	99	99	99	99	99	99	2
29	IANNONE	99	26	29	29	93	93	93	93	93	93	93	93	46	46	46	46	46	46	46	46	46	46	3
38	SMITH	26	4	46	93	46	46	46	46	46	46	46	46	93	93	93	93	93	93	93	93	93	93	4
26	PEDROSA	93	46	93	46	29	29	29	29	29	29	29	29	29	29	29	4	4	4	29	29	29	29	5
99	LORENZO	46	93	4	4	4	4	4	4	4	4	4	4	4	4	4	29	29	29	4	4	4	4	6
46	ROSSI	44	44	6	6	6	6	6	6	6	6	6	6	6	6	6	6	6	6	6	6	6	6	7
6	BRADL	6	6	44	44	44	44	41	41	41	41	41	41	41	41	41	41	41	41	41	41	41	41	8
44	P. ESPARGARO	38	38	41	41	41	41	38	38	38	38	38	38	38	38	38	38	38	38	38	38	38	38	9
41	A. ESPARGARO	41	41	38	38	38	38	19	19	19	19	19	19	19	19	19	19	19	19	19	19	19	19	10
35	CRUTCHLOW	35	68	68	19	19	19	51	51	51	51	51	51	51	51	51	51	51	51	45	45	45	45	11
68	HERNANDEZ	68	51	19	51	51	51	45	45	45	45	45	45	45	45	45	45	45	45	51	51	51	51	12
51	PIRRO	51	45	51	68	45	45	7	7	7	7	7	7	7	7	7	7	7	7	7	7	7	7	13
19	BAUTISTA	45	19	45	45	2	7	2	17	17	17	17	17	17	17	17	2	2	2	17	17	17	17	14
45	REDDING	19	2	2	2	7	2	17	2	2	2	2	2	2	2	2	17	17	17	2	2	2	2	15
7	AOYAMA	2	7	7	7	17	17	15	15	15	9	9	9	15	15	15	15	15	9	9	15	15		
17	ABRAHAM	7	17	17	17	15	9	9	9	9	15	15	15	9	9	9	9	15	15	8	8	8		
2	CAMIER	17	15	15	15	9	8	8	8	8	8	8	8	8	8	8	8	8	8	8	63	63		
9	PETRUCCI	15	9	9	9	8	8	63	63	63	63	63	63	63	63	63	63	63	63	63	23	23		
15	DE ANGELIS	8	8	8	8	63	63	23	23	23	23	23	23	23	23	23	23	23	23					
8	BARBERA	9	63	63	63	70	70	35																
70	LAVERTY	63	23	23	23	23	23																	
23	PARKES	23	70	70	70	68	35																	
63	DI MEGLIO	70	35	35	35	35																		

35 Pit stop

Moto2

RACE DISTANCE: 20 laps, 67.145 miles/108.060km · RACE WEATHER: Dry (air 17°C, humidity 66%, track 26°C)

Pos.	Rider	Nat.	No.	Entrant	Machine	Laps	Time & Speed
1	**Esteve Rabat**	SPA	53	Marc VDS Racing Team	Kalex	20	41m 05.058s 98.1mph/ 157.8km/h
2	**Mika Kallio**	FIN	36	Marc VDS Racing Team	Kalex	20	41m 08.332s
3	**Sandro Cortese**	GER	11	Dynavolt Intact GP	Kalex	20	41m 11.285s
4	**Thomas Luthi**	SWI	12	Interwetten Paddock Moto2	Suter	20	41m 13.141s
5	**Dominique Aegerter**	SWI	77	Technomag carXpert	Suter	20	41m 13.203s
6	**Maverick Vinales**	SPA	40	Paginas Amarillas HP 40	Kalex	20	41m 14.450s
7	**Julian Simon**	SPA	60	Italtrans Racing Team	Kalex	20	41m 15.727s
8	**Franco Morbidelli**	ITA	21	Italtrans Racing Team	Kalex	20	41m 19.619s
9	**Johann Zarco**	FRA	5	AirAsia Caterham	Caterham Suter	20	41m 20.300s
10	**Marcel Schrotter**	GER	23	Tech 3	Tech 3	20	41m 22.228s
11	**Axel Pons**	SPA	49	AGR Team	Kalex	20	41m 26.386s
12	**Simone Corsi**	ITA	3	NGM Forward Racing	Kalex	20	41m 26.592s
13	**Hafizh Syahrin**	MAL	55	Petronas Raceline Malaysia	Kalex	20	41m 26.744s
14	**Xavier Simeon**	BEL	19	Federal Oil Gresini Moto2	Suter	20	41m 27.043s
15	**Jonas Folger**	GER	94	AGR Team	Kalex	20	41m 27.202s
16	Louis Rossi	FRA	96	SAG Team	Kalex	20	41m 28.646s
17	Mattia Pasini	ITA	54	NGM Forward Racing	Kalex	20	41m 28.923s
18	Jordi Torres	SPA	81	Mapfre Aspar Team Moto2	Suter	20	41m 29.018s
19	Takaaki Nakagami	JPN	30	IDEMITSU Honda Team Asia	Kalex	20	41m 30.425s
20	Ricard Cardus	SPA	88	Tech 3	Tech 3	20	41m 30.777s
21	Josh Herrin	USA	2	AirAsia Caterham	Caterham Suter	20	41m 38.531s
22	Anthony West	AUS	95	QMMF Racing Team	Speed Up	20	41m 38.948s
23	Riccardo Russo	ITA	84	Tasca Racing Moto2	Suter	20	41m 39.210s
24	Randy Krummenacher	SWI	4	Octo IodaRacing Team	Suter	20	41m 39.365s
25	Nicolas Terol	SPA	18	Mapfre Aspar Team Moto2	Suter	20	41m 39.633s
26	Gino Rea	GBR	8	AGT REA Racing	Suter	20	41m 41.879s
27	Roman Ramos	SPA	97	QMMF Racing Team	Speed Up	20	41m 55.805s
28	Azlan Shah	MAL	25	IDEMITSU Honda Team Asia	Kalex	20	42m 06.704s
29	Thitipong Warokorn	THA	10	APH PTT The Pizza SAG	Kalex	20	42m 06.823s
30	Robin Mulhauser	SWI	70	Technomag carXpert	Suter	20	42m 44.420s
31	Lucas Mahias	FRA	90	Promoto Sport	Transfiormers	20	43m 05.868s
	Luis Salom	SPA	39	Paginas Amarillas HP 40	Kalex	15	DNF
	Miroslav Popov	CZE	59	Montaze Broz Racing Team	Suter	8	DNF
	Sam Lowes	GBR	22	Speed Up	Speed Up	7	DNF
	Tetsuta Nagashima	JPN	45	Teluru Team JiR Webike	TSR	3	DNF
	Lorenzo Baldassarri	ITA	7	Gresini Moto2	Suter	0	DNF

Fastest lap: Esteve Rabat, on lap 5, 2m 2.383s, 98.7mph/158.9km/h (record).
Previous lap record: Johann Zarco, FRA (Suter), 2m 2.605s, 98.5mph/158.6km/h (2013).
Event best maximum speed: Hafizh Syahrin, 162.2mph/261.1km/h (race).

Qualifying

Weather: Dry
Air Temp: 20° **Track Temp:** 36°
Humidity: 55%

1	Rabat	2m 01.911s
2	Luthi	2m 02.143s
3	Cortese	2m 02.307s
4	Lowes	2m 02.322s
5	Corsi	2m 02.514s
6	Kallio	2m 02.517s
7	Aegerter	2m 02.528s
8	Schrotter	2m 02.684s
9	Folger	2m 02.846s
10	Morbidelli	2m 02.888s
11	Simon	2m 02.961s
12	Zarco	2m 03.095s
13	Pasini	2m 03.097s
14	Salom	2m 03.214s
15	Pons	2m 03.216s
16	Cardus	2m 03.370s
17	Vinales	2m 03.414s
18	Rossi	2m 03.441s
19	Torres	2m 03.482s
20	Simeon	2m 03.494s
21	Syahrin	2m 03.548s
22	Nakagami	2m 03.584s
23	Mahias	2m 03.824s
24	Baldassarri	2m 03.873s
25	Krummenacher	2m 03.887s
26	Russo	2m 03.990s
27	Rea	2m 04.016s
28	West	2m 04.076s
29	Terol	2m 04.208s
30	Mulhauser	2m 04.449s
31	Ramos	2m 04.557s
32	Shah	2m 04.798s
33	Herrin	2m 04.867s
34	Nagashima	2m 04.897s
35	Popov	2m 05.210s
36	Warokorn	2m 05.827s

Fastest race laps

1	Rabat	2m 02.383s
2	Kallio	2m 02.561s
3	Cortese	2m 02.783s
4	Aegerter	2m 02.816s
5	Luthi	2m 02.869s
6	Lowes	2m 02.995s
7	Morbidelli	2m 03.031s
8	Vinales	2m 03.068s
9	Simon	2m 03.166s
10	Folger	2m 03.198s
11	Zarco	2m 03.223s
12	Syahrin	2m 03.381s
13	Schrotter	2m 03.382s
14	Corsi	2m 03.433s
15	Simeon	2m 03.439s
16	Salom	2m 03.492s
17	Nakagami	2m 03.495s
18	Pons	2m 03.520s
19	Pasini	2m 03.573s
20	Rossi	2m 03.608s
21	Torres	2m 03.635s
22	Cardus	2m 03.695s
23	West	2m 03.821s
24	Terol	2m 03.866s
25	Herrin	2m 03.887s
26	Russo	2m 03.995s
27	Krummenacher	2m 04.009s
28	Rea	2m 04.175s
29	Ramos	2m 04.524s
30	Popov	2m 04.770s
31	Mulhauser	2m 04.842s
32	Shah	2m 05.228s
33	Nagashima	2m 05.228s
34	Warokorn	2m 05.315s
35	Mahias	2m 05.764s

Championship Points

1	Rabat	208
2	Kallio	196
3	Vinales	150
4	Aegerter	123
5	Corsi	100
6	Luthi	81
7	West	65
8	Salom	62
9	Zarco	59
10	Cortese	58
11	Folger	48
12	Schrotter	44
13	Simeon	39
14	De Angelis	37
15	Lowes	33
16	Morbidelli	33
17	Cardus	28
18	Torres	27
19	Simon	24
20	Pasini	22
21	Syahrin	21
22	Krummenacher	19
23	Nakagami	16
24	Pons	15
25	Rossi	13
26	Baldassarri	12
27	Rea	5
28	Terol	2

Constructor Points

1	Kalex	265
2	Suter	168
3	Speed Up	85
4	Caterham Suter	59
5	Tech 3	54
6	Forward KLX	33

Moto3

RACE DISTANCE: 19 laps, 63.788 miles/102.657km · RACE WEATHER: Dry (air 16°C, humidity 68%, track 23°C)

Pos.	Rider	Nat.	No.	Entrant	Machine	Laps	Time & Speed
1	**Alexis Masbou**	FRA	10	Ongetta-Rivacold	Honda	19	40m 59.759s 93.3mph/ 150.2km/h
2	**Enea Bastianini**	ITA	33	Junior Team GO&FUN Moto3	KTM	19	40m 59.916s
3	**Danny Kent**	GBR	52	Red Bull Husqvarna Ajo	Husqvarna	19	40m 59.946s
4	**Alex Marquez**	SPA	12	Estrella Galicia 0,0	Honda	19	40m 59.959s
5	**Jack Miller**	AUS	8	Red Bull KTM Ajo	KTM	19	40m 59.976s
6	**Brad Binder**	RSA	41	Ambrogio Racing	Mahindra	19	41m 00.069s
7	**Miguel Oliveira**	POR	44	Mahindra Racing	Mahindra	19	41m 00.229s
8	**Efren Vazquez**	SPA	7	SaxoPrint-RTG	Honda	19	41m 00.308s
9	**Alex Rins**	SPA	42	Estrella Galicia 0,0	Honda	19	41m 00.669s
10	**Isaac Vinales**	SPA	32	Calvo Team	KTM	19	41m 00.768s
11	**Romano Fenati**	ITA	5	SKY Racing Team VR46	KTM	19	41m 00.801s
12	**Niklas Ajo**	FIN	31	Avant Tecno Husqvarna Ajo	Husqvarna	19	41m 00.820s
13	**Niccolo Antonelli**	ITA	23	Junior Team GO&FUN Moto3	KTM	19	41m 00.950s
14	**Jakub Kornfeil**	CZE	84	Calvo Team	KTM	19	41m 01.568s
15	**Karel Hanika**	CZE	98	Red Bull KTM Ajo	KTM	19	41m 01.597s
16	Juanfran Guevara	SPA	58	Mapfre Aspar Team Moto3	Kalex KTM	19	41m 01.703s
17	Francesco Bagnaia	ITA	21	SKY Racing Team VR46	KTM	19	41m 12.523s
18	Jules Danilo	FRA	95	Ambrogio Racing	Mahindra	19	41m 14.518s
19	Scott Deroue	NED	9	RW Racing GP	Kalex KTM	19	41m 14.938s
20	Matteo Ferrari	ITA	3	San Carlo Team Italia	Mahindra	19	41m 14.952s
21	Alessandro Tonucci	ITA	19	CIP	Mahindra	19	41m 15.017s
22	Zulfahmi Khairuddin	MAL	63	Ongetta-AirAsia	Honda	19	41m 21.418s
23	Bryan Schouten	NED	51	CIP	Mahindra	19	41m 21.480s
24	Philipp Oettl	GER	65	Interwetten Paddock Moto3	Kalex KTM	19	41m 26.551s
25	Andrea Locatelli	ITA	55	San Carlo Team Italia	Mahindra	19	41m 26.587s
26	Arthur Sissis	AUS	61	Mahindra Racing	Mahindra	19	41m 26.792s
27	Eric Granado	BRA	57	Calvo Team	KTM	19	41m 36.511s
28	Hafiq Azmi	MAL	38	SIC-AJO	KTM	19	42m 04.156s
29	Gabriel Ramos	VEN	4	Kiefer Racing	Kalex KTM	19	42m 06.046s
	Luca Grunwald	GER	43	Kiefer Racing	Kalex KTM	12	DNF
	Ana Carrasco	SPA	22	RW Racing GP	Kalex KTM	12	DNF
	Gabriel Rodrigo	ARG	91	RBA Racing Team	KTM	11	DNF
	John McPhee	GBR	17	SaxoPrint-RTG	Honda	1	DNF
	Jorge Navarro	SPA	99	Marc VDS Racing Team	Kalex KTM	1	DNF

Fastest lap: Romano Fenati, on lap 3, 2m 8.064s, 94.3mph/151.8km/h (record).
Previous lap record: Luis Salom, SPA (KTM), 2m 8.307s, 94.1mph/151.5km/h (2013).
Event best maximum speed: Efren Vazquez, 140.4mph/226.0km/h (race).

Qualifying

Weather: Dry
Air Temp: 18° **Track Temp:** 30°
Humidity: 55%

1	Marquez	2m 07.691s
2	Vinales	2m 07.914s
3	Antonelli	2m 08.006s
4	Rins	2m 08.051s
5	Oliveira	2m 08.095s
6	Miller	2m 08.122s
7	Masbou	2m 08.210s
8	Vazquez	2m 08.337s
9	Bastianini	2m 08.396s
10	Fenati	2m 08.461s
11	McPhee	2m 08.542s
12	Kent	2m 08.560s
13	Kornfeil	2m 08.649s
14	Binder	2m 08.714s
15	Tonucci	2m 08.771s
16	Ajo	2m 08.791s
17	Hanika	2m 08.861s
18	Guevara	2m 08.925s
19	Navarro	2m 09.004s
20	Bagnaia	2m 09.127s
21	Granado	2m 09.306s
22	Khairuddin	2m 09.435s
23	Locatelli	2m 09.457s
24	Azmi	2m 09.493s
25	Deroue	2m 09.498s
26	Ferrari	2m 09.681s
27	Rodrigo	2m 09.773s
28	Grunwald	2m 09.776s
29	Danilo	2m 09.780s
30	Schouten	2m 09.953s
31	Sissis	2m 10.063s
32	Oettl	2m 10.436s
33	Carrasco	2m 11.946s
34	Ramos	2m 12.814s

Fastest race laps

1	Fenati	2m 08.064s
2	Kornfeil	2m 08.251s
3	Kent	2m 08.300s
4	Binder	2m 08.341s
5	Guevara	2m 08.414s
6	Ajo	2m 08.427s
7	Oliveira	2m 08.480s
8	Rins	2m 08.487s
9	Khairuddin	2m 08.491s
10	Vinales	2m 08.492s
11	Miller	2m 08.493s
12	Masbou	2m 08.541s
13	Hanika	2m 08.577s
14	Bastianini	2m 08.596s
15	Vazquez	2m 08.604s
16	Bagnaia	2m 08.612s
17	Tonucci	2m 08.679s
18	Antonelli	2m 08.705s
19	Marquez	2m 08.714s
20	Granado	2m 08.759s
21	Danilo	2m 08.830s
22	Rodrigo	2m 08.861s
23	Deroue	2m 08.957s
24	Ferrari	2m 09.011s
25	Locatelli	2m 09.071s
26	Grunwald	2m 09.206s
27	Schouten	2m 09.365s
28	Azmi	2m 09.389s
29	Oettl	2m 09.494s
30	Sissis	2m 09.678s
31	Ramos	2m 10.476s
32	Carrasco	2m 12.011s

Championship Points

1	Miller	169
2	Marquez	146
3	Vazquez	145
4	Fenati	135
5	Rins	125
6	Masbou	117
7	Vinales	96
8	Bastianini	71
9	Oliveira	71
10	Binder	66
11	Kent	66
12	Kornfeil	56
13	McPhee	45
14	Bagnaia	42
15	Ajo	39
16	Guevara	31
17	Antonelli	21
18	Hanika	20
19	Loi	17
20	Tonucci	15
21	Khairuddin	14
22	Ferrari	12
23	Oettl	10
24	Iwema	4
25	Sissis	3
26	Granado	2
27	Navarro	2

Constructor Points

1	KTM	246
2	Honda	228
3	Mahindra	101
4	Husqvarna	86
5	Kalex KTM	43
6	FTR KTM	4

Out of my way! Sequence shows the moment. Lorenzo was aiming for the apex, but Marquez got there first.
Photos: Gold & Goose

NOT even the cold brisk winds of Friday and Saturday could blow away the thought that hung everywhere in the paddock and around the long lap – that this was possibly the last visit to Silverstone. The Circuit of Wales had the contract from 2015, and while there was more than just serious doubt that the circuit would be ready in time, there was already talk of an alternative venue. Silverstone was clearly a candidate; but there were many who thought that Donington was at least equally likely. They would soon turn out to be right.

A feeling of disappointment was more universal. Silverstone's longest lap of the year is unique, combining elements of the fast old circuit with inlays of a more modern fashion, and most especially offering three substantial straights. In this respect especially, according Bradley Smith, "It is one of the only tracks where you get to stretch the legs of a MotoGP bike and actually get rolling. So I like to ride there."

Smith was *de facto* star of the show, Cal Crutchlow having been obliged to cede the position thanks to his continuing Ducati sleepwalk. He did so rather pointedly at the pre-event conference, a response to Smith's earlier reference to "carnage in our pit" at the previous year's event, when they were team-mates: Crutchlow had a second crash-strewn British GP, and a second heroic strong finish.

In 2014, he qualified a typically downbeat 15th while team-mate Dovi put the other red Ducati on the front row. Asked thereafter if at least it was a crumb of comfort that he was unhurt, he gave another Eeyore-like response: "There's still tomorrow."

Smith was ready to run and held sixth after a strong start, against all odds on an increasingly wayward bike. Eventually he slowed and pitted: a cracked rear rim had lowered rear tyre pressure from 1.8 bar to 0.6.

Now it was up to Scott Redding to play home hero, a role he took on with relish: easily fastest production Honda, in the top ten and only five seconds away from beating Aleix Espargaro's semi-factory 'Open' Yamaha. It was a useful performance, at a time when his career was in the balance.

The other reward for the 67,500-strong crowd was a sunny day on Sunday. Important also for the riders: the cooler temperatures and the three straights had made it hard to keep temperature in the tyres, although thankfully Bridgestone had added their softest compound to the allocation of front tyres.

Less easily solved was the bumpy surface and the lack of grip. "We need to stop F1 cars wrecking it for us – two years after a resurface and it's like motocross already," complained Crutchlow."

The Movistar Yamahas were seriously inconvenienced, neither getting into the top ten on day one – had it rained the next morning for FP3, both Lorenzo and Rossi would have been obliged to get themselves out of Q1. It didn't rain, and by day two, most riders had managed to find a way around the worst ripples, or dial in suspension to suit. According to Pedrosa, the best way to cope was "by changing your line", while Marquez said philosophically, "They are the same bumps for everybody."

For Rossi, they worked against a promising change of setting emphasis the team had discovered at Brno. "We found a modification to improve tyre life, but for this track it is not good. We need to have enough feeling in the front for the bumps … they are a crucial part of the fast corners."

The fast and mainly open track, interspersed with pack-shuffling twirls, yielded fine racing not only in Moto 3 as usual and MotoGP (the result was much as expected, but Lorenzo really made Marquez work for it), but also in Moto2. For once, there was a race up front with variety, remorseless pursuit and a sting in the tail for race-long leader Kallio.

The most historic names on the grid played no part in it. Randy Mamola's son, Dakota, had a difficult debut, falling in free practice and again in the race, thereafter in and out of the pits to finish three laps down. Jeremy McWilliams, returned as a wild-card at the age of 50, suffered a nose-breaking encounter with his own bike's back wheel in qualifying, but raced on regardless. He was just one lap down.

The oldest name of all was emblazoned across his motorcycle: Brough Superior. But while the roadgoing retro-model of the same name bears a strong family resemblance to the inter-war 'Rolls-Royce of motorcycles', the eponymous Moto2 bike could hardly have been different from Lawrence of Arabia's steed. Wrought in carbon-fibre monocoque and with a rear-mounted radiator, the bike had raced under the name Taylormade in the US, with some success. At GP level, and with a GP rider on board, it fell woefully short, suffering severe chatter and qualifying only by virtue of a time in free practice, after McWilliams crashed twice in qualifying, the second time being badly beaten up when the Brough hit him.

The newest name in Moto3 released some news: Mahindra Racing announced that it would disband its own team at the end of the season, having established the marque with currently eight on the grid, to concentrate on development for its customers. At the same time, the Indian company

took more direct control of technical development, although still working closely with Suter, and out of Switzerland. The news was greeted with dismay in Mahindra's home country.

Gresini's deadline for ordering Hondas for 2015 was extended again, but it was common knowledge that he would be switching to Aprilia for 2015; Redding had the steadfast support of HRC and was being steered either to the Aspar team or back to Marc VDS, should they move up to MotoGP.

Japanese Moto2 rookie Tetsuta Nagashima was helicoptered to hospital after a heavy crash in FP3, which brought out the red flags. He had tangled with Malaysian Azlan Shah, who escaped unhurt. Suffering from leg and hip fractures among other heavy injuries, Nagashima would be out for the rest of the year.

MOTOGP RACE – 20 laps

While the Yamahas took a day to get going, the Ducatis were fast throughout (Crutchlow excepted, sadly), with Dovizioso qualifying second for a third race in a row. Marquez claimed a clear pole number ten with his usual assurance, giving the front row an increasingly familiar feel. Lorenzo moved up when it mattered, to a close third.

Aleix Espargaro and Rossi sandwiched Pedrosa on row two; Smith led the third from team-mate Espargaro and Bradl. Iannone had been challenging for a second succes-

sive front-row start when he crashed at the end of his best lap, doing a lot of damage to his Ducati and ending up tenth. Then came the pair through from Q1, Redding and Bautista, the production-Honda rider consistently faster than the doldrum-struck factory-mounted Bautista.

On race morning, Bautista's team found a setting that ameliorated the rear-grip problems on his exclusively Showa-suspended RC213V and he ran up to a respectable sixth – but it came to naught again, with his sixth race crash.

Lorenzo made a brilliant start, "for once", and led away; Marquez tucked in behind him. Dovi closed a bit on the second lap, with Rossi now ahead of Espargaro, and on lap three slow-away Pedrosa also got by the Open Yamaha.

On lap five, Rossi finally got the better of Dovi, but in the time it took, the front pair had escaped. Jorge and Marc were alone together, again.

"I rode like an animal," said Lorenzo, striving to preserve the pace, and succeeding to the extent of surprising his pursuer, who looked close to the edge just staying in touch. Then, just after half-distance, the Yamaha opened up a little gap, almost half a second.

Marquez, however, becomes happier when the tyres start to slide more; the Yamaha becomes more unsettled. "Marc is very good at braking, and now I started to lose my advantage accelerating earlier out of the corners," said Lorenzo.

Marquez took the lead for the first time on lap 14 of 20,

Above: Rossi, Pedrosa and Dovizioso waged a race-long battle for third. The Yamaha prevailed.

Left: Old names in action: popular veteran McWilliams made it to the finish with the Brough Superior.

Below left: GP first-timer Dakota Mamola had a single Moto2 outing.

Far left: Bradley Smith was fast all weekend. Sadly, his race was wrecked by broken wheel.

Photos: Gold & Goose

Above: Crutchlow's Ducati crew have little to smile about, before another forgettable outing. His previous home GPs had been very different.

Photo: Gold & Goose

but it was not cut and dried. Two laps later, Lorenzo was in front again, and he stayed there next time around as well.

It was fierce. Marquez was obliged to bring back contact racing. His earlier pass had been smooth and easy. Now it was hand-to-hand combat, at the Village complex, turns 12 through 15, a fast left, a slower right, then a very slow left, where they had already swapped earlier in the race. Lorenzo came back from the first pass and cut across to the apex of the final left. As he got there, Marquez appeared in his way. He had to lift suddenly. It was the decisive encounter.

They touched at least once, earning Lorenzo's criticism, though he said, "It is not for me to judge. It is Race Direction … but I don't think they will do anything."

Three seconds behind at half-distance and three times that at the end, the next trio had been trading blows most of the race. Rossi had most of the lead, and Dovi was mostly at the back, but not always; Pedrosa led the gang for three laps after half-distance, only for both to pass him when he suffered a small slide. Rossi hung on to the end; Pedrosa regained fourth into the first corner at the start of the last lap.

Behind them, as Aleix Espargaro lost ground, home-boy Smith had come through to take sixth by lap five, soon joined by Iannone's hastily rebuilt Ducati.

The Italian was ahead before half-distance, Aleix hanging on behind, and brother Pol had joined in and was cutting through. He was ahead of Smith when the Briton suddenly slowed and cruised to the pits, his rear tyre steadily deflating.

By then, Bautista had caught up; and also Bradl, after running wide and dropping to tenth on lap one.

It was a lively group, closing on Iannone, with Pol the first to catch and pass the Ducati. Next came the Hondas, but Bautista slipped off again with two laps to go; Bradl took seventh off Iannone on the last lap.

With Aleix now a distant ninth, Redding was tenth, barely five seconds down and top production Honda again after another strong race; he had passed the fading Hernandez on lap 17.

Crutchlow had yet another race to forget on the factory Ducati, finishing 12th; then came Abraham and Aoyama, pressed hard by 15th-placed de Angelis, who claimed the last point as he got to grips with the Forward Yamaha.

Camier was 16th, followed by Barbera, di Meglio, Parkes and (one lap down) Smith.

With Marquez stretching away again, the battle for second remained tense, Rossi just ten points down on Pedrosa.

MOTO2 RACE – 18 laps

The top 15 were typically close in qualifying, except for the first one. Zarco claimed his first Moto2 pole by an impressive 0.373 second. "I put on a new tyre, and suddenly I had a good lap time. I stopped for a rest, and then I was able to improve again. I hope I can keep this pace for the race."

Kallio was alongside, fastest of the rest, then Corsi. Rabat led row two from rookie Folger and old hand Luthi; Vinales was in the middle of row three, between GP beginner Lowes and Cortese.

Long straights and good slipstreaming opportunities yielded an exciting race for once, decided only at the last gasp, the front three over the line inside just over two-tenths. Only the name of the winner was a little predictable. Rabat chased and caught team-mate Kallio to claim his sixth win of the year.

Zarco led away, and for the early laps he and Kallio exchanged the lead, while Rabat was held up in a harrying gang, led first by Corsi and then Folger.

When Zarco was also subsumed by the brawl, Kallio made the most of the situation and by lap 12 had a lead of almost two seconds.

By then, Folger had crashed out, along with Corsi, who broke his left arm and damaged his wrist so badly that he would miss the next five races.

Vinales, meanwhile, had forced his way through to set about Rabat. He seemed to have the upper hand, but Rabat has the trick of speeding up towards the end of a race, while Kallio was running out of steam.

Rabat passed Kallio on lap 17; Kallio got him back before the end of it, and the trio started the last lap locked together. Any of them could have won, but only if Rabat hadn't been the strongest when it mattered. He pushed past Kallio again and proved impossible to pass, the antics of the title rivals ensuring that Vinales never had a chance to pass either.

Zarco was a couple of seconds away in fourth; five seconds further back, Luthi finally managed to outpace rookie Morbidelli, who then fell into the clutches of Lowes, but managed to stay narrowly ahead.

A long way back, a big group was at it for eighth, with Syahrin finally getting narrowly ahead of Pasini, Pons, Torres, Simon, Krummenacher, Schrotter and last points-scorer Nakagami. There were more in the group, eighth to 17th covered by five seconds.

Aegerter was an early casualty, having crashed on the first lap, after tagging Vinales in the crush. Simeon and Baldassari also crashed out.

In the standings, Rabat stretched his lead over Kallio back to 17 points.

MOTO3 RACE – 17 laps

Rins returned from his Brno blunder for his third pole of the year. Team-mate Marquez was on the far end of the front row, Antonelli's KTM between them. Binder's Mahindra was sandwiched by Bastianini and Masbou on row two; official Mahindra rider Oliveira headed row three –only then came Miller, a full second off pole.

Unusually last race of the day, it was a fitting finale, with a first-in-2014 win for Rins; Marquez was second, Bastianini and Oliveira as close as paint – four over the line inside 0.123 second.

The first three had been at it from the start, at the head of the unusual enormous melee. When Oliveira joined them at half-distance, the quartet pulled away convincingly.

Each took at least one turn up front; Rins's well-judged last sprint was much as it had been at Brno two weeks before. The difference this time was that he had waited for the final lap.

Less than five seconds behind, the street-fight had continued unabated, Antonelli playing a leading role, but with other hopefuls taking turns up front, if only for a corner.

Miller was in the thick of it; Fenati at the back, with fifth to 17th over the line covered by less than two seconds.

Miller explained later how the KTM development pair had been disadvantaged compared with Bastianini up front. "The new chassis doesn't seem to work when it's a bit bumpy. Fenati also struggled here. Bastianini is on the same chassis we had at Qatar, and all the other races I won. We need to go back to square one."

He was sixth to Kornfeil's fifth; then came Antonelli, Masbou and Kent, with Ajo completing the top ten. McPhee was narrowly 11th, while the rest of the points went to Hanika, Vinales, Guevara and Binder.

Indy winner Vazquez went out on the first lap, after a collision left him with a broken gearshift.

Above: A jubilant Rins atoned for his Brno mistake.

Photo: Clive Challinor Motorsport Photography

Above left: Close as you like: Marquez looks across at team-mate Rins. Bastianini tucks in close, as they head for the line.

Top: Rabat reeled in team-mate Kallio to strengthen his Moto2 points lead.

Photos: Gold & Goose

HERTZ BRITISH GRAND PRIX

29–31 AUGUST, 2014

SILVERSTONE GRAND PRIX CIRCUIT
20 laps
Length: 5.900km / 3.666 miles
Width: 17m

Key
96/60 kph/mph
Gear

- Club 225/140
- Vale 95/59
- Abbey 160/99
- Stowe 199/124
- Farm 160/99
- Hangar straight 312/194
- The Loop 87/54
- Chapel 211/131
- Becketts 249/155
- Maggotts 291/181
- Copse 287/178
- Woodcote 265/165
- Brooklands 96/60
- Wellington Straight
- Luffield 111/69

MotoGP

RACE DISTANCE: 20 laps, 73.322 miles/118.000km · RACE WEATHER: Dry (air 18°C, humidity 67%, track 29°C)

Pos.	Rider	Nat.	No.	Entrant	Machine	Tyres	Race tyre choice	Laps	Time & speed
1	**Marc Marquez**	SPA	93	Repsol Honda Team	Honda RC213V	B	F: Medium/R: Medium	20	40m 51.835s / 107.6mph / 173.2km/h
2	**Jorge Lorenzo**	SPA	99	Movistar Yamaha MotoGP	Yamaha YZR-M1	B	F: Medium/R: Medium	20	40m 52.567s
3	**Valentino Rossi**	ITA	46	Movistar Yamaha MotoGP	Yamaha YZR-M1	B	F: Medium/R: Medium	20	41m 00.354s
4	**Dani Pedrosa**	SPA	26	Repsol Honda Team	Honda RC213V	B	F: Medium/R: Medium	20	41m 00.529s
5	**Andrea Dovizioso**	ITA	4	Ducati Team	Ducati Desmosedici	B	F: Medium/R: Medium	20	41m 01.073s
6	**Pol Espargaro**	SPA	44	Monster Yamaha Tech 3	Yamaha YZR-M1	B	F: Medium/R: Medium	20	41m 16.581s
7	**Stefan Bradl**	GER	6	LCR Honda MotoGP	Honda RC213V	B	F: Medium/R: Medium	20	41m 18.552s
8	**Andrea Iannone**	ITA	29	Pramac Racing	Ducati Desmosedici	B	F: Soft/R: Medium	20	41m 18.745s
9	**Aleix Espargaro**	SPA	41	NGM Forward Racing	Forward Yamaha	B	F: Medium/R: Soft	20	41m 25.290s
10	**Scott Redding**	GBR	45	GO&FUN Honda Gresini	Honda RCV1000R	B	F: Soft/R: Soft	20	41m 30.929s
11	**Yonny Hernandez**	COL	68	Energy T.I. Pramac Racing	Ducati Desmosedici	B	F: Soft/R: Soft	20	41m 32.090s
12	**Cal Crutchlow**	GBR	35	Ducati Team	Ducati Desmosedici	B	F: Medium/R: Medium	20	41m 34.862s
13	**Karel Abraham**	CZE	17	Cardion AB Motoracing	Honda RCV1000R	B	F: Soft/R: Soft	20	41m 44.080s
14	**Hiroshi Aoyama**	JPN	7	Drive M7 Aspar	Honda RCV1000R	B	F: Soft/R: Soft	20	41m 50.816s
15	**Alex de Angelis**	RSM	15	NGM Forward Racing	Forward Yamaha	B	F: Soft/R: Medium	20	41m 50.999s
16	Leon Camier	GBR	2	Drive M7 Aspar	Honda RCV1000R	B	F: Soft/R: Soft	20	41m 57.515s
17	Michael Laverty	GBR	70	Paul Bird Motorsport	PBM-ART	B	F: Soft/R: Soft	20	42m 02.774s
18	Danilo Petrucci	ITA	9	Octo IodaRacing Team	ART	B	F: Soft/R: Soft	20	42m 08.669s
19	Hector Barbera	SPA	8	Avintia Racing	Avintia	B	F: Soft/R: Soft	20	42m 08.739s
20	Mike di Meglio	FRA	63	Avintia Racing	Avintia	B	F: Soft/R: Soft	20	42m 26.774s
21	Broc Parkes	AUS	23	Paul Bird Motorsport	PBM-ART	B	F: Soft/R: Soft	20	42m 30.277s
22	Bradley Smith	GBR	38	Monster Yamaha Tech 3	Yamaha YZR-M1	B	F: Soft/R: Medium	19	42m 39.042s
	Alvaro Bautista	SPA	19	GO&FUN Honda Gresini	Honda RC213V	B	F: Medium/R: Medium	18	DNF-crash
	Nicky Hayden	USA	69	Drive M7 Aspar	Honda RCV1000R	B	–	–	Absent-injured

Fastest lap: Marc Marquez, on lap 13, 2m 1.980s, 108.2mph/174.1km/h.

Lap record: Dani Pedrosa, SPA (Honda), 2m 1.941s, 108.2mph/174.1km/h (2013).

Event best maximum speed: Andrea Dovizioso, 204.2mph/328.6km/h (race).

Qualifying

Weather: Dry
Air Temp: 17° **Track Temp:** 22°
Humidity: 70%

1	Marquez	2m 00.829s
2	Dovizioso	2m 01.140s
3	Lorenzo	2m 01.175s
4	A. Espargaro	2m 01.448s
5	Pedrosa	2m 01.464s
6	Rossi	2m 01.550s
7	Smith	2m 01.593s
8	P. Espargaro	2m 01.747s
9	Bradl	2m 01.973s
10	Iannone	2m 02.064s
11	Redding	2m 02.116s
12	Bautista	2m 03.618s
13	Hernandez	2m 03.046s
14	Abraham	2m 03.206s
15	Crutchlow	2m 03.407s
16	Aoyama	2m 03.563s
17	De Angelis	2m 03.686s
18	Camier	2m 03.696s
19	Petrucci	2m 04.755s
20	Laverty	2m 04.836s
21	Barbera	2m 04.957s
22	Di Meglio	2m 05.451s
23	Parkes	2m 06.106s

Fastest race laps

1	Marquez	2m 01.980s
2	Dovizioso	2m 02.006s
3	Pedrosa	2m 02.013s
4	Rossi	2m 02.043s
5	Lorenzo	2m 02.066s
6	Bradl	2m 02.916s
7	Smith	2m 02.935s
8	Iannone	2m 02.947s
9	A. Espargaro	2m 03.037s
10	Bautista	2m 03.146s
11	P. Espargaro	2m 03.209s
12	Redding	2m 03.273s
13	Hernandez	2m 03.409s
14	Crutchlow	2m 03.708s
15	Abraham	2m 04.169s
16	De Angelis	2m 04.641s
17	Aoyama	2m 04.655s
18	Camier	2m 04.793s
19	Laverty	2m 05.417s
20	Barbera	2m 05.495s
21	Petrucci	2m 05.697s
22	Di Meglio	2m 05.974s
23	Parkes	2m 06.119s

Championship Points

1	Marquez	288
2	Pedrosa	199
3	Rossi	189
4	Lorenzo	157
5	Dovizioso	129
6	A. Espargaro	92
7	P. Espargaro	88
8	Iannone	81
9	Bradl	74
10	Smith	65
11	Bautista	56
12	Redding	51
13	Crutchlow	40
14	Aoyama	39
15	Hernandez	32
16	Hayden	29
17	Abraham	28
18	Edwards	11
19	Pirro	11
20	Parkes	7
21	Di Meglio	4
22	Petrucci	4
23	Laverty	2
24	Barbera	2
25	De Angelis	1
26	Camier	1

Constructor Points

1	Honda	300
2	Yamaha	214
3	Ducati	136
4	Forward Yamaha	95
5	PBM	8
6	Avintia	6
7	ART	4

Grid order	1	2	3	4	5	6	7	8	9	10	11	12	13	14	15	16	17	18	19	20	
93 MARQUEZ	99	99	99	99	99	99	99	99	99	99	99	99	99	93	93	99	99	93	93	93	1
4 DOVIZIOSO	93	93	93	93	93	93	93	93	93	93	93	93	93	99	99	93	93	99	99	99	2
99 LORENZO	4	4	4	4	46	46	46	46	26	26	26	26	46	46	46	46	46	46	46	46	3
41 A. ESPARGARO	41	46	46	46	4	4	26	26	46	46	46	46	4	4	4	4	4	4	4	26	4
26 PEDROSA	46	26	26	26	26	26	4	4	4	4	4	4	26	26	26	26	26	26	26	4	5
46 ROSSI	26	41	41	41	38	38	29	29	29	29	29	29	29	29	29	44	44	44	44	44	6
38 SMITH	38	38	38	38	29	29	38	38	38	44	44	44	44	44	44	29	29	29	29	6	7
44 P. ESPARGARO	29	29	29	29	41	41	41	41	44	38	41	41	19	19	19	19	19	6	29		8
6 BRADL	44	6	6	44	44	19	44	44	41	41	19	19	41	6	6	6	6	41	41		9
29 IANNONE	6	44	44	19	19	44	19	19	19	19	6	6	6	41	41	41	41	41	45	45	10
45 REDDING	68	68	19	68	68	68	68	6	6	6	68	68	68	68	68	68	45	45	68	68	11
19 BAUTISTA	19	19	68	45	6	6	6	68	68	68	45	45	45	45	45	45	68	68	35	35	12
68 HERNANDEZ	45	45	45	6	45	45	45	45	45	45	35	35	35	35	35	35	35	35	17	17	13
17 ABRAHAM	35	35	35	35	35	35	35	35	35	35	17	17	17	17	17	17	17	7	7	7	14
35 CRUTCHLOW	2	2	17	17	17	17	17	17	17	7	7	7	7	7	7	7	7	15	15	15	15
7 AOYAMA	70	17	2	2	7	7	7	7	7	15	15	15	15	15	15	15	15	2	2		
15 DE ANGELIS	17	7	7	7	2	2	15	15	15	2	2	2	2	2	2	2	2	70	70		
2 CAMIER	7	70	15	15	15	15	2	2	2	70	70	70	70	70	70	70	9	9			
9 PETRUCCI	63	15	70	70	70	70	70	70	70	70	8	8	9	9	9	9	9	8			
70 LAVERTY	9	9	9	9	9	9	9	9	8	9	9	9	8	8	8	8	63	63			
8 BARBERA	15	8	8	8	8	8	8	8	9	63	63	63	63	63	63	63	23	23			
63 DI MEGLIO	8	63	63	63	63	63	63	63	63	23	23	23	23	23	23	23	38				
23 PARKES	23	23	23	23	23	23	23	23	23	38	38	38	38	38	38	38					

38 Pit stop · 38 Lapped rider

Moto2

RACE DISTANCE: 18 laps, 65.990 miles/106.200km · RACE WEATHER: Dry (air 16°C, humidity 75%, track 26°C)

Pos.	Rider	Nat.	No.	Entrant	Machine	Laps	Time & Speed
1	**Esteve Rabat**	SPA	53	Marc VDS Racing Team	Kalex	18	38m 29.795s 102.8mph/ 165.5km/h
2	**Mika Kallio**	FIN	36	Marc VDS Racing Team	Kalex	18	38m 29.858s
3	**Maverick Vinales**	SPA	40	Paginas Amarillas HP 40	Kalex	18	38m 29.998s
4	**Johann Zarco**	FRA	5	AirAsia Caterham	Caterham Suter	18	38m 32.569s
5	**Thomas Luthi**	SWI	12	Interwetten Paddock Moto2	Suter	18	38m 37.824s
6	**Franco Morbidelli**	ITA	21	Italtrans Racing Team	Kalex	18	38m 40.324s
7	**Sam Lowes**	GBR	22	Speed Up	Speed Up	18	38m 40.359s
8	**Hafizh Syahrin**	MAL	55	Petronas Raceline Malaysia	Kalex	18	38m 47.508s
9	**Mattia Pasini**	ITA	54	NGM Forward Racing	Kalex	18	38m 47.597s
10	**Axel Pons**	SPA	49	AGR Team	Kalex	18	38m 47.830s
11	**Jordi Torres**	SPA	81	Mapfre Aspar Team Moto2	Suter	18	38m 47.893s
12	**Julian Simon**	SPA	60	Italtrans Racing Team	Kalex	18	38m 48.085s
13	**Randy Krummenacher**	SWI	4	Octo IodaRacing Team	Suter	18	38m 48.615s
14	**Marcel Schrotter**	GER	23	Tech 3	Tech 3	18	38m 49.346s
15	**Takaaki Nakagami**	JPN	30	IDEMITSU Honda Team Asia	Kalex	18	38m 50.665s
16	Ricard Cardus	SPA	88	Tech 3	Tech 3	18	38m 51.115s
17	Louis Rossi	FRA	96	SAG Team	Kalex	18	38m 52.492s
18	Sandro Cortese	GER	11	Dynavolt Intact GP	Kalex	18	38m 59.637s
19	Luis Salom	SPA	39	Paginas Amarillas HP 40	Kalex	18	39m 03.282s
20	Gino Rea	GBR	8	AGT REA Racing	Suter	18	39m 03.587s
21	Dominique Aegerter	SWI	77	Technomag carXpert	Suter	18	39m 17.356s
22	Anthony West	AUS	95	QMMF Racing Team	Speed Up	18	39m 17.455s
23	Riccardo Russo	ITA	84	Tasca Racing Moto2	Suter	18	39m 17.661s
24	Josh Herrin	USA	2	AirAsia Caterham	Caterham Suter	18	39m 17.777s
25	Azlan Shah	MAL	25	IDEMITSU Honda Team Asia	Kalex	18	39m 18.002s
26	Roman Ramos	SPA	97	QMMF Racing Team	Speed Up	18	39m 18.310s
27	Robin Mulhauser	SWI	70	Technomag carXpert	Suter	18	39m 19.494s
28	Thitipong Warokorn	THA	10	APH PTT The Pizza SAG	Kalex	18	39m 37.284s
29	Jeremy McWilliams	GBR	9	Brough Superior Racing	Taylor Made	17	38m 58.567s
30	Dakota Mamola	BEL	80	Mapfre Aspar Team Moto2	Suter	15	38m 46.742s
	Lorenzo Baldassarri	ITA	7	Gresini Moto2	Suter	14	DNF
	Jonas Folger	GER	94	AGR Team	Kalex	12	DNF
	Simone Corsi	ITA	3	NGM Forward Racing	Kalex	12	DNF
	Xavier Simeon	BEL	19	Federal Oil Gresini Moto2	Suter	9	DNF

Fastest lap: Esteve Rabat, on lap 15, 2m 7.253s, 103.7mph/166.9km/h.

Lap record: Esteve Rabat, SPA (Kalex), 2m 7.186s, 103.7mph/166.9km/h (2013).

Event best maximum speed: Thomas Luthi, 169.3mph/272.5km/h (race).

Qualifying

Weather: Dry

Air Temp: 17° **Track Temp:** 23°

Humidity: 69%

1	Zarco	2m 07.094s
2	Kallio	2m 07.467s
3	Corsi	2m 07.487s
4	Rabat	2m 07.632s
5	Folger	2m 07.906s
6	Luthi	2m 07.979s
7	Lowes	2m 08.014s
8	Vinales	2m 08.055s
9	Cortese	2m 08.102s
10	Morbidelli	2m 08.123s
11	Pons	2m 08.185s
12	Nakagami	2m 08.189s
13	Simon	2m 08.276s
14	Pasini	2m 08.301s
15	Rossi	2m 08.331s
16	Salom	2m 08.424s
17	Simeon	2m 08.433s
18	Torres	2m 08.495s
19	Aegerter	2m 08.516s
20	Cardus	2m 08.676s
21	Syahrin	2m 08.697s
22	Schrotter	2m 08.750s
23	Baldassarri	2m 08.770s
24	Krummenacher	2m 08.946s
25	West	2m 09.064s
26	Rea	2m 09.134s
27	Russo	2m 09.576s
28	Herrin	2m 10.206s
29	Ramos	2m 10.228s
30	Mulhauser	2m 10.333s
31	Shah	2m 10.381s
32	Warokorn	2m 11.471s
33	Mamola	2m 12.190s
	McWilliams	2m 16.102s
	Nagashima	No Time

Fastest race laps

1	Rabat	2m 07.253s
2	Vinales	2m 07.432s
3	Zarco	2m 07.640s
4	Folger	2m 07.787s
5	Kallio	2m 07.858s
6	Luthi	2m 07.944s
7	Corsi	2m 08.000s
8	Aegerter	2m 08.037s
9	Morbidelli	2m 08.038s
10	Lowes	2m 08.164s
11	Torres	2m 08.182s
12	Cortese	2m 08.213s
13	Krummenacher	2m 08.242s
14	Simon	2m 08.276s
15	Pasini	2m 08.290s
16	Schrotter	2m 08.322s
17	Pons	2m 08.342s
18	Nakagami	2m 08.371s
19	Syahrin	2m 08.431s
20	Cardus	2m 08.489s
21	Rossi	2m 08.507s
22	Simeon	2m 08.574s
23	Salom	2m 08.771s
24	Baldassarri	2m 08.830s
25	Rea	2m 08.884s
26	Herrin	2m 09.325s
27	Mulhauser	2m 09.447s
28	Russo	2m 09.447s
29	Ramos	2m 09.787s
30	West	2m 09.900s
31	Shah	2m 09.915s
32	Warokorn	2m 11.144s
33	Mamola	2m 11.436s
34	McWilliams	2m 15.141s

Championship Points

1	Rabat	233
2	Kallio	216
3	Vinales	166
4	Aegerter	123
5	Corsi	100
6	Luthi	92
7	Zarco	72
8	West	65
9	Salom	62
10	Cortese	58
11	Folger	48
12	Schrotter	46
13	Morbidelli	43
14	Lowes	42
15	Simeon	39
16	De Angelis	37
17	Torres	32
18	Pasini	29
19	Syahrin	29
20	Simon	28
21	Cardus	28
22	Krummenacher	22
23	Pons	21
24	Nakagami	17
25	Rossi	13
26	Baldassarri	12
27	Rea	5
28	Terol	2

Constructor Points

1	Kalex	290
2	Suter	179
3	Speed Up	94
4	Caterham Suter	72
5	Tech 3	56
6	Forward KLX	33

Moto3

RACE DISTANCE: 17 laps, 62.324 miles/100.300km · RACE WEATHER: Dry (air 19°C, humidity 56%, track 28°C)

Pos.	Rider	Nat.	No.	Entrant	Machine	Laps	Time & Speed
1	**Alex Rins**	SPA	42	Estrella Galicia 0,0	Honda	17	38m 11.330s 97.9mph/ 157.5km/h
2	**Alex Marquez**	SPA	12	Estrella Galicia 0,0	Honda	17	38m 11.341s
3	**Enea Bastianini**	ITA	33	Junior Team GO&FUN Moto3	KTM	17	38m 11.402s
4	**Miguel Oliveira**	POR	44	Mahindra Racing	Mahindra	17	38m 11.453s
5	**Jakub Kornfeil**	CZE	84	Calvo Team	KTM	17	38m 15.930s
6	**Jack Miller**	AUS	8	Red Bull KTM Ajo	KTM	17	38m 16.031s
7	**Niccolo Antonelli**	ITA	23	Junior Team GO&FUN Moto3	KTM	17	38m 16.097s
8	**Alexis Masbou**	FRA	10	Ongetta-Rivacold	Honda	17	38m 16.923s
9	**Danny Kent**	GBR	52	Red Bull Husqvarna Ajo	Husqvarna	17	38m 16.989s
10	**Niklas Ajo**	FIN	31	Avant Tecno Husqvarna Ajo	Husqvarna	17	38m 17.001s
11	**John McPhee**	GBR	17	SaxoPrint-RTG	Honda	17	38m 17.079s
12	**Karel Hanika**	CZE	98	Red Bull KTM Ajo	KTM	17	38m 17.270s
13	**Isaac Vinales**	SPA	32	Calvo Team	KTM	17	38m 17.352s
14	**Juanfran Guevara**	SPA	58	Mapfre Aspar Team Moto3	Kalex KTM	17	38m 17.534s
15	**Brad Binder**	RSA	41	Ambrogio Racing	Mahindra	17	38m 17.656s
16	Romano Fenati	ITA	5	SKY Racing Team VR46	KTM	17	38m 17.819s
17	Philipp Oettl	GER	65	Interwetten Paddock Moto3	Kalex KTM	17	38m 38.493s
18	Zulfahmi Khairuddin	MAL	63	Ongetta-AirAsia	Honda	17	38m 39.156s
19	Andrea Locatelli	ITA	55	San Carlo Team Italia	Mahindra	17	38m 39.656s
20	Hafiq Azmi	MAL	38	SIC-AJO	KTM	17	38m 39.704s
21	Francesco Bagnaia	ITA	21	SKY Racing Team VR46	KTM	17	38m 40.497s
22	Alessandro Tonucci	ITA	19	CIP	Mahindra	17	38m 40.552s
23	Jasper Iwema	NED	13	KRP Abbink Racing	FTR KTM	17	38m 40.955s
24	Matteo Ferrari	ITA	3	San Carlo Team Italia	Mahindra	17	38m 41.576s
25	Jules Danilo	FRA	95	Ambrogio Racing	Mahindra	17	38m 44.052s
26	Eric Granado	BRA	57	Calvo Team	KTM	17	38m 51.002s
27	Jorge Navarro	SPA	99	Marc VDS Racing Team	Kalex KTM	17	38m 52.072s
28	Gabriel Ramos	VEN	4	Kiefer Racing	Kalex KTM	17	38m 54.399s
29	Ana Carrasco	SPA	22	RW Racing GP	Kalex KTM	17	39m 13.399s
	Scott Deroue	NED	9	RW Racing GP	Kalex KTM	13	DNF
	Andrea Migno	ITA	16	Mahindra Racing	Mahindra	2	DNF
	Efren Vazquez	SPA	7	SaxoPrint-RTG	Honda	0	DNF
	Joe Irving	GBR	66	Redline Motorcycles/KTM UK	KTM	0	DNF

Fastest lap: Jakub Kornfeil, on lap 5, 2m 13.664s, 98.7mph/158.9km/h(record).

Previous lap record: Alex Rins, SPA (KTM), 2m 14.093s, 98.4mph/158.3km/h (2013).

Event best maximum speed: John McPhee, 145mph/233.4km/h (race).

Qualifying

Weather: Dry

Air Temp: 16° **Track Temp:** 24°

Humidity: 74%

1	Rins	2m 13.112s
2	Antonelli	2m 13.224s
3	Marquez	2m 13.450s
4	Bastianini	2m 13.711s
5	Binder	2m 13.768s
6	Masbou	2m 13.855s
7	Oliveira	2m 13.888s
8	Miller	2m 14.184s
9	Vinales	2m 14.324s
10	Ajo	2m 14.384s
11	Guevara	2m 14.416s
12	Kent	2m 14.500s
13	Hanika	2m 14.531s
14	Deroue	2m 14.544s
15	Vazquez	2m 14.556s
16	Kornfeil	2m 14.686s
17	McPhee	2m 14.726s
18	Bagnaia	2m 14.845s
19	Ferrari	2m 14.853s
20	Azmi	2m 14.886s
21	Migno	2m 14.990s
22	Fenati	2m 15.002s
23	Khairuddin	2m 15.099s
24	Tonucci	2m 15.151s
25	Oettl	2m 15.312s
26	Navarro	2m 15.405s
27	Granado	2m 15.683s
28	Iwema	2m 15.709s
29	Schouten	2m 15.925s
30	Locatelli	2m 15.939s
31	Danilo	2m 16.889s
32	Irving	2m 16.942s
33	Carrasco	2m 17.418s
34	Ramos	2m 18.608s
	Grunwald	No Time

Fastest race laps

1	Kornfeil	2m 13.664s
2	Vinales	2m 13.791s
3	McPhee	2m 13.819s
4	Oliveira	2m 13.921s
5	Guevara	2m 13.937s
6	Hanika	2m 13.965s
7	Masbou	2m 14.007s
8	Marquez	2m 14.026s
9	Antonelli	2m 14.027s
10	Bastianini	2m 14.051s
11	Binder	2m 14.104s
12	Kent	2m 14.155s
13	Rins	2m 14.158s
14	Fenati	2m 14.230s
15	Miller	2m 14.234s
16	Ajo	2m 14.385s
17	Khairuddin	2m 14.841s
18	Migno	2m 14.906s
19	Ferrari	2m 15.079s
20	Azmi	2m 15.191s
21	Deroue	2m 15.218s
22	Iwema	2m 15.235s
23	Tonucci	2m 15.269s
24	Oettl	2m 15.325s
25	Granado	2m 15.362s
26	Navarro	2m 15.446s
27	Danilo	2m 15.485s
28	Locatelli	2m 15.515s
29	Bagnaia	2m 15.708s
30	Ramos	2m 15.714s
31	Carrasco	2m 16.689s

Championship Points

1	Miller	179
2	Marquez	166
3	Rins	150
4	Vazquez	145
5	Fenati	135
6	Masbou	125
7	Viñales	99
8	Bastianini	87
9	Oliveira	84
10	Kent	73
11	Binder	67
12	Kornfeil	67
13	McPhee	50
14	Ajo	45
15	Bagnaia	42
16	Guevara	33
17	Antonelli	30
18	Hanika	24
19	Loi	17
20	Tonucci	15
21	Khairuddin	14
22	Ferrari	12
23	Oettl	10
24	Iwema	4
25	Sissis	3
26	Granado	2
27	Navarro	2

Constructor Points

1	KTM	262
2	Honda	253
3	Mahindra	114
4	Husqvarna	93
5	Kalex KTM	45
6	FTR KTM	4

FIM WORLD CHAMPIONSHIP · ROUND 13

SAN MARINO GRAND PRIX

MISANO WORLD CIRCUIT

Main: The crucial moment. Marquez slipped, he stumbled, he fell.

Insets, above: The fans were fervent; Rossi repaid them, proving that an old god can learn new tricks.

Inset, above right: Lorenzo rolls on by as Marquez picks up his bike, the engine stopped. He recovered to win a single point.
Photos: Gold & Goose

Above: "The best Valentino": Rossi crosses the line to take his and Yamaha's first win of the year.

Opposite page, clockwise from top left: Petrucci braves the Friday floods; Phil Read was on hand to mark the 50th anniversary of his and Yamaha's first world championship; Marc van der Straten celebrates his Moto2 team's one-two; Aleix Espargaro heads the midfield gang from Smith, Crutchlow and Hernandez.

Right: Cuzari and Poncharal part of the Yamaha clan.

Centre right: Bowing out gracefully? Race runner-up Alex Marquez lost his chance of a front-row start with this qualifying crash.

Bottom centre: Remy Gardner, son of 1987 champion Wayne, made a respectable one-off Moto3 debut.

Photos: Gold & Goose

"I AM," said the Misano winner after a triumphant re-turn, "the best Valentino I have ever been. I am riding better than when I won eleven races in a season. The difference now is the competition is stronger, younger, and more professional."

He might have added that the bikes and especially the tyres were also very different, and this was the most remarkable aspect of his first win in five years at the circuit within walking distance (if you're an avid fan) of his home town, Tavullia. He had not only been required to ride better, but also to ride differently. The improvement in his form in 2014 compared to the season before demonstrated an ability to adapt his style, to smooth out his braking, to balance the bike and to use the throttle differently to suit the latest Bridgestones.

This, as Colin Edwards had demonstrated, is harder for an older rider. As the American double Superbike champion had explained, earlier in the year, "in a crisis, you tend to go back to default mode."

The crisis at Misano did not happen to Rossi, but to the hitherto all-but-perfect Marquez, eager to win to gain a chance of securing title number two with victory at Aragon a fortnight later. His crash was simple: following Rossi and bidding his time, he ran a little far over the inside paint, lost the front and slipped off at low speed. It wouldn't have been so bad if the engine hadn't stopped. By the time he got it going again, losing a minute and ten seconds, everyone was long gone. It was his first race crash since Mugello early in 2013, but he gave the back-markers something to think about as he came storming through, stealing the last point off Camier (in his last GP subbing for Hayden) on the final lap.

The weather was at its worst at the track adjacent to the Adriatic coast, storms and rain spoiling one scheduled pre-event publicity stunt – a riders' pedallo race – because of the stormy sea on Thursday. Another one, a go-kart race on one of the many tracks in the area, was led throughout by Dovizioso, until Rossi barged him aside. "It was a clean fair race … until the last corner," said the good-natured loser. Both of them, and the many other GP racers from the area, had cut their teeth racing minibikes on these tracks.

It was still raining on Friday, leading to a possible one-day record of 62 crashes in all classes. None was serious, most the result of locking the front under braking, but some famous names were involved, including Rossi and Marquez, one of several to fall twice. By Saturday, it had cleared, although there were still damp patches for the first Moto3 session, leaving them especially short of set-up time. The all-time crash record, set at Estoril in Portugal in 2010, is 128 for the weekend.

Unsurprisingly, this led to criticism of the lack of wet grip on the somewhat polished surface; it reminded older fans of the infamous 1989 event, when top riders pulled in after the start to leave a tearful victory to the sole remaining works rider, Pierfrancesco Chili, strike-breaking out of obligation to his Italian sponsors.

There was another flurry of announcements, although nothing really unexpected, as fall-out from Gresini's sponsorship problems. The respected team owner confirmed that he would be running the returning factory Aprilia in 2015; while Belgian brewing magnate Marc van der Straten was on hand to finalise the long-standing, but often deferred plan to add MotoGP to his Motos 2 and 3 portfolio. This also rescued Scott Redding; as was confirmed on social media late on Sunday night. Rather prematurely, it seemed, breaking HRC protocol in the process.

The week before, there had been another Marc VDS announcement: Alex Marquez would be joining their Moto2 team. Team-mate Alex Rins would also move up, replacing the departing Maverick Vinales in Sito Pons's Paginas Amarillas Moto2 squad.

The most stunning announcement (in the following week) also confirmed long-standing rumours: Jack Miller would leapfrog directly from Moto3 to MotoGP, to join LCR on an upgraded production-racer Honda RCV1000R.

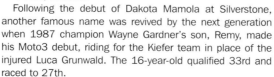

Rossi also confirmed that his current ex-Ducati Moto3 team chief, Vittoriano Guareschi, was on the way out, after "we did not agree on technical issues", to be replaced by current Calvo team chief Pablo Nieto. Guareschi had favoured a switch from KTM to Honda. "We still have good relations. We have been friends for a long time," said Rossi. There was another reminder of his ruthless streak, however, in a probably mischievous rumour that his dumped long-time crew chief, Jerry Burgess, would be returning in 2015 to take the same role with Jack Miller. "I can't say anything," commented Burgess from Australia.

There were mixed feelings about the British GP moving from Silverstone to Donington Park in 2015, announced in the week after that race. Crutchlow was one who viewed the move with some trepidation, particularly concerned about the risks of the long downhill right-hander Craner Curves that start the lap, with the potential warm-up problems of Bridgestone tyres. "Maybe we should have an agreement that nobody races through that section," he joked. Rossi was among those relishing a return to the swooping parkland circuit, where he had recorded five premier-class wins.

Electronic limitations drew a little closer at Misano, with a new rule requiring factory teams to cease software development on 30th June in 2015. From the next day, they would be required to switch development to the 2016 'unified' software. New manufacturers Suzuki and Aprilia would not be restricted, however.

Following the debut of Dakota Mamola at Silverstone, another famous name was revived by the next generation when 1987 champion Wayne Gardner's son, Remy, made his Moto3 debut, riding for the Kiefer team in place of the injured Luca Grunwald. The 16-year-old qualified 33rd and raced to 27th.

Eight-times world champion Phil Read was at Misano, celebrating 50 years to the day since his and Yamaha's first championship. Read had won the Nations GP at Monza in 1964, riding a factory RD56 Yamaha 250, which ushered in a new era of racing. He had some pithy comments about modern racing, and about Marquez's tactics in particular – with reference to his attacks on Lorenzo at Jerez in 2013 and at Silverstone two weeks before. "I think he should be punished, or at least warned," he said. "When you force the guy to pick the bike up, it's too much." If that had happened in the old days, he said, the remedy would have been simple. "You find the guy in the paddock later, and punch him."

MOTOGP RACE – 28 laps

Foul weather meant Friday was lost, leaving just one morning session not only to try to find the right settings for the bumpy and tortuous circuit, but also to slot into the crucial top ten. Iannone, back from two wet crashes on Friday, led the way; Rossi was sixth and Bautista scraped in at tenth, leaving Bradl and Hernandez (fastest in the first wet session) to find their way through to Q2; Crutchlow was left behind after bike trouble scotched his second run.

Times were close – ten inside just over three-quarters of a second, the order a little different, confirming the view that this at last was a track that suited Yamaha better than Honda. Lorenzo took his first pole of the year and Rossi was third, with Iannone sandwiched between them.

Marquez was fourth, off the front row for the first time in the season, if only just over a tenth off pole; then came Pedrosa and Dovizioso, his hopes of a fourth successive front row scuppered by bike trouble in FP4, spoiling his schedule.

The Espargaro Bros led an all-Yamaha row three, Pol ahead of Aleix, Smith alongside. Next came Bradl, Hernandez and Bautista, with Crutchlow and Redding best of the rest.

Jorge made the jump from the start; Marquez bullied his way through the first corners to secure third behind Rossi. Pedrosa was seventh, behind not only the Ducatis of Iannone and Dovizioso, but also Pol Espargaro. It would take him until the eighth lap to get free, by which time any chance of joining the front battle was long gone.

The front three laid on a hell of a show, with Valentino clearly utterly determined, fighting back at once every time Marquez attacked, and for once "with a small advantage over the Hondas", evident when he even passed Marquez in a straight line, which he credited to better corner exit traction.

On laps two and three, it was Marquez versus Rossi; then on lap four, Rossi versus Lorenzo – they changed places five times, but by the end of it both Rossi and Marquez were ahead, and Lorenzo's fight was over. He alone had chosen the harder front tyre. "In Brno, it was a good decision. Here it was my mistake. I was slower than last year, and slower even than on the 800." He would be alone from then on.

Marquez now decided to "cool down a bit and follow" for the next five laps, still thinking he had a chance to win. Until the headstrong crash. Asked if he shouldn't now start riding carefully, since he didn't need to win another race, he laughed: "I think now is the time to change tactics ... but with the exception of Aragon in two weeks."

That was it up front, but nobody could call the race dull as Rossi stretched steadily away, riding at 35 with all the vigour of his youth.

Iannone succumbed to both Pedrosa and Dovizioso on lap eight, and soon afterwards lost touch. But Dovi was a thorn in the side of the Honda to the flag, rather to the Spanish rider's surprise. "In a few corners, I was losing, so had to go over the limit in sections where I was better," said the Ducati rider. "I was locking the front and sliding. I took a lot of risks, more than usual." He was just over a second adrift at the flag, and a landmark 5.5 off the lead.

Pol Espargaro had dropped away behind Iannone and finished sixth; team-mate Smith was another four seconds away, having lost touch by running wide on lap two. He surrendered two positions, but by the time he got them back, the rest had gone.

There'd been a lively battle for eighth, Crutchlow tussling with Aleix Espargaro and then also Bautista, the trio catching and passing fast-starter Hernandez.

Crutchlow lost touch when a tyre shifted on its rim; Espargaro also dropped back, but then caught and passed Bautista, only to crash on the final lap.

Hernandez was tenth; a long way back, Abraham had caught Aoyama, getting ahead to be top RCV1000R for the first time, and also first Open bike. Redding was next, never in touch after "a disastrous weekend, with three crashes."

De Angelis was 14th, in the points in his third race on the ex-Colin Edwards bike, and just two seconds ahead of Marquez. The latter grabbed the last point off Camier on the final lap.

Laverty was 17th, team-mate Parkes next, a lap down, having defeated Barbera by two-tenths. Bradl crashed out in the early stages, by which time di Meglio and Petrucci had already fallen.

Rossi's win put him within one point of Pedrosa for second place overall.

MOTO2 RACE – 26 laps

Equally stricken by the weather, the front positions in the smaller classes also went to those who already had good base settings for the bumpy, twisty track, or in some cases perhaps stumbled upon them. Kallio took his third pole, with Rabat second, then Luthi: Kalex, Kalex, Suter. "It was a difficult day for everyone," said Kallio. "Thanks to the team, the bike was already good in the morning. But we need to improve, and everyone else will improve, too."

Vinales led the second row from Aegerter and Zarco; Cardus headed the third.

Silverstone's result was repeated, but not so much the excitement, in another largely processional race.

Kallio took off at speed, taking a one-second lead over Rabat on the first lap and adding another six-tenths over the next two: "We know I am faster in the early laps, so I tried to build a gap and then manage it."

But it didn't last, once Rabat got his head down, and before half-distance he had closed right up, "took a little breather", and finally pounced to take the lead on the 18th lap. Kallio's hopes of fighting back came to naught after he made a mistake, and they carried on in that order to the finish, Rabat finally 2.2 seconds ahead for his seventh win of the season, which extended his title lead to more than 20 points.

Cardus took a flier from the third row to hold third for three laps, but then succumbed to both Zarco and Aegerter. The next to pass him was Vinales, and shortly afterwards, on lap 11, also Luthi. Two laps later, the Tech 3 rider slipped off, rejoining at the back.

The only other changes up front came as Aegerter dropped steadily back, being passed first by Vinales and three laps later by Luthi.

This was the order: Zarco third, then Vinales, Luthi and Aegerter, respectfully spaced apart.

There was a bit of a battle for seventh, with rookie Morbidelli taking the position back from team-mate Simon on the last lap; Pons was a few tenths behind, and Nakagami another second adrift at the end.

Folger had been ahead of this group, but had failed to

lose one position as required after "exceeding the track limits"; he was called in for a ride-through penalty and finally finished 19th.

There wasn't much action behind this, with Schrotter, Cortese, Pasini, Krummenacher and Salom wrapping up the rest of the points. Simeon and West narrowly missed out.

Corsi was absent, injured; Popov and Shah crashed out; the returned Terol retired.

MOTO3 RACE – 23 laps

The factory-backed KTM Red Bull Ajo team had ditched the 'development' chassis that had cost Miller dear at Silverstone, and he came through right at the end of qualifying to take his seventh pole of the year, by just 0.004 second from latecomer Ajo, pushing Rins to third.

Marquez was fourth after a late tumble, Mahindra's Oliveira alongside, complaining that a potential pole lap had been ruined when Miller slowed in front of him. Kent completed row two; Antonelli led the third from Vinales and Vazquez.

Miller dashed off, but the breakaway didn't work, and Rins led team-mate Marquez past on lap four.

Oliveira was with the Hondas as they moved away, while Miller dropped into a gang, and on lap five was behind Vazquez and Vinales. He regained fourth next time around and escaped over the ensuing laps, but the gap to the front kept growing.

Then Oliveira slipped off, a loss of rear tyre pressure the culprit, promoting Miller to third. At the same time, Rins had stretched away by better than a second, only for Marquez to peg him back. He was right on him by lap 17 and attacked on the second-last lap to lead for the first time.

It was one lap too early, however, and Rins was able to reverse the positions after a fraught final lap, crossing the line an almost notional 0.042 second ahead.

Miller was four seconds down and a second ahead of a battling trio: Vinales, Bastianini and Binder.

Seventh to 11th was covered by seven-tenths, the group led over the line by Masbou, after a remarkable charge through from 24th on the grid. Perhaps even more remarkably, Andrea Migno, in his second GP on the ex-Sissis Mahindra, had followed Masbou through and even led the gang, losing seventh only on the final lap. The rookie had beaten a couple of current GP winners, with Guevara next, then title contenders Vazquez and Fenati. Kent, McPhee, Khairuddin and Navarro rounded out the points.

Miller's title lead was coming under increasing threat from both Marquez and Rins, the former only nine points adrift.

GP TIM
DI SAN MARINO E
DELLA RIVIERA DI RIMINI

12-14 SEPTEMBER, 2014

MISANO WORLD CIRCUIT

28 laps
Length: 4.226 km / 2.626 miles
Width: 14m

Key
96/60 kph/mph
Gear

Tramonto 75/47
Turn 9
Rio 75/47
Turn 5
Turn 6 120/75
Rimini 265/165
Quercia 90/56
Curvone 260/161
Turn 12
Turn 2
Misano 105/65
Variante del Parco 155/71
Turn 1 132/82
Turn 15 135/84
Carro 80/50
Turn 13 162/101

MotoGP

RACE DISTANCE: 28 laps, 73.526 miles/118.328km · **RACE WEATHER:** Dry (air 25°C, humidity 45%, track 37°C)

Pos.	Rider	Nat.	No.	Entrant	Machine	Tyres	Race tyre choice	Laps	Time & speed
1	**Valentino Rossi**	ITA	46	Movistar Yamaha MotoGP	Yamaha YZR-M1	B	F: Medium/R: Medium	28	44m 14.586s / 99.7mph / 160.4km/h
2	**Jorge Lorenzo**	SPA	99	Movistar Yamaha MotoGP	Yamaha YZR-M1	B	F: Hard/R: Medium	28	44m 16.164s
3	**Dani Pedrosa**	SPA	26	Repsol Honda Team	Honda RC213V	B	F: Medium/R: Medium	28	44m 18.862s
4	**Andrea Dovizioso**	ITA	4	Ducati Team	Ducati Desmosedici	B	F: Medium/R: Medium	28	44m 20.096s
5	**Andrea Iannone**	ITA	29	Pramac Racing	Ducati Desmosedici	B	F: Medium/R: Medium	28	44m 26.357s
6	**Pol Espargaro**	SPA	44	Monster Yamaha Tech 3	Yamaha YZR-M1	B	F: Medium/R: Medium	28	44m 33.585s
7	**Bradley Smith**	GBR	38	Monster Yamaha Tech 3	Yamaha YZR-M1	B	F: Medium/R: Medium	28	44m 37.686s
8	**Alvaro Bautista**	SPA	19	GO&FUN Honda Gresini	Honda RC213V	B	F: Medium/R: Medium	28	44m 51.044s
9	**Cal Crutchlow**	GBR	35	Ducati Team	Ducati Desmosedici	B	F: Medium/R: Medium	28	44m 53.066s
10	**Yonny Hernandez**	COL	68	Energy T.I. Pramac Racing	Ducati Desmosedici	B	F: Medium/R: Soft	28	45m 00.464s
11	**Karel Abraham**	CZE	17	Cardion AB Motoracing	Honda RCV1000R	B	F: Soft/R: Soft	28	45m 09.351s
12	**Hiroshi Aoyama**	JPN	7	Drive M7 Aspar	Honda RCV1000R	B	F: Soft/R: Soft	28	45m 11.361s
13	**Scott Redding**	GBR	45	GO&FUN Honda Gresini	Honda RCV1000R	B	F: Soft/R: Medium	28	45m 17.320s
14	**Alex de Angelis**	RSM	15	NGM Forward Racing	Forward Yamaha	B	F: Soft/R: Medium	28	45m 28.132s
15	**Marc Marquez**	SPA	93	Repsol Honda Team	Honda RC213V	B	F: Soft/R: Soft	28	45m 30.534s
16	Leon Camier	GBR	2	Drive M7 Aspar	Honda RCV1000R	B	F: Soft/R: Soft	28	45m 35.346s
17	Michael Laverty	GBR	70	Paul Bird Motorsport	PBM-ART	B	F: Soft/R: Soft	28	45m 41.008s
18	Broc Parkes	AUS	23	Paul Bird Motorsport	PBM-ART	B	F: Soft/R: Soft	27	44m 17.702s
19	Hector Barbera	SPA	8	Avintia Racing	Avintia	B	F: Soft/R: Soft	27	44m 17.921s
	Aleix Espargaro	SPA	41	NGM Forward Racing	Forward Yamaha	B	F: Soft/R: Soft	27	DNF-crash
	Stefan Bradl	GER	6	LCR Honda MotoGP	Honda RC213V	B	F: Medium/R: Medium	6	DNF-crash
	Danilo Petrucci	ITA	9	Octo IodaRacing Team	ART	B	F: Soft/R: Soft	1	DNF-crash
	Mike di Meglio	FRA	63	Avintia Racing	Avintia	B	F: Soft/R: Soft	0	DNF-crash
	Nicky Hayden	USA	69	Drive M7 Aspar	Honda RCV1000R	B	–	–	Absent-injured

Fastest lap: Marc Marquez, on lap 4, 1m 34.108s, 100.4mph/161.6km/h.

Lap record: Jorge Lorenzo, SPA (Yamaha), 1m 33.906s, 100.7mph/162.0km/h (2011).

Event best maximum speed: Pol Espargaro, 179.8mph/289.3km/h (free practice 3).

Qualifying

Weather: Dry
Air Temp: 24° **Track Temp:** 36°
Humidity: 55%

1	Lorenzo	1m 33.238s
2	Iannone	1m 33.289s
3	Rossi	1m 33.302s
4	Marquez	1m 33.360s
5	Pedrosa	1m 33.439s
6	Dovizioso	1m 33.439s
7	P. Espargaro	1m 33.557s
8	A. Espargaro	1m 33.713s
9	Smith	1m 33.761s
10	Bradl	1m 33.995s
11	Hernandez	1m 34.283s
12	Bautista	1m 34.640s
13	Crutchlow	1m 34.495s
14	Redding	1m 34.919s
15	Aoyama	1m 34.966s
16	Camier	1m 35.275s
17	Abraham	1m 35.292s
18	Laverty	1m 35.589s
19	De Angelis	1m 35.679s
20	Parkes	1m 36.317s
21	Barbera	1m 36.689s
22	Di Meglio	1m 42.497s
23	Petrucci	No Time

Fastest race laps

1	Marquez	1m 34.108s
2	Rossi	1m 34.165s
3	Lorenzo	1m 34.295s
4	Pedrosa	1m 34.320s
5	Dovizioso	1m 34.330s
6	Bradl	1m 34.591s
7	Iannone	1m 34.751s
8	P. Espargaro	1m 34.888s
9	Smith	1m 34.981s
10	A. Espargaro	1m 35.108s
11	Hernandez	1m 35.279s
12	Bautista	1m 35.293s
13	Crutchlow	1m 35.390s
14	Abraham	1m 35.826s
15	Aoyama	1m 35.954s
16	Redding	1m 36.040s
17	De Angelis	1m 36.478s
18	Laverty	1m 36.996s
19	Camier	1m 37.012s
20	Barbera	1m 37.314s
21	Parkes	1m 37.314s

Championship Points

1	Marquez	289
2	Pedrosa	215
3	Rossi	214
4	Lorenzo	177
5	Dovizioso	142
6	P. Espargaro	98
7	A. Espargaro	92
8	Iannone	92
9	Bradl	74
10	Smith	74
11	Bautista	64
12	Redding	54
13	Crutchlow	47
14	Aoyama	43
15	Hernandez	38
16	Abraham	33
17	Hayden	29
18	Edwards	11
19	Pirro	11
20	Parkes	7
21	Di Meglio	4
22	Petrucci	4
23	De Angelis	3
24	Laverty	2
25	Barbera	2
26	Camier	1

Grid order

Grid order	1	2	3	4	5	6	7	8	9	10	11	12	13	14	15	16	17	18	19	20	21	22	23	24	25	26	27	28
99 LORENZO	99	99	99	46	46	46	46	46	46	46	46	46	46	46	46	46	46	46	46	46	46	46	46	46	46	46	46	46
29 IANNONE	46	46	46	93	93	93	93	93	93	99	99	99	99	99	99	99	99	99	99	99	99	99	99	99	99	99	99	99
46 ROSSI	93	93	93	99	99	99	99	99	99	26	26	26	26	26	26	26	26	26	26	26	26	26	26	26	26	26	26	26
93 MARQUEZ	29	29	29	29	29	29	29	26	26	4	4	4	4	4	4	4	4	4	4	4	4	4	4	4	4	4	4	4
26 PEDROSA	4	4	26	26	26	26	26	4	29	29	29	29	29	29	29	29	29	29	29	29	29	29	29	29	29	29	29	29
4 DOVIZIOSO	44	44	26	4	4	4	29	29	44	44	44	44	44	44	44	44	44	44	44	44	44	44	44	44	44	44	44	44
44 P. ESPARGARO	26	26	44	44	44	44	44	44	38	38	38	38	38	38	38	38	38	38	38	38	38	38	38	38	38	38	38	38
41 A. ESPARGARO	38	41	6	6	6	6	38	38	35	35	35	35	19	19	35	19	19	19	19	19	19	41	41	41	19			
38 SMITH	41	6	41	41	38	38	41	35	35	68	19	19	35	35	19	19	35	41	41	41	41	19	19	19	35			
6 BRADL	6	38	38	38	41	41	35	68	68	19	68	68	68	68	41	41	41	35	35	35	35	35	35	35	68			
68 HERNANDEZ	68	68	68	35	35	35	68	41	19	41	41	41	41	41	68	68	68	68	68	68	68	68	68	68	17			
19 BAUTISTA	35	35	35	68	68	68	19	19	41	7	7	7	7	7	7	7	7	7	7	17	17	17	17	7				
35 CRUTCHLOW	2	19	19	19	19	19	7	7	17	17	17	17	17	17	17	17	17	17	7	7	7	7	45					
45 REDDING	19	7	7	7	7	17	17	45	45	45	45	45	45	45	45	45	45	45	45	45	45	45	15					
7 AOYAMA	7	45	17	17	17	15	15	15	15	15	15	15	15	15	15	15	15	15	15	15	15	93	93					
2 CAMIER	45	17	15	15	15	15	45	45	15	2	2	2	2	2	2	2	2	2	2	2	2	2	2	93	2			
17 ABRAHAM	17	15	2	2	2	2	2	2	2	70	70	70	70	70	70	70	70	70	70	70	70	70	93	2	70			
70 LAVERTY	15	2	70	70	45	45	70	70	70	23	8	23	8	23	23	23	23	23	93	93	93	93	70	70				
15 DE ANGELIS	70	70	45	45	70	70	23	23	23	8	8	8	23	8	8	8	8	8	23	23	23	23	23	23				
23 PARKES	9	23	23	23	23	23	8	8	8	93	93	93	93	93	93	93	93	93	8	8	8	8	8	8				
8 BARBERA	23	8	8	8	8	8																						
63 DI MEGLIO	8																											
9 PETRUCCI																												

23 Lapped rider

Constructor Points

1	Honda	316
2	Yamaha	239
3	Ducati	149
4	Forward Yamaha	97
5	PBM	8
6	Avintia	6
7	ART	4

Moto2

RACE DISTANCE: 26 laps, 68.274 miles/109.876km · **RACE WEATHER:** Dry (air 24°C, humidity 48%, track 34°C)

Pos.	Rider	Nat.	No.	Entrant	Machine	Laps	Time & Speed
1	**Esteve Rabat**	SPA	53	Marc VDS Racing Team	Kalex	26	42m 48.724s 95.6mph/ 153.9km/h
2	**Mika Kallio**	FIN	36	Marc VDS Racing Team	Kalex	26	42m 50.995s
3	**Johann Zarco**	FRA	5	AirAsia Caterham	Caterham Suter	26	42m 52.992s
4	**Maverick Vinales**	SPA	40	Paginas Amarillas HP 40	Kalex	26	42m 56.172s
5	**Thomas Luthi**	SWI	12	Interwetten Paddock Moto2	Suter	26	42m 58.403s
6	**Dominique Aegerter**	SWI	77	Technomag carXpert	Suter	26	43m 00.311s
7	**Franco Morbidelli**	ITA	21	Italtrans Racing Team	Kalex	26	43m 10.623s
8	**Julian Simon**	SPA	60	Italtrans Racing Team	Kalex	26	43m 11.127s
9	**Axel Pons**	SPA	49	AGR Team	Kalex	26	43m 11.468s
10	**Takaaki Nakagami**	JPN	30	IDEMITSU Honda Team Asia	Kalex	26	43m 12.768s
11	**Marcel Schrotter**	GER	23	Tech 3	Tech 3	26	43m 14.435s
12	**Sandro Cortese**	GER	11	Dynavolt Intact GP	Kalex	26	43m 18.197s
13	**Mattia Pasini**	ITA	54	NGM Forward Racing	Kalex	26	43m 20.653s
14	**Randy Krummenacher**	SWI	4	Octo IodaRacing Team	Suter	26	43m 23.791s
15	**Luis Salom**	SPA	39	Paginas Amarillas HP 40	Kalex	26	43m 24.018s
16	Xavier Simeon	BEL	19	Federal Oil Gresini Moto2	Suter	26	43m 26.137s
17	Anthony West	AUS	95	QMMF Racing Team	Speed Up	26	43m 26.552s
18	Sam Lowes	GBR	22	Speed Up	Speed Up	26	43m 27.027s
19	Jonas Folger	GER	94	AGR Team	Kalex	26	43m 31.524s
20	Hafizh Syahrin	MAL	55	Petronas Raceline Malaysia	Kalex	26	43m 31.660s
21	Jordi Torres	SPA	81	Mapfre Aspar Team Moto2	Suter	26	43m 32.717s
22	Gino Rea	GBR	8	AGT REA Racing	Suter	26	43m 33.100s
23	Ratthapark Wilairot	THA	14	AirAsia Caterham	Caterham Suter	26	43m 39.263s
24	Florian Marino	FRA	20	NGM Forward Racing	Kalex	26	43m 37.021s
25	Lorenzo Baldassarri	ITA	7	Gresini Moto2	Suter	26	43m 37.757s
26	Louis Rossi	FRA	96	SAG Team	Kalex	26	43m 41.527s
27	Roman Ramos	SPA	97	QMMF Racing Team	Speed Up	26	43m 51.039s
28	Federico Caricasulo	ITA	64	Teluru Team JiR Webike	TSR	26	43m 51.141s
29	Robin Mulhauser	SWI	70	Technomag carXpert	Suter	26	43m 51.767s
30	Thitipong Warokorn	THA	10	APH PTT The Pizza SAG	Kalex	26	43m 55.045s
31	Federico Fuligni	ITA	32	Ciatti	Suter	26	43m 54.530s
32	Azlan Shah	MAL	25	IDEMITSU Honda Team Asia	Kalex	25	43m 22.564s
	Ricard Cardus	SPA	88	Tech 3	Tech 3	13	DNF
	Riccardo Russo	ITA	84	Tasca Racing Moto2	Suter	12	DNF
	Nicolas Terol	SPA	18	Mapfre Aspar Team Moto2	Suter	10	DNF
	Miroslav Popov	CZE	59	Montaze Broz Racing Team	Suter	3	DNF

Fastest lap: Esteve Rabat, on lap 4, 1m 38.265s, 96.2mph/154.8km/h.
Lap record: Pol Espargaro, SPA (Kalex), 1m 38.070s, 96.4mph/155.1km/h (2013).
Event best maximum speed: Sandro Cortese, 152.3mph/245.1km/h (warm up).

Qualifying
Weather: Dry
Air Temp: 24° **Track Temp:** 37°
Humidity: 55%

1	Kallio	1m 38.043s
2	Rabat	1m 38.110s
3	Luthi	1m 38.114s
4	Vinales	1m 38.202s
5	Aegerter	1m 38.236s
6	Zarco	1m 38.413s
7	Cardus	1m 38.499s
8	Nakagami	1m 38.506s
9	Krummenacher	1m 38.522s
10	Pons	1m 38.626s
11	Schrotter	1m 38.671s
12	Folger	1m 38.706s
13	Simon	1m 38.729s
14	Cortese	1m 38.784s
15	Salom	1m 38.865s
16	Terol	1m 39.028s
17	Simeon	1m 39.040s
18	Morbidelli	1m 39.081s
19	Baldassarri	1m 39.148s
20	Torres	1m 39.177s
21	Rossi	1m 39.235s
22	Pasini	1m 39.355s
23	West	1m 39.510s
24	Lowes	1m 39.598s
25	Syahrin	1m 39.670s
26	Marino	1m 39.746s
27	Shah	1m 39.832s
28	Rea	1m 39.878s
29	Wilairot	1m 39.898s
30	Warokorn	1m 40.056s
31	Ramos	1m 40.088s
32	Russo	1m 40.096s
33	Fuligni	1m 40.135s
34	Caricasulo	1m 40.416s
35	Mulhauser	1m 40.742s
36	Popov	1m 40.865s

Fastest race laps

1	Rabat	1m 38.265s
2	Kallio	1m 38.267s
3	Vinales	1m 38.429s
4	Zarco	1m 38.441s
5	Luthi	1m 38.454s
6	Aegerter	1m 38.559s
7	Folger	1m 38.649s
8	Morbidelli	1m 38.680s
9	Cortese	1m 38.807s
10	Pons	1m 38.841s
11	Cardus	1m 38.859s
12	Schrotter	1m 38.886s
13	Salom	1m 38.897s
14	Simon	1m 38.944s
15	Rossi	1m 38.960s
16	Nakagami	1m 39.038s
17	Pasini	1m 39.049s
18	Lowes	1m 39.193s
19	Rea	1m 39.382s
20	Simeon	1m 39.395s
21	West	1m 39.407s
22	Krummenacher	1m 39.431s
23	Wilairot	1m 39.525s
24	Syahrin	1m 39.567s
25	Terol	1m 39.581s
26	Baldassarri	1m 39.736s
27	Marino	1m 39.769s
28	Torres	1m 39.793s
29	Mulhauser	1m 40.134s
30	Ramos	1m 40.218s
31	Russo	1m 40.225s
32	Caricasulo	1m 40.244s
33	Warokorn	1m 40.287s
34	Fuligni	1m 40.362s
35	Shah	1m 40.723s
36	Popov	1m 44.339s

Championship Points

1	Rabat	258
2	Kallio	236
3	Vinales	179
4	Aegerter	133
5	Luthi	103
6	Corsi	100
7	Zarco	88
8	West	65
9	Salom	63
10	Cortese	62
11	Morbidelli	52
12	Schrotter	51
13	Folger	48
14	Lowes	42
15	Simeon	39
16	De Angelis	37
17	Simon	36
18	Pasini	32
19	Torres	32
20	Syahrin	29
21	Cardus	28
22	Pons	28
23	Krummenacher	24
24	Nakagami	23
25	Rossi	13
26	Baldassarri	12
27	Rea	5
28	Terol	2

Constructor Points

1	Kalex	315
2	Suter	190
3	Speed Up	94
4	Caterham Suter	88
5	Tech 3	61
6	Forward KLX	33

Moto3

RACE DISTANCE: 23 laps, 60.396 miles/97.198km · **RACE WEATHER:** Dry (air 23°C, humidity 53%, track 30°C)

Pos.	Rider	Nat.	No.	Entrant	Machine	Laps	Time & Speed
1	**Alex Rins**	SPA	42	Estrella Galicia 0,0	Honda	23	39m 50.694s 90.9mph/ 146.3km/h
2	**Alex Marquez**	SPA	12	Estrella Galicia 0,0	Honda	23	39m 50.736s
3	**Jack Miller**	AUS	8	Red Bull KTM Ajo	KTM	23	39m 54.097s
4	**Isaac Vinales**	SPA	32	Calvo Team	KTM	23	39m 55.153s
5	**Enea Bastianini**	ITA	33	Junior Team GO&FUN Moto3	KTM	23	39m 55.179s
6	**Brad Binder**	RSA	41	Ambrogio Racing	Mahindra	23	39m 55.365s
7	**Alexis Masbou**	FRA	10	Ongetta-Rivacold	Honda	23	40m 00.100s
8	**Andrea Migno**	ITA	16	Mahindra Racing	Mahindra	23	40m 00.237s
9	**Juanfran Guevara**	SPA	58	Mapfre Aspar Team Moto3	Kalex KTM	23	40m 00.400s
10	**Efren Vazquez**	SPA	7	SaxoPrint-RTG	Honda	23	40m 00.737s
11	**Romano Fenati**	ITA	5	SKY Racing Team VR46	KTM	23	40m 00.802s
12	**Danny Kent**	GBR	52	Red Bull Husqvarna Ajo	Husqvarna	23	40m 03.246s
13	**John McPhee**	GBR	17	SaxoPrint-RTG	Honda	23	40m 05.108s
14	**Zulfahmi Khairuddin**	MAL	63	Ongetta-AirAsia	Honda	23	40m 06.179s
15	**Jorge Navarro**	SPA	99	Marc VDS Racing Team	Kalex KTM	23	40m 06.869s
16	Niccolo Antonelli	ITA	23	Junior Team GO&FUN Moto3	KTM	23	40m 11.648s
17	Jakub Kornfeil	CZE	84	Calvo Team	KTM	23	40m 12.823s
18	Alessandro Tonucci	ITA	19	CIP	Mahindra	23	40m 12.851s
19	Philipp Oettl	GER	65	Interwetten Paddock Moto3	Kalex KTM	23	40m 28.066s
20	Bryan Schouten	NED	51	CIP	Mahindra	23	40m 33.489s
21	Eric Granado	BRA	57	Calvo Team	KTM	23	40m 34.017s
22	Miguel Oliveira	POR	44	Mahindra Racing	Mahindra	23	40m 34.655s
23	Hafiq Azmi	MAL	38	SIC-AJO	KTM	23	40m 45.906s
24	Ana Carrasco	SPA	22	RW Racing GP	Kalex KTM	23	40m 45.963s
25	Lorenzo Petrarca	ITA	77	Team Ciatti	KTM	23	40m 46.125s
26	Jules Danilo	FRA	95	Ambrogio Racing	Mahindra	23	40m 46.688s
27	Remy Gardner	AUS	2	Kiefer Racing	Kalex KTM	23	40m 48.806s
28	Gabriel Ramos	VEN	4	Kiefer Racing	Kalex KTM	23	40m 57.508s
	Scott Deroue	NED	9	RW Racing GP	Kalex KTM	19	DNF
	Andrea Locatelli	ITA	55	San Carlo Team Italia	Mahindra	18	DNF
	Niklas Ajo	FIN	31	Avant Tecno Husqvarna Ajo	Husqvarna	11	DNF
	Gabriel Rodrigo	ARG	91	RBA Racing Team	KTM	11	DNF
	Karel Hanika	CZE	98	Red Bull KTM Ajo	KTM	8	DNF
	Francesco Bagnaia	ITA	21	SKY Racing Team VR46	KTM	7	DNF
	Matteo Ferrari	ITA	3	San Carlo Team Italia	Mahindra	3	DNF

Fastest lap: Juanfran Guevara, on lap 4, 1m 43.196s, 91.6mph/147.4km/h (record).
Previous lap record: Alex Marquez, SPA (KTM), 1m 43.293s, 91.5mph/147.2km/h (2013).
Event best maximum speed: Efren Vazquez, 131mph/210.9km/h (race).

Qualifying
Weather: Dry
Air Temp: 22° **Track Temp:** 33°
Humidity: 56%

1	Miller	1m 42.974s
2	Ajo	1m 42.978s
3	Rins	1m 43.012s
4	Marquez	1m 43.163s
5	Oliveira	1m 43.298s
6	Kent	1m 43.491s
7	Antonelli	1m 43.546s
8	Vinales	1m 43.547s
9	Vazquez	1m 43.553s
10	Binder	1m 43.676s
11	Fenati	1m 43.698s
12	Guevara	1m 43.956s
13	Navarro	1m 43.978s
14	Bagnaia	1m 43.986s
15	McPhee	1m 44.039s
16	Kornfeil	1m 44.154s
17	Bastianini	1m 44.201s
18	Khairuddin	1m 44.281s
19	Hanika	1m 44.286s
20	Rodrigo	1m 44.302s
21	Tonucci	1m 44.367s
22	Migno	1m 44.370s
23	Granado	1m 44.381s
24	Masbou	1m 44.435s
25	Ferrari	1m 44.456s
26	Locatelli	1m 44.595s
27	Danilo	1m 44.908s
28	Deroue	1m 45.122s
29	Oettl	1m 45.280s
30	Schouten	1m 45.398s
31	Petrarca	1m 45.719s
32	Azmi	1m 46.065s
33	Gardner	1m 46.264s
34	Carrasco	1m 46.477s
35	Ramos	1m 47.183s

Fastest race laps

1	Guevara	1m 43.196s
2	Rins	1m 43.206s
3	Oliveira	1m 43.225s
4	Binder	1m 43.227s
5	Vinales	1m 43.273s
6	Marquez	1m 43.289s
7	Miller	1m 43.310s
8	Masbou	1m 43.311s
9	Vazquez	1m 43.335s
10	Bastianini	1m 43.416s
11	McPhee	1m 43.463s
12	Kent	1m 43.464s
13	Fenati	1m 43.506s
14	Migno	1m 43.525s
15	Ajo	1m 43.544s
16	Khairuddin	1m 43.578s
17	Navarro	1m 43.585s
18	Kornfeil	1m 43.704s
19	Hanika	1m 43.802s
20	Antonelli	1m 43.871s
21	Ferrari	1m 43.912s
22	Tonucci	1m 43.941s
23	Locatelli	1m 44.155s
24	Rodrigo	1m 44.196s
25	Oettl	1m 44.260s
26	Bagnaia	1m 44.341s
27	Danilo	1m 44.452s
28	Schouten	1m 44.574s
29	Granado	1m 44.637s
30	Deroue	1m 44.749s
31	Azmi	1m 45.105s
32	Gardner	1m 45.134s
33	Carrasco	1m 45.153s
34	Petrarca	1m 45.348s
35	Ramos	1m 45.425s

Championship Points

1	Miller	195
2	Marquez	186
3	Rins	175
4	Vazquez	151
5	Fenati	140
6	Masbou	134
7	Vinales	112
8	Bastianini	98
9	Oliveira	84
10	Binder	77
11	Kent	77
12	Kornfeil	67
13	McPhee	53
14	Ajo	45
15	Bagnaia	42
16	Guevara	40
17	Antonelli	30
18	Hanika	24
19	Loi	17
20	Khairuddin	16
21	Tonucci	15
22	Ferrari	12
23	Oettl	10
24	Migno	8
25	Iwema	4
26	Sissis	3
27	Navarro	3
28	Granado	2

Constructor Points

1	KTM	278
2	Honda	278
3	Mahindra	124
4	Husqvarna	97
5	Kalex KTM	52
6	FTR KTM	4

ARAGON GRAND PRIX

MOTORLAND ARAGON

Main: One down, one to go: Pedrosa falls behind Marquez, who managed one more lap.

Inset, top: High flier: Lorenzo is applauded by first-time podium companions Espargaro and Crutchlow.

Inset, below left: Dazed and confused, Rossi was taken away in an ambulance.

Inset, bottom left: Iannone's race was abbreviated, and so was his new Ducati. He was lucky the bike did not land on him.

Photos: Gold & Goose

Above: Crutchlow, Smith, Bradl and Bautista were early callers in the pits for a bike swap.

Top right: Too tall to tango? Loris Baz was hired, then fired by the Aspar team – and immediately taken up by Forward Racing.

Above centre right: A feast of mutual gratitude between Forward team boss Giovanni Cuzari and Yamaha's Kouichi Tsuji and Lin Jarvis was justified by Sunday's podium finish.

Above right: Maverick Vinales celebrates his second Moto2 win.

Right: Lorenzo's gamble earned him a first win in almost a year.

Photos: Gold & Goose

PERFECTION was undone at Misano, through over-enthusiasm – Marquez admitted that he had crashed because he had been anxious to put himself in a position to tie up the championship at Aragon, in front of his home crowd.

It was undone again by a completely different agency in the arid Aragon landscape, in the 800th grand prix. It rained, which brought havoc – and not only to the formerly invincible title leader.

In the case of Marquez and Pedrosa, both erstwhile race leaders, it was a matter of making the wrong decision.

For Iannone and Rossi, both of whom had very narrow escapes from being hit by their own somersaulting bikes, it was down to the track verge being lined with a strip of artificial grass, lethally wet.

For Dovizioso, with a potential victory in his sights, it was just a matter of timing. He'd been planning to pit at the end of lap 19, but a patch of damp ensured he didn't get that far.

Gambling can go both ways, of course. The first rider to pit for a bike change was Aleix Espargaro, who had battled through after being pushed off track on lap one. He needed the opposite of the Repsol Honda pair – for the rain to become heavier rather than lighter. His particular flip of the coin landed the right way up: second place.

It helped, of course, having little to lose. Much the same applied to Lorenzo, long since an afterthought in the championship battle. He pitted two laps after Espargaro. The reward? His first win of the year. And for Crutchlow, on the rostrum after timing his stop perfectly as well.

In the pause after the race, however, it became even clearer just how hard the decision making process must have been, given the calibre of the riders who went the wrong way. Racing your peers on the world's fastest bikes requires a lot of attention. Add in mental arithmetic, weather forecasting and the inability to toss a coin while travelling at speed, and you can see how easy it is to get it wrong.

With a good crowd of more than 66,500, the race started dry. By the mid-point, it was spitting, the white 'Wet Race' flags out after 11 of 23 laps, but it was still not really wet enough to stop. With slick tyres still warm and lap times at first dropping only to about the same level as on wet tyres, the temptation to press on was underlined by the unwillingness to lose the 20–25 seconds that a pit stop would cost. The situation deteriorated; at the same time, the decision became more fraught, a stop more costly.

Moto2 had a dry race, but it had rained in the morning, and for the first of the day, Moto3, conditions were also dire. Most came to the line on wet tyres, but changed to dries on the grid. No choice, really, because there was a dry line. It was rather narrow, however, and it was this that caused the incident that meant the championship lead, held all season by Jack Miller, changed hands.

Alex Marquez had pushed into the lead on lap four; Miller wanted it back immediately and used his famous late braking at the end of the long straight. They were almost side by side into the fast final corner, but as the line narrowed they touched. Miller, on the outside, was pitched off the inside of his bike, his foot went under the back wheel and the bike

was airborne. "If not for that, I probably could have saved it," he said. Admitting it had been a headstrong move at an early stage of the race, he was generous enough to say that Marquez had no choice but to run wide, to avoid the wet, though study of the TV images suggest otherwise. Race Direction was also generous, however, after investigation, and applied no penalty.

Miller was much in the spotlight after the announcement of his impending MotoGP move, repeating his mantra that "It's only a motorbike, with an engine and two tyres." It's only relatively recently that a spell in the intermediate class has become the norm: every premier-class champion but one (Hayden) since Criville in 1999 has done so, but before that the last to serve this apprenticeship was 1982 champion Uncini. From 1983 to 1998, champions Spencer, Lawson, Gardner, Schwantz and Doohan skipped it. Rainey did an isolated 250 year, but like the others came effectively direct not from 125s, but big-bore Superbikes.

Hayden was back at last, his depleted wrist surviving both practice and the race better than an outsider might have expected: for the rider, "I never thought about it being career ending"; and he was rewarded with a careful top-ten finish.

Ducati brought an update, only for the two Andreas. It was dubbed the GP14.2, and the major difference, according to Dovizioso, was that it was generally slimmer, most importantly around the footrests and dummy tank, making it more comfortable to ride; it also offered a better range of setting adjustments. The understeer, however, remained unchanged. They also had an extra bike for Barbera, whose Avintia team was scheduled to switch to Ducati in 2015. It turned out to be more than one extra bike, in terms of replacement chassis, bodywork and engine parts, after a failed fuel union caused it to catch fire on the first day. The rider suffered painful burns to his arm before he was able to jump off, making "barbecued Barbera" jokes somewhat tasteless. He crashed again the next day.

Announcements continued, led by a cloying mutually grateful session (rather justified in the race) at the NGM Forward hospitality unit, which confirmed that Yamaha would continue supplying them Open bikes for 2015. The riders would be Stefan Bradl and (confirmed the next week) Loris Baz, who had thought he would be joining the Aspar Drive M7 team, only for the handshake deal to be repudiated because the team judged the Frenchman "too tall"! The Aspar production Honda seat went instead to Eugene Laverty, while it soon followed that the place occupied by factory-bound Iannone at Pramac Ducati would go to Danilo Petrucci.

MOTOGP RACE – 23 laps

There seemed little doubt that Aragon was a Honda track. But which Honda? Pedrosa topped the list – until Marquez noticed, "took some risks on a cold tyre" and claimed pole number 11 by a quarter of a second.

The Yamahas were at sea, with a tyre grip problem that prevented them from making up the difference with their better corner speed; the main opposition in qualifying came instead from Ducati, with Dovizioso fastest of all on day one (a first for Ducati since the Stoner days), but ending up ninth after a rare crash in qualifying. Instead it was Iannone on the front row, for a fourth time in the season; while Cal Crutchlow slotted into the middle of row two in fifth, his best of the year.

He had a Yamaha on each side, the faster ridden by Pol Espargaro, with Rossi sixth after being obliged, for the first time, to get through Q1 to join Q2, blaming a "defective" tyre. Similarly tyre troubled, Lorenzo headed row three from Bradl and Dovizioso – then Aleix Espargaro, Smith and Barbera, through from Q1 for the first time. Hernandez was best of the rest, followed by Aoyama and Bautista; the returned Hayden was 18th.

For the first 16 laps, it was a lively race, up front and in the midfield.

Iannone made a blazing start and was second when he fell

on lap two. Marquez had pushed into the lead by that point, but Lorenzo stayed right up close, with Pedrosa on his heels. On lap nine, to the surprise of all, Lorenzo took the lead for three laps and kept on attacking after Marquez had seized it back. On the 15th, the rain now spotting harder, Marquez motioned him past on the pit straight. "I didn't know if he was scared from the spitting or if he had engine trouble," said Lorenzo; he soon realised that at least the latter wasn't the case when Marc passed him once again.

On lap 17, Dani took the lead, but by then the lap times were stretching, from the 1m 49s in the dry to almost ten seconds slower. The trend would continue – three seconds slower the next lap, another five seconds next time around. But as long as they all stayed out, who could afford to lose the time of making a pit stop to change bikes?

The crashes, on lap 20 for Dani and 21 for Marc, would provide the answer to that; but Lorenzo had already cast his dice. Dropping back, he had watched the Hondas continue and decided to gamble on doing it differently. As he leapt on to his wet-shod bike, Pedrosa crashed under brakes at the far end of the pit straight. The difficulty of warming up the tyres was no barrier to success, as he took the lead when Marquez tumbled next time around.

Behind this battle, Dovizioso had been a strong fourth, only three seconds behind the slowing Lorenzo when he too was caught out by the damp, with a high-side that left his bike too badly damaged to continue. "I was going to pit at the end of that lap," he later said, ruefully.

Pol Espargaro was next, having run wide in the dry phase to fall behind the next group, then passing them again. That left Aleix engaged with Crutchlow, Smith (recovering from a near run-off on lap one), Bautista and Bradl – until Aleix was the first into the pits.

Now it became confusing as other riders followed into the pits and the order shuffled. Aleix gained two places when Pedrosa crashed and brother Pol pitted from an erstwhile fourth; another when Marquez fell. Now he was second.

Behind him, Crutchlow and Bradl were closely engaged, until the final lap when the Briton was faster than anyone ex-cept Lorenzo, in a late surge that brought him alongside Aleix on the run to the line. They clashed; Crutchlow later grinned: "We were so close, I couldn't change gear. I crossed the line in third instead of fifth." Espargaro hung on to second by less than two-hundredths.

Bradl was a close, but lone fourth; Smith a couple of tenths ahead of Pol after besting him with two laps left, then Bautista now out of touch.

Aoyama was another eight seconds down in eighth; returned team-mate Hayden was ninth. "All things considered, away three months, rebuilt wrist – a top-ten finish and good points, I've got to be happy," he said. "Maybe I could have taken a few more chances in the damp, made up a position or two, but I wanted to be smart this weekend."

The rest trailed in: Redding tenth; then Petrucci and de Angelis, still well clear of Marquez and Pedrosa, with Hernandez taking the last point, the last rider not to be lapped.

The result had little effect on the championship, beyond *increasing* Marquez's lead while possibly prolonging the decision for one more race, and giving Lorenzo a sniff of a possible second.

MOTO2 RACE – 21 laps

Points leader Rabat slipped off in the closing stages of qualifying, missing his chance in a final flurry that resulted in Moto3 champ Vinales displacing Zarco to claim his first pole in the class. At the same time, Kallio put in a flyer to knock rookie Morbidelli off the front row. Rabat was fifth, Luthi sixth; Nakagami headed row three.

The only dry race of the day started in familiar style, with Kallio taking off in the lead from the front row. One difference was his immediate companion, Vinales – and after five laps he pounced, to take a lead he would never lose, stretching it to 2.6 seconds until the closing stages.

There was a lively battle for second, as both Rabat and Aegerter managed to get ahead of Zarco, while Morbidelli tagged on behind.

After one-third distance, Kallio started to drop back in

this gang, with first Aegerter and then Zarco taking over the chase, the latter for three laps.

But as Kallio's pace dropped, in another familiar pattern, Rabat was gaining strength, and on lap 12 he was at the head of the group; after four more, he'd gained a little gap.

Now he started chipping away at Vinales's lead, a few tenths each lap. On the 18th, it was less than two seconds, and just over one second as they started the last. But reigning Moto3 champion Vinales had it under control, for his second win of his first season in the class. And his only season – in 2015, he was scheduled to join the Suzuki MotoGP team.

By now, Luthi had caught the pursuit pack and worked his way through it to attack front-man Zarco in the final stages. Zarco hung on to third by less than two-tenths.

Aegerter had narrowly lost touch, with Kallio and then Morbidelli chasing along. The rookie proved the strongest, passing both for a best-yet fifth, half a second clear of Aegerter, who was just a tenth ahead of Kallio.

Torres was a distant eighth, managing to stay in front of Lowes by less than a second – the Briton had picked his way through strongly from 16th on lap one.

Schrotter was tenth, having pulled clear of his group only on the last lap, to leave Syahrin to take 11th off Cortese, also on the last lap. Salom was still close. Then came Cardus and Nakagami; West was the only faller in the race, remounting only to retire.

Placing seventh was a blow to Kallio's title hopes; Rabat was now 33 points clear.

MOTO3 RACE – 20 laps

Honda narrowly prevailed in qualifying, Rins taking his fourth pole by just over a tenth from Kent's Husqvarna; Guevara was third, his first front row. The top 17 were within one second; title leader Miller was fourth, heading row two from Marquez and rookie Bastianini.

It was another tiddler thriller, in about the worst imaginable conditions – the track wet but for a narrow dry line. It made for a race of wildly changing fortunes, most of all for Miller, who handed over the championship top spot by refusing to concede an early race lead to Marquez.

Kent led away, but Miller had taken over by the end of the first lap, lost the place to Rins next time around, taken it back on the third, then met his fate at the end of the long straight on the fourth.

Kornfeil and McPhee were well up in the front pack, the latter even threatening to lead before he fell victim to the damp on the edge of the narrow line on lap 12.

Marquez and Rins had exchanged the lead until lap ten, when Rins ran wide, narrowly saving the crash; Kent was still part of the mix. But nemesis was coming from behind.

Fenati had finished the first lap 19th, but by half-distance he was up to fifth, and two laps later he took the lead for the first time.

He and Marquez scrapped it out, the decisive move coming last time down the long straight. He drafted past the Spaniard, staying ahead over the line by 0.06 second for his fourth win; Kent was a couple of tenths back.

Rins was more than ten seconds adrift; then came Kornfeil and Bastianini. Another five seconds down, Oliveira beat fellow Mahindra rider Binder by a second after a canny ride from 20th on the grid, including a pause to open his fogged-up visor.

Antonelli was ninth, a couple of seconds clear of Masbou and Ono, with Vinales, Vazquez and Danilo crossing the line almost side by side. Khairuddin took the last point.

Left: Crutchlow and Espargaro clash on the run to the line.

Below left: Vinales, leading Kallio and Rabat, was uncatchable.

Below: Miller's battered KTM was hastily repaired, and he went out "to get time on used tyres", three laps down.

Below centre: Winner Romano Fenati and third-placed Danny Kent on the Moto3 podium.

Bottom: Alex Marquez chases Fenati: the victory margin was 0.057 second.

Photos: Gold & Goose

GRAN PREMIO
IVECO
DE ARAGON

26-28 SEPTEMBER, 2014

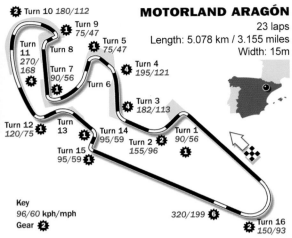

MOTORLAND ARAGÓN

23 laps
Length: 5.078 km / 3.155 miles
Width: 15m

Turn 10 180/112
Turn 9 75/47
Turn 8
Turn 5 75/47
Turn 11 270/168
Turn 7 90/56
Turn 4 195/121
Turn 6
Turn 3 182/113
Turn 12 120/75
Turn 13
Turn 14 95/59
Turn 1 90/56
Turn 15 95/59
Turn 2 155/96
320/199
Turn 16 150/93

Key
96/60 kph/mph
Gear

MotoGP · RACE DISTANCE: 23 laps, 72.572 miles/116.794km · RACE WEATHER: Dry-wet (air 18°C, humidity 93%, track 20°C)

Pos.	Rider	Nat.	No.	Entrant	Machine	Tyres	Race tyre choice*	Laps	Time & speed
1	Jorge Lorenzo	SPA	99	Movistar Yamaha MotoGP	Yamaha YZR-M1	B	F: Soft/R: Medium	23	44m 20.406s 98.2mph/ 158.0km/h
2	Aleix Espargaro	SPA	41	NGM Forward Racing	Forward Yamaha	B	F: Medium/R: Medium	23	44m 30.701s
3	Cal Crutchlow	GBR	35	Ducati Team	Ducati Desmosedici	B	F: Medium/R: Medium	23	44m 30.718s
4	Stefan Bradl	GER	6	LCR Honda MotoGP	Honda RC213V	B	F: Medium/R: Hard	23	44m 32.124s
5	Bradley Smith	GBR	38	Monster Yamaha Tech 3	Yamaha YZR-M1	B	F: Medium/R: Medium	23	44m 49.889s
6	Pol Espargaro	SPA	44	Monster Yamaha Tech 3	Yamaha YZR-M1	B	F: Medium/R: Medium	23	44m 50.092s
7	Alvaro Bautista	SPA	19	GO&FUN Honda Gresini	Honda RC213V	B	F: Soft/R: Medium	23	44m 50.169s
8	Hiroshi Aoyama	JPN	7	Drive M7 Aspar	Honda RCV1000R	B	F: Soft/R: Medium	23	44m 58.247s
9	Nicky Hayden	USA	69	Drive M7 Aspar	Honda RCV1000R	B	F: Soft/R: Soft	23	45m 03.363s
10	Scott Redding	GBR	45	GO&FUN Honda Gresini	Honda RCV1000R	B	F: Medium/R: Soft	23	45m 14.343s
11	Danilo Petrucci	ITA	9	Octo IodaRacing Team	ART	B	F: Medium/R: Soft	23	45m 20.230s
12	Alex de Angelis	RSM	15	NGM Forward Racing	Forward Yamaha	B	F: Soft/R: Medium	23	45m 21.124s
13	Marc Marquez	SPA	93	Repsol Honda Team	Honda RC213V	B	F: Medium/R: Hard	23	45m 35.633s
14	Dani Pedrosa	SPA	26	Repsol Honda Team	Honda RC213V	B	F: Medium/R: Hard	23	45m 44.932s
15	Yonny Hernandez	COL	68	Energy T.I. Pramac Racing	Ducati Desmosedici	B	F: Soft/R: Medium	23	45m 58.661s
16	Michael Laverty	GBR	70	Paul Bird Motorsport	PBM-ART	B	F: Medium/R: Soft	22	44m 37.129s
17	Mike Di Meglio	FRA	63	Avintia Racing	Avintia	B	F: Medium/R: Soft	22	45m 02.913s
18	Broc Parkes	AUS	23	Paul Bird Motorsport	PBM-ART	B	F: Medium/R: Soft	22	45m 02.992s
19	Hector Barbera	SPA	8	Avintia Racing	Ducati Desmosedici	B	F: Medium/R: Soft	22	45m 59.305s
	Andrea Dovizioso	ITA	4	Ducati Team	Ducati Desmosedici	B	F: Medium/R: Medium	18	DNF-crash
	Valentino Rossi	ITA	46	Movistar Yamaha MotoGP	Yamaha YZR-M1	B	F: Soft/R: Medium	3	DNF-crash
	Andrea Iannone	ITA	29	Pramac Racing	Ducati Desmosedici	B	F: Medium/R: Medium	1	DNF-crash
	Karel Abraham	CZE	17	Cardion AB Motoracing	Honda RCV1000R	B	F: Medium/R: Medium	1	DNF-mechanical

* At start of race.

Fastest lap: Jorge Lorenzo, on lap 5, 1m 49.107s, 104.1mph/167.5km/h.

Lap record: Dani Pedrosa, SPA (Honda), 1m 48.565s, 104.6mph/168.3km/h (2013).

Event best maximum speed: Andrea Iannone, 210.6mph/339.0km/h (free practice 2).

Qualifying

Weather: Dry
Air Temp: 24° Track Temp: 36°
Humidity: 55%

1	Marquez	1m 47.187s
2	Pedrosa	1m 47.549s
3	Iannone	1m 47.685s
4	P. Espargaro	1m 47.865s
5	Crutchlow	1m 47.897s
6	Rossi	1m 48.226s
7	Lorenzo	1m 48.246s
8	Bradl	1m 48.368s
9	Dovizioso	1m 48.542s
10	A. Espargaro	1m 48.568s
11	Smith	1m 48.810s
12	Barbera	No Time
13	Hernandez	1m 49.051s
14	Aoyama	1m 49.209s
15	Bautista	1m 49.274s
16	Redding	1m 49.703s
17	Abraham	1m 49.790s
18	Hayden	1m 49.835s
19	De Angelis	1m 50.263s
20	Petrucci	1m 50.635s
21	Laverty	1m 51.280s
22	Parkes	1m 51.489s
23	Di Meglio	1m 52.181s

Fastest race laps

1	Lorenzo	1m 49.107s
2	Marquez	1m 49.133s
3	Pedrosa	1m 49.174s
4	Rossi	1m 49.386s
5	Dovizioso	1m 49.553s
6	P. Espargaro	1m 49.690s
7	A. Espargaro	1m 49.775s
8	Bradl	1m 49.826s
9	Smith	1m 49.978s
10	Crutchlow	1m 49.994s
11	Bautista	1m 50.032s
12	Redding	1m 50.634s
13	Aoyama	1m 50.832s
14	Hernandez	1m 50.850s
15	Barbera	1m 51.040s
16	Hayden	1m 51.199s
17	Petrucci	1m 51.325s
18	De Angelis	1m 51.330s
19	Parkes	1m 52.105s
20	Laverty	1m 52.144s
21	Di Meglio	1m 53.168s

Championship Points

1	Marquez	292
2	Pedrosa	217
3	Rossi	214
4	Lorenzo	202
5	Dovizioso	142
6	A. Espargaro	112
7	P. Espargaro	108
8	Iannone	92
9	Bradl	87
10	Smith	85
11	Bautista	73
12	Crutchlow	63
13	Redding	60
14	Aoyama	51
15	Hernandez	39
16	Hayden	36
17	Abraham	33
18	Edwards	11
19	Pirro	11
20	Petrucci	9
21	Parkes	7
22	De Angelis	7
23	Di Meglio	4
24	Laverty	2
25	Barbera	2
26	Camier	1

Grid order		1	2	3	4	5	6	7	8	9	10	11	12	13	14	15	16	17	18	19	20	21	22	23	
93	MARQUEZ	29	93	93	93	93	93	93	93	99	99	99	93	93	93	99	93	26	26	93	93	99	99	99	1
26	PEDROSA	93	99	99	99	99	99	99	99	93	93	93	99	99	99	93	26	93	93	26	99	41	41	41	2
29	IANNONE	99	26	26	26	26	26	26	26	26	26	26	26	26	26	99	99	99	99	41	35	35	35		3
44	P. ESPARGARO	26	46	46	44	44	44	44	4	4	4	4	4	4	4	4	4	4	44	35	6	6	6		4
35	CRUTCHLOW	44	44	44	4	4	4	4	6	6	6	44	44	44	44	44	44	44	41	6	44	38	38		5
46	ROSSI	46	4	4	6	6	6	6	35	44	44	6	35	41	41	35	35	44	38	44	44	44		6
99	LORENZO	4	6	6	35	35	35	35	44	35	19	19	19	19	35	38	35	6	38	19	19	19		7
6	BRADL	35	35	35	19	19	19	19	19	35	35	35	6	35	41	35	38	19	6	38	19	7	7	7	8
4	DOVIZIOSO	6	19	19	41	41	41	41	41	41	41	41	41	6	6	19	6	19	19	7	69	69	69		9
41	A. ESPARGARO	68	8	41	45	45	38	38	38	38	38	38	38	38	6	41	7	9	69	93	45	45		10
38	SMITH	19	45	8	68	38	45	45	45	45	45	45	68	68	68	9	7	45	45	9	9	11
8	BARBERA	8	68	45	38	68	68	68	68	68	68	68	68	68	45	7	7	41	69	26	15	15	15		12
68	HERNANDEZ	69	41	68	8	8	8	8	8	8	8	8	8	7	7	45	45	45	15	9	93	93		13
7	AOYAMA	45	69	38	69	69	69	69	7	7	7	7	7	8	8	9	9	8	15	9	26	26	26		14
19	BAUTISTA	15	38	69	7	7	7	7	69	69	69	69	69	69	69	8	68	68	68	68	68	68		15
45	REDDING	9	15	9	9	9	9	9	15	9	9	9	15	15	15	69	69	8	70	70	70		
17	ABRAHAM	17	9	7	15	15	15	15	15	15	15	15	9	15	15	15	15	15	23	23	23	63		
69	HAYDEN	7	7	15	23	23	23	23	23	23	23	23	23	23	23	23	23	70	63	63	23		
15	DE ANGELIS	41	23	23	63	63	63	63	70	70	70	70	70	70	70	70	70	70	63	8	8	8		
9	PETRUCCI	38	63	63	70	70	70	70	63	63	63	63	63	63	63	63	63	63					
70	LAVERTY	23	70	70																					
23	PARKES	63																							
63	DI MEGLIO	70																							

99 Pit stop · 70 Lapped rider

Constructor Points

1	Honda	329
2	Yamaha	264
3	Ducati	165
4	Forward Yamaha	117
5	ART	9
6	PBM	8
7	Avintia	6

Moto2

RACE DISTANCE: 21 laps, 66.262 miles/206.638km · RACE WEATHER: Dry (air 19°C, humidity 89%, track 21°C)

Pos.	Rider	Nat.	No.	Entrant	Machine	Laps	Time & Speed
1	**Maverick Vinales**	SPA	40	Paginas Amarillas HP 40	Kalex	21	40m 16.321s 98.7mph/ 158.8km/h
2	**Esteve Rabat**	SPA	53	Marc VDS Racing Team	Kalex	21	40m 17.606s
3	**Johann Zarco**	FRA	5	AirAsia Caterham	Caterham Suter	21	40m 21.197s
4	**Thomas Luthi**	SWI	12	Interwetten Sitag	Suter	21	40m 21.354s
5	**Franco Morbidelli**	ITA	21	Italtrans Racing Team	Kalex	21	40m 22.281s
6	**Dominique Aegerter**	SWI	77	Technomag carXpert	Suter	21	40m 22.726s
7	**Mika Kallio**	FIN	36	Marc VDS Racing Team	Kalex	21	40m 22.846s
8	**Jordi Torres**	SPA	81	Mapfre Aspar Team Moto2	Suter	21	40m 33.634s
9	**Sam Lowes**	GBR	22	Speed Up	Speed Up	21	40m 34.469s
10	**Marcel Schrotter**	GER	23	Tech 3	Tech 3	21	40m 36.014s
11	**Hafizh Syahrin**	MAL	55	Petronas Raceline Malaysia	Kalex	21	40m 37.269s
12	**Sandro Cortese**	GER	11	Dynavolt Intact GP	Kalex	21	40m 37.431s
13	**Luis Salom**	SPA	39	Paginas Amarillas HP 40	Kalex	21	40m 38.986s
14	**Ricard Cardus**	SPA	88	Tech 3	Tech 3	21	40m 40.724s
15	**Takaaki Nakagami**	JPN	30	IDEMITSU Honda Team Asia	Kalex	21	40m 40.786s
16	Julian Simon	SPA	60	Italtrans Racing Team	Kalex	21	40m 43.723s
17	Gino Rea	GBR	8	AGT REA Racing	Suter	21	40m 55.981s
18	Roman Ramos	SPA	97	QMMF Racing Team	Speed Up	21	40m 56.183s
19	Azlan Shah	MAL	25	IDEMITSU Honda Team Asia	Kalex	21	40m 56.394s
20	Louis Rossi	FRA	96	SAG Team	Kalex	21	40m 56.506s
21	Mattia Pasini	ITA	54	NGM Forward Racing	Kalex	21	40m 57.072s
22	Ratthapark Wilairot	THA	14	AirAsia Caterham	Caterham Suter	21	40m 57.385s
23	Jonas Folger	GER	94	AGR Team	Kalex	21	40m 57.579s
24	Riccardo Russo	ITA	84	Tasca Racing Moto2	Suter	21	40m 58.502s
25	Lorenzo Baldassarri	ITA	7	Gresini Moto2	Suter	21	40m 58.596s
26	Robin Mulhauser	SWI	70	Technomag carXpert	Suter	21	40m 58.731s
27	Randy Krummenacher	SWI	4	Octo IodaRacing Team	Suter	21	41m 00.681s
28	Florian Marino	FRA	20	NGM Forward Racing	Kalex	21	41m 03.886s
29	Nicolas Terol	SPA	18	Mapfre Aspar Team Moto2	Suter	21	41m 06.064s
30	Thitipong Warokorn	THA	10	APH PTT The Pizza SAG	Kalex	21	41m 21.991s
	Axel Pons	SPA	49	AGR Team	Kalex	12	DNF
	Kenny Noyes	USA	9	Teluru Team JiR Webike	TSR	6	DNF
	Xavier Simeon	BEL	19	Federal Oil Gresini Moto2	Suter	4	DNF
	Anthony West	AUS	95	QMMF Racing Team	Speed Up	4	DNF

Fastest lap: Thomas Luthi, on lap 17, 1m 54.254s, 99.4mph/160.0km/h.
Lap record: Marc Marquez, SPA (Suter), 1m 53.956s, 99.7mph/160.4km/h (2011).
Event best maximum speed: Sandro Cortese, 173.2mph/278.7km/h (race).

Qualifying
Weather: Dry
Air Temp: 25° **Track Temp:** 37°
Humidity: 50%

1	Vinales	1m 54.073s
2	Zarco	1m 54.124s
3	Kallio	1m 54.130s
4	Morbidelli	1m 54.183s
5	Rabat	1m 54.224s
6	Luthi	1m 54.341s
7	Nakagami	1m 54.390s
8	Aegerter	1m 54.391s
9	Cortese	1m 54.475s
10	Schrotter	1m 54.508s
11	Simon	1m 54.650s
12	Folger	1m 54.786s
13	Torres	1m 54.786s
14	Simeon	1m 54.798s
15	Salom	1m 54.800s
16	Pasini	1m 54.827s
17	Syahrin	1m 54.843s
18	Pons	1m 54.866s
19	Cardus	1m 54.916s
20	Lowes	1m 54.983s
21	Rossi	1m 55.057s
22	Terol	1m 55.182s
23	West	1m 55.280s
24	Rea	1m 55.298s
25	Baldassarri	1m 55.401s
26	Marino	1m 55.429s
27	Wilairot	1m 55.438s
28	Mulhauser	1m 55.487s
29	Ramos	1m 55.814s
30	Russo	1m 55.859s
31	Krummenacher	1m 55.978s
32	Shah	1m 56.069s
33	Warokorn	1m 56.447s
34	Noyes	1m 57.046s

Fastest race laps

1	Luthi	1m 54.254s
2	Rabat	1m 54.276s
3	Vinales	1m 54.425s
4	Kallio	1m 54.446s
5	Zarco	1m 54.611s
6	Morbidelli	1m 54.620s
7	Aegerter	1m 54.694s
8	Syahrin	1m 54.932s
9	Salom	1m 54.996s
10	Folger	1m 55.133s
11	Lowes	1m 55.157s
12	Nakagami	1m 55.159s
13	Pons	1m 55.163s
14	Schrotter	1m 55.190s
15	Torres	1m 55.266s
16	Cortese	1m 55.287s
17	Cardus	1m 55.423s
18	Simon	1m 55.450s
19	Rea	1m 55.706s
20	Pasini	1m 55.754s
21	Shah	1m 55.862s
22	West	1m 55.863s
23	Wilairot	1m 55.877s
24	Krummenacher	1m 55.907s
25	Ramos	1m 55.912s
26	Baldassarri	1m 55.917s
27	Terol	1m 55.939s
28	Rossi	1m 55.952s
29	Russo	1m 55.962s
30	Mulhauser	1m 56.015s
31	Marino	1m 56.171s
32	Simeon	1m 56.195s
33	Warokorn	1m 57.190s
34	Noyes	1m 58.468s

Championship Points

1	Rabat	278
2	Kallio	245
3	Vinales	204
4	Aegerter	143
5	Luthi	116
6	Zarco	104
7	Corsi	100
8	Salom	66
9	Cortese	66
10	West	65
11	Morbidelli	63
12	Schrotter	57
13	Lowes	49
14	Folger	48
15	Torres	40
16	Simeon	39
17	De Angelis	37
18	Simon	36
19	Syahrin	34
20	Pasini	32
21	Cardus	30
22	Pons	28
23	Krummenacher	24
24	Nakagami	24
25	Rossi	13
26	Baldassarri	12
27	Rea	5
28	Terol	2

Constructor Points

1	Kalex	340
2	Suter	203
3	Caterham Suter	104
4	Speed Up	101
5	Tech 3	67
6	Forward KLX	33

Moto3

RACE DISTANCE: 20 laps, 63.106 miles/101.560km · RACE WEATHER: Wet (air 17°C, humidity 100%, track 20°C)

Pos.	Rider	Nat.	No.	Entrant	Machine	Laps	Time & Speed
1	**Romano Fenati**	ITA	5	SKY Racing Team VR46	KTM	20	40m 52.209s 92.6mph/ 149.0km/h
2	**Alex Marquez**	SPA	12	Estrella Galicia 0,0	Honda	20	40m 52.266s
3	**Danny Kent**	GBR	52	Red Bull Husqvarna Ajo	Husqvarna	20	40m 52.492s
4	**Alex Rins**	SPA	42	Estrella Galicia 0,0	Honda	20	41m 03.840s
5	**Jakub Kornfeil**	CZE	84	Calvo Team	KTM	20	41m 10.591s
6	**Enea Bastianini**	ITA	33	Junior Team GO&FUN Moto3	KTM	20	41m 11.468s
7	**Miguel Oliveira**	POR	44	Mahindra Racing	Mahindra	20	41m 15.915s
8	**Brad Binder**	RSA	41	Ambrogio Racing	Mahindra	20	41m 16.982s
9	**Niccolo Antonelli**	ITA	23	Junior Team GO&FUN Moto3	KTM	20	41m 29.232s
10	**Alexis Masbou**	FRA	10	Ongetta-Rivacold	Honda	20	41m 31.253s
11	**Hiroki Ono**	JPN	50	Honda Team Asia	Honda	20	41m 31.793s
12	**Isaac Vinales**	SPA	32	Calvo Team	KTM	20	41m 54.224s
13	**Efren Vazquez**	SPA	7	SaxoPrint-RTG	Honda	20	41m 54.270s
14	**Jules Danilo**	FRA	95	Ambrogio Racing	Mahindra	20	41m 54.447s
15	**Zulfahmi Khairuddin**	MAL	63	Ongetta-AirAsia	Honda	20	41m 57.477s
16	Jasper Iwema	NED	13	CIP	Mahindra	20	41m 57.491s
17	Eric Granado	BRA	57	Calvo Team	KTM	20	41m 58.695s
18	Andrea Locatelli	ITA	55	San Carlo Team Italia	Mahindra	20	42m 04.283s
19	Hafiq Azmi	MAL	38	SIC-AJO	KTM	20	42m 14.039s
20	Gabriel Rodrigo	ARG	91	RBA Racing Team	KTM	20	42m 17.335s
21	Gabriel Ramos	VEN	4	Kiefer Racing	Kalex KTM	20	42m 17.451s
22	Ana Carrasco	SPA	22	RW Racing GP	Kalex KTM	20	42m 27.253s
23	Karel Hanika	CZE	98	Red Bull KTM Ajo	KTM	20	42m 29.577s
24	Francesco Bagnaia	ITA	21	SKY Racing Team VR46	KTM	19	41m 35.056s
25	Niklas Ajo	FIN	31	Avant Tecno Husqvarna Ajo	Husqvarna	19	41m 37.120s
26	Luca Grunwald	GER	43	Kiefer Racing	Kalex KTM	18	41m 24.388s
27	Jack Miller	AUS	8	Red Bull KTM Ajo	KTM	17	41m 40.090s
	John McPhee	GBR	17	SaxoPrint-RTG	Honda	12	DNF
	Andrea Migno	ITA	16	Mahindra Racing	Mahindra	9	DNF
	Philipp Oettl	GER	65	Interwetten Paddock Moto3	Kalex KTM	8	DNF
	Jorge Navarro	SPA	99	Marc VDS Racing Team	Kalex KTM	5	DNF
	Alessandro Tonucci	ITA	19	CIP	Mahindra	5	DNF
	Juanfran Guevara	SPA	58	Mapfre Aspar Team Moto3	Kalex KTM	3	DNF
	Scott Deroue	NED	9	RW Racing GP	Kalex KTM	2	DNF
	Matteo Ferrari	ITA	3	San Carlo Team Italia	Mahindra	0	DNF

Fastest lap: Romano Fenati, on lap 19, 2m 0.176s, 94.5mph/152.1km/h.
Lap record: Philipp Oettl, GER (Kalex KTM), 1m 59.681s, 94.9mph/152.7km/h (2013).
Event best maximum speed: Efren Vazquez, 148.2mph/238.5km/h (qualifying).

Qualifying
Weather: Dry
Air Temp: 22° **Track Temp:** 31°
Humidity: 55%

1	Rins	1m 58.318s
2	Kent	1m 58.434s
3	Guevara	1m 58.470s
4	Miller	1m 58.476s
5	Marquez	1m 58.510s
6	Bastianini	1m 58.647s
7	Vinales	1m 58.707s
8	McPhee	1m 58.743s
9	Antonelli	1m 58.770s
10	Vazquez	1m 58.828s
11	Navarro	1m 58.969s
12	Kornfeil	1m 58.999s
13	Fenati	1m 59.032s
14	Migno	1m 59.187s
15	Binder	1m 59.208s
16	Masbou	1m 59.224s
17	Hanika	1m 59.314s
18	Khairuddin	1m 59.374s
19	Ono	1m 59.422s
20	Oliveira	1m 59.626s
21	Granado	1m 59.636s
22	Bagnaia	1m 59.718s
23	Tonucci	2m 00.027s
24	Ferrari	2m 00.046s
25	Danilo	2m 00.087s
26	Ajo	2m 00.260s
27	Deroue	2m 00.289s
28	Azmi	2m 00.329s
29	Rodrigo	2m 00.384s
30	Locatelli	2m 00.765s
31	Iwema	2m 00.805s
32	Carrasco	2m 00.878s
33	Grunwald	2m 01.044s
34	Oettl	2m 01.107s
35	Ramos	2m 02.112s

Fastest race laps

1	Fenati	2m 00.176s
2	Kent	2m 00.203s
3	Marquez	2m 00.431s
4	Kornfeil	2m 00.513s
5	Binder	2m 00.970s
6	Oliveira	2m 01.002s
7	Miller	2m 01.011s
8	Masbou	2m 01.053s
9	Rins	2m 01.102s
10	Bastianini	2m 01.278s
11	Vinales	2m 01.283s
12	Khairuddin	2m 01.618s
13	McPhee	2m 01.644s
14	Granado	2m 01.704s
15	Antonelli	2m 01.844s
16	Ono	2m 01.912s
17	Vazquez	2m 02.042s
18	Ajo	2m 02.143s
19	Iwema	2m 02.624s
20	Azmi	2m 02.957s
21	Locatelli	2m 03.189s
22	Danilo	2m 03.440s
23	Migno	2m 03.558s
24	Grunwald	2m 03.622s
25	Ramos	2m 03.716s
26	Rodrigo	2m 03.731s
27	Carrasco	2m 03.983s
28	Oettl	2m 04.103s
29	Hanika	2m 04.375s
30	Navarro	2m 04.431s
31	Guevara	2m 05.112s
32	Bagnaia	2m 05.664s
33	Tonucci	2m 06.206s
34	Deroue	2m 08.770s

Championship Points

1	Marquez	206
2	Miller	195
3	Rins	188
4	Fenati	165
5	Vazquez	154
6	Masbou	140
7	Viñales	116
8	Bastianini	108
9	Kent	93
10	Oliveira	93
11	Binder	85
12	Kornfeil	78
13	McPhee	53
14	Ajo	45
15	Bagnaia	42
16	Guevara	40
17	Antonelli	37
18	Hanika	24
19	Loi	17
20	Khairuddin	17
21	Tonucci	15
22	Ferrari	12
23	Oettl	10
24	Migno	8
25	Ono	5
26	Iwema	4
27	Sissis	3
28	Navarro	3
29	Danilo	2
30	Granado	2

Constructor Points

1	KTM	303
2	Honda	298
3	Mahindra	133
4	Husqvarna	113
5	Kalex KTM	52
6	FTR KTM	4

JAPANESE GRAND PRIX

TWIN RING MOTEGI

Awash with cava, Marquez and his crew celebrate the first time Honda had tied up a premier-class title at its own circuit.
Photo: Gold & Goose

Above: The moment Marquez made sure: he passes Rossi to cement his second championship.

Top: Soft tyre, hard acceleration: Dovizioso put the Ducati on pole at Honda's home.

Top right: Track inspection: rear wheel in the air, Pedrosa sets an inadvertent MotoGP stunt record.

Above right: Double return – 1982 500cc champion Franco Uncini was on hand to demonstrate Suzuki's 2015 MotoGP machine.

Above far right: Marquez and his HRC boss Shuhei Nakamoto had plenty to smile about.

Right: Lorenzo was in unbeatable form for a second straight win of the season.

Photos: Gold & Goose

THE Japanese GP was run not under a cloud, but under the threat of a number of clouds. Typhoon Phanfong had played havoc with F1 at Suzuka the weekend before, and now Typhoon Vonfong was waiting in the wings. By some mercy, this superstorm, biggest of the year so far, slowed compared to earlier predictions and struck only in the far south of Japan on race day. On Monday, it played havoc with transport arrangements on the necessarily quick run down to Australia. Both of these storms questioned the wisdom of holding Japanese rounds in typhoon season.

MotoGP got away with it, however, with two sunny days of practice and qualifying, and a dry and only partially overcast race Sunday. It was a day of celebration for circuit owners Honda, since for the first time in Motegi's 15-year history, a Honda rider clinched a championship on home soil.

It meant yet more records for Marquez, who achieved a second successive title while still at a younger age than the previous youngest ever, 1983 champion Freddie Spencer. He also undercut the previous youngest rider to win back-to-back titles: Mike Hailwood, in 1963. Meanwhile, the family had another potential landmark in sight, as brother Alex won the Moto3 race and extended his title lead. Never before have brothers won titles, let alone in the same year.

It was celebration also for Yamaha, whose efforts to match the mighty H seemed at last to be bearing fruit, with a third race win of the year, and third in succession. Lorenzo was at his imperious best. Then again, Marquez needed only to finish ahead of Rossi and Pedrosa, but above all he needed to finish, so perhaps the tables were somewhat skewed.

The new double champion had earlier run true to high-risk form, starting out with a crash early in the very first practice session after his brake pads had been knocked off by a violent headshake out of turn four. On arriving at the next

corner, by the time he'd pumped the front brake back into action, it was too late, and he ran across the gravel for a luckily harmless crash.

The consensus was that he should have known better; the excuse was a lack of experience with the large 340mm front carbon discs that had become optional for all at Mugello, but that were compulsory at Motegi. This followed several instances of brake problems at the stop-and-go (especially stop) track; the bigger brakes cope with temperature better than the usual 320mm units, being thicker as well as larger. Rather surprisingly, both factory Hondas started the weekend with the discs shrouded to avoid over-cooling, though these were not seen again after Marquez's crash. By contrast, some Yamahas and the Ducatis went the other way, with air-scoops delivering cooling air to the callipers.

Pedrosa's brakes seemed powerful enough anyway, as the rider set a probable, if inadvertent, stunting record for MotoGP with a 'stoppie' of more than 100m, back wheel so high in the air at the end of the downhill straight that "I thought I would go over the handlebars".

The riders' Safety Commission meeting was lively, after the crashes suffered by Rossi and Iannone on wet artificial grass at Aragon. Originally, the use of this material had been requested by MotoGP, but the lethal lack of grip when wet had changed everyone's minds. Dorna's Javier Alonso emerged with the promise that they would start to remove it, especially from danger points, from then on. Lorenzo proposed a different approach, to ensure that running off the track would still incur a penalty, but without being dangerous – a higher step off the outside of the kerbing.

Lorenzo also had ideas to prevent the evident risk of the current flag-to-flag bike-change system, although it had worked to his advantage at Aragon, suggesting that bike

changes should be made compulsory, under the control of a safety car. This revived an idea rejected several years ago, but it found little support.

Rossi had a hangover from his crash: a fracture to his right-hand little finger, already injured at Brno. This was painful, he admitted, "but when the adrenalin comes, it is not a problem." Doubtless the same hormone was working its magic for Nicky Hayden, whose second race back after his wrist had been comprehensively stripped and reassembled was at the most punishing of circuits. Again he gritted his teeth and finished in the points, saying afterwards, "I'm glad to get the first two out of the way."

Fellow American Colin Edwards, who had retired at Indianapolis and at once accepted a role as Yamaha test rider for the Michelin tyres to be introduced in 2017, was back in the news, as the NGM Forward team confirmed that he would make a final GP appearance after all, riding a third bike alongside regulars Espargaro and de Angelis at Valencia. Talking of Michelin, Honda planned two days of tests with the French tyres after the Motegi race. The typhoon put paid to that.

Redding and the Marc VDS team's move to MotoGP with a factory Honda was finally confirmed officially; while Suzuki officially launched their GSX1000RR racer, with Franco Uncini and Kevin Schwantz (Suzuki champions in 1982 and 1993) doing demonstration laps; an interesting concession by circuit owners Honda, who generally prefer to exercise some of their own classic bikes to entertain the fervent fans, 42,856 of whom were there on race day.

The rumoured return of legendary crew chief Jerry Burgess (Gardner, Doohan, Rossi) to spanner for Jack Miller in 2015 was put to bed, when it emerged that in fact Stoner's ex-crew chief, Cristian Gabarrini, would fill the role.

MOTOGP RACE – 24 laps

Motegi is Honda's track, but in some ways also Ducati's: four wins in the past nine races, three in a row for Capirossi and one for Stoner. Ducati claimed another little piece with Dovizioso's first pole of the year. Although his fifth front row, it was his and Ducati's first since 2010, and only the second pole in his career, achieved at the same track as the first.

Soft tyres helped the lap time. Another question: would four extra litres of fuel help over race distance, at the most fuel-hungry track of the year?

Rossi was second by half a tenth – he too had not been on pole since 2010, but it might have been different, if third fastest Pedrosa had not slipped off on the second-last corner at the end of the session on a blazing lap of his own.

Marquez was fourth, his second time all year off the front row; Lorenzo was fifth, then Iannone. Pol Espargaro, Crutchlow and Bradl were on row three. The first five were inside three-tenths, the top 11 within a second.

Rossi took a flyer off the line ahead of Dovizioso, Iannone likewise to lead Lorenzo into the first corner, Marquez outside of him. The last-named lifted cautiously; Lorenzo pushed through the inside, admitting, "I took a lot of risks in the first corners." This put him second, where he stayed for four laps before noting that Rossi's pace was dropping a bit. Once past, he delivered a trademark needle-sharp race, setting a new lap record.

Marquez had dropped to seventh in the first corner, behind not only Iannone, but also Pedrosa and jack-rabbit Pol Espargaro, though he was ahead of the pair by the end of the lap. After two consecutive race errors, "If I made another one here, it would be too much. I was riding a little bit more stiff. But I am human…"

It took him two more laps to pass the first Ducati, and until the ninth to deal with Dovi, whose pace was starting to drop as the tyres wore.

He didn't need to beat Lorenzo, but he did need to beat Rossi. On lap 15, he pounced; Rossi passed him straight back on the next corner. Next time around, however, the Honda was through. Second was enough; he finished 1.6 seconds off the winning Yamaha, one ahead of Rossi. The job was done.

Pedrosa had disposed of Iannone, but was stuck behind Dovi until after half-distance, spiking any hopes of the ros-

trum. He closed on Rossi and was only half a second down over the line, but that was as close as he ever got.

Dovi's hopes of a possible win were dashed, and a 14-second gap at the end told its own story; "The fact is, we're still not ready," he said.

Iannone was just another two adrift. He had spent most of the race fending off a persistent Bradl, but the German faded towards the end, to come under pressure from Pol Espargaro and Smith, the latter losing touch after a little slip with two laps to go.

Comfortably behind, Hernandez had been holding off Bautista, only succumbing to the factory bike on lap 18. The Colombian had trouble coming, however, as Aleix Espargaro had broken free from the next gang and by the last lap was ready to fight for 11th. His attack was successful, but it caused Hernandez to crash – an action that earned him a reprimand and one penalty point.

More than ten seconds back by the end, wild-card Katsuyuki Nakasuga, the factory Yamaha tester, had his hands very full with Aoyama's top Open Honda, finishing less than a tenth ahead.

Five seconds down, Hayden was a brave 14th, coping with the braking, but discomposed when Redding ran off ahead of him in the early stages, throwing up rocks that smashed his screen, spoiling his aerodynamics.

Three seconds away, Barbera's second Ducati race yielded a single point after he passed Redding on the last lap, the Briton complaining about a queasy front-end feeling that spoiled his braking and corner entry, causing at least one further run-off.

De Angelis was out of touch. Laverty narrowly prevailed over di Meglio; Parkes had been with them, but was four seconds down at the end.

Crutchlow was back to Ducati nightmare mode, messing up his start, then crashing out on lap two while trying to make up for it. Abraham also crashed out, blaming a return of brake failure; Petrucci retired.

The result may have settled first place in the championship, but it set up a thriller for second, likely to go all the way to Valencia.

MOTO2 RACE – 23 laps

It was heartbreak for Luthi, firmly on top with an upgraded Suter chassis until the last seconds of qualifying. Then came Rabat, who had been struggling until then, claiming his eighth pole of the year by three-hundredths.

Zarco joined them, his third front row in three races; less than a tenth down, Vinales led a relatively slow Kallio, almost half a second adrift, and Nakagami.

Again the race was a bit of a procession, but with some refreshing differences – Rabat didn't come through to win. He could do no better than third; Luthi led from start to finish. "I made two mistakes," he said, "missing a gear once, and braking a bit late another time." That aside, he was almost perfect, with enough in hand to resist a fierce lap-record attack from Vinales in the closing laps.

He led into the first corner and soon began stretching clear, helped because Zarco was second and holding up the pursuit for the first nine laps. By then, he had Vinales, Rabat, Kallio and Simon all piled up behind him, and Luthi was two seconds clear.

Once Vinales found his way past on lap ten, they started to stretch out a bit. Rabat went with his fellow Spaniard and was leaning on him hard on lap 15, but to no avail. Vinales was flying and even looked like he might catch Luthi in the closing stages, but he was still just under a second down as they started the last lap, and 1.2 by the end of it.

Rabat was third, another 1.2 seconds down.

Kallio had faded by the end, leaving Zarco to a safe fourth, while the Finn was busy fending off Simon, whose teammate, rookie Morbidelli, had closed right up, only to drop away again by the end.

More than five seconds away, Aegerter had finally caught and passed Cardus, only to slip off with three laps to go, remounting to finish 18th, a costly no-score.

By the finish, Malaysian thruster Syahrin had also got past Cardus for eighth, the pair comfortably ahead of Simeon and Torres, who was pressed at the end by Jonas Folger. Nakagami's strong qualifying had again flattered to deceive, but he passed Gino Rea with a couple of laps to go, the Briton's

Above: Conformist *tifosi*, Japanese style: the Honda stand was packed with fans with flags.

Top: Luthi leads Zarco (half hidden), Kallio (36) and Vinales (40), first time into turn three. He was never headed.

Right: Joy in the morning: Motegi brought Luthi's first win since 2012.

Far right: Vazquez, Binder and McPhee chase Alex Marquez on the last run out of Victory Corner. The win handsomely boosted his title chances.

Photos: Gold & Goose

Above: Lorenzo and Rossi did Yamaha proud at Honda's home track.
Photo: Movistar Yamaha

Left: Malaysian Hafizh Syahrin over-takes Simeon on his way to eighth place, his third top ten of the year.

Below: Former Motegi winner Danny Kent earned a first ever pole position for Husqvarna.
Photos: Gold & Goose

first finish in the points in seven races. Salom succeeded in retaining the last point from a pressing Louis Rossi.

Sam Lowes was an early faller, joined on the crash list by Cortese (twice!), Pasini, West, Schrotter and Pons.

Rabat stretched his lead over Kallio, 294 to 256; Vinales was closing on 224. Aegerter was out of touch on 143, with compatriot Luthi closing on 141.

MOTO3 RACE – 20 laps

All three Moto3 title contenders crashed over the three days, Rins and Miller in qualifying. The Australian's prang, going into the first underpass, was spectacular, high-siding and ending up with the bike on top of him.

This left a career second pole (and Husqvarna's first ever) to former Motegi winner Kent. It was an unusual front row, with Antonelli and then McPhee, best Honda and also his own personal best.

Oliveira's Mahindra had led the session earlier, and he ended up heading row two from Miller and Vinales. Only then came the usual top Honda riders, Marquez seventh and Rins ninth, with Binder between them.

Kent led away, and when Miller took over on lap five, a lead group of six added Oliveira, Marquez, Binder and McPhee. Miller stayed ahead until lap 11, by which point Vazquez had worked through the next pack and caught up. Almost immediately Oliveira was gone, in a huge thumping high-side.

Marquez led one more lap, then it was Miller again, the pack shuffling constantly as the laps counted down.

The crucial moment came at the end of the downhill straight on the last corner. Kent dived inside to lead into the corner, only to run out wide. Marquez was on the other side of Miller when the Australian found neutral instead of first gear and also ran wide.

He collided with Kent as they regained the track, but by then Marquez was gone, with Vazquez on his heels. Binder was third and McPhee a career-best fourth, the first four over the line within less than seven-tenths.

Miller was only another four-tenths away in fifth, Kent right behind. Fenati led the next group for seventh, from Bastianini, Antonelli, Rins and Vinales, seventh to 11th within just over a second.

It was costly to the title chances of both Fenati and Rins, who had been batted off track on the first corner by a wide-running Ajo (who subsequently high-sided when he tried to rejoin) and had battled through from 20th, but couldn't escape from the brawl.

The two Japanese wild-cards crashed out on the first corner; Ferrari brought down fellow Italian and Migno at the other end of lap one, with Guevara, Kornfeil, Navarro and Masbou swelling the crash list.

Marquez gained a 25-point lead over Miller, now seriously threatening to make it a first-time brother double act for the championship.

MOTUL
GRAND PRIX OF JAPAN

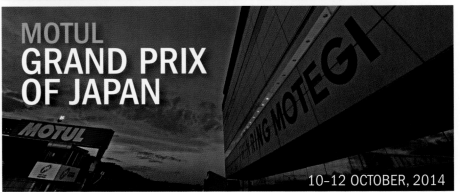

10-12 OCTOBER, 2014

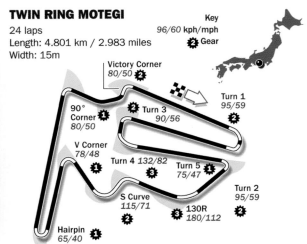

TWIN RING MOTEGI
24 laps
Length: 4.801 km / 2.983 miles
Width: 15m

Key
96/60 kph/mph
Gear

Victory Corner 80/50
Turn 1 95/59
90° Corner 80/50
Turn 3 90/56
V Corner 78/48
Turn 4 132/82
Turn 5 75/47
Turn 2 95/59
S Curve 115/71
130R 180/112
Hairpin 65/40

MotoGP RACE DISTANCE: 24 laps, 71.597 miles/115.224km · RACE WEATHER: Dry (air 19°C, humidity 57%, track 27°C)

Pos.	Rider	Nat.	No.	Entrant	Machine	Tyres	Race tyre choice	Laps	Time & speed
1	Jorge Lorenzo	SPA	99	Movistar Yamaha MotoGP	Yamaha YZR-M1	B	F: Medium/R: Soft	24	42m 21.259s 101.4mph/ 163.2km/h
2	Marc Marquez	SPA	93	Repsol Honda Team	Honda RC213V	B	F: Medium/R: Soft	24	42m 22.897s
3	Valentino Rossi	ITA	46	Movistar Yamaha MotoGP	Yamaha YZR-M1	B	F: Medium/R: Soft	24	42m 23.861s
4	Dani Pedrosa	SPA	26	Repsol Honda Team	Honda RC213V	B	F: Medium/R: Soft	24	42m 24.416s
5	Andrea Dovizioso	ITA	4	Ducati Team	Ducati Desmosedici	B	F: Medium/R: Soft	24	42m 35.612s
6	Andrea Iannone	ITA	29	Pramac Racing	Ducati Desmosedici	B	F: Medium/R: Soft	24	42m 37.912s
7	Stefan Bradl	GER	6	LCR Honda MotoGP	Honda RC213V	B	F: Medium/R: Soft	24	42m 40.790s
8	Pol Espargaro	SPA	44	Monster Yamaha Tech	Yamaha YZR-M1	B	F: Medium/R: Soft	24	42m 41.074s
9	Bradley Smith	GBR	38	Monster Yamaha Tech	Yamaha YZR-M1	B	F: Medium/R: Soft	24	42m 44.834s
10	Alvaro Bautista	SPA	19	GO&FUN Honda Gresini	Honda RC213V	B	F: Medium/R: Soft	24	42m 56.946s
11	Aleix Espargaro	SPA	41	NGM Forward Racing	Forward Yamaha	B	F: Medium/R: Soft	24	43m 01.927s
12	Katsuyuki Nakasuga	JPN	21	YAMALUBE Racing Team with YSP	Yamaha YZR-M1	B	F: Medium/R: Soft	24	43m 12.286s
13	Hiroshi Aoyama	JPN	7	Drive M7 Aspar	Honda RCV1000R	B	F: Medium/R: Extra-Soft	24	43m 12.352s
14	Nicky Hayden	USA	69	Drive M7 Aspar	Honda RCV1000R	B	F: Medium/R: Extra-Soft	24	43m 17.051s
15	Hector Barbera	SPA	8	Avintia Racing	Ducati Desmosedici	B	F: Medium/R: Soft	24	43m 20.348s
16	Scott Redding	GBR	45	GO&FUN Honda Gresini	Honda RCV1000R	B	F: Medium/R: Soft	24	43m 20.767s
17	Alex de Angelis	RSM	15	NGM Forward Racing	Forward Yamaha	B	F: Medium/R: Extra-Soft	24	43m 37.806s
18	Michael Laverty	GBR	70	Paul Bird Motorsport	PBM-ART	B	F: Medium/R: Extra-Soft	24	43m 49.280s
19	Mike di Meglio	FRA	63	Avintia Racing	Avintia	B	F: Medium/R: Extra-Soft	24	43m 50.729s
20	Broc Parkes	AUS	23	Paul Bird Motorsport	PBM-ART	B	F: Medium/R: Extra-Soft	24	43m 54.512s
	Yonny Hernandez	COL	68	Energy T.I. Pramac Racing	Ducati Desmosedici	B	F: Medium/R: Soft	23	DNF-crash
	Karel Abraham	CZE	17	Cardion AB Motoracing	Honda RCV1000R	B	F: Medium/R: Extra-Soft	14	DNF-crash
	Danilo Petrucci	ITA	9	Octo IodaRacing Team	ART	B	F: Medium/R: Extra-Soft	4	DNF-mechanical
	Cal Crutchlow	GBR	35	Ducati Team	Ducati Desmosedici	B	F: Medium/R: Soft	1	DNF-crash

Fastest lap: Jorge Lorenzo, on lap 8, 1m 45.350s, 101.9mph/164.0km/h (record).

Previous lap record: Dani Pedrosa, SPA (Honda), 1m 45.589s, 101.7mph/163.7km/h (2012).

Event best maximum speed: Marc Marquez, 192.2mph/309.3km/h (race).

Qualifying

Weather: Dry
Air Temp: 23° **Track Temp:** 36°
Humidity: 50%

1	Dovizioso	1m 44.502s
2	Rossi	1m 44.557s
3	Pedrosa	1m 44.755s
4	Marquez	1m 44.775s
5	Lorenzo	1m 44.784s
6	Iannone	1m 44.854s
7	P. Espargaro	1m 44.867s
8	Crutchlow	1m 44.898s
9	Bradl	1m 45.005s
10	Smith	1m 45.044s
11	A. Espargaro	1m 45.315s
12	Bautista	1m 45.677s
13	Hernandez	1m 45.971s
14	Hayden	1m 46.465s
15	Redding	1m 46.499s
16	Barbera	1m 46.796s
17	Nakasuga	1m 46.876s
18	Aoyama	1m 46.915s
19	Abraham	1m 46.948s
20	De Angelis	1m 47.092s
21	Petrucci	1m 47.757s
22	Laverty	1m 48.144s
23	Di Meglio	1m 48.185s
24	Parkes	1m 48.261s

Fastest race laps

1	Lorenzo	1m 45.350s
2	Pedrosa	1m 45.381s
3	Marquez	1m 45.389s
4	Rossi	1m 45.545s
5	Dovizioso	1m 45.557s
6	Bradl	1m 45.772s
7	Iannone	1m 45.880s
8	Smith	1m 46.147s
9	P. Espargaro	1m 46.183s
10	A. Espargaro	1m 46.605s
11	Bautista	1m 46.660s
12	Hernandez	1m 46.735s
13	Barbera	1m 46.898s
14	Nakasuga	1m 47.066s
15	Aoyama	1m 47.104s
16	Hayden	1m 47.230s
17	Redding	1m 47.289s
18	Abraham	1m 47.690s
19	De Angelis	1m 48.168s
20	Laverty	1m 48.613s
21	Petrucci	1m 48.651s
22	Di Meglio	1m 48.934s
23	Parkes	1m 49.004s

Championship Points

1	Marquez	312
2	Rossi	230
3	Pedrosa	230
4	Lorenzo	227
5	Dovizioso	153
6	A. Espargaro	117
7	P. Espargaro	116
8	Iannone	102
9	Bradl	96
10	Smith	92
11	Bautista	79
12	Crutchlow	63
13	Redding	60
14	Aoyama	54
15	Hernandez	39
16	Hayden	38
17	Abraham	33
18	Edwards	11
19	Pirro	11
20	Petrucci	9
21	Parkes	7
22	De Angelis	7
23	Di Meglio	4
24	Nakasuga	4
25	Barbera	3
26	Laverty	2
27	Camier	1

Constructor Points

1	Honda	349
2	Yamaha	289
3	Ducati	176
4	Forward Yamaha	122
5	ART	9
6	PBM	8
7	Avintia	6

Grid order		1	2	3	4	5	6	7	8	9	10	11	12	13	14	15	16	17	18	19	20	21	22	23	24	
4	DOVIZIOSO	46	46	46	46	99	99	99	99	99	99	99	99	99	99	99	99	99	99	99	99	99	99	99	99	1
46	ROSSI	99	99	99	99	46	46	46	46	46	46	46	46	46	46	46	93	93	93	93	93	93	93	93	93	2
26	PEDROSA	4	4	4	4	4	4	4	4	93	93	93	93	93	93	93	46	46	46	46	46	46	46	46	46	3
93	MARQUEZ	29	29	93	93	93	93	93	93	4	4	4	4	4	26	26	26	26	26	26	26	26	26	26	26	4
99	LORENZO	93	93	29	29	26	26	26	26	26	26	26	26	26	4	4	4	4	4	4	4	4	4	4	4	5
29	IANNONE	26	26	26	26	29	29	29	29	29	29	29	29	29	29	29	29	29	29	29	29	29	29	29	29	6
44	P. ESPARGARO	44	44	6	6	6	6	6	6	6	6	6	6	6	6	6	6	6	6	6	6	6	6	6	6	7
35	CRUTCHLOW	6	6	44	44	44	44	44	44	44	44	44	44	44	44	44	44	44	44	44	44	44	44	44	44	8
6	BRADL	38	38	38	38	38	38	38	38	38	38	38	38	38	38	38	38	38	38	38	38	38	38	38	38	9
38	SMITH	35	68	68	68	68	68	68	68	68	68	68	68	68	68	68	68	19	19	19	19	19	19	19	19	10
41	A. ESPARGARO	68	19	19	19	19	19	19	19	19	19	19	19	19	19	19	19	68	68	68	68	68	68	41	41	11
19	BAUTISTA	19	45	45	45	45	41	41	41	41	41	41	41	41	41	41	41	41	41	41	41	41	41	21	21	12
68	HERNANDEZ	41	69	21	21	21	21	21	21	21	21	21	21	21	21	21	21	21	21	21	21	21	7	7	7	13
69	HAYDEN	45	21	69	41	41	45	7	7	7	7	7	7	7	7	7	7	7	7	7	7	7	69	69	69	14
45	REDDING	69	7	7	7	7	7	45	69	69	69	45	45	69	69	69	69	69	69	69	69	69	8	8	15
8	BARBERA	7	41	41	69	69	69	69	45	45	45	69	69	45	45	45	45	45	45	45	45	45	45	45	
21	NAKASUGA	21	17	17	17	17	17	8	17	17	17	17	17	15	15	15	15	15	15	15	15	8	45	15	
7	AOYAMA	8	8	8	8	17	17	17	8	17	17	17	17	17	17	15	15	15	15	15	15	15	15	70	
17	ABRAHAM	17	9	9	70	70	15	15	15	15	15	15	15	70	70	70	70	70	70	70	70	70	63	
15	DE ANGELIS	9	70	70	15	15	63	63	63	63	63	63	70	63	63	63	63	63	63	63	63	23	
9	PETRUCCI	63	63	15	63	63	70	70	70	70	70	70	63	23	23	23	23	23	23	23	23	
70	LAVERTY	70	15	63	23	23	23	23	23	23	23	23	23									
63	DI MEGLIO	23	23	23	9																	
23	PARKES	15																				

Inset, left: And the ever popular winner was...? "It was me!"
Photo: Movistar Yamaha

Insets, far and centre left: Body language: frustration from crasher Marquez in the grass; jubilation from rostrum finisher Smith.

Main: Lorenzo and Smith made the best starts, with cannonball Iannone and Pol Espargaro half hidden, and Marquez looking for a way to take over. Note Crutchlow (35), soon to be knocked sideways by Iannone, and Rossi poised to take the benefit.
Photos: Gold & Goose

Above: Down and out. Marquez showed how easy it was, on the wrong tyre, to crash under braking.

Above right: Iannone led away after his second and more serious collision, rear-ending an innocent Pedrosa out of the race.

Photos: Gold & Goose

Top: Rossi would get the upper hand in a long struggle. Note the exaggerated right wear on Lorenzo's front Bridgestone.

Photo: Movistar Yamaha

THERE are all sorts of ways to fall off a motorcycle. At grand prix level, unless it is wet, falls nearly all take place when the bike is leaned over. It was different at Phillip Island, clearly the most challenging track of them all for tyre constructors.

The dreams of three top riders ended in the grass lining the scenic seaside circuit, where a midday change of wind direction to a sea breeze off the icy Bass Strait sent track and air temperatures plummeting. That was enough to undermine the measures taken by Bridgestone to correct 2013's tyre debacle (the race cut by almost a third and split into two for a change to fresh rubber). And to undo the hopes of race leader Marquez – until then, on target to equal Doohan's record of 12 wins in a season; of Crutchlow – who had overturned his Ducati misfortunes and was barely a mile from a resounding second place; of the younger Espargaro – on target to equal his career-best fourth. And in practice the equilibrium of the resurgent Lorenzo.

All of these crashes took place when the motorcycles were bolt upright, when the front wheels locked under braking for one or the other of the track's pair of slow right-hand corners. (There were, by the way, a number of other crashes on Dunlops in the smaller classes, 34 on the first day alone, but none quite like this.)

The results were simple, but the background complex. All of these crashes happened on Bridgestone's new asymmetric front tyre, available for the first time; but this was somewhat coincidental. The tyre was the same as the soft option, paradoxically the harder available, with a strip of extra-soft

rubber around the right-hand side. To preserve braking integrity, a problem with previous attempts at dual-compound fronts, riders only gained benefit from this strip once they had reached 30 degrees of lean.

For both Marquez and Crutchlow, the crashes came when they had slackened off slightly, their objectives gained, their wish to reduce the risk. The circuit's almost continuous curves and the cool conditions allowed the centre of the tyre to cool too much.

Bridgestone took most of the blame, but that too was not so simple. It is Dorna, aiming to cut costs, that imposed a control tyre, bringing to an end the tyre wars that had forced the pace of development; and also imposed severe restrictions on testing. Bridgestone were working in a vacuum.

Furthermore, Dorna had imposed a time schedule that was two hours later than normal, with the big race starting at 4pm, so that European viewers could switch on their TVs at 7am rather than 5am. Had this not been the case, MotoGP would have avoided the cold conditions that caused so much havoc.

It left the way clear for a momentous second win of the year by Rossi, in his 250th GP, after winning every race at Phillip Island from 2001 to 2005. Almost ten years later, back on top, he said, "What a race! To come back and win again at one of the most beautiful and favourite circuits after so long."

The winners had chosen the extra-soft front, although this in itself was a risk, and it played badly for Lorenzo, who said this was "my luckiest second place". The left-hand side of

Left: Miller was the centre of attention, and duly delivered.

Below left: The busts and the not-busts: Phillip Island honoured past Australian heroes Doohan, Gardner and Stoner.

Below centre left: Soon to be ex-crew chief Mike Leitner, in vehement consultation with an impassive Pedrosa.

Below: Already ex-crew chief Jerry Burgess was a cheery presence at his home GP.

Bottom: Crutchlow was suddenly back to full fighting form, only to lose a certain second place on the last lap.

Photos: Gold & Goose

his front tyre had suffered such graining that his lap times had dropped by 2.5 seconds by the end. He was unable to defend himself against Crutchlow, and with a lap or two more would have succumbed also to Smith. He blamed a faulty tyre, pointing out that the same had happened to Rossi at Austin: "You work so hard to get the best set-up and in qualifying, and everything seems well. Sometimes you get this type of tyre, that is a complete disaster."

Pedrosa's weekend started badly, at a pre-race publicity event in Melbourne, where he dropped his U-turning Honda because his legs are too short and he was blown the wrong way. It got worse when news broke that his crew chief of 11 years, ever since ever since his double 250 title, had decided to quit. Former racer Mike Leitner was dismayed that two of the team's mechanics were to be dismissed and said, "It's time for me to draw a line." The final indignity was retirement, after being clouted from behind by Iannone in the race, a blow to his chances of second overall.

Australia's grand prix heroes Wayne Gardner, Mick Doohan and Casey Stoner were on hand for the unveiling of bronze busts of each of them in the paddock; news broke also that Stoner was to test again at Motegi for Honda at the end of October, one day on Bridgestones and the next on the 2016 Michelins. He had done the same in 2013, but the exercise had been hit by bad weather.

Did this mean a return? Will we see Stoner versus Marquez? "Not in this lifetime," he said.

Gardner recalled his role in bringing bike GPs to Australia, after winning the nation's first premier-class title in 1987. This sparked unprecedented public interest, and two years later came the first GP at Phillip Island. He won it. And the next one. Doohan expressed the hope that soon there would be more bronze busts – perhaps Jack Miller's. The white hope obliged with an epic win in a breathtakingly close Moto3 race.

Race Direction had a field day with penalty points, dishing out 11 over the weekend, a record since the system was introduced in the previous season. Moto3 rider Vazquez received two, one for practising a start outside the zone, a second for punting Fenati off in the race; Bradl one for his race attack on Espargaro; Smith one for passing under a yellow flag. The remaining seven were for Moto3 riders in an attempt to crack down on the dangerous, but prevalent practice of gangs of riders loitering on track in qualifying, waiting to pick up a worthwhile tow. Those punished were McPhee, Deroue, Ferrari, Vinales, Navarro, Tonucci and wildcard Remy Gardner.

MOTOGP RACE – 27 laps

After two sunny days, out of nowhere a sudden squall abbreviated Q1, and threatened Q2. It dried at once, however, and Marquez promptly equalled Stoner's record of 12 poles in a season – by almost a quarter of a second. A similar interval covered the next six; Crutchlow a surprise second, ahead of Lorenzo. Smith led row two from Pedrosa – obliged to go through Q1 for the first time.

Rossi was eighth and started well enough to hold his position into the first corner, and to take the benefit as Iannone tipped Crutchlow out wide. The drama was up front, where Smith had taken a flier and all but led into the first turn, where the better-placed Lorenzo took over.

From third, Marquez swung around the outside of Smith through the left-hand Southern Loop, then cut inside Lorenzo on the exit. He had taken control, though Lorenzo didn't give up easily.

While the satellite Yamaha pair were scrapping over fourth, Rossi carefully lined up Smith over Lukey Heights on lap two to ease past into the next tight right; then he picked off Espargaro at the far end of the main straight.

Pedrosa was being shuffled back in a brawl, with both factory Ducatis ahead and Iannone behind, poised for his fateful attack at the hairpin on lap six. He missed his braking, clob-

Above: Smith will outpace Dovizioso and stay wheels-down for a well-earned career-best third.

Top right: Barbera leads an early skirmish from Hernandez, Bautista and Aoyama. He would take the Ducati to sixth, easily his best of the year.

Photos: Gold & Goose

Above right: Lorenzo and Rossi: one got the champagne, the other sucked a lemon.

Photo: Movistar Yamaha

Right: Maverick Vinales was too strong for Rabat in the Moto2 race.

Below right: Ten Moto3 bikes, just one parking space. There would still be six as close at the flag. Winner Miller leads Binder (41), Kent (obscured). Rins, Vazquez, Masbou (10), Fenati (blue-white helmet), Marquez, Vinales (obscured) and McPhee.

Photos: Gold & Goose

bered Pedrosa and went flying. Pedrosa slowed directly, then pitted, his rear wheel dangerously buckled.

The front three pulled away, Marquez by a second on that same lap. Rossi set fastest lap on the ninth, 1.5 seconds off Marquez's 2013 record, set on the infamous ten-lap tyres, and was closing on Lorenzo: "I concentrated on him, because Marc was too fast." They engaged in a spirited battle from the ninth lap until the 17th, changing places several times. Then it was won. Rossi was second. Marquez was just under two seconds ahead, and the gap would grow steadily. Until lap 18.

By then, the champion was better than four seconds clear. He was heading for victory, until he hit the brakes on the downhill run into MG Corner, then he was heading for the grass with the bike on its side. Front wheel lock-up had caught out even the seemingly invincible. Rossi led.

Crutchlow had emerged from the chase group, depleted by the loss of Iannone and Pedrosa, but still including the Monster Yamahas, Dovizioso and Aleix Espargaro. They would soon be joined by Bradl, stuck at the back until his costly lunge on Espargaro on lap 20. It was almost a copy of Iannone/Pedrosa; the German passed inside Smith and Dovizioso, but piled into the Forward Yamaha just ahead. Bradl fell heavily. Espargaro's bike lost its tailpiece, and he coasted to a stop with many strong gestures.

That left brother Pol with a little breathing space, and looking good for fourth for five laps until he fell suddenly, just like Marquez, at the other hard braking area. He, too, was using the harder asymmetric front.

Now Smith, using an extra-soft, was fourth, after keeping his place without excessive risk, and managing also to get to the end of the race. By then, fourth had become an emotional first podium. Well earned.

This final promotion came on the last lap, at the expense of compatriot Crutchlow. He'd cleared the pursuit and closed rapidly on Lorenzo. Fortuitously, for it was the Yamaha rider's pace dropping off as he skated around the fast corners with the left of his front tyre shredding and graining.

Crutchlow was safely past and drawing away, with five laps left and second within his grasp. At the hairpin, halfway around the last one, he fell into the same braking trap as Marquez, in the same place as Espargaro.

Dovi was a lonely and disappointed fourth; a long way

back, another big battle – at one stage involving seven riders – was finally resolved on the run to the line. Redding led the surviving trio into the last corners, but Barbera and Bautista had blown past the production Honda by the finish line, fifth to seventh covered by seven-hundredths.

Having fallen behind, Aoyama led de Angelis and Nicky Hayden for eighth in an equally tight gang. Hernandez had been with them, but was well down by the end, with Petrucci, Laverty and eventually di Meglio wrapping up the last points.

Parkes had retired early, badly battered after a massive practice crash; Abraham had crashed out on lap four.

No score, but no worries for Marquez; but plenty for no-score team-mate Pedrosa (Repsol's first such double since 2010). Rossi had pulled 25 points clear, and Lorenzo 17.

MOTO2 RACE – 25 laps

Long-life Dunlops notwithstanding, Rabat's ninth pole of the year was a new best lap. Zarco was alongside and then Kallio. It should have been a good omen for the title leader, who ran full race distance non-stop in the first three practices: every Phillip Island Moto2 race victory had gone to the pole-sitter. Ominously, however, Vinales was leading row two from Luthi and Cortese – previous champions all – and there were 20 within one second.

A third win went to blazing class rookie Vinales, who emerged invincible from a fraught five-way battle, with four of the riders leading at least once, and three of them making errors from which they were lucky to escape wheels down.

It was the sudden change of wind direction that did it, and that became obvious before half a lap was done.

Rabat shrieked off the line, tailed by Kallio and Zarco, got to Honda Hairpin ... and promptly ran wide, bamboozled by wind blowing in the opposite direction from morning warm-up. That handed the lead to Kallio; Rabat dropped to sixth.

Vinales was already second, and one lap later Zarco would be fading while GP rookie Lowes was now second, and Motegi winner Luthi fourth.

Kallio led for eight laps; Rabat came back to pass him again on the seventh, only to repeat his hairpin trick. Vinales, Luthi and Lowe were still with them, changing places here and there. All except Lowes would lead again over the line.

On lap 17, it was Kallio's turn to be caught out by the hair-

pin, going from first to fifth, a second behind. Vinales picked this moment to put the hammer down.

Rabat tried to go with him until another major wobble. "After this, I said: 'Tito, do your best. The important thing is to finish in front of Mika.'"

Three laps later, Luthi finally got ahead of the hard-braking Lowes, and as Vinales pulled out a lead that was over a second at the finish, he took over second.

Rabat was third, less than two-tenths behind Luthi and some three ahead of Kallio, after a strong recovery. Lowes lost touch by 1.5 seconds over the line.

Zarco fell back into the clutches of an on-form Schrotter; at the same time, Cortese had pushed through from tenth on lap one. They were fighting it out when Zarco crashed; Cortese eventually got the better of Schrotter for sixth by just eight-hundredths.

Five or so seconds behind, Aegerter passed Simeon and Torres only on the last lap; Nakagami was on their heels, by inches from Rossi, Morbidelli and Folger, eighth to 15th covered by just over a second.

Pasini, Warokorn and Wilairot also crashed out, while Syahrin retired.

Rabat did extend his points lead, but he would have to wait at least one more race before he could call himself champion; Vinales was now challenging Kallio for second, while Aegerter's disappointing run meant he lost fourth overall to the resurgent Luthi.

MOTO3 RACE – 23 laps

Another Dunlop-shod best lap for Marquez, his third pole, a fraction clear of Rins, with Guevara alongside for a career-second front row. Kent, McPhee (battered from a heavy day-one crash) and Vazquez filled the second; Miller matched Rossi in eighth.

The fast track assured a super-close race, with a lead pack 11-strong until lap nine, and still six-strong at the end, after sundry collisions and other disputes had sent five of the riders packing.

The first to go were Guevara and Vinales, tangling together on lap ten.

Now there were nine, swooping and swerving and slip-streaming and diving. A false move could easily lose five or more places, a well-timed lunge gain that number.

The lap chart records that Marquez led 14 laps, Miller seven, Vazquez and Romano Fenati (Sky VR46 KTM) one each – but that was only over the line, and by the time they got to the first corner, it was almost guaranteed that at least one rider would have drafted past.

Numbers were cut by another three on the second-last lap. Fenati was nudged off on the second corner by Vazquez; on the way into Honda Hairpin, Binder and Kent were squeezed by Miller and crashed out together – Binder had been up to second on the previous two laps.

It was all a matter of last-lap tactics, and home hero Miller had taken tips from good friend Maverick Vinales, who had come off second-best in a seven-bike Moto3 gang the year before, having tried to win it by slipstreaming.

"He told me to get the lead at turn four, then make sure nobody came past down the straight," said Miller.

In fact, he regained the lead from title leader Marquez earlier than that, using all his late-braking skills to stay there until the last corners, then a bit of swerving to preserve it to the line.

Marquez was second by 0.029 second, then came Rins; Vazquez, McPhee and Masbou were almost alongside, the top six covered by 0.242 of a second!

Oliveira had failed to catch them, finishing a second down, having been delayed in a prolonged skirmish with Kornfeil, just over half a second away over the line.

Wild-card Remy Gardner had to start from the pit lane after stalling before the warm-up lap.

OFFICIAL TIMEKEEPER · *moto* · **TISSOT**

PHILLIP ISLAND
27 laps
Length: 4.448 km / 2.764 miles
Width: 13m

Key
96/60 kph/mph
⚙ Gear

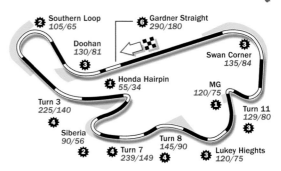

- Southern Loop 105/65
- Gardner Straight 290/180
- Doohan 130/81
- Swan Corner 135/84
- Honda Hairpin 55/34
- MG 120/75
- Turn 3 225/140
- Turn 11 129/80
- Siberia 90/56
- Turn 8 145/90
- Turn 7 239/149
- Lukey Hieghts 120/75

TISSOT AUSTRALIAN GRAND PRIX

17–19 OCTOBER, 2014

MotoGP

RACE DISTANCE: 27 laps, 74.624 miles/120.096km · **RACE WEATHER:** Dry (air 16°C, humidity 84%, track 29°C)

Pos.	Rider	Nat.	No.	Entrant	Machine	Tyres	Race tyre choice	Laps	Time & speed
1	**Valentino Rossi**	ITA	46	Movistar Yamaha MotoGP	Yamaha YZR-M1	B	F: Extra-Soft/R: Medium	27	40m 46.405s / 109.8mph/ 176.7km/h
2	**Jorge Lorenzo**	SPA	99	Movistar Yamaha MotoGP	Yamaha YZR-M1	B	F: Extra-Soft/R: Medium	27	40m 57.241s
3	**Bradley Smith**	GBR	38	Monster Yamaha Tech 3	Yamaha YZR-M1	B	F: Extra-Soft/R: Medium	27	40m 58.699s
4	**Andrea Dovizioso**	ITA	4	Ducati Team	Ducati Desmosedici	B	F: Soft-Asym/R: Medium	27	41m 01.298s
5	**Hector Barbera**	SPA	8	Avintia Racing	Ducati Desmosedici	B	F: Soft-Asym/R: Medium	27	41m 16.494s
6	**Alvaro Bautista**	SPA	19	GO&FUN Honda Gresini	Honda RC213V	B	F: Extra-Soft/R: Medium	27	41m 16.559s
7	**Scott Redding**	GBR	45	GO&FUN Honda Gresini	Honda RCV1000R	B	F: Extra-Soft/R: Medium	27	41m 16.563s
8	**Hiroshi Aoyama**	JPN	7	Drive M7 Aspar	Honda RCV1000R	B	F: Extra-Soft/R: Soft	27	41m 19.571s
9	**Alex de Angelis**	RSM	15	NGM Forward Racing	Forward Yamaha	B	F: Extra-Soft/R: Soft	27	41m 19.982s
10	**Nicky Hayden**	USA	69	Drive M7 Aspar	Honda RCV1000R	B	F: Soft-Asym/R: Medium	27	41m 20.549s
11	**Yonny Hernandez**	COL	68	Energy T.I. Pramac Racing	Ducati Desmosedici	B	F: Soft-Asym/R: Medium	27	41m 25.873s
12	**Danilo Petrucci**	ITA	9	Octo IodaRacing Team	ART	B	F: Soft-Asym/R: Soft	27	41m 43.089s
13	**Michael Laverty**	GBR	70	Paul Bird Motorsport	PBM-ART	B	F: Soft-Asym/R: Soft	27	41m 59.218s
14	**Mike di Meglio**	FRA	63	Avintia Racing	Avintia	B	F: Soft/R: Soft	27	42m 14.455s
	Cal Crutchlow	GBR	35	Ducati Team	Ducati Desmosedici	B	F: Soft-Asym/R: Medium	26	DNF-crash
	Pol Espargaro	SPA	44	Monster Yamaha Tech 3	Yamaha YZR-M1	B	F: Soft-Asym/R: Medium	24	DNF-crash
	Aleix Espargaro	SPA	41	NGM Forward Racing	Forward Yamaha	B	F: Extra-Soft/R: Soft	20	DNF-crash
	Stefan Bradl	GER	6	LCR Honda MotoGP	Honda RC213V	B	F: Soft-Asym/R: Medium	19	DNF-crash
	Marc Marquez	SPA	93	Repsol Honda Team	Honda RC213V	B	F: Soft-Asym/R: Medium	17	DNF-crash
	Broc Parkes	AUS	23	Paul Bird Motorsport	PBM-ART	B	F: Extra-Soft/R: Soft	13	DNF-Injured
	Dani Pedrosa	SPA	26	Repsol Honda Team	Honda RC213V	B	F: Soft-Asym/R: Medium	6	DNF-crash
	Andrea Iannone	ITA	29	Pramac Racing	Ducati Desmosedici	B	F: Extra-Soft/R: Medium	5	DNF-crash
	Karel Abraham	CZE	17	Cardion AB Motoracing	Honda RCV1000R	B	F: Soft/R: Soft	4	DNF-crash

Fastest lap: Valentino Rossi, on lap 9, 1m 29.605s, 111.0mph/178.7km/h.

Lap record: Marc Marquez, SPA (Honda), 1m 28.108s, 112.9mph/181.7km/h (2013).

Event best maximum speed: Marc Marquez, 215.1mph/346.2km/h (qualifying 2).

Qualifying

Weather: Dry
Air Temp: 20° **Humidity:** 25%
Track Temp: 51°

1	Marquez	1m 28.408s
2	Crutchlow	1m 28.642s
3	Lorenzo	1m 28.650s
4	Smith	1m 28.656s
5	Pedrosa	1m 28.675s
6	A. Espargaro	1m 28.866s
7	Iannone	1m 28.887s
8	Rossi	1m 28.956s
9	P. Espargaro	1m 28.968s
10	Dovizioso	1m 29.088s
11	Bradl	1m 29.155s
12	Aoyama	1m 29.955s
13	Redding	1m 30.280s
14	Barbera	1m 30.348s
15	Hayden	1m 30.542s
16	Abraham	1m 30.569s
17	Bautista	1m 30.635s
18	Hernandez	1m 30.729s
19	Petrucci	1m 30.812s
20	Di Meglio	1m 31.431s
21	Laverty	1m 31.492s
22	Parkes	1m 31.730s
23	De Angelis	1m 32.595s

Fastest race laps

1	Rossi	1m 29.605s
2	Marquez	1m 29.608s
3	Lorenzo	1m 29.771s
4	Crutchlow	1m 30.014s
5	Bradl	1m 30.119s
6	Iannone	1m 30.265s
7	Dovizioso	1m 30.363s
8	P. Espargaro	1m 30.382s
9	Pedrosa	1m 30.385s
10	A. Espargaro	1m 30.419s
11	Smith	1m 30.437s
12	Hernandez	1m 30.712s
13	Redding	1m 30.757s
14	Aoyama	1m 30.780s
15	Hayden	1m 30.821s
16	Bautista	1m 30.847s
17	Barbera	1m 30.888s
18	De Angelis	1m 31.001s
19	Abraham	1m 31.130s
20	Petrucci	1m 31.594s
21	Laverty	1m 32.409s
22	Parkes	1m 32.722s
23	Di Meglio	1m 32.851s

Championship Points

1	Marquez	312
2	Rossi	255
3	Lorenzo	247
4	Pedrosa	230
5	Dovizioso	166
6	A. Espargaro	117
7	P. Espargaro	116
8	Smith	108
9	Iannone	102
10	Bradl	96
11	Bautista	89
12	Redding	69
13	Crutchlow	63
14	Aoyama	62
15	Hayden	44
16	Hernandez	44
17	Abraham	33
18	Barbera	14
19	De Angelis	14
20	Petrucci	13
21	Edwards	11
22	Pirro	11
23	Parkes	7
24	Di Meglio	6
25	Laverty	5
26	Nakasuga	4
27	Camier	1

Grid order	1	2	3	4	5	6	7	8	9	10	11	12	13	14	15	16	17	18	19	20	21	22	23	24	25	26	27	
93 MARQUEZ	93	93	93	93	93	93	93	93	93	93	93	93	93	93	93	93	93	46	46	46	46	46	46	46	46	46	46	1
35 CRUTCHLOW	99	99	99	99	99	99	99	99	99	46	46	46	46	99	99	99	46	99	99	99	99	99	35	35	35	35	99	2
99 LORENZO	38	44	46	46	46	46	46	46	46	99	99	99	99	46	46	46	99	35	35	35	35	35	99	99	99	99	38	3
38 SMITH	44	46	44	44	44	35	35	35	35	35	35	35	35	35	35	35	35	41	41	44	44	44	44	44	38	38	4	4
26 PEDROSA	46	38	38	38	35	44	44	44	41	41	4	4	4	41	41	41	41	44	44	41	38	38	38	38	4	4	8	5
41 A. ESPARGARO	26	4	35	35	38	4	4	41	44	4	41	41	41	4	44	44	44	4	4	4	4	4	4	8	8	19	6
29 IANNONE	4	35	4	4	41	41	4	38	44	38	44	44	44	4	4	4	38	38	38	19	19	19	19	8	45	45	7
46 ROSSI	41	41	41	41	41	38	38	38	4	38	44	38	38	38	6	6	6	6	6	45	45	45	8	45	45	19	7	8
44 P. ESPARGARO	35	26	26	26	26	6	6	6	6	6	6	6	6	38	38	38	45	45	19	8	8	45	8	7	7	15	9
4 DOVIZIOSO	6	6	6	6	6	8	8	8	68	68	68	8	45	45	45	45	45	19	19	8	68	69	7	7	69	15	69	10
6 BRADL	29	29	29	29	29	68	68	68	8	8	7	19	19	19	68	19	8	8	69	69	68	69	69	15	69	68	11
7 AOYAMA	19	19	19	19	19	19	19	19	7	19	45	68	68	68	19	68	68	68	15	7	68	15	68	68	9	12
45 REDDING	8	8	68	68	8	7	7	7	19	8	7	7	7	8	8	15	69	69	15	7	15	15	68	9	9	70	13
8 BARBERA	68	68	8	8	68	69	69	69	45	69	8	8	8	7	15	8	15	15	7	9	9	9	70	70	63	14
69 HAYDEN	45	45	7	7	15	15	45	45	69	45	15	15	15	7	69	7	7	9	70	70	70	70	63	63
17 ABRAHAM	7	7	15	15	7	45	45	15	15	15	69	69	69	69	7	9	9	70	63	63	63	63
19 BAUTISTA	15	15	69	69	15	26	9	9	9	9	9	9	9	9	9	9	70	70	63
68 HERNANDEZ	9	9	9	17	45	9	70	70	70	70	70	70	70	70	70	70	63	63
9 PETRUCCI	69	69	17	9	9	70	23	23	63	63	23	63	63	63	63	63	63
63 DI MEGLIO	70	17	45	45	70	23	63	63	23	23	63	23	23
70 LAVERTY	63	70	70	70	23	63
23 PARKES	23	63	63	63	63
15 DE ANGELIS	17	23	23	23

26 Pit stop

Constructor Points

1	Honda	359
2	Yamaha	314
3	Ducati	189
4	Forward Yamaha	129
5	ART	13
6	PBM	11
7	Avintia	8

Moto2

RACE DISTANCE: 25 laps, 69.096 miles/111.200km · RACE WEATHER: Dry (air 16°C, humidity 84%, track 29°C)

Pos.	Rider	Nat.	No.	Entrant	Machine	Laps	Time & Speed
1	Maverick Vinales	SPA	40	Paginas Amarillas HP 40	Kalex	25	39m 10.419s / 105.8mph / 170.3km/h
2	Thomas Luthi	SWI	12	Interwetten Sitag	Suter	25	39m 11.748s
3	Esteve Rabat	SPA	53	Marc VDS Racing Team	Kalex	25	39m 11.923s
4	Mika Kallio	FIN	36	Marc VDS Racing Team	Kalex	25	39m 12.262s
5	Sam Lowes	GBR	22	Speed Up	Speed Up	25	39m 13.711s
6	Sandro Cortese	GER	11	Dynavolt Intact GP	Kalex	25	39m 22.116s
7	Marcel Schrotter	GER	23	Tech 3	Tech 3	25	39m 22.196s
8	Dominique Aegerter	SWI	77	Technomag carXpert	Suter	25	39m 28.695s
9	Xavier Simeon	BEL	19	Federal Oil Gresini Moto2	Suter	25	39m 28.701s
10	Jordi Torres	SPA	81	Mapfre Aspar Team Moto2	Suter	25	39m 28.897s
11	Takaaki Nakagami	JPN	30	IDEMITSU Honda Team Asia	Kalex	25	39m 28.933s
12	Louis Rossi	FRA	96	SAG Team	Kalex	25	39m 28.979s
13	Franco Morbidelli	ITA	21	Italtrans Racing Team	Kalex	25	39m 29.253s
14	Lorenzo Baldassarri	ITA	7	Gresini Moto2	Suter	25	39m 29.643s
15	Jonas Folger	GER	94	AGR Team	Kalex	25	39m 29.856s
16	Ricard Cardus	SPA	88	Tech 3	Tech 3	25	39m 43.657s
17	Luis Salom	SPA	39	Paginas Amarillas HP 40	Kalex	25	39m 44.195s
18	Nicolas Terol	SPA	18	Mapfre Aspar Team Moto2	Suter	25	39m 46.835s
19	Randy Krummenacher	SWI	4	Octo IodaRacing Team	Suter	25	39m 50.993s
20	Julian Simon	SPA	60	Italtrans Racing Team	Kalex	25	39m 51.049s
21	Gino Rea	GBR	8	AGT REA Racing	Suter	25	40m 01.644s
22	Anthony West	AUS	95	QMMF Racing Team	Speed Up	25	40m 01.700s
23	Roman Ramos	SPA	97	QMMF Racing Team	Speed Up	25	40m 01.867s
24	Tomoyoshi Koyama	JPN	71	Teluru Team JiR Webike	NTS	25	40m 01.915s
25	Florian Marino	FRA	20	NGM Forward Racing	Kalex	25	40m 05.685s
26	Aiden Wagner	AUS	41	Marc VDS Racing Team	Kalex	25	40m 12.702s
27	Max Croker	AUS	42	Tasca Racing Moto2	Suter	24	40m 22.533s
	Mattia Pasini	ITA	54	NGM Forward Racing	Kalex	18	DNF
	Johann Zarco	FRA	5	AirAsia Caterham	Caterham Suter	17	DNF
	Hafizh Syahrin	MAL	55	Petronas Raceline Malaysia	Kalex	15	DNF
	Ratthapark Wilairot	THA	14	AirAsia Caterham	Caterham Suter	12	DNF
	Thitipong Warokorn	THA	10	APH PTT The Pizza SAG	Kalex	4	DNF

Fastest lap: Maverick Vinales, on lap 25, 1m 33.066s, 106.9mph/172.0km/h.
Lap record: Alex de Angelis, RSM (Speed Up), 1m 32.814s, 107.2mph/172.5km/h (2013).
Event best maximum speed: Louis Rossi, 181.3mph/291.8km/h (warm up).

Qualifying
Weather: Dry
Air: 20° Track: 26°
Humidity: 53%

1	Rabat	1m 32.470s
2	Zarco	1m 32.485s
3	Kallio	1m 32.698s
4	Vinales	1m 32.712s
5	Luthi	1m 32.757s
6	Cortese	1m 32.824s
7	Lowes	1m 32.938s
8	Torres	1m 32.941s
9	Simeon	1m 32.960s
10	Schrotter	1m 32.964s
11	Cardus	1m 32.968s
12	Morbidelli	1m 33.083s
13	Pasini	1m 33.111s
14	Folger	1m 33.198s
15	Krummenacher	1m 33.252s
16	Aegerter	1m 33.253s
17	Syahrin	1m 33.349s
18	Baldassarri	1m 33.379s
19	Nakagami	1m 33.391s
20	Rossi	1m 33.420s
21	Wilairot	1m 33.480s
22	Salom	1m 33.566s
23	Terol	1m 33.609s
24	Marino	1m 33.841s
25	West	1m 34.000s
26	Simon	1m 34.042s
27	Rea	1m 34.367s
28	Pons	1m 34.414s
29	Warokorn	1m 34.458s
30	Koyama	1m 34.862s
31	Wagner	1m 35.172s
32	Ramos	1m 35.373s
33	Mulhauser	1m 38.203s
34	Croker	1m 38.619s
	Shah	No Time

Fastest race laps

1	Vinales	1m 33.066s
2	Kallio	1m 33.104s
3	Lowes	1m 33.203s
4	Rabat	1m 33.235s
5	Luthi	1m 33.273s
6	Cortese	1m 33.377s
7	Pasini	1m 33.523s
8	Morbidelli	1m 33.605s
9	Schrotter	1m 33.627s
10	Rossi	1m 33.699s
11	Zarco	1m 33.787s
12	Baldassarri	1m 33.841s
13	Nakagami	1m 33.847s
14	Simeon	1m 33.865s
15	Salom	1m 33.970s
16	Torres	1m 33.987s
17	Folger	1m 34.008s
18	Aegerter	1m 34.021s
19	West	1m 34.061s
20	Cardus	1m 34.143s
21	Wilairot	1m 34.320s
22	Krummenacher	1m 34.336s
23	Simon	1m 34.359s
24	Terol	1m 34.443s
25	Syahrin	1m 34.482s
26	Koyama	1m 34.857s
27	Rea	1m 34.927s
28	Ramos	1m 35.002s
29	Marino	1m 35.134s
30	Wagner	1m 35.297s
31	Warokorn	1m 35.626s
32	Croker	1m 39.759s

Championship Points

1	Rabat	310
2	Kallio	269
3	Vinales	249
4	Luthi	161
5	Aegerter	151
6	Zarco	117
7	Corsi	100
8	Cortese	76
9	Morbidelli	75
10	Salom	67
11	Schrotter	66
12	West	65
13	Lowes	60
14	Folger	53
15	Simeon	52
16	Torres	51
17	Simon	46
18	Syahrin	42
19	De Angelis	37
20	Cardus	37
21	Pasini	32
22	Nakagami	32
23	Pons	28
24	Krummenacher	24
25	Rossi	17
26	Baldassarri	14
27	Rea	7
28	Terol	2

Constructor Points

1	Kalex	385
2	Suter	248
3	Caterham Suter	117
4	Speed Up	112
5	Tech 3	83
6	Forward KLX	33

Moto3

RACE DISTANCE: 23 laps, 63.569 miles/102.304km · RACE WEATHER: Dry (air 24°C, humidity 33%, track 27°C)

Pos.	Rider	Nat.	No.	Entrant	Machine	Laps	Time & Speed
1	Jack Miller	AUS	8	Red Bull KTM Ajo	KTM	23	37m 25.209s / 101.9mph / 164.0km/h
2	Alex Marquez	SPA	12	Estrella Galicia 0,0	Honda	23	37m 25.238s
3	Alex Rins	SPA	42	Estrella Galicia 0,0	Honda	23	37m 25.241s
4	Efren Vazquez	SPA	7	SaxoPrint-RTG	Honda	23	37m 25.253s
5	John McPhee	GBR	17	SaxoPrint-RTG	Honda	23	37m 25.343s
6	Alexis Masbou	FRA	10	Ongetta-Rivacold	Honda	23	37m 25.451s
7	Miguel Oliveira	POR	44	Mahindra Racing	Mahindra	23	37m 27.962s
8	Jakub Kornfeil	CZE	84	Calvo Team	KTM	23	37m 28.664s
9	Niklas Ajo	FIN	31	Avant Tecno Husqvarna Ajo	Husqvarna	23	37m 43.327s
10	Niccolo Antonelli	ITA	23	Junior Team GO&FUN Moto3	KTM	23	37m 43.328s
11	Francesco Bagnaia	ITA	21	SKY Racing Team VR46	KTM	23	37m 43.413s
12	Jorge Navarro	SPA	99	Marc VDS Racing Team	Kalex KTM	23	37m 43.435s
13	Karel Hanika	CZE	98	Red Bull KTM Ajo	KTM	23	37m 43.487s
14	Alessandro Tonucci	ITA	19	CIP	Mahindra	23	37m 43.753s
15	Brad Binder	RSA	41	Ambrogio Racing	Mahindra	23	37m 45.677s
16	Jasper Iwema	NED	13	CIP	Mahindra	23	37m 48.643s
17	Andrea Migno	ITA	16	Mahindra Racing	Mahindra	23	37m 51.101s
18	Hafiq Azmi	MAL	38	SIC-AJO	KTM	23	37m 51.103s
19	Luca Grunwald	GER	43	Kiefer Racing	Kalex KTM	23	38m 00.780s
20	Danny Kent	GBR	52	Red Bull Husqvarna Ajo	Husqvarna	23	38m 01.811s
21	Philipp Oettl	GER	65	Interwetten Paddock Moto3	Kalex KTM	23	38m 05.500s
22	Jules Danilo	FRA	95	Ambrogio Racing	Mahindra	23	38m 05.521s
23	Scott Deroue	NED	9	RW Racing GP	Kalex KTM	23	38m 05.723s
24	Matteo Ferrari	ITA	3	San Carlo Team Italia	Mahindra	23	38m 17.240s
25	Juanfran Guevara	SPA	58	Mapfre Aspar Team Moto3	Kalex KTM	23	38m 21.442s
26	Remy Gardner	AUS	2	Team Laglisse Calvo	KTM	23	38m 21.483s
27	Gabriel Ramos	VEN	71	Kiefer Racing	Kalex KTM	23	38m 22.211s
28	Olly Simpson	AUS	45	Olly Simpson Racing	KTM	23	38m 22.549s
	Romano Fenati	ITA	5	SKY Racing Team VR46	KTM	21	DNF
	Isaac Vinales	SPA	32	Calvo Team	KTM	16	DNF
	Enea Bastianini	ITA	33	Junior Team GO&FUN Moto3	KTM	12	DNF
	Andrea Locatelli	ITA	55	San Carlo Team Italia	Mahindra	1	DNF
	Zulfahmi Khairuddin	MAL	63	Ongetta-AirAsia	Honda	1	DNF

Fastest lap: Jack Miller, on lap 3, 1m 36.302s, 103.3mph/166.2km/h (record).
Previous lap record: Alex Marquez, SPA (KTM), 1m 37.073s, 102.5mph/164.9km/h (2013).
Event best maximum speed: Juanfran Guevara, 157.1mph/252.8km/h (race).

Qualifying:
Weather: Dry
Air: 20° Track: 28°
Humidity: 53%

1	Marquez	1m 36.050s
2	Rins	1m 36.064s
3	Guevara	1m 36.389s
4	Kent	1m 36.419s
5	McPhee	1m 36.521s
6	Vazquez	1m 36.572s
7	Iwema	1m 36.640s
8	Miller	1m 36.672s
9	Masbou	1m 36.688s
10	Fenati	1m 36.692s
11	Navarro	1m 36.753s
12	Binder	1m 36.766s
13	Antonelli	1m 36.771s
14	Vinales	1m 36.773s
15	Oliveira	1m 36.865s
16	Tonucci	1m 36.898s
17	Kornfeil	1m 36.953s
18	Hanika	1m 37.158s
19	Ajo	1m 37.201s
20	Bastianini	1m 37.203s
21	Grunwald	1m 37.228s
22	Azmi	1m 37.285s
23	Locatelli	1m 37.440s
24	Gardner	1m 37.472s
25	Khairuddin	1m 37.614s
26	Migno	1m 37.699s
27	Bagnaia	1m 37.729s
28	Granado	1m 38.017s
29	Deroue	1m 38.026s
30	Oettl	1m 38.467s
31	Ferrari	1m 38.707s
32	Danilo	1m 38.852s
33	Simpson	1m 38.993s
34	Ramos	1m 39.047s

Fastest race laps

1	Miller	1m 36.302s
2	Masbou	1m 36.434s
3	Vazquez	1m 36.531s
4	Kent	1m 36.536s
5	Vinales	1m 36.632s
6	McPhee	1m 36.646s
7	Rins	1m 36.700s
8	Binder	1m 36.705s
9	Marquez	1m 36.728s
10	Fenati	1m 36.731s
11	Oliveira	1m 36.849s
12	Kornfeil	1m 36.912s
13	Tonucci	1m 37.000s
14	Guevara	1m 37.004s
15	Ajo	1m 37.227s
16	Antonelli	1m 37.261s
17	Navarro	1m 37.319s
18	Bastianini	1m 37.322s
19	Hanika	1m 37.380s
20	Bagnaia	1m 37.426s
21	Iwema	1m 37.490s
22	Azmi	1m 37.777s
23	Grunwald	1m 37.929s
24	Deroue	1m 37.952s
25	Migno	1m 37.995s
26	Danilo	1m 38.383s
27	Oettl	1m 38.538s
28	Gardner	1m 38.635s
29	Ramos	1m 38.658s
30	Simpson	1m 38.768s
31	Ferrari	1m 38.788s

Championship Points

1	Marquez	251
2	Miller	231
3	Rins	210
4	Vazquez	187
5	Fenati	174
6	Masbou	150
7	Vinales	121
8	Bastianini	116
9	Kent	103
10	Binder	102
11	Oliveira	102
12	Kornfeil	86
13	McPhee	77
14	Ajo	52
15	Bagnaia	50
16	Antonelli	50
17	Guevara	40
18	Hanika	31
19	Khairuddin	19
20	Tonucci	18
21	Loi	17
22	Ferrari	12
23	Oettl	10
24	Migno	8
25	Navarro	7
26	Ono	5
27	Iwema	4
28	Sissis	3
29	Granado	2
30	Danilo	2

Constructor Points

1	Honda	343
2	KTM	339
3	Mahindra	158
4	Husqvarna	130
5	Kalex KTM	56
6	FTR KTM	4

The Green versus the Evergreen.
Rossi pressured Marquez hard in an
absorbing battle.
Photo: Gold & Goose

MALAYSIAN GRAND PRIX

SEPANG CIRCUIT

Above: Bradl had a strong race, resisting a late challenge from Smith to hold on to fourth.

Top right: "No you don't." Marquez finds Miller in his way again in a fierce Moto3 contest.

Above right: Pre-race favourite Dani Pedrosa fell, remounted, then fell again, losing any chance of finishing runner-up to Marquez.

Right: A punctured oil radiator triggered a fiery and painful crash for Pol Espargaro. He came back for a brave race to sixth.

Photos: Gold & Goose

RACE, pack, fly; race, pack, fly; race. The third flyaway in as many weeks added blazing heat, sapping humidity and a warm welcome from a record crowd of almost 82,000, proving the growing significance of MotoGP not just in Malaysia, but also in the whole of South-East Asia. A matter of great importance to the factories, in a vast and expanding market.

It was underlined by the support race: final round of the fledgling Shell Advance Asia Talent Cup, modelled on the Red Bull Rookies project, overseen by ex-GP winner, management luminary and accomplished talent scout Alberto Puig.

And by no fewer than five Moto2 riders, three from Thailand and two from Malaysia, only one of them a wild-card. Series regular Syahrin rewarded the home fans best, charging through to eighth after starting from 18th, before crashing out.

There were other rewards, in a day of racing mercifully not visited by one of the region's frequent 4pm downpours, since a second successive adjustment of the timing schedule in the interests of European TV viewers meant that the main race of the day started at that hour.

Just such a downpour had struck on Friday, shortly after the end of Moto3's second free practice, flooding the track and delaying the subsequent MotoGP session by almost half an hour. Although the track dries quickly in the heat, a remaining rivulet was blamed for an accident that some attributed to karma for Iannone, after his collision with Pedrosa in Australia. He had been fit enough to go before Race Direction, asserting that the crash had been the consequence of getting neutral instead of first gear, but he was given a penalty point anyway. On track, he was turning in to the tight final corner just as Marquez arrived, aquaplaned over the standing water and slammed into him hard enough to put him out of the race. He flew home early for further medical investigation.

There would be no karmic recompense for Pedrosa, however, strong throughout practice and widely tipped to take a third successive Sepang win. Instead he crashed twice in the race. Zero points for a second race condemned him to fourth overall, leaving the battle for second to Yamaha team-mates Rossi and Lorenzo. The first part of a fine race was between them also, the older rider gaining the upper hand. Marquez was only biding his time behind them, however, and went on to take win number 12. This equalled Mick Doohan's 1997 record. It's worth recording that Mick did it in a year with only 15 rounds, a rate of 80 per cent. Marquez took 17 races, or 70.5 per cent. With one race left, a record-breaking 13 wins remained possible.

Rossi's resurgence at his team-mate's expense continued to delight. Jorge blamed his own fitness, as well as the loss of a rubber knee-grip from his tank, which meant "I was sliding forward in the brakings". Since Rossi had been struggling by comparison in practice and in qualifying, his prolonged attack on Marquez was doubly impressive: it came after setting changes on Sunday had robbed him of precision and turning, but "made a bike that loved the tyres". In the end, though, the Honda loved its tyres better. From Rossi's seat, Marquez only lost rear traction and acceleration, whereas he lost front fidelity as well, chatter and sliding finally blunting his attack.

Moto2 was settled, with no surprises. Tito Rabat's seniors praised the work and dedication over a career that had begun in 2005, and so far had spanned 143 GPs. His first win came only in 2013, but his work ethic – exemplified by a habit of running full race distance non-stop in free practices – made the difference. As Lorenzo said, "He is not the most talented rider, but he shows that with hard work you can improve that." Quite so, and throughout 2014 he had made most of the rest of the Moto2 mob look fairly average.

But it was Moto3 that grabbed the interest, the headlines and the controversy, in a stirring fightback by Miller. He had said, before the race, "There's no tactics in Moto3," but gave the lie with a race of forceful cunning. Though it did not result in victory, it gave a boost to his title chances.

On six occasions in the race, he and Marquez had touched, or nearly touched, every time to the Spaniard's disadvantage. Miller said later, "If I'd wanted to, I could have run into the side of his bike and he'd have been down. But I wanted a clean race." What he did was "to put my bike where he wanted to put his". No mean feat, considering there were six or more other riders in very close proximity.

The last lap was the key. Miller was swamped on the run into the first bend, but had eyes only for Marquez. Braking late, he put his KTM right in the way. Marquez had to pick up, run wide, drop to fifth. As Miller battled up front, fellow Ajo teamster Danny Kent kept Marquez behind him.

Revenge for Aragon? Or unfair tactics? Marquez's team thought the latter, and put in an official protest against both Miller and Kent. To the relief at least of the Anglophone faction, to whom Miller is a breath of fresh non-Spanish air, Race Direction disagreed.

The other Moto3 controversy came in qualifying, a week after seven riders had been punished in Australia, with at least half the field dawdling on the long straights waiting for a tow, some barely at walking pace. A sorry spectacle, resembling a slow bicycle race, but unpunishable, according to "incensed" Race Director Mike Webb, because the rules only prevented riders from obstructing others, and "I strive for consistency". New rules, he promised, would follow.

Pol Espargaro suffered a heavy crash in FP4, after both Dovizioso and Redding, spattered by oil when behind him, had warned the rider. "I couldn't see or feel anything wrong, because the leak was very small", he explained. Big enough, however, to contaminate his rear tyre and precipitate a fiery crash at turn one. He suffered a broken bone in his left foot, but was passed fit to ride the next day, for an exceedingly brave race.

Provisional entry lists for 2015 were published in the interim, with few surprises, except that Moto3's soon-to-become double race winner Efren Vazquez was absent from it. So too Caterham in Moto2; while in MotoGP the major casualty was Hiro Aoyama.

MOTOGP RACE – 20 laps

Marquez's 50th career pole and his 13th of the year broke the record of 12, set by Doohan (in a shorter season) in 1997 and equalled by Stoner in 2011. More importantly, he was the first to break the two-minute barrier at an official meeting – it had been done in pre-season testing.

Shortly afterwards, Pedrosa, strong all weekend, became the second to do so.

Lorenzo joined the Hondas on the front row; a troubled Rossi was on the far end of the second, slower than Bradl and Dovizioso, and a full second down.

Aleix Espargaro led row three from Crutchlow and Smith; Bautista was tenth after coming through from Q1; Aoyama (11th) had done the same; Pol missed the session and would start from 12th. Hernandez was best of the rest to lead row five from Hayden and Abraham.

For a second weekend, it was a race of attrition, with only 14 finishers.

Two went at the start of lap two, when Aleix Espargaro messed up his braking into the first corner and crashed into the ever-misfortunate Bautista. At the end of it, Pedrosa – lying second to Lorenzo – peeled into the final corner well within himself, and to his surprise folded the front wheel and slid out. He remounted at the back.

Crutchlow was also an early casualty, coasting to a stop trackside from sixth after only four laps, with another electronic failure.

Pedrosa had led into the first corner, but a determined Lorenzo, taking "many risks" dived in, pushing Marquez out wide and down to an erstwhile eighth in the process. The Yamaha rider dropped behind Dovizioso, but had passed the Ducati before half a lap was done, and then Pedrosa as well to lead on to the back straight.

Marquez recovered positions quickly, setting a new record on lap two as he passed Bradl then took third off Dovizioso. Rossi also passed the Ducati on the same lap, and the front three rapidly moved clear together. Before half-distance, Rossi was leaning hard on his team-mate. His first attack at turn nine was repulsed; next time around, he made it stick, with Marquez following past the discombobulated Lorenzo directly. Within two laps, he was losing touch.

Rossi pushed and pushed, and Marquez – skating the front wheel on corner entries – appeared to be feeling the pressure. The crowd responded as Rossi made light of the 14-year age gap, the evergreen versus the green. It was a stirring effort, and another demonstration of how the veteran, in his 19th year of GP racing, had been able to rejuvenate his motivation and adapt to changing times and machines.

But as the tyres wore, Marquez proved the stronger, and over the last laps he pulled out a commanding lead, to win by 2.4 seconds.

At an ever increasing distance, Dovi had been keeping his Ducati a couple of seconds clear of Bradl's LCR Honda. Then his fuel pump started to play up. "Every time I opened the gas, the engine stuttered." He began a rapid slide backwards, losing five seconds a lap.

Smith had been holding station a couple of seconds adrift of Bradl. Towards the end, the German was having tyre trouble on the ever greasy and overheated surface. Smith closed rapidly, making his final lunge at the last corner, but he ran wide and finished a close fifth.

A plucky sixth for Pol Espargaro came after a good early battle with an on-form Hernandez, who would finish seventh, and top Ducati after passing the troubled Dovizioso two laps from the end. He'd faced a challenge from Aoyama, but the Japanese had suffered a problem with his camel-back drinks system, and blamed dehydration for running wide and dropping back.

One more lap and Dovizioso would have surrendered eighth to Barbera.

Hayden had crashed out, folding the front, on lap seven, leaving top production Honda spot to tenth-placed Redding after a steady, but undistinguished race, with Aoyama 11th. De Angelis had been with Redding, but retired on the last lap; Abraham had crashed out earlier.

It might have been different, if Pedrosa's shocking luck hadn't remained bad. He had been lapping at the same speed and even faster than the leaders, and had cut through to 11th and still been making progress when once again the front folded under braking, leaving the Honda rider baffled and disconsolate.

The high casualty rate left points for the usual back-markers, with Laverty only two seconds off Aoyama, 12th his best

finish. Di Meglio was another ten seconds down, and then Parkes – still suffering the after-effects of his heavy Phillip Island tumble.

Rossi would go to the last race with a 12-point advantage over Lorenzo, and while Honda had secured the constructors' title, Yamaha's resurgence meant that the teams' trophy was far from settled.

MOTO2 RACE – 19 laps

Pole number ten for Rabat extended the record he had set a week before in Australia and underlined his regular assertion – although should Kallio win, he need finish only seventh to secure the title, "for me it is the same as every race: I will try to win."

Likewise Kallio, qualified second just over a tenth slower, victory the only option, plus the need to beat class rookie Vinales, to protect second overall.

Cortese completed row one; Vinales led the second from Luthi and latecomer Nakagami; Simon, Zarco and Aegerter were poised behind.

A Marc VDS team champion was assured, but there is always a Maverick to spoil the party.

Above and above right: New champion Rabat and double champion Marquez train together in Spain, celebrate separately in Malaysia.

Top left: Points for all. Laverty, di Meglio and Parkes picked up the crumbs in a depleted MotoGP race.

Top: Rabat leads Kallio; eventual winner Vinales bides his time.

Right: No tactics? Moto3 yielded another game of inches, between (*from left*) winner Vazquez, Rins, Miller, McPhee and Marquez.

Photos: Gold & Goose

Cortese, Simon and Zarco broke free together; Syahrin crashed out on lap 11.

In the last laps, Aegerter's tyres were sliding badly and the pursuit closing rapidly. On the last, Zarco got through for fourth, Simon a close sixth. Cortese was off the back; then came Luthi, fending off a late threat from Folger, after having broken free from a big gang behind and passed Schrotter five laps from the end.

Salom made impressive progress from 31st on lap one to 11th. He took control of the next group with two laps to go, then left Cardus, Pasini and 33-year-old returnee substitute Rolfo. Torres, off the back by the finish, was 15th for the last point.

Gino Rea crashed out on the first corner, suffering right foot fractures. Morbidelli, Lowes, Krummenacher, Nakagami and Wilairot also crashed out.

MOTO3 RACE – 18 laps

Miller managed to find a way through the mooching mob at the end of qualifying, and a tow down both straights, to secure pole number eight, displacing surprise leader McPhee by half a second. Kornfeil was third; Marquez fifth behind Vazquez after falling late in the session. Fenati completed row two; Kent, Vinales and Oliveira were next.

All but Oliveira would take part in a trademark Moto3 leading bunch – the Mahindra rider fell on the second corner. More would join, including Binder on a second Mahindra, until sidelined by a deflating tyre, plus Honda-mounted Masbou, in yet another remarkable ride from 21st on lap one.

At half-distance, it was 11-strong, although fairly loose-knit, with Kent having a canny tyre-preserving ride near the back. Soon afterwards, Vinales would crash out.

They would bunch up once more, and at the finish there were still eight, over the line in a couple of seconds.

All of the top five except for Kent had led over the line, Miller seven times, but Vazquez eight, including when it mattered. McPhee had a heartbreaking crash on the last lap.

Although he didn't win, it had been a commanding performance by Miller, whose last corner had been occupied in keeping Rins back, which let Vazquez through for a second win of the season. Kent was fourth, an upset Marquez fifth and Masbou a tenth behind. Then Antonelli, with Kornfeil on his back wheel.

Hanika was a lone ninth, Bastianini tenth. Remy Gardner, son of Wayne, took his first point for 15th, at the head of a gang of four regulars.

Fenati retired after 11 laps.

Valencia, predicted Miller, will be "like the last round of a boxing match. Gloves off."

The race was typically Moto2: somewhat processional. But tense all the same, because the stakes were so high.

Rabat took off, Kallio and Vinales following close, Aegerter busting through from the third row in close pursuit.

By lap six, it was the three of them, Kallio and his Spanish shadow closing on Rabat's early lead. As they started the tenth lap, Rabat ran wide into the first corner, and three corners later he was third. He would stay there, under no threat from behind.

Within three more laps, Vinales was leaning heavily on Kallio. They swapped once, and straight back again, but on the 15th lap the Spaniard was past. He drew steadily clear to win by 2.7 seconds.

Kallio: "Everything on the bike was okay, and I hoped to win. But he was just faster."

As for the ever improving Vinales: "I was intelligent in the first part of the race, saving up for the last laps. We made that plan and the plan worked," the 19-year-old said.

The win took him within 15 points of Kallio for second overall – but third was more than enough for Rabat to secure his first title. "I tried to do my best all season, and I tried very well," he commented.

Aegerter was alone for much of the race, while a lively group behind was led until after half-distance by Cortese, from Simon, home star Syahrin – having pushed through heroically from 18th on the grid – Luthi and Zarco.

SHELL ADVANCE
MALAYSIAN MOTORCYCLE GRAND PRIX

24-26 OCTOBER, 2014

SEPANG INTERNATIONAL CIRCUIT
20 laps
Length: 5.548 km / 3.447 miles
Width: 25m

Key
96/60 kph/mph
Gear ⚙

Langkawi curve 90/56
Genting Curve 145/90
Turn 2 65/40
Turn 3 179/112
Turn 5 155/96
Hairpin 75/47
Turn 7 124/77
Pangkor Laut Chicane 70/43
KLIA Curve 130/81
Berjaya Tioman Corner 65/40
Sunway Lagoon Corner 90/56
Turn 12 155/96
Kenyir Lake 105/65

MotoGP	RACE DISTANCE: 20 laps, 68.885 miles/110.860km · RACE WEATHER: Dry (air 36°C, humidity 50%, track 54°C)

Pos.	Rider	Nat.	No.	Entrant	Machine	Tyres	Race tyre choice	Laps	Time & speed
1	**Marc Marquez**	SPA	93	Repsol Honda Team	Honda RC213V	B	F: Medium/R: Medium	20	40m 45.523s 101.3mph/ 163.1km/h
2	**Valentino Rossi**	ITA	46	Movistar Yamaha MotoGP	Yamaha YZR-M1	B	F: Medium/R: Medium	20	40m 47.968s
3	**Jorge Lorenzo**	SPA	99	Movistar Yamaha MotoGP	Yamaha YZR-M1	B	F: Hard/R: Medium	20	40m 49.031s
4	**Stefan Bradl**	GER	6	LCR Honda MotoGP	Honda RC213V	B	F: Medium/R: Medium	20	41m 06.757s
5	**Bradley Smith**	GBR	38	Monster Yamaha Tech 3	Yamaha YZR-M1	B	F: Medium/R: Medium	20	41m 07.806s
6	**Pol Espargaro**	SPA	44	Monster Yamaha Tech 3	Yamaha YZR-M1	B	F: Medium/R: Medium	20	41m 20.191s
7	**Yonny Hernandez**	COL	68	Energy T.I. Pramac Racing	Ducati Desmosedici	B	F: Hard/R: Medium	20	41m 23.958s
8	**Andrea Dovizioso**	ITA	4	Ducati Team	Ducati Desmosedici	B	F: Hard/R: Medium	20	41m 34.362s
9	**Hector Barbera**	SPA	8	Avintia Racing	Ducati Desmosedici	B	F: Hard/R: Soft	20	41m 36.315s
10	**Scott Redding**	GBR	45	GO&FUN Honda Gresini	Honda RCV1000R	B	F: Medium/R: Medium	20	41m 44.611s
11	**Hiroshi Aoyama**	JPN	7	Drive M7 Aspar	Honda RCV1000R	B	F: Medium/R: Medium	20	42m 01.472s
12	**Michael Laverty**	GBR	70	Paul Bird Motorsport	PBM-ART	B	F: Medium/R: Soft	20	42m 03.489s
13	**Mike di Meglio**	FRA	63	Avintia Racing	Avintia	B	F: Hard/R: Soft	20	42m 13.296s
14	**Broc Parkes**	AUS	23	Paul Bird Motorsport	PBM-ART	B	F: Hard/R: Soft	20	42m 29.767s
	Alex de Angelis	RSM	15	NGM Forward Racing	Forward Yamaha	B	F: Medium/R: Medium	19	DNF-mechanical
	Danilo Petrucci	ITA	9	Octo IodaRacing Team	ART	B	F: Medium/R: Soft	14	DNF-mechanical
	Dani Pedrosa	SPA	26	Repsol Honda Team	Honda RC213V	B	F: Medium/R: Medium	12	DNF-crash
	Karel Abraham	CZE	17	Cardion AB Motoracing	Honda RCV1000R	B	F: Medium/R: Soft	11	DNF-crash
	Nicky Hayden	USA	69	Drive M7 Aspar	Honda RCV1000R	B	F: Medium/R: Soft	6	DNF-crash
	Cal Crutchlow	GBR	35	Ducati Team	Ducati Desmosedici	B	F: Hard/R: Medium	4	DNF-mechanical
	Aleix Espargaro	SPA	41	NGM Forward Racing	Forward Yamaha	B	F: Hard/R: Medium	1	DNF-crash
	Alvaro Bautista	SPA	19	GO&FUN Honda Gresini	Honda RC213V	B	F: Medium/R: Medium	1	DNF-crash
	Andrea Iannone	ITA	29	Pramac Racing	Ducati Desmosedici	B	–	–	DNS-injured

Fastest lap: Marc Marquez, on lap 2, 2m 1.150s, 102.3mph/164.7km/h (record).
Previous lap record: Marc Marquez, SPA (Honda), 2m 1.415s, 102.2mph/164.5km/h (2013).
Event best maximum speed: Andrea Dovizioso, 204.8mph/329.6km/h (free practice 4).

Qualifying
Weather: Dry
Air Temp: 35° Track Temp: 56°
Humidity: 51%

1	Marquez	1m 59.791s
2	Pedrosa	1m 59.973s
3	Lorenzo	2m 00.203s
4	Bradl	2m 00.472s
5	Dovizioso	2m 00.703s
6	Rossi	2m 00.740s
7	A. Espargaro	2m 00.801s
8	Crutchlow	2m 01.119s
9	Smith	2m 01.263s
10	Bautista	2m 02.294s
11	Aoyama	2m 10.568s
12	P. Espargaro	No Time
13	Hernandez	2m 02.184s
14	Hayden	2m 02.330s
15	Abraham	2m 02.548s
16	Barbera	2m 02.682s
17	Redding	2m 02.874s
18	De Angelis	2m 03.165s
19	Petrucci	2m 03.874s
20	Laverty	2m 04.539s
21	Di Meglio	2m 04.784s
22	Parkes	2m 05.208s
23	Iannone	No Time

Fastest race laps

1	Marquez	2m 01.150s
2	Rossi	2m 01.315s
3	Lorenzo	2m 01.556s
4	Pedrosa	2m 01.653s
5	Crutchlow	2m 02.106s
6	Dovizioso	2m 02.295s
7	Bradl	2m 02.313s
8	Smith	2m 02.519s
9	Hernandez	2m 02.739s
10	P. Espargaro	2m 02.854s
11	Aoyama	2m 03.175s
12	Hayden	2m 03.308s
13	Barbera	2m 03.694s
14	Redding	2m 03.743s
15	Abraham	2m 04.151s
16	De Angelis	2m 04.171s
17	Petrucci	2m 04.790s
18	Laverty	2m 05.305s
19	Di Meglio	2m 05.392s
20	Parkes	2m 05.891s

Championship Points

1	Marquez	337
2	Rossi	275
3	Lorenzo	263
4	Pedrosa	230
5	Dovizioso	174
6	P. Espargaro	126
7	Smith	119
8	A. Espargaro	117
9	Bradl	109
10	Iannone	102
11	Bautista	89
12	Redding	75
13	Aoyama	67
14	Crutchlow	63
15	Hernandez	53
16	Hayden	44
17	Abraham	33
18	Barbera	21
19	De Angelis	14
20	Petrucci	13
21	Edwards	11
22	Pirro	11
23	Parkes	9
24	Laverty	9
25	Di Meglio	9
26	Nakasuga	4
27	Camier	1

Constructor Points

1	Honda	384
2	Yamaha	334
3	Ducati	198
4	Forward Yamaha	129
5	PBM	15
6	ART	13
7	Avintia	11

Grid order	1	2	3	4	5	6	7	8	9	10	11	12	13	14	15	16	17	18	19	20	
93 MARQUEZ	99	99	99	99	99	99	99	99	99	46	93	93	93	93	93	93	93	93	93	93	1
26 PEDROSA	26	46	46	46	46	46	46	46	46	93	46	46	46	46	46	46	46	46	46	46	2
99 LORENZO	4	93	93	93	93	93	93	93	93	99	99	99	99	99	99	99	99	99	99	99	3
6 BRADL	46	4	4	4	4	4	4	4	4	4	4	4	4	4	4	6	6	6	6	6	4
4 DOVIZIOSO	6	6	6	6	6	6	6	6	6	6	6	6	6	6	6	38	38	38	38	38	5
46 ROSSI	93	35	35	35	38	38	38	38	38	38	38	38	38	38	38	4	4	44	44	44	6
41 A. ESPARGARO	35	38	38	38	68	68	44	44	44	44	44	44	44	44	44	68	68	68	68	68	7
35 CRUTCHLOW	38	68	68	68	44	44	68	68	68	68	68	68	68	68	68	44	4	4	4	4	8
38 SMITH	68	44	44	44	7	7	7	7	7	7	7	7	7	7	7	8	8	8	8	8	9
19 BAUTISTA	44	7	7	7	69	69	8	8	8	8	8	8	8	8	8	45	45	45	45		10
7 AOYAMA	41	15	69	69	45	8	45	45	45	45	45	26	45	45	45	45	15	15	15	7	11
44 P. ESPARGARO	19	69	15	45	8	45	15	15	15	15	15	45	15	15	15	15	7	7	7	70	12
68 HERNANDEZ	15	45	45	15	15	15	17	17	17	17	26	15	9	9	70	70	70	70	70	63	13
69 HAYDEN	7	17	8	8	17	17	9	9	9	26	17	9	70	70	63	63	63	63	63	23	14
17 ABRAHAM	45	8	17	17	9	9	70	70	26	9	9	70	63	63	23	23	23	23	23		
8 BARBERA	69	9	9	9	70	70	63	63	70	70	63	23	23								
45 REDDING	17	70	70	70	63	63	26	26	63	63	63	23									
15 DE ANGELIS	8	63	63	63	23	23	23	23	23	23											
9 PETRUCCI	9	23	23	23	26	26															
70 LAVERTY	70	26	26	26																	
63 DI MEGLIO	63																				
23 PARKES	23																				

Moto2

RACE DISTANCE: 19 laps, 65.441 miles/105.317km · RACE WEATHER: Dry (air 34°C, humidity 56%, track 55°C)

Pos.	Rider	Nat.	No.	Entrant	Machine	Laps	Time & Speed
1	**Maverick Vinales**	SPA	40	Paginas Amarillas HP 40	Kalex	19	40m 46.754s 96.3mph/ 154.9km/h
2	**Mika Kallio**	FIN	36	Marc VDS Racing Team	Kalex	19	40m 49.448s
3	**Esteve Rabat**	SPA	53	Marc VDS Racing Team	Kalex	19	40m 54.808s
4	**Johann Zarco**	FRA	5	AirAsia Caterham	Caterham Suter	19	40m 57.344s
5	**Dominique Aegerter**	SWI	77	Technomag carXpert	Suter	19	40m 57.417s
6	**Julian Simon**	SPA	60	Italtrans Racing Team	Kalex	19	40m 57.523s
7	**Sandro Cortese**	GER	11	Dynavolt Intact GP	Kalex	19	41m 02.411s
8	**Thomas Luthi**	SWI	12	Interwetten Sitag	Suter	19	41m 05.593s
9	**Jonas Folger**	GER	94	AGR Team	Kalex	19	41m 06.240s
10	**Marcel Schrotter**	GER	23	Tech 3	Tech 3	19	41m 11.641s
11	**Luis Salom**	SPA	39	Paginas Amarillas HP 40	Kalex	19	41m 14.988s
12	**Ricard Cardus**	SPA	88	Tech 3	Tech 3	19	41m 17.092s
13	**Mattia Pasini**	ITA	54	NGM Forward Racing	Kalex	19	41m 17.287s
14	**Roberto Rolfo**	ITA	44	Tasca Racing Moto2	Suter	19	41m 17.302s
15	**Jordi Torres**	SPA	81	Mapfre Aspar Team Moto2	Suter	19	41m 21.523s
16	Florian Marino	FRA	20	NGM Forward Racing	Kalex	19	41m 23.367s
17	Lorenzo Baldassarri	ITA	7	Gresini Moto2	Suter	19	41m 25.623s
18	Anthony West	AUS	95	QMMF Racing Team	Speed Up	19	41m 28.955s
19	Xavier Simeon	BEL	19	Federal Oil Gresini Moto2	Suter	19	41m 34.630s
20	Azlan Shah	MAL	25	IDEMITSU Honda Team Asia	Kalex	19	41m 39.704s
21	Thitipong Warokorn	THA	10	APH PTT The Pizza SAG	Kalex	19	41m 39.917s
22	Roman Ramos	SPA	97	QMMF Racing Team	Speed Up	19	41m 46.753s
23	Tomoyoshi Koyama	JPN	71	Teluru Team JiR Webike	NTS	19	41m 50.085s
24	Nicolas Terol	SPA	18	Mapfre Aspar Team Moto2	Suter	19	41m 55.029s
25	Decha Kraisart	THA	46	Singha Eneos Yamaha Tech 3	Tech 3	19	42m 03.750s
26	Randy Krummenacher	SWI	4	Octo IodaRacing Team	Suter	18	42m 00.977s
	Franco Morbidelli	ITA	21	Italtrans Racing Team	Kalex	15	DNF
	Sam Lowes	GBR	22	Speed Up	Speed Up	14	DNF
	Axel Pons	SPA	49	AGR Team	Kalex	12	DNF
	Hafizh Syahrin	MAL	55	Petronas Raceline Malaysia	Kalex	10	DNF
	Louis Rossi	FRA	96	SAG Team	Kalex	8	DNF
	Takaaki Nakagami	JPN	30	IDEMITSU Honda Team Asia	Kalex	6	DNF
	Ratthapark Wilairot	THA	14	AirAsia Caterham	Caterham Suter	6	DNF
	Gino Rea	GBR	8	AGT REA Racing	Suter	0	DNF

Fastest lap: Mika Kallio, on lap 5, 2m 7.949s, 96.9mph/155.9km/h (record).
Previous lap record: Mika Kallio, FIN (Kalex), 2m 7.959s, 96.9mph/155.9km/h (2013).
Event best maximum speed: Azlan Shah, 168.5mph/271.2km/h (warm up).

Qualifying

Weather: Dry
Air Temp: 33° **Track Temp:** 56°
Humidity: 56%

1	Rabat	2m 07.429s
2	Kallio	2m 07.587s
3	Cortese	2m 07.706s
4	Vinales	2m 07.754s
5	Luthi	2m 07.849s
6	Nakagami	2m 07.875s
7	Simon	2m 07.886s
8	Zarco	2m 07.956s
9	Aegerter	2m 08.133s
10	Pons	2m 08.144s
11	Schrotter	2m 08.169s
12	Folger	2m 08.225s
13	Morbidelli	2m 08.338s
14	Simeon	2m 08.344s
15	Lowes	2m 08.359s
16	Salom	2m 08.398s
17	Rossi	2m 08.503s
18	Syahrin	2m 08.558s
19	Rolfo	2m 08.669s
20	Marino	2m 08.759s
21	Rea	2m 08.832s
22	Torres	2m 08.835s
23	Baldassarri	2m 08.865s
24	Cardus	2m 09.254s
25	Krummenacher	2m 09.335s
26	West	2m 09.409s
27	Terol	2m 09.441s
28	Koyama	2m 09.710s
29	Shah	2m 09.782s
30	Warokorn	2m 09.813s
31	Ramos	2m 09.829s
32	Kraisart	2m 10.699s
33	Wilairot	2m 15.599s
	Pasini	No Time
	Mulhauser	No Time

Fastest race laps

1	Kallio	2m 07.949s
2	Vinales	2m 08.001s
3	Rabat	2m 08.150s
4	Aegerter	2m 08.403s
5	Folger	2m 08.447s
6	Zarco	2m 08.475s
7	Simon	2m 08.550s
8	Cortese	2m 08.589s
9	Syahrin	2m 08.720s
10	Luthi	2m 08.796s
11	Cardus	2m 08.856s
12	Lowes	2m 08.993s
13	Pons	2m 09.060s
14	Schrotter	2m 09.068s
15	Salom	2m 09.102s
16	Pasini	2m 09.167s
17	Simeon	2m 09.375s
18	Torres	2m 09.396s
19	Rolfo	2m 09.405s
20	Rossi	2m 09.460s
21	Marino	2m 09.519s
22	Morbidelli	2m 09.587s
23	Wilairot	2m 09.607s
24	Baldassarri	2m 09.680s
25	Nakagami	2m 09.857s
26	West	2m 09.920s
27	Terol	2m 10.091s
28	Shah	2m 10.113s
29	Warokorn	2m 10.174s
30	Ramos	2m 10.183s
31	Koyama	2m 10.586s
32	Krummenacher	2m 10.851s
33	Kraisart	2m 11.009s

Championship Points

1	Rabat	326
2	Kallio	289
3	Vinales	274
4	Luthi	169
5	Aegerter	162
6	Zarco	130
7	Corsi	100
8	Cortese	85
9	Morbidelli	75
10	Salom	72
11	Schrotter	72
12	West	65
13	Folger	60
14	Lowes	60
15	Simon	56
16	Simeon	52
17	Torres	52
18	Syahrin	42
19	Cardus	41
20	De Angelis	37
21	Pasini	35
22	Nakagami	32
23	Pons	28
24	Krummenacher	24
25	Rossi	17
26	Baldassarri	14
27	Rea	7
28	Terol	2
29	Rolfo	2

Constructor Points

1	Kalex	410
2	Suter	259
3	Caterham Suter	130
4	Speed Up	112
5	Tech 3	89
6	Forward KLX	33

Moto3

RACE DISTANCE: 18 laps, 61.997 miles/99.774km · RACE WEATHER: Dry (air 33°C, humidity 56%, track 49°C)

Pos.	Rider	Nat.	No.	Entrant	Machine	Laps	Time & Speed
1	**Efren Vazquez**	SPA	7	SaxoPrint-RTG	Honda	18	40m 41.002s 91.4mph/ 147.1km/h
2	**Jack Miller**	AUS	8	Red Bull KTM Ajo	KTM	18	40m 41.215s
3	**Alex Rins**	SPA	42	Estrella Galicia 0,0	Honda	18	40m 41.387s
4	**Danny Kent**	GBR	52	Red Bull Husqvarna Ajo	Husqvarna	18	40m 41.805s
5	**Alex Marquez**	SPA	12	Estrella Galicia 0,0	Honda	18	40m 41.833s
6	**Alexis Masbou**	FRA	10	Ongetta-Rivacold	Honda	18	40m 42.075s
7	**Niccolo Antonelli**	ITA	23	Junior Team GO&FUN Moto3	KTM	18	40m 42.918s
8	**Jakub Kornfeil**	CZE	84	Calvo Team	KTM	18	40m 43.091s
9	**Karel Hanika**	CZE	98	Red Bull KTM Ajo	KTM	18	40m 48.338s
10	**Enea Bastianini**	ITA	33	Junior Team GO&FUN Moto3	KTM	18	40m 50.522s
11	**Juanfran Guevara**	SPA	58	Mapfre Aspar Team Moto3	Kalex KTM	18	40m 58.409s
12	**Jorge Navarro**	SPA	99	Marc VDS Racing Team	Kalex KTM	18	40m 58.612s
13	**Hafiq Azmi**	MAL	38	SIC-AJO	KTM	18	41m 10.594s
14	**Alessandro Tonucci**	ITA	19	CIP	Mahindra	18	41m 10.747s
15	**Remy Gardner**	AUS	2	Calvo Team	KTM	18	41m 18.469s
16	Luca Grunwald	GER	43	Kiefer Racing	Kalex KTM	18	41m 18.507s
17	Jules Danilo	FRA	95	Ambrogio Racing	Mahindra	18	41m 18.794s
18	Philipp Oettl	GER	65	Interwetten Paddock Moto3	Kalex KTM	18	41m 19.775s
19	Gabriel Ramos	VEN	4	Kiefer Racing	Kalex KTM	18	41m 36.585s
20	Hafiza Rofa	MAL	88	SIC-AJO	KTM	18	42m 17.172s
	John McPhee	GBR	17	SaxoPrint-RTG	Honda	17	DNF
	Francesco Bagnaia	ITA	21	SKY Racing Team VR46	KTM	12	DNF
	Isaac Vinales	SPA	32	Calvo Team	KTM	11	DNF
	Romano Fenati	ITA	5	SKY Racing Team VR46	KTM	11	DNF
	Scott Deroue	NED	9	RW Racing GP	Kalex KTM	8	DNF
	Matteo Ferrari	ITA	3	San Carlo Team Italia	Mahindra	8	DNF
	Andrea Locatelli	ITA	55	San Carlo Team Italia	Mahindra	7	DNF
	Brad Binder	RSA	41	Ambrogio Racing	Mahindra	6	DNF
	Niklas Ajo	FIN	31	Avant Tecno Husqvarna Ajo	Husqvarna	4	DNF
	Zulfahmi Khairuddin	MAL	63	Ongetta-AirAsia	Honda	1	DNF
	Andrea Migno	ITA	16	Mahindra Racing	Mahindra	1	DNF
	Jasper Iwema	NED	13	CIP	Mahindra	1	DNF
	Ramdan Rosli	MAL	93	Petronas AHM Malaysia	KTM	1	DNF
	Miguel Oliveira	POR	44	Mahindra Racing	Mahindra	0	DNF

Fastest lap: Alex Rins, on lap 2, 2m 13.731s, 92.7mph/149.2km/h (record).
Previous lap record: Miguel Oliveira, POR (Mahindra), 2m 14.339s, 92.3mph/148.6km/h (2013).
Event best maximum speed: Efren Vazquez, 144.2mph/232.1km/h (free practice 3).

Qualifying

Weather: Dry
Air Temp: 32° **Track Temp:** 52°
Humidity: 54%

1	Miller	2m 12.450s
2	McPhee	2m 12.909s
3	Kornfeil	2m 13.016s
4	Vazquez	2m 13.040s
5	Marquez	2m 13.315s
6	Fenati	2m 13.434s
7	Kent	2m 13.529s
8	Vinales	2m 13.556s
9	Oliveira	2m 13.679s
10	Bastianini	2m 13.709s
11	Masbou	2m 13.822s
12	Hanika	2m 13.884s
13	Antonelli	2m 13.990s
14	Ajo	2m 14.155s
15	Bagnaia	2m 14.290s
16	Azmi	2m 14.413s
17	Rins	2m 14.444s
18	Migno	2m 14.796s
19	Guevara	2m 14.799s
20	Navarro	2m 15.277s
21	Rosli	2m 15.455s
22	Khairuddin	2m 15.498s
23	Ferrari	2m 15.509s
24	Grunwald	2m 15.595s
25	Binder	2m 15.619s
26	Danilo	2m 15.656s
27	Locatelli	2m 15.750s
28	Tonucci	2m 15.828s
29	Gardner	2m 15.875s
30	Oettl	2m 16.057s
31	Rofa	2m 16.104s
32	Iwema	2m 16.253s
33	Deroue	2m 16.326s
34	Ramos	2m 16.929s

Fastest race laps

1	Rins	2m 13.731s
2	Kornfeil	2m 13.777s
3	Marquez	2m 13.901s
4	McPhee	2m 13.977s
5	Binder	2m 14.000s
6	Fenati	2m 14.130s
7	Miller	2m 14.206s
8	Antonelli	2m 14.277s
9	Vazquez	2m 14.286s
10	Navarro	2m 14.312s
11	Bagnaia	2m 14.327s
12	Vinales	2m 14.403s
13	Masbou	2m 14.409s
14	Guevara	2m 14.443s
15	Hanika	2m 14.483s
16	Bastianini	2m 14.516s
17	Kent	2m 14.564s
18	Ajo	2m 15.183s
19	Azmi	2m 15.299s
20	Tonucci	2m 15.519s
21	Locatelli	2m 15.906s
22	Danilo	2m 16.019s
23	Rofa	2m 16.044s
24	Gardner	2m 16.158s
25	Ferrari	2m 16.164s
26	Deroue	2m 16.165s
27	Grunwald	2m 16.167s
28	Oettl	2m 16.345s
29	Ramos	2m 16.590s

Championship Points

1	Marquez	262
2	Miller	251
3	Rins	226
4	Vazquez	212
5	Fenati	174
6	Masbou	160
7	Bastianini	122
8	Vinales	121
9	Kent	116
10	Binder	102
11	Oliveira	102
12	Kornfeil	94
13	McPhee	77
14	Antonelli	59
15	Ajo	52
16	Bagnaia	50
17	Guevara	45
18	Hanika	38
19	Tonucci	20
20	Khairuddin	19
21	Loi	17
22	Ferrari	12
23	Navarro	11
24	Oettl	10
25	Migno	8
26	Ono	5
27	Iwema	4
28	Azmi	3
29	Sissis	3
30	Danilo	2
31	Granado	2
32	Gardner	1

Constructor Points

1	Honda	368
2	KTM	359
3	Mahindra	160
4	Husqvarna	143
5	Kalex KTM	61
6	FTR KTM	4

FIM WORLD CHAMPIONSHIP · ROUND 18

VALENCIA GRAND PRIX

VALENCIA CIRCUIT

Inset, far left: Monkey business: new Moto2 champion Rabat apes the Caped Crusader for his home fans.

Inset, left: Brothers in history: Moto3 winner Alex Marquez's team celebrate his victory, joined by MotoGP champion Marc and Honda's Shuhei Nakamoto.
Photos: Gold & Goose

Main: Jack and the gang: Miller leads Marquez and a Moto3 maelstrom – Vinales, Vasquez, Rins, Kent, McPhee, Antonelli, Ajo...
Photo: Gold & Goose

GRAN PREMIO
GENERALI DE LA
COMUNITAT
VALENCIANA

Comunitat Valenciana
Ricardo Tormo 2014

Above: When a picture is worth a thousand words. Jack Miller admires the new Moto3 champion's T-shirt.

Top right: Dovi and Crutchlow duked it out for a final time as team-mates.

Above right: A Marquez moment – the double champion came to win.

Above far right: Marco Melandri was about to return to the MotoGP fold.

Right: Scott Redding goes to ground for the photographers. Later, he touched down his helmet.

Below right: Aoyama, in his last race for Honda, battles with de Puniet, in his first and last for Suzuki.

Photos: Gold & Goose

WHILE neighbouring Catalunya voted for independence in a 'non-binding' referendum, Catalunyan riders cemented a second successive Spanish clean sweep at Valencia. The margin was much narrower than the breakaway majority. Just two points made the difference in the last remaining title to be settled.

It was yet more history for the Marquez family, on a day that sent 101,000 fans home happy. While elder brother Marc's 13th win outranked Doohan's dozen in 1997, sibling Alex had the help of a horde of Hondas to finish third in a high-intensity Moto3 race. KTM's Jack Miller took his sixth win of the season, double the number of his Spanish rival. It was all he could do, but it was not quite enough, with a shortage of allies in a front group with an intriguing landscape of conflicting loyalties.

Pre-race, both Rins and McPhee had said they would help Marquez; and Honda could count on the support also of Vazquez, in return for the promise of finding the until-now unemployed double GP winner a top-level berth for 2015.

Miller's potential backing was less predictable. Team-mate Hanika was not really fast enough to influence the front group. Hopes that good friend Rins might settle his own grudge against team-mate Marquez came to naught, when Rins nudged him wide. Meanwhile, fast KTM/Husqvarna 'colleague' Danny Kent was also to join Honda for 2015. Only Isaac Vinales would be staying with the Austrian bikes, and he was a steadfast ally, finishing second to Miller after having seized and then ceded a commanding lead. But Kent did his best: a threatening last-lap lunge on Marquez only failed when he ran wide through the final switchback. Had he taken third place, Miller would have been champion.

It was a dramatic finale to a second successive nail-biting year in the smallest class, on a weekend when there was plenty of background drama, starting with a flawed, but welcome return by Suzuki, and running on to a flurry of new signings, contracts and adventures. Especially for Miller, whose day of defeat would be followed directly by his first ride on a MotoGP bike.

The Suzuki proved to be handsome and raucous, and

not disgracefully slow, considering the marque's three-year absence, a difficult year of weather-hit testing and a race-rusty rider. With Randy de Puniet on board, it fairly matched the production Hondas, equally short of top speed (20km/h down) and setting similar lap times to qualify 20th. The day after the race, 2015 rider Aleix Espargaro circulated a couple of tenths faster. However, it did fall crucially short in reliability. On Friday, the bike expired on track in a plume of smoke: a top-end failure. On Saturday, de Puniet pottered back to the pits in free practice; and likewise in the race, due to gear selection problems.

It was rather more surprising to see Aoyama's struggles. He had the prototype of the 2015 Open Honda RC213VS, with pneumatic valve springs, although lacking the seamless-shift gearbox. He qualified 18th and managed one point for 15th, last but one Open Honda. The problems, he said, were to do with electronic set-up: the bike had plenty of top speed, but with no experience they were fumbling in the dark and suffering poor acceleration as they looked for the right ECU balance, as well as seeking gearing to suit the broader rev range.

With Aoyama set to retire to a role as Honda factory tester, the single bike would be shared by the other production Honda riders in testing over the next three days. The pneumatic-valve-spring Aprilia was also on hand for the tests, and it was finally confirmed that Marco Melandri would join Alvaro Bautista in the Gresini team as second rider. Loris Baz (Forward Yamaha) and Eugene Laverty (Drive M7 Honda) were also on hand to begin their MotoGP careers.

Another last jigsaw piece was put into place with the announcement that the Marc VDS team's entry to the premier class would be in conjunction with Estrella Galicia, linked to Emilio Alzamora's already very influential Monlau technical and riding academy, with both Marquez brothers already in the fold. Finally, Wayne Gardner's son, Remy, was signed up by the CIP Moto3 team, after rider Jakub Kornfeil abandoned plans to join the Mahindra-equipped team for a KTM berth with a new Sepang-sponsored team.

Bridgestone's asymmetric front tyre returned, in more fa-

vourable circumstances than its tricky introduction in Australia. Crutchlow was one of three riders who had crashed there on the tyre, and he robustly affirmed that "I'm not going near it", but generally it found more favour; team-mate Dovi gave it the thumbs-up after first Friday trials. Hayden was another fan, having raced it and finished with it at Phillip Island. On race day, more riders chose it than the standard tyre, on a ratio of 14:11. Among factory bikes, however, it was 9:5 against, with the top five finishers all sticking with the symmetric soft front.

For all riders, the weekend began with a wigging. Race Director Mike Webb assembled all three classes separately to explain "a new interpretation" of rules concerning loitering on track waiting for a faster rider. It was, he said, mainly aimed at Moto3, after a dismal slow bicycle race at Sepang and a more serious situation at the much narrower Phillip Island track.

There were no rules against following, but "the super-slow riding has to stop," he said. Apart from looking silly, there are obvious collision dangers, a type of accident with the risk of very serious injury. From this race onwards, any slow riding would be scrutinised and penalties applied case by case, whether or not any obstruction had been involved. It would be subjective, and some might get away with it; they were working on a system whereby a maximum section time could be instituted. Any rider exceeding this without good reason (an out- or in-lap, for example, or because of mechanical problems) would be in trouble.

At Valencia, four riders fell foul, all in Moto3, with a penalty point each for Jasper Iwema, Hafiq Azmi, Gabriel Rodrigo and John McPhee, the last named for a second time, after being similarly punished in Australia.

MOTOGP RACE – 30 laps

Second place was the focus of the big class, and Rossi took the high ground with his first pole since the French GP in 2010. Cheekily, his time came, after a bit of a struggle in free practice, by following Lorenzo after slowing to save his rear tyre, having botched his previous attempt. It was inadvertent, but amusing, he said. Further indignity followed for the Spaniard, who had been third fastest last time he passed the pits and accordingly wheeled into *parc ferme*, only to be wheeled out again: Pedrosa had just gone fractionally quicker.

Iannone was second; Marquez and Pol Espargaro were alongside Lorenzo, times very close on the short track, with six-tenths covering the top ten.

As the race started, the weather turned, with light spots of rain and the white flags out at the end of the first lap. The rain, such as it was, stopped directly, only to begin again after 17 laps, slightly more seriously.

It led to wildly varying lap times, and effectively did for Lorenzo, who (like Miller) needed to win, and hope that Rossi was no higher than fourth. Unsettled by the risky surface, which became quite wet in some sections, he repeated his successful Aragon tactics and called in to swap bikes, followed by Iannone. Instead, it mostly dried within four laps. He was ten seconds off the pace and pitted to retire. "I played my last card," he said. "To come third or fourth – there was no reason."

Iannone led off the line, Rossi in pursuit and Marquez pushing past Lorenzo to take third. In the semi-wet conditions, the early laps were spread out, brave boy Iannone up to almost 1.5 seconds clear after five laps, and Marquez a similar distance behind Rossi.

The factory Ducatis had pushed through and pounced on Pedrosa, Crutchlow currently ahead and even challenging Marquez; Dovizioso was behind Dani.

Pedrosa would escape, and the Ducatis were soon passed by Lorenzo, Dovizioso now ahead as they continued a race-long battle.

Above: MotoGP midfield on lap three: the Espargaro brothers head Bradl, Redding, Smith, Bautista, Pirro and Hayden, then de Angelis, Barbera, Petrucci, the Suzuki at the back.

Top right: Great joy. Rossi's second meant he beat Lorenzo for best of the rest.

Above right: Zarco (5) was freed from Morbidelli's challenge for third when the Italian fell off.

Top far right: Vinales messed it up and took out rival Kallio.

Above far right: Luthi (35) and Rabat (53) waged a race-long battle.

Centre right: Luthi was surprised and delighted by his last-gasp win.

Centre far right: Double-top for the first world championship-winning brothers, let alone in the same year.

Right: Jack Miller comfortably leads Vinales and Antonelli, and the stalking Marquez (12).

Photos: Gold & Goose

With the track drying, the front three closed up. On lap ten, Marquez slipped cleanly past Rossi and set about Iannone. He proved a hard nut to crack, immediately regaining the lead after the first attempt. But by the end of lap 11, Marquez was ahead, and next time around not only Rossi was past the Ducati, but also Pedrosa.

Marquez gradually pulled clear; Rossi and Pedrosa were together, Lorenzo a couple of seconds behind. Then on lap 17, it started to rain again, a bit harder, mechanics again warming up wet-shod bikes in the pit lane.

Marquez: "Now I had some doubts. I remembered Aragon, but there were only three or four corners where it was really wet. One lap, I made a signal to my team I was coming in. But then the rain stopped and I carried on."

With lap times up by five seconds or more, Rossi closed again, able to use the leader as a guide, but also concerned. "A lot of times I thought about coming in." Only Lorenzo and Iannone did so, to their cost.

Soon it was mainly dry again. Marquez pulled clear once more to win his 13th of the year by 3.5 seconds. A cautious Pedrosa was third, another ten seconds down.

The Ducati pair fought to the end, Crutchlow briefly ahead a couple of times in the closing laps in a replay of their Tech 3 battles of two years before. Dovizioso took fifth by less than a tenth.

A long way back, Pol Espargaro finally got the better of brother Aleix, Bradl dropping away at the end in eighth.

Smith had moved clear of this group, only to run off on lap 18. He rejoined for an eventual 14th, but stormed off to Race Control to complain that a marshal had pushed him off his bike as he tried to restart.

Wild-card Pirro came past Redding for ninth. Another six seconds away, a three-bike gang had been trading blows in the latter stages. On the final lap, Barbera managed to out-power the persistent Petrucci and Hayden.

Smith was next, storming past Aoyama and a fading Bautista, with the Japanese rider taking 15th on the final lap.

The Suzuki's return race ended early. De Puniet had diced with Aoyama until he cruised into the pits to retire after 11 laps with reported gearshift problems.

Rossi's fine second in both race and championship were well deserved, underlining his remarkable rebirth. Marquez's win number 13 broke the record, but he had the good grace to say it didn't mean much, because Doohan had done it in

just 15 races. In percentage terms, Doohan had 80, Marc 72.2. Less than Mike Hailwood's 1963 best of 87.5 per cent. But both John Surtees and Giacomo Agostini had won every race, the only two hundred-per-centers in history.

MOTO2 RACE – 27 laps

Rabat waited until the end before extending his record run of Moto2 poles. It was the new champion's 11th, taken from an earlier dominant Zarco. Rookie Morbidelli celebrated the close of his first season with his first front row in third.

The focus was on the rivals for second overall: Vinales in the middle of the third row, Kallio alongside in ninth.

Their battle was also the focus of the race. After three wins in the previous four rounds, Vinales was just 15 points behind. Kallio needed not merely to finish, but to finish strongly.

The sting went out of the thing on the very first lap, when Vinales missed his braking point going into the last tight turn. Out of control, he went piling into the back of Kallio. Both went down in a heap, and while Vinales managed to restart – Kallio waving him off with a classic one-finger salute – it was only to retire.

But there would be another sting, in the tail of an otherwise typically processional race for the leaders.

Rabat led away, with Luthi in pursuit. The Motegi winner was glued to the Spaniard's back wheel, one- or two-tenths behind every lap. They started the last lap the same way, and Luthi finally attacked in the early tight turns.

It went wrong; he ran wide, and Rabat was back in control. All the way to the exit from the final corner.

As he accelerated away, pulling a little wheelie, his bike suddenly slowed; a surprised and delighted Luthi flew past, for his second win of the year.

The cause, Rabat explained, was fuel starvation, caused by a surge in a near-empty tank as the bike reared up. "The track temperature was lower and I was sliding more, and used more fuel," he said.

He still set a record points total of 346.

Zarco was ten seconds adrift for a lone third, a position he had held from the first lap to the last, but there was something of a tussle for fourth in the closing stages.

Aegerter had inherited the position after Morbidelli slipped off after five laps; and the Swiss rider held it until there were four laps to go.

Now Simeon took over, only to lose it on the last lap to Salom. The trio crossed the line within less than two seconds.

World Supersport champion Lowes was seventh; Schrotter won a four-bike battle for eighth, from West, Baldassarri and Torres. Cardus narrowly beat Folger, Nakagami, Rossi and Syahrin, the last missing out on points.

Cortese fell on the first lap, thereby ceding eighth overall to Salom. Simon and Pons also crashed out; likewise Lucas Mahias on the unconventional Transfiormers, with its wishbone front end.

MOTO3 RACE – 24 laps

Close qualifying yielded a maiden pole for Antonelli, from Miller and Marquez; Vinales, Rins and Hanika were behind.

Miller made a flying start, with Vinales taking second off Antonelli at the end of the lap. Miller would lead almost every lap over the line, but there were a couple of key moments.

On lap 15, the Australian managed to stuff it up inside Marquez and push him wide. The Spaniard fell back to fourth in a large and growing lead pack.

Then on lap 20, Rins did the same thing to Miller. He dropped briefly to sixth, though he had recovered to fourth by the end of the lap.

This opened the way for Vinales to lead, and he opened a gap of more than 1.5 seconds over new second-placer Kent.

Now Miller showed all his strength as he forged back to second within one lap, then slashed away at a lead of more than 1.5 seconds. "I left no stone unturned – I was stretching the throttle cable, that's for sure," he said.

He was in front again as they started the last lap, Vinales riding shotgun in second – but Marquez was third, which was all he needed.

The final drama came from Kent, who mounted a spirited attack in the last lap, ready to pounce on Marquez into the last corner, only to run wide.

Marquez was almost a second adrift at the end, but it was enough. Kent was fourth, then came Rins, Vazquez (who had set a new record early on) and Antonelli.

The lead group had grown considerably in the closing stages, but was interrupted when McPhee again crashed on the last lap. In the confusion, Oliveira was able to pounce on Binder for eighth, securing tenth overall in the process – they had arrived equal on points. Kornfeil completed the top ten.

GP GENERALI DE LA COMUNITAT VALENCIANA

7–9 NOVEMBER, 2014

CIRCUITO DE LA COMUNITAT VALENCIANA

30 laps
Length: 4.005 km / 2.489 miles
Width: 12m

Key
96/60 kph/mph
⚙ Gear

Angel Nieto 96/60 ⚙
Afición 210/130 ⚙
Mick Doohan 80/50 ⚙
Turn 8 95/59
Turn 11 80/50 ⚙
Turn 13 194/120 ⚙
Champi Herreros 130/81 ⚙
Turn 5 105/65 ⚙
Turn 4 105/65 ⚙
Adrian Campos 90/56 ⚙
Jorge Martinez Aspar 136/84 ⚙

MotoGP

RACE DISTANCE: 30 laps, 74.658 miles/120.150km · RACE WEATHER: Dry (air 18°C, humidity 45%, track 22°C)

Pos.	Rider	Nat.	No.	Entrant	Machine	Tyres	Race tyre choice	Laps	Time & speed
1	Marc Marquez	SPA	93	Repsol Honda Team	Honda RC213V	B	F: Soft/R: Medium	30	46m 39.627s
									95.9mph/
									154.4km/h
2	Valentino Rossi	ITA	46	Movistar Yamaha MotoGP	Yamaha YZR-M1	B	F: Soft/R: Medium	30	46m 43.143s
3	Dani Pedrosa	SPA	26	Repsol Honda Team	Honda RC213V	B	F: Soft/R: Medium	30	46m 53.667s
4	Andrea Dovizioso	ITA	4	Ducati Team	Ducati Desmosedici	B	F: Soft/R: Medium	30	46m 56.332s
5	Cal Crutchlow	GBR	35	Ducati Team	Ducati Desmosedici	B	F: Soft/R: Medium	30	46m 56.400s
6	Pol Espargaro	SPA	44	Monster Yamaha Tech 3	Yamaha YZR-M1	B	F: Soft-Asym/R: Medium	30	47m 17.511s
7	Aleix Espargaro	SPA	41	NGM Forward Racing	Forward Yamaha	B	F: Soft-Asym/R: Soft	30	47m 17.795s
8	Stefan Bradl	GER	6	LCR Honda MotoGP	Honda RC213V	B	F: Soft/R: Medium	30	47m 21.430s
9	Michele Pirro	ITA	51	Ducati Team	Ducati Desmosedici	B	F: Soft/R: Medium	30	47m 25.337s
10	Scott Redding	GBR	45	GO&FUN Honda Gresini	Honda RCV1000R	B	F: Soft-Asym/R: Soft	30	47m 30.818s
11	Hector Barbera	SPA	8	Avintia Racing	Ducati Desmosedici	B	F: Soft-Asym/R: Soft	30	47m 36.139s
12	Danilo Petrucci	ITA	9	Octo IodaRacing Team	ART	B	F: Soft-Asym/R: Medium	30	47m 36.627s
13	Nicky Hayden	USA	69	Drive M7 Aspar	Honda RCV1000R	B	F: Soft-Asym/R: Soft	30	47m 36.889s
14	Bradley Smith	GBR	38	Monster Yamaha Tech 3	Yamaha YZR-M1	B	F: Soft-Asym/R: Medium	30	47m 37.144s
15	Hiroshi Aoyama	JPN	7	Drive M7 Aspar	Honda RC213V-RS	B	F: Soft-Asym/R: Medium	30	47m 38.402s
16	Alvaro Bautista	SPA	19	GO&FUN Honda Gresini	Honda RC213V	B	F: Soft-Asym/R: Medium	30	47m 38.491s
17	Karel Abraham	CZE	17	Cardion AB Motoracing	Honda RCV1000R	B	F: Extra-Soft/R: Soft	30	47m 42.016s
18	Alex de Angelis	RSM	15	NGM Forward Racing	Forward Yamaha	B	F: Soft-Asym/R: Soft	30	47m 55.422s
19	Michael Laverty	GBR	70	Paul Bird Motorsport	PBM-ART	B	F: Soft-Asym/R: Soft	30	48m 05.936s
20	Broc Parkes	AUS	23	Paul Bird Motorsport	PBM-ART	B	F: Soft-Asym/R: Soft	30	48m 16.839s
21	Mike di Meglio	FRA	63	Avintia Racing	Avintia	B	F: Soft/R: Soft	29	46m 40.210s
22	Andrea Iannone	ITA	29	Pramac Racing	Ducati Desmosedici	B	F: Soft-Asym/R: Medium	29	47m 55.140s
	Jorge Lorenzo	SPA	99	Movistar Yamaha MotoGP	Yamaha YZR-M1	B	F: Soft/R: Medium	24	DNF-retired
	Randy de Puniet	FRA	14	Team Suzuki MotoGP	Suzuki GSX-RR	B	F: Soft-Asym/R: Soft	12	DNF-mechanical
	Yonny Hernandez	COL	68	Energy T.I. Pramac Racing	Ducati Desmosedici	B	F: Soft/R: Medium	9	DNF-mechanical

Fastest lap: Marc Marquez, on lap 8, 1m 31.515s, 97.9mph/157.5km/h (record).

Previous lap record: Dani Pedrosa, SPA (Honda), 1m 31.628s, 97.7mph/157.3km/h (2013).

Event best maximum speed: Cal Crutchlow, 206.5mph/332.4km/h (qualifying 2).

Qualifying

Weather: Dry
Air Temp: 20° **Track Temp:** 27°
Humidity: 39%

1	Rossi	1m 30.843s
2	Iannone	1m 30.975s
3	Pedrosa	1m 30.999s
4	Lorenzo	1m 31.049s
5	Marquez	1m 31.144s
6	P. Espargaro	1m 31.307s
7	Smith	1m 31.324s
8	Crutchlow	1m 31.359s
9	Dovizioso	1m 31.426s
10	Bradl	1m 31.443s
11	A. Espargaro	1m 31.486s
12	Pirro	1m 32.617s
13	Bautista	1m 32.160s
14	Redding	1m 32.315s
15	Hernandez	1m 32.321s
16	Barbera	1m 32.395s
17	Barbera	1m 32.443s
18	Aoyama	1m 32.449s
19	De Angelis	1m 32.453s
20	De Puniet	1m 32.509s
21	Petrucci	1m 32.683s
22	Laverty	1m 32.808s
23	Abraham	1m 33.019s
24	Parkes	1m 33.972s
25	Di Meglio	1m 34.510s

Fastest race laps

1	Marquez	1m 31.515s
2	Rossi	1m 31.688s
3	Pedrosa	1m 31.715s
4	Lorenzo	1m 31.817s
5	Dovizioso	1m 31.966s
6	Smith	1m 31.989s
7	Crutchlow	1m 32.019s
8	Iannone	1m 32.054s
9	P. Espargaro	1m 32.104s
10	A. Espargaro	1m 32.446s
11	Bradl	1m 32.500s
12	Bautista	1m 32.538s
13	Barbera	1m 32.918s
14	Hayden	1m 32.989s
15	De Angelis	1m 33.013s
16	Pirro	1m 33.094s
17	Redding	1m 33.127s
18	Aoyama	1m 33.399s
19	De Puniet	1m 33.445s
20	Hernandez	1m 33.511s
21	Petrucci	1m 33.552s
22	Abraham	1m 33.627s
23	Laverty	1m 33.636s
24	Parkes	1m 34.071s
25	Di Meglio	1m 34.640s

Championship Points

1	Marquez	362
2	Rossi	295
3	Lorenzo	263
4	Pedrosa	246
5	Dovizioso	187
6	P. Espargaro	136
7	A. Espargaro	126
8	Smith	121
9	Bradl	117
10	Iannone	102
11	Bautista	89
12	Redding	81
13	Crutchlow	74
14	Aoyama	68
15	Hernandez	53
16	Hayden	47
17	Abraham	33
18	Barbera	26
19	Pirro	18
20	Petrucci	17
21	De Angelis	14
22	Edwards	11
23	Parkes	9
24	Laverty	9
25	Di Meglio	9
26	Nakasuga	4
27	Camier	1

Grid Order

		1	2	3	4	5	6	7	8	9	10	11	12	13	14	15	16	17	18	19	20	21	22	23	24	25	26	27	28	29	30	
46	ROSSI	29	29	29	29	29	29	29	29	29	29	93	93	93	93	93	93	93	93	93	93	93	93	93	93	93	93	93	93	93	93	1
29	IANNONE	46	46	46	46	46	46	46	46	46	93	29	46	46	46	46	46	46	46	46	46	46	46	46	46	46	46	46	46	46	46	2
26	PEDROSA	93	93	93	93	93	93	93	93	93	46	46	26	26	26	26	26	26	26	26	26	26	26	26	26	26	26	26	26	26	26	3
99	LORENZO	99	26	35	35	35	26	26	26	26	26	26	29	29	29	99	99	99	99	4	4	4	4	4	4	35	4	4	4	4	4	4
93	MARQUEZ	26	35	26	26	26	35	4	99	99	99	99	99	99	99	4	4	35	35	35	35	35	35	35	35	4	35	35	35			5
44	P. ESPARGARO	35	4	4	4	4	4	99	99	4	4	4	4	4	4	35	35	4	99	41	41	41	41	41	41	41	44	44	44	44		6
38	SMITH	4	99	99	99	99	99	35	35	35	35	35	35	35	35	29	29	29	29	44	44	44	44	44	44	44	41	41	41	41		7
35	CRUTCHLOW	44	44	68	41	41	41	38	38	38	38	38	38	38	38	44	38	38	44	41	6	6	6	6	6	6	6	6	6	6		8
4	DOVIZIOSO	6	41	41	45	38	38	41	41	41	41	41	41	41	44	44	44	44	45	45	45	45	51	51	51	51	51	51	51			9
6	BRADL	41	6	44	68	45	45	44	44	44	44	41	41	41	41	41	41	6	6	19	51	51	51	45	45	45	45	45	45			10
41	A. ESPARGARO	38	68	6	38	68	68	44	44	45	6	6	6	6	6	6	6	19	19	51	19	19	19	9	9	9	9	9	8			11
51	PIRRO	68	38	38	6	44	44	6	6	45	19	19	19	19	19	45	45	69	69	69	8	8	69	69	8	8	9					12
19	BAUTISTA	51	19	45	44	6	6	68	19	19	45	45	45	45	45	51	51	8	8	8	69	69	8	8	69	69	69					13
45	REDDING	45	51	19	19	19	19	19	69	69	69	69	69	69	69	69	9	9	9	9	19	19	19	19	19	7	38					14
68	HERNANDEZ	19	45	51	69	69	69	69	51	51	8	8	8	8	8	8	69	8	17	17	17	17	17	7	7	19	7					15
69	HAYDEN	15	15	69	8	8	51	51	51	8	51	51	51	51	51	51	15	15	7	7	7	7	7	17	17	38	19					
8	BARBERA	69	69	15	15	51	8	8	15	15	15	15	15	15	15	9	9	15	15	38	38	38	38	38	17	17						
7	AOYAMA	8	8	51	15	15	15	7	7	7	7	7	7	7	7	7	7	7	99	38	38	15	15	15	15	15	15					
15	DE ANGELIS	7	7	9	9	9	14	7	14	14	14	9	9	9	9	17	17	29	99	70	70	70	70	70	70	70	70					
14	DE PUNIET	17	17	7	7	7	14	7	14	9	9	17	17	17	17	38	38	38	70	99	99	23	23	23	23	23	23					
9	PETRUCCI	9	9	17	17	14	9	9	70	70	17	70	70	70	70	70	70	70	23	29	29	23	63	63	63	63	63					
70	LAVERTY	70	14	14	14	17	70	70	17	17	70	23	23	23	23	23	23	63	99	29	29	29	29	29								
17	ABRAHAM	14	70	63	63	70	70	17	17	68	23	23	63	63	63	63	63	63	29	29												
23	PARKES	63	63	70	70	63	63	63	23	63	63	14																				
63	DI MEGLIO	23	23	23	23	23	23	23	23	63																						

68 Pit stop   63 Lapped rider

Constructor Points

1	Honda	409
2	Yamaha	354
3	Ducati	211
4	Forward Yamaha	138
5	ART	17
6	PBM	15
7	Avintia	11

Moto2

RACE DISTANCE: 27 laps, 67.192 miles/108.135km · RACE WEATHER: Dry (air 18°C, humidity 48%, track 22°C)

Pos.	Rider	Nat.	No.	Entrant	Machine	Laps	Time & Speed
1	**Thomas Luthi**	SWI	12	Interwetten Sitag	Suter	27	43m 08.366s 93.4mph/ 150.3km/h
2	**Esteve Rabat**	SPA	53	Marc VDS Racing Team	Kalex	27	43m 08.499s
3	**Johann Zarco**	FRA	5	AirAsia Caterham	Caterham Suter	27	43m 19.094s
4	**Luis Salom**	SPA	39	Paginas Amarillas HP 40	Kalex	27	43m 21.380s
5	**Xavier Simeon**	BEL	19	Federal Oil Gresini Moto2	Suter	27	43m 22.055s
6	**Dominique Aegerter**	SWI	77	Technomag carXpert	Suter	27	43m 23.072s
7	**Sam Lowes**	GBR	22	Speed Up	Speed Up	27	43m 27.191s
8	**Marcel Schrotter**	GER	23	Tech 3	Tech 3	27	43m 38.551s
9	**Anthony West**	AUS	95	QMMF Racing Team	Speed Up	27	43m 38.593s
10	**Lorenzo Baldassarri**	ITA	7	Gresini Moto2	Suter	27	43m 38.970s
11	**Jordi Torres**	SPA	81	Mapfre Aspar Team Moto2	Suter	27	43m 38.981s
12	**Ricard Cardus**	SPA	88	Tech 3	Tech 3	27	43m 41.788s
13	**Jonas Folger**	GER	94	AGR Team	Kalex	27	43m 41.960s
14	**Takaaki Nakagami**	JPN	30	IDEMITSU Honda Team Asia	Kalex	27	43m 42.363s
15	**Louis Rossi**	FRA	96	SAG Team	Kalex	27	43m 42.373s
16	Hafizh Syahrin	MAL	55	Petronas Raceline Malaysia	Kalex	27	43m 43.944s
17	Robin Mulhauser	SWI	70	Technomag carXpert	Suter	27	43m 44.057s
18	Nicolas Terol	SPA	18	Mapfre Aspar Team Moto2	Suter	27	43m 55.362s
19	Ratthapark Wilairot	THA	14	AirAsia Caterham	Caterham Suter	27	43m 59.016s
20	Roberto Rolfo	ITA	44	Tasca Racing Moto2	Suter	27	44m 00.243s
21	Franco Morbidelli	ITA	21	Italtrans Racing Team	Kalex	27	44m 01.174s
22	Randy Krummenacher	SWI	4	Octo IodaRacing Team	Suter	27	44m 01.794s
23	Florian Marino	FRA	20	NGM Forward Racing	Kalex	27	44m 01.801s
24	Gino Rea	GBR	8	AGT REA Racing	Suter	27	44m 16.070s
25	Roman Ramos	SPA	97	QMMF Racing Team	Speed Up	27	44m 21.979s
26	Tetsuta Nagashima	JPN	45	Teluru Team JiR Webike	NTS	27	44m 23.343s
27	Azlan Shah	MAL	25	IDEMITSU Honda Team Asia	Kalex	27	44m 23.504s
28	Thitipong Warokorn	THA	10	APH PTT The Pizza SAG	Kalex	25	44m 07.885s
	Mattia Pasini	ITA	54	NGM Forward Racing	Kalex	7	DNF
	Lucas Mahias	FRA	90	Promoto Sport	Transfiormers	4	DNF
	Julian Simon	SPA	60	Italtrans Racing Team	Kalex	2	DNF
	Axel Pons	SPA	49	AGR Team	Kalex	2	DNF
	Maverick Vinales	SPA	40	Paginas Amarillas HP 40	Kalex	2	DNF
	Mika Kallio	FIN	36	Marc VDS Racing Team	Kalex	0	DNF
	Sandro Cortese	GER	11	Dynavolt Intact GP	Kalex	0	DNF

Fastest lap: Thomas Luthi, on lap 18, 1m 35.312s, 94.0mph/151.2km/h (record).
Previous lap record: Jordi Torres, SPA (Suter), 1m 35.694s, 93.6mph/150.6km/h (2013).
Event best maximum speed: Esteve Rabat, 170.3mph/274.0km/h (qualifying).

Qualifying
Weather: Dry
Air Temp: 19° **Track Temp:** 23°
Humidity: 39%

1	Rabat	1m 35.199s
2	Zarco	1m 35.242s
3	Morbidelli	1m 35.420s
4	Luthi	1m 35.532s
5	Simeon	1m 35.566s
6	Schrotter	1m 35.630s
7	Folger	1m 35.639s
8	Vinales	1m 35.653s
9	Kallio	1m 35.670s
10	Salom	1m 35.711s
11	Aegerter	1m 35.732s
12	Simon	1m 35.772s
13	Pons	1m 35.823s
14	Lowes	1m 35.830s
15	Rossi	1m 35.880s
16	Cortese	1m 35.947s
17	Baldassarri	1m 36.036s
18	Pasini	1m 36.082s
19	Syahrin	1m 36.105s
20	Cardus	1m 36.214s
21	Krummenacher	1m 36.254s
22	Nakagami	1m 36.263s
23	West	1m 36.345s
24	Mahias	1m 36.385s
25	Torres	1m 36.475s
26	Mulhauser	1m 36.480s
27	Marino	1m 36.481s
28	Wilairot	1m 36.638s
29	Terol	1m 36.752s
30	Rolfo	1m 36.809s
31	Warokorn	1m 36.923s
32	Rea	1m 36.925s
33	Ramos	1m 37.152s
34	Shah	1m 37.551s
35	Nagashima	1m 38.326s

Fastest race laps

1	Luthi	1m 35.312s
2	Rabat	1m 35.327s
3	Salom	1m 35.521s
4	Zarco	1m 35.535s
5	Morbidelli	1m 35.573s
6	Aegerter	1m 35.662s
7	Simeon	1m 35.733s
8	Lowes	1m 35.761s
9	Folger	1m 35.792s
10	Torres	1m 35.955s
11	Cardus	1m 36.034s
12	Baldassarri	1m 36.160s
13	West	1m 36.169s
14	Schrotter	1m 36.194s
15	Syahrin	1m 36.262s
16	Krummenacher	1m 36.280s
17	Nakagami	1m 36.355s
18	Rossi	1m 36.378s
19	Mulhauser	1m 36.508s
20	Wilairot	1m 36.520s
21	Terol	1m 36.612s
22	Ramos	1m 36.655s
23	Pasini	1m 36.662s
24	Rea	1m 36.774s
25	Rolfo	1m 36.924s
26	Marino	1m 36.931s
27	Pons	1m 37.079s
28	Simon	1m 37.190s
29	Shah	1m 37.397s
30	Mahias	1m 37.598s
31	Nagashima	1m 37.658s
32	Warokorn	1m 38.120s

Championship Points

1	Rabat	346
2	Kallio	289
3	Vinales	274
4	Luthi	194
5	Aegerter	172
6	Zarco	146
7	Corsi	100
8	Salom	85
9	Cortese	85
10	Schrotter	80
11	Morbidelli	75
12	West	72
13	Lowes	69
14	Simeon	63
15	Folger	63
16	Torres	57
17	Simon	56
18	Cardus	45
19	Syahrin	42
20	De Angelis	37
21	Pasini	35
22	Nakagami	34
23	Pons	28
24	Krummenacher	24
25	Baldassarri	20
26	Rossi	18
27	Rea	7
28	Terol	2
29	Rolfo	2

Constructor Points

1	Kalex	430
2	Suter	284
3	Caterham Suter	146
4	Speed Up	121
5	Tech 3	97
6	Forward KLX	33

Moto3

RACE DISTANCE: 24 laps, 59.726 miles/96.120km · RACE WEATHER: Dry (air 16°C, humidity 61%, track 18°C)

Pos.	Rider	Nat.	No.	Entrant	Machine	Laps	Time & Speed
1	**Jack Miller**	AUS	8	Red Bull KTM Ajo	KTM	24	40m 10.983s 89.2mph/ 143.5km/h
2	**Isaac Vinales**	SPA	32	Calvo Team	KTM	24	40m 11.138s
3	**Alex Marquez**	SPA	12	Estrella Galicia 0,0	Honda	24	40m 11.938s
4	**Danny Kent**	GBR	52	Red Bull Husqvarna Ajo	Husqvarna	24	40m 12.555s
5	**Alex Rins**	SPA	42	Estrella Galicia 0,0	Honda	24	40m 13.234s
6	**Efren Vazquez**	SPA	7	SaxoPrint-RTG	Honda	24	40m 13.491s
7	**Niccolo Antonelli**	ITA	23	Junior Team GO&FUN Moto3	KTM	24	40m 14.603s
8	**Miguel Oliveira**	POR	44	Mahindra Racing	Mahindra	24	40m 15.199s
9	**Brad Binder**	RSA	41	Ambrogio Racing	Mahindra	24	40m 15.231s
10	**Karel Hanika**	CZE	98	Red Bull KTM Ajo	KTM	24	40m 15.346s
11	**Enea Bastianini**	ITA	33	Junior Team GO&FUN Moto3	KTM	24	40m 16.445s
12	**Alexis Masbou**	FRA	10	Ongetta-Rivacold	Honda	24	40m 16.763s
13	**Jakub Kornfeil**	CZE	84	Calvo Team	KTM	24	40m 16.942s
14	**Romano Fenati**	ITA	5	SKY Racing Team VR46	KTM	24	40m 17.192s
15	**Juanfran Guevara**	SPA	58	Mapfre Aspar Team Moto3	Kalex KTM	24	40m 17.709s
16	Francesco Bagnaia	ITA	21	SKY Racing Team VR46	KTM	24	40m 22.758s
17	John McPhee	GBR	17	SaxoPrint-RTG	Honda	24	40m 27.646s
18	Andrea Migno	ITA	16	Mahindra Racing	Mahindra	24	40m 35.902s
19	Zulfahmi Khairuddin	MAL	63	Ongetta-AirAsia	Honda	24	40m 39.021s
20	Jasper Iwema	NED	13	CIP	Mahindra	24	40m 39.387s
21	Alessandro Tonucci	ITA	19	CIP	Mahindra	24	40m 39.473s
22	Luca Grunwald	GER	43	Kiefer Racing	Kalex KTM	24	40m 51.756s
23	Hafiq Azmi	MAL	38	SIC-AJO	KTM	24	40m 51.767s
24	Gabriel Ramos	VEN	4	Kiefer Racing	Kalex KTM	24	41m 00.312s
25	Matteo Ferrari	ITA	3	San Carlo Team Italia	Mahindra	24	41m 00.338s
26	Andrea Locatelli	ITA	55	San Carlo Team Italia	Mahindra	24	41m 03.845s
27	Maria Herrera	SPA	6	Junior Team Estrella Galicia 0,0	Honda	24	41m 03.862s
28	Albert Arenas	SPA	14	Calvo Team	KTM	24	41m 40.775s
	Niklas Ajo	FIN	31	Avant Tecno Husqvarna Ajo	Husqvarna	20	DNF
	Jorge Navarro	SPA	99	Marc VDS Racing Team	Kalex KTM	9	DNF
	Scott Deroue	NED	9	RW Racing GP	Kalex KTM	8	DNF
	Jules Danilo	FRA	95	Ambrogio Racing	Mahindra	7	DNF
	Gabriel Rodrigo	ARG	91	RBA Racing Team	KTM	1	DNF
	Philipp Oettl	GER	65	Interwetten Paddock Moto3	Kalex KTM	1	DNF

Fastest lap: Efren Vazquez, on lap 7, 1m 39.400s, 90.1mph/145.0km/h (record).
Previous lap record: Luis Salom, SPA (KTM), 1m 39.744s, 89.8mph/144.5km/h (2013).
Event best maximum speed: Efren Vazquez, 146.8mph/236.2km/h (free practice 3).

Qualifying
Weather: Dry
Air Temp: 20° **Track Temp:** 26°
Humidity: 40%

1	Antonelli	1m 39.183s
2	Miller	1m 39.251s
3	Marquez	1m 39.556s
4	Vinales	1m 39.637s
5	Rins	1m 39.716s
6	Hanika	1m 39.731s
7	Ajo	1m 39.750s
8	McPhee	1m 39.775s
9	Vazquez	1m 39.869s
10	Guevara	1m 39.884s
11	Kent	1m 39.923s
12	Kornfeil	1m 39.969s
13	Migno	1m 40.018s
14	Fenati	1m 40.022s
15	Masbou	1m 40.038s
16	Binder	1m 40.045s
17	Oliveira	1m 40.053s
18	Navarro	1m 40.097s
19	Tonucci	1m 40.334s
20	Bagnaia	1m 40.379s
21	Bastianini	1m 40.412s
22	Arenas	1m 40.447s
23	Iwema	1m 40.780s
24	Azmi	1m 40.875s
25	Rodrigo	1m 40.950s
26	Khairuddin	1m 41.040s
27	Ferrari	1m 41.051s
28	Grunwald	1m 41.137s
29	Danilo	1m 41.336s
30	Locatelli	1m 41.378s
31	Herrera	1m 41.474s
32	Oettl	1m 41.671s
33	Deroue	1m 41.701s
34	Ramos	1m 42.209s

Fastest race laps

1	Vazquez	1m 39.400s
2	Miller	1m 39.482s
3	Marquez	1m 39.537s
4	Guevara	1m 39.573s
5	McPhee	1m 39.587s
6	Bastianini	1m 39.689s
7	Kent	1m 39.723s
8	Bagnaia	1m 39.742s
9	Oliveira	1m 39.767s
10	Rins	1m 39.771s
11	Antonelli	1m 39.794s
12	Vinales	1m 39.802s
13	Ajo	1m 39.809s
14	Fenati	1m 39.819s
15	Binder	1m 39.831s
16	Navarro	1m 39.858s
17	Hanika	1m 39.911s
18	Masbou	1m 39.918s
19	Kornfeil	1m 39.990s
20	Migno	1m 40.035s
21	Tonucci	1m 40.625s
22	Grunwald	1m 40.633s
23	Khairuddin	1m 40.648s
24	Danilo	1m 40.805s
25	Azmi	1m 40.893s
26	Iwema	1m 40.968s
27	Ramos	1m 41.109s
28	Ferrari	1m 41.228s
29	Arenas	1m 41.540s
30	Herrera	1m 41.584s
31	Locatelli	1m 41.713s
32	Deroue	1m 43.126s

Championship Points

1	Marquez	278
2	Miller	276
3	Rins	237
4	Vazquez	222
5	Fenati	176
6	Masbou	164
7	Vinales	141
8	Kent	129
9	Bastianini	127
10	Oliveira	110
11	Binder	109
12	Kornfeil	97
13	McPhee	77
14	Antonelli	68
15	Ajo	52
16	Bagnaia	50
17	Guevara	46
18	Hanika	44
19	Tonucci	20
20	Khairuddin	19
21	Loi	17
22	Ferrari	12
23	Navarro	11
24	Oettl	10
25	Migno	8
26	Ono	5
27	Iwema	4
28	Azmi	3
29	Sissis	3
30	Danilo	2
31	Granado	2
32	Gardner	1

Constructor Points

1	KTM	384
2	Honda	384
3	Mahindra	168
4	Husqvarna	156
5	Kalex KTM	62
6	FTR KTM	4

WORLD CHAMPIONSHIP POINTS 2014

Compiled by PETER McLAREN

MotoGP – Riders

Position	Rider	Nationality	Machine	Qatar	Texas	Argentina	Spain	France	Italy	Catalunya	Netherlands	Germany	Indianapolis	Czech Republic	Great Britain	San Marino	Aragon	Japan	Australia	Malaysia	Valencia	Points total
1	**Marc Marquez**	SPA	Honda	25	25	25	25	25	25	25	25	25	25	13	25	1	3	20	–	25	25	**362**
2	**Valentino Rossi**	ITA	Yamaha	20	8	13	20	20	16	20	11	13	16	16	16	25	–	16	25	20	20	**295**
3	**Jorge Lorenzo**	SPA	Yamaha	–	6	16	13	10	20	13	3	16	20	20	20	20	25	25	20	16	–	**263**
4	**Dani Pedrosa**	SPA	Honda	16	20	20	16	11	13	16	16	20	13	25	13	16	2	13	–	–	16	**246**
5	**Andrea Dovizioso**	ITA	Ducati	11	16	7	11	8	10	8	20	8	9	10	11	13	–	11	13	8	13	**187**
6	**Pol Espargaro**	SPA	Yamaha	–	10	8	7	13	11	9	–	9	11	–	10	10	10	–	10	10	10	**136**
7	**Aleix Espargaro**	SPA	Forward Yamaha	13	7	1	9	7	7	10	13	10	–	8	7	–	20	5	–	–	9	**126**
8	**Bradley Smith**	GBR	Yamaha	–	11	9	8	6	–	6	8	–	10	7	–	9	11	7	16	11	2	**121**
9	**Stefan Bradl**	GER	Honda	–	13	11	6	9	–	11	6	–	–	9	9	–	13	–	13	8		**117**
10	**Andrea Iannone**	ITA	Ducati	6	9	10	–	–	9	7	10	11	–	11	8	11	–	10	–	–	–	**102**
11	**Alvaro Bautista**	SPA	Honda	–	–	–	10	16	8	–	9	7	–	6	–	8	9	6	10	–	–	**89**
12	**Scott Redding**	GBR	Honda	9	–	2	3	4	3	3	4	5	7	5	6	3	6	–	9	6	6	**81**
13	**Cal Crutchlow**	GBR	Ducati	10	–	–	–	5	–	7	6	8	–	4	7	16	–	–	–	11		**74**
14	**Hiroshi Aoyama**	JPN	Honda	5	4	6	4	2	2	1	–	4	6	3	2	4	8	3	8	5	1	**68**
15	**Yonny Hernandez**	COL	Ducati	4	3	4	2	3	6	5	–	–	5	6	1	–	5	9	–			**53**
16	**Nicky Hayden**	USA	Honda	8	5	5	5	–	4	–	2	–	–	–	7	2	6	–	3			**47**
17	**Karel Abraham**	CZE	Honda	3	2	3	–	1	4	–	2	3	5	2	3	5	–	–	–	–		**33**
18	**Hector Barbera**	SPA	Avintia/Ducati	–	1	–	1	–	–	–	–	–	–	–	–	1	11	7	5			**26**
19	**Michele Pirro**	ITA	Ducati	–	–	–	–	–	5	2	–	–	4	–	–	–	–	7				**18**
20	**Danilo Petrucci**	ITA	ART	2	–	–	–	–	–	1	1	–	–	–	5	–	4	–	4			**17**
21	**Alex de Angelis**	RSM	Forward Yamaha	–	–	–	–	–	–	–	–	–	1	2	4	–	7	–	–			**14**
22	**Colin Edwards**	USA	Forward Yamaha	7	–	–	–	1	–	–	–	3	–	–	–	–	–	–				**11**
23	**Broc Parkes**	AUS	PBM	1	–	–	–	–	5	–	1	–	–	–	–	2	–					**9**
24	**Michael Laverty**	GBR	PBM	–	–	–	–	–	–	–	2	–	–	–	3	4	–					**9**
25	**Mike di Meglio**	FRA	Avintia	–	–	–	–	–	–	–	4	–	–	–	2	3	–					**9**
26	**Katsuyuki Nakasuga**	JPN	Yamaha	–	–	–	–	–	–	–	–	–	–	–	4	–	–					**4**
27	**Leon Camier**	GBR	Honda	–	–	–	–	–	–	–	–	1	–	–	–	–	–					**1**

MotoGP - Teams

Position	Team	Qatar	Texas	Argentina	Spain	France	Italy	Catalunya	Netherlands	Germany	Indianapolis	Czech Republic	Great Britain	San Marino	Aragon	Japan	Australia	Malaysia	Valencia	Points total
1	**Repsol Honda Team**	41	45	45	41	36	38	41	41	45	38	38	38	17	5	33	–	25	41	**608**
2	**Movistar Yamaha MotoGP**	20	14	29	33	30	36	33	14	29	36	36	36	45	25	41	45	36	20	**558**
3	**Ducati Team**	21	16	7	11	13	10	8	27	14	17	10	15	20	16	11	13	8	24	**261**
4	**Monster Yamaha Tech 3**	–	21	17	15	19	11	15	8	9	21	7	10	19	21	15	16	21	12	**257**
5	**GO&FUN Honda Gresini**	9	–	2	13	20	11	3	13	12	7	11	6	11	15	6	19	6	6	**170**
6	**Pramac Racing**	10	12	14	2	3	15	12	10	11	–	11	13	17	1	10	5	9	–	**155**
7	**NGM Forward Racing**	20	7	1	9	7	8	10	13	10	3	8	8	2	24	5	7	–	9	**151**
8	**LCR Honda MotoGP**	–	13	11	6	9	–	11	6	–	–	9	9	–	13	–	13	8		**117**
9	**Drive M7 Aspar**	13	9	11	9	2	2	5	–	6	6	4	2	4	15	5	14	5	4	**116**
10	**Avintia Racing**	–	1	–	1	–	–	–	–	–	4	–	–	–	1	13	10	5		**35**
11	**Cardion AB Motoracing**	3	2	3	–	1	4	–	2	3	5	2	3	5	–	–	–	–		**33**
12	**Paul Bird Motorsport**	1	–	–	–	–	–	5	–	3	–	–	–	–	3	6	–			**18**
13	**Octo Iodaracing Team**	2	–	–	–	–	–	1	1	–	–	–	5	–	4	–	4			**17**

Moto2

Position	Rider	Nationality	Machine	Qatar	Texas	Argentina	Spain	France	Italy	Catalunya	Netherlands	Germany	Indianapolis	Czech Republic	Great Britain	San Marino	Aragon	Japan	Australia	Malaysia	Valencia	Points total
1	Esteve Rabat	SPA	Kalex	25	20	25	13	16	25	25	8	13	13	25	25	25	20	16	16	16	20	346
2	Mika Kallio	FIN	Kalex	20	13	9	25	25	10	13	16	20	25	20	20	20	9	11	13	20	–	289
3	Maverick Vinales	SPA	Kalex	13	25	–	11	13	7	20	20	11	20	10	16	13	25	20	25	25	–	274
4	Thomas Luthi	SWI	Suter	16	10	–	6	8	–	11	10	7	–	13	11	11	13	25	20	8	25	194
5	Dominique Aegerter	SWI	Suter	–	16	13	20	9	11	2	–	25	16	11	–	10	10	–	8	11	10	172
6	Johann Zarco	FRA	Caterham Suter	–	–	–	8	–	9	16	13	3	6	7	13	16	16	10	–	13	16	146
7	Simone Corsi	ITA	Forward KLX/Kalex	11	11	11	–	–	20	13	–	3	16	11	4	–	–	–	–	–	–	100
8	Luis Salom	SPA	Kalex	2	–	16	10	11	20	–	1	2	–	–	–	1	3	1	–	5	13	85
9	Sandro Cortese	GER	Kalex	9	2	7	7	4	3	–	–	–	10	16	–	4	4	–	10	9	–	85
10	Marcel Schrotter	GER	Tech 3	–	7	5	–	5	4	7	4	4	2	6	2	5	6	–	9	6	8	80
11	Franco Morbidelli	ITA	Kalex	–	–	3	–	6	6	–	–	10	–	8	10	9	11	9	3	–	–	75
12	Anthony West	AUS	Speed Up	7	9	4	5	2	–	6	25	–	7	–	–	–	–	–	–	–	7	72
13	Sam Lowes	GBR	Speed Up	10	–	8	–	7	8	–	–	–	–	–	9	–	7	–	11	–	9	69
14	Xavier Simeon	BEL	Suter	–	–	20	9	–	2	–	–	6	–	2	–	–	–	6	7	–	11	63
15	Jonas Folger	GER	Kalex	5	–	–	16	10	16	–	–	–	–	1	–	–	4	1	7	3	–	63
16	Jordi Torres	SPA	Suter	8	–	6	4	–	5	–	–	4	–	5	–	8	5	6	1	5	–	57
17	Julian Simon	SPA	Kalex	–	–	–	2	–	–	4	9	–	–	9	4	8	–	10	–	10	–	56
18	Ricard Cardus	SPA	Tech 3	4	6	–	3	–	–	9	–	5	1	–	–	2	7	–	4	4	–	45
19	Hafizh Syahrin	MAL	Kalex	1	1	–	–	1	–	–	6	–	9	3	8	–	5	8	–	–	–	42
20	Alex de Angelis	RSM	Suter	–	8	10	–	–	–	–	11	–	8	–	–	–	–	–	–	–	–	37
21	Mattia Pasini	ITA	Forward KLX/Kalex	–	4	–	–	–	–	10	–	8	–	–	7	3	–	–	3	–	–	35
22	Takaaki Nakagami	JPN	Kalex	–	5	1	–	–	–	3	–	–	5	–	1	6	1	3	5	2	2	34
23	Axel Pons	SPA	Kalex	–	–	–	–	1	8	–	1	–	5	6	7	–	–	–	–	–	–	28
24	Randy Krummenacher	SWI	Suter	3	–	–	1	3	–	–	–	9	–	–	3	2	3	–	–	–	–	24
25	Lorenzo Baldassarri	ITA	Suter	–	–	–	–	–	5	7	–	–	–	–	–	–	–	2	–	–	6	20
26	Louis Rossi	FRA	Kalex	6	–	–	–	–	1	–	3	3	–	–	–	–	4	–	–	1	–	18
27	Gino Rea	GBR	Suter	–	–	–	–	–	5	–	–	–	–	–	–	2	–	–	–	–	–	7
28	Nicolas Terol	SPA	Suter	–	–	2	–	–	–	–	–	–	–	–	–	–	–	–	–	–	–	2
29	Roberto Rolfo	ITA	Suter	–	–	–	–	–	–	–	–	–	–	–	–	–	–	–	–	2	–	2

Moto3

Position	Rider	Nationality	Machine	Qatar	Texas	Argentina	Spain	France	Italy	Catalunya	Netherlands	Germany	Indianapolis	Czech Republic	Great Britain	San Marino	Aragon	Japan	Australia	Malaysia	Valencia	Points total
1	Alex Marquez	SPA	Honda	20	–	20	9	11	–	25	25	13	10	13	20	20	20	25	20	11	16	278
2	Jack Miller	AUS	KTM	25	25	16	13	25	–	13	–	25	16	11	10	16	–	11	25	20	25	276
3	Alex Rins	SPA	Honda	11	13	11	16	20	16	–	20	–	11	7	25	25	13	6	16	16	11	237
4	Efren Vazquez	SPA	Honda	16	16	10	20	10	4	16	10	10	25	8	–	6	3	20	13	25	10	222
5	Romano Fenati	ITA	KTM	4	–	20	25	25	–	25	11	–	–	20	5	–	5	25	9	–	2	176
6	Alexis Masbou	FRA	Honda	9	10	5	4	7	10	5	13	16	13	25	8	9	6	–	10	10	4	164
7	Isaac Vinales	SPA	KTM	8	–	9	11	16	20	9	9	8	–	6	3	13	4	5	–	–	20	141
8	Danny Kent	GBR	Husqvarna	3	8	7	5	3	1	–	8	11	4	16	7	4	16	10	–	13	13	129
9	Enea Bastianini	ITA	KTM	–	3	6	7	9	–	20	–	1	5	20	16	11	10	8	–	6	5	127
10	Miguel Oliveira	POR	Mahindra	13	1	–	2	4	13	4	16	–	9	9	13	–	9	–	9	–	8	110
11	Brad Binder	RSA	Mahindra	1	–	2	–	2	7	10	7	20	7	10	1	10	8	16	1	–	7	109
12	Jakub Kornfeil	CZE	KTM	10	11	–	10	6	–	1	5	5	6	2	11	–	11	–	8	8	3	97
13	John McPhee	GBR	Honda	5	7	–	3	8	–	6	9	–	–	5	3	7	–	13	11	–	–	77
14	Niccolo Antonelli	ITA	KTM	7	–	–	–	–	–	–	11	–	–	3	9	–	7	7	6	9	9	68
15	Niklas Ajo	FIN	Husqvarna	–	2	8	6	–	11	8	–	–	–	4	6	–	–	7	–	–	–	52
16	Francesco Bagnaia	ITA	KTM	6	9	–	8	13	–	6	–	–	–	–	–	–	–	3	5	–	–	50
17	Juanfran Guevara	SPA	Kalex KTM	–	5	4	–	–	8	–	–	6	8	–	2	7	–	–	–	5	1	46
18	Karel Hanika	CZE	KTM	2	6	–	–	–	6	2	–	–	–	3	1	4	4	–	3	7	6	44
19	Alessandro Tonucci	ITA	Mahindra	–	–	3	–	–	9	3	–	–	–	–	–	–	–	1	2	2	–	20
20	Zulfahmi Khairuddin	MAL	Honda	–	–	1	–	5	5	–	2	–	1	–	–	2	1	2	–	–	–	19
21	Livio Loi	BEL	Kalex KTM	–	4	13	–	–	–	–	–	–	–	–	–	–	–	–	–	–	–	17
22	Matteo Ferrari	ITA	Mahindra	–	–	–	–	–	2	–	3	7	–	–	–	–	–	–	–	–	–	12
23	Jorge Navarro	SPA	Kalex KTM	–	–	–	–	–	–	–	–	–	2	–	–	1	–	–	4	4	–	11
24	Philipp Oettl	GER	Kalex KTM	–	–	–	1	1	3	–	1	4	–	–	–	–	–	–	–	–	–	10
25	Andrea Migno	ITA	Mahindra	–	–	–	–	–	–	–	–	–	–	–	–	–	8	–	–	–	–	8
26	Hiroki Ono	JPN	Honda	–	–	–	–	–	–	–	–	–	–	–	–	–	–	5	–	–	–	5
27	Jasper Iwema	NED	FTR KTM/Mahindra	–	–	–	–	–	–	–	4	–	–	–	–	–	–	–	–	–	–	4
28	Hafiq Azmi	MAL	KTM	–	–	–	–	–	–	–	–	–	–	–	–	–	–	–	–	3	–	3
29	Arthur Sissis	AUS	Mahindra	–	–	–	–	–	–	–	–	3	–	–	–	–	–	–	–	–	–	3
30	Jules Danilo	FRA	Mahindra	–	–	–	–	–	–	–	–	–	–	–	–	–	–	–	2	–	–	2
31	Eric Granado	BRA	KTM	–	–	–	–	–	–	–	–	2	–	–	–	–	–	–	–	–	–	2
32	Remy Gardner	AUS	Kalex KTM/KTM	–	–	–	–	–	–	–	–	–	–	–	–	–	–	–	–	1	–	1

MARTIN MAKES THE GRADE

By PETER CLIFFORD

Above: Typical close combat at the Sachsenring. Razgatlioglu (54), Manzi (29) and Mir (36) narrowly lead Gutierrez (17), Mihara (74) and Ray (28).

Above right: Jorge Martin, Spain's first Rookies champion.

Above far right: Dutch 15-year-old Bo Bendsneyder was fast, consistent and a home-race winner.

Right: Martin thought that this convincing win at Mugello was his best of the year.

Far right: Runner-up Mir lofts his trophy at Brno.

Photos: Gold & Goose

IT was another great year of teenage battles. Jorge Martin considered his lights-to-flag win in Mugello as the crucial victory in his Red Bull MotoGP Rookies Cup-winning season. That is certainly valid, and the manner of the 16-year-old's victory was very impressive. He was the first Spaniard to win the Cup in eight seasons.

The Italian Grand Prix was also the event where Martin's closest rival, Joan Mir, suffered a points loss he could not make up, having pulled off the track with nine laps to go while in the podium battle. He thought he had a gearbox failure, but there was nothing wrong with the engine of his KTM RC 250 R; a missed down-change must have momentarily confused the 16-year-old Spaniard.

As usual, the global entry produced a range of winners, including then 14-year-old Japanese Soushi Mihara, 17-year-old Turk Toprak Razgatlioglu, Dutch 15-year-old Bo Bendsneyder and Italian 15-year-old Stefano Manzi. The last named put in an impressively consistent season with a total of nine podiums, including victory at home in Misano.

Manzi had been putting pressure on Mir for second in the points table at the end of the season, but his worst finish of the year, eighth, in a very wet and slippery final race in Aragon was not enough to take the position, even though Mir fell. Martin had clinched the title the day before with a perfectly judged fourth in the dry, while Mir had won his third race. Then Martin took all the chances he had avoided on Saturday for his sixth victory in the 14-race season.

"It was the perfect end for the year for me," enthused Martin after his tenth podium appearance. "Coming here, I really wanted to take the Cup yesterday, so that I could concentrate on winning today and that is what happened. You really want to end the season on the top of the podium."

He had only made a mess of things twice, falling after trying to make up for a start-line incident in race one at the Sachsenring and coming together with Bendsneyder starting the last lap of race two in Brno. The pair crashed out of the lead group. On both occasions, Martin won the other race that weekend.

"For me, though, my best win was in Mugello. To win that one so convincingly, I think said something to the Moto3 teams, and of course that is where I hope to be next year," he concluded. On the Monday after Aragon, the Martinez team announced that Martin had been signed to their Moto3 GP squad for 2015. Manzi was also headed to the world championship, while it appeared that Mir would probably be in the Spanish championship.

The majority of Martin's wins were not runaway affairs, a very rare thing in Rookies Cup, and for the most part he had to deal with the elbow clashing eight- or ten-man battles for the lead that are the norm and an essential preparation for the rigours of the Moto3 World Championship.

After his Sachsenring fall, he remounted to finish 12th, so he only failed to score in that one race in Brno, a superb consistency that was matched by few, one being Brad Ray,

who scored in every round bar Mugello, where he was let down by a very rare mechanical problem.

Ray finished the season fourth; he missed out on a race win, not helped by the fact that he had grown from the weedy little kid who had joined the Cup in 2012 into an athletic young man who struggled to tuck himself away on a Moto3 bike. He had won in Texas the previous year and continued to show his talent at the front of the field in 2014.

Razgatlioglu is every bit as tall as Ray, but he won race one at the Sachsenring in brilliant style and also managed a podium in race two. Considering his stature, his future probably doesn't lie in Moto3; he contested the final Superstock 600 round at Magny-Cours and won. Just ahead of him in the Rookies Cup points, in fifth, was Manuel Pagliani. The 18-year-old Italian didn't win a race, but was second four times. However, he did win the Italian Moto3 title.

Matching Martin for the ability to score points regularly were newcomers Bendsneyder and Italian 15-year-old Fabio di Giannantonio. The latter finished every race, only failing to score with 16th in the final race of the year. A fine third the previous day in Aragon and an excellent second after leading on to the final lap in Brno race two put him eighth in the points table.

He is bound to be a title contender in 2015, as is Bendsneyder, who won at home in Assen. The Dutch youngster wisely held back when uncertain, as he was in the wet in race one in Assen and race two in Aragon, but on both occasions he got going once he had tested the conditions. Gaining experience in such a sensible manner is a very useful quality.

He didn't score in race two in Brno, due to the coming together with Martin, and missed the Sachsenring races thanks to an injury in a non-Cup event. Otherwise he was fast and consistent, taking ninth in the final reckoning.

Marc Garcia also finished every race, and while tenth place in the points table is a fair reflection of the season's performance, he is certainly a man for 2015. The 14-year-old Spaniard enjoyed a model first season. He got inside the top ten for the first time in the fourth round – the wet and slippery race one in Assen – and he kept his head while those about him were losing theirs.

A couple of races later, he was solidly in the top ten at the Sachsenring, but he produced his finest ride at the end of the season when he led the final wet race very strongly. Even better, he accepted that Martin still had the edge and an extra two seasons' experience, eventually letting him go to pick up a superb second.

The Rookies Cup has yet to find a new world champion. Johann Zarco (second in 2011) and Luis Salom (second in 2012, third in 2013) have come close, but there is a constant stream of talented youngsters who flow from the Cup to follow their dreams in the World Championship. Martín and Manzi are the latest.

SUPERBIKE WORLD CHAMPIONSHIP
REVIEW OF 2014

By GORDON RITCHIE

SPLIT DECISION

A ASSUMING all of Dorna's wishes for a healthier SBK come to fruition sometime in the future, then some may look back to 2014 as the nadir of the series, in terms of public perception. From the outside, the series looked like a shadow of its former self. From the inside, it felt a bit more substantial most of the time.

From the riders' seats, the empty grandstands at far too many rounds must have been heartbreaking. For the fans watching, the action and interest were at their usual high level. There were more different manufacturers than ever, and the championship was decided at the final round.

So were things really so bad?

The many minor rules that came into effect in 2014 made little difference to lap times. And – surprise, surprise – the most successful manufacturers were the ones who put the most time and effort into their campaigns.

The once-only Evo season, instigated by Dorna, was a great success numerically – praise is deserved for a positive initiative that underwrote the bottom half of the grid. However, it was quite clear that the rules would only allow two or maybe three manufacturers to be truly competitive in any given season.

In the more liberal full SBK class, there were five different winners, on four different machines, and in terms of podiums, there were five manufacturers and ten unique riders who scored a top three at some stage of the season.

The Evo champion – again, surprise, surprise – was on the most direct factory bike of all, the KRT Ninja. The only real opposition came from the semi-supported bikes from BMW and Ducati. Any other choice of Evo machine apparently was not up to muster because nobody opted to use them for a season. Translate that to the full Superbike class for the next few years and the series really would be in trouble.

Be happy then that in 2015 we shall go back to everybody being on more or less full Superbikes, with no more Evo machines. Only this time around, the Superbikes will have limited engine tuning, cost-capped race parts again, but relatively free electronics, manufacturer by manufacturer. Crucially, the electronics hardware and software will be cost capped and made available to all those who compete on the same models.

The best of all worlds, then?

Only time, podium statistics and the size of the regular grid will tell.

Photo: Gold & Goose

AGAINST THE ODDS

By GORDON RITCHIE

Photo: Gold & Goose

A T the penultimate round of the championship, in his native France, Sylvain Guintoli said of his battle with Tom Sykes that they were playing poker. As the weeks went by, they kept on backing themselves with even greater stakes. And neither was folding.

In winning both the final races of the year, to scoop the title by six points, Guintoli found the royal flush that some had said he never had in his deck.

The ability to win, rather than settle for a podium, was not what he had been known for. The need to succeed more than the next man seemed to be missing. Nice guys don't win, so the old racing adage goes, and few are more popular and friendly than Guintoli. Funny with it.

But in racing, winning is the only thing that really counts.

Over 100 SBK race starts at the beginning of the 2014 season, but only four race wins for Sylvain? Difficult to see a potential champion in those stats. He didn't seem to have quite what it takes to lift the crown.

Without doubt, 32-year-old Guintoli made the necessary leap in self-belief towards the end of the season, starting in the aftermath of Laguna Seca. Faced with a 44-point deficit and staring at another 'nearly there' year, both rider and Aprilia works team determined that whatever it took, they would make every race count.

There were wholesale changes behind the scenes within Aprilia in 2014, after the exit of legendary race manager Luigi Dall'Igna. The predictions of the collapse of their SBK operations appeared less than outlandish at one point, as the anointed champion in many people's eyes, Marco Melandri, could not convince Aprilia to go with his settings. All this just as the rumours of Aprilia quitting SBK to move to MotoGP one year earlier than planned were slipping into reality.

Everybody was talking about Aprilia's ineffectual SBK season, while overlooking the year-long work of Guintoli. He had been piling on points, in his own quiet unobtrusive way. He was proving to be the one who could really challenge Sykes, even if few thought he could overcome him.

Part of Guintoli's ultimate success was just to keep his head down and keep taking podium finishes. Often, he had no option, as he usually found one or other of his rivals faster over full race distance each weekend. This limited his overall win total to five (including one inherited from his team-mate in France, thanks to the imposition of team orders). In all, he picked up 16 podium places.

When Melandri got his RSV-4 working the way he had wanted all along, he did a season's worth of winning on it in only a few races. Guintoli was often there with him, but never ahead.

With both Aprilia works riders having become competitive every weekend, despite their very different styles and builds, the team learned more lessons about a bike that had been around since 2009.

All this extra knowledge, and revamped working practices initiated by new race boss Romano Albesiano, helped both riders move to and occasionally right above the works Kawasaki level, starting at Sepang.

All the old Aprilia dogs had obviously learned new tricks.

As a result, Guintoli managed to outperform Sykes in every race after Laguna, dealing with the long gaps between the final three rounds better than his rival or Kawasaki appeared to do.

Guintoli's refusal to accept that he could not win paid off, sliding around Jerez like a 500GP rider of old, even if he was still having to give best to Melandri. Slithering at full-risk pace in the rain to take second again behind Marco in France, inheriting a win there as well.

But it was the final round in Losail that underlined why Sylvain should be considered a worthy champion.

Twelve points behind on race day, he won both races, lifting his winning total to five for the year. He needed no help from Melandri this time, pulling off his usual trick of looking smooth, but not exactly fastest, and all the while laying into the stopwatches and points scores.

Guintoli made himself champion against the odds, as an underdog in his own team, by playing the perfect hand of poker when required.

Even Sykes, the previous champion and only beaten at the last, had nothing but good things to say about the new FIM Superbike World Champion.

TOM SYKES

MARCO MELANDRI

EUGENE LAVERTY

DAVID SALOM

SYLVAIN BARRIER

IMRE TOTH

CLAUDIO CORTI

ALEX LOWES

NICCOLO CANEPA

TONI ELIAS

SUPERBIKE WORLD CHAMPIONSHIP
2014 TEAMS &RIDERS

By GORDON RITCHIE

APRILIA

Aprilia Racing Team
Sylvain Guintoli (32) lost one formidable riding partner, but gained another in the shape of Marco Melandri (32) as the Aprilia Racing Team continued with full factory presence. The new top man, replacing Luigi Dall'Igna, was Romano Albesiano, and it was business as usual at races at least, with so many long-term race staff remaining in situ to aid the transition.

Red Devils Roma
Toni Elias (31) proved an astute choice for the only remaining Aprilia privateers on the grid as they struggled on in the face of so many full factory bikes. Elias rewarded them with some great rides.

BIMOTA

Team Alstare Bimota EVO
After splitting from Ducati a year early, Francis Batta formed a new alliance, and Ayrton Badovini (28) and Christian Iddon (29) joined one of the most successful team names in SBK history with one of the iconic names from SBK racing's early history in tow. No points

were scored, as they missed homologation deadlines, but phantom results were good amd they often 'beat' many of their main Evo rivals. The roadbike project's inability to get off the ground in sufficient homologation numbers resulted in the last track action in America.

BMW

BMW Motorrad Italia SBK EVO
Sylvain Barrier (25) was desperately unlucky with first a broken pelvis after a race crash, and then a car crash back in Europe wrecking his good hopes of being the Evo champion, as he won races when he came back into play. He was replaced in Australia by local rider Glenn Allerton (33) and then for a greater length of time by occasional Evo race winner Leon Camier (28). Andrea Buzzoni from BMW Italia continued his push as if his team were still the semi-official BMW effort from 2013.

BMW Team Toth
Imre Toth (29) fielded himself on a full Superbike S1000RR, but he also had younger Hungarian compatriot Peter Sebestyen (20) on an Evo bike. He was replaced later in the year by Gabor Rizmayer (32).

DUCATI

Ducati Superbike Team
The former kings of SBK, Ducati moved ahead after staring into the abyss in 2013. They deliberately chose two ambitious and relatively young riders in Chaz Davies (27) and Davide Giugliano (24), and got some rewards. Still under the close control of Ernesto Marinelli from Ducati Corse, and with the Feel Racing effort Ducati's partners as in the glory days, it was factory and faster every weekend.

Althea Racing EVO
Niccolo Canepa (26) had a good stab at being Evo champion early in the season, but it was too tough later in the year, as it was evident that one-lap speed could not be translated into similar high-level race results. Genesio Bevilacqua's privateers ran a small, but tight ship again.

Barni Racing EVO
Wild-cards from the CIV and Superbike Class, Barni Racing has ambitions to compete at the highest level in 2015 and fielded Ivan Goi (34) in the Italian rounds.

Grandi Corse by A.P. Racing EVO
Matteo Baiocco (30) and Michael Savary (27) each rode for the same team, but on different bikes. Baiocco took part in the Misano round on a Ducati Panigale, and Savary practised, but did not race, at Misano on an MV Agusta F4.

3C Racing Team Ducati
Imperious IDM trio Max Neukirchner (31), Javier Fores (29) and old SBK winner Lorenzo Lanzi (33) joined in the fun at Magny-Cours. All were fast on their full-SBK-spec Ducati Panigale machines.

JONATHAN REA

CHAZ DAVIES

SYLVAIN GUINTOLI

JEREMY GUARNONI

AYRTON BADOVINI

LEON CAMIER

SHERIDAN MORAIS

LEON HASLAM

DAVIDE GIUGLIANO

LORIS BAZ

EBR

Team Hero EBR
Supported by Indian manufacturer Hero, with machinery made in America by EBR, and run in Europe by Italians and Americans, the Team Hero EBR squad performed minor logistical miracles to meet the homologation numbers. Then another set of unholy efforts to get on track on time. Then a season trying to make up for that lack of preparation. It was an impossible task for Erik Buell, Giulio Bardi and company, but it was a Heroic effort in all possible ways.

Foremost Insurance EBR
Larry Pegram (41) was a popular wild-card rider at Laguna, on the bike he competes with in AMA racing.

HONDA

Pata Honda World Superbike Team
Honda Europe's own team, if not an HRC team, the Ten Kate-operated and Pata-sponsored Honda squad was a lone CBR entry again. Ronald ten Kate controlled the overall team, with input from Honda Europe's Carlo Fiorani.

With a new bike to sell in the CBR1000RR SP, the effort had a bit more pep to it and the same riding line-up from 2013 of Jonathan Rea (27) and Leon Haslam (31). Rea soared at times; Haslam battled always.

Injury free for the most part in 2014, Rea was able to mount a more serious challenge, but Haslam was still not physically 100 per cent. Consistency was still an issue with set-up and electronics, but less so than 2013.

Winteb LiquidRubber Racing Team EVO
Kervin Bos (27) rode at the Assen round as a wild-card on his relatively stock Ten Kate CBR1000RR.

GEICO Motorcycle Road Racing Honda
Chris Ulrich (34) competed at his home round in Laguna Seca with a best of 17th place in race two.

KAWASAKI

Kawasaki Racing Team
Tom Sykes (30) and Loris Baz (21) once more carried on the Ninja attack, from the front on most occasions. David Salom (30) formed a one-man KRT Evo effort, and often rode almost one-handed after injury, but still won heaps of races. Toni Alfosea looked after the Evo side after many years in the GP paddock.

A direct factory team, it was run from Barcelona by Provec, with Guim Roda the Team Manager and Ichiro Yoda the KHI controller.

Team Pedercini
The most populous and tenacious team in SBK, the Pedercini family firm went for the Evo class in a big way. Regulars Alessandro Andreozzi (23) and Lucca Scassa (31) had contrasting fortunes, with Scassa injured for much of the year and replaced by Riccardo Russo (21), while Andreozzi ended up scoring points from Imola onwards. Romain Lanusse (20) popped up from Superstock for a couple of rounds, and at the last event Aussie Alex Cudlin (28) took the second bike due to Scassa's continuing injury.

MAHI Racing Team India EVO
Fabien Foret (41) was a lone competitor for the frequently embroiled Mahi team, which eventually stopped as a WSS effort and then as an Evo force, too. A frustrating year for Foret with the team, and the former WSS champion ended up heading to Magny-Cours with Pedercini in Evo, replacing the still injured Scassa.

MRS Kawasaki EVO
Jeremy Guarnoni (21) was a one-man band in Evo, making a good show of it as second-best Kawasaki rider and best of all on occasion for French riding guru Adrien Morillas' team.

IRON BRAIN Grillini Kawasaki EVO
Sheridan Morais (29) and Michel Fabrizio (30) started the season together, but Fabrizio left early and was replaced by Bryan Staring (27). Low-order points scoring was the realistic and oft-realised ambition.

MV AGUSTA

MV Agusta Reparto Corse
An official MV Reparto Corse was how it ended the season, but you could have added a Yakhnich Motorsport suffix at the first few rounds, until the money and political will gave out for the partner of the works team.

Claudio Corti (27) was the man charged with riding the often-too-stock machine. When he was sidelined by injury, Leon Camier (28) was drafted in after his BMW adventures. Brian Gillen oversaw the team as it grew in experience over the year. At Magny-Cours wild-card Nicolas Salchaud (27) rode his private F4-RR to 16th place in race one.

SUZUKI

Voltcom Crescent Suzuki
Eugene Laverty (28) and new British champion Alex Lowes (24) joined forces to sharpen the attack of the only Suzukis in the entire championship. Run from the UK by Paul Denning's Crescent concern and teamed up with Yoshimura again, they proved the GSX-R still had what it takes.

Aprilia RSV4

BMW S1000RR

THE SUPERBIKES OF 2014

DUCATI 1199R

HERO EBR 1190RX

APRILIA RSV4 FACTORY

Of all the machines in the 2014 World Superbike paddock, the Aprilia was still the most pointedly aimed at the track as an overall design, even though it was far from a new model.

New regulation meant that the advantage of having a cassette gearbox was negated by the choice of three possible gearbox sets, or two alternate primary gears and two gearbox options, with limited opportunities to change them.

The RSV4's 65-degree DOHC V4 engine, with bore and stroke of 78 x 52.3mm, was densely packaged inside the twin-spar aluminium chassis.

Engine performance was increased in 2014, to 229.2bhp at a reduced 15,000rpm. The main focus on work over the winter months had been to make the full-race engines reliable within the eight-engines-per-rider rule and still be competitive. A less radical initial 'hit' of the cams on the valves did the trick and along the way a couple more horses were corralled.

With variable intake trumpets, ride-by-wire of their own making, and software and electronics hardware still controlled in-house, Aprilia concentrated efforts on the most important stuff in 2014.

Once again, more experiments were completed with swing-arms, providing more support as the rider moved up from full lean into harder acceleration. Suspension was Öhlins.

Variable-thickness front discs, not just variable-diameter rotors, were adopted, but still within the cost-capping rules.

BMW S1000RR

Now in privateer guise, the BMW S1000RR Team Toth ran full Superbike. It was a 2012 semi-official machine from Feel Racing, with the new cost-reducing tech applied.

BMW's main Evo effort came from the BMW Motorrad Italia squad and the oft-injured Sylvain Barrier.

For the Toth team's Superbike, the capped-price suspension from Öhlins and brakes from Brembo were allied with the alloy, twin-spar bridge-style chassis, a stock swing-arm being used simply because the latest OZ wheels did not match the full-race item.

Originally, it ran top-spec BMW electronics to match the ex-works-level engine. However, these were swapped for a Motec system from Misano onward. For a smaller team, they were declared easy to use, and with so much power on tap, managing the peaky output was a priority at every race. The Motec unit was also claimed to be a kilo lighter than the car derived BMW with its larger connectors.

The 999cc engine had a bore and stroke of 80 x 49.7mm, which gave its radical power and delivery. The engine spun up and down very quickly, and with a claimed 234.6bhp on tap, it was not short of outright power.

The Toth team also ran an Evo machine, which delivered the same engine performance as the full Superbike between around 8,000 and 11,000rpm, where the full-spec engine comes alive.

DUCATI 1199R

This was another unique design, still *avant-garde* in its second season. Up front, the monocoque chassis formed the headstock tube holder, airbox and top engine mount, while the mono-shock rear suspension and single swing-arm were mounted on brackets attached to the engine and the top subframe.

An Öhlins rear shock sat at a jaunty, almost horizontal angle on the left side of the rear cylinder, worked by a triangulated link. A unique design, the chassis was improved in performance all year, but tyre life could still be an issue if the settings were off.

Lots of effort had been put into electronics and engine management, to tame the radical bore and stroke of 112 x 60.8mm.

With no restrictors all year because of the balancing rules, the power output went to and possibly above 217bhp at 11,500rpm, driven through an EVR clutch. Despite still having to retain more stock engine components than the fours, the main V-twin caught up a lot in terms of top speed in 2014 – although not at every track.

In the braking department, Ducati finally opted for the more expensive, but much more modern, T-type Brembo brakes. OZ wheels completed the rolling chassis.

The Althea Ducati squad ran in the Evo class. Initially, their 1199RR was competitive, but as the season wore on it lost out to the Kawasakis and BMW.

HERO EBR 1190RX

EBR went from a possible to a participant in breathless fashion, neither team nor manufacturer having had much preparation time.

A 106 x 67.5mm, 72-degree V-twin engine needed all the buzz-kill of its balance shafts, but at the start of the season it also needed much more than its probable 190bhp. With work on the Marelli 4.5 EFI system and some tuning, particularly towards the very end of the year, power was squeezed out more gradually in some regards, and at short tracks like Jerez the speed differential narrowed.

Maverick chassis design allowed fuel to be carried inside the chassis spars, with an additional alloy tank under the seat to make up the 24-litre maximum.

Kit suspension was from Öhlins, but at the rear the challenge for all was obvious. The link-free rear suspension made for settings that were way off the beaten track and not easy for anyone to resolve. A semi-cast and semi-fabricated rear swing-arm featured a rear section that had no 'skin' on the inside spars, again in a departure from the SBK norm.

Up front, the kit Öhlins suspension was conventional, but the wheel and braking system were unique. A giant perimeter single disc was gripped by a bulky single calliper, on the right-hand side. This mirrored the road bike, but nothing in the rules prevented a more conventional system from being tried.

KAWASAKI NINJA ZX-10R

MV AGUSTA F4 RR

By GORDON RITCHIE

HONDA CBR1000RR SP

SUZUKI GSX-R1000K14

Photos: Gold & Goose

HONDA CBR1000RR SP

There was a new road model to base things on, but almost everything that updated the roadbike was replaced for racing. There were some core changes, too, most obviously to the electronics.

After a serious attempt to move towards MotoGP tech in 2013, it was back to their own Cosworth and Pectel systems in 2014. Ride-by-wire was already there, but the sophistication went up a notch.

One main advance was the split throttle system, which helped make the Honda yet another growling four/twin at low revs, but cut engine life from 1900km to 1500 – still enough to make all eight engines from the official allocation last more than all year.

The 76 x 55.1mm engine was worked on over the winter, and the claimed power went up to 228bhp, at undisclosed revs.

As a team partner, Nissin still supplied Rea with 330/335mm brakes, and they were paired with Yutaka discs on occasion, of 335mm diameter. Haslam persevered with Brembo up front and Nissin at the rear.

When the advances in electronics worked to plan, the Honda won races.

KAWASAKI NINJA ZX-10R

The 2013 championship winner was back again in the same basic guise, but with more restrictions inside and out.

The 76 x 55mm engine appeared to have lost some performance at the top, but it was still a full factory beast, with maybe a little less than the 236.6bhp it had in 2013. It appeared a well-balanced engine through the rev range, helped by its relatively conservative bore and stroke dimensions.

A Marelli MHT ECU controlled the split ride-by-wire throttle bodies, which were 47mm in diameter.

Uniquely, the KHI team used Showa suspension front and back, and despite the cost cap the new 48mm front forks (with twin-tube 25mm cartridges) worked well after a winter experiment with Öhlins. A Showa T5512 BFR was incorporated in Kawasaki's horizontal back link rear suspension. It was exposed on top to liberate space for the exhaust routing, and also to make it easier to adjust and replace.

In almost all circumstances, the 336mm Brembo H-type discs were used with the kit Brembo callipers.

MV AGUSTA F4 RR

The inheritor of long-ago GP legend, the WSB MV Agusta RR was true to its heritage in being an across-the-frame four, and the upper half of the chassis was even made from tubular steel. Aside from that, it was very much a modern unit, but not conventionally.

On the engine side, a Marvel 4 EFI pushed air and fuel down variable inlet tracts into a radial cylinder head, with four valves per cylinder (79 x 50.9mm bore and stroke). With titanium inlet and exhaust valves as stock, and 201bhp at the crank in roadbike form, the engine was a great base to build on, and some said it ended up with 240bhp at the crank by season's end.

At maybe 170kg, it was not the lightest bike on the track, but it was unique in its chassis design, the tubular top chassis section being mated to two alloy side plates that carried the single swing-arm. This operated the rear shock by a cantilever; being pushed by an adjustable rod at the top and another link at the bottom, the Öhlins unit was squeezed from both ends. Six designs of swing-arm had been tried by the time Jerez came around, all made or modified in-house.

With Brembo brakes and Marchesini wheels, it was a riot of Italian flair and technology, wrapped in a skin of the finest fairings.

SUZUKI GSX-R1000K14

Another old-stager, on the right day the Suzuki was still a race winner. With almost conservative 74.5 x 57.3mm engine architecture, there were some limits, and with only eight engines per season, each tuning step or component change counted double compared to many other years.

Over 217bhp at 14,000rpm was the quoted 2014 engine figure, but maybe it was nearer 226 than ever before. Again, Yoshimura were tuning partners, with engine development a joint effort, but engine refreshes were done in house. A Yoshimura 4-into-1 exhaust was in a conventional position on the right side.

The electronics were provided by a Motec M170 once again, which ran a digital dash up front with a separate ECU. A twin-throttle set-up had one set of throttle butterflies controlled by the rider and another under full control of the ECU, allowing for rider aids, but also more direct rider input.

Öhlins suspension and Brembo callipers were of the kit variety, but in one important area of braking Suzuki differed from the herd by using Sunstar disc rotors. The forks were FGR200 Öhlins units, in 42mm diameter, with the rear shock an RSP40.

A new underslung swing-arm arrived in 2014, being adjustable at first. It was first used by Laverty and then eventually also Lowes. It liberated so much space under the seat that plans were made to expand the fuel tank base into that area.

SUPERBIKE WORLD CHAMPIONSHIP
PHILLIP ISLAND
ROUND 1 · AUSTRALIA

Above: Eugene Laverty gave the Crescent Suzuki squad a real boost with a win in the opening round of the 2014 SBK series.

Centre right: Tyre wear was a matter of concern for Pirelli's Matteo Giusti and Giorgio Barbier.

Below right: Guintoli leads Baz, Rea, Laverty, Melandri, Giugliano, Davies and Haslam.

Opposite page, from top: Guintoli and Baz celebrate their race-two success; Giugliani raced his Ducati to two fourth-place finishes; Paul Denning looks suitably pleased with Laverty's unexpected victory.

Opposite page, bottom right: Baz leads Rea and Sykes in race one.

Photos: Gold & Goose

WHEN is a miracle not really a miracle? When it is only nearly impossible in the first place. As Eugene Laverty (Voltcom Crescent Suzuki) won the opening race of the new season at Phillip Island, on the least fancied of the current traditional SBK machines and having been down in seventh position early on, everybody could only look on in awe.

Once he got going, as his tyres became nicely warm while his opponents found them too warm, he skipped over them all like a stone being skimmed at the nearby Surfers' Beach. PI is a tyre killer, with all those fast lefts and rights, and many riders complained of blistering and overheating on the relatively new and still abrasive track surface.

Laverty admitted that even though he and his new team had made a lot of set-up and performance improvements pre-race, the top Aprilia riders should have been too hard to beat. In fact, he made it look easy, in a measured way. It may well have been one of the best wins ever seen in SBK racing. Perhaps due to the more limited 2014 technical rules having an immediate effect?

Despite the fact that Aprilias usually run up front at PI – it was a 1-2, 1-2 for the V4 in 2013 – the Irishman had the legs on both of the RSV-4s in the corners, no seeming disadvantage in recorded top speed, and he pulled away to win by almost three seconds. In race one at least, he made use of a chassis package he really rated to deliver Crescent and new sponsor Voltcom a first ever SBK race win first time out.

Behind Laverty, a battle between Marco Melandri and Sylvain Guintoli only just went to Melandri, but more surprising still, after the 2013 woes of the Ducati Panigale, was that the reformed official Ducati World Superbike Team had a rider take fourth in the opening race.

Recently retired Carlos Checa had put the Panigale on pole at PI in 2013, but that was about as good as it got in dry conditions. First time out in 2014, Davide Giugliano was second in PI Superpole (behind Guintoli) and then only six seconds back on Laverty after 22 laps.

Loris Baz (KRT) and Jonathan Rea (Pata Honda World Superbike) rounded out the top six places in the first race, with troubled reigning champion Tom Sykes (KRT) seventh.

In race two, there would be no fairytale double for miracle man Laverty, just a dramatic smokescreen when the Suzuki's engine blew while he was battling for the lead with Guintoli, Baz and Sykes. The last had not been happy about team-mate Baz's overtakes, and felt he could and would have won race two had it not been red-flagged after 14 laps.

It finished in the order Guintoli, Baz and Sykes within 1.1 seconds. Melandri had run wide approaching Honda corner and lost lots of time in the slip road. He was ninth.

In a fluke-free opening performance for Ducati, Giugliano repeated his fourth place from race one in the second; Rea lifted himself to fifth and 0.6 second ahead of team-mate Leon Haslam.

It was the first weekend of action for the all-new Evo class (with Superstock engines and electronics packages, but full Superbike chassis), and three bikes were rated capable enough to compete in the new category: the Kawasaki Ninja ZX-10R, the Ducati Panigale R and the BMW S1000RR.

In the first ever Evo 'race within a race', the best Kawasaki (from David Salom and KRT) just beat the best Ducati (from Niccolo Canepa and Althea), and both were just ahead of stand-in rider Glenn Allerton on a BMW (from Motorrad Italia). Salom was ninth overall in the opening race; he also won Evo 'race' two, this time with an overall tenth.

ARAGON

ROUND 2 · SPAIN

Above: Badovini (86) ran the Bimota, but as it was not yet homologated, it could not contest the Evo championship with Salom's (44) Kawasaki.

Far left: A one-two double for Sykes and Baz on their dominant Kawasakis.

Below: Supersub Leon Camier stood in for Barrier and won the race-one Evo class.

Below right: Toni Elias and Leon Haslam were less than a second apart at the finish of race two, albeit only in front of the Evo-class runners

Photos: Gold & Goose

MOTORLAND Aragon, with its giant straight and rises and falls – plus chicanes and hairpins of varying intensities – is a circuit where power counts. But so do manoeuvrability, and corner exit and entry prowess. It was a surprise then that Kawasaki not only beat Aprilia hands down in the first race of the day, but that even when they had made a recovery in race two, it was still a Kawasaki one-two, with Sykes twice just ahead of team-mate Baz.

In the first race, Sykes had stretched out an advantage of 4.2 seconds, while Baz was also over four seconds up on third-placed rider Jonathan Rea, on the first Pata Honda home. Lots of testing had helped Honda's early-season cause.

Sykes posted a new lap record on lap two of the opener as he tried to escape, his 1m 57.664s beating his own previous best by just over 0.3 second.

Chaz Davies, even on his relatively less pokey Ducati, was only a few km/h down this weekend and was one place from third, albeit nearly eight seconds back. Davies loves Aragon: his previous record underlines it, but this was real SBK springtime for Ducati after 2013's pain and PI's promising finishes from Davide Giugliano.

PI race winner Eugene Laverty came in nearly 20 seconds behind Sykes, with factory Aprilia rider and top local Toni Elias (Red Devils Aprilia) seventh.

Giugliano could have been third, not eighth, had he not tried to recover his long-held podium place from Rea, after the Honda rider had dived inside going into the final corner. Giugliano took the inside line and accelerated to try to pass Rea as they came out of the hairpin, but he was at an angle and only succeeded in colliding with the Honda rider. He came off worse and fell, while Rea continued to third.

Sykes just ran away from the start of the opener, and some said that Kawasaki had a real advantage when the conditions were cooler. That was important in 2014, because the points scoring action had started at 10.30 in the morning, under Dorna's new, but not always consistently delivered European timetable of races.

Race two was off at 13.10, when the track temperature had almost doubled, which did help the factory Aprilia pairing, but not enough to prevent Sykes and Baz from taking another one-two. The second race was closer and more combative, with Sykes only 0.338 second up on Baz, while Melandri was only 0.470 second from his first win for Aprilia.

Baz had hassled Sykes at every opportunity, while Melandri had made up ground to Sykes at the end and made a bold last-lap attempt at an inside pass at the final hairpin. In running wide, he had allowed Baz and Sykes back through. An open-air lunchtime theatrical thriller.

Behind these three combatants, Guintoli slotted into fourth, with Rea some distance behind him, and Laverty throwing an unsatisfying double sixth.

There was a curious first sight at Motorland Aragon: the as-yet not homologated Bimota BB3 arrived, in the care of SBK powerhouse Alstare. Their two riders, Ayrton Badovini and Christian Iddon, were highly visible on their red-and-white BMW-powered bikes at the front of the Evo field, but they became instantly invisible in the results when each rider was disqualified after each race, for not having a homologated machine.

The small-scale Rimini phoenix that is Bimota could run, if not compete, in SBK for a while, but only if they made the required 125 bikes before the end of August.

The Evo 'races' were won by Leon Camier (BMW Motorrad Italia), standing in for Barrier, and David Salom (KRT SBK EVO).

Above left: Melandri took third place for Aprilia in race two.

Above far left: Thumbs up from a delighted Sykes.

Far left and left: Giugliano and Rea collide in race two, putting the Italian on the deck.

Photos: Gold & Goose

IT was the proverbial game of two halves – two shortened races, but way too much extra time, even before the second race had started. It was a difficult day for everyone, but competition and clashes abounded.

Assen provided a patchy, but drying 16-lapper (instead of the planned 21 laps) in race one. It was red-flagged after the engine of Geoff May's Hero EBR blew up.

In a ten-lap second race, held in horribly wet conditions, the first attempted start had been halted by astonishing rain and the risk of aquaplaning. There was an initial contest of sorts, but that was also red-flagged by worsening rain and track conditions.

The real second race, much shortened compared to the original 21-lap plan, got under way two hours after the scheduled 13.10 start. It was organised chaos, and the real stars of the show were race winners Guintoli and Rea, plus the Dutch fans, who stuck with the action to the end.

In the opening event of the day, Guintoli seemed prepared to take most risks, and he was duly rewarded with his second win of the year. He ignored the early damp patches, and his uncanny ability in such conditions told in the end, but it was an early end, which perhaps was lucky.

Sykes finished second after the red flag came out, but he had been closing down Guintoli, even though he had run off the track early in the race and had to re-pass eventual third-place rider Rea, and team-mate Baz.

With more laps, Sykes knew he could have caught Guintoli, who also knew it, but neither was prepared to say definitely that he would have won if the race had gone full distance. Baz was fourth and only 4.459 seconds down, but top riders like Laverty and Giugliano fell. In all, six riders did not finish race one, while the two Bimota riders, who were present until the end of each race, had their places and points struck from the record.

In the race two, the weather attacked just at the wrong time and after the first restart, which Guintoli stopped by raising his hand as the track became submerged. Delays and track inspections came and went. The long wait terminated in a soaking ten-lap sprint, so risk as well as restraint were needed.

Rea was an eventually convincing winner, after Guintoli fell at the start-finish chicane while chasing him. The Frenchman got going again to take ninth.

Only six races into his full SBK career, Alex Lowes placed second in the wet, 2.222 seconds away from Rea, clearly showing his BSB champion's credentials. Usefully, he had raced a Superbike around the circuit at Assen before, during the 2013 BSB series.

Wet weather suits Giugliano, who duly finished third, after a typical race of full commitment on his Ducati. Sykes made a solid fourth-place finish look like a wise choice as others slid off; even Melandri ran wide, having to settle for sixth, one place behind a resurgent Haslam.

In six races, there had been four different race winners, on four different bikes; the latest revised technical regulations and a new rider line-up had kick-started Suzuki's unfancied challenge for year-one SBK rider Lowes.

Wild-card Kervin Bos took his Winteb LiquidRubber Honda to 11th and second place in the Evo classification at his home track. After all the rain, race delays, red flags and widely differing fortunes, it was still a good day to be Dutch.

The crowd stayed with it to the end, despite their displeasure at shortened and delayed races, and with Michael van der Mark winning in WSS, they had a double Ten Kate victory rainbow to ride home under.

Above: Lowes, Rea and Giugliano shone in the wet and earned their appearance on the race-two podium.

Left: Both races were shortened, to 16 and ten laps, thanks to an oil spill and an ill-timed weather attack.

Above left: Rea mastered the conditions in race two, but Guintoli was caught out.

Top: Guintoli goes into orbit, but he got back on his Aprilia for ninth.

Far left: Lowes leads Elias (hidden), Davies and Baz in race two.

Left: Althea's Canepa held sway in the Evo class.

Right: A big crowd endured depressing weather and a three-hour delay.

Photos: Gold & Goose

Above: A shocked looking Melandri was at odds with his Aprilia.

Above left: Leon Camier was top Evo runner in both races.

Left: Guintoli made it to the podium in race two, reducing Aprilia's woes.

Right: Sykes leads Davies and Baz in race two.

Photos: Gold & Goose

Far left: Eventual double winner Rea leads Guintoli, Melandri, Giugliano and Davies at the start of race two.

Left: Chaz Davies took a fine second place for Ducati in each race.

Below left: Giugliano loosens up with stretching exercises.

Bottom right: A podium selfie for Davies, Rea and Guintoli.

Photos: Gold & Goose

THE endlessly undulating and often unforgiving Imola has both light and dark elements to its character, but it was the light that shone on race weekend this time around.

Rea and his dazzlingly white Pata Honda held everyone's attention as he won not only both 19-lap races, but also Superpole. He steamrollered the opposition. Yet again, he had shown that he was the only rider in recent times who could master the venerable Honda Fireblade. He led the championship at the end of the day, for the first time since joining SBK, so Imola was significant in so many ways for him and the team's Italian sponsor.

'JR' led over the stripe on every lap, winning each race by over four seconds, from Chaz Davies and Ducati each time. His pole positions, just like his fastest laps in each race, were not at record pace, but his race-day work remained flawless.

It was a good weekend for the resurrection men in general. Ducati had gone through agonies in 2013 with Checa and the Panigale. At Imola in 2014, they took two runner-up spots that were as close to wins as they could possibly have been at this stage of development.

At a circuit just down the *autostrada* from Borgo Panigale, it was a good day to be decked out in red. Only Davide Giugliano's late fall in race one, followed by a distant sixth in race two, nearly spoiled the party.

Sykes had doubled at the circuit in 2013, but he could do no better than third in race one, then fifth in race two. In reasonable track temperatures, after a scorching Saturday, he slipped behind Rea, both in the points tally and in terms of his season's race wins. His main problem appeared to be understeer, and he struggled to turn the bike into the several chicanes.

Race one delivered the first all-British podium since 2010.

Baz placed fourth in race one, beaten by Sykes, but he reversed that order with fourth in race two. His problem was not being able to transfer his bike's obvious power to the ground in the opener. That was sorted to an extent: in race two, he was less than a second from podium man Guintoli. The factory Aprilia rider had recovered from a race-one fifth place to take third in race two, 1.5 seconds behind Davies.

Melandri, the other factory Aprilia man, was going through a painful rite of passage that almost every new Aprilia works rider has had to endure: a period of adjustment, then too many setting changes, then disillusionment when the SBK dream ride suddenly turns sour.

He left Imola in near silence, stony faced and hurting. A home race equalled nothing less than humiliation as he struggled even to be 14 seconds back and sixth in race one. It got worse. He was 37 seconds from the win in race two and a dreary 11th.

Marco's bike set-up, however, dictated by his team until this stage, would soon satisfy his apparently unusual tastes, which the team had felt were out of any normal range.

Haslam's flowering for a time at Assen was subverted in dry conditions in Italy: he placed tenth and eighth, while his team-mate inconveniently won both races.

Suzuki's previous podium pairing of Laverty and Lowes struggled with race-day track temperatures that were only in the low-30°C region. Perhaps they needed more asphalt heat to do better than seventh and eighth in race one, then ninth and tenth respectively in race two.

In Evo-land, Camier made the most of his latest opportunity to take 11th in race one and 12th in race two, and win each stock-engined contest on the BMW Motorrad Italia machine. After Sylvain Barrier's latest injury, he was proving a super-sub.

BACK in 1988, Donington Park provided the birthplace for the brand-new Superbike World Championship. Thus at the most spectator-friendly circuit imaginable, in the heart of England, with plenty of British talent desperate to show off their undoubted brilliance to a home crowd, you would think that Donington 2014 would have been an unmissable event for home fans.

Sadly, that was not the case. Hardly anybody came to watch reigning champion Tom Sykes (from Yorkshire) take a double win, or BSB hero Alex Lowes (Lincolnshire) score his first dry-weather podium.

The weekend schedule had changed to another format, the first race getting under way at noon, not 10.30, and the second due to start at 15.00, not the traditional 15.30 of years gone by. Noon for race one made the normal 2014 race-two start time of 13.10 impossible, of course. Lack of consistency was not confined to rider performance in this 'anything goes' first year under Dorna.

A Sykes double on such a 'Jekyll and Hyde' track as Donington sounds like a visual bore as far as action is concerned. Ultimately, however, it was a thriller, perhaps because he was way down in 11th place in the early stages of race one, after qualifying seventh and departing off the third row.

Although he did not set any new lap records, the number-one plate holder was still too hot to handle for all the others. Some say that Sykes can't scrap once he has been passed, but this was cage fighting to win, against multiple opponents.

Some of his main rivals, including a new one in Lowes, competed strongly up front for most of the first race, but Sykes still blitzed away to what he thought may have been the best race win of his career. He married head to heart to lead by lap 20 and emerge victorious with 1.5 seconds to spare over team-mate Baz.

Lowes had been combative and more than competent as he tussled up front in race one, adding a great dry-weather third to his wet second spot at Assen. He ended up lonely, however, as he was four seconds up on fourth-placed Melandri. Lowes was one of a quartet of riders who led the race, the others being Guintoli, Baz and Sykes.

Davies in fifth and Rea in sixth were in a fight, but the Honda rider was comparatively well off the pace after his recent trio of wins.

Guintoli rounded out race one in seventh after a crash in Superpole on Saturday. From a good position, he crashed again in race one. Laverty also fell and was not able to rejoin.

In the second race, Sykes was up to the lead by lap 11, and the result was not in serious doubt thereafter. Baz was second again, this time 3.8 seconds back. A spread-out podium had Guintoli third and seven seconds adrift, despite having led for ten laps.

Giugliano kept it together to finish fourth, and five seconds or so ahead of team-mate Davies. Rea once again was relatively nowhere in sixth, after a race where tough passes and contact in the braking zones seemed almost inevitable. This reality would prove costly for both Melandri and Lowes in race two. The latter's push inside into the Melbourne hairpin failed and he caught the rear wheel of the Aprilia rider's machine quite solidly. Both fell.

Laverty soon had his own off, at the next corner, remounting for 13th. Melandri just couldn't get a break at a circuit where he has an enviable record, and not just because it is one of his old MotoGP haunts. His promising noontime fourth and potentially better race two ended in no points for 17th. Salom took the double Evo win for KRT.

Above: Baz, Sykes and Guintoli make for a happy race-two rostrum.

Above left: Under the sunny Donington skies, Sykes led Baz to a Kawasaki one-two in both races.

Right: Post-race packing, in readiness for the long haul to Sepang.

Top: As Baz leaves the chicane in race one, Giugliano falls in front of Lowes.

Left: Lowes impressed in race one to take third place. Here he leads the Aprilia pair of Melandri and Guintoli.

Right: Guintoli heads the race-one field through the Craner Curves.

Photos: Gold & Goose

Above left and above: Both Lowes and Sykes were lucky to avoid serious injury after Baz's indiscretion.

Left: The Aprilias of Melandri and Guintoli were in complete control.

Right: Toni Elias and Chaz Davies battle it out in race one. Laverty, trailing them here, would overtake them both for third.

Photos: Gold & Goose

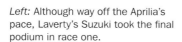

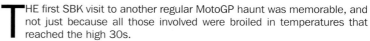

Left: Although way off the Aprilia's pace, Laverty's Suzuki took the final podium in race one.

Far left: Disaster at the start for Kawasaki as Baz takes out Lowes and team-mate Sykes.

Below left: Baz cools off before the start. Soon it would become very hot for the Frenchman.

Below: Sykes rode through the pain to take a vital podium in race two.

Bottom right: Melandri finally delivered for Aprilia, with two race wins.

Photos: Gold & Goose

THE first SBK visit to another regular MotoGP haunt was memorable, and not just because all those involved were broiled in temperatures that reached the high 30s.

Sepang gave Melandri his first win for Aprilia, and a few hours after that his second, as the RSV4 came good in emphatic fashion because of higher track temperatures. It took an emergency meeting on Saturday and study of data gathered over several seasons to get there, but the results were dramatically good for Aprilia.

With the track at 52°C in race one and almost 60°C for race two, Melandri and Superpole winner Guintoli had two close fights for the wins, but the latter had to give way to the former each time.

In race one, over 16 laps, Melandri was eventually 0.620 second ahead, but most telling was that Laverty's Suzuki was a fighting third, if still over 12 seconds behind – an age in SBK, in this year or any other.

More than this slightly unpredictable, but emphatic podium order, the first race at Sepang will be remembered for a first-lap incident involving both KRT riders, Sykes and Baz, and Voltcom Crescent Suzuki rookie Alex Lowes.

As Baz made an ill-advised attempted move inside of Lowes at the horribly tight and downhill turn two, he misjudged the pace, ran over the paint and lost the front, his sliding bike taking out both Lowes and Sykes. Sykes became tangled with and trapped by Lowes's machine, suffering an enduring hand injury and only just escaping a substantial leg injury.

It looked as though the day was over for Sykes and his previously swelling points lead, but he had other ideas.

Fourth in the first race was Davies, who had previous GP experience of Sepang. He had to use all of it to keep former MotoGP winner and Moto2 champion Elias behind him, on yet another Aprilia.

Rea, run off track by the first-lap melee, was a massive 31 seconds down in fifth; his wins at Imola and Assen seemed a long way in the past. Only 16 riders finished race one; Salom, the Evo 'race' winner, was ninth.

Sykes and Baz nearly came to blows in their pit garage as the former brushed aside the latter's attempted apology, complaining about several previous instances when he felt Baz had gone too far.

Thus Baz was also charged up as they lined up on the grid for race two.

The first attempt was halted by a substantial oil leak from Corti's MV Agusta, and in the race proper – now ten-lap sprint – the two Aprilias fought it out at the end, after Melandri had run wide early on and had to re-pass Baz and Sykes. After a last-corner decider, Melandri passed inside to win by only 0.166 second from Guintoli.

Despite his pain, Sykes took a more-than-decent third place, in the manner expected of a world champion. Elias finished fourth, underlining the importance of having an Aprilia and experience of Sepang on the day. He just held off Baz.

Rea was less happy in sixth, 7.073 seconds off the win, while Laverty was seventh, albeit only a shade behind Rea.

Davies was eighth and Giugliano tenth on a very non-Ducati day in the Malaysian heat.

The Evo competition went to Camier in race two, by considerable margin over Salom.

Near disaster in race one for Sykes became disaster averted, but he still lost a host of points to the Aprilia riders. Luckily for him, most went to the rider who posed the least immediate threat in the standings.

Above: Sykes was in control at Misano, taking Superpole and both race wins.

Right: It was retro gear for Guintoli and Team Aprilia.

Centre right: Canepa on the Althea Racing Ducati.

Below right: The Voltcom Suzuki pair of Laverty and Lowes ran in close convoy, but finished some 20 seconds adrift of the winner in race two.

Opposite page, from top: Salom, once again the winner of the Evo class; Goi returned to action and scored points on his Evo Ducati; Barrier leads Foret and Goi in race one; Baz and Melandri in race-two action; Giugliano leads Sykes and the rest at the start of race two.

Opposite page, bottom right: Sykes celebrates with Melandri.

Photos: Gold & Goose

OM SYKES had only a few days to recover from the first-lap crash at Sepang, which had been caused by team-mate Loris Baz. And he used that time to brood. He knew that he had to regain his championship advantage at almost all costs in Misano – at the home of Aprilia and Melandri.

The weekend started well with a Superpole win on Saturday and a new track best of 1m 34.883s. It also went perfectly to plan in race one, where he led every lap, set a new lap record of 1m 35.629s and added 25 more points to his total. He looked imperious again, being five seconds ahead of the next best rider, and he seemed set for another double – barring disaster.

Race two was considerably harder than the opener, as his bike moved around a lot more. With three seconds of winning advantage, however, he still looked uncatchable.

To cheer him up all the more, Baz delivered two second places. Although the team-mates had not been the best of friends after Sepang, a Kawasaki rider in second place meant that the best Aprilia could do no better than third. Again, that most potent Aprilia points harvester on race-day was Melandri, 1.4 seconds behind Baz in race one.

Melandri and Guintoli sported retro leather designs and paint jobs on their bikes, while their mechanics wore 1987-era Aprilia dungarees and white shirts – to celebrate Aprilia's first 250GP race win with Loris Reggiani all those years before at Misano.

Ducati remained in red as usual, and only the push from Melandri and some drop-off in grip for Davies kept the Welshman in fourth place in race one. He was the only one of the non-podium riders in the same orbit as the leading three, with seven seconds covering them all.

Guintoli lost his bearings slightly in fifth, 16 seconds down on the wrong tyre option. Elias placed sixth, just a second or so behind him. Rea was seventh and Giugliano eighth, commenting about a strange vibration from his bike, which would also plague Davies in race two.

In the second full-distance 21-lap race, Sykes was almost as dominant as in the opener, but Baz had to work even harder to keep Melandri behind him. There was less than 0.4 second in it at the flag from second to third, but it was *déjà vu* for the fans with an identical one-two-three.

Guintoli was fourth, 1.5 seconds back from Melandri. The top four were just that in race two, with just over five seconds covering them all. The next nearest rider was Rea, some 18 seconds back from the win on his Honda. Seemingly excellent one weekend, then off the pace the next, the 2014 Honda was a better bike than most, but still not quite as consistent as the Kawasaki or Aprilia. Rea was paying the price in points again, or so it appeared.

He beat the Aprilia of Elias in going fifth in race two, with Laverty, another one-time 2014 race winner, suffering the mid-season blues. Lowes was right behind his Irish team-mate in race two, but Giugliano jump-started and had to enter the pits, finally recovering to ninth.

The Evo geniuses did battle again, and once more Salom was a double winner for Kawasaki. The early-season prowess of Canepa on the Althea Ducati Evo entry was beginning to abate as the championship progressed, but Salom was not short of competition with Barrier back on the grid and in fine form for BMW.

With half of the – planned – season gone, it was all to play for, but it would be over 12 rounds, not the intended 14. With six wins in the 14 races so far, Sykes was still riding high.

Above: Rea and his PATA Honda dominated in the wet in race two.

Above right: New and old faces. Peter Sebestyen (*left*), at just 21, promoted from the Euro Cup to the Toth team; and 41-year-old Aaron Yates, trying his luck in SBK after a long AMA career.

Top: Sykes's win in race one helped maintain his championship lead.

Right: Haslam, Lowes and Davies battle for the final podium place in race two.

Photos: Gold & Goose

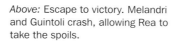

Above: Escape to victory. Melandri and Guintoli crash, allowing Rea to take the spoils.

Left and below left: Baz and Guintoli trade paint in their race-one duel.

Below: Giugliano took his Ducati into second place in race two.

Bottom: Rea accepts the plaudits after his win.

Bottom right: Chaz Davies comes under attack from the Aprilias of Guintoli (50) and Melandri (33).

Photos: Gold & Goose

A N intense ribbon of tarmac wrapped around a hillside in the Algarve, Portimao is a mini-rollercoaster that can suffer weird weather, despite the well-founded reputation for sunshine enjoyed by the south coast of Portugal. Race-day produced this changeable aspect of its character to the full, just at the wrong time for many riders.

After a Misano double, a single win for Sykes in the first race kept him at the top of the standings in the hunt for the SBK crown.

A good start by Rea had pole-winner Sykes behind for three laps, but after he had taken the initiative up front, he led over the stripe each time from then on, to win by 2.539 seconds from a resurgent Guintoli.

In an essentially dry race that had the white flags out for more than a few spots of rain in the middle, Sykes had to pass team-mate Baz on his way to the front and keep his tall French team-mate there, by just over half a second at the flag. Almost a second behind Baz, Melandri slotted into fourth, one second per position behind Sykes. It would become worse for him and Guintoli shortly afterwards.

Rea slowly dropped back to finish fifth in the opener, but he was well clear of the next bunch of riders, who were involved in a scrap of epic proportions for the final places in the top eight. Lowes, Giugliano and Laverty finished in that order, but were separated by less than two-tenths.

Davies and Haslam came into contact entering the downhill hairpin across from the pits, just as the white flags for rain were shown. Both fell, but got going again, Haslam to finish 11th. Davies was 18th and last, which was doubly irritating, as he had put his Ducati on the front row alongside Sykes and Rea.

Salom just held off Barrier for ninth and the Evo class win, in a close chase for the line.

Things would improve not only for Davies, but also Ducati, as both official Panigale riders made it to the podium in race two, in second and third places respectively.

It was wet in race two, suddenly and horribly, which had a definite impact on the championship fight for one top rider, while giving another a real confidence boost that he could carry forward.

Rea was a convincing race-two winner, ending up over six seconds ahead of Giugliano and eight better than Davies. Lowes underlined his wet-weather credentials once more with fourth place, and this time Haslam got around cleanly to secure a top five, ahead of normally rapid wet-weather rider Baz.

In the second Evo 'race', Barrier and BMW were victorious with 11th; Salom found the wet a real disadvantage, finishing 17th.

It was an altogether more dramatic race two for another French rider, Guintoli. With 12 laps gone and in third position behind Melandri, he saw his team-mate leave a small gap going into the infamous infield hairpin. He dived inside, then saw Melandri moving back over, not having noticed the initial attack. The collision was inevitable, albeit truly avoidable. Each of the riders had been rapidly catching Rea, and with six laps left to run, there was plenty of time to take an Aprilia one-two.

The result was a non-finish for Melandri, but a remarkable recovery for Guintoli. He even got back ahead of Sykes to finish seventh.

Sykes was in real difficulty in the rain. His bike seemed to have either a strong wet setting or a strong dry one, but the two seemed alien to each other without many adjustments and recalibrations. It seems it had moved too far from the optimum setting for the wet. Eighth was not a disaster, however, as he still left with an enhanced points lead.

A strange season was steadily becoming an unfathomable one.

SUPERBIKE WORLD CHAMPIONSHIP
LAGUNA SECA
ROUND 9 · UNITED STATES

Above: Pegram leads May and Sebestyen in race one.

Left: Salom was again the class of the Evo field in both races.

Below left: Guintoli had to accept second-place finishes behind Melandri and Sykes.

Below: Melandri threw his Aprilia down the road in the second race.

Far left: Sykes leads the field away at the start of race two.

Photos: Gold & Goose

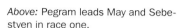

Left: After third in race one, a delighted Sykes took victory in race two.

Right: Rizmayer leads May and Ulrich as the trio chase the points in race one.

Far left: Melandri leads Sykes and the rest through the Corkscrew early in race two.

Photos: Gold & Goose

P OLE-MAN Sykes, with a new track best of 1m 21.811s, and his peers shared a tough race-day in the sun at Laguna Seca, with many delays and two races of very different lengths.

The first ran the full 25 laps and started on time at 11.00. It proved to be an Aprilia love-in at the very top of the podium, as Melandri had found his winning mojo again. He was almost a second up on Guintoli, despite the French rider having set a short-lived new lap record of 1m 23.559s on lap seven.

Sykes, with a spinning rear, was back in damage limitation mode and was unerringly adept at it, securing a safe third, 6.627 seconds from the lead. He had led at the very beginning, but ran off track entering the Corkscrew and had to work hard to avoid a crash, losing two places.

Giugliano and Ducati won an off-podium final-corner duel with Elias and his privateer Aprilia for fourth, with tenth-placed qualifier Rea down in sixth and 15 seconds from the win. His resurgent team-mate, Haslam, was only three seconds behind him in seventh. Davies crashed out of race one after a front-row start and concussion ruled him out of race two. He had fancied his chances of a first win on the Panigale.

The second race, eventually just seven laps, but delivering full points, had three attempts at completion.

The first start, of a planned 25-laps, was halted when Lowes crashed into Baz entering the Corkscrew. The British rider fell hard for the second time that day: he had suffered a fast wipe-out after suffering a brake problem entering turn two in morning warm-up, at around 150mph.

The restart lasted as long as it took Barrier to crash coming out of the final corner, his bike pitching towards the pit-lane wall on the inside. The stricken rider cracked his heel and foot, which kept him out of the final running of the second race.

There should really have been yet another red flag after new lap-record setter Giugliano (1m 23.403s) crashed at the Corkscrew and his machine lay on the exit line, with bikes whizzing past uncomfortably close.

Melandri appeared to have the short race wrapped up with his front-running pace, but he was over-eager and fell at the entry to turn 11. He could have run wide, but he opted to try to make the corner, and that ruled him out.

With a clear track ahead and champagne in the offing, Sykes pushed on to win race two, by just over a second from Guintoli.

Rea earned a popular second-race podium for third, in his first ever visit to Laguna. He had missed the round in 2013 because of injury. Less than three seconds back was race-one non-scorer Laverty in fourth. Privateer Elias was fifth.

It was a woeful weekend for Baz, with ninth in race one and sixth – a second a lap off team-mate Sykes – in race two.

Salom won both Evo races. He had been tenth in the opener, and only three seconds behind the toiling Baz on the full-power version of his stock-engined official KRT machine.

As Claudio Corti had been injured at the previous round in Portugal, the versatile Camier returned to action, riding the MV Agusta F4 to 15th and then tenth.

It had been another horribly disturbed race-day in the SBK paddock, with injuries, red flags and delays, but thankfully the fans saw two races – even if one had been only about a quarter of the full helping.

SUPERBIKE WORLD CHAMPIONSHIP
JEREZ
ROUND 10 · SPAIN

Above: Sykes had to fend off Laverty in their battle for fifth in race one.

Above right: The Aprilia pair were dominant in both races.

Top: Guintoli and Melandri lead the field at the start of race one.

Right: Melandri celebrates his second win of the day; Guintoli and Sykes had kept their championship battle alive.

Photos: Gold & Goose

Above: Little autumnal growth in Dorna's very own backyard.

Left: Guarnoni, in the thick of the battle among the Evo-class Kawasakis.

Below left: Corti on the still-developing MV Agusta.

Below: Elias keeps his private Aprilia ahead of Barrier's Evo-BMW.

Bottom: Laverty struggles to keep Rea at bay in race two.

Below right: Davies put the Ducati on the podium in race one.

Photos: Gold & Goose

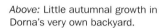

I T was a very long time between the Laguna Seca round on 13th July and Jerez on 7th September, but few riders showed any rustiness with so much still to play for. They all knew that now Jerez would be the third-to-last round, following the cancellation of the proposed Phakisa weekend in South Africa and the confirmation of Qatar as the finale. No more extra races at those rounds either, as had been proposed to make up for losing Phakisa.

Thus Jerez would be more pivotal than previously expected and, not for the first time in 2014, an SBK contest proved to be a straight fight between Aprilia and Kawasaki.

Pre-race, pole-man Baz and third-placed Sykes appeared set for a jolly green day, but the race pace indications told a different story. The Jerez podiums duly featured a one-two for the factory Aprilia riders, with nobody else involved in a curiously internecine fight.

Melandri pushed hard to make sure he won both races, and with no team orders, much less damage was done to Sykes's championship lead than might otherwise have been the case.

Guintoli, the only realistic Aprilia world champion prospect, seemed unsurprised, though less than impressed at leaving Spain 31 points behind Sykes when the gap could easily have been 21. For some, his riding style seems casual, but he rode his heart out in pursuit of wins, taking risks up front that meant he could have fallen and lost even more championship ground.

Post-race chatter was about little else than posing the question of whether Aprilia had blown it by playing fair with their riders, or whether they had been admirable in their sporting neutrality by rejecting team orders, consistently abhorred by fans.

Either way, despite suffering a relative nightmare weekend in fifth and third, Sykes was the one to benefit from Aprilia's race-day finishing order – and he knew it.

He had said pre-race that Jerez was a difficult place, despite the positive emotion of returning to the track where he had lifted the trophy in 2013. Even after winter testing at Jerez, and more speed that KRT had found there, Sykes was unable to challenge for a podium in race one.

His recovery to finish third in race two (if still significantly behind the winner) was almost a recurring theme after the same kind of one-down/one-up results in the previous couple of rounds.

In the first race, Baz and Guintoli fought it out, then Baz and Melandri. The Kawasaki rider touched handlebars with Melandri's bike with seven laps left and fell to earth to no-score. Then Melandri caught Guintoli, passed him comfortably and won by 1.397 seconds.

Early podium contestant Giugliano had fallen, which left Davies to take third on his Ducati, only four seconds from the victory.

He and Honda-man Rea were close, but the latter seemed more concerned to keep Sykes behind him, which he did successfully. Sykes eventually held Laverty at bay for fifth.

Melandri, down the order in the early stages of race two, came through in imperious fashion for a double that impressed all who saw it. He finished 2.845 seconds ahead of Guintoli, whom he passed with ease again into his favourite turn one. Riding flat out, Sykes was third and just over a second-and-a-half up on Davies.

The Welsh rider showed that he was getting over his dislike of Jerez; at a circuit with no massive straights, the Ducati demonstrated a more consistent high level of performance. He was over a second ahead of Rea at the end, with Laverty a lonely sixth.

Melandri's resurgence meant that the Aprilia rider had won half of the ten most recent races.

MAGNY-COURS
ROUND 11 · FRANCE

Above: Sykes waves a leg at Baz after his team-mate allowed him to take fourth in race one.

Above right: Lanzi had lots of previous form at Magny-Cours, and the Italian wild-card took fifth in race two.

Top: Aprilias on top again as Melandri leads Guintoli in race two.

Right: Haslam was determined to take third in race two and did so in dramatic fashion.

Photos: Gold & Goose

Left: Wild-card rider Neukirchner took two strong top-ten places on his IDM-spec Ducati.

Below left: Having ceded the win to Guintoli in race one, Melandri was in no mood to surrender in the second.

Below: Guintoli kept his title chances alive at his home round.

Bottom: Haslam had waited two years to taste champagne again in SBK.

Below right: Rea took third place for Honda in race one, keeping Sykes off the podium.

Photos: Gold & Goose

FROM opening sunshine to final splash, Magny-Cours was an appropriate catalyst to ensure that there would be a *dénouement* in the desert. The season-ending Qatari round in November would not be a dreaded dead rubber for Dorna.

Even though Sykes finished on top of the positively balmy October practice and Superpole sessions at Magny-Cours, and with a new track best of 1m 36.366s, Sunday would prove a different matter.

A free-practice fall on Saturday could have derailed his subsequent Superpole win through bike or rider damage, but he was quick-witted enough to ensure a safer low-side exit.

A change from dry to wet conditions on race day produced a situation that no amount of quick thinking or rider input could overcome for Sykes, as Kawasaki once more found some wet woes on Sunday.

Aprilia riders Guintoli and Melandri had no such worries; it was a home round for Guintoli to boot.

In front of soaked, but enthusiastic fans (large numbers of them as usual), Guintoli had no answer to an eventually fleeing Melandri in race one – but his team did. Having missed the chance to claw back significant points to Sykes at the previous round in Spain, because of a Melandri double win over Guintoli, Aprilia had issued team orders. Melandri was shown a yellow-faced emoticon on his pitboard – with a frown replacing the smile – and then a subsequent downward arrow to indicate he really should drop a place.

He allowed Guintoli to pass, in a very public and visible manner, which meant the championship could not now be closed out in France after all.

Kawasaki had no answer to Aprilia in the conditions, even with wet specialist Loris Baz, so the KRT squad followed suit and Sykes duly inherited a fourth-place finish from Baz right at the end.

With so much at stake and a chance for Aprilia to wreck Sykes's points lead not once, but twice, it was no wonder that team orders had been issued. In race two, however, leader Melandri completely ignored the frowny face, and although Aprilia took a one-two again, it was in the wrong order. Guintoli finished over two seconds behind Melandri and ended up 12 points adrift of Sykes, rather than a much more significant seven.

For Sykes, two fourth places, even if he had been gifted the first, were worthy rides for a world champion, as the surface at Magny-Cours was treacherous. Track temperatures were only 13°C in race one and 16°C in race two. Add in the rain and the fact that only 13 riders finished race two, and it became clear that Sykes had put in two hard rides. Naturally he was quietly seething about how his imperfect wet set-up had limited his pace.

There were other big stories, too.

Finally there were positives on both sides of the Pata Honda garage, with Jonathan Rea posting third in race one. Then Leon Haslam gained his first Pata Honda podium in two years of injury and electronic frustrations. He had disposed of a determined Sykes by riding around the outside of him – in the wet, well off the racing line…

Baz, a fated fifth in race one, slipped back to a puzzled seventh in race two, as the wild-card 3C Ducati team, regular IDM competitors, eclipsed the struggling factory boys, thanks to Lorenzo Lanzi and Max Neukirchner.

In Evo, Salom was missing after a flare up of his hand injury; Sylvain Barrier and then Niccolo Canepa took the honours for BMW and Ducati respectively.

Above: Fully focused, Guintoli heads for the championship.

Right: Tears of joy: the Guintoli family were all on hand to share the relief.

Top right: Loris Baz bust team orders to take second in race one, piling more pressure on team-mate Sykes.

Above centre right: The face of a championship won: Sylvain Guintoli.

Centre right: The face of a championship lost: Tom Sykes.

Far right: Jonathan Rea leads Sykes and Guintoli early in race two.

Photos: Gold & Goose

DEFYING the vast cloak of the surrounding darkness, the Losail night race made a suitably floodlit stage on which to play out the championship's deciding dramas.

The final night of the 12-event run even went to the last act, and then to the very last scene. Rows between the key cast members carried on long after the floodlights had been switched off, however.

Friday had seen Kawasaki well off the pace and worried, but with Baz second and Sykes third in Superpole, and Guintoli only fifth and Melandri eighth, the pendulum swung towards Sykes being champion for a second time.

In warm-up on race day, it was looking good for two battling races at least, and that is what the crowd was treated to. Or at least two tense affairs and verbal fights after race one and then race two.

Guintoli eventually romped away out front in the opener, after overcoming a determined Baz. Behind, Sykes was running as fast as his set-up could carry him, but it was not enough to make an impression on the front two.

As the first race approached its end, Sykes was watching the handy 12-point lead he had carried into Losail being seriously eroded. However, it could be kept to a seven-point advantage with one race to go if Baz dropped a place. In that circumstance, Sykes could still finish second behind Guintoli in race two and be champion by two points.

The 'Lose 1P' sign duly came out, but Baz ran across the line second anyway, leaving Sykes third – and livid with his young team-mate.

Sykes had struggled to find Guintoli's pace, but he was still only just under four seconds down after 15 laps – and he had managed to hold Rea down to fourth. Giugliano's Ducati was fifth.

The problem for Sykes was that now he had only a three-point advantage going into race two, meaning he had to make sure he could win the race. That said, if anybody could, he could. After all, with valuable tyre and suspension data from race one, things would be better for him in race two, surely. And he had won eight races already, more than anybody else.

However, in a five-second-faster race two, Guintoli found depths of focus and a sheer pace that he did not know he possessed. Riding almost on autopilot, he was in control in a relaxed way he had never felt before. 'Guinters' set a new lap record on lap eight and earned his first SBK double victory at the very moment it mattered most.

Behind, with Baz down the field after running off at the first corner, Rea shadowed and harried Sykes. The Honda rider had the better final pace, and he burst through to take second.

Thus Sykes, in third, would not have been champion, even if he had been gifted the four points by his team-mate in race one. Had the pressure of needing to beat Guintoli got to him?

He lambasted Baz, who returned the compliment with interest, leading to a spiral of recrimination and insult.

Nonetheless Sykes paid tribute to Guintoli for his two great rides and the fantastic final push that had allowed the Frenchman to overturn a 44-point deficit in the last six individual races since Laguna. He had outscored Sykes in every race since then.

Rea's race-two second place gave him an overall third in the standings. He ended up just a single point ahead of an off-form Melandri, who scored an eighth and a fourth.

Melandri had had to employ all of his Aprilia's power to keep Davies and his Ducati behind him across the line in race two, with Elias making it a fighting trio.

2014 WORLD SUPERBIKE CHAMPIONSHIP RESULTS

Compiled by Peter McLaren

Round 1 — PHILLIP ISLAND, Australia · 23 February, 2014 · 2.762-mile/4.445km circuit · WEATHER: Race 1 · Dry · Track 32°C · Air 21°C; Race 2 · Dry · Track 48°C · Air 22°C

Race 1: 22 laps, 60.764 miles/97.790km

Time of race: 33m 39.440s · Average speed: 108.322mph/174.328km/h

Pos.	Rider	Nat.	No.	Entrant	Machine	Tyres	Time & Gap	Laps
1	Eugene Laverty	IRL	58	Voltcom Crescent Suzuki	Suzuki GSX-R1000	P		22
2	Marco Melandri	ITA	33	Aprilia Racing Team	Aprilia RSV4 Factory	P	2.959s	22
3	Sylvain Guintoli	FRA	50	Aprilia Racing Team	Aprilia RSV4 Factory	P	3.034s	22
4	Davide Giugliano	ITA	34	Ducati Superbike Team	Ducati 1199 Panigale R	P	6.972s	22
5	Loris Baz	FRA	76	Kawasaki Racing Team	Kawasaki ZX-10R	P	11.132s	22
6	Jonathan Rea	GBR	65	PATA Honda World Superbike	Honda CBR1000RR	P	11.718s	22
7	Tom Sykes	GBR	1	Kawasaki Racing Team	Kawasaki ZX-10R	P	15.612s	22
8	Chaz Davies	GBR	7	Ducati Superbike Team	Ducati 1199 Panigale R	P	25.724s	22
9	David Salom	ESP	44	Kawasaki Racing Team	Kawasaki ZX-10R EVO	P	37.407s	22
10	Niccolo Canepa	ITA	59	Althea Racing	Ducati 1199 Panigale R EVO	P	37.468s	22
11	Glen Allerton	AUS	14	BMW Motorrad Italia SBK	BMW S1000 RR EVO	P	39.271s	22
12	Fabien Foret	FRA	9	MAHI Racing Team India	Kawasaki ZX-10R EVO	P	45.212s	22
13	Claudio Corti	ITA	71	MV Agusta RC-Yakhnich M.	MV Agusta F4 RR	P	50.249s	22
14	Jeremy Guarnoni	FRA	11	MRS Kawasaki	Kawasaki ZX-10R EVO	P	1m 17.134s	22
15	Sheridan Morais	RSA	32	IRON BRAIN Kawasaki SBK	Kawasaki ZX-10R EVO	P	1m 23.686s	22
16	Imre Toth	HUN	10	BMW Team Toth	BMW S1000 RR	P	1m 30.651s	22
17	Aaron Yates	USA	20	Team Hero EBR	EBR 1190 RX	P	1 Lap	21
	Alessandro Andreozzi	ITA	21	Team Pedercini	Kawasaki ZX-10R EVO	P	DNF	14
	Leon Haslam	GBR	91	PATA Honda World Superbike	Honda CBR1000RR	P	DNF	4
	Alex Lowes	GBR	22	Voltcom Crescent Suzuki	Suzuki GSX-R1000	P	DNF	3
	Toni Elias	ESP	24	Red Devils Roma	Aprilia RSV4 Factory	P	DNF	3

Race 2: 14 laps, 38.668 miles/62.230km

Time of race: 35m 36.814s · Average speed: 107.574mph/173.124km/h

Pos.	Rider	Time & Gap	Laps
1	Sylvain Guintoli		14
2	Loris Baz	0.283s	14
3	Tom Sykes	1.103s	14
4	Davide Giugliano	2.052s	14
5	Jonathan Rea	4.951s	14
6	Leon Haslam	5.673s	14
7	Chaz Davies	9.664s	14
8	Marco Melandri	10.574s	14
9	Toni Elias	11.682s	14
10	David Salom	15.065s	14
11	Niccolo Canepa	16.294s	14
12	Fabien Foret	16.919s	14
13	Alex Lowes	19.694s	14
14	Sheridan Morais	27.266s	14
15	Glen Allerton	27.845s	14
16	Jeremy Guarnoni	29.431s	14
17	Alessandro Andreozzi	36.393s	14
18	Claudio Corti	37.018s	14
19	Imre Toth	54.093s	14
20	Aaron Yates	1m 13.385s	14
	Eugene Laverty	DNF	14

Superpole

1	Guintoli	1m 30.038s
2	Giugliano	1m 30.135s
3	Melandri	1m 30.332s
4	Laverty	1m 30.385s
5	Lowes	1m 30.421s
6	Rea	1m 30.660s
7	Baz	1m 30.796s
8	Sykes	1m 30.835s
9	Haslam	1m 31.138s
10	Canepa	1m 31.274s
11	Davies	1m 31.281s
12	Salom	1m 31.950s
13	Elias	1m 32.107s
14	Corti	1m 32.187s
15	Foret	1m 32.248s
16	Andreozzi	1m 32.902s
17	Guarnoni	1m 33.146s
18	Morais	1m 33.404s
19	Allerton	1m 33.605s
20	Toth	1m 34.137s

Fastest race lap: Chaz Davies on lap 2, 1m 30.949s, 109.327mph/175.945km/h (record).
Previous lap record: Eugene Laverty, IRL (Aprilia), 1m 31.168s, 109.064mph/175.522km/h (2013).

Fastest race lap: Sylvain Guintoli on lap 12, 1m 31.421s, 108.762mph/175.036km/h.

Points

1, Guintoli 41; 2, Baz 31; 3, Melandri 28; 4, Giugliano 26; 5, Laverty 25; 6, Sykes 25; 7, Rea 21; 8, Davies 17; 9, Salom 13; 10, Canepa 11; 11, Haslam 10; 12, Foret 8; 13, Elias 7; 14, Allerton 6; 15, Lowes 3; 16, Corti 3; 17, Morais 3; 18, Guarnoni 2.

Round 2 — ARAGON, Spain · 13 April, 2014 · 3.321-mile/5.344km circuit · WEATHER: Race 1 · Dry · Track 16°C · Air 16°C; Race 2 · Dry · Track 32°C · Air 19°C

Race 1: 17 laps, 56.450 miles/90.848km

Time of race: 33m 38.583s · Average speed: 100.675mph/162.021km/h

Pos.	Rider	Nat.	No.	Entrant	Machine	Tyres	Time & Gap	Laps
1	Tom Sykes	GBR	1	Kawasaki Racing Team	Kawasaki ZX-10R	P		17
2	Loris Baz	FRA	76	Kawasaki Racing Team	Kawasaki ZX-10R	P	4.275s	17
3	Jonathan Rea	GBR	65	PATA Honda World Superbike	Honda CBR1000RR	P	8.418s	17
4	Chaz Davies	GBR	7	Ducati Superbike Team	Ducati 1199 Panigale R	P	15.715s	17
5	Eugene Laverty	IRL	58	Voltcom Crescent Suzuki	Suzuki GSX-R1000	P	19.305s	17
6	Sylvain Guintoli	FRA	50	Aprilia Racing Team	Aprilia RSV4 Factory	P	21.998s	17
7	Toni Elias	ESP	24	Red Devils Roma	Aprilia RSV4 Factory	P	24.018s	17
8	Davide Giugliano	ITA	34	Ducati Superbike Team	Ducati 1199 Panigale R	P	27.894s	17
9	Leon Haslam	GBR	91	PATA Honda World Superbike	Honda CBR1000RR	P	29.077s	17
10	Alex Lowes	GBR	22	Voltcom Crescent Suzuki	Suzuki GSX-R1000	P	29.863s	17
11	Marco Melandri	ITA	33	Aprilia Racing Team	Aprilia RSV4 Factory	P	34.820s	17
12	Leon Camier	GBR	19	BMW Motorrad Italia SBK	BMW S1000 RR EVO	P	35.255s	17
13	David Salom	ESP	44	Kawasaki Racing Team	Kawasaki ZX-10R EVO	P	43.975s	17
14	Jeremy Guarnoni	FRA	11	MRS Kawasaki	Kawasaki ZX-10R EVO	P	46.721s	17
15	Sheridan Morais	RSA	32	IRON BRAIN Grillini Kawasaki	Kawasaki ZX-10R EVO	P	56.619s	17
16	Luca Scassa	ITA	23	Team Pedercini	Kawasaki ZX-10R EVO	P	1m 16.469s	17
17	Aaron Yates	USA	20	Team Hero EBR	EBR 1190 RX	P	1m 35.047s	17
18	Imre Toth	HUN	10	BMW Team Toth	BMW S1000 RR	P	1m 48.427s	17
19	Alessandro Andreozzi	ITA	21	Team Pedercini	Kawasaki ZX-10R EVO	P	1m 51.222s	17
20	Peter Sebestyen	HUN	56	BMW Team Toth	BMW S1000 RR EVO	P	2m 01.152s	17
	Michel Fabrizio	ITA	84	IRON BRAIN Grillini Kawasaki	Kawasaki ZX-10R EVO	P	DNF	9
	Niccolo Canepa	ITA	59	Althea Racing	Ducati 1199 Panigale R EVO	P	DNF	4
	Geoff May	USA	99	Team Hero EBR	EBR 1190 RX	P	DNF	3
	Claudio Corti	ITA	71	MV Agusta RC-Yakhnich M.	MV Agusta F4 RR	P	DNF	1
	Fabien Foret	FRA	9	MAHI Racing Team India	Kawasaki ZX-10R EVO	P	DNF	0
	Ayrton Badovini	ITA	86	Team Alstare	Bimota BB3 EVO	P	NC	17
	Christian Iddon	GBR	2	Team Alstare	Bimota BB3 EVO	P	NC	17

Race 2: 17 laps, 56.450 miles/90.848km

Time of race: 33m 37.223s · Average speed: 100.743mph/162.130km/h

Pos.	Rider	Time & Gap	Laps
1	Tom Sykes		17
2	Loris Baz	0.338s	17
3	Marco Melandri	0.470s	17
4	Sylvain Guintoli	5.429s	17
5	Jonathan Rea	8.861s	17
6	Eugene Laverty	15.986s	17
7	Davide Giugliano	18.206s	17
8	Leon Haslam	25.513s	17
9	Toni Elias	25.823s	17
10	David Salom	38.949s	17
11	Niccolo Canepa	39.413s	17
12	Leon Camier	41.486s	17
13	Sheridan Morais	1m 02.587s	17
14	Luca Scassa	1m 09.720s	17
15	Fabien Foret	1m 14.046s	17
16	Alessandro Andreozzi	1m 14.233s	17
17	Aaron Yates	1m 35.195s	17
18	Imre Toth	1m 37.781s	17
19	Peter Sebestyen	1m 54.547s	17
20	Geoff May	1m 57.166s	17
	Michel Fabrizio	DNF	12
	Jeremy Guarnoni	DNF	9
	Claudio Corti	DNF	5
	Chaz Davies	DNF	3
	Alex Lowes	DNF	1
	Ayrton Badovini	NC	17
	Christian Iddon	NC	10

Superpole

1	Sykes	1m 56.479s
2	Baz	1m 56.675s
3	Guintoli	1m 56.769s
4	Giugliano	1m 56.825s
5	Rea	1m 56.972s
6	Davies	1m 56.977s
7	Melandri	1m 57.063s
8	Laverty	1m 57.736s
9	Lowes	1m 57.975s
10	Elias	1m 58.180s
11	Camier	1m 59.326s
12	Haslam	No Time
13	Canepa	1m 59.255s
14	Salom	1m 59.486s
15	Badovini	1m 59.596s
16	Corti	1m 59.747s
17	Morais	2m 00.415s
18	Iddon	2m 01.102s
19	Fabrizio	2m 01.862s
20	Guarnoni	No Time

Fastest race lap: Tom Sykes on lap 2, 1m 57.664s, 101.596mph/163.503km/h (record).
Previous lap record: Tom Sykes, GBR (Kawasaki), 1m 57.973s, 101.330mph/163.075km/h (2013).

Fastest race lap: Chaz Davies on lap 2, 1m 57.982s, 101.322mph/163.062km/h.

Points

1, Sykes 75; 2, Baz 71; 3, Guintoli 64; 4, Melandri 49; 5, Rea 48; 6, Laverty 46; 7, Giugliano 43; 8, Davies 30; 9, Haslam 25; 10, Elias 23; 11, Salom 22; 12, Canepa 16; 13, Lowes 9; 14, Foret 9; 15, Camier 8; 16, Morais 7; 17, Allerton 6; 18, Guarnoni 4; 19, Corti 3; 20, Scassa 2.

WORLD SUPERBIKE CHAMPIONSHIP · 2014

Race 1: 16 laps, 45.156 miles/72.672km

Time of race: 25m 56.636s · **Average speed:** 104.432mph/168.067km/h

Pos.	Rider	Nat.	No.	Entrant	Machine	Tyres	Time & Gap	Laps
1	**Sylvain Guintoli**	FRA	50	Aprilia Racing Team	Aprilia RSV4 Factory	P		16
2	**Tom Sykes**	GBR	1	Kawasaki Racing Team	Kawasaki ZX-10R	P	1.259s	16
3	**Jonathan Rea**	GBR	65	PATA Honda World Superbike	Honda CBR1000RR	P	4.116s	16
4	**Loris Baz**	FRA	76	Kawasaki Racing Team	Kawasaki ZX-10R	P	4.459s	16
5	**Toni Elias**	ESP	24	Red Devils Roma	Aprilia RSV4 Factory	P	23.728s	16
6	**Marco Melandri**	ITA	33	Aprilia Racing Team	Aprilia RSV4 Factory	P	25.478s	16
7	**Chaz Davies**	GBR	7	Ducati Superbike Team	Ducati 1199 Panigale R	P	26.533s	16
8	**Leon Haslam**	GBR	91	PATA Honda World Superbike	Honda CBR1000RR	P	26.696s	16
9	**Alex Lowes**	GBR	22	Voltcom Crescent Suzuki	Suzuki GSX-R1000	P	27.971s	16
10	**Niccolo Canepa**	ITA	59	Althea Racing	Ducati 1199 Panigale R EVO	P	33.479s	16
11	**Luca Scassa**	ITA	23	Team Pedercini	Kawasaki ZX-10R EVO	P	40.689s	16
12	**David Salom**	ESP	44	Kawasaki Racing Team	Kawasaki ZX-10R EVO	P	40.803s	16
13	**Leon Camier**	GBR	19	BMW Motorrad Italia SBK	BMW S1000 RR EVO	P	41.086s	16
14	**Claudio Corti**	ITA	71	MV Agusta RC-Yakhnich M.	MV Agusta F4 RR	P	41.410s	16
15	**Jeremy Guarnoni**	FRA	11	MRS Kawasaki	Kawasaki ZX-10R EVO	P	41.977s	16
16	Sheridan Morais	RSA	32	IRON BRAIN Grillini Kawasaki	Kawasaki ZX-10R EVO	P	1m 08.454s	16
17	Alessandro Andreozzi	ITA	21	Team Pedercini	Kawasaki ZX-10R EVO	P	1m 19.067s	16
18	Kervin Bos	NED	77	Winteb LiquidRubber Racing T.	Honda CBR1000RR EVO	P	1m 19.076s	16
19	Geoff May	USA	99	Team Hero EBR	EBR 1190 RX	P	1m 29.475s	16
20	Imre Toth	HUN	10	BMW Team Toth	BMW S1000 RR	P	1 Lap	15
	Michel Fabrizio	ITA	84	IRON BRAIN Grillini Kawasaki	Kawasaki ZX-10R EVO	P	DNF	9
	Eugene Laverty	IRL	58	Voltcom Crescent Suzuki	Suzuki GSX-R1000	P	DNF	6
	Aaron Yates	USA	20	Team Hero EBR	EBR 1190 RX	P	DNF	6
	Peter Sebestyen	HUN	56	BMW Team Toth	BMW S1000 RR EVO	P	DNF	2
	Davide Giugliano	ITA	34	Ducati Superbike Team	Ducati 1199 Panigale R	P	DNF	0
	Fabien Foret	FRA	9	MAHI Racing Team India	Kawasaki ZX-10R EVO	P	DNS	0
	Ayrton Badovini	ITA	86	Team Bimota Alstare	Bimota BB3 EVO	P	STH	16
	Christian Iddon	GBR	2	Team Bimota Alstare	Bimota BB3 EVO	P	STH	8

Fastest race lap: Sylvain Guintoli on lap 3, 1m 36.440s, 105.352mph/169.548km/h.

Lap record: Tom Sykes, GBR (Kawasaki), 1m 35.893s, 105.956mph/170.520km/h (2013).

Race 2: 10 laps, 28.223 miles/45.420km

Time of race: 19m 9.464s · **Average speed:** 88.391mph/142.251km/h

Pos.	Rider	Time & Gap	Laps
1	**Jonathan Rea**		10
2	**Alex Lowes**	2.222s	10
3	**Davide Giugliano**	4.955s	10
4	**Tom Sykes**	13.089s	10
5	**Leon Haslam**	13.639s	10
6	**Marco Melandri**	18.041s	10
7	**Loris Baz**	21.837s	10
8	**Chaz Davies**	26.919s	10
9	**Sylvain Guintoli**	32.766s	10
10	**Niccolo Canepa**	37.965s	10
11	**Kervin Bos**	44.141s	10
12	**Luca Scassa**	1m 23.769s	10
13	**Sheridan Morais**	1m 45.062s	10
14	**Michel Fabrizio**	1 Lap	9
15	**David Salom**	1 Lap	9
16	Imre Toth	1 Lap	9
	Eugene Laverty	DNF	7
	Claudio Corti	DNF	6
	Leon Camier	DNF	6
	Alessandro Andreozzi	DNF	4
	Toni Elias	DNF	2
	Fabien Foret	DNF	2
	Jeremy Guarnoni	DNF	0
	Christian Iddon	STH	10
	Ayrton Badovini	STH	0

	Superpole	
1	Baz	1m 34.357s
2	Guintoli	1m 34.845s
3	Sykes	1m 35.311s
4	Melandri	1m 35.333s
5	Rea	1m 35.361s
6	Giugliano	1m 35.476s
7	Canepa	1m 35.500s
8	Laverty	1m 35.646s
9	Lowes	1m 35.684s
10	Elias	1m 36.203s
11	Haslam	1m 36.284s
12	Davies	1m 36.288s
13	Camier	1m 36.434s
14	Badovini	1m 36.547s
15	Salom	1m 36.749s
16	Iddon	1m 36.772s
17	Corti	1m 36.888s
18	Guarnoni	1m 37.141s
19	Morais	1m 37.280s
20	Scassa	1m 37.343s

Fastest race lap: Alex Lowes on lap 9, 1m 52.975s, 89.933mph/144.733km/h.

Points

1, Sykes 108; 2,Guintoli 96; 3, Baz 93; 4, Rea 89; 5, Melandri 69; 6, Giugliano 59; 7, Davies 47; 8, Laverty 46; 9, Haslam 44; 10, Lowes 36; 11, Elias 34; 12, Canepa 28; 13, Salom 27; 14, Scassa 11; 15, Camier 11; 16, Morais 10; 17, Foret 9; 18, Allerton 6; 19, Bos 5; 20, Corti 5; 21, Guarnoni 5; 22, Fabrizio 2.

Race 1: 19 laps, 58.275 miles/93.784km

Time of race: 34m 14.829s · **Average speed:** 102.096mph/164.307km/h

Pos.	Rider	Nat.	No.	Entrant	Machine	Tyres	Time & Gap	Laps
1	**Jonathan Rea**	GBR	65	PATA Honda World Superbike	Honda CBR1000RR	P		19
2	**Chaz Davies**	GBR	7	Ducati Superbike Team	Ducati 1199 Panigale R	P	4.511s	19
3	**Tom Sykes**	GBR	1	Kawasaki Racing Team	Kawasaki ZX-10R	P	6.492s	19
4	**Loris Baz**	FRA	76	Kawasaki Racing Team	Kawasaki ZX-10R	P	8.434s	19
5	**Sylvain Guintoli**	FRA	50	Aprilia Racing Team	Aprilia RSV4 Factory	P	9.134s	19
6	**Marco Melandri**	ITA	33	Aprilia Racing Team	Aprilia RSV4 Factory	P	14.925s	19
7	**Eugene Laverty**	IRL	58	Voltcom Crescent Suzuki	Suzuki GSX-R1000	P	19.973s	19
8	**Alex Lowes**	GBR	22	Voltcom Crescent Suzuki	Suzuki GSX-R1000	P	21.582s	19
9	**Toni Elias**	ESP	24	Red Devils Roma	Aprilia RSV4 Factory	P	28.781s	19
10	**Leon Haslam**	GBR	91	PATA Honda World Superbike	Honda CBR1000RR	P	31.245s	19
11	**Leon Camier**	GBR	19	BMW Motorrad Italia SBK	BMW S1000 RR EVO	P	40.996s	19
12	**David Salom**	ESP	44	Kawasaki Racing Team	Kawasaki ZX-10R EVO	P	55.372s	19
13	**Luca Scassa**	ITA	23	Team Pedercini	Kawasaki ZX-10R EVO	P	55.899s	19
14	**Jeremy Guarnoni**	FRA	11	MRS Kawasaki	Kawasaki ZX-10R EVO	P	1m 04.402s	19
15	**Alessandro Andreozzi**	ITA	21	Team Pedercini	Kawasaki ZX-10R EVO	P	1m 23.074s	19
16	Fabien Foret	FRA	9	MAHI Racing Team India	Kawasaki ZX-10R EVO	P	1m 23.324s	19
17	Sheridan Morais	RSA	32	IRON BRAIN Grillini Kawasaki	Kawasaki ZX-10R EVO	P	1m 36.763s	19
18	Claudio Corti	ITA	71	MV Agusta RC-Yakhnich M.	MV Agusta F4 RR	P	1m 36.942s	19
19	Peter Sebestyen	HUN	56	BMW Team Toth	BMW S1000 RR EVO	P	1m 43.545s	19
20	Imre Toth	HUN	10	BMW Team Toth	BMW S1000 RR	P	1m 43.819s	19
	Davide Giugliano	ITA	34	Ducati Superbike Team	Ducati 1199 Panigale R	P	DNF	11
	Michel Fabrizio	ITA	84	IRON BRAIN Grillini Kawasaki	Kawasaki ZX-10R EVO	P	DNF	8
	Aaron Yates	USA	20	Team Hero EBR	EBR 1190 RX	P	DNF	7
	Niccolo Canepa	ITA	59	Althea Racing	Ducati 1199 Panigale R EVO	P	DNF	5
	Ivan Goi	ITA	112	BARNI Racing Team	Ducati 1199 Panigale R EVO	P	DNF	0
	Geoff May	USA	99	Team Hero EBR	EBR 1190 RX	P	DNS	0
	Christian Iddon	GBR	2	Team Bimota Alstare	Bimota BB3 EVO	P	STH	19
	Ayrton Badovini	ITA	86	Team Bimota Alstare	Bimota BB3 EVO	P	STH	7

Fastest race lap: Jonathan Rea on lap 6, 1m 47.532s, 102.681mph/165.249km/h.

Lap record: Tom Sykes, GBR (Kawasaki), 1m 47.274s, 102.928mph/165.647km/h (2013).

Race 2: 19 laps, 58.275 miles/93.784km

Time of race: 34m 14.255s · **Average speed:** 102.124mph/164.353km/h

Pos.	Rider	Time & Gap	Laps
1	**Jonathan Rea**		19
2	**Chaz Davies**	4.095s	19
3	**Sylvain Guintoli**	5.546s	19
4	**Loris Baz**	6.285s	19
5	**Tom Sykes**	7.147s	19
6	**Davide Giugliano**	22.054s	19
7	**Toni Elias**	25.811s	19
8	**Leon Haslam**	26.127s	19
9	**Eugene Laverty**	26.306s	19
10	**Alex Lowes**	33.046s	19
11	**Marco Melandri**	37.788s	19
12	**Leon Camier**	42.415s	19
13	**David Salom**	52.114s	19
14	**Luca Scassa**	59.001s	19
15	**Fabien Foret**	1m 04.364s	19
16	Jeremy Guarnoni	1m 18.512s	19
17	Alessandro Andreozzi	1m 34.487s	19
18	Geoff May	1 Lap	18
19	Imre Toth	1 Lap	18
	Niccolo Canepa	DNF	15
	Sheridan Morais	DNF	10
	Michel Fabrizio	DNF	8
	Peter Sebestyen	DNF	8
	Aaron Yates	DNF	8
	Claudio Corti	DNF	6
	Ivan Goi	DNS	0
	Ayrton Badovini	STH	19
	Christian Iddon	STH	19

	Superpole	
1	Rea	1m 46.289s
2	Guintoli	1m 46.554s
3	Giugliano	1m 46.555s
4	Davies	1m 46.678s
5	Melandri	1m 46.740s
6	Sykes	1m 46.767s
7	Baz	1m 47.014s
8	Laverty	1m 47.715s
9	Canepa	1m 48.240s
10	Haslam	1m 48.242s
11	Camier	1m 48.371s
12	Lowes	No Time
13	Goi	1m 48.632s
14	Salom	1m 48.743s
15	Elias	1m 48.882s
16	Badovini	1m 48.909s
17	Scassa	1m 49.732s
18	Morais	1m 49.781s
19	Iddon	1m 49.997s
20	Fabrizio	1m 50.936s

Fastest race lap: Jonathan Rea on lap 2, 1m 47.356s, 102.849mph/165.520km/h.

Points

1, Rea 139; 2, Sykes 135; 3, Guintoli 123; 4, Baz 119; 5, Davies 87; 6, Melandri 84; 7, Giugliano 69; 8, Laverty 62; 9, Haslam 58; 10, Lowes 50; 11, Elias 50; 12, Salom 34; 13, Canepa 28; 14, Camier 20; 15, Scassa 16; 16,Foret 10; 17, Morais 10; 18, Guarnoni 7; 19, Allerton 6; 20, Bos 5; 21, Corti 5; 22, Fabrizio 2; 23, Andreozzi 1.

Round 5 — DONINGTON PARK, Great Britain · 25 May, 2014 · 2.500-mile/4.023km circuit · WEATHER: Race 1 · Dry · Track 22°C · Air 16°C; Race 2 · Dry · Track 28°C · Air 18°C

Race 1: 23 laps, 57.495 miles/92.529km
Time of race: 34m 23.929s · Average speed: 100.285mph/161.393km/h

Pos.	Rider	Nat.	No.	Entrant	Machine	Tyres	Time & Gap	Laps
1	**Tom Sykes**	GBR	1	Kawasaki Racing Team	Kawasaki ZX-10R	P		23
2	**Loris Baz**	FRA	76	Kawasaki Racing Team	Kawasaki ZX-10R	P	1.538s	23
3	**Alex Lowes**	GBR	22	Voltcom Crescent Suzuki	Suzuki GSX-R1000	P	6.394s	23
4	**Marco Melandri**	ITA	33	Aprilia Racing Team	Aprilia RSV4 Factory	P	11.875s	23
5	**Chaz Davies**	GBR	7	Ducati Superbike Team	Ducati 1199 Panigale R	P	14.514s	23
6	**Jonathan Rea**	GBR	65	PATA Honda World Superbike	Honda CBR1000RR	P	14.708s	23
7	**Sylvain Guintoli**	FRA	50	Aprilia Racing Team	Aprilia RSV4 Factory	P	18.483s	23
8	**Leon Haslam**	GBR	91	PATA Honda World Superbike	Honda CBR1000RR	P	29.295s	23
9	**Toni Elias**	ESP	24	Red Devils Roma	Aprilia RSV4 Factory	P	31.291s	23
10	David Salom	ESP	44	Kawasaki Racing Team	Kawasaki ZX-10R EVO	P	46.953s	23
11	**Niccolo Canepa**	ITA	59	Althea Racing	Ducati 1199 Panigale R EVO	P	47.170s	23
12	**Fabien Foret**	FRA	9	MAHI Racing Team India	Kawasaki ZX-10R EVO	P	1m 02.583s	23
13	Jeremy Guarnoni	FRA	11	MRS Kawasaki	Kawasaki ZX-10R EVO	P	1m 06.195s	23
14	Alessandro Andreozzi	ITA	21	Team Pedercini	Kawasaki ZX-10R EVO	P	1m 11.244s	23
15	**Claudio Corti**	ITA	71	MV Agusta RC-Yakhnich M.	MV Agusta F4 RR	P	1m 12.643s	23
16	Romain Lanusse	FRA	98	Team Pedercini	Kawasaki ZX-10R EVO	P	1m 22.209s	23
17	Aaron Yates	USA	20	Team Hero EBR	EBR 1190 RX	P	1 Lap	22
18	Imre Toth	HUN	10	BMW Team Toth	BMW S1000 RR	P	1 Lap	22
19	Sheridan Morais	RSA	32	IRON BRAIN Grillini Kawasaki	Kawasaki ZX-10R EVO	P	2 Laps	21
	Davide Giugliano	ITA	34	Ducati Superbike Team	Ducati 1199 Panigale R	P	DNF	16
	Eugene Laverty	IRL	58	Voltcom Crescent Suzuki	Suzuki GSX-R1000	P	DNF	4
	Ayrton Badovini	ITA	86	Team Bimota Alstare	Bimota BB3 EVO	P	STH	23
	Christian Iddon	GBR	2	Team Bimota Alstare	Bimota BB3 EVO	P	STH	4

Race 2: 23 laps, 57.495 miles/92.529km
Time of race: 34m 14.134s · Average speed: 100.763mph/162.163km/h

Pos.	Rider	Time & Gap	Laps
1	**Tom Sykes**		23
2	**Loris Baz**	3.678s	23
3	**Sylvain Guintoli**	7.376s	23
4	**Davide Giugliano**	10.827s	23
5	**Chaz Davies**	15.140s	23
6	**Jonathan Rea**	17.975s	23
7	**Leon Haslam**	33.737s	23
8	**Toni Elias**	40.362s	23
9	**Alex Lowes**	41.465s	23
10	**David Salom**	48.929s	23
11	**Niccolo Canepa**	49.229s	23
12	**Claudio Corti**	57.984s	23
13	**Eugene Laverty**	1m 00.751s	23
14	**Jeremy Guarnoni**	1m 01.697s	23
15	**Alessandro Andreozzi**	1m 03.349s	23
16	Sheridan Morais	1m 03.820s	23
17	Marco Melandri	1m 05.485s	23
18	Fabien Foret	1m 11.049s	23
19	Romain Lanusse	1m 15.943s	23
20	Imre Toth	1 Lap	22
	Aaron Yates	DNF	9
	Ayrton Badovini	STH	23
	Christian Iddon	STH	23

Superpole (Wet)

1	Giugliano	1m 44.903s
2	Haslam	1m 45.009s
3	Melandri	1m 45.111s
4	Lowes	1m 45.258s
5	Guintoli	1m 45.839s
6	Baz	1m 46.058s
7	Sykes	1m 46.241s
8	Rea	1m 46.306s
9	Elias	1m 46.326s
10	Laverty	1m 47.963s
11	Davies	1m 50.099s
12	Badovini	No Time
13	Iddon	1m 49.541s
14	Corti	1m 49.961s
15	Andreozzi	1m 50.509s
16	Canepa	1m 51.062s
17	Salom	1m 53.656s
18	Camier	No Time
19	Foret	No Time
20	Guarnoni	No Time

Fastest race lap: Tom Sykes on lap 16, 1m 28.779s, 101.366mph/163.133km/h.
Lap record: Tom Sykes, GBR (Kawasaki), 1m 28.074s, 102.178mph/164.439km/h (2013).

Points

1, Sykes185; 2, Rea 159; 3, Baz 159; 4, Guintoli 148; 5, Davies 109; 6, Melandri 97; 7, Giugliano 82; 8, Haslam75; 9, Lowes 73; 10, Laverty 65; 11, Elias 65; 12, Salom 46; 13, Canepa 38; 14, Camier 20; 15, Scassa 16; 16, Foret 14; 17, Guarnoni 12; 18, Corti 10; 19, Morais 10; 20, Allerton 6; 21, Bos 5; 22, Andreozzi 4; 23, Fabrizio 2.

Round 6 — SEPANG, MALAYSIA · 6–8 June, 2014 · 3.447-mile/5.548km circuit · WEATHER: Race 1 · Dry · Track 52°C · Air 32°C; Race 2 · Dry · Track 59°C · Air 36°C

Race 1: 16 laps, 55.158 miles/88.768km
Time of race: 33m 42.359s · Average speed: 98.187mph/158.016km/h

Pos.	Rider	Nat.	No.	Entrant	Machine	Tyres	Time & Gap	Laps
1	**Marco Melandri**	ITA	33	Aprilia Racing Team	Aprilia RSV4 Factory	P		16
2	**Sylvain Guintoli**	FRA	50	Aprilia Racing Team	Aprilia RSV4 Factory	P	0.620s	16
3	**Eugene Laverty**	IRL	58	Voltcom Crescent Suzuki	Suzuki GSX-R1000	P	12.865s	16
4	**Chaz Davies**	GBR	7	Ducati Superbike Team	Ducati 1199 Panigale R	P	15.437s	16
5	**Toni Elias**	ESP	24	Red Devils Roma	Aprilia RSV4 Factory	P	15.723s	16
6	**Jonathan Rea**	GBR	65	PATA Honda World Superbike	Honda CBR1000RR	P	31.304s	16
7	**Leon Haslam**	GBR	91	PATA Honda World Superbike	Honda CBR1000RR	P	34.093s	16
8	**Davide Giugliano**	ITA	34	Ducati Superbike Team	Ducati 1199 Panigale R	P	35.804s	16
9	**David Salom**	ESP	44	Kawasaki Racing Team	Kawasaki ZX-10R EVO	P	42.031s	16
10	**Leon Camier**	GBR	19	BMW Motorrad Italia SBK	BMW S1000 RR EVO	P	49.465s	16
11	**Jeremy Guarnoni**	FRA	11	MRS Kawasaki	Kawasaki ZX-10R EVO	P	53.715s	16
12	**Alessandro Andreozzi**	ITA	21	Team Pedercini	Kawasaki ZX-10R EVO	P	1m 07.783s	16
13	**Bryan Staring**	AUS	67	IRON BRAIN Grillini Kawasaki	Kawasaki ZX-10R EVO	P	1m 10.746s	16
14	**Imre Toth**	HUN	10	BMW Team Toth	BMW S1000 RR	P	1m 18.143s	16
15	**Romain Lanusse**	FRA	98	Team Pedercini	Kawasaki ZX-10R EVO	P	1m 21.026s	16
16	Aaron Yates	USA	20	Team Hero EBR	EBR 1190 RX	P	1m 49.054s	16
	Niccolo Canepa	ITA	59	Althea Racing	Ducati 1199 Panigale R EVO	P	DNF	13
	Sheridan Morais	RSA	32	IRON BRAIN Grillini Kawasaki	Kawasaki ZX-10R EVO	P	DNF	7
	Peter Sebestyen	HUN	56	BMW Team Toth	BMW S1000 RR EVO	P	DNF	6
	Claudio Corti	ITA	71	MV Agusta RC-Yakhnich M.	MV Agusta F4 RR	P	DNF	6
	Fabien Foret	FRA	9	MAHI Racing Team India	Kawasaki ZX-10R EVO	P	DNF	4
	Alex Lowes	GBR	22	Voltcom Crescent Suzuki	Suzuki GSX-R1000	P	DNF	0
	Loris Baz	FRA	76	Kawasaki Racing Team	Kawasaki ZX-10R	P	DNF	0
	Tom Sykes	GBR	1	Kawasaki Racing Team	Kawasaki ZX-10R	P	DNF	0
	Ayrton Badovini	ITA	86	Team Bimota Alstare	Bimota BB3 EVO	P	STH	16
	Christian Iddon	GBR	2	Team Bimota Alstare	Bimota BB3 EVO	P	STH	8

Race 2: 10 laps, 34.474 miles/55.480km
Time of race: 21m 0.424s · Average speed: 98.463mph/158.461km/h

Pos.	Rider	Time & Gap	Laps
1	**Marco Melandri**		10
2	**Sylvain Guintoli**	0.166s	10
3	**Tom Sykes**	2.689s	10
4	**Toni Elias**	5.386s	10
5	**Loris Baz**	5.514s	10
6	**Jonathan Rea**	7.073s	10
7	**Eugene Laverty**	7.476s	10
8	**Chaz Davies**	11.057s	10
9	**Alex Lowes**	15.866s	10
10	**Davide Giugliano**	16.206s	10
11	**Leon Haslam**	16.488s	10
12	**Leon Camier**	23.820s	10
13	**David Salom**	30.653s	10
14	**Jeremy Guarnoni**	31.266s	10
15	**Niccolo Canepa**	43.009s	10
16	Bryan Staring	46.127s	10
17	Sheridan Morais	58.167s	10
18	Imre Toth	1m 00.017s	10
19	Peter Sebestyen	1m 03.574s	10
20	Aaron Yates	1m 13.522s	10
	Romain Lanusse	DNF	5
	Alessandro Andreozzi	DNF	2
	Fabien Foret	DNF	0
	Ayrton Badovini	STH	10
	Christian Iddon	STH	10

Superpole

1	Guintoli	2m 03.002s
2	Sykes	2m 03.108s
3	Giugliano	2m 03.137s
4	Elias	2m 03.160s
5	Melandri	2m 03.971s
6	Baz	2m 04.027s
7	Laverty	2m 04.263s
8	Davies	2m 04.343s
9	Lowes	2m 04.433s
10	Rea	2m 04.514s
11	Haslam	2m 05.202s
12	Salom	2m 06.388s
13	Canepa	2m 05.771s
14	Corti	2m 05.859s
15	Iddon	2m 06.012s
16	Camier	2m 06.184s
17	Morais	2m 06.631s
18	Badovini	2m 06.808s
19	Foret	2m 07.081s
20	Guarnoni	2m 07.220s

Fastest race lap: Marco Melandri on lap 2, 2m 4.884s, 99.377mph/159.931km/h (record).
Previous lap record: New circuit.

Fastest race lap: Marco Melandri on lap 6, 2m 4.991s, 99.291mph/159.794km/h.

Points

1, Sykes 201; 2, Guintoli 188; 3, Rea 179; 4, Baz 170; 5, Melandri 147; 6, Davies 130; 7, Giugliano 96; 8, Laverty 90; 9, Elias 89; 10, Haslam 89; 11, Lowes 80; 12, Salom 56; 13, Canepa 39; 14, Camier 30; 15, Guarnoni 19; 16, Scassa 16; 17, Foret 14; 18, Corti 10; 19, Morais 10; 20, Andreozzi 8; 21, Allerton 6; 22, Bos 5; 23, Staring 3; 24, Toth 2; 25, Fabrizio 2; 26, Lanusse 1.

WORLD SUPERBIKE CHAMPIONSHIP · 2014

Round 7 | **MISANO, Italy** · 22 June, 2014 · 2.626-mile/4.226km circuit · WEATHER: Race 1 · Dry · Track 38°C · Air 29°C; Race 2 · Dry · Track 44°C · Air 28°C

Race 1: 21 laps, 55.144 miles/88.746km

Time of race: 33m 46.932s · **Average speed:** 97.941mph/157.620km/h

Pos.	Rider	Nat.	No.	Entrant	Machine	Tyres	Time & Gap	Laps
1	**Tom Sykes**	GBR	1	Kawasaki Racing Team	Kawasaki ZX-10R	P		21
2	**Loris Baz**	FRA	76	Kawasaki Racing Team	Kawasaki ZX-10R	P	5.012s	21
3	**Marco Melandri**	ITA	33	Aprilia Racing Team	Aprilia RSV4 Factory	P	6.417s	21
4	**Chaz Davies**	GBR	7	Ducati Superbike Team	Ducati 1199 Panigale R	P	7.783s	21
5	**Sylvain Guintoli**	FRA	50	Aprilia Racing Team	Aprilia RSV4 Factory	P	16.248s	21
6	**Toni Elias**	ESP	24	Red Devils Roma	Aprilia RSV4 Factory	P	17.399s	21
7	**Jonathan Rea**	GBR	65	PATA Honda World Superbike	Honda CBR1000RR	P	21.162s	21
8	**Davide Giugliano**	ITA	34	Ducati Superbike Team	Ducati 1199 Panigale R	P	26.393s	21
9	**Eugene Laverty**	IRL	58	Voltcom Crescent Suzuki	Suzuki GSX-R1000	P	26.842s	21
10	**Leon Haslam**	GBR	91	PATA Honda World Superbike	Honda CBR1000RR	P	40.600s	21
11	**David Salom**	ESP	44	Kawasaki Racing Team	Kawasaki ZX-10R EVO	P	42.064s	21
12	**Niccolo Canepa**	ITA	59	Althea Racing	Ducati 1199 Panigale R EVO	P	46.804s	21
13	**Claudio Corti**	ITA	71	MV Agusta Reparto Corse	MV Agusta F4 RR	P	48.909s	21
14	**Ivan Goi**	ITA	112	BARNI Racing Team	Ducati 1199 Panigale R EVO	P	50.429s	21
15	**Sylvain Barrier**	FRA	52	BMW Motorrad Italia SBK	BMW S1000 RR EVO	P	52.452s	21
16	Jeremy Guarnoni	FRA	11	MRS Kawasaki	Kawasaki ZX-10R EVO	P	1m 02.476s	21
17	Riccardo Russo	ITA	48	Team Pedercini	Kawasaki ZX-10R EVO	P	1m 11.815s	21
18	Bryan Staring	AUS	67	IRON BRAIN Grillini Kawasaki	Kawasaki ZX-10R EVO	P	1m 23.649s	21
19	Peter Sebestyen	HUN	56	BMW Team Toth	BMW S1000 RR EVO	P	1 Lap	20
	Sheridan Morais	RSA	32	IRON BRAIN Grillini Kawasaki	Kawasaki ZX-10R EVO	P	DNF	18
	Alex Lowes	GBR	22	Voltcom Crescent Suzuki	Suzuki GSX-R1000	P	DNF	12
	Aaron Yates	USA	20	Team Hero EBR	EBR 1190 RX	P	DNF	10
	Fabien Foret	FRA	9	MAHI Racing Team India	Kawasaki ZX-10R EVO	P	DNF	9
	Matteo Baiocco	ITA	15	Grandi Corse by A.P. Racing	Ducati 1199 Panigale R EVO	P	DNF	7
	Alessandro Andreozzi	ITA	21	Team Pedercini	Kawasaki ZX-10R EVO	P	DNF	5
	Geoff May	USA	99	Team Hero EBR	EBR 1190 RX	P	DNF	4
	Ayrton Badovini	ITA	86	Team Bimota Alstare	Bimota BB3 EVO	P	STH	21
	Christian Iddon	GBR	2	Team Bimota Alstare	Bimota BB3 EVO	P	STH	21

Fastest race lap: Tom Sykes on lap 5, 1m 35.629s, 98.854mph/159.090km/h (record).
Previous lap record: Carlos Checa, ESP (Ducati), 1m 36.080s, 98.388mph/158.340km/h (2012).

Race 2: 21 laps, 55.144 miles/88.746km

Time of race: 33m 55.695s · **Average speed:** 97.519mph/156.942km/h

Pos.	Rider	Time & Gap	Laps		Superpole	
1	**Tom Sykes**		21	1	Sykes	1m 34.883s
2	**Loris Baz**	3.083s	21	2	Giugliano	1m 35.079s
3	**Marco Melandri**	3.413s	21	3	Guintoli	1m 35.106s
4	**Sylvain Guintoli**	5.092s	21	4	Baz	1m 35.254s
5	**Jonathan Rea**	18.975s	21	5	Melandri	1m 35.316s
6	**Toni Elias**	19.365s	21	6	Elias	1m 35.404s
7	**Eugene Laverty**	20.177s	21	7	Davies	1m 35.602s
8	**Alex Lowes**	20.439s	21	8	Rea	1m 35.675s
9	**Davide Giugliano**	33.820s	21	9	Laverty	1m 36.043s
10	**David Salom**	42.156s	21	10	Canepa	1m 36.404s
11	**Sylvain Barrier**	43.581s	21	11	Lowes	1m 36.489s
12	**Leon Haslam**	51.993s	21	12	Haslam	1m 36.515s
13	**Ivan Goi**	53.714s	21			
14	**Riccardo Russo**	59.316s	21	13	Salom	1m 36.843s
15	**Alessandro Andreozzi**	1m 00.914s	21	14	Baiocco	1m 36.931s
16	Niccolo Canepa	1m 01.839s	21	15	Badovini	1m 37.038s
17	Claudio Corti	1m 07.178s	21	16	Corti	1m 37.351s
18	Bryan Staring	1m 13.510s	21	17	Barrier	1m 37.499s
19	Peter Sebestyen	1m 31.715s	21	18	Goi	1m 37.540s
	Jeremy Guarnoni	DNF	17	19	Morais	1m 37.807s
	Geoff May	DNF	16	20	Foret	1m 38.008s
	Chaz Davies	DNF	15			
	Sheridan Morais	DNF	10			
	Matteo Baiocco	DNS	0			
	Fabien Foret	DNS	0			
	Ayrton Badovini	STH	21			
	Christian Iddon	STH	2			

Fastest race lap: Davide Giugliano on lap 2, 1m 36.033s, 98.438mph/158.421km/h.

Points

1, Sykes 251; 2, Guintoli 212; 3, Baz 210; 4, Rea 199; 5, Melandri 179; 6, Davies 143; 7, Giugliano 111; 8, Elias 109; 9, Laverty 106; 10, Haslam 99; 11, Lowes 88; 12, Salom 67; 13, Canepa 43; 14, Camier 30; 15, Guarnoni 19; 16, Scassa 16; 17, Foret 14; 18, Corti 13; 19, Morais 10; 20, Andreozzi 9; 21, Barrier 6; 22, Allerton 6; 23, Bos 5; 24, Goi 5; 25, Staring 3; 26, Russo 2; 27, Toth 2; 28, Fabrizio 2; 29, Lanusse 1.

Round 8 | **PORTIMAO, Portugal** · 6 July, 2014 · 2.853-mile/4.592km circuit · WEATHER: Race 1 · Dry · Track 29°C · Air 21°C; Race 2 · Wet · Track 27°C · Air 21°C

Race 1: 20 laps, 57.067 miles/91.840km

Time of race: 34m 45.568s · **Average speed:** 98.505mph/158.529km/h

Pos.	Rider	Nat.	No.	Entrant	Machine	Tyres	Time & Gap	Laps
1	**Tom Sykes**	GBR	1	Kawasaki Racing Team	Kawasaki ZX-10R	P		20
2	**Sylvain Guintoli**	FRA	50	Aprilia Racing Team	Aprilia RSV4 Factory	P	2.539s	20
3	**Loris Baz**	FRA	76	Kawasaki Racing Team	Kawasaki ZX-10R	P	3.175s	20
4	**Marco Melandri**	ITA	33	Aprilia Racing Team	Aprilia RSV4 Factory	P	4.042s	20
5	**Jonathan Rea**	GBR	65	PATA Honda World Superbike	Honda CBR1000RR	P	7.791s	20
6	**Alex Lowes**	GBR	22	Voltcom Crescent Suzuki	Suzuki GSX-R1000	P	14.772s	20
7	**Davide Giugliano**	ITA	34	Ducati Superbike Team	Ducati 1199 Panigale R	P	14.877s	20
8	**Eugene Laverty**	IRL	58	Voltcom Crescent Suzuki	Suzuki GSX-R1000	P	14.941s	20
9	**David Salom**	ESP	44	Kawasaki Racing Team	Kawasaki ZX-10R EVO	P	26.018s	20
10	**Sylvain Barrier**	FRA	52	BMW Motorrad Italia SBK	BMW S1000 RR EVO	P	26.032s	20
11	**Leon Haslam**	GBR	91	PATA Honda World Superbike	Honda CBR1000RR	P	33.041s	20
12	**Jeremy Guarnoni**	FRA	11	MRS Kawasaki	Kawasaki ZX-10R EVO	P	38.385s	20
13	**Niccolo Canepa**	ITA	59	Althea Racing	Ducati 1199 Panigale R EVO	P	42.237s	20
14	**Riccardo Russo**	ITA	48	Team Pedercini	Kawasaki ZX-10R EVO	P	47.908s	20
15	**Alessandro Andreozzi**	ITA	21	Team Pedercini	Kawasaki ZX-10R EVO	P	1m 03.502s	20
16	Aaron Yates	USA	20	Team Hero EBR	EBR 1190 RX	P	1 Lap	19
17	Gabor Rizmayer	HUN	16	BMW Team Toth	BMW S1000 RR	P	1 Lap	19
18	Chaz Davies	GBR	7	Ducati Superbike Team	Ducati 1199 Panigale R	P	5 Laps	15
	Bryan Staring	AUS	67	IRON BRAIN Grillini Kawasaki	Kawasaki ZX-10R EVO	P	DNF	13
	Peter Sebestyen	HUN	56	BMW Team Toth	BMW S1000 RR EVO	P	DNF	12
	Sheridan Morais	RSA	32	IRON BRAIN Grillini Kawasaki	Kawasaki ZX-10R EVO	P	DNF	6
	Toni Elias	ESP	24	Red Devils Roma	Aprilia RSV4 Factory	P	DNF	5
	Fabien Foret	FRA	9	MAHI Racing Team India	Kawasaki ZX-10R EVO	P	DNF	4
	Geoff May	USA	99	Team Hero EBR	EBR 1190 RX	P	DNF	4
	Ayrton Badovini	ITA	86	Team Bimota Alstare	Bimota BB3 EVO	P	STH	20
	Christian Iddon	GBR	2	Team Bimota Alstare	Bimota BB3 EVO	P	STH	20

Fastest race lap: Tom Sykes on lap 4, 1m 43.167s, 99.567mph/160.237km/h.
Lap record: Tom Sykes, GBR (Kawasaki), 1m 42.475s, 100.239mph/161.319km/h (2013).

Race 2: 18 laps, 51.360 miles/82.656km

Time of race: 34m 55.154s · **Average speed:** 88.250mph/142.024km/h

Pos.	Rider	Time & Gap	Laps		Superpole	
1	**Jonathan Rea**		18	1	Sykes	1m 42.484s
2	**Davide Giugliano**	6.817s	18	2	Rea	1m 42.765s
3	**Chaz Davies**	8.676s	18	3	Davies	1m 42.924s
4	**Alex Lowes**	9.740s	18	4	Melandri	1m 43.038s
5	**Leon Haslam**	11.289s	18	5	Baz	1m 43.048s
6	**Loris Baz**	11.808s	18	6	Guintoli	1m 43.076s
7	**Sylvain Guintoli**	14.169s	18	7	Laverty	1m 43.245s
8	**Tom Sykes**	17.164s	18	8	Giugliano	1m 43.317s
9	**Eugene Laverty**	26.406s	18	9	Haslam	1m 43.475s
10	**Toni Elias**	30.168s	18	10	Barrier	1m 43.754s
11	**Sylvain Barrier**	41.820s	18	11	Lowes	1m 43.840s
12	**Sheridan Morais**	47.434s	18	12	Salom	1m 44.361s
13	**Jeremy Guarnoni**	50.045s	18			
14	**Bryan Staring**	1m 17.436s	18	13	Badovini	1m 44.472s
15	**Riccardo Russo**	1m 24.500s	18	14	Canepa	1m 44.590s
16	Alessandro Andreozzi	1m 30.563s	18	15	Iddon	1m 44.971s
17	David Salom	1m 34.242s	18	16	Morais	1m 45.198s
18	Niccolo Canepa	1m 34.647s	18	17	Staring	1m 45.543s
19	Gabor Rizmayer	1m 47.422s	18	18	Andreozzi	1m 45.805s
	Marco Melandri	DNF	12	19	Corti	No Time
	Geoff May	DNF	6	20	Elias	No Time
	Aaron Yates	DNF	0			
	Peter Sebestyen	DNS	0			
	Ayrton Badovini	STH	18			
	Christian Iddon	STH	18			

Fastest race lap: Chaz Davies on lap 18, 1m 54.118s, 90.012mph/144.861km/h.

Points

1, Sykes 284; 2, Guintoli 241; 3, Baz 236; 4, Rea 235; 5, Melandri 192; 6, Davies 159; 7, Giugliano 140; 8, Laverty 121; 9, Elias 115; 10, Haslam 115; 11, Lowes 111; 12, Salom 74; 13, Canepa 46; 14, Camier 30; 15, Guarnoni 26; 16, Barrier 17; 17, Scassa 16; 18, Foret 14; 19, Morais 14; 20, Corti 13; 21, Andreozzi 10; 22, Allerton 6; 23, Bos 5; 24, Staring 5; 25, Goi 5; 26, Russo 5; 27, Toth 2; 28, Fabrizio 2; 29, Lanusse 1.

Round 9 — **LAGUNA SECA, USA** · 13 July, 2014 · 2.243-mile/3.610km circuit · WEATHER: Race 1 · Dry · Track 38°C · Air 21°C; Race 2 · Dry · Track 49°C · Air 20°C

Race 1: 25 laps, 56.079 miles/90.250km

Time of race: 35m 7.782s · **Average speed:** 95.780mph/154.143km/h

Pos.	Rider	Nat.	No.	Entrant	Machine	Tyres	Time & Gap	Laps
1	**Marco Melandri**	ITA	33	Aprilia Racing Team	Aprilia RSV4 Factory	P		25
2	**Sylvain Guintoli**	FRA	50	Aprilia Racing Team	Aprilia RSV4 Factory	P	0.905s	25
3	**Tom Sykes**	GBR	1	Kawasaki Racing Team	Kawasaki ZX-10R	P	6.627s	25
4	**Davide Giugliano**	ITA	34	Ducati Superbike Team	Ducati 1199 Panigale R	P	13.574s	25
5	**Toni Elias**	ESP	24	Red Devils Roma	Aprilia RSV4 Factory	P	13.855s	25
6	**Jonathan Rea**	GBR	65	PATA Honda World Superbike	Honda CBR1000RR	P	15.575s	25
7	**Leon Haslam**	GBR	91	PATA Honda World Superbike	Honda CBR1000RR	P	18.820s	25
8	**Alex Lowes**	GBR	22	Voltcom Crescent Suzuki	Suzuki GSX-R1000	P	20.184s	25
9	**Loris Baz**	FRA	76	Kawasaki Racing Team	Kawasaki ZX-10R	P	34.479s	25
10	**David Salom**	ESP	44	Kawasaki Racing Team	Kawasaki ZX-10R EVO	P	37.463s	25
11	**Niccolo Canepa**	ITA	59	Althea Racing	Ducati 1199 Panigale R EVO	P	45.440s	25
12	**Sylvain Barrier**	FRA	52	BMW Motorrad Italia SBK	BMW S1000 RR EVO	P	47.538s	25
13	**Bryan Staring**	AUS	67	IRON BRAIN Grillini Kawasaki	Kawasaki ZX-10R EVO	P	49.750s	25
14	**Jeremy Guarnoni**	FRA	11	MRS Kawasaki	Kawasaki ZX-10R EVO	P	55.420s	25
15	**Leon Camier**	GBR	19	MV Agusta Reparto Corse	MV Agusta F4 RR	P	58.449s	25
16	Alessandro Andreozzi	ITA	21	Team Pedercini	Kawasaki ZX-10R EVO	P	1m 08.922s	25
17	Gabor Rizmayer	HUN	16	BMW Team Toth	BMW S1000 RR	P	1m 17.853s	25
18	Geoff May	USA	99	Team Hero EBR	EBR 1190 RX	P	1m 18.084s	25
19	Chris Ulrich	USA	18	GEICO Motorcycle Road Rac.	Honda CBR1000RR	P	1 Lap	24
20	Sheridan Morais	RSA	32	IRON BRAIN Grillini Kawasaki	Kawasaki ZX-10R EVO	P	3 Laps	22
	Larry Pegram	USA	72	Foremost Insurance EBR	EBR 1190 RX	P	DNF	22
	Peter Sebestyen	HUN	56	BMW Team Toth	BMW S1000 RR EVO	P	DNF	15
	Aaron Yates	USA	20	Team Hero EBR	EBR 1190 RX	P	DNF	13
	Eugene Laverty	IRL	58	Voltcom Crescent Suzuki	Suzuki GSX-R1000	P	DNF	7
	Chaz Davies	GBR	7	Ducati Superbike Team	Ducati 1199 Panigale R	P	DNF	1
	Christian Iddon	GBR	2	Team Bimota Alstare	Bimota BB3 EVO	P	STH	25
	Ayrton Badovini	ITA	86	Team Bimota Alstare	Bimota BB3 EVO	P	STH	7

Fastest race lap: Sylvain Guintoli on lap 7, 1m 23.559s, 96.642mph/155.531km/h.
Previous lap record: Davide Giugliano, ITA (Ducati), 1m 23.707s, 96.472mph/155.256km/h (2013).

Race 2: 7 laps, 15.702 miles/25.270km

Time of race: 9m 51.346s · **Average speed:** 95.591mph/153.839km/h

Pos.	Rider	Time & Gap	Laps		Superpole	
1	**Tom Sykes**		7	1	Sykes	1m 21.811s
2	**Sylvain Guintoli**	1.014s	7	2	Guintoli	1m 22.339s
3	**Jonathan Rea**	2.793s	7	3	Davies	1m 22.384s
4	**Eugene Laverty**	3.681s	7	4	Giugliano	1m 22.422s
5	**Toni Elias**	4.165s	7	5	Melandri	1m 22.704s
6	**Loris Baz**	7.160s	7	6	Laverty	1m 22.725s
7	**Leon Haslam**	7.331s	7	7	Haslam	1m 23.181s
8	**David Salom**	15.061s	7	8	Baz	1m 23.242s
9	**Alessandro Andreozzi**	15.674s	7	9	Elias	1m 23.358s
10	**Leon Camier**	17.015s	7	10	Rea	1m 23.501s
11	**Jeremy Guarnoni**	18.338s	7	11	Lowes	1m 23.562s
12	**Bryan Staring**	19.270s	7	12	Canepa	1m 23.924s
13	**Sheridan Morais**	20.040s	7			
14	**Larry Pegram**	23.845s	7	13	Barrier	1m 23.840s
15	**Gabor Rizmayer**	25.592s	7	14	Iddon	1m 24.024s
16	Geoff May	26.688s	7	15	Salom	1m 24.227s
17	Chris Ulrich	31.893s	7	16	Badovini	1m 24.301s
	Davide Giugliano	DNF	2	17	Staring	1m 24.986s
	Marco Melandri	DNF	2	18	Morais	1m 25.021s
	Niccolo Canepa	DNF	0	19	Camier	1m 25.157s
	Sylvain Barrier	DNS	0	20	Andreozzi	1m 25.383s
	Alex Lowes	DNS	0			
	Peter Sebestyen	DNS	0			
	Chaz Davies	DNS	0			
	Aaron Yates	DNS	0			
	Ayrton Badovini	STH	7			
	Christian Iddon	STH	7			

Fastest race lap: Davide Giugliano on lap 2, 1m 23.403s, 96.823mph/155.822km/h (record).

Points

1, Sykes 325; 2, Guintoli 281; 3, Rea 261; 4, Baz 253; 5, Melandri 217; 6, Davies 159; 7, Giugliano 153; 8, Elias 137; 9, Laverty 134; 10, Haslam 133; 11, Lowes 119; 12, Salom 88; 13, Canepa 51; 14, Camier 37; 15, Guarnoni 33; 16, Barrier 21; 17, Andreozzi 17; 18, Morais 17; 19, Scassa 16; 20, Foret 14; 21, Corti 13; 22, Staring 12; 23, Allerton 6; 24, Bos 5; 25, Goi 5; 26, Russo 5; 27, Pegram 2; 28, Toth 2; 29, Fabrizio 2; 30, Rizmayer 1; 31, Lanusse 1.

Round 10 — **JEREZ, Spain** · 7 September, 2014 · 2.748-mile/4.423km circuit · WEATHER: Race 1 · Dry · Track 26°C · Air 23°C; Race 2 · Dry · Track 40°C · Air 28°C

Race 1: 20 laps, 54.966 miles/88.460km

Time of race: 34m 20.164s · **Average speed:** 96.050mph/154.578km/h

Pos.	Rider	Nat.	No.	Entrant	Machine	Tyres	Time & Gap	Laps
1	**Marco Melandri**	ITA	33	Aprilia Racing Team	Aprilia RSV4 Factory	P		20
2	**Sylvain Guintoli**	FRA	50	Aprilia Racing Team	Aprilia RSV4 Factory	P	1.397s	20
3	**Chaz Davies**	GBR	7	Ducati Superbike Team	Ducati 1199 Panigale R	P	4.283s	20
4	**Jonathan Rea**	GBR	65	PATA Honda World Superbike	Honda CBR1000RR	P	5.705s	20
5	**Tom Sykes**	GBR	1	Kawasaki Racing Team	Kawasaki ZX-10R	P	6.979s	20
6	**Eugene Laverty**	IRL	58	Voltcom Crescent Suzuki	Suzuki GSX-R1000	P	7.342s	20
7	**Leon Haslam**	GBR	91	PATA Honda World Superbike	Honda CBR1000RR	P	14.868s	20
8	**Toni Elias**	ESP	24	Red Devils Roma	Aprilia RSV4 Factory	P	23.853s	20
9	**David Salom**	ESP	44	Kawasaki Racing Team	Kawasaki ZX-10R EVO	P	25.886s	20
10	**Sylvain Barrier**	FRA	52	BMW Motorrad Italia SBK	BMW S1000 RR EVO	P	26.536s	20
11	**Jeremy Guarnoni**	FRA	11	MRS Kawasaki	Kawasaki ZX-10R EVO	P	41.308s	20
12	**Alessandro Andreozzi**	ITA	21	Team Pedercini	Kawasaki ZX-10R EVO	P	46.672s	20
13	**Sheridan Morais**	RSA	32	IRON BRAIN Grillini Kawasaki	Kawasaki ZX-10R EVO	P	48.742s	20
14	**Niccolo Canepa**	ITA	59	Althea Racing	Ducati 1199 Panigale R EVO	P	50.131s	20
15	**Claudio Corti**	ITA	71	MV Agusta Reparto Corse	MV Agusta F4 RR	P	1m 03.677s	20
16	Gabor Rizmayer	HUN	16	BMW Team Toth	BMW S1000 RR EVO	P	1m 14.881s	20
17	Geoff May	USA	99	Team Hero EBR	EBR 1190 RX	P	1m 22.832s	20
18	Imre Toth	HUN	10	BMW Team Toth	BMW S1000 RR EVO	P	1m 35.170s	20
	Aaron Yates	USA	20	Team Hero EBR	EBR 1190 RX	P	DNF	16
	Loris Baz	FRA	76	Kawasaki Racing Team	Kawasaki ZX-10R	P	DNF	13
	Alex Lowes	GBR	22	Voltcom Crescent Suzuki	Suzuki GSX-R1000	P	DNF	13
	Davide Giugliano	ITA	34	Ducati Superbike Team	Ducati 1199 Panigale R	P	DNF	11
	Bryan Staring	AUS	67	IRON BRAIN Grillini Kawasaki	Kawasaki ZX-10R EVO	P	DNF	7

Fastest race lap: Davide Giugliano on lap 2, 1m 41.939s, 97.058mph/156.199km/h.
Lap record: Tom Sykes, GBR (Kawasaki), 1m 41.691s, 97.294mph/156.580km/h (2013).

Race 2: 20 laps, 54.966 miles/88.460km

Time of race: 34m 25.940s · **Average speed:** 95.782mph/154.146km/h

Pos.	Rider	Time & Gap	Laps		Superpole	
1	**Marco Melandri**		20	1	Baz	1m 40.298s
2	**Sylvain Guintoli**	2.845s	20	2	Giugliano	1m 40.533s
3	**Tom Sykes**	6.097s	20	3	Sykes	1m 40.561s
4	**Chaz Davies**	7.749s	20	4	Melandri	1m 40.822s
5	**Jonathan Rea**	7.935s	20	5	Guintoli	1m 40.877s
6	**Eugene Laverty**	10.510s	20	6	Laverty	1m 41.092s
7	**Loris Baz**	16.078s	20	7	Davies	1m 41.199s
8	**Leon Haslam**	16.098s	20	8	Haslam	1m 41.338s
9	**Alex Lowes**	16.554s	20	9	Lowes	1m 41.421s
10	**Toni Elias**	25.840s	20	10	Rea	1m 41.447s
11	**Sylvain Barrier**	36.839s	20	11	Elias	1m 41.882s
12	**Sheridan Morais**	55.531s	20	12	Barrier	1m 42.928s
13	**Jeremy Guarnoni**	55.980s	20			
14	**Gabor Rizmayer**	1m 18.354s	20	13	Salom	1m 42.329s
15	**Niccolo Canepa**	1m 26.338s	20	14	Canepa	1m 42.356s
16	Aaron Yates	1m 31.468s	20	15	Andreozzi	1m 42.622s
	Alessandro Andreozzi	DNF	12	16	Morais	1m 43.380s
	Imre Toth	DNF	11	17	Guarnoni	1m 43.628s
	Geoff May	DNF	10	18	Staring	1m 43.640s
	Claudio Corti	DNF	6	19	Corti	1m 43.651s
	Davide Giugliano	DNF	2	20	Toth	1m 44.633s
	David Salom	DNF	1			
	Bryan Staring	DNS	0			

Fastest race lap: Sylvain Guintoli on lap 3, 1m 42.223s, 96.788mph/155.765km/h.

Points

1, Sykes 352; 2, Guintoli 321; 3, Rea 285; 4, Melandri 267; 5, Baz 262; 6, Davies 188; 7, Laverty 154; 8, Giugliano 153; 9, Elias 151; 10, Haslam 150; 11, Lowes 126; 12, Salom 95; 13, Canepa 54; 14, Guarnoni 41; 15, Camier 37; 16, Barrier 32; 17, Morais 24; 18, Andreozzi 21; 19, Scassa 16; 20, Foret 14; 21, Corti 14; 22, Staring 12; 23, Allerton 6; 24, Bos 5; 25, Goi 5; 26, Russo 5; 27, Rizmayer 3; 28, Pegram 2; 29, Toth 2; 30, Fabrizio 2; 31, Lanusse 1.

SBK OFFICIAL TIMEKEEPER · TISSOT

Round 11	MAGNY-COURS, France · 5 October, 2014 · 2.741-mile/4.411km circuit · WEATHER: Race 1 · Wet · Track 13°C · Air 14°C; Race 2 · Wet · Track 16°C · Air 14°C

Race 1: 19 laps, , 52.076 miles/83.809km

Time of race: 36m 45.206s · **Average speed:** 85.015mph/136.818km/h

Pos.	Rider	Nat.	No.	Entrant	Machine	Tyres	Time & Gap	Laps
1	Sylvain Guintoli	FRA	50	Aprilia Racing Team	Aprilia RSV4 Factory	P		19
2	Marco Melandri	ITA	33	Aprilia Racing Team	Aprilia RSV4 Factory	P	2.257s	19
3	Jonathan Rea	GBR	65	PATA Honda World Superbike	Honda CBR1000RR	P	5.954s	19
4	Tom Sykes	GBR	1	Kawasaki Racing Team	Kawasaki ZX-10R	P	15.670s	19
5	Loris Baz	FRA	76	Kawasaki Racing Team	Kawasaki ZX-10R	P	16.149s	19
6	Leon Haslam	GBR	91	PATA Honda World Superbike	Honda CBR1000RR	P	29.411s	19
7	Davide Giugliano	ITA	34	Ducati Superbike Team	Ducati 1199 Panigale R	P	57.319s	19
8	Lorenzo Lanzi	ITA	57	3C Racing Team	Ducati 1199 Panigale R	P	59.306s	19
9	Max Neukirchner	GER	27	3C Racing Team	Ducati 1199 Panigale R	P	1m 12.274s	19
10	Sylvain Barrier	FRA	52	BMW Motorrad Italia SBK	BMW S1000 RR EVO	P	1m 22.931s	19
11	Niccolo Canepa	ITA	59	Althea Racing	Ducati 1199 Panigale R EVO	P	1m 39.670s	19
12	Jeremy Guarnoni	FRA	11	MRS Kawasaki	Kawasaki ZX-10R EVO	P	1m 42.886s	19
13	Claudio Corti	ITA	71	MV Agusta Reparto Corse	MV Agusta F4 RR	P	2m 03.253s	19
14	Bryan Staring	AUS	67	IRON BRAIN Grillini Kawasaki	Kawasaki ZX-10R EVO	P	1 Lap	18
15	Fabien Foret	FRA	9	Team Pedercini	Kawasaki ZX-10R EVO	P	1 Lap	18
16	Nicolas Salchaud	FRA	74	Dream Team Company	MV Agusta F4 RR	P	1 Lap	18
17	Sheridan Morais	RSA	32	IRON BRAIN Grillini Kawasaki	Kawasaki ZX-10R EVO	P	2 Laps	17
18	Geoff May	USA	99	Team Hero EBR	EBR 1190 RX	P	2 Laps	17
19	Eugene Laverty	IRL	58	Voltcom Crescent Suzuki	Suzuki GSX-R1000	P	2 Laps	17
20	Imre Toth	HUN	10	BMW Team Toth	BMW S1000 RR	P	3 Laps	16
	Gabor Rizmayer	HUN	16	BMW Team Toth	BMW S1000 RR EVO	P	DNF	7
	Aaron Yates	USA	20	Team Hero EBR	EBR 1190 RX	P	DNF	7
	Xavi Fores	ESP	212	3C Racing Team	Ducati 1199 Panigale R	P	DNF	5
	Alessandro Andreozzi	ITA	21	Team Pedercini	Kawasaki ZX-10R EVO	P	DNF	3
	Toni Elias	ESP	24	Red Devils Roma	Aprilia RSV4 Factory	P	DNF	2
	Alex Lowes	GBR	22	Voltcom Crescent Suzuki	Suzuki GSX-R1000	P	DNF	2
	Chaz Davies	GBR	7	Ducati Superbike Team	Ducati 1199 Panigale R	P	DNF	1

Race 2: 19 laps, 52.076 miles/83.809km

Time of race: 36m 25.402s · **Average speed:** 85.785mph/138.058km/h

Pos.	Rider	Time & Gap	Laps
1	Marco Melandri		19
2	Sylvain Guintoli	2.669s	19
3	Leon Haslam	16.450s	19
4	Tom Sykes	20.759s	19
5	Lorenzo Lanzi	46.689s	19
6	Max Neukirchner	58.490s	19
7	Loris Baz	1m 03.100s	19
8	Claudio Corti	1m 24.699s	19
9	Chaz Davies	1m 27.899s	19
10	Niccolo Canepa	1m 51.706s	19
11	Fabien Foret	1 Lap	18
12	Gabor Rizmayer	2 Laps	17
13	Imre Toth	2 Laps	17
	Bryan Staring	DNF	16
	Eugene Laverty	DNF	14
	Xavi Fores	DNF	12
	Jeremy Guarnoni	DNF	12
	Jonathan Rea	DNF	11
	Sylvain Barrier	DNF	6
	Sheridan Morais	DNF	4
	Davide Giugliano	DNF	3
	Geoff May	DNF	2
	Alex Lowes	DNF	1
	Aaron Yates	DNF	1
	Toni Elias	DNF	0
	Nicolas Salchaud	DNF	0
	Alessandro Andreozzi	DNS	0

	Superpole	
1	Sykes	1m 36.366s
2	Giugliano	1m 36.593s
3	Rea	1m 36.906s
4	Davies	1m 37.021s
5	Guintoli	1m 37.184s
6	Melandri	1m 37.190s
7	Baz	1m 37.215s
8	Lowes	1m 37.270s
9	Laverty	1m 37.407s
10	Haslam	1m 37.575s
11	Fores	1m 37.673s
12	Neukirchner	1m 37.877s
13	Barrier	1m 38.415s
14	Elias	1m 38.621s
15	Lanzi	1m 38.883s
16	Canepa	1m 39.367s
17	Salom	1m 39.452s
18	Corti	1m 39.518s
19	Morais	1m 39.701s
20	Foret	1m 39.850s

Fastest race lap: Marco Melandri on lap 11, 1m 54.013s, 86.544mph/139.279km/h.

Lap record: Tom Sykes, GBR (Kawasaki), 1m 37.932s, 100.755mph/162.149km/h (2013).

Fastest race lap: Sylvain Guintoli on lap 10, 1m 53.660s, 86.812mph/139.711km/h.

Points

1, Sykes 378; 2, Guintoli 366; 3, Melandri 312; 4, Rea 301; 5, Baz 282; 6, Davies 195; 7, Haslam 176; 8, Giugliano 162; 9, Laverty 154; 10, Elias 151; 11, Lowes 126; 12, Salom 95; 13, Canepa 65; 14, Guarnoni 45; 15, Barrier 38; 16, Camier 37; 17, Corti 25; 18, Morais 24; 19, Andreozzi 21; 20, Foret 20; 21, Lanzi 19; 22, Neukirchner 17; 23, Scassa 16; 24, Staring 14; 25, Rizmayer 7; 26, Allerton 6; 27, Bos 5; 28, Toth 5; 29, Goi 5; 30, Russo 5; 31, Pegram 2; 32, Fabrizio 2; 33, Lanusse 1.

Round 12	LOSAIL, Qatar · 2 November, 2014 · 3.343-mile/5.380km circuit · WEATHER: Race 1 · Dry · Track 30°C · Air 27°C; Race 2 · Dry · Track 28°C · Air 25°C

Race 1: 17 laps, 56.831 miles/91.460km

Time of race: 33m 46.738s · **Average speed:** 100.945mph/162.456km/h

Pos.	Rider	Nat.	No.	Entrant	Machine	Tyres	Time & Gap	Laps
1	Sylvain Guintoli	FRA	50	Aprilia Racing Team	Aprilia RSV4 Factory	P		17
2	Loris Baz	FRA	76	Kawasaki Racing Team	Kawasaki ZX-10R	P	2.650s	17
3	Tom Sykes	GBR	1	Kawasaki Racing Team	Kawasaki ZX-10R	P	3.955s	17
4	Jonathan Rea	GBR	65	PATA Honda World Superbike	Honda CBR1000RR	P	4.805s	17
5	Davide Giugliano	ITA	34	Ducati Superbike Team	Ducati 1199 Panigale R	P	7.861s	17
6	Toni Elias	ESP	24	Red Devils Roma	Aprilia RSV4 Factory	P	8.192s	17
7	Chaz Davies	GBR	7	Ducati Superbike Team	Ducati 1199 Panigale R	P	8.991s	17
8	Marco Melandri	ITA	33	Aprilia Racing Team	Aprilia RSV4 Factory	P	10.512s	17
9	Eugene Laverty	IRL	58	Voltcom Crescent Suzuki	Suzuki GSX-R1000	P	15.978s	17
10	Alex Lowes	GBR	22	Voltcom Crescent Suzuki	Suzuki GSX-R1000	P	21.456s	17
11	Leon Haslam	GBR	91	PATA Honda World Superbike	Honda CBR1000RR	P	25.977s	17
12	Niccolo Canepa	ITA	59	Althea Racing	Ducati 1199 Panigale R EVO	P	29.085s	17
13	David Salom	ESP	44	Kawasaki Racing Team	Kawasaki ZX-10R EVO	P	29.096s	17
14	Sylvain Barrier	FRA	52	BMW Motorrad Italia SBK	BMW S1000 RR EVO	P	39.270s	17
15	Bryan Staring	AUS	67	IRON BRAIN Grillini Kawasaki	Kawasaki ZX-10R EVO	P	43.360s	17
16	Jeremy Guarnoni	FRA	11	MRS Kawasaki	Kawasaki ZX-10R EVO	P	46.206s	17
17	Geoff May	USA	99	Team Hero EBR	EBR 1190 RX	P	1m 16.323s	17
18	Imre Toth	HUN	10	BMW Team Toth	BMW S1000 RR	P	1 Lap	16
	Alessandro Andreozzi	ITA	21	Team Pedercini	Kawasaki ZX-10R EVO	P	DNF	7
	Gabor Rizmayer	HUN	16	BMW Team Toth	BMW S1000 RR EVO	P	DNF	6
	Alex Cudlin	AUS	95	Team Pedercini	Kawasaki ZX-10R EVO	P	DNF	2
	Aaron Yates	USA	20	Team Hero EBR	EBR 1190 RX	P	DNF	2
	Claudio Corti	ITA	71	MV Agusta Reparto Corse	MV Agusta F4 RR	P	DNF	1

Race 2: 17 laps, 56.831mi/91.460km

Time of race: 33m 41.803s · **Average speed:** 101.192mph/162.853km/h

Pos.	Rider	Time & Gap	Laps
1	Sylvain Guintoli		17
2	Jonathan Rea	3.568s	17
3	Tom Sykes	5.092s	17
4	Marco Melandri	8.305s	17
5	Chaz Davies	8.390s	17
6	Toni Elias	8.654s	17
7	Loris Baz	9.115s	17
8	Davide Giugliano	13.015s	17
9	Alex Lowes	13.478s	17
10	Leon Haslam	25.471s	17
11	David Salom	37.964s	17
12	Niccolo Canepa	38.001s	17
13	Bryan Staring	46.248s	17
14	Claudio Corti	51.926s	17
15	Alessandro Andreozzi	56.331s	17
16	Geoff May	1m 23.937s	17
17	Imre Toth	1 Lap	16
18	Alex Cudlin	1 Lap	16
	Sylvain Barrier	DNF	5
	Aaron Yates	DNF	4
	Jeremy Guarnoni	DNF	3
	Eugene Laverty	DNF	2

	Superpole	
1	Giugliano	1m 57.033s
2	Baz	1m 57.281s
3	Sykes	1m 57.468s
4	Davies	1m 57.562s
5	Guintoli	1m 57.833s
6	Haslam	1m 58.005s
7	Rea	1m 58.190s
8	Melandri	1m 58.355s
9	Laverty	1m 58.379s
10	Elias	1m 58.583s
11	Lowes	1m 58.919s
12	Salom	1m 59.015s
13	Barrier	1m 58.918s
14	Canepa	1m 59.492s
15	Andreozzi	1m 59.601s
16	Cudlin	2m 00.439s
17	Staring	2m 00.638s
18	Guarnoni	2m 00.817s
19	May	2m 01.860s
20	Morais	No Time

Fastest race lap: Loris Baz on lap 2, 1m 58.096s, 101.906mph/164.002km/h.

Previous lap record: Ben Spies, USA (Yamaha), 1m 59.041s, 101.097mph/162.700km/h (2009).

Fastest race lap: Sylvain Guintoli on lap 8, 1m 57.906s, 102.070mph/164.266km/h (record).

Points

1, Guintoli 416; 2, Sykes 410; 3, Rea 334; 4, Melandri 333; 5, Baz 311; 6, Davies 215; 7, Haslam 187; 8, Giugliano 181; 9, Elias 171; 10, Laverty 161; 11, Lowes 139; 12, Salom 103; 13, Canepa 73; 14, Guarnoni 45; 15, Barrier 40; 16, Camier 37; 17, Corti 27; 18, Morais 24; 19, Andreozzi 22; 20, Foret 20; 21, Lanzi 19; 22, Staring 18; 23, Neukirchner 17; 24, Scassa 16; 25, Rizmayer 7; 26, Allerton 6; 27, Bos 5; 28, Toth 5; 29, Goi 5; 30, Russo 5; 31, Pegram 2; 32, Fabrizio 2; 33, Lanusse 1.

2014 FINAL POINTS TABLE

Position	Rider	Nationality	Machine	Phillip Island/1	Phillip Island/2	Aragon/1	Aragon/2	Assen/1	Assen/2	Imola/1	Imola/2	Donington/1	Donington/2	Sepang/1	Sepang/2	Misano/1	Misano/2	Portimão/1	Portimão/2	Laguna Seca/1	Laguna Seca/2	Jerez/1	Jerez/2	Magny-Cours/1	Magny-Cours/2	Losail/1	Losail/2	Total Points
1	**Sylvain Guintoli**	FRA	Aprilia	16	25	10	13	25	7	11	16	9	16	20	20	11	13	20	9	20	20	20	20	25	20	25	25	**416**
2	**Tom Sykes**	GBR	Kawasaki	9	16	25	25	20	13	16	11	25	25	–	16	25	8	16	25	25	25	11	16	13	13	16	16	**410**
3	**Jonathan Rea**	GBR	Honda	10	11	16	11	16	25	25	25	10	10	10	10	9	11	11	25	10	16	13	11	16	–	13	20	**334**
4	**Marco Melandri**	ITA	Aprilia	20	8	5	–	10	10	10	5	13	–	25	25	16	16	13	16	–	25	25	25	20	25	8	13	**333**
5	**Loris Baz**	FRA	Kawasaki	11	20	20	20	20	9	13	13	20	20	–	11	20	20	16	10	7	10	–	9	11	9	20	9	**311**
6	**Chaz Davies**	GBR	Ducati	8	9	13	–	9	8	20	20	11	11	13	8	13	–	–	16	–	–	16	13	–	7	9	11	**215**
7	**Leon Haslam**	GBR	Honda	–	10	7	8	8	11	6	8	8	9	9	5	6	4	5	11	9	9	9	8	10	16	5	6	**187**
8	**Davide Giugliano**	ITA	Ducati	13	13	8	9	–	16	–	10	–	13	8	6	8	7	9	20	13	–	–	9	–	–	11	8	**181**
9	**Toni Elias**	ESP	Aprilia	–	7	9	7	11	–	7	9	7	8	11	13	10	10	–	6	11	11	8	6	–	–	10	10	**171**
10	**Eugene Laverty**	IRL	Suzuki	25	–	11	10	–	–	9	7	–	3	16	9	7	9	8	7	–	13	10	10	–	–	7	–	**161**
11	**Alex Lowes**	GBR	Suzuki	–	3	6	–	7	20	8	6	16	7	–	7	–	8	10	13	8	–	–	7	–	–	6	7	**139**
12	**David Salom**	ESP	Kawasaki	7	6	3	6	4	1	4	3	6	6	7	3	5	6	7	–	6	8	7	–	–	–	3	5	**103**
13	**Niccolo Canepa**	ITA	Ducati	6	5	–	5	6	6	–	–	5	5	–	1	4	–	3	–	5	–	2	1	5	6	4	4	**73**
14	**Jeremy Guarnoni**	FRA	Kawasaki	2	–	2	1	2	3	–	2	3	2	5	2	–	–	4	3	2	5	5	3	4	–	–	–	**45**
15	**Sylvain Barrier**	FRA	BMW	–	–	–	–	–	–	–	–	–	–	1	5	6	5	4	–	–	–	6	5	6	2	–	–	**40**
16	**Leon Camier**	GBR	BMW/MV Agusta	–	4	4	3	–	5	4	–	–	6	4	–	–	–	–	–	1	6	–	–	–	–	–	–	**37**
17	**Claudio Corti**	ITA	MV Agusta	3	–	–	–	2	–	–	1	4	–	3	–	–	–	–	–	1	–	3	–	3	8	–	2	**27**
18	**Sheridan Morais**	RSA	Kawasaki	1	2	1	3	–	3	–	–	–	–	–	–	–	–	–	–	4	3	3	4	–	–	–	–	**24**
19	**Alessandro Andreozzi**	ITA	Kawasaki	–	–	–	–	1	–	2	1	4	–	1	1	–	7	4	–	–	–	–	–	–	–	–	1	**22**
20	**Fabien Foret**	FRA	Kawasaki	4	4	–	1	–	–	1	4	–	–	–	–	–	–	–	–	1	5	–	–	–	–	–	–	**20**
21	**Lorenzo Lanzi**	ITA	Ducati	–	–	–	–	–	–	–	–	–	–	–	–	–	–	–	–	–	–	–	–	8	11	–	–	**19**
22	**Bryan Staring**	AUS	Kawasaki	–	–	–	–	–	–	–	–	–	–	3	–	–	2	3	4	–	–	–	–	2	–	1	3	**18**
23	**Max Neukirchner**	GER	Ducati	–	–	–	–	–	–	–	–	–	–	–	–	–	–	–	–	–	–	–	–	7	10	–	–	**17**
24	**Luca Scassa**	ITA	Kawasaki	–	–	–	2	5	4	3	2	–	–	–	–	–	–	–	–	–	–	–	–	–	–	–	–	**16**
25	**Gabor Rizmayer**	HUN	BMW	–	–	–	–	–	–	–	–	–	–	–	–	–	–	–	–	1	–	–	2	–	4	–	–	**7**
26	**Glenn Allerton**	AUS	BMW	5	1	–	–	–	–	–	–	–	–	–	–	–	–	–	–	–	–	–	–	–	–	–	–	**6**
27	**Kervin Bos**	NED	Honda	–	–	–	–	5	–	–	–	–	–	–	–	–	–	–	–	–	–	–	–	–	–	–	–	**5**
28	**Imre Toth**	HUN	BMW	–	–	–	–	–	–	–	–	–	–	2	–	–	–	–	–	–	–	–	–	–	3	–	–	**5**
29	**Ivan Goi**	ITA	Ducati	–	–	–	–	–	–	–	–	–	–	2	3	–	–	–	–	–	–	–	–	–	–	–	–	**5**
30	**Riccardo Russo**	ITA	Kawasaki	–	–	–	–	–	–	–	–	–	–	–	2	2	1	–	–	–	–	–	–	–	–	–	–	**5**
31	**Larry Pegram**	USA	EBR	–	–	–	–	–	–	–	–	–	–	–	–	–	–	–	–	–	2	–	–	–	–	–	–	**2**
32	**Michel Fabrizio**	ITA	Kawasaki	–	–	–	–	–	2	–	–	–	–	–	–	–	–	–	–	–	–	–	–	–	–	–	–	**2**
33	**Romain Lanusse**	FRA	Kawasaki	–	–	–	–	–	–	–	–	–	–	1	–	–	–	–	–	–	–	–	–	–	–	–	–	**1**

THE MAGIC OF MICHAEL

By GORDON RITCHIE

Above: Champion van der Mark leads Cluzel and Rolfo in Malaysia, on his way to one of six wins.

Top right: Cluzel was the only serious challenger to Magic Mikey; he took MV Agusta's first win since Agostini.

Above right: Florian Marino was third overall, and best Kawasaki.

Right: Kev Coghlan was top Yamaha; he placed fifth.

Far right: America's 'PJ' Jacobsen made a solid switch from BSB to race for podiums in WSS.

Photos: Gold & Goose

AFTER a straight Yamaha-versus-Kawasaki and man-to-man fight the previous year, 2014's Supersport World Championship was a riot of new winners, machine variety and a vainglorious mass pursuit of the lone consistent front-runner.

On the whole, it was joyous, anarchic, mischievous and all of the things WSS racing really should be in any season. Not only that, but the average age of the top competitors was still low compared to most previous seasons.

The championship was decided in favour of the Ten Kate-operated Pata Honda team and its 21-year-old rider, Michael van der Mark, with no fewer than two rounds to go. He won five of the first nine rounds, but despite his final supremacy, 2014 was filled by dramas and close competition, causing a resurgence in the status of the whole category.

Van der Mark led the race-win count from the front, but in the first four rounds there were four different winners.

In Australia, at such a difficult track for DOT tyres on a 150bhp 600, Jack Kennedy's (CIA Insurance Honda) engine cried enough, his sudden stop bringing out the red flags after just over half-distance. Following a clean-up, the restarted race, controversially, was just five laps long, but with full points awarded.

In just under eight minutes of mayhem, Jules Cluzel (MV Agusta RC Yakhnich Motorsport), Kev Coghlan (Yamaha DMC-Panavto Yamaha) and Raffaele de Rosa (CIA Insurance Honda) hoovered up the podium points. Early pack leaders Kenan Sofuoglu (Kawasaki Mahi Racing Team India) and Michael van der Mark fell independently of each other at the same turn two left-hander.

The opportunity left by the exit of pole-sitter Sofuoglu and second qualifier van der Mark led to the ambitious next tier of talent finishing almost as one. Cluzel, Coghlan, de Rosa and Florian Marino (Kawasaki Intermoto PonyExpres) were all within 0.347 second of each other, while Roberto Tamburini (San Carlo Puccetti Racing Kawasaki) was only 0.822 second down.

It was MV's first full FIM race win since the last days of Agostini and aggressively earned by Frenchman Cluzel.

At round two in Motorland Aragon, Spain, the results produced a more familiar one-two, with Sofuoglu taking the win and van der Mark second, just 0.869 second back. Cluzel had fallen trying one of his trademark lunges under braking as he vied to keep his triple in touch with the fastest fours at the end of the runway-like straight.

Marino was a massive nine seconds back in third place. Coghlan had been looking for his first win until the over-eager Cluzel took his bike from under him. The Scot recovered to finish fifth, behind the ever improving Lorenzo Zanetti (Pata Honda World Supersport).

At Assen, van der Mark won for the first time at this level, and by almost ten seconds from the chasing Marino. Cluzel

Above: Top three at Assen, and top three in the standings: Marino, van der Mark and Cluzel.

Top right: The fourth man, Zanetti, took a home win at Imola.

Above right: Former champion Sofuoglu had a torrid season, but still won in Motorland Aragon.

Right: The clear winner of the seven-round Superstock 600 Championship was Marco Faccani.

Below right: Ducati rider Leandro Mercado survived atrocious conditions to snatch the Superstock 1000 FIM Cup at Magny-Cours.

Photos: Gold & Goose

was third, but almost 15 seconds down. Coghlan was fourth, Zanetti fifth, but Sofuoglu retired with a technical problem on lap 13. Two DNFs in three rounds? The three-times champion's season was nearly over before it had begun.

More was forthcoming after Sofuoglu had led from lap two to lap 12 at the following round in Imola. His bike ceased normal operations, driving him into the pits and the pit of despair. His cash-strapped team were already running into problems with the expected engine allocation, and the Turk ended his day ninth in the championship standings.

For Zanetti, who led from lap 13 to the very emotional end, Imola was a home win, which he dedicated to the family and memory of his sadly missed countryman, Andrea Antonelli, who had died in the Moscow WSS race in 2013.

Van der Mark was just over two seconds back, while Marino and the rapidly learning American rider Patrick 'PJ' Jacobsen took third and fourth for Kawasaki Intermoto PonyExpres.

Donington was a test of riding ability as usual, but picking up some track debris held back the final push of early leader Sofuoglu, who slid back to fourth, albeit only 1.556 seconds from race winner van der Mark. Cluzel was only 0.114 second off the winner, while Coghlan had led for two laps of his home race and clambered on to the podium with great relief in third.

Zanetti's bike suffered a technical problem and he had to stop with only a few laps left.

There was a marked contrast between the 16°C of the UK and the steamy 32°C of Sepang next time out, but the top two remained van der Mark and Cluzel, with Sofuoglu managing to get on the podium in third, after battling the Go Eleven Kawasaki of Roby Rolfo. The cracks in the Mahi effort had become fissures, however, and they would not see the end of the season.

Zanetti was fifth, and the South-East Asian fans had a semi-local to cheer, as Thailand's Ratthapark Wilairot (Core PTR Honda) took a career-best sixth. Malaysian M. Zaidi (SIC Racing Team) secured ninth in a race that had been wel-

comed on to the calendar for the very first time.

The once annual pilgrimage of the WSS Championship to the seaside at Misano was reinstated, with three different makes of bike on the podium again. Off track, MV had split from the Russian Yakhnich part of the team.

With van der Mark in a more-than-useful 33-point lead, Cluzel was a convincing first-to-last leader, despite van der Mark catching him rapidly in the final few laps. Only 1.5 seconds back at the line, the championship damage was minor for the Dutchman. Jacobsen, third and on the podium for the first time in his short WSS career, was one up on Sofuoglu and two ahead of Tamburini.

As a contest, the championship effectively, if unofficially, came to an end at Portimao, after Cluzel suffered some gearbox issues that made him run off track; he returned to the pits to retire. The race was finished early, after only 12 laps, because of rain, but it included some great fights between the top men. Van der Mark was 1.6 seconds ahead of yet another new podium rider, in the shape of Ireland's Kennedy. A mass of potential and push, he rode with confidence and determination to keep Sofuoglu 0.3 second behind him before the race was stopped.

PI podium rider de Rosa took fourth place, with Jacobsen right with him across the line.

Without the usual WSS race at Laguna, there was a two-month break in the action. Van der Mark filled his time by winning the Suzuka 8 Hours – again – as he brooded about his chances of winning the championship in Spain. He was 53 points ahead of French rival Cluzel, but the battle ended up with far more than two riders trading shots and paint.

There were six changes of lead across the line in the 19 laps at Jerez, but the only one that counted was the last one. Cluzel had attacked the leading duo of Marino and Jacobsen at the final corner of the penultimate lap, but had fallen and run Marino off.

That allowed van der Mark to cut inside and finish off what had begun as a very nervous race for him. Luckily, he got his

head sorted, after almost crashing when he ran wide early on, but he needed all his concentration. The passing and pressure of riders on each other was relentless.

After a breathless race, the four leading riders crossed the line within 0.960 second of each other, in the order van der Mark, Jacobsen, a recovered Marino and Kennedy, all zipping across faster than you could list their names.

Thus Supersport's hall of fame received a new name and a new nationality in champion Michael van der Mark from the Netherlands.

With a month to the next race, at Cluzel's home track in Magny-Cours, you might have thought that he could have gone off the boil, but now his fight was for second overall.

For a while, he was forced to ride like a man possessed in treacherous conditions, just to stay in sight of eight-lap leader Sofuoglu, now on a San Carlo Puccetti Racing Kawasaki. The Turk was setting 1m 58s while the rest were well over two minutes a lap. He seemed headed for win number two and an extension of his all-time record until the most prosaic of issues ended his race on lap nine.

His visor had misted up, he thought because his helmet was still wet inside from its morning warm-up soaking, and he kept lifting and dropping it as the race progressed. Finally he lost his concentration and fell under braking into the hairpin.

While pole-man Cluzel charged on to take the win by over 20 seconds, van der Mark slid off, remounted and fought back through from fifth to go second, four seconds up on veteran Rolfo. The former 250cc winner had shown class and cleverness when it mattered most, which was all the time on a surface that was like polished glass.

Zanetti just missed out on a podium by half a second, and Marino ended his home round fifth.

The fight for the remaining top five championship places was very much on. It may have been no surprise that a rider with vast recent experience of Losail in Moto2's darkness, Ratthapark Wilairot (Core PTR Honda), was the shadow that ensured van der Mark was kept honest to the last.

The new champion duly scored his sixth win of the year, more than half of all the races. Second place was hardly less pleasing for Wilairot, who took his first WSS podium in utterly assured style.

Cluzel rounded out his often-brilliant MV season with another podium and second place overall.

Superstock 1000 FIM Cup

It took a dramatic and soaking finale in France to determine the winner of the seven-round Stock 1000 championship. When sitting in second place at Magny-Cours, Lorenzo Savadori (Kawasaki Team Pedercini) fell and then remounted to finish the race sixth. That result gave the championship to two-times race winner Leandro Mercado (Barni Racing Ducati), who had hung on to finish fourth and won the title by eight points.

Matthieu Lussiana (Garner by ASPI Kawasaki) won the final race and was third overall. Other single race victories were taken by Kevin Valk (MTM Racing Team Kawasaki) and Ondrej Jezek (Barni Racing Team Ducati)

Superstock 600 FIM European Championship

The clear winner of the seven-round Superstock 600 Championship was Marco Faccani (San Carlo Team Italia Kawasaki). He ended his year 43 points ahead of Wayne Tessels (Wayne Racing Team Suzuki) and 53 in front of his teammate, Andrea Tucci.

Faccani took five wins and one no-score at the final round. Finland's Niki Tulli (Kallio Racing Yamaha) finished fourth after a race win at Assen, and one-off rider Toprak Razgatioglu (Bike Service Racing Kawasaki), who had been a regular Turkish representative in the MotoGP Red Bull Rookies Cup, took the final Stock 600 victory in France.

ISLE OF MAN TT
SPEED DATES
By RUPERT PAUL

Above: Michael Dunlop aviates his BMW at Barregarrow, ahead of Brookes and Anstey. It was his first of four wins, also the first for BMW for 75 years.

Photo: Gavan Caldwell

Right: Peter Hickman, fastest newcomer in TT history.

Far right: A new Mountain to climb for Danny Webb.

Photos: David Collister/photocycles.com

Below far right: North-West victim Simon Andrew was remembered on Mad Sunday.

Photo: Gavan Caldwell

FOR 48 weeks of the year, Gorse Lea in the Isle of Man is an indistinct right-hand kink at the western end of Greeba village, just before the famous TT landmark of Ballacraine. But the opening night of TT Superbike practice turns it into a fifth-gear, knee-down borehole through space and time. The precise, violent manner in which the top riders dived into this ultra-high-speed corner – not to mention the 160mph shock wave of displaced air that followed them in – made every fan sitting on the outside wall that first evening flinch. And that's before they saw Michael Dunlop.

Straight-lining the S-bends from the bottom of the village on his Hawk BMW S1000RR, he arrived at the crest outside the old farmhouse with one foot dangling, the front pawing the air and the bike veering across the central white line. For a lesser rider, it might have been a fatal incident. The Irishman merely looked irritated as he reasserted control over the most powerful motorcycle the course has ever seen. Barely shutting off, he wrenched it back on line and hurtled around the bend as if nothing had happened.

"It was a bit of a handful on the first night," he said later.

Thanks largely to dramas like that, the TT continues its breakneck self-reinvention as a global sporting spectacle. In 2013, with North One's TV coverage, it reached an independently audited record 24.4 million viewers. For 2014, new broadcasting deals increased that number again to a record of almost 26 million, an increase on the previous year of 5.7 per cent. The numbers have more than tripled from the 8.1 million start point in 2010, the first year of broadcasting. One hundred and thirty countries around the world now take TT coverage.

It's the same story for the fans who make the considerable effort to visit the races: 39,224 people attended the 2013 event (the latest year for which figures are available), up from 30,787 in 2010. By the end of 2014's TT fortnight, vehicle ferry crossings for the 2015 races were already booked solid

back to the Wednesday before practice week. How many people would go to a MotoGP event if they knew it would rain, that getting there involved a three-and-a-half-hour sea crossing, and that you had to buy your ticket a year in advance? (In August, the Steam Packet Company announced it would be adding an extra deck for bikes to its catamaran ferry, the *Manannan*.)

Yet it's not hard to understand the interest. The drama of Dunlop, Anstey or McGuinness fighting a Superbike at top speed on a 38-mile public road is, quite simply, unavailable anywhere else on earth. Even Valentino Rossi described the TT as "unbelievable".

The 2014 event presented an outstanding mix of established riders and hungry young talent. The big news was that Michael Dunlop had signed to ride a factory BMW, run by Stuart Hicken's seasoned Hawk Racing BSB squad. After a poisonous split with Honda, with whom he'd won four TTs in 2013, Dunlop had talked of taking a year off. But BMW UK's Lee Nicholls had persuaded the German factory to mount a serious effort for the 75th anniversary of Georg Meier's 1939 TT win, and Dunlop (who'd already won TTs on Hondas, Kawasakis and Yamahas) loved the idea of a serious go on a new make of bike.

He arrived in the island with a 225bhp factory WSB motor and an undeveloped (for the TT) S1000RR running Metzeler tyres. Although he had won one of the Superbike races at the North West, in the other he'd been duffed up by his brother, William, prompting a now-famous post-race threat made in the heat of the moment: "You ever do that again..."

By Thursday of practice week, the bike was on Dunlops. It was a PR disaster for the Pirelli-owned Metzeler, but Michael was interested in winning races, and his style needed the full-lean grip of his namesake tyres.

Michael's former Honda team-mate, John McGuinness, was less well placed. He'd broken his scaphoid on a dirt bike

in March – the worst injury of his racing career – and was not back to full fitness. He'd pulled in on the final lap of both Superbike races at the North West. By the end of practice week at the TT, he'd managed 129.79mph on a CBR1000RR Superbike, but six laps at that pace still looked a big ask.

Other fast qualifiers on the Superbikes were Bruce Anstey (Valvoline Padgetts Honda Fireblade) and Guy Martin (Tyco Suzuki GSX-R), both of whom exceeded 130mph laps in practice. Dan Kneen (BE Racing Suzuki GSX-R), Michael Rutter (Bathams BMW S1000RR), Conor Cummins (Honda Racing Fireblade), William Dunlop (Tyco Suzuki GSX-R) and Gary Johnson (Honda Racing Fireblade) all qualified faster than 128mph.

In Superstock, the rapidly improving Dean Harrison, son of sidecar veteran Conrad, was on a practice-week roll after an imperious win on a ZXR750 in the Billown Pre-TT classic races. His 128.622mph lap, on a more or less standard Kawasaki ZX-10R with trick suspension, was only beaten by Michael Dunlop (BMW, 129.333mph) and Gary Johnson (Kawasaki, 130.207mph).

Johnson looked even stronger in the Supersport class, where his Smiths Triumph 675 Daytona was on pole at 125.934mph. The Dunlop brothers (Michael on a Honda, William on a Suzuki), Dean Harrison (Yamaha R6) and the newly-unretired Keith Amor (Honda) were just behind him.

The paddock's darkest mutterings were reserved for the 650cc-twin Lightweight class. Now in its third year, the supposedly low-cost formula had developed to the point where humble ER-6 Kawasakis were being turned into mini superbikes, with trick gearboxes, special ECUs, super-finished crankshafts and fragile 95+bhp engines. A meeting between Lightweight riders and new TT Technical Director Adrian Gorst revealed that 75 per cent of the bikes were, at best, making highly creative use of the rules. There was also the question of the new-for-2014 Italian Paton S1 Strada, which used a Kawasaki 650 engine in a lightweight racing chassis. Paton had obtained the necessary homologation to classify the S1

as a production road bike and hoped to sell replicas after the TT. But up to the beginning of practice week, the only complete S1 on earth was Olie Linsdell's TT racer.

The Lightweight class has become the route most new riders follow to get into TT racing. The 2013 winner, James Hillier, is now an established 130+mph lapper. In 2014, the top qualifiers included three old hands: Ryan Farquhar (back from retirement on one of his own KMR ER-6 Kawasakis), Keith Amor (also KMR) and Linsdell (Flitwick Motorcycles Paton S1).

There were also young guns Jamie Hamilton and James Cowton (Stewart Smith Kawasakis), and Ivan Lintin (McKinstry Kawasaki). Not far behind in qualifying was former 125cc GP and Moto3 racer Danny Webb (KMR Kawasaki). After failing to make a living in grands prix, Webb had switched to the TT as a long-term career. "I race because I love motorbikes, and going to the TT was the best opportunity I had," he said. "It's a new experience and a new challenge."

Webb wasn't the only high-profile short-circuit racer to start in 2014. BSB riders Peter Hickman and Martin Jessopp tried their hands, too. Jessopp had managed an impressive 123.470mph lap by the end of the fortnight. But Hickman ended race week as the fastest newcomer in TT history, lapping at 129.104mph, and beating the record of another BSB star, Josh Brookes – 127.726mph, set in 2013. "I look at someone like Bruce Anstey and I can imagine going around here like him in another 20 years," said Hickman afterwards.

It's easy to imagine short-circuit riders getting to the TT and just going nuts. The truth is they're a lot more methodical. At the TT launch in March, Josh Brookes talked politely to journalists in the bar until 3am, then went out for a lap. "It's the only time the roads are really clear," he said. All the newcomers get their speed from hundreds of laps in cars, on road bikes and on screen.

Yet another newcomer, multiple club champion and former motocrosser Phil Crowe, recorded a 121.593mph lap in the Senior. But more compelling was a video taken by a specta-

Above: Gary Johnson put Triumph back on the top step in the Supersport TT.
Photo: David Collister/photocycles.com

Above right: Michael Dunlop took a second BMW win in Superstock.

Top and top right: The notorious Barregarrow. Guy Martin's Suzuki has both wheels in the air on the approach; Bruce Anstey's Honda is fully bottomed out at the apex. Anstey set a new outright lap record in the Superbike race.
Photos: Gavan Caldwell

Right: Josh Brookes askew exiting Ballaugh in the Supersport race.
Photo: David Collister/photocycles.com

tor of his near miss with the pub at Ballaugh. A tank-slapper had forced him to jump the bridge at around 80mph. The landing bent the footrests of his BMW S1000RR, but he kept going. The video is on his Facebook page.

In a repeat of 2013, TT fortnight demonstrated its grim side. Two riders – well-known Karl Harris (33) and long-time Island racer Bob Price (65) – died in races. Their deaths followed that of factory Honda rider Simon Andrews (29), who passed away in hospital on 19th May from injuries sustained in a crash at the North West. Although that accident was nothing to do with the TT, Andrews was such a charismatic figure that several thousand TT fans joined a remembrance ride around the course, led by James Hillier. And that wasn't the end of it: during TT fortnight, at least three more riders – newcomer Laurent Hoffman, racer Joe Faragher and travelling marshal Paul Hunt – were badly injured.

As is now the norm, four MotoGP riders were due to visit the TT: Bradley Smith, Michael Laverty, Scott Redding and Isle of Man resident Cal Crutchlow. Redding knew Bob Price well; the older man had helped him in his earliest days of racing, and in a passionately worded statement, he announced that he would not attend the races. The online abuse he received from some TT fans for his decision was disgraceful.

Norton's bizarre TT adventure continued for a third year, this time with a top rider, Cameron Donald, riding the Aprilia V4-engined, Spondon-framed superbike. The team suffered several setbacks, and even in Donald's hands the beautiful machine only managed 124.058mph – about the same as a quick 600. It didn't finish a race.

SUPERBIKE

These days, TTs are often won or lost by seconds, so everything depends on being able to set off at lap-record pace. Dunlop did exactly that, using the horsepower of his BMW to catch Anstey before Ramsey and shoot past the Honda in a straight line. By the end of the first lap, the Ulsterman had set a new lap record from a standing start: 131.7mph. Martin (Suzuki) was second, followed by Conor Cummins (Honda), Hillier (Kawasaki), 24-year-old Dean Harrison (Kawasaki) and 27-year-old Manxman Dan Kneen (Suzuki).

Lap two saw McGuinness, Hillier, Martin and Michael Dunlop circulating together over the mountain, and Dunlop breaking his own lap record at 131.89mph. They were still together after their first fuel stops. Ian Hutchinson's Milwaukee Yamaha blew on lap three, and team-mate Josh Brookes wasn't much better off, his R1 clearly wobbling everywhere.

By mid-race, the less experienced riders were beginning to drop back; the order was now Michael Dunlop, Martin, Cummins, Hillier and Michael Rutter on another very fast BMW.

By the second pit stop, at the end of lap four, Anstey (who'd made a rare error on lap one) was still – by his standards – just getting out of bed. Meanwhile, fans were treated to the sight of Martin and Michael Dunlop riding in close formation over the Mountain. Martin had caught Dunlop on the road, but didn't want to risk a pass on a rider who was 25 seconds ahead on corrected time. Anstey finally got going on lap five, charging hard to fourth place, ahead of Rutter and McGuinness, and behind Martin and Cummins. The New Zealander's final lap was simply astonishing: 17 minutes 6.68 seconds meant a new outright TT record of 132.298mph.

But it was too late. Dunlop's early pace had given him total control over the race, and he beat second-placed Guy Martin by 20.6 seconds. It was BMW's first TT win on a big bike for 75 years. "Great job," a delighted Dunlop said afterwards. "We haven't had a lot of time on it, so there's still more to come."

With ten TT podiums, Martin became the most consistent finisher of modern times not to have won a race. "I couldn't have done any more," he said.

Cummins was third, followed by Anstey, Rutter and William Dunlop. McGuinness's wrist, and the slowing effect of backmarkers, dropped him to seventh. "I was in the hunt for fourth before I got held up and I finished the race, so I didn't disgrace myself," was his assessment. Dean Harrison was eighth. One to watch.

SUPERSTOCK

Although overshadowed by the Superbike races, the Superstock formula (trick suspension, stock brakes and engine) is a truer reflection of a streetbike's performance. Michael Dunlop entered on a BMW S1000RR in his own MDR team's colours, but helped by BMW Germany. He'd not ridden it much in practice, and Gary Johnson (Kawasaki) had set the fastest lap – a sizzling 130.207mph.

The race began in sensational style as four riders – Dunlop, Dean Harrison, Gary Johnson and James Hillier (these last three on Kawasakis) – set a similar pace. Unfortunately, the hoped-for titanic scrap failed to materialise. Accelerating through the right-hand kink after Ramsey Hairpin on lap one, Johnson hit a damp patch and flew over the edge of the road into one of the gardens below. The bike burned to a crisp; he escaped with a broken collarbone and neck injuries.

Dunlop kept his head down, and once he had caught Bruce Anstey on the road, he used his information boards around the circuit to keep the hard-charging Dean Harrison at bay.

Dunlop's opening lap was 129.6mph. Behind him at that point were Harrison, Anstey (Honda), Hillier, Cummins (Honda) and Martin (Suzuki). On lap two, there was a big crash at Joey's, just past the Gooseneck, but the race continued. Dunlop's time was almost exactly the same as his first: 127.8mph. Michael Rutter (BMW) made a move on lap three, up to sixth, ahead of the fading Hillier.

Martin was in fifth when a photographer, Janice Ayers, accidentally captured his rear wheel nut flying off on the Cronk-y-Voddy straight. She told a marshal and he was black-flagged, pulling in safely at Ramsey.

Dunlop finished the race unchallenged, with Dean Harrison a superb second, 20 seconds behind, and Anstey third, 24 seconds further back. Australian David Johnson (Kawasaki) was fourth, with Lee Johnston (Honda) and Michael Rutter less than two-tenths apart in sixth and seventh. Dan Kneen (Suzuki) was seventh and newcomer Peter Hickman (BMW) an impressive eighth.

Conor Cummins, who originally placed fourth, was docked two minutes after a race suspension linkage, intended for a Superbike, was spotted on his Honda.

Dunlop was delighted with the performance of his S1000RR: "Nine wins is the same as Bruce and some other great names, and I'm only a young lad." It was only after the celebrations that news of Karl Harris's death hit the paddock. Starting last after a difficult practice week, he'd been carving through backmarkers. At Joey's, he and Joe Faragher had come together. Faragher survived with a broken leg and severe neck lacerations; Harris was not so fortunate.

SUPERSPORT – Races One & Two

In 2014, Supersport was the most hotly contested TT class. The top 20 qualifiers featured an outstanding depth of talent, though not necessarily going as well as they'd have liked. Bruce Anstey (Padgetts Honda), for instance, was ninth, Guy Martin (Tyco Suzuki) tenth and Ian Hutchinson (Milwaukee Yamaha) a depressing 16th. Michael Dunlop (MDR Honda), forced to prioritise setting up his BMW Superbike, was 'only' second quickest. The fastest was Gary Johnson, on a Smiths Triumph 675 Daytona.

After lap one, just ten seconds separated the top five. After lap two, the top three of Johnson, Anstey and Michael Dunlop were still only six seconds apart. Johnson's 126.732mph would be the fastest lap of the race, but the lead fluctuated constantly, particularly as damp conditions on the mountain made the limit very hard to judge. At the finish, Johnson led Anstey by just 1.5 seconds, with Dunlop ten seconds further back. Weather apart, it was as good as the TT gets: relentless pressure to concentrate for four laps, and an uncertain winner until the last possible moment.

Johnson's win was Triumph's first since 2003, when Anstey had been victorious. The post-race celebrations featured large helpings of mutual admiration and respect.

For race two, Michael Dunlop was in determined mood. As well as winning the Superstock race in the previous 48 hours, he had rebuilt the Honda with tuner Chris Mehew and mechanic Mark Kelly. He led from the off, hunting down main rival Bruce Anstey, who'd set off ten seconds in front.

An early retirement by Ian Hutchinson at Glen Darragh Road resulted in the Yorkshireman assaulting his Yamaha R6 in frustration, much to the amusement of the few onlookers.

After Dunlop had caught Anstey, the two circulated closely, initially with Michael's brother, William (Tyco Suzuki), and Harrison (Mar Train Yamaha). By lap two, Michael had dropped those two. By lap three, even Anstey was nine seconds adrift – a gap that had grown by a second on the final lap. In a typical display of sportsmanship, Anstey let Michael Dunlop cross the line first. The race was overshadowed by the death of Bob Price, who was killed at Ballaugh. He had been racing at the Isle of Man for many years.

SIDECAR – Races One & Two

Walk among the sidecar teams in the paddock and before long you'll meet Conrad Harrison. An archetypal Yorkshire engineer, he's been an enormous TT character for 21 years. But in all that time, without winning a race. Or at least he hadn't done until race one in 2014.

The opening lap had Ben and Tom Birchall leading, just, from John Holden and Andy Winkle, and Dave Molyneux and Patrick Farrance. Harrison and passenger Mike Aylott were fourth, closely pursued by 2013's winner, Tim Reeves, this time partnered by Gregory Cluze.

By lap two, Harrison and Aylott were up to third, after the Birchalls, who had extended their lead to ten seconds, crashed at Black Dub (Tom without serious harm; Ben with a nasty hand injury).

When Molyneux and Farrance retired on lap three, Harrison and Aylott were now in second and only just behind the new leaders, Holden and Winkle. Sensing destiny, Harrison put in the fastest lap of his life (114.674mph) to take the win from Holden and Winkle by 17 seconds. Reeves and Cluze were third.

Bad weather meant that race two, scheduled for Wednesday, was held over until Thursday. With occasional damp patches on the course, the lap-one order was Holden/Winkle, Molyneux/Farrance, Harrison/Aylott and an increasingly distant Reeves/Cluze. Lap two produced no change, but on the final lap Holden and Winkle's motor began to slow. Molyneux and Farrance seized the chance to win, with Harrison and Aylott second. Holden and Winkle held on to third, just over five seconds ahead of Reeves and Cluze.

It was Molyneux's 17th TT win, and Farrance's third. Molyneux, who had first raced a sidecar at the TT in 1985, had now won using Honda, Suzuki, Yamaha and Kawasaki engines. For some, it was the greatest achievement by any rider at the 2014 TT.

TT ZERO

Anstey vs McGuinness! The most expensive and advanced bikes on the island! A global showcase for new technology!

Well, yes. At the top end of the leaderboard, the electric race was fought by the best riders and a very clever factory spending millions. And as far as John McGuinness was concerned, it was a proper TT. But there were only ten bikes in the one-lap race. Sending them off took just 90 seconds, and then four broke down.

Factory Mugen riders McGuinness and Anstey had spent a week in Japan testing, and they dominated practice with respective speeds of 115.597mph and 113.642mph. The race went much the same way, with McGuinness – injured scaphoid untroubled by the lower speeds – appearing to have the better bike. He did 154.3mph through the Sulby speed trap and recrossed the line in 19 minutes 17.3 seconds – 117.366mph. Anstey was 23 seconds back, still at an amazing 115.048mph.

The inaugural 2009 electric TT, won by Rob Barber at 85mph, seemed a long time ago. This time, Barber had to settle for third on the Buckeye Current RW-2.x and 95.531mph. Robert Wilson came in just 0.27 second later on the Belgian Sarolea.

In Japan, new battery research holds out the prospect of an electric bike that, pound for pound, could deliver three-quarters of a petrol bike's rear wheel energy (currently it's about a tenth). But right now TT Zero needs more competition. Throwing the race open to other low-carbon technologies would be a start.

LIGHTWEIGHT

Winner in 2013 James Hillier (Quattro Plant Kawasaki) had been strangely slow during practice week. In a master stroke, his crew chief, Bournemouth Kawasaki's Phil Biggs,

had reasoned that the class's ubiquitous road-bike fairings were aerodynamically poor, so he'd fitted an Aprilia 250cc GP fairing and seat. A protest from another team, however, had forced him to use a stock ECU, and it took all week to set up the motor. The team took the bike to the line with fingers crossed.

Fastest qualifier Ivan Lintin (McKinstry Kawasaki) went out almost immediately with an engine problem. Hillier's bike was fast, but Dean Harrison's (RC Express Kawasaki) was slightly faster, with James Cowton (Stewart Smith Kawasaki) in third. Jamie Hamilton (Stewart Smith Kawasaki), Olie Linsdell (Flitwick Motorcycles Paton) and Keith Amor (KMR Kawasaki) completed the top six by the first fuel stop after lap one.

The next two laps saw the leaders stretch out, old hand Amor moving from sixth to finish fourth. Harrison (25) eventually was able to control the race from the front, and with second-placed Hiller (28) and Cowton (22), it was the youngest TT podium for years. Deano also made history by being the son of sidecar winner Conrad Harrison. It was the first time in TT history that a father and son had won races in the same week. Short-circuit newcomers Martin Jessopp and Danny Webb were 11th and 14th respectively.

Speed was down on 2013, when Hillier had lapped at 119.130mph; Harrison's fastest was 118.666mph. Nevertheless, the organisers are trying to address the runaway cost of the top bikes. Conrad mischievously said on Manx Radio that Dean had "built the bike in a shed for five grand". In fact, it had been built by mechanic Danny Horne for £22,000, which included a week at Arrow in Italy having a custom exhaust developed. TT technical director Adrian Gorst, the hugely experienced crew chief who helped Colin Edwards to his 2002 WSB title, had the job of refining the rules for 2015.

SENNIOR

TT first-timers sometimes wonder why the Senior is such a big deal. After all, it's contested by virtually the same bods and bikes as the opening Superbike race. The difference is that it's a last chance to shine, and the riders' brains have spent two weeks at TT speed. It's the event's ultimate sort-out, and there are usually quite a few guys who are convinced they can win it.

This time, however, Dunlop was the clear favourite. "The Superbike race win was for BMW, but the Senior was my personal goal," he said. Changes he and the team had made to the bike hadn't worked, however, and by the first timing point he was seventh. Ahead of him lay Hillier (Quattro Plant Kawasaki) in sixth, McGuinness (Honda Racing), Harrison (RC Express Kawasaki), Martin (Tyco Suzuki), Cummins (Honda Racing) and his brother, William (Tyco Suzuki).

By the time he got back to Douglas, he'd overhauled them all on corrected time, but there were still fewer than three seconds between the top five, all of whom had done 130+mph laps from a standing start.

After two laps, William Dunlop was second, but Michael's new race record lap of 131.668mph kept him eight seconds ahead. Next came Martin, Cummins, Harrison and the warming Bruce Anstey, trying to recover from the disadvantage of starting just in front of Michael.

Lap three produced a terrible dilemma when William Dunlop lost the front going into the super-fast left before the Bungalow. Amazingly, he escaped with a fractured leg, but when Michael saw the wreckage, he had to assume the worst. His next pit stop was longer than usual as he asked his crew, "Is he okay? Is he all right?" "He's fine, he's fine," was the reply.

Harrison, now a member of the 130 club, blew his motor and pulled in at Sulby Glen for a pint.

By lap five, fans were being treated to a freight train of the top TT riders – Martin, Hillier, McGuinness and Michael Dunlop, revised within half a lap to Dunlop, Martin, Hillier, McGuinness. The lead shrank to a few seconds at times as Michael struggled to regain his rhythm after his brother's crash and Cummins piled on the pressure. But the Irishman won his 11th TT by 14 seconds – a wafer-thin margin after two pit stops and an hour-and-three-quarters of racing.

Martin was just nine seconds further back, followed by Anstey, Hillier and McGuinness. It was a fabulous race, rounded off by William Dunlop's reappearance in the paddock with a leg cast and crutches later in the afternoon.

Above: Michael Dunlop lofts the Senior trophy, his fourth win of the year, 11 in total. Guy Martin's Herculean efforts again were not quite enough.
Photo: BMW Press Club

Top left: Veteran Sidecar race one winners Conrad Harrison and Mike Aylott lift off at Ballaugh Bridge.
Photo: Gavan Caldwell

Above left: Concentration in action: Dave Molyneux and Patrick Farrance's race-two win was the driver's 17th.
Photo: Mark Walters

Left: Despite niggling injury, John McGuinness notched up his 21st IOM win in the TT Zero race.
Photo: Gavan Caldwell

Below left: Village roads, and victory beckons for Dean Harrison (Kawasaki) in the Lightweight.
Photo: David Collister/photocycles.com

BRITISH SUPERBIKE REVIEW
BYRNE'S FANTASTIC FOUR
By OLLIE BARSTOW

Above: Shane Byrne leads Brookes, Bridewell and Ellison at the Brands Hatch Showdown.
Photo: Gavan Caldwell

Top right: Veteran Chris Walker made the Title Showdown and enjoyed his best BSB campaign since 2000.

Above right: Milwaukee Yamaha's Tommy Bridewell pipped team-mate Brookes to take third overall.
Photos: Clive Challinor Motorsport Photography

Right: Shake on it, Shakey: Kyonari congratulates Byrne on taking his fourth BSB title.
Photo: Gavan Caldwell

WHEN is dominance not dominant? When do ten wins, 23 podiums and never once being headed between the first flickers of a green light to the 26th and final chequered flag not result in a rider holding the title trophy aloft well before the season's close?

Indeed, on paper, there is little reason to suggest that Shane 'Shakey' Byrne's run to a record-breaking fourth British Superbike Championship title in 2014 was anything other than comprehensive.

However, while six wins in the first eight races should have been enough to signal a call to end all bets, the much discussed Title Showdown format once again served its purpose by maintaining a shred of unpredictability throughout, even when the Rapid Solicitors Kawasaki rider's advantage swelled to three figures.

Indeed, though the spectre of the controversial, but now well-established three-round, seven-race title chase format continues to generate debate among teams, riders and fans alike, the sheer quality and consistency of Byrne's quest to inscribe his name in the history books made it difficult to justify how he could – or should – be denied by anyone, anything or any format.

Yet whether you sided with the purists or preferred the spectacle of a six-way showdown, few could begrudge the rise of Byrne's closest challenger, Japanese rider Ryuichi Kiyonari.

In what can only be described as a veritable career about-turn, Kiyonari's re-emergence as a title contender on the

Buildbase BMW, after most had written him off as an enigma past his prime, was arguably the story of 2014.

Kiyo's invigoration was such that even the most steadfast naysayers found themselves relishing the coined 'War for Four' between – statistically at least – the sport's most successful and respected protagonists, artificially engineered or otherwise.

That's not to say the 2014 British Superbike Championship was ever merely about two riders. With the usual intriguing cross-section of experienced stalwarts, returning headliners and exciting prospects, British Superbikes reinforced its billing as the most competitive domestic Superbike series in the world.

In fact, Byrne almost singled himself out by staying put at Paul Bird Motorsport, casually brushing off absurd suggestions that he might have hung up his leathers in the wake of his 2013 final-race title defeat at the hands of Alex Lowes. The remainder of the field was almost entirely made up of familiar faces in unfamiliar places.

Byrne's omnipresent rival for title glory since 2010, twice BSB 'bridesmaid' Josh Brookes, brought his tenure with Suzuki to an end and moved to Milwaukee Yamaha, alongside Tommy Bridewell, while his 'Gixxer' was taken over by 2011 runner-up and fan favourite John Hopkins, the embattled American having returned to BSB in another effort to rekindle former glories.

Beyond Byrne, Kawasaki certainly had the advantage in terms of sheer numbers, the ZX-10R emerging as the bike of

choice for more than half of the riders on the 30-strong grid, most notably Stuart Easton (Rapid Solicitors PBM), James Ellison and Chris Walker (GBmoto), Dan Linfoot (Quattro Plant), Ben Wilson (Gearlink) and Richard Cooper (TAG).

Missing from the entry list, however, was Honda. Remarkably, despite their 2013 title win, with Lowes having gone on to international success in World Superbikes and ties having been severed with perennial Honda man Kiyonari, the difficulties of finding a new title sponsor and a drought of what it described as "riders capable of mounting a title challenge", the manufacturer's involvement was whittled down to just the odd wild-card appearance with Julien da Costa and a couple of privateer bikes.

However, Honda plan to return in 2015. Their withdrawal could have dealt a massive blow to the series, but their absence was all but forgotten as BSB 2014 fired into action with its traditional Easter weekend opener at Brands Hatch.

With no Lowes or Honda to defend their respective titles, the season may have begun in the knowledge that there would be new champions to hail in 2014, but there was nothing novel about the front-runners during the initial rounds, with the likes of Byrne, Brookes, Walker and Ellison marking their presence.

With 680 starts, 87 wins and 112 years between them, the first 2014 podium of Byrne, Walker and Ellison took on a pleasingly nostalgic form, the last named rider in particular proving that there is no substitute for sheer experience by notching up Lloyds British GBmoto's first ever top-three re-

Above: A resurgent Kiyonari heads Byrne on his way to victory at Donington.

Right: Kiyonari went on to take a double in Derbyshire. He shares the podium with Byrne and Brookes.

Photos: Clive Challinor Motorsport Photography

sult. The team were reaping immediate dividends from their decision to switch from Honda to Kawasaki over the winter.

Even so, the Brands Hatch opener was still only about one man. Not only did Byrne live up to his billing as the pre-season favourite by taking a maximum haul of points, but also the result suggested that a winter spent reflecting on the loss of the 2013 title to Lowes had spurred him on to come back stronger than ever.

It was a double success that ultimately would set the tone for the coming events as Byrne continued to stamp his authority on proceedings, a third consecutive win at Oulton Park being followed by another dominant double win in round three at Snetterton. His five wins from six races gave him a points haul of 145, from a maximum of 150.

Perhaps more significantly, his lead over the opposition stood at a full 60 points after just three rounds and a quarter of the season completed.

Fortunately for his fellow competitors, the Title Showdown format at least held out the prospect of a second chance further down the line; relief no doubt for Australian rider Brookes, who emerged as Byrne's closest rival in terms of outright speed.

Brookes had switched to Shaun Muir's Milwaukee Yamaha team over the winter in a concerted bid to secure his elusive first BSB title, but costly crashes at Brands Hatch and Snetterton contributed to the gulf in points to Byrne. Three second places and a win at Oulton Park, however, suggested that at least he had found his form on the notoriously tricky Yamaha YZF-R1, if not quite the limit.

If Byrne and Brookes had marked their territory on the first and second steps of the podium, step three had become home for Ellison, the 2009 runner-up displaying painstaking

consistency on the GBmoto Kawasaki to reel off five consecutive third-place finishes in five races, before graduating to a new personal best of second around Snetterton, at the expense of a high-siding Brookes.

As the championship headed north of the border to the breezy Knockhill circuit, it seemed that the top three had already been firmly established...

Until Kiyonari turned the tables with his first win in three years at the Scottish venue, the Japanese rider kicking off his championship bid with an unexpected bang courtesy of a lights-to-flag performance that harked back to the very best days of his 2006, 2007 and 2010 title campaigns.

Notably happier with Stuart Hicken's Buildbase operation, having become visibly jaded during the final stages of an increasingly strained relationship with Honda, Kiyonari's Knockhill performance was the measure of a man who had finally found his comfort zone on the BMW S1000RR. Flashes of form in the early races had matured into a fully rounded affinity with the bike.

More than that, his success even delivered BMW's first win (and podium for that matter) in BSB after four years of trying and would pave the way for the feat to be matched repeatedly thereafter.

Kiyonari might have been in with a chance of a double at Knockhill, had a squirrelly moment out of the hairpin not opened the door for Byrne to capitalise decisively. Another win for him, though, gave him six from eight races, his advantage in the overall standings swelling to 79 points over Brookes, after the Australian lost ground during an unusually off-form weekend in the Scottish Lowlands.

By contrast, as Kiyonari brimmed with new-found confidence on the BMW, a second visit of the season to Brands

Hatch underlined the fact that Byrne faced a renewed threat from the only other rider capable of beating him to the record of a fourth BSB title. And so it proved: Kiyonari beat Byrne to a second win in three races on his rival's home turf.

The Japanese rider's relentless form was brought to an abrupt halt, however, by technical issues during the second Brands Hatch race, the form-man slipping more than 100 points off an overall lead that, in any other championship, would have put him all but out of the title fight. Significantly, though, his rise to the fore had coincided with the elimination of Ellison from the running for the Showdown, his hopes of mounting a bid for the title scuppered by a minor mistake at Brands Hatch. The former MotoGP rider left with a broken hip after being flicked spectacularly from his Kawasaki when he ran wide on to wet grass at Dingle Dell.

It was a bitter blow, for Ellison was leading at the time. His dramatic exit overshadowed an unexpected first win for Josh Waters around the Kent circuit, the Australian carving his way to the first of two damp victories for Tyco Suzuki.

Ellison was now out of contention for one of the six Showdown spots, despite a remarkable fight to fitness that put him back on a bike in little more than a month. That made another position available alongside the existing certainties of Byrne, Brookes and Kiyonari.

Tommy Bridewell, Chris Walker and Dan Linfoot were best placed to capitalise on Ellison's misfortune, the first two declaring their intentions with podiums at Snetterton and Brands Hatch respectively, while the last named had unwavering consistency to thank for his provisional top-six placing.

From the crests and troughs of Brands Hatch, the series moved on to the fast, flat sweeps of Thruxton, the fastest track on the calendar, where the year's first convincing face-off took place between the three leading protagonists.

Elbows out and slipstreaming down the back straight, Brookes, Byrne and Kiyonari fought for advantage. They finished in the same order in both races, with Brookes defying his Yamaha's relative lack of straight-line speed to secure a confidence boosting double win, a welcome respite for the Aussie after a run of disappointing results.

The emphasis for the Showdown turned to gaining podium credits – and psychological victories – as the series returned to Oulton Park for the annual triple-header, Byrne leading Brookes and Kiyonari by 82 and 122 points respectively.

The trio would prove rather more closely matched on track, with Kiyonari powering back from a row-four start to win the first race, before doubling up in race two. Brookes – having finished second in the opening races – ended the weekend with his third win in five races, while Byrne gathered up the remaining podium places.

For all of his dominance during the initial rounds and his unwavering consistency throughout the year, Byrne now had not won since Knockhill two months earlier. While there was certainly no possibility of him not making the Title Showdown, it at least raised anticipation that he could have met his match ahead of the impending shootout.

Byrne's victory drought continued into round eight at Cadwell Park, though his pair of second places at least proved more lucrative than Brookes's fourth and exclusion (for falling on the warm-up lap and restarting, thus breaking the no-remount regulation), and Kiyonari's double DNF (one technical, one self-inflicted).

Instead, the day belonged to two first-time winners: Tommy Bridewell and Peter Hickman. Bridewell's success came in particularly unusual circumstances – he was declared victorious by a mere 0.005 second from Byrne after the race had been red-flagged early and the result determined on count-back. Despite Bridewell never really having led on the road, having only momentarily nosed ahead by virtue of a better run out of the final corner, the unscheduled stoppage handed him an emotional maiden BSB win.

Local rider Hickman's triumph was similarly unexpected. In an extraordinary performance in sodden conditions on the RAF Reserves Honda, he dominated from start to finish.

The result struck a poignant note in the BSB paddock, for Hickman had been drafted into the team to replace the late Simon Andrews, a former BSB podium finisher, tragically killed at the North West 200. Shortly afterwards, another well-known BSB competitor, Karl Harris, succumbed to inju-

Above: Brookes heads Byrne to win at a damp Brands Hatch.

Top right: Howie Mainwaring took a breakthrough win at the Brands Hatch Showdown finale.

Top far right: Stuart Easton missed the Showdown, but took the BSB Cup for seventh overall.

Above right: Peter Hickman, on the RAF Reserves Honda, took a victory at Cadwell Park.

Above far right: Josh Waters had his good days. The Australian Superbike champion took two wins for Suzuki.

Photos: Clive Challinor Motorsport Photography

Right: Kawasaki-mounted Dan Linfoot, here leading Waters (Suzuki) and Da Costa (Honda), was a surprise of the 2014 season.

Photo: Bryn Williams

ries at the Isle of Man TT. Their passing left an indelible mark on the racing community in 2014.

Only honour and podium credits were at stake for Byrne, Kiyonari and Brookes at Donington Park, the last event before the three-round shootout. With this in mind, it was Kiyonari who could take the greatest confidence forward, as he dismissed Byrne's challenge to notch up a double win. His fifth and sixth triumphs also brought him into line with his main rival in terms of victories; Byrne had now contested five events without a win. With the points equalised and podium credits tallied, he would begin the Title Showdown with a total of 562 points, ahead of Brookes on 536 and Kiyonari on 535. Under normal circumstances, he would have had mammoth 107- and 141-point advantages; with the margins slashed to 26 and 27, the momentum seemed to be swinging towards his increasingly confident contemporaries. The 2014 BSB title fight was most definitely still on.

Completing the Showdown six were Bridewell, thanks to his Cadwell win and Donington podiums; the ever-consistent Linfoot, who had earned his place with an unfaltering run of finishes in the points, topped by a long awaited maiden podium at Oulton Park; and wily veteran Chris Walker, the fitting beneficiary of sidelined GBmoto team-mate Ellison. They started the Title Showdown on 508, 501 and 505 points respectively.

Following successful trips across the North Sea to the Netherlands in 2012 and 2013, the iconic TT circuit at Assen was charged once again with kicking off the three crucial rounds. The Cathedral lived up to its reputation for intense racing, not least when the elements threw a timely challenge into a finely poised title tussle, with a light, but consequential sprinkling of rain.

Only Kiyonari handled Mother Nature's curve ball with aplomb; Brookes and Byrne fumbled in the Dutch drizzle, the former eliminating himself with a tumble on the opening lap. Byrne followed suit rather more dramatically a few laps later, caught out while pushing on.

Faced with an open goal, Kiyonari favoured caution when it came down to a heart-stopping last lap head-to-head with rain man Waters – who once again found his form when the

going became treacherous. The former champion's second against his main rivals' DNFs put him well into the title fight.

With a dry track in race two, Byrne and Kiyonari locked horns once more, the former increasingly desperate in the wake of a winless streak that now stretched to six events. His early dominance was a distant memory, all but wiped out by his race-one *faux pas*.

Showing a true champion's response, however, Byrne shrugged off any hint of increasing pressure by taking the fight all the way to the notorious final chicane on the final lap. He confidently dipped the Kawasaki beneath his rival's BMW to come out on top for his first win in three months.

If Byrne and Kiyonari had reason to be satisfied with their overseas exploits, Brookes suffered different emotions as his title dreams were snuffed out by a technical problem and a double DNF at a critical moment. His title bid ended on the European mainland.

With one leading protagonist out of the frame, the much-vaunted six-way battle became a straight fight between only Byrne and Kiyonari. This gave rise again to the term 'War for Four', originally coined in 2013, when the battle to become the first man to win a record four British Superbike titles was a possibility. Though quickly forgotten at the time as Kiyonari's form paled by comparison with Byrne's, a year later it was taking on a new relevance.

The battle-lines had been drawn heading to the penultimate Silverstone round, and though Shakey and Kiyo's mutual respect was evident on and off track, it wouldn't diminish the bar-to-bar action. The duo gave spectators a tremendous show with an exemplary display of precision racing.

With one win apiece and barely a moment spent out of one another's company around the Northamptonshire circuit, the two races proved a fitting showcase of quality riding by two of the sport's best competitors, the honours-even result being a suitably fitting outcome.

It also proved that either rider was worthy of the BSB title, regardless of early-season form, setting up an enticing end-of-season championship showdown at Brands Hatch. Byrne had the upper hand by 12 points.

Above: James Ellison powers to the Silverstone podium – the Kawasaki rider's season was wrecked by injury.

Top: Josh Waters and John Hopkins suffered during Suzuki's worst season for years.

Top right: Emotion overflowed for Shane Byrne after clinching his fourth BSB crown.

Photos: Clive Challinor Motorsport Photography

This was the head-to-head BSB fans had been waiting for, Byrne and Kiyonari having notched up 108 race wins between them and six titles over the previous eight years. Byrne may have had the edge on victories, but the three races at Brands Hatch would prove – for the time being at least – who was the best BSB rider of all time...

At least they would have done if the championship hadn't been cruelly determined by a sprinkling of rain, a slight over-eagerness on the throttle and an awkward landing. Unfortunately, a relatively low-speed fall in slippery conditions during FP3 had led to Kiyonari suffering a collarbone injury serious enough to scupper his title dreams.

Despite keeping the hopes of fans alive by vowing to race if favourable circumstances prevailed, ultimately Kiyonari was forced to admit defeat, the final-round Showdown shown up by a small mistake with a big cost.

Not that Byrne made things entirely easy for himself, fluffing his first attempt to seal the title by crashing out of race one, which handed a surprise win to Quattro Plant Kawasaki's Howie Mainwaring. He made amends in style, however, by winning race two – and with it a historic fourth British Superbike Championship crown.

He wrapped up the year in fitting fashion with his tenth win of the season in race three. His route to the title may have concluded more smoothly than many may have hoped for, but no one could use that to belittle the record-breaking achievements of the rider, who is not only still in his prime, but also seemingly capable of becoming even greater.

Despite his forced absence, Kiyonari held on to the runner-up spot. The crushing disappointment of his costly late error aside, second overall was an almost unthinkable result 12 months after most had conceded his career was in decline. It also represents a landmark performance for the Buildbase team and BMW in BSB.

Behind them, the battle for third went to the wire. Brookes's dismal end to the year – which included another DNF at Silverstone – was typified by him being pipped to the bronze in the final race by team-mate Bridewell. The latter's podiums at Assen and Brands Hatch allowed him to win out in the tussle for Milwaukee Yamaha supremacy.

Though unable to build on his podium tally, the ever-consistent Linfoot still became embroiled in the fight for third, but fell just short. Fifth overall remains a huge validation for an almost faultless campaign on the Quattro Plant bike. Kawasaki counterpart Walker, meanwhile, ended the year sixth, his form dwindling when it mattered. Even so, he scored his best overall BSB finish since 2000.

Outside the top six, Stuart Easton clinched the BSB Riders Cup for the best placed non-Showdown rider, though the Scotsman's season never really sparkled. Despite only regaining full fitness in the closing stages of the campaign, the unfortunate Ellison's three podiums in the final four races at least gave him cause for optimism.

Two wins and a podium in the wet aside, Waters's dry-weather form was never strong enough for him to mount a consistent challenge beyond ninth overall, while tenth-placed Hopkins failed to mount the podium during his much anticipated comeback as Suzuki suffered its worst BSB season for several years.

Race winner Hickman, Jon Kirkham – who had started the season with Tsingtao Kawasaki before switching to Halsall Kawasaki, an injury-hampered Westmoreland (Buildbase BMW), race winner Mainwaring and Jakub Smrz (Millsport Ducati) rounded out the top 15.

Motorpoint British Supersport Championship

Australian rider Billy McConnell had forged a reputation as something of a nearly-man at this level, but even the most partisan of supporters would have been hard pressed to begrudge him his first Motorsport British Supersport Championship title in 2014.

McConnell came into the season as arguably the most decorated British Supersport rider without a title trophy, second place in 2009 still his career best. However, after previous campaigns typified by inconsistencies, crashes and technical dramas, his stars finally aligned in 2014 on the Smiths Triumph, with a winning blend of victories, podiums and limited DNFs that prevailed over his talented rivals.

He was one of several candidates tipped for success pre-season, in the absence of defending champion Stuart Easton, who had joined Ben Wilson and Richard Cooper in stepping up to Superbikes in 2014. Former champion Glen Richards was a notable absentee, having retired.

Having just missed out on the 2013 title with Gearlink Kawasaki, Supersport superstar Alastair Seeley looked ominously threatening on the Mar-Train Yamaha that Easton had taken to glory that year, while McConnell's own Smiths Triumph team-mate, Graeme Gowland, arrived with something to prove after a 2013 season in which he had displayed flashes of speed on unfavourable machinery.

McConnell hit his stride first, though, double victory on the Triumph 675R at Oulton Park putting him on top overall. It was a position he would cede on only three occasions, to Seeley and Gowland, over the course of the year, but it was telling that he never slipped more than two points off the lead.

The second-round rout arguably proved McConnell's crowning moment, the Australian thereafter trading race wins for outright consistency. He wouldn't stand atop the podium again until round eight, once again at Oulton Park.

Nonetheless, while he certainly didn't allow himself to become too fond of the taste of champagne, his methodical approach reaped dividends over the long term. So much so that while both Seeley and Gowland spent the mid-season period tallying their wins, the odd DNF meant they never did more than nose ahead of their more consistent rival.

In fact, despite notching up five wins in nine rounds, Seeley was all but out of the title fight with three rounds remain-

ing, after four further DNFs. The Ulsterman was 59 points shy of the lead.

The title battle was set to go the way of one of the two Smiths Triumph riders: McConnell, who had added a fourth win of the year at Cadwell Park; and Gowland, also a four-times race winner and similarly reliable when it came to notching up the podium results.

With only the double-headers at Assen, Silverstone and Donington Park remaining, the two riders would enter the final stretch separated by just a single point. As they headed for the Netherlands, honours were almost even and the scene should have been set for a thrilling inter-team showdown. But when Gowland fell at Assen and then was sidelined by technical issues at Silverstone, he was well on the back foot going into the final event.

A comfortable 18-point advantage meant that McConnell simply needed to keep his nose clean and the bike upright at Brands Hatch, an objective he duly fulfilled with intentionally modest runs to ninth and eighth places.

By contrast, Gowland's all-out last-gasp effort ended with him picking himself up off the floor, his final race misdemeanour also losing Smiths Triumph an overall one-two, as Seeley nipped in to grab second. In fact, after a strong end to the year, Seeley was just four points shy of overhauling McConnell, but eight wins weren't enough to make up for lost ground elsewhere.

On his route to the title, McConnell won fewer races than Seeley and stood on the podium on fewer occasions than Gowland. Ultimately, however, that single DNF in 24 races made the difference.

Behind the top three, Glenn Irwin came of age on the Gearlink Kawasaki, his five wins a fine return on the team's decision to give the youngster a shot in 2014; while Luke Jones and Luke Stapleford took notable steps forward on the T3 Triumph and Profile Triumph respectively.

Luke Mossey won twice, but couldn't string together enough consistency to finish higher than seventh overall, ahead of Macadam Appleyard Yamaha's Luke Jones and American James Rispoli, riding for Keith Flint's Team Traction Control. Tyco Suzuki's Taylor Mackenzie rounded out the top ten.

In the Evo class, Alex Olsen was the overwhelmingly dominant winner, notching up 14 wins to finish more than 200 points clear of Tim Hastings and Josh Corner.

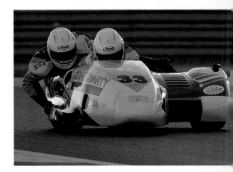

Pirelli National Superstock 1000 Championship

Danny Buchan bounced back from his ill-fated move into the British Superbike class in 2013 by comprehensively dominating the Pirelli National Superstock 1000 Championship in 2014.

Riding the Tsingtao WK Kawasaki ZX-10R, Buchan barely put a wheel wrong during a remarkable season that yielded eight wins and three second places over 12 races, with just a DNF at Donington Park blotting an otherwise exemplary campaign.

He wrapped up the title with one round in hand, and might have taken the opportunity to relax even earlier but for the persistent presence of Jason O'Halloran, who returned to the class in 2014 to spearhead Honda Racing's challenge.

However, though the Australian was off the podium just twice in 2014 and he saw the chequered flag in each race, his two wins paled in comparison to Buchan's success, and he had to settle for the runner-up spot.

Tempering his season with the odd Superbike outing, Lee Jackson brought home the 'bronze' for Buildbase BMW, peaking with a victory at Thruxton; while reigning champion Hudson Kennaugh couldn't quite replicate the highs of 2013 en route to fourth overall on the Linxcel BMW.

Adam Jenkinson's quest for an SSTK 1000 title continued into 2014 as he went winless in fifth place for Northern Escalator Kawasaki, ahead of Josh Elliot (GA Kawasaki) and Filip Backlund (SMT Kawasaki). The last named probably would have finished higher than seventh, had he not switched to the Superbike class for the final rounds.

Joe Burns (JG Speedfit Kawasaki), Daniel Johnson (Morello Kawasaki) and David Johnson (PR Kawasaki) completed the top ten.

Pirelli National Superstock 600 Championship

A thrilling Pirelli National Superstock 600 Championship went to the wire, with three riders tussling for title honours right to the final corner at Brands Hatch.

With just four points separating Joe Collier, Andy Reid and Kyle Ryde, victory for any one of the three at Brands Hatch would have assured them the title. In a fittingly thrilling three-way tussle, Pacedayz Yamaha's Ryde prevailed, his fifth win of the season proving most timely.

Let down by costly errors that otherwise negated his five wins over the course of the season, runner-up Reid nonetheless made his mark in 2014 with an eye-catching effort on the FFX Yamaha. Be Wiser Kawasaki's Collier displayed unwavering consistency against just a single win to thank for making him a stealthy title contender right to the end of the year.

Motul British Motostar Championship

Seventeen-year-old Jordan Weaving wrapped up the 2014 Motul British Motostar Moto3 Championship with one round to spare in a season of speed and consistency that belied his age.

Indeed, though Weaving's three wins on the Jordan Racing KTM were comfortably bettered by Joe Irving's seven on the Redline KTM, ultimately seven second-place finishes made the difference when set against his rival's two DNFs.

Edward Rendell was the more convincing title winner in the 125GP class, taking victories on five occasions to defeat Taz Taylor and Bradley Ray.

Ducati TriOptions Cup

Dennis Hobbs was crowned champion in the one-make Ducati TriOptions Cup after a stronger end to his season allowed him finally to overhaul year-long rival Leon Morris. Having led from the opening races, Morris ceded his advantage to Hobbs at the penultimate round before the P&H/Carl Cox Motorsports rider prevailed in a final-round showdown to clinch the crown.

TriStar R&G Triple Challenge

After finishing runner-up in 2013, Freddy Pett progressed to title glory in the Triumph-supported TriStar R&G Triple Challenge. In a dominant campaign, he led from the opening race to the last. Eight wins from 20 races proved more than sufficient to see off the challenge from runner-up Scott Pitchers and third-placed Philip Atkinson.

Eastern Airways British Sidecar Challenge

The popular Eastern Airways British Sidecar Championship continued its support billing in 2014, with Sean Hegarty and James Neave taking 13 wins from 20 races to lead from start to finish.

Above: Supersport champion Kyle Read heads runner-up Andy Reid at Donington Park.

Top: Speed and consistency gave 17-year-old Jordan Weaving the Moto3 title with one race to spare.
Photos: Clive Challinor Motorsport Photography

Top left: Danny Buchan (Kawasaki) won a dominant Superstock crown.

Opposite, above far left: Australian Billy McConnell finally came out on top in British Supersport.
Photo: Gavan Caldwell

Opposite, above left: Close runner-up Alastair Seeley leads the applause as McConnell succumbs to ecstasy.
Photo: Clive Challinor Motorsport Photography

Opposite, from top: Freddy Pett took the Triumph Triple title; Sean Hegarty and passenger James Neave dominated on three wheels; with 14 wins, Alex Olsen was the runaway Supersport Evo Class winner; veteran Dennis Hobbs took the honours in the one-make Ducati 848 series.
Photos: Clive Challinor Motorsport Photography

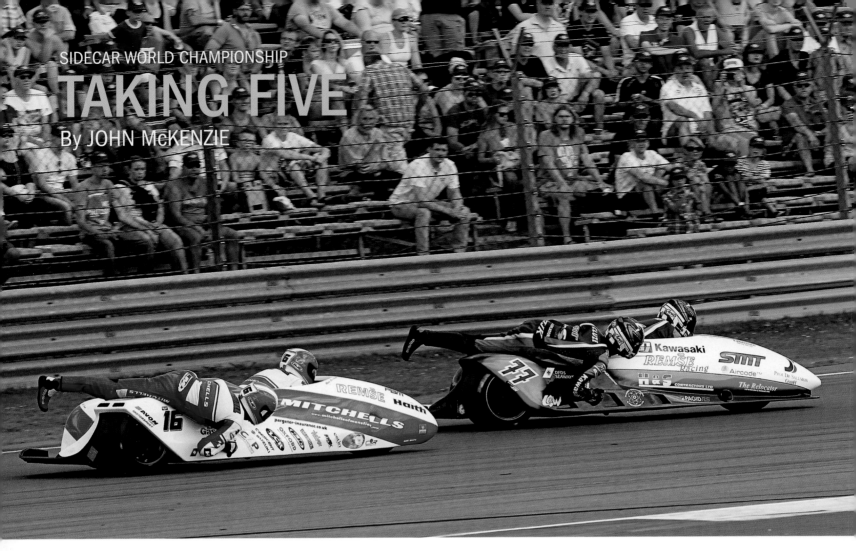

TAKING FIVE

By JOHN McKENZIE

REIGNING world champions Pekka Paivarinta and Adolf Haenni had decided not to defend their title in 2014, so it was heartening to see four-times world champion Tim Reeves, partnered by Greg Cluze, return after a year-long sabbatical.

With BMW-powered Jorg Steinhausen and the Birchall brothers on a seven-win bounce with their Mitchells of Mansfield LCR Suzuki absolutely flying, it appeared that it would be another very close-fought year.

Round 1 – 13 April, Aragon, Spain

With clear blue skies above the 5.344km circuit, Ben and Tom Birchall put their red-and-white outfit on pole with a time of 2m 07.229s; Reeves and Steinhausen completed the front row.

After Reeves was excluded from his preferred British championship by a rule change, his decision to return to the world stage came so late that the outfit arrived unpainted. On top of that, they'd installed a previously untried – at this level – Kawasaki ZX10 motor in their eight-year-old LCR chassis.

With just 11 outfits on the grid, Reeves made the initial race pace, with favourite Birchall enmeshed in the pack after a poor start. By the end of the first lap, Reeves led from Steinhausen and new partner Axel Kolsch, while Birchall had fought through to third. Over the course of the 15 laps, all three outfits, as predicted, took a turn at the front, until Birchall increased the pace. With six laps to go, he was four seconds clear and pulling away at a searing pace. At the flag, the advantage was eight seconds over Steinhausen, while Reeves had shown his mettle by putting his virtually untested Kawasaki outfit in third.

Round 2 – 25 May, Donington Park, Great Britain

It was a welcome return to the Leicestershire track for the first time since 2008, with the grid bolstered by an entry from the British championship series.

With rain threatening practice, Reeves was quickly out, finding a fast disappearing dry line and posting 1m 54.05s for pole. With Birchall second, the front row was completed by veteran Andy Peach before heavy rain red-flagged the session.

The sun came out for the 19-lap race, however, and top qualifier Reeves was first into Redgate, but with Birchall in close company. By lap six, Birchall was pegging him back, then took the lead and managed to build a slight gap until back-markers allowed Reeves back into contention.

The battle intensified and they swapped back and forth. Exiting Goddard's on the last lap, almost side by side, Reeves just managed to get the traction to take the win by the tiniest margin of 0.099 second. Half a minute back in third was Steinhausen, who had managed to catch and pass Hock and Becker after they went wide.

Round 3 – 14–15 June, Rijeka, Croatia

On to Croatia and the first two-race, 50-point weekend of the year. Before the races had even started, however, two major events occurred that ultimately would define the outcome of the series.

First, title leaders Ben and Tom Birchall had crashed at the Isle of Man TT, and their injuries were sufficient to prevent them from making the trip to Rijeka.

Second, any advantage that title challenger Jorg Steinhausen might then have hoped for was lost when he crashed heavily at the end of the home straight in practice, totally wrecking his beautifully prepared LCR BMW outfit. Passenger Axel Kolsch was lucky to escape with a broken ankle.

"Nothing can be salvaged from the bike. I estimate a high five-figure sum for the repairs. I'll sleep on it and decide how to proceed, but at the moment I'm thinking about giving up. Obviously, a sportsman doesn't want to say goodbye like this," said the disconsolate German. But having slept on it, the popular Steiny effectively quit the sport, taking no further

part in the championship, his dreams of emulating his father's title successes of the mid-1970s shattered.

With Jakob Remse and Jamie Biggs having crashed out, and Kurt Hock also out with injury, it was a much depleted field that started the ten-lap sprint race. Pole man Reeves shot away and was never seriously challenged, taking the flag by 12 seconds from Bennie Streuer and Geert Koerts in second, with Petri Makkula third. It was a best ever result for Streuer, and the first time the famous name had appeared on a sidecar rostrum since his luxuriantly bearded father and triple world champion Egbert had taken second place in his last ever race at Assen in 1992.

High winds threatened cancellation of Sunday's Gold race, but conditions were deemed safe after Streuer and French driver Philippe Gallerne put in some laps before confirming that conditions were acceptable. The late start meant the race was shortened to 14 laps.

Once again, Reeves set the pace and was never headed. Streuer appeared likely to take another second until his final-drive sprocket sheared off, forcing him out. That left the remaining rostrum places for either Uwe Gurck and Manfred Wechselberger on the ex-Steinhausen 2013 LCR BMW, or Finnish pair Petri Makkula and Harri Asumanie. Makkula won the battle, second his best ever result.

Fifty points picked up without a serious challenge gave Reeves a total of 91, ahead of Gurck (51), with the absent Birchall stuck on 45. For a seasoned veteran and four-times champion like Reeves, it wasn't an advantage he would relinquish.

Round 4 – 27 June, Assen, Netherlands

The sidecars were back to support the MotoGP weekend at Assen for their biggest meeting of the year. A third consecutive pole position for Reeves, with a blistering 1m 40.969s, ahead of the returned Birchalls, boosted his confidence; local boy Streuer qualified third with his fastest ever lap of his home track. Just

Left: Tim Reeves returned after a year away to win a fifth title, with new passenger Gregory Cluze.

Far left: Ben and Tom Birchall battle with Reeves and Cluze at Assen.

Below left: Jakob Rutz and Thomas Hofer lead Uwe Gurck and Manfred Wechselberger, with Bennie Streuer and Geert Koerts in pursuit in the final round at Le Mans.

Photos: Mark Walters

flag knowing that they were world champions again. Although the Birchalls took the 50 points, Reeves had comfortably done enough to seal the campaign.

It was Tim Reeves's fifth title, but the first for Greg Cluze, and a first for a French passenger. It was also a first for a Kawasaki-powered machine, ending an 11-year run for Suzuki.

Round 8 – 20 September, Le Mans, France

With the title decided, there was nothing at stake at Le Mans, except burning personal pride and the consuming obsessions of the world's two best sidecar racers. Birchall's place as number two had also been sealed, but third place in the table was still up for grabs, by either Uwe Gurck or Bennie Streuer.

The task was 18 laps of the Bugatti circuit, with the added frisson of the return of 2013 world champion Pekka Paivarinta with a new BMW-powered outfit, but accompanied by an old passenger, Timmo Karttialla.

Once again, Birchall, from pole, and Reeves made the pace, swapping the lead – and also a bit of paint – as they jostled and jockeyed for the advantage.

On lap three, their battle for the same piece of tarmac let Paivarinta through, knocking Birchall back to third. Then Reeves tried to make a gap, but his exhaust had been damaged in the melee and was filling the cockpit with intense heat and fumes. By lap nine, he could take no more and was forced to retire.

Meanwhile, the Birchalls had got the better of the returning Finnish world champion and took their third consecutive win – their 22nd – after posting another fastest lap at 1m 43.893s.

Seb Delannoy was very happy with third at his home race. Uwe Gurck took eighth, which was enough to confirm his third place in the championship. Final positions gave Reeves 201 points, Birchall 185 and Gurck 112.

And so ended the 2014 sidecar championship, a season with more than its fair share of ups and downs. As always, there were so many 'what ifs' – but that, as they say, is racing.

There can be no doubt, however, that missing the 50-pointer at Rijeka – for the second season in a row – cost Birchall's title hopes dearly, but what an amazing performance from Reeves, who also took the inaugural FIM F2 Sidecar world title in a busy weekend at Oschersleben. After a full season out, to come back at the last minute with an untried motor, and take four poles and five race wins for a fifth title shows him to be a great battler. The racing between him and Birchall was the closest week-in, week-out that we had seen for many a year, but they needed some further competition. Too often, it was a two-horse race.

As ever, money was the issue, and at some events the grids were quite low, but if four-times champion Paivarinta can secure a deal for 2015, he has the pedigree to challenge both Birchall and Reeves. If that happens, a series with three engines – Kawasaki, Suzuki and BMW – and three world champions on the grid is surely something to look forward to.

---

an hour before the race start time, however, there was a huge downpour.

With parts of the track still wet, an extra warm-up lap was run to determine conditions, the race being shortened by one lap to 15. Everyone decided to start on slicks, the damp track apparently drying.

Reeves blew his pole advantage with a bad start, allowing Birchall, still not 100 per cent fit, to escape. The former eventually managed to pass Streuer for second, then set about catching and passing Birchall.

He built up a three-second advantage, which was enough to hold off Birchall's late fastest-lap charge by better than two seconds. Streuer and the Dutch crowd were overjoyed with third, which gave him a rostrum at home.

Round 5 – 13 July, Sachsenring, Germany

Tragedy struck at the Sachsenring when local German heroes Kurt Hock and Enrico Becker crashed badly in practice. Sadly, passenger Becker succumbed at the scene, while Hock was airlifted to hospital with very serious injuries. Although the incident shook the closely-knit sidecar community, the race would go ahead at the request of both families.

Reeves and Birchall had another very close wheel-to-wheel race, with Birchall getting the verdict at the very last corner to win by 0.145 second. Robert Zimmerman made his first rostrum appearance in third, but there were no celebrations.

"We had a great race with Tim and Greg, but the events yesterday really hit you. It is a real loss to sidecar racing; we are all a big family in the sidecar paddock. We would like to dedicate this race to Enrico and hope that Kurt recovers well," said Ben Birchall.

Round 6 – 3 August, Assen, Netherlands

It was back to Assen, but in a reversal of the previous visit, Birchall was fastest qualifier, from Reeves. French pair Seb Delannoy and Kevin Rousseau made a welcome return to the world scene, putting themselves third on the grid.

Another huge Assen crowd greeted race day and 17 sunny laps of the famous track. Reeves made the first turn with Birchall on his rear wheel, giving another superb display of incredibly close racing, the lead being swapped continuously. Again, back-markers played a part, allowing Reeves to pull half-a-dozen lengths by half-distance, and a tenacious Reeves and Cluze managed to hold on and beat Birchall by just half a second. Fastest lap again was set by Birchall in his efforts to catch up.

Delannoy was overjoyed to get the better of Streuer for third. A maximum score for Reeves in his 38th GP win was enough to extend his lead to 51 points. With just three races and 75 points left, it was starting to look cut and dried.

Round 7 – 23–24 August, Oschersleben, Germany

With two races to fight over, and nothing to lose, Birchall's only chance was to lead from the front, and even though he may have realised that his title hopes rested on an unlikely mechanical disaster befalling Reeves, he wasn't going out without a fight. A pole position, two wins and the lap record comprehensively underlined that notion.

In the 12-lap Sprint race on Saturday, Reeves grabbed a holeshot once again, before another battle with Birchall. By lap three, Birchall was ahead, and he gradually built a lead to take the flag, while Reeves limped over the line in second place with a broken gear change. However, Reeves now only needed a mere five points from the Gold Race on Sunday to clinch the title.

Again, Reeves had got away quickest, and again by lap three, Birchall had grabbed the lead, managing to build up a buffer of ten seconds as once more gear-change problems slowed the former. But Reeves and Cluze knew what was needed, and they took the

US RACING REVIEW

END OF AN ERA

By PAUL CARRUTHERS

Above: Over the hill at Elkhart Lake, champion Hayes (4) leads Cardenas (36), Roger Lee Hayden (95), Pegram (72) and Anthony (25).

Above right: Hayes and team-mate Cameron Beaubier shared the top two podium places at four races.

Right: Hayes (4), Hayden (95) and Beaubier (2) were the outstanding trio of 2014.

Photos: AMA Pro Series

IT'S often said that sometimes you have to hit rock bottom before you can rebound into doing great things. In 2014, the AMA Pro Racing Superbike Series might not have hit the bottom, but it was definitely within arm's reach.

The series consisted of just six rounds, television coverage was non-existent, rider and team participation was less than normal, and fan interest had waned to the point of losing even the hardcore enthusiast. But at season's end, the series was thrown a lifeline in the form of new ownership from a group called KRAVE. More importantly, the group was led by a man with a history in the sport. A man named Wayne Rainey – armed with the backing of both the FIM and Dorna.

Suddenly everything seemed instantly better. But more on that later.

First things first, let's review the season on the racetrack. After all, that's where the good stuff was still taking place.

The story line coming into the 2014 season was all about rookie Cameron Beaubier, America's hope for future international stardom. At the tender age of 21, Beaubier was coming off a season in the 600cc-based Daytona SportBike class, where not only did he win the title, but also every race bar one. He had been fast in all his previous tests on a

Superbike, so he seemed almost destined to come in, strut his stuff and take the Superbike title with him in his debut season on the factory Yamaha R1.

The problem was... well someone forgot to send that memo to Josh Hayes.

Hayes, who turned 39 during the '14 season, came in as a three-times AMA Superbike champion, who had lost out in his bid for title number four to young team-mate Josh Herrin the season before – despite doubling Herrin's amount of race wins, eight to four. Herrin wouldn't be around to defend his title, however, as he was off to Moto2 for what would be a dismal international debut – he was relieved of his duties mid-season.

But Hayes was faced with the prospect of battling with a young team-mate again – only he knew this one would present an even bigger challenge. This Beaubier kid was the real deal, and Hayes knew it. But ultimately he did what he does best: dug in his heels and refused to give way. Preseason hype be damned, Hayes came in prepared for battle. As he always does.

While Beaubier was impressive in his rookie Superbike season, with three victories (two of them in the first three

rounds), the title went to the masterful Hayes. And he did it in style, winning seven times in the 11 races (five of the rounds were double-headers) to take the title by a whopping 54 points.

And when all was said and done, it wasn't Beaubier who ended up second in the title chase. Instead that spot went to Roger Lee Hayden in his first season on the Yoshimura Suzuki. The youngest of the racing Hayden family won a race at the final round in New Jersey and finished on the podium a further seven times to take the runner-up spot behind Hayes.

Beaubier ended up third, with three wins in a season when he had started like gangbusters, lost confidence in the middle, regained it, then ended on a low. But he will be back with a year of experience under his belt in 2015, and the season will likely begin with him at least a co-favourite to take the crown.

Hayes (7), Beaubier (3) and Hayden (1) were the only three riders to take wins in 2014, and they were head and shoulders above the rest. Even Martin Cardenas, a race winner in 2013 on the factory Yoshimura Suzuki, struggled in 2014, with a best finish of second at Barber Motorsports Park and a dismal sixth when all the points were added up at season's end.

Chris Clark ended the series fourth on his paid-for Yoshimura Suzuki ride, the young rider from Las Vegas showing promise and landing on the podium for the first time in his career in the fifth round. He parlayed consistent finishes to fourth in the title chase – one point better than impressive Aussie privateer David Anthony.

The season started as it always has done at Daytona International Speedway (though it won't do so in 2015, MotoAmerica not having concluded a deal with Daytona). The Superbikes served as a support race to the Daytona 200, which had switched to running 600cc motorcycles in 2005.

Above: Class rookie Beaubier took three early wins, but eventually finished third overall.

Top right: Australian privateer David Anthony was consistently impressive.

Above right: Fourth in the overall standings, Chris Clark heads the pack on the Yoshimura Suzuki.

Right: Roger Lee Hayden leads the Yamaha pair and team-mate Cardenas, on his way to a contentious wet-race win at the New Jersey finale.

Photos: AMA Pro Series

Again, the factory Graves Motorsports Yamaha team came in as the favourites, with arguably the two best riders on the two best bikes. Hayes was the leader of the team – with three titles and 41 Superbike race wins on his resume – and rookie Beaubier joined him, fresh from his magical 2014 season in the 600cc class.

The only other factory team was the Yoshimura Suzuki squad of Cardenas and Clark, the pair being joined late by off-season signee Hayden. In 2013, Hayden had ridden for Michael Jordan's Suzuki team, but the basketball legend wasn't happy with the direction the Daytona Motorsports Group (DMG)-run series was headed, so he pulled out. That left Hayden without a ride until Yoshimura tossed him a life jacket and brought him back to the deep end of the pool. He repaid them by being the team's best hope for victory week in and week out.

KTM was again represented by Chris Fillmore and the HMC team, this time going it alone in a one-man effort. Fillmore's best result was a fourth, and he ended up eighth in the series, losing gobs of points in the last two races at New Jersey with two non-finishes.

Larry Pegram had his family-run team in the series again, this time with EBRs, having traded his BMWs for Yamahas in 2013. The bikes weren't up to the challenge, but Pegram did finish the season on a high with a podium in the rain at the final round in New Jersey. Another highlight came at the World Superbike round at Laguna Seca, where he sat out the AMA race to compete with the big boys and promptly earned EBR its first ever world championship points. Pegram was joined on the EBRs by Cory West, who topped the veteran in the final points tally after ending the season seventh to Pegram's ninth.

Anthony was always the best of the non-factory riders on his privateer Suzukis, the Australian just missing out on fourth in the title chase by a single point to Clark.

For once, Hayes's season didn't start with a nightmare at

Daytona, though it was at least a bit nightmarish. He won the first of the two races, but his Daytona luck reared its ugly head in race two when his R1's engine failed. Still, he left Florida in much better shape than a year earlier, when he had failed to finish either race.

Beaubier had finished third in the first race at Daytona after making a few rookie mistakes in his Superbike debut. A day later and he showed he was a quick study, ending the race on top with his first career Superbike victory.

"It means everything," Beaubier said after winning. "I've worked really hard to get here."

So he was on his way, leaving Daytona with a win and a third place in his first two Superbike races.

Hayden also was off to a good start, with two second-place finishes in his Yoshimura Suzuki debut. He'd been in the fight in both races, but ultimately his GSX-R1000 didn't have the horsepower to beat the Yamahas at a racetrack that values horsepower more than any other. Hayden's team-mate Clark left Daytona smiling, with two fourth-place finishes – career bests for the youngster.

Then the series went on hiatus with a two-month break in the action before round two set things rolling again at Road America in Elkhart Lake, Wisconsin.

Beaubier backed up his Daytona success with a victory in race one over Hayes, but the rookie made his first big mistake of the season in race two when he crashed early, losing the front and losing confidence in the front end at the same time.

The race went on without him, but it turned into a debacle. Though the race was declared wet, the track was too dry to use rain tyres, and 99 per cent of the field started on slicks. Then the rain came and the crashes began. Hayes tiptoed around on his slicks better than anyone else, and finally it came to a close – with a red flag and tons of riders pissed-off that it hadn't come sooner.

After seeing the white flag, Hayes was in disbelief: "I

thought, 'My god, they're really going to make me ride this thing around another lap. Are they not watching this? Are they not seeing what's happening right now?'"

After the race, he was fuming. "If you care about your show, if you care about your athletes, how do you make this decision?" he said.

Cardenas left Road America second best to Hayes after finishing third in both races, while team-mate Hayden ended up fourth and third. Anthony, meanwhile, enjoyed his career-best finish of second in Sunday's wet race.

After a few more weeks off, the series ventured to the pristine Barber Motorsports Park for its third-round double-header, and Hayes was in fine mid-season form, sweeping to victories in both races. The Yamaha man went into Barber third in the title chase and came out of it with the points lead. Boom!

Beaubier's struggles, meanwhile, continued in race one at Barber, the youngster crashing out for the second race in a row as he continued to battle a front-end feel problem. He bounced back to finish third in the second race, behind Hayes and the surprising Anthony, the Aussie getting back-to-back second-place finishes in Alabama.

The AMA Series joined up with the World Superbike Championship for round four at Mazda Raceway Laguna Seca on California's Monterey Peninsula, and it was Hayes marching to his fourth straight win and fifth of the season. He was impressive in this one, taking a three-second win over Beaubier for the 46th AMA Superbike win of his career. Even the master himself was somewhat surprised that he'd been able to get away from his pupil in this one, especially with Beaubier having earned pole position for the race.

"I thought it might come down to a cat-and-mouse game towards the end of the race, depending on who would get the most out of the tyre," Hayes said.

Although Beaubier ended up second, the gap in the standings had grown to a yawning 40 points.

Above: Top-ten battle. Pegram (72) leads Knapp (44), Christie (20), Ulrich (18) and Clark (6) in New Jersey.

Top right: Daytona Sportbike champion Jake Gagne took his Yamaha to a trio of wins.

Above right: Hayden Gillim, Sportbike champion.

Above far right: Dustin Dominguez won more races than Gillim; lost the title by two points.

Centre right: Consistency, and just one win, earned Danny Eslick the Vance & Hines Harley-Davidson crown.

Photos: AMA Pro Series

Centre far right: Triple world champion, and potential saviour of US racing, Wayne Rainey.

Photo: Gold & Goose

Right: A rumble of Harleys led by Tyler O'Hara at Mid-Ohio.

Photo: AMA Pro Series

Third place went to Hayden, who even made a run at Beaubier once he'd disposed of team-mate Cardenas. But it was too little too late, and the Yamahas were again one-two in the race.

The series made its annual trek to the Mid-Ohio Sports Car Course in July, and it ended up a split decision between the two Yamaha men in what was the closest battle of the season – and one that put Hayes and Beaubier well clear of their Suzuki rivals in both races. Race one went to young Beaubier, but old man Hayes reversed that result in race two. It was a case of no harm, no foul in the points chase as the gap between the Yamaha men remained at 40.

Hayden was hopeful of much more at Mid-Ohio, since he'd pressured Hayes for victory in the two races there the season before. But this time he was forced to settle for third in both races, beating team-mate Cardenas in race one, with Fillmore riding the KTM to a season-best fourth in race two after the Colombian crashed out.

The abbreviated season came to a close at New Jersey Motorsports Park almost a month later, when Hayes earned his fourth AMA Superbike championship by taking second- and first-place finishes in the two races. That put him in a tie with Mat Mladin as the only men to have won four US Superbike titles.

Race one was held in a rainstorm, and it was Hayes who crossed the line first after a scintillating battle with Hayden. Later the AMA reversed the decision, however, with a ruling that Hayes had passed Hayden under a yellow caution flag. That gave Hayden the win – his first of the year – and prevented the Monster Graves Yamaha team from having a perfect season. Pegram also had his best outing of 2014 on the underpowered EBR, finishing third in the iffy conditions.

The next day, the weather was perfect and Hayes romped to victory, catching and passing Beaubier, who crashed out just after mid-race. Hayden was able to beat Cardenas to the flag for second, the two Yosh Suzuki riders joining the new four-times champion on the podium.

DAYTONA SPORTBIKE

In 2013, Jake Gagne was the only rider to beat Cameron Beaubier in the Daytona SportBike class, his lone victory coming mid-season at Road America. Thus with Beaubier moving to the Superbike class in 2014, he was the pre-season choice to take the SportBike title.

And he didn't disappoint.

Although he didn't dominate in the manner Beaubier had done, Gagne and his Red Bull Roadrace Factory Yamaha R6 did what was necessary. He won three races, finished second four times, third once and fourth once, while suffering only one bad race when he was caught up in a crash in race one at Barber.

In the end, he beat Mees Motorsports Yamaha's Jake Lewis (who rides under the watchful eye of Earl Hayden and the Hayden brothers) by 44 points, the 18-year-old having somewhat of a breakout season with two victories and four podium finishes.

Third overall went to Dane Westby, the Yamalube/Westby Racing Yamaha rider having swept to his first ever series wins at round three at Barber, with another victory at the season finale in New Jersey.

Daytona 200 winner Danny Eslick rode a Triumph to fourth in the series, though his campaign was highlighted with that opening-round victory in Florida. Gagne's team-mate, JD Beach, ended the series ranked fifth.

The fifth rider to win a race in the Daytona SportBike Series in 2014 was Jason DiSalvo, the New Yorker having taken first place in race one at Mid-Ohio in what otherwise was a pretty mediocre season for the Triumph-mounted veteran.

SPORTBIKE

The 2014 Sportbike Series was brought together as one, rather than as in previous years when it was split into East/West series. That meant one champion, and that champion

was Hayden Gillim, the cousin of the Haydens ending up with three wins in a series that went to the bitter end. After two rounds in New Jersey, Gillim had topped Dustin Dominguez by just two points, 246–244. Dominguez had the satisfaction of knowing he'd won more races, the Oklahoman having taken four wins to Gillim's three.

Corey Alexander looked to be the racer to beat early in the season as he ripped off three straight wins to get things rolling. After finishing second in the fourth race, his season went downhill, however, as he suffered crashes, injuries and bad luck. He ended up fourth in the series standings, one position behind Celtic Racing team-mate Wyatt Farris.

HARLEY-DAVIDSON

Five riders won Vance & Hines Harley-Davidson races in 2014 – including Irishman Jeremy McWilliams in a one-off ride in the series at Indianapolis Motor Speedway. Three riders won two races – Tyler O'Hara, Steve Rapp and Kyle Wyman – but the other rider, who won just once, came away with the title. That was Danny Eslick.

Eslick's lone win came at Laguna Seca in July, but his four second-place finishes put him at the top when the points were added up. Ben Carlson, who went winless in the series, was second by virtue of five podium finishes.

THE RAINEY ERA

At season's end, it was announced that a group led by three-times 500cc World Champion Wayne Rainey had purchased the marketing and promotional rights to the American Road Racing Championships, had obtained AMA and FIM sanction, and had the blessing of Dorna, the rights holders of MotoGP. The series would start in 2015 under the name MotoAmerica, with riders set to compete for national championships.

And the world of American road racing suddenly became a better place.

Rainey is well respected worldwide and especially so in his homeland. He started his career as a dirt-tracker, travelling the country in a van with his bikes in the back. Then he moved on to road racing, serving his apprenticeship as a privateer before being given factory rides and winning championships. He parlayed his success in the United States into three world championships. In other words, he's a racer who has been there, done that. And with all that comes heaps of respect, especially from fellow racers.

Rainey became involved in KRAVE – the group behind MotoAmerica – because he wanted to see American road racing flourish again. And he wanted American road racers to have a path back to MotoGP and World Superbike.

"When I raced, the grand prix teams were looking for talent coming out of America," Rainey said. "Whether that was because of our background or because we were Americans and we were competitive. For whatever reason, Americans dominated that landscape. And you can basically say that the Europeans have taken our blueprint and adopted that – and maybe even done a better job than what we were doing, because they were working on the younger-aged kids to get them more prepared to be racing road-race bikes. As a whole, I think our goal is to get our championship competitive to where it will be seen one day in the not too distant future as a strong series again."

Rainey's class structure is similar to what was already in place, with a few tweaks here and there – namely adopting World Superbike-type rules for Superbike, Superstock and Supersport classes. There will also be two spec-bike classes in 2015 – probably the Harley-Davidson class and a smaller class using something along the lines of the new KTM 390s.

In the future, Rainey wants to work a Moto2 class into the programme, but negotiations to purchase the series from the Daytona Motorsports Group were protracted and the group ran out of time to try to make a Moto2 class work in year one.

MAJOR RESULTS

OTHER CHAMPIONSHIP RACING SERIES WORLDWIDE

Compiled by PETER McLAREN

AMA Championship Road Race Series (Superbike)

DAYTONA INTERNATIONAL SPEEDWAY, Daytona Beach, Florida, 14–15 March, 2014, 44.300 miles/70.006km

Race 1

1 Josh Hayes (Yamaha); **2** Roger Hayden (Suzuki); **3** Cameron Beaubier (Yamaha); **4** Chris Clark (Suzuki); **5** David Anthony (Suzuki); **6** Chris Fillmore (KTM); **7** Diego Pierluigi (Suzuki); **8** Taylor Knapp (Suzuki); **9** Cory West (EBR); **10** Stefano Mesa (Kawasaki)

Race 2

1 Cameron Beaubier (Yamaha); **2** Roger Hayden (Suzuki); **3** Martin Cardenas (Suzuki); **4** Chris Clark (Suzuki); **5** David Anthony (Suzuki); **6** Chris Fillmore (KTM); **7** Diego Pierluigi (Suzuki); **8** Taylor Knapp (Suzuki); **9** Cory West (EBR); **10** Chris Urlich (Honda)

ROAD AMERICA, Elkhart Lake, Wisconsin, 31 May–1 June, 2014, 52.000 miles/83.686km

Race 1

1 Cameron Beaubier (Yamaha); **2** Josh Hayes (Yamaha); **3** Martin Cardenas (Suzuki); **4** Roger Hayden (Suzuki); **5** David Anthony (Suzuki); **6** Chris Clark (Suzuki); **7** Chris Fillmore (KTM); **8** Chris Ulrich (Honda); **9** Cory West (EBR); **10** Jason Farrell (Kawasaki)

Race 2

1 Josh Hayes (Yamaha); **2** David Anthony (Suzuki); **3** Roger Hayden (Suzuki); **4** Chris Clark (Suzuki); **5** Chris Fillmore (KTM); **6** Larry Pegram (EBR); **7** Martin Cardenas (Suzuki); **8** Bernat Martinez (Yamaha); **9** Trent Gibson (Kawaski); **10** Francois Dumas (BMW)

BARBER MOTORSPORTS PARK, Birmingham, Alabama, 21–22 June, 2014, 49.890 miles/80.435km

Race 1

1 Josh Hayes (Yamaha); **2** David Anthony (Suzuki); **3** Chris Clark (Suzuki); **4** Larry Pegram (EBR); **5** Cory West (EBR); **6** Sean Dwyer (Suzuki); **7** Reese Wacker (Suzuki); **8** Trent Gibson (Kawasaki); **9** Johnny Rock Page (Suzuki); **10** Frankie Babuska (Suzuki)

Race 2

1 Josh Hayes (Yamaha); **2** Martin Cardenas (Suzuki); **3** Cameron Beaubier (Yamaha); **4** David Anthony (Suzuki); **5** Roger Hayden (Suzuki); **6** Chris Clark (Suzuki); **7** Chris Ulrich (Honda); **8** Cory West (EBR); **9** Larry Pegram (EBR); **10** Sean Dwyer (Suzuki)

MAZDA RACEWAY LAGUNA SECA, Monterey, California, 13 July, 2014, 41.400 miles/66.627km

1. Josh Hayes (Yamaha); **2** Cameron Beaubier (Yamaha); **3** Roger Hayden (Suzuki); **4** Martin Cardenas (Suzuki); **5** Chris Fillmore (KTM); **6** David Anthony (Suzuki); **7** Cory West (EBR); **8** Bernat Martinez (Yamaha); **9** Chris Clark (Suzuki); **10** Sebastiao Ferreira (Kawasaki)

MID-OHIO SPORTS CAR COURSE, Lexington, Ohio, 19–20 July, 2014, 50.400 miles/81.100km

Race 1

1 Cameron Beaubier (Yamaha); **2** Josh Hayes (Yamaha) **3** Roger Hayden (Suzuki); **4** Martin Cardenas (Suzuki); **5** Chris Fillmore (KTM); **6** Chris Clark (Suzuki); **7** David Anthony (Suzuki); **8** Larry Pegram (EBR); **9** Chris Ulrich (Honda); **10** Frankie Babuska (Suzuki)

Race 2

1 Josh Hayes (Yamaha); **2** Cameron Beaubier (Yamaha); **3** Roger Hayden (Suzuki); **4** Chris Fillmore (KTM); **5** Chris Clark (Suzuki); **6** Taylor Knapp (Suzuki); **7** David Anthony (Suzuki); **8** Chris Ulrich (Honda); **9** Cory West (EBR); **10** Frankie Babuska (Suzuki)

NEW JERSEY MOTORSPORTS PARK, Millville, New Jersey, 13–14 September, 2014, 51.750 miles/82.284km

Race 1

1 Roger Hayden (Suzuki); **2** Josh Hayes (Yamaha); **3** Larry Pegram (EBR); **4** Sean Dwyer (Suzuki); **5** Cameron Beaubier (Yamaha); **6** Marcel Irnie (BMW); **7** Chris Clark (Suzuki); **8** Cory West (EBR); **9** Chris Ulrich (Honda); **10** Taylor Knapp (Suzuki)

Race 2

1 Josh Hayes (Yamaha); **2** Roger Hayden (Suzuki); **3** Martin Cardenas (Suzuki); **4** Bernat Martinez (Yamaha); **5** David Anthony (Suzuki); **6** Jodi Christie (Honda); **7** Chris Clark (Suzuki); **8** Larry Pegram (EBR); **9** Chris Ulrich (Honda) **10** Taylor Knapp (Suzuki)

Final Championship Points

1	Josh Hayes	285
2	Roger Hayden	231
3	Cameron Beaubier	206
4	Chris Clark	176
5	David Anthony	175
6	Martin Cardenas	147

7 Cory West, 124; **8** Chris Fillmore, 119; **9** Larry Pegram, 105; **10** Benrat Martinez, 98.

Endurance World Championship

BOL D'OR (24 HOURS), Magny-Cours, France, 26–27 April, 2014.
FIM Endurance World Championship, Round 1. 743 laps of the 2.741-mile/4.411km circuit, 2036.500 miles/3277.400km

1 SRC Kawasaki: Leblanc/Lagrive/Salchaud (Kawasaki ZX-10R), 24h 0m 16.395s, 84.800mph/136.500km/h.

2 Yamaha Racing GMT 94 Michelin: Checa/Foray/Gines (Yamaha YZF-R1), 738 laps; **3** Junior Team LMS Suzuki: Guittet/Masson/Black (Suzuki GSX-R1000), 732 laps; **4** Team Bolliger Switzerland: Saiger/Stamm/Sutter (Kawasaki ZX-10R), 731 laps; **5** Team Motors Events April Moto: Fastre/Savary/Storrar (Suzuki GSX-R1000), 730 laps; **6** National Motos: Tizon/Four/Junod (Honda CBR1000RR), 725 laps; **7** Team R2CL: Jones/Martin/Giabbani (Suzuki GSX-R1000), 722 laps; **8** Yamaha Viltaïs Experience: Bardet/Carrillo/Nigon (Yamaha YZF-R1), 714 laps; **9** METISS JLC MOTO: Holub/Ayer/Cheron (METISS 1000), 709 laps; **10** AM Moto Racing Competition: Loiseau/Maitre/Buisson (Suzuki GSX-R1000), 703 laps; **11** TMC City Bike TRT 27: Aynie/Billega/Diard (Suzuki GSX-R1000), 698 laps; **12** BMRT 3D Endurance: Burlin/Romanens/Guyot (Kawasaki ZX-10R), 696 laps; **13** Völpker NRT 48 Schubert Motors: Stuppi/Takada/Nadalet (BMW S1000RR), 691 laps; **14** Penz13.com Franks Autowelt Racing Team: Pridmore/Vallcaneras/Mackels (BMW S1000RR), 691 laps; **15** AZ Motos-April: Napoleone/Dumain/Mezard (Suzuki GSX-R1000), 690 laps.

Fastest lap: Honda Racing: Da Costa/Foray/Gimbert, 1m 41.680s, 97.100mph/156.200km/h, on lap 145.

Endurance World Championship (EWC) points: 1 SRC Kawasaki, 55; **2** Yamaha Racing GMT 94 Michelin, 50; **3** Team Bolliger Switzerland, 37; **4** Team Motors Events April Moto, 35; **5** National Motos, 32; **6** Team R2CL, 24.

SUZUKA 8 HOURS, Suzuka, Japan, 27 July, 2014.
FIM Endurance World Championship, Round 2. 172 laps of the 3.617-mile/5.821km circuit, 622.100 miles/1001.200km

1 Musashi RT Harc Pro: Takahashi/Haslam/Van der Mark (Honda CBR1000RR), 6h 56m 13.056s, 89.680mph/144.330km/h.

2 Yoshimura Suzuki Shell Advance: Tsuda/Waters/De Puniet (Suzuki GSX-R1000), +59.844s; **3** Team Kagayama & Verity: Haga/Aegerter/Kagayama (Suzuki GSX-R1000), 171 laps; **4** Monster Energy Yamaha with YSP: Nakasuga/Parkes/Brookes (Yamaha YZF-R1), 171 laps; **5** Toho Racing with Moriwaki: Kunikawa/Yamaguchi/Kobayashi (Honda CBR1000RR), 170 laps; **6** Honda Suzuka Racing Team: Hiura/Morii/Yasuda (Honda CBR1000RR), 170 laps; **7** Honda Team Asia: Hook/Zamri Baba/Ekky Pratama (Honda CBR1000RR), 169 laps; **8** Suzuki Endurance Racing Team: Delhalle/Nigon/Cudlin (Suzuki GSX-R1000), 169 laps; **9** Yamaha Racing GMT 94 Michelin: Foray/Gines/Checa (Yamaha YZF-R1), 168 laps; **10** Monster Energy Yamaha YART: Bridewell/Maxwell/Olson (Yamaha YZF-R1), 168 laps; **11** Honda Kumamoto Racing: Yoshida/Kojima/Tokudome (Honda CBR1000RR), 168 laps; **12** Team Green: Yanagawa/Watanabe/Fujiwara (Kawasaki ZX-10R), 167 laps; **13** Team Bolliger Switzerland: Saiger/Stamm/Sutter (Kawasaki ZX-10R), 166 laps; **14** Confia Flex Motorrad39: Sakai/Takeishi/Oonishi (BMW S1000RR), 166 laps; **15** Honda Escargot & PGR: Kuboyama/Nakatsuhara (Honda CBR1000RR), 166 laps.

Fastest lap: Musashi RT Harc Pro: Takahashi/Haslam/Van der Mark, 2m 8.620s, 101.2mph/163.0km/h, on lap 141.

Endurance World Championship (EWC) points:

1 Yamaha Racing GMT 94 Michelin, 62; **2** SRC Kawasaki, 55; **3** Team Bolliger Switzerland, 45; **4** Musashi RT Harc Pro, 35; **5** Team Motors Events April Moto, 35; **6** National Motos, 32.

8 HOURS OF OSCHERSLEBEN, Oschersleben, Germany, 23 August, 2014.
FIM Endurance World Championship, Round 3. 291 laps of the 2.279-mile/3.667km circuit, 663.100 miles/1067.100km

1 Honda Racing: Da Costa/Gimbert/Foray (Honda CBR1000RR), 8h 0m 19.304s, 82.830mph/133.000km/h.

2 Yamaha Racing GMT 94 Michelin: Checa/Foray/Gines (Yamaha YZF-R1), 289 laps; **3** Team Bolliger Switzerland: Saiger/Stamm/Sutter (Kawasaki ZX-10R), 288 laps; **4** Penz13.com Franks Autowelt Racing Team: Vallcaneras/Mackels/Reiterberger (BMW S1000RR), 288 laps; **5** Qatar Endurance Racing Team: West/Cudlin/Al Naimi (Kawasaki ZX-10R), 288 laps; **6** Suzuki Endurance Racing Team: Philippe/Delhalle/Nigon (Suzuki GSX-R1000), 287 laps; **7** Team 18 Sapeurs-Pompiers: Maurin/Egea/Alarcos (Kawasaki ZX-10R), 285 laps; **8** Junior Team LMS Suzuki: Guittet/Masson/Black (Suzuki GSX-R1000), 285 laps; **9** Monster Energy Yamaha YART: Morais/Olson/Jerman (Yamaha YZF-R1), 284 laps; **10** SRC Kawasaki: Leblanc/Lagrive/Foret (Kawasaki ZX-10R), 282 laps; **11** Starteam PAM-Racing: Lucas/Hardt/Longearet (Suzuki GSX-R1000), 280 laps; **12** AM Moto Racing Competition: Loiseau/Thibaut/Buisson (Suzuki GSX-R1000), 279 laps; **13** Flembbo Leader Team: Prosenik/Bellucci/Derine (Kawasaki ZX-10R), 279 laps; **14** National Motos: Tizon/Junod/Debise (Honda CBR1000RR), 278 laps; **15** ECS1 - Ecurie Chrono Sport 1: Cudeville/Auger/Maccio (Kawasaki ZX-10R), 277 laps.

Fastest lap: Monster Energy Yamaha with YSP: Parkes/M. Laverty, 1m 27.266s, 94.000mph/151.300km/h, on lap 89.

Endurance World Championship (EWC) points:

1 Yamaha Racing GMT 94 Michelin, 91; **2** Team Bolliger Switzerland, 70; **3** SRC Kawasaki, 69; **4** Honda Racing, 54; **5** Suzuki Endurance Racing Team, 44; **6** Team Motors Events April Moto, 44.

24 HOURS OF LE MANS, Le Mans Bugatti Circuit, France, 20–21 September, 2014.
FIM Endurance World Championship, Round 4. 812 laps of the 2.600-mile/4.185km circuit, 2111.600 miles/3398.200km

1 Suzuki Endurance Racing Team: Philippe/Delhalle/Nigon (Suzuki GSXR-1000), 24h 0m 42.444s, 87.900mph/141.500km/h.

2 Yamaha Racing GMT 94 Michelin: Checa/Foray/Gines (Yamaha YZF-R1), 810 laps; **3** Monster Energy Yamaha YART: Parkes/M. Laverty/Morais (Yamaha YZF-R1), 804 laps; **4** Qatar Endurance Racing Team: West/Cudlin/Al Naimi (Kawasaki ZX-10R), 802 laps; **5** Junior Team LMS Suzuki: Guittet/Masson/Black (Suzuki GSXR-1000), 800 laps; **6** National Motos: Junod/Tizon/Four (Honda CBR1000RR), 794 laps; **7** Penz13.com Racing Team: Pridmore/Barrier/Allerton (BMW S1000RR), 792 laps; **8** Team R2CL: Jones/Martin/Giabbani (Suzuki GSXR-1000), 790 laps; **9** Metiss JLC Moto: Michel/Huvier/Cheron (Metiss 1000), 788 laps; **10** Starteam PAM-Racing: Lucas/Hardt/Longearet (Suzuki GSXR-1000), 788 laps; **11** Team Traqueur Louit Moto 33: Pilot/Perret/Jonchiere (Kawasaki ZX-10R), 787 laps; **12** AM Moto Racing Competition: Loiseau/Maitre/Ayer (Suzuki GSXR-1000), 783 laps; **13** Tati Team Beaujolais Racing: Enjolras/Chevaux/Prulhiere (Kawasaki ZX-10R), 780 laps; **14** Team Bolliger Switzerland: Saiger/Sutter/Wildisen (Kawasaki ZX-10R), 774 laps; **15** Penz13.com Franks Autowelt Racing Team: Vallcaneras/Mercer/Van Keymeulen (BMW S1000RR), 767 laps.

Fastest lap: Penz13.com Racing Team: Pridmore/Barrier/Allerton, 1m 38.133s, 95.380mph/153.500km/h, on lap 116.

Endurance World Championship (EWC) Final points:

1	Yamaha Racing GMT 94 Michelin,	141
2	Suzuki Endurance Racing Team,	104
3	Team Bolliger Switzerland,	100
4	National Motos,	80
5	SRC Kawasaki,	72
6	Monster Energy Yamaha YART,	70

7 Honda Racing, 63; **8** Team Motors Events April Moto, 60; **9** Team R2CL, 54; **10** Flembbo Leader Team, 47; **11** Musashi RT Harc Pro, 35; **12** Team 18 Sapeurs-Pompiers, 35; **13** Team Space Moto 37, 34; **14** Maco Racing Team, 32; **15** TMC City Bike TRT 27, 30.

Riders' World Championship Final points:

1	David Checa,	141
1	Kenny Foray,	141
1	Mathieu Gines,	141

4 Anthony Delhalle, 104; **4** Erwan Nigon, 104; **6** Daniel Sutter, 100; **6** Horst Saiger, 100; **8** Vincent Philippe, 91; **9** Arturo Tizon, 80; **9** Grégory Junod, 80; **11** Mathieu Lagrive, 74; **12** Gregory Leblanc, 72; **13** Roman Stamm, 70; **14** Olivier Four, 68; **15** Broc Parkes, 64.

Isle of Man Tourist Trophy Races

ISLE OF MAN TOURIST TROPHY COURSE, 31 May–6 June, 2014, 37.73-mile/60.72km circuit.

Dainese Superbike TT (6 laps, 226.380 miles/364.320km)

1 Michael Dunlop (BMW), 1h 45m 46.384s, 128.415mph/206.664km/h.

2 Guy Martin (Suzuki), 1h 46m 6.954s; **3** Conor Cummins (Honda), 1h 46m 9.934s; **4** Bruce Anstey (Honda), 1h 46m 31.687s; **5** Michael Rutter (BMW), 1h 46m 48.186s; **6** William Dunlop (Suzuki), 1h 46m 57.992s; **7** John McGuinness (Honda), 1h 46m 58.772s; **8** Dean Harrison (Kawasaki), 1h 47m 39.797s; **9** James Hillier (Kawasaki), 1h 48m 4.777s; **10** Joshua Brookes (Yamaha), 1h 48m 5.487s; **11** Dan Kneen (Suzuki), 1h 48m 20.997s; **12** David Johnson (Kawasaki), 1h 49m 9.248s; **13** Lee Johnston (Honda), 1h 49m 10.958s; **14** Peter Hickman (BMW), 1h 50m 58.103s; **15** Dan Stewart (Honda), 1h 52m 11.142s.

Fastest lap & new Outright TT record: Bruce Anstey (Honda), 17m 6.682s, 132.298mph/212.913km/h, on lap 6.

Previous Superbike TT lap record: John McGuinness (Honda), 17m 11.572s, 131.671mph/211.904km/h (2013).

Sure Sidecar TT Race 1 (3 laps, 113.190 miles/182.160km)

1 Conrad Harrison/Mike Aylott (Shelbourne Honda), 59m 34.820s, 113.987mph/183.444km/h.

2 John Holden/Andrew Winkle (LCR), 59m 51.823s; **3** Tim Reeves/Gregory Cluze (DMR), 1h 0m 8.410s; **4** Ian Bell/Carl Bell (Yamaha), 1h 1m 31.122s; **5** Karl Bennett/Lee Cain (Kawasaki), 1h 1m 32.236s; **6** Wayne Lockey/Mark Sayers (Ireson Honda), 1h 1m 58.646s; **7** Darren Hope/Paul Bumfrey (Kawasaki), 1h 2m 28.986s; **8** Gregory Lambert/Kenny Cole (Honda), 1h 2m 39.691s; **9** Roy Hanks/Kevin Perry (Molyneux Rose TB), 1h 2m 46.954s; **10** Gordon Shand/Phil Hyde (Shand F2), 1h 2m 54.414s; **11** Alan Founds/Tom Peters (LCR Suzuki), 1h 3m 9.981s; **12** John Saunders/Robert Lunt (Shelbourne), 1h 3m 17.376s; **13** Tony Baker/Fiona Baker-Milligan (Suzuki), 1h 3m 23.139s; **14** Nicholas Dukes/William Moralee (BLR), 1h 3m 26.068s; **15** Mike Cookson/Alun Thomas (Honda), 1h 3m 26.682s.

Fastest lap: Dave Molyneux/Patrick Farrance (DMR), 19m 35.612s, 115.538mph/185.940km/h, on lap 2.

Sidecar lap record: Nick Crowe/Daniel Sayle (LCR Honda), 19m 24.24s, 116.667mph/187.757km/h (2007).

Monster Energy Supersport TT Race 1 (4 laps, 150.920 miles/242.880km)
1 Gary Johnson (Triumph), 1h 12m 43.035s, 124.526mph/200.405km/h.
2 Bruce Anstey (Honda), 1h 12m 44.537s; **3** Michael Dunlop (Honda), 1h 12m 54.719s; **4** Dean Harrison (Yamaha), 1h 13m 24.656s; **5** William Dunlop (Suzuki), 1h 13m 37.324s; **6** Guy Martin (Suzuki), 1h 13m 44.591s; **7** James Hillier (Kawasaki), 1h 14m 30.983s; **8** Lee Johnston (Honda), 1h 14m 32.414s; **9** Michael Rutter (Triumph), 1h 14m 38.907s; **10** Keith Amor (Honda), 1h 14m 48.288s; **11** Ian Hutchinson (Yamaha), 1h 14m 49.313s; **12** Ivan Lintin (Honda), 1h 14m 57.448s; **13** Dan Stewart (Honda), 1h 15m 1.217s; **14** Dan Kneen (Honda), 1h 15m 9.314s; **15** John McGuinness (Honda), 1h 15m 10.703s.
Fastest lap: Gary Johnson (Triumph), 17m 51.771s, 126.732mph/203.955km/h, on lap 2.
Supersport lap record: Michael Dunlop (Honda), 17m 35.659s, 128.666mph/207.069km/h (2013).

Royal London 360 Superstock TT (4 laps, 150.920 miles/242.880km)
1 Michael Dunlop (BMW), 1h 11m 10.773s, 127.216mph/204.734km/h.
2 Dean Harrison (Kawasaki), 1h 11m 30.882s; **3** Bruce Anstey (Honda), 1h 11m 54.197s; **4** David Johnson (Kawasaki), 1h 12m 11.802s; **5** Lee Johnston (Honda), 1h 12m 18.017s; **6** Michael Rutter (BMW), 1h 12m 18.305s; **7** Dan Kneen (Suzuki), 1h 12m 52.351s; **8** Peter Hickman (BMW), 1h 13m 13.249s; **9** John McGuinness (Honda), 1h 13m 15.099s; **10** James Hillier (Kawasaki), 1h 13m 24.822s; **11** Horst Saiger (Kawasaki), 1h 13m 46.555s; **12** Russ Mountford (Kawasaki), 1h 13m 51.100s; **13** James Cowton (Honda), 1h 14m 1.169s; **14** Ivan Lintin (Honda), 1h 14m 2.371s; **15** Jimmy Storrar (BMW), 1h 14m 2.830s.
Fastest lap: Michael Dunlop (BMW), 17m 26.621s, 129.778mph/208.857km/h, on lap 2.
Superstock lap record: Michael Dunlop (Honda), 17m 15.114s, 131.220mph/211.178km/h (2013).

SES TT Zero (1 lap, 37.730 miles/60.720km)
1 John McGuinness (Shinden San), 19m 17.300s, 117.366mph/188.882km/h (record).
2 Bruce Anstey (Shinden San), 19m 40.625s; **3** Robert Barber (Buckeye Current RW-2.x), 24m 12.230s; **4** Robert Wilson (Sarolea), 24m 12.600s; **5** Mark Miller (VercarMoto), 26m 22.562s; **6** Timothee Monot (TT Zero), 29m 2.378s.
Previous TT Zero lap record: Michael Rutter (2013 MotoCzysz E1PC), 20m 38.461s, 109.675mph/176.505km/h (2013).

Monster Energy Supersport TT Race 2 (4 laps, 150.920 miles/242.880km)
1 Michael Dunlop (Honda), 1h 12m 23.794s, 125.078mph/201.294km/h.
2 Bruce Anstey (Honda), 1h 12m 33.883s; **3** William Dunlop (Suzuki), 1h 12m 47.678s; **4** Dean Harrison (Yamaha), 1h 13m 3.459s; **5** James Hillier (Kawasaki), 1h 13m 37.712s; **6** Keith Amor (Honda), 1h 13m 49.580s; **7** Ivan Lintin (Honda), 1h 13m 59.555s; **8** Dan Kneen (Honda), 1h 14m 9.289s; **9** Dan Stewart (Honda), 1h 14m 11.141s; **10** Guy Martin (Suzuki), 1h 14m 30.161s; **11** Russ Mountford (Triumph), 1h 14m 45.755s; **12** Jamie Hamilton (Honda), 1h 15m 5.814s; **13** Steve Mercer (Suzuki), 1h 15m 39.061s; **14** Michal Dokoupil (Yamaha), 1h 15m 39.699s; **15** Sam Wilson (Kawasaki), 1h 15m 54.719s.
Fastest lap: Michael Dunlop (Honda), 17m 46.129s, 127.403mph/205.035km/h, on lap 2.
Supersport lap record: Michael Dunlop (Honda), 17m 35.659s, 128.667mph/207.069km/h (2013).

Sure Sidecar TT Race 2 (3 laps, 113.190 miles/182.16km)
1 Dave Molyneux/Patrick Farrance (DMR), 1h 0m 1.355s, 113.147mph/182.092km/h.
2 Conrad Harrison/Mike Aylott (Shelbourne Honda), 1h 0m 45.285s; **3** John Holden/Andrew Winkle (LCR), 1h 1m 21.282s; **4** Tim Reeves/Gregory Cluze (DMR), 1h 1m 26.906s; **5** Karl Bennett/Lee Cain (Kawasaki), 1h 1m 36.566s; **6** Alan Founds/Tom Peters (LCR Suzuki), 1h 3m 3.517s; **7** Gregory Lambert/Kenny Cole (GLR Honda), 1h 3m 12.024s; **8** Wayne Lockey/Mark Sayers (Ireson Honda), 1h 3m 13.207s; **9** John Saunders/Robert Lunt (Shelbourne), 1h 3m 42.483s; **10** Robert Handcock/Basil Bevan (Baker), 1h 3m 47.042s; **11** Mike Cookson/Alun Thomas (Honda), 1h 3m 50.616s; **12** Dwight Beare/Noel Beare (LCR), 1h 4m 3.938s; **13** Gordon Shand/Phil Hyde (Shand F2), 1h 4m 13.303s; **14** Matt Dix/Shaun Parker (Baker), 1h 4m 21.176s; **15** Howard Baker/Mike Killingworth (Shelbourne Honda), 1h 4m 24.116s.
Fastest lap: Dave Molyneux/Patrick Farrance (DMR), 19m 54.027s, 113.756mph/183.073km/h, on lap 3.
Sidecar lap record: Nick Crowe/Daniel Sayle (LCR Honda), 19m 24.24s, 116.667mph/187.757km/h (2007).

Bikenation Lightweight TT (3 laps, 113.190 miles/182.160km)
1 Dean Harrison (Kawasaki), 57m 49.129s, 117.460mph/189.034km/h.
2 James Hillier (Kawasaki), 58m 3.755s; **3** James Cowton (Kawasaki), 58m 12.754s; **4** Keith Amor (Kawasaki), 58m 16.164s; **5** Jamie Hamilton (Kawasaki), 58m 44.190s; **6** Oliver Linsdell (Paton), 59m 14.516s; **7** Ryan Farquhar (Kawasaki), 59m 33.625s; **8** Daniel Cooper (Kawasaki), 59m 41.580s; **9** Connor Behan (Kawasaki), 1h 0m 24.584s; **10** Michal Dokoupil (Kawasaki), 1h 0m 31.019s; **11** Martin Jessopp (Kawasaki), 1h 0m 32.703s; **12** David Johnson (Kawasaki), 1h 0m 34.291s; **13** Daniel Webb (Kawasaki), 1h 0m 42.544s; **14** Michael Sweeney (Kawasaki), 1h 0m 55.739s; **15** Adrian Harrison (Kawasaki), 1h 1m 14.732s.
Fastest lap: Keith Amor (Kawasaki), 19m 1.514s, 118.989mph/191.494km/h, on lap 3.
Lightweight TT record: James Hillier (Kawasaki), 19m 0.168s, 119.130mph/191.721km/h (2013).

PokerStars Senior TT (6 laps, 226.380 miles/364.320km)
1 Michael Dunlop (BMW), 1h 45m 33.291s, 128.680mph/207.090km/h.
2 Conor Cummins (Honda), 1h 45m 47.291s; **3** Guy Martin (Suzuki), 1h 45m 56.962s; **4** Bruce Anstey (Honda), 1h 46m 20.814s; **5** James Hillier (Kawasaki), 1h 46m 22.262s; **6** John McGuinness (Honda), 1h 46m 38.179s; **7** Joshua Brookes (Yamaha), 1h 46m 43.877s; **8** Dan Kneen (Suzuki), 1h 47m 28.519s; **9** Michael Rutter (BMW), 1h 47m 34.561s; **10** David Johnson (Kawasaki), 1h 48m 11.127s; **11** Peter Hickman (BMW), 1h 48m 19.976s; **12** Dan Stewart (Honda), 1h 48m 33.673s; **13** Ian Hutchinson (Yamaha), 1h 50m 4.848s; **14** Daniel Cooper (Kawasaki), 1h 50m 59.232s; **15** Ian Mackman (Suzuki), 1h 51m 13.305s.
Fastest lap: Michael Dunlop (BMW), 17m 11.591s, 131.668mph/211.899km/h, on lap 2 (record).
Previous Senior TT lap record: John McGuinness (Honda), 17m 12.30s, 131.578mph/211.754km/h (2009).

British Championships

BRANDS HATCH INDY, 21 April, 2014, 1.208-mile/1.944km circuit.
MCE British Superbike Championship With Pirelli, Round 1
Race 1 (12 laps, 14.484 miles/23.310km)
1 Shane Byrne (Kawasaki), 9m 20.872s, 93.030mph/149.720km/h.
2 Chris Walker (Kawasaki); **3** James Ellison (Kawasaki); **4** Ben Wilson (Kawasaki); **5** John Hopkins (Suzuki); **6** Stuart Easton (Kawasaki); **7** Tommy Bridewell (Yamaha); **8** Richard Cooper (Kawasaki); **9** Jakub Smrz (Ducati); **10** James Westmoreland (BMW); **11** Dan Linfoot (Kawasaki); **12** Michael Rutter (BMW); **13** Martin Jessopp (BMW); **14** Patric Muff (BMW); **15** Josh Waters (Suzuki).
Fastest lap: Ellison, 46.063s, 94.400mph/151.930km/h.

Race 2 (30 laps, 36.210 miles/58.274km)
1 Shane Byrne (Kawasaki), 23m 17.781s, 93.330mph/150.200km/h.
2 Josh Brookes (Yamaha); **3** James Ellison (Kawasaki); **4** Ryuichi Kiyonari (BMW); **5** Chris Walker (Kawasaki); **6** Stuart Easton (Kawasaki); **7** James Westmoreland (BMW); **8** Dan Linfoot (Kawasaki); **9** Tommy Bridewell (Yamaha); **10** Ben Wilson (Kawasaki); **11** John Hopkins (Suzuki); **12** Martin Jessopp (BMW); **13** Harry Hartley (Kawasaki); **14** Patric Muff (BMW); **15** Richard Cooper (Kawasaki).
Fastest lap: Ellison, 46.007s, 94.520mph/152.110km/h.
Championship points: **1** Byrne, 50; **2** Ellison, 32; **3** Walker, 31; **4** Easton, 20; **5** Brookes, 20; **6** Wilson, 19.

Motorpoint British Supersport Championship & Supersport Evo, Round 1
Race 1 (18 laps, 21.744 miles/34.994km)
1 Glenn Irwin (Kawasaki), 16m 24.873s, 79.470mph/127.890km/h.
2 Luke Jones (Triumph); **3** Alastair Seeley (Yamaha); **4** Alex Olsen (Triumph); **5** Luke Hedger (Kawasaki); **6** Billy McConnell (Triumph); **7** Callan Cooper (Yamaha); **8** Bjorn Estment (Yamaha); **9** Samuel Hornsey (Triumph); **10** Daniel Cooper (Kawasaki); **11** James Rispoli (Suzuki); **12** Luke Stapleford (Triumph); **13** David Allingham (Yamaha); **14** Josh Daley (Kawasaki); **15** Juha Kallio (Suzuki).
Fastest lap: Jones, 53.143s, 81.820mph/131.680km/h.

Race 2 (20 laps, 24.160 miles/38.882km)
1 Alastair Seeley (Yamaha), 15m 49.719s, 91.570mph/147.370km/h.
2 Graeme Gowland (Triumph); **3** Billy McConnell (Triumph); **4** Luke Stapleford (Triumph); **5** Glenn Irwin (Kawasaki); **6** Luke Jones (Triumph); **7** Jake Dixon (Yamaha); **8** Taylor Mackenzie (Suzuki); **9** Bjorn Estment (Yamaha); **10** Samuel Hornsey (Triumph); **11** Alex Olsen (Triumph); **12** Sam Coventry (Kawasaki); **13** James Rispoli (Suzuki); **14** Daniel Cooper (Kawasaki); **15** Steve Mercer (Suzuki).
Fastest lap: Seeley, 46.775s, 92.960mph/149.610km/h.
Championship points: **1** Seeley, 41; **2** Irwin, 36; **3** Jones, 30; **4** McConnell, 26; **5** Gowland, 20; **6** Olsen, 18.

Motul British Motostar Championship, Round 1 (16 laps, 19.328 miles/31.105km)
1 Joe Irving (KTM), 13m 41.293s, 84.710mph/136.330km/h.
2 Ryan Saxelby (Honda); **3** Jordan Weaving (KTM); **4** Jayson Uribe (Honda); **5** Edward Rendell (Honda); **6** Bradley Ray (EE125); **7** Taz Taylor (Luyten Honda); **8** Daniel Costilla (Repli-Cast); **9** Charlie Nesbitt (Repli-Cast); **10** James Flitcroft (Nykos); **11** Alex Persson (Honda); **12** Anthony Alonso (Honda); **13** Chris Taylor (Honda); **14** Brian Slooten (Honda); **15** Georgina Polden (Honda).
Fastest lap: Irving, 50.470s, 86.160mph/138.660km/h.
Moto3 points: **1** Irving, 25; **2** Weaving, 20; **3** Uribe, 16; **4** Costilla, 13; **5** Nesbitt, 11; **6** Taylor, 10.
125GP points: **1** Saxelby, 25; **2** Rendell, 20; **3** Ray, 16; **4** Taylor, 13; **5** Flitcroft, 11; **6** Persson, 10.

OULTON PARK, 5 May, 2014, 2.692-mile/4.332km circuit.
MCE British Superbike Championship With Pirelli, Round 2 (2 x 18 laps, 48.456 miles/77.982km)
Race 1
1 Shane Byrne (Kawasaki), 30m 15.190s, 96.100mph/154.660km/h.
2 Josh Brookes (Yamaha); **3** James Ellison (Kawasaki); **4** Tommy Bridewell (Yamaha); **5** Stuart Easton (Kawasaki); **6** Dan Linfoot (Kawasaki); **7** Richard Cooper (Kawasaki); **8** James Westmoreland (BMW); **9** Jon Kirkham (Kawasaki); **10** Jakub Smrz (Ducati); **11** Michael Rutter (BMW); **12** Martin Jessopp (BMW); **13** Josh Waters (Suzuki); **14** Patric Muff (BMW); **15** Ben Wilson (Kawasaki).
Fastest lap: Brookes, 1m 35.411s, 101.570mph/163.460km/h.

Race 2
1 Josh Brookes (Yamaha), 28m 50.237s, 100.820mph/162.250km/h.
2 Shane Byrne (Kawasaki); **3** James Ellison (Kawasaki); **4** Stuart Easton (Kawasaki); **5** Tommy Bridewell (Yamaha); **6** James Westmoreland (BMW); **7** Dan Linfoot (Kawasaki); **8** Chris Walker (Kawasaki); **9** John Hopkins (Suzuki); **10** Jon Kirkham (Kawasaki); **11** Jakub Smrz (Ducati); **12** Michael Rutter (BMW); **13** Josh Waters (Suzuki); **14** Martin Jessopp (BMW); **15** Patric Muff (BMW).
Fastest lap: Brookes, 1m 35.466s, 101.510mph/163.370km/h.
Championship points: **1** Byrne, 95; **2** Brookes, 65; **3** Ellison, 64; **4** Easton, 44; **5** Bridewell, 40; **6** Walker, 39.

Motorpoint British Supersport Championship & Supersport Evo, Round 2
Race 1 (12 laps, 32.304 miles/51.988km)
1 Billy McConnell (Triumph), 19m 48.318s, 97.860mph/157.490km/h.
2 Luke Stapleford (Triumph); **3** Glenn Irwin (Kawasaki); **4** Luke Jones (Triumph); **5** Jake Dixon (Yamaha); **6** Taylor Mackenzie (Suzuki); **7** Callan Cooper (Yamaha); **8** Dean Hipwell (Triumph); **9** James Rispoli (Suzuki); **10** Sam Coventry (Kawasaki); **11** Grant Whitaker (Yamaha); **12** Ben Field (Yamaha); **13** Alex Olsen (Triumph); **14** Paul Curran (Triumph); **15** Carl Phillips (Yamaha).
Fastest lap: Seeley, 1m 37.563s, 99.330mph/159.860km/h.

Race 2 (16 laps, 43.072 miles/69.318km)
1 Billy McConnell (Triumph), 26m 22.012s, 98.010mph/157.730km/h.
2 Alastair Seeley (Yamaha); **3** Graeme Gowland (Triumph); **4** Luke Stapleford (Triumph); **5** Glenn Irwin (Kawasaki); **6** Luke Mossey (Triumph); **7** Luke Jones (Triumph); **8** Jake Dixon (Yamaha); **9** Samuel Hornsey (Triumph); **10** Taylor Mackenzie (Suzuki); **11** Callan Cooper (Yamaha); **12** James Rispoli (Suzuki); **13** Alex Olsen (Triumph); **14** Sam Coventry (Kawasaki); **15** Paul Curran (Triumph).
Fastest lap: Seeley, 1m 37.918s, 98.970mph/159.280km/h.
Championship points: **1** McConnell, 76; **2** Irwin, 63; **3** Seeley, 61; **4** Jones, 52; **5** Stapleford, 50; **6** Gowland, 36.

Motul British Motostar Championship, Round 2 (14 laps, 37.688 miles/60.653km)
1 Jordan Weaving (KTM), 25m 7.334s, 90.010mph/144.860km/h.
2 Edward Rendell (Honda); **3** Jayson Uribe (Honda); **4** Taz Taylor (Luyten Honda); **5** James Flitcroft (Nykos); **6** Anthony Alonso (Honda); **7** Arnie Shelton (Honda); **8** Ryan Saxelby (Honda); **9** Chris Taylor (Honda); **10** Mike Brouwers (Honda); **11** Josh Owens (Honda); **12** James Hobson (Honda); **13** Joseph Thomas (Honda); **14** Kai Johnson (Nykos); **15** Asher Durham (Honda).
Fastest lap: Weaving, 1m 46.665s, 90.850mph/146.220km/h.
Moto3 points: **1** Weaving, 45; **2** Uribe, 36; **3** Taylor, 26; **4** Irving, 25; **5** Brouwers, 21; **6** Booth-Amos, 17.
125GP points: **1** Rendell, 45; **2** Saxelby, 35; **3** Taylor, 33; **4** Flitcroft, 27; **5** Alonso, 22; **6** Shelton, 18.

SNETTERTON, 15 June, 2014, 2.969-mile/4.778km circuit.
MCE British Superbike Championship With Pirelli, Round 3 (2 x 16 laps, 47.504 miles/76.450km)
Race 1
1 Shane Byrne (Kawasaki), 30m 13.693s, 94.280mph/151.730km/h.
2 Josh Brookes (Yamaha); **3** James Ellison (Kawasaki); **4** Tommy Bridewell (Yamaha); **5** Ryuichi Kiyonari (BMW); **6** Chris Walker (Kawasaki); **7** Dan Linfoot (Kawasaki); **8** Patric Muff (BMW); **9** John Hopkins (Suzuki); **10** Josh Waters (Suzuki); **11** Barry Burrell (Kawasaki); **12** Richard Cooper (Kawasaki); **13** Ian Hutchinson (Yamaha); **14** Keith Farmer (Kawasaki); **15** Aaron Zanotti (Suzuki).
Fastest lap: Byrne, 1m 48.119s, 98.850mph/159.090km/h.

Race 2
1 Shane Byrne (Kawasaki), 29m 0.693s, 98.240mph/158.100km/h.
2 James Ellison (Kawasaki); **3** Tommy Bridewell (Yamaha); **4** Ryuichi Kiyonari (BMW); **5** Julien da Costa (Honda); **6** Dan Linfoot (Kawasaki); **7** John Hopkins (Suzuki); **8** Jakub Smrz (Ducati); **9** Richard Cooper (Kawasaki); **10** Josh Waters (Suzuki); **11** Barry Burrell (Kawasaki); **12** Ian Hutchinson (Yamaha); **13** Stuart Easton (Kawasaki); **14** Michael Rutter (BMW); **15** Ben Wilson (Kawasaki).
Fastest lap: Brookes, 1m 47.882s, 99.070mph/159.440km/h.
Championship points: **1** Byrne, 145; **2** Ellison, 100; **3** Brookes, 85; **4** Bridewell, 69; **5** Linfoot, 51; **6** Walker, 49.

Motorpoint British Supersport Championship & Supersport Evo, Round 3
Race 1 (10 laps, 29.690 miles/47.781km)
1 Graeme Gowland (Triumph), 18m 46.658s, 94.860mph/152.660km/h.
2 Alastair Seeley (Yamaha); **3** Billy McConnell (Triumph); **4** Luke Jones (Triumph); **5** Glenn Irwin (Kawasaki); **6** Luke Mossey (Triumph); **7** Taylor Mackenzie (Suzuki); **8** James Rispoli (Suzuki); **9** Luke Stapleford (Triumph); **10** Samuel Hornsey (Triumph); **11** Dean Hipwell (Triumph); **12** Callan Cooper (Yamaha); **13** David Allingham (Yamaha); **14** Alex Olsen (Triumph); **15** Josh Corner (Kawasaki).
Fastest lap: Gowland, 1m 51.137s, 96.170mph/154.770km/h.

Race 2 (15 laps, 44.535 miles/71.672 km)
1 Graeme Gowland (Triumph), 28m 2.661s, 95.270mph/153.320km/h.
2 Billy McConnell (Triumph); **3** Luke Mossey (Triumph); **4** Luke Stapleford (Triumph); **5** Taylor Mackenzie (Suzuki); **6** Glenn Irwin (Kawasaki); **7** Samuel Hornsey (Triumph); **8** Jake Dixon (Yamaha); **9** Callan Cooper (Yamaha); **10** Dean Hipwell (Triumph); **11** Alex Olsen (Triumph); **12** Grant Whitaker (Yamaha); **13** Tim Hastings (Kawasaki); **14** Steve Mercer (Suzuki); **15** Dan Helyer (Yamaha).
Fastest lap: Stapleford, 1m 51.273s, 96.050mph/154.580km/h.
Championship points: **1** McConnell, 112;

2 Gowland, 86; **3** Irwin, 84; **4** Seeley, 81; **5** Stapleford, 70; **6** Jones, 65.

Motul British Motostar Championship, Round 3 (12 laps, 35.628 miles/57.338km)
1 Joe Irving (KTM), 24m 29.238s, 87.290mph/140.480km/h.
2 Bradley Ray (EE125); **3** Jordan Weaving (KTM); **4** Ernst Dubbink (Honda); **5** Edward Rendell (Honda); **6** Jayson Uribe (Honda); **7** Charlie Nesbitt (Repli-Cast); **8** James Hobson (Honda); **9** Taz Taylor (Luyten Honda); **10** Mike Brouwers (Honda); **11** Anthony Alonso (Honda); **12** Chris Taylor (Honda); **13** Arnie Shelton (Honda); **14** Asher Durham (Honda); **15** Elliot Lodge (Honda).
Fastest lap: Weaving, 2m 0.433s, 88.740mph/142.820km/h.
Moto3 points: 1 Weaving, 65; **2** Irving, 50; **3** Uribe, 49; **4** Taylor, 34; **5** Brouwers, 30; **6** Hobson, 27.
125GP points: 1 Rendell, 65; **2** Taylor, 49; **3** Ray, 41; **4** Saxelby, 35; **5** Alonso, 35; **6** Shelton, 29.

KNOCKHILL, 29 June, 2014, 1.267-mile/2.039km circuit.
MCE British Superbike Championship With Pirelli, Round 4 (2 x 30 laps, 38.010 miles/61.171km)
Race 1
1 Ryuichi Kiyonari (BMW), 24m 26.947s, 93.270mph/150.100km/h.
2 Shane Byrne (Kawasaki); **3** Stuart Easton (Kawasaki); **4** Josh Brookes (Yamaha); **5** Chris Walker (Kawasaki); **6** Tommy Bridewell (Yamaha); **7** Dan Linfoot (Kawasaki); **8** Barry Burrell (Kawasaki); **9** John Hopkins (Suzuki); **10** James Westmoreland (BMW); **11** Richard Cooper (Kawasaki); **12** Jakub Smrz (Ducati); **13** Michael Rutter (BMW); **14** Peter Hickman (Honda); **15** Keith Farmer (Kawasaki).
Fastest lap: Byrne, 48.435s, 94.160mph/151.550km/h.

Race 2
1 Shane Byrne (Kawasaki), 24m 24.655s, 93.420mph/150.340km/h.
2 Ryuichi Kiyonari (BMW); **3** Chris Walker (Kawasaki); **4** Josh Brookes (Yamaha); **5** Stuart Easton (Kawasaki); **6** Dan Linfoot (Kawasaki); **7** Tommy Bridewell (Yamaha); **8** James Ellison (Kawasaki); **9** Richard Cooper (Kawasaki); **10** Michael Rutter (BMW); **11** John Hopkins (Suzuki); **12** Jakub Smrz (Ducati); **13** Peter Hickman (Honda); **14** Keith Farmer (Kawasaki); **15** Ian Hutchinson (Yamaha).
Fastest lap: Kiyonari, 48.253s, 94.520mph/152.120km/h.
Championship points: 1 Byrne, 190; **2** Brookes, 111; **3** Ellison, 108; **4** Bridewell, 88; **5** Kiyonari, 82; **6** Walker, 76.

Motorpoint British Supersport Championship & Supersport Evo, Round 4
Race 1 (12 laps, 15.204 miles/24.468km)
1 Graeme Gowland (Triumph), 10m 2.980s, 90.770mph/146.080km/h.
2 Billy McConnell (Triumph); **3** Luke Stapleford (Triumph); **4** Luke Jones (Triumph); **5** Jake Dixon (Yamaha); **6** Alastair Seeley (Yamaha); **7** Luke Mossey (Triumph); **8** Samuel Hornsey (Triumph); **9** Taylor Mackenzie (Suzuki); **10** Glenn Irwin (Kawasaki); **11** James Rispoli (Suzuki); **12** Bjorn Estment (Yamaha); **13** Dean Hipwell (Triumph); **14** Tim Hastings (Kawasaki); **15** Alex Olsen (Triumph).
Fastest lap: Stapleford, 49.653s, 91.850mph/147.830km/h.

Race 2 (26 laps, 32.942 miles/53.015km)
1 Luke Mossey (Triumph), 22m 43.288s, 86.980mph/139.980km/h.
2 Billy McConnell (Triumph); **3** Luke Stapleford (Triumph); **4** Jake Dixon (Yamaha); **5** Alastair Seeley (Yamaha); **6** Glenn Irwin (Kawasaki); **7** Luke Jones (Triumph); **8** Bjorn Estment (Yamaha); **9** Dean Hipwell (Triumph); **10** Alex Olsen (Triumph); **11** James Rispoli (Suzuki); **12** Tim Hastings (Kawasaki); **13** Ben Field (Yamaha); **14** Danny Webb (Kawasaki); **15** Grant Whitaker (Yamaha).
Fastest lap: Mossey, 49.889s, 91.420mph/147.130km/h.
Championship points: 1 McConnell, 152; **2** Gowland, 111; **3** Seeley, 102; **4** Stapleford, 102; **5** Irwin, 100; **6** Jones, 87.

Motul British Motostar Championship, Round 4 (22 laps, 27.874 miles/44.859km)
1 Jordan Weaving (KTM), 20m 2.423s, 83.450mph/134.300km/h.
2 Joe Irving (KTM); **3** Jayson Uribe (Honda); **4** James Hobson (Honda); **5** Edward Rendell (Honda); **6** Charlie Nesbitt (Repli-Cast); **7** Arnie Shelton (Honda); **8** Elliot Lodge (Honda); **9** Josh Owens (Honda); **10** Asher Durham (Honda); **11** Kai Johnson (Nykos); **12** Sam Burman (Honda); **13** Joseph Thomas (Honda); **14** Joe Thompson (Repli-Cast); **15** Louis Valleley (KTM).
Fastest lap: Irving, 54.006s, 84.450mph/135.910km/h.
Moto3 points: 1 Weaving, 90; **2** Irving, 70; **3** Uribe, 65; **4** Hobson, 40; **5** Taylor, 34; **6** Nesbitt, 33.
125GP points: 1 Rendell, 90; **2** Taylor, 49; **3** Shelton, 49; **4** Ray, 41; **5** Saxelby, 35; **6** Alonso, 35.

BRANDS HATCH GP, 19–20 July, 2014, 2.433-mile/3.916km circuit.
MCE British Superbike Championship With Pirelli, Round 5
Race 1 (19 laps, 46.227 miles/74.395km)
1 Ryuichi Kiyonari (BMW), 28m 21.703s, 97.800mph/157.390km/h.
2 Shane Byrne (Kawasaki); **3** James Ellison (Kawasaki); **4** Chris Walker (Kawasaki); **5** Dan Linfoot (Kawasaki); **6** Josh Brookes (Yamaha); **7** Jakub Smrz (Ducati); **8** Richard Cooper (Kawasaki); **9** John Hopkins (Suzuki); **10** Stuart Easton (Kawasaki); **11** Howie Mainwaring (Kawasaki); **12** Peter Hickman (Honda); **13** Jon Kirkham (Kawasaki); **14** Josh Waters (Suzuki); **15** Patric Muff (BMW).
Fastest lap: Byrne, 1m 26.751s, 100.970mph/162.500km/h.

Race 2 (15 laps, 36.495 miles/58.733km)
1 Josh Waters (Suzuki), 24m 55.675s, 87.850mph/141.380km/h.
2 Richard Cooper (Kawasaki); **3** Keith Farmer (Kawasaki); **4** Tommy Bridewell (Yamaha); **5** Shane Byrne (Kawasaki); **6** Jon Kirkham (Kawasaki); **7** Dan Linfoot (Kawasaki); **8** Josh Brookes (Yamaha); **9** Chris Walker (Kawasaki); **10** John Hopkins (Suzuki); **11** Gary Mason (Kawasaki); **12** John Ingram (Kawasaki); **13** Peter Hickman (Honda); **14** Stuart Easton (Kawasaki); **15** Ben Wilson (Kawasaki).
Fastest lap: Farmer, 1m 37.336s, 89.990mph/144.830km/h.
Championship points: 1 Byrne, 221; **2** Brookes, 129; **3** Ellison, 124; **4** Kiyonari, 107; **5** Bridewell, 101; **6** Walker, 96.

Motorpoint British Supersport Championship & Supersport Evo, Round 5
Race 1 (12 laps, 29.196 miles/46.986km)
1 Alastair Seeley (Yamaha), 17m 56.178s, 97.670mph/157.180km/h.
2 Graeme Gowland (Triumph); **3** Luke Jones (Triumph); **4** Jake Dixon (Yamaha); **5** Luke Stapleford (Triumph); **6** Luke Mossey (Triumph); **7** Glenn Irwin (Kawasaki); **8** James Rispoli (Yamaha); **9** Taylor Mackenzie (Suzuki); **10** Luke Hedger (Kawasaki); **11** Bjorn Estment (Yamaha); **12** Alex Olsen (Triumph); **13** Tim Hastings (Kawasaki); **14** Samuel Hornsey (Triumph); **15** Danny Webb (Kawasaki).
Fastest lap: Jones, 1m 28.943s, 98.480mph/158.500km/h.

Race 2 (18 laps, 43.794 miles/70.480km)
1 Alastair Seeley (Yamaha), 26m 42.648s, 98.380mph/158.330km/h.
2 Graeme Gowland (Triumph); **3** Luke Jones (Triumph); **4** Jake Dixon (Yamaha); **5** Luke Stapleford (Triumph); **6** Billy McConnell (Triumph); **7** Glenn Irwin (Kawasaki); **8** Luke Mossey (Triumph); **9** Taylor Mackenzie (Suzuki); **10** Luke Hedger (Kawasaki); **11** Bjorn Estment (Yamaha); **12** James Rispoli (Yamaha); **13** Samuel Hornsey (Triumph); **14** Alex Olsen (Triumph); **15** Danny Webb (Kawasaki).
Fastest lap: Gowland, 1m 28.294s, 99.210mph/159.660km/h.
Championship points: 1 McConnell, 162; **2** Seeley, 152; **3** Gowland, 151; **4** Stapleford, 124; **5** Jones, 119; **6** Irwin, 118.

Motul British Motostar Championship, Round 5 (12 laps, 29.196 miles/46.986km)
1 Olly Simpson (KTM), 19m 10.865s, 91.330mph/146.980km/h.
2 Jordan Weaving (KTM); **3** Joe Irving (KTM); **4** Bradley Ray (EE125); **5** Taz Taylor (Luyten Honda); **6** Ernst Dubbink (Honda); **7** Edward Rendell (Honda); **8** Jayson Uribe (Honda); **9** James Hobson (Honda); **10** Charlie Nesbitt (Repli-Cast); **11** Brian Slooten (Honda); **12** Arnie Shelton (Honda); **13** Alex Persson (Honda); **14** Elliot Lodge (Honda); **15** Chris Taylor (Honda).
Fastest lap: Irving, 1m 54.006s, 84.450mph/135.910km/h.
Moto3 points: 1 Weaving, 110; **2** Irving, 86; **3** Uribe, 76; **4** Hobson, 50; **5** Nesbitt, 42; **6** Taylor, 41.
125GP points: 1 Rendell, 106; **2** Taylor, 69; **3** Ray, 66; **4** Shelton, 62; **5** Lodge, 40; **6** Saxelby, 35.

THRUXTON, 3 August, 2014, 2.356-mile/3.792km circuit.
MCE British Superbike Championship With Pirelli, Round 6
Race 1 (20 laps, 47.120 miles/75.832km)
1 Josh Brookes (Yamaha), 25m 39.249s, 110.200mph/177.350km/h.
2 Shane Byrne (Kawasaki); **3** Ryuichi Kiyonari (BMW); **4** Dan Linfoot (Kawasaki); **5** Tommy Bridewell (Yamaha); **6** Jakub Smrz (Ducati); **7** Chris Walker (Kawasaki); **8** John Hopkins (Suzuki); **9** Michael Rutter (BMW); **10** Patric Muff (BMW); **11** Jon Kirkham (Kawasaki); **12** Peter Hickman (Honda); **13** Barry Burrell (Kawasaki); **14** Keith Farmer (Kawasaki); **15** Lee Jackson (BMW).
Fastest lap: Linfoot, 1m 15.930s, 111.700mph/179.760km/h.

Race 2 (15 laps, 35.340 miles/56.874km)
1 Josh Brookes (Yamaha), 19m 11.792s, 110.450mph/177.750km/h.
2 Shane Byrne (Kawasaki); **3** Ryuichi Kiyonari (BMW); **4** Dan Linfoot (Kawasaki); **5** Chris Walker (Kawasaki); **6** Jon Kirkham (Kawasaki); **7** Stuart Easton (Kawasaki); **8** John Hopkins (Suzuki); **9** Howie Mainwaring (Kawasaki); **10** Peter Hickman (Honda); **11** Patric Muff (BMW); **12** Josh Waters (Suzuki); **13** Jakub Smrz (Ducati); **14** Barry Burrell (Kawasaki); **15** Aaron Zanotti (Suzuki).
Fastest lap: Kiyonari, 1m 16.015s, 111.570mph/179.560km/h.
Championship points: 1 Byrne, 261; **2** Brookes, 179; **3** Kiyonari, 139; **4** Ellison, 124; **5** Walker, 116; **6** Linfoot, 116.

Motorpoint British Supersport Championship & Supersport Evo, Round 6
Race 1 (12 laps, 28.272 miles/45.499km)
1 Alastair Seeley (Yamaha), 15m 38.412s, 108.450mph/174.530km/h.
2 Luke Jones (Triumph); **3** Graeme Gowland (Triumph); **4** Billy McConnell* (Triumph); **5** Glenn Irwin (Kawasaki); **6** Luke Mossey (Triumph); **7** Luke Stapleford (Triumph); **8** Taylor Mackenzie (Suzuki); **9** James Rispoli (Yamaha); **10** Jake Dixon (Yamaha); **11** Bjorn Estment (Yamaha); **12** Luke Hedger (Kawasaki); **13** Alex Olsen (Triumph); **14** Tim Hastings (Kawasaki); **15** Danny Webb (Kawasaki).
** Received two-place post-race penalty.*
Fastest lap: Mossey, 1m 17.322s, 109.690mph/176.530km/h.

Race 2 (18 laps, 42.408 miles/68.249km)
1 Graeme Gowland (Triumph), 23m 29.530s, 108.310mph/174.310km/h.
2 Luke Mossey (Triumph); **3** Billy McConnell (Triumph); **4** Luke Jones (Triumph); **5** Alastair Seeley (Yamaha); **6** Luke Stapleford (Triumph); **7** Glenn Irwin (Kawasaki); **8** James Rispoli (Yamaha); **9** Bjorn Estment (Yamaha); **10** Jake Dixon (Yamaha); **11** Luke Hedger (Kawasaki); **12** Alex Olsen (Triumph); **13** David Allingham (Yamaha); **14** Samuel Hornsey (Triumph); **15** Dean Hipwell (Triumph).
Fastest lap: Irwin, 1m 17.200s, 109.860mph/176.810km/h.
Championship points: 1 Gowland, 192; **2** McConnell, 191; **3** Seeley, 188; **4** Jones, 152; **5** Stapleford, 143; **6** Irwin, 138.

Motul British Motostar Championship, Round 6 (14 laps, 32.984 miles/53.083km)
1 Joe Irving (KTM), 19m 15.404s, 102.770mph/165.390km/h.
2 Jordan Weaving (KTM); **3** Edward Rendell (Honda); **4** James Hobson (Honda); **5** Taz Taylor (Luyten Honda); **6** Jayson Uribe (Honda); **7** Mike Brouwers (Honda); **8** Charlie Nesbitt (Repli-Cast); **9** Georgina Polden (Honda); **10** Arnie Shelton (Honda); **11** Alex Persson (Honda); **12** Chris Taylor (Honda); **13** Asher Durham (Honda); **14** Sam Burman (Honda); **15** Joe Thompson (Repli-Cast).
Fastest lap: Weaving, 1m 21.844s, 103.630mph/166.770km/h.
Moto3 points: 1 Weaving, 130; **2** Irving, 111; **3** Uribe, 89; **4** Hobson, 66; **5** Nesbitt, 52; **6** Taylor, 50.
125GP points: 1 Rendell, 131; **2** Taylor, 89; **3** Shelton, 75; **4** Ray, 66; **5** Durham, 41; **6** Lodge, 40.

OULTON PARK, 9–10 August, 2014, 2.692-mile/4.332km circuit.
MCE British Superbike Championship With Pirelli, Round 7
Race 1 (15 laps, 40.380 miles/64.985km)
1 Ryuichi Kiyonari (BMW), 24m 11.609s, 100.140mph/161.160km/h.
2 Josh Brookes (Yamaha); **3** Shane Byrne (Kawasaki); **4** Tommy Bridewell (Yamaha); **5** Dan Linfoot (Kawasaki); **6** John Hopkins (Suzuki); **7** Peter Hickman (Honda); **8** Josh Waters (Suzuki); **9** Stuart Easton (Kawasaki); **10** Howie Mainwaring (Kawasaki); **11** Jakub Smrz (Ducati); **12** Patric Muff (BMW); **13** Barry Burrell (Kawasaki); **14** Jon Kirkham (Kawasaki); **15** Lee Jackson (BMW).
Fastest lap: Brookes, 1m 35.877s, 101.080mph/162.670km/h.

Race 2 (18 laps, 48.456 miles/77.982km)
1 Ryuichi Kiyonari (BMW), 29m 33.324s, 98.370mph/158.310km/h.
2 Josh Brookes (Yamaha); **3** Shane Byrne (Kawasaki); **4** Dan Linfoot (Kawasaki); **5** Chris Walker (Kawasaki); **6** Stuart Easton (Kawasaki); **7** Tommy Bridewell (Yamaha); **8** Jon Kirkham (Kawasaki); **9** Josh Waters (Suzuki); **10** Patric Muff (BMW); **11** Michael Rutter (BMW); **12** Jakub Smrz (Ducati); **13** Keith Farmer (Kawasaki); **14** Glen Richards (Kawasaki); **15** Scott Smart (Kawasaki);
Fastest lap: Byrne, 1m 36.241s, 100.690mph/162.050km/h.

Race 3 (18 laps, 48.456 miles/77.982km)
1 Josh Brookes (Yamaha), 29m 30.630s, 98.520mph/158.550km/h.
2 Shane Byrne (Kawasaki); **3** Dan Linfoot (Kawasaki); **4** Ryuichi Kiyonari (BMW); **5** Stuart Easton (Kawasaki); **6** Josh Waters (Suzuki); **7** Chris Walker (Kawasaki); **8** Tommy Bridewell (Yamaha); **9** Jon Kirkham (Kawasaki); **10** Jakub Smrz (Ducati); **11** Michael Rutter (BMW); **12** Glen Richards (Kawasaki); **13** Peter Hickman (Honda); **14** Scott Smart (Kawasaki); **15** Howie Mainwaring (Kawasaki).
Fastest lap: Kiyonari, 1m 36.002s, 100.940mph/162.460km/h.
Championship points: 1 Byrne, 313; **2** Brookes, 244; **3** Kiyonari, 202; **4** Linfoot, 156; **5** Bridewell, 142; **6** Walker, 136.

Motorpoint British Supersport Championship & Supersport Evo, Round 7
Race 1 (10 laps, 26.920 miles/43.324km)
1 Billy McConnell (Triumph), 16m 33.317s, 97.560mph/157.010km/h.
2 Graeme Gowland (Triumph); **3** Luke Mossey (Triumph); **4** Jake Dixon (Yamaha); **5** Alastair Seeley (Yamaha); **6** Luke Jones (Triumph); **7** Luke Hedger (Kawasaki); **8** Taylor Mackenzie (Suzuki); **9** James Rispoli (Yamaha); **10** Samuel Hornsey (Triumph); **11** Dean Hipwell (Triumph); **12** David Allingham (Yamaha); **13** Danny Webb (Kawasaki); **14** Bjorn Estment (Yamaha); **15** Alex Olsen (Triumph).
Fastest lap: Gowland, 1m 38.178s, 98.710mph/158.860km/h.

Race 2 (15 laps, 40.380 miles/64.985km)
1 Alastair Seeley (Yamaha), 28m 42.197s, 84.400mph/135.830km/h.
2 Glenn Irwin (Kawasaki); **3** Graeme Gowland (Triumph); **4** Luke Jones (Triumph); **5** Billy McConnell (Triumph); **6** James Rispoli (Yamaha); **7** Luke Stapleford (Triumph); **8** Luke Hedger (Kawasaki); **9** Samuel Hornsey (Triumph); **10** Taylor Mackenzie (Suzuki); **11** Danny Webb (Kawasaki); **12** Luke Mossey (Triumph); **13** Dean Hipwell (Triumph); **14** Josh Corner (Kawasaki); **15** Alex Olsen (Triumph).
Fastest lap: Seeley, 1m 45.329s, 92.000mph/148.070km/h.
Championship points: 1 Gowland, 228; **2** McConnell, 227; **3** Seeley, 224; **4** Jones, 175; **5** Irwin, 158; **6** Stapleford, 152.

Motul British Motostar Championship, Round 7 (10 laps, 26.920 miles/43.324km)
1 Joe Irving (KTM), 19m 46.385s, 81.680mph/131.450km/h.
2 Edward Rendell (Honda); **3** Jordan Weaving (KTM); **4** Jayson Uribe (Honda); **5** Chris Taylor (Honda); **6** Mike Brouwers (Honda); **7** Joe Thompson (Repli-Cast); **8** Vasco van der Valk (Honda); **9** Josh Owens (Honda); **10** Daniel Hermansson (TSR Luyten); **11** Jake Archer (Honda); **12** Greg Greenwood (Luyten Honda); **13** Asher Durham (Honda); **14** Sam Burman (Honda); **15** Louis Valleley (KTM).
Fastest lap: Irving, 1m 56.913s, 82.890mph/133.400km/h.
Moto3 points: 1 Weaving, 150; **2** Irving, 136; **3** Uribe, 105; **4** Hobson, 73; **5** Taylor, 63; **6** Nesbitt, 52.
125GP points: 1 Rendell, 156; **2** Taylor, 89; **3** Shelton, 75; **4** Ray, 66; **5** Durham, 51; **6** Owens, 50.

CADWELL PARK, 25 August, 2014, 2.180-mile/3.508km circuit.
MCE British Superbike Championship With Pirelli, Round 8
Race 1 (10 laps, 21.800 miles/35.084km)
1 Tommy Bridewell (Yamaha), 15m 2.868s, 86.920mph/139.880km/h.
2 Shane Byrne (Kawasaki); **3** Chris Walker (Ka-

wasaki); **4** Josh Brookes (Yamaha); **5** Josh Waters (Suzuki); **6** Peter Hickman (Honda); **7** Dan Linfoot (Kawasaki); **8** Jon Kirkham (Kawasaki); **9** Stuart Easton (Kawasaki); **10** Glen Richards (Kawasaki); **11** James Westmoreland (BMW); **12** Ben Wilson (Kawasaki); **13** John Hopkins (Suzuki); **14** Patric Muff (BMW); **15** Howie Mainwaring (Kawasaki).
Fastest lap: Kiyonari, 1m 28.796s, 88.380mph/142.230km/h.

Race 2 (15 laps, 32.700 miles/52.626km)
1 Peter Hickman (Honda), 25m 16.852s, 77.600mph/124.890km/h.
2 Shane Byrne (Kawasaki); **3** Tommy Bridewell (Yamaha); **4** Gary Mason (Kawasaki); **5** Josh Waters (Suzuki); **6** Jon Kirkham (Kawasaki); **7** Glen Richards (Kawasaki); **8** Chris Walker (Kawasaki); **9** Ben Wilson (Kawasaki); **10** Michael Rutter (BMW); **11** Dan Linfoot (Kawasaki); **12** Howie Mainwaring (Kawasaki); **13** Patric Muff (BMW); **14** John Ingram (Kawasaki); **15** Scott Smart (Kawasaki).
Fastest lap: Byrne, 1m 38.889s, 79.360mph/127.720km/h.
Championship points: **1** Byrne, 353; **2** Brookes, 257; **3** Kiyonari, 202; **4** Bridewell, 183; **5** Linfoot, 170; **6** Walker, 160.

Motorpoint British Supersport Championship & Supersport Evo, Round 8
Race 1 (12 laps, 26.160 miles/42.100km)
1 Billy McConnell (Triumph), 17m 59.996s, 87.200mph/140.330km/h.
2 Graeme Gowland (Triumph); **3** Luke Stapleford (Triumph); **4** Glenn Irwin (Kawasaki); **5** Luke Jones (Triumph); **6** Alastair Seeley (Yamaha); **7** Luke Hedger (Kawasaki); **8** James Rispoli (Yamaha); **9** Samuel Hornsey (Triumph); **10** Bjorn Estment (Yamaha); **11** Dean Hipwell (Triumph); **12** Alex Olsen (Triumph); **13** Ben Field (Triumph); **14** Taylor Mackenzie (Suzuki); **15** Josh Corner (Kawasaki).
Fastest lap: McConnell, 1m 28.891s, 88.280mph/142.080km/h.

Race 2 (14 laps, 30.520 miles/49.117km)
1 Glenn Irwin (Kawasaki), 23m 31.644s, 77.830mph/125.260km/h.
2 Billy McConnell (Triumph); **3** Graeme Gowland (Triumph); **4** Luke Stapleford (Triumph); **5** Samuel Hornsey (Triumph); **6** Dean Hipwell (Triumph); **7** Taylor Mackenzie (Suzuki); **8** Josh Corner (Kawasaki); **9** Tim Hastings (Kawasaki); **10** Grant Whitaker (Yamaha); **11** Ben Field (Triumph); **12** James Henry (Kawasaki); **13** DNF; **14** DNF; **15** DNF.
Fastest lap: Dixon, 1m 38.802s, 79.430mph/127.830km/h.
Championship points: **1** McConnell, 272; **2** Gowland, 264; **3** Seeley, 234; **4** Irwin, 196; **5** Jones, 186; **6** Stapleford, 181.

Motul British Motostar Championship, Round 8
Postponed until Donington Park due to weather conditions.

DONINGTON PARK, 7 September, 2014, 2.487-mile/4.002km circuit.
MCE British Superbike Championship With Pirelli, Round 9 (2 x 20 laps, 49.740 miles/80.049km
Race 1
1 Ryuichi Kiyonari (BMW), 31m 0.650s, 96.250mph/154.900km/h.
2 Shane Byrne (Kawasaki); **3** Tommy Bridewell (Yamaha); **4** Josh Brookes (Yamaha); **5** Stuart Easton (Kawasaki); **6** Josh Waters (Suzuki); **7** Peter Hickman (Honda); **8** Dan Linfoot (Kawasaki); **9** Patric Muff (BMW); **10** James Westmoreland (BMW); **11** Chris Walker (Kawasaki); **12** Jon Kirkham (Kawasaki); **13** Howie Mainwaring (Kawasaki); **14** James Ellison (Kawasaki); **15** Julien da Costa (Honda).
Fastest lap: Waters, 1m 30.064s, 99.420mph/160.000km/h.

Race 2
1 Ryuichi Kiyonari (BMW), 30m 8.256s, 99.030mph/159.370km/h.
2 Shane Byrne (Kawasaki); **3** Josh Brookes (Yamaha); **4** Stuart Easton (Kawasaki); **5** Josh Waters (Suzuki); **6** Julien da Costa (Honda); **7** Peter Hickman (Honda); **8** James Westmoreland (BMW); **9** John Hopkins (Suzuki); **10** Chris Walker (Kawasaki); **11** James Ellison (Kawasaki); **12** Howie Mainwaring (Kawasaki); **13** Jon Kirkham (Kawasaki); **14** Dan Linfoot (Kawasaki); **15** Filip Backlund (Yamaha).
Fastest lap: Kiyonari, 1m 29.803s, 99.710mph/160.470km/h.

The top six BSB riders in points after Donington Park qualified for 'The Showdown', to decide the championship over the last three rounds. These six title fighters had their points equalised at 500 and then podium credits added from their main season results (5 points for each 1st place, 3 points for 2nd, 1 point for 3rd).

Championship points for start of Showdown: **1** Byrne, 562; **2** Brookes, 536; **3** Kiyonari, 535; **4** Bridewell, 508; **5** Walker, 505; **6** Linfoot, 501.

Motorpoint British Supersport Championship & Supersport Evo, Round 9
Race 1 (10 laps, 24.870 miles/40.024km)
1 Glenn Irwin (Kawasaki), 15m 23.367s, 96.970mph/156.060km/h.
2 Luke Mossey (Triumph); **3** Graeme Gowland (Triumph); **4** Billy McConnell (Triumph); **5** Luke Hedger (Kawasaki); **6** Samuel Hornsey (Triumph); **7** Luke Stapleford (Triumph); **8** Alastair Seeley (Yamaha); **9** Luke Jones (Triumph); **10** Taylor Mackenzie (Suzuki); **11** Jake Dixon (Yamaha); **12** Alex Olsen (Triumph); **13** Tim Hastings (Kawasaki); **14** Dean Hipwell (Triumph); **15** Josh Corner (Kawasaki).
Fastest lap: Gowland, 1m 31.454s, 97.910mph/157.570km/h.

Race 2 (18 laps, 44.766 miles/72.044km)
1 Luke Mossey (Triumph), 28m 22.757s, 94.650mph/152.320km/h.
2 Graeme Gowland (Triumph); **3** Billy McConnell (Triumph); **4** Luke Stapleford (Triumph); **5** Glenn Irwin (Kawasaki); **6** Luke Jones (Triumph); **7** Jake Dixon (Yamaha); **8** James Rispoli (Yamaha); **9** Alex Olsen (Triumph); **10** Josh Corner (Kawasaki); **11** Dean Hipwell (Triumph); **12** Lee Johnston (Honda); **13** Paul Curran (Triumph); **14** Jamie Perrin (Yamaha); **15** Ben Field (Triumph).
Fastest lap: McConnell, 1m 31.807s, 97.530mph/156.960km/h.
Championship points: **1** McConnell, 301; **2** Gowland, 300; **3** Seeley, 242; **4** Irwin, 232; **5** Jones, 203; **6** Stapleford, 203.

Motul British Motostar Championship, Rounds 8 & 9
Race 1 (10 laps, 24.870 miles/40.024km)
1 Joe Irving (KTM), 16m 27.474s, 90.680mph/145.940km/h.
2 Bradley Ray (EE125); **3** Jordan Weaving (KTM); **4** Taz Taylor (Luyten Honda); **5** Olly Simpson (KTM); **6** Edward Rendell (Honda); **7** Arnie Shelton (Honda); **8** James Hobson (KTM); **9** Asher Durham (Honda); **10** Georgina Polden (Honda); **11** Mike Brouwers (Honda); **12** Brian Slooten (Honda); **13** Chris Taylor (Honda); **14** Sam Burman (Honda); **15** Joe Thompson (Repli-Cast).
Fastest lap: Irving, 1m 37.502s, 91.830mph/147.800km/h.

Race 2 (14 laps, 34.818 miles/56.034km)
1 Bradley Ray (EE125), 23m 15.918s, 89.800mph/144.520km/h.
2 Jordan Weaving (KTM); **3** Taz Taylor (Luyten Honda); **4** Asher Durham (Honda); **5** Edward Rendell (Honda); **6** Charlie Nesbitt (Repli-Cast); **7** Jayson Uribe (Honda); **8** James Hobson (KTM); **9** Brian Slooten (Honda); **10** Chris Taylor (Honda); **11** Elliot Lodge (Honda); **12** Daniel Hermansson (TSR Luyten); **13** Greg Greenwood (Luyten Honda); **14** Kai Johnson (Aprilia); **15** Sam Burman (Honda).
Fastest lap: Irving, 1m 38.252s, 91.130mph/146.670km/h.
Moto3 points: **1** Weaving, 195; **2** Irving, 161; **3** Uribe, 118; **4** Hobson, 97; **5** Taylor, 80; **6** Nesbitt, 68.
125GP points: **1** Rendell, 188; **2** Taylor, 129; **3** Ray, 116; **4** Shelton, 88; **5** Lodge, 61; **6** Greenwood, 59.

ASSEN, 21 September, 2014, 2.822-mile/4.452km circuit.
MCE British Superbike Championship With Pirelli, Round 10
Race 1 (17 laps, 47.974 miles/77.207km)
1 Josh Waters (Suzuki), 31m 59.961s, 89.960mph/144.780km/h.
2 Ryuichi Kiyonari (BMW); **3** Stuart Easton (Kawasaki); **4** James Ellison (Kawasaki); **5** Christian Iddon (Bimota); **6** Dan Linfoot (Kawasaki); **7** Jed Metcher (Kawasaki); **8** Howie Mainwaring (Kawasaki); **9** Tommy Bridewell (Yamaha); **10** Lee Jackson (BMW); **11** Gary Mason (Kawasaki); **12** Peter Hickman (Honda); **13** Ben Wilson (Kawasaki); **14** James Westmoreland (BMW); **15** Aaron Zanotti (Suzuki).
Fastest lap: Kirkham, 1m 48.285s, 93.820mph/151.000km/h.

Race 2 (18 laps, 50.796 miles/81.748km)
1 Shane Byrne (Kawasaki), 29m 33.013s, 103.140mph/165.990km/h.
2 Ryuichi Kiyonari (BMW); **3** Tommy Bridewell (Yamaha); **4** Dan Linfoot (Kawasaki); **5** John Hopkins (Suzuki); **6** Stuart Easton (Kawasaki); **7** James Ellison (Kawasaki); **8** Josh Waters (Suzuki); **9** Filip Backlund (Yamaha); **10** James Westmoreland (BMW); **11** Kevin Valk (Kawasaki); **12** Lee Jackson (BMW); **13** Jed Metcher (Kawasaki); **14** Martin Jessopp (BMW); **15** Barry Burrell (Kawasaki).
Fastest lap: Linfoot, 1m 37.586s, 104.110mph/167.550km/h.
Championship points: **1** Byrne, 587; **2** Kiyonari, 575; **3** Brookes, 536; **4** Bridewell, 531; **5** Linfoot, 524; **6** Walker, 505.

Motorpoint British Supersport Championship & Supersport Evo, Round 10
Race 1 (11 laps, 31.042 miles/49.957km)
1 Alastair Seeley (Yamaha), 20m 26.371s, 91.130mph/146.660km/h.
2 James Rispoli (Yamaha); **3** Luke Jones (Triumph); **4** Glenn Irwin (Kawasaki); **5** Kervin Bos (Honda); **6** Jake Dixon (Yamaha); **7** Kyle Ryde (Yamaha); **8** Dean Hipwell (Triumph); **9** Luke Mossey (Triumph); **10** Chris Nobel (Suzuki); **11** Billy McConnell (Triumph); **12** Luke Stapleford (Triumph); **13** Taylor Mackenzie (Suzuki); **14** Rob Hartog (Suzuki); **15** Samuel Hornsey (Triumph).
Fastest lap: Hornsey, 1m 45.668s, 96.150mph/154.740km/h.

Race 2 (12 laps, 33.864 miles/54.499km)
1 Billy McConnell (Triumph), 20m 12.604s, 100.540mph/161.800km/h.
2 Graeme Gowland (Triumph); **3** Luke Mossey (Triumph); **4** Luke Stapleford (Triumph); **5** Luke Jones (Triumph); **6** Alastair Seeley (Yamaha); **7** Kyle Ryde (Yamaha); **8** Kervin Bos (Honda); **9** Samuel Hornsey (Triumph); **10** Luke Hedger (Kawasaki); **11** Jake Dixon (Yamaha); **12** James Rispoli (Yamaha); **13** Sam Coventry (Kawasaki); **14** Alex Olsen (Triumph); **15** Chris Nobel (Suzuki).
Fastest lap: Stapleford, 1m 39.478s, 102.130mph/164.370km/h.
Championship points: **1** McConnell, 332; **2** Gowland, 320; **3** Seeley, 277; **4** Irwin, 245; **5** Jones, 230; **6** Stapleford, 221.

Motul British Motostar Championship, Round 10 (9 laps, 25.398 miles/40.874km)
1 Bo Bendsneyder (FTR Honda), 16m 6.965s, 94.560mph/152.180km/h.
2 Olly Simpson (KTM); **3** Ernst Dubbink (Ten Kate Honda); **4** Thomas Van Leeuwen (KTM); **5** Joe Irving (KTM); **6** Jordan Weaving (KTM); **7** Taz Taylor (Luyten Honda); **8** Jayson Uribe (Honda); **9** Arnie Shelton (Honda); **10** Edward Rendell (Honda); **11** Mike Brouwers (Honda); **12** Charlie Nesbitt (Repli-Cast); **13** Felix Nassi (Honda); **14** Alex Persson (Honda); **15** Asher Durham (Honda).
Fastest lap: Bendsneyder, 1m 46.144s, 95.720mph/154.040km/h.
Moto3 points: **1** Weaving, 205; **2** Irving, 172; **3** Uribe, 127; **4** Hobson, 97; **5** Taylor, 83; **6** Nesbitt, 75.
125GP points: **1** Rendell, 204; **2** Taylor, 154; **3** Ray, 116; **4** Shelton, 108; **5** Lodge, 68; **6** Greenwood, 62.

SILVERSTONE, 5 October, 2014, 3.667-mile/5.902km circuit.
MCE British Superbike Championship With Pirelli, Round 11 (2 x 14 laps, 51.338 miles/82.621km)
Race 1
1 Shane Byrne (Kawasaki), 29m 41.657s, 103.740mph/166.950km/h.
2 Ryuichi Kiyonari (BMW); **3** Josh Brookes (Yamaha); **4** Dan Linfoot (Kawasaki); **5** Stuart Easton (Kawasaki); **6** Julien da Costa (Honda); **7** Josh Waters (Suzuki); **8** James Westmoreland (BMW); **9** Peter Hickman (Honda); **10** Tommy Bridewell (Yamaha); **11** James Ellison (Kawasaki); **12** Chris Walker (Kawasaki); **13** Filip Backlund (Yamaha); **14** Patric Muff (BMW); **15** Gary Mason (Kawasaki).
Fastest lap: Byrne, 2m 6.576s, 104.300mph/167.860km/h.

Race 2
1 Ryuichi Kiyonari (BMW), 29m 35.185s, 104.120mph/167.560km/h.
2 Shane Byrne (Kawasaki); **3** James Ellison (Kawasaki); **4** Tommy Bridewell (Yamaha); **5** Josh Waters (Suzuki); **6** Stuart Easton (Kawasaki); **7** Dan Linfoot (Kawasaki); **8** Julien da Costa (Honda); **9** Peter Hickman (Honda); **10** James Westmoreland (BMW); **11** Filip Backlund (Yamaha); **12** Chris Walker (Kawasaki); **13** Patric Muff (BMW);14 Howie Mainwaring (Kawasaki); **15** Jon Kirkham (Kawasaki).
Fastest lap: Kiyonari, 2m 6.326s, 104.510mph/168.190km/h.
Championship points: **1** Byrne, 632; **2** Kiyonari, 620; **3** Brookes, 552; **4** Bridewell, 550; **5** Linfoot, 546; **6** Walker, 513.

Motorpoint British Supersport Championship & Supersport Evo, Round 11
Race 1 (9 laps, 33.003 miles/53.113km)
1 Alastair Seeley (Yamaha), 19m 53.994s, 99.510mph/160.150km/h.
2 Taylor Mackenzie (Suzuki); **3** James Rispoli (Yamaha); **4** Luke Mossey (Triumph); **5** Samuel Hornsey (Triumph); **6** Luke Jones (Triumph); **7** Luke Stapleford (Triumph); **8** Billy McConnell (Triumph); **9** Alex Olsen (Triumph); **10** Luke Hedger (Kawasaki); **11** James Rose (Kawasaki); **12** Josh Day (Triumph); **13** Paul Curran (Triumph); **14** Ben Field (Triumph); **15** Josh Corner (Kawasaki).
Fastest lap: Seeley, 2m 10.631s, 101.060mph/162.650km/h.

Race 2 (12 laps, 44.004 miles/70.818km)
1 Glenn Irwin (Kawasaki), 25m 59.662s, 101.570mph/163.460km/h.
2 Luke Stapleford (Triumph); **3** Luke Mossey (Triumph); **4** Alastair Seeley (Yamaha); **5** Graeme Gowland (Triumph); **6** James Rispoli (Yamaha); **7** Billy McConnell (Triumph); **8** Luke Hedger (Kawasaki); **9** Luke Jones (Triumph); **10** Taylor Mackenzie (Suzuki); **11** Samuel Hornsey (Triumph); **12** Alex Olsen (Triumph); **13** James Rose (Kawasaki); **14** Josh Day (Triumph); **15** Dean Hipwell (Triumph).
Fastest lap: Stapleford, 2m 9.072s, 102.280mph/164.610km/h.
Championship points: **1** McConnell, 349; **2** Gowland, 331; **3** Seeley, 315; **4** Irwin, 270; **5** Stapleford, 250; **6** Jones, 247.

Motul British Motostar Championship, Round 11 (9 laps, 33.003 miles/53.113km)
1 Bradley Ray (EE125), 20m 56.822s, 94.540mph/152.150km/h.
2 Joe Irving (KTM); **3** Taz Taylor (Luyten Honda); **4** Jordan Weaving (KTM); **5** Jayson Uribe (Honda); **6** Asher Durham (Honda); **7** Edward Rendell (Honda); **8** Arnie Shelton (Honda); **9** Chris Taylor (Honda); **10** Mike Brouwers (Honda); **11** Brian Slooten (Honda); **12** Elliot Lodge (Honda); **13** Georgina Polden (Honda); **14** Joe Thompson (Repli-Cast); **15** Cat Green (Honda).
Fastest lap: Ray, 2m 18.757s, 95.140mph/153.120km/h.
Moto3 points: **1** Weaving, 225; **2** Irving, 197; **3** Uribe, 143; **4** Hobson, 97; **5** Taylor, 94; **6** Brouwers, 80.
125GP points: **1** Rendell, 220; **2** Taylor, 174; **3** Ray, 141; **4** Shelton, 121; **5** Lodge, 79; **6** Greenwood, 69.

BRANDS HATCH GP, 18–19 October, 2014, 2.433-mile/3.916km circuit.
MCE British Superbike Championship With Pirelli, Round 12
Race 1 (18 laps, 43.798 miles/70.486km)
1 Howie Mainwaring (Kawasaki), 29m 39.251s, 88.610mph/142.600km/h.
2 Josh Waters (Suzuki); **3** Jon Kirkham (Kawasaki); **4** Dan Linfoot (Kawasaki); **5** Tommy Bridewell (Yamaha); **6** Stuart Easton (Kawasaki); **7** James Ellison (Kawasaki); **8** Josh Brookes (Yamaha); **9** James Westmoreland (BMW); **10** Chris Walker (Kawasaki); **11** Gary Mason (Kawasaki); **12** Ben Wilson (Kawasaki); **13** Peter Hickman (Honda); **14** Jakub Smrz (Ducati); **15** Julien da Costa (Honda).
Fastest lap: Waters, 1m 37.021s, 90.280mph/145.300km/h.

Race 2 (20 laps, 48.664 miles/78.317km)
1 Shane Byrne (Kawasaki), 29m 17.545s, 99.680mph/160.420km/h.
2 James Ellison (Kawasaki); **3** Howie Mainwaring (Kawasaki); **4** Josh Brookes (Yamaha); **5** Stuart Easton (Kawasaki); **6** Tommy Bridewell (Yamaha); **7** Jon Kirkham (Kawasaki); **8** Dan Linfoot (Kawasaki); **9** James Westmoreland (BMW); **10** John Hopkins (Suzuki); **11** Peter Hickman (Honda); **12** Jakub Smrz (Ducati); **13** Patric Muff (BMW); **14** Julien da Costa (Honda); **15** Filip Backlund (Yamaha).
Fastest lap: Brookes, 1m 26.864s, 100.840mph/162.290km/h.

Race 3 (17 laps, 41.364 miles/66.569km)
1 Shane Byrne (Kawasaki), 25m 28.986s, 97.390mph/156.730km/h.
2 James Ellison (Kawasaki); **3** Tommy Bridewell (Yamaha); **4** Stuart Easton (Kawasaki); **5** Josh Brookes (Yamaha); **6** Dan Linfoot (Kawasaki); **7** Jon Kirkham (Kawasaki); **8** John Hopkins (Suzuki); **9** Peter Hickman (Honda); **10** Chris Walker (Kawasaki); **11** Jakub Smrz (Ducati); **12** Filip Backlund (Yamaha); **13** Patric Muff (BMW); **14** James Westmoreland (BMW); **15** Josh Waters (Suzuki).
Fastest lap: Bridewell, 1m 26.567s, 101.190mph/162.850km/h.

Motorpoint British Supersport Championship & Supersport Evo, Round 12
Race 1 (10 laps, 24.332 miles/39.159km)
1 Glenn Irwin (Kawasaki), 16m 35.301s, 88.010mph/141.640km/h.
2 Alastair Seeley (Yamaha); **3** Luke Jones (Triumph); **4** Luke Hedger (Kawasaki); **5** Taylor Mackenzie (Suzuki); **6** Graeme Gowland (Triumph); **7** Jake Dixon (Yamaha); **8** Samuel Hornsey (Triumph); **9** Billy McConnell (Triumph); **10** Josh Day (Triumph); **11** Bjorn Estment (Yamaha); **12** Alex Olsen (Triumph); **13** James Rispoli (Yamaha); **14** Dean Hipwell (Triumph); **15** Luke Stapleford (Triumph).
Fastest lap: Jones, 1m 37.901s, 89.470mph/143.990km/h.

Race 2 (18 laps, 43.798 miles/70.486km)
1 Alastair Seeley (Yamaha), 26m 48.904s, 98.000mph/157.720km/h.
2 Glenn Irwin (Kawasaki); **3** Luke Jones (Triumph); **4** Jake Dixon (Yamaha); **5** Luke Stapleford (Triumph); **6** Luke Hedger (Kawasaki); **7** Luke Mossey (Triumph); **8** Billy McConnell (Triumph); **9** Dean Hipwell (Triumph); **10** Bjorn Estment (Yamaha); **11** Josh Day (Triumph); **12** Ben Field (Triumph); **13** Taylor Mackenzie (Suzuki); **14** Sam Coventry (Kawasaki); **15** Tim Hastings (Kawasaki).
Fastest lap: Stapleford, 1m 28.517s, 98.960mph/159.260km/h.

Motul British Motostar Championship, Round 12 (12 laps, 29.198 miles/46.990km)
1 Joe Irving (KTM), 19m 16.471s, 90.890mph/146.270km/h.
2 Edward Rendell (Honda); **3** Jayson Uribe (Honda); **4** Charlie Nesbitt (Repli-Cast); **5** Arnie Shelton (Honda); **6** Jorel Boerboom (Suter Honda); **7** Asher Durham (Honda); **8** Georgina Polden (Honda); **9** Elliot Lodge (Honda); **10** James Hobson (KTM); **11** Greg Greenwood (Luyten Honda); **12** Peter Sutherland (Aprilia); **13** Joe Thompson (Repli-Cast); **14** Daniel Hermansson (TSR Luyten); **15** Cat Green (Honda).
Fastest lap: Taylor, 1m 34.848s, 92.350mph/148.630km/h.

British Superbike Championship
Final points:

1	Shane Byrne,	682
2	Ryuichi Kiyonari,	620
3	Tommy Bridewell,	587
4	Josh Brookes,	584
5	Dan Linfoot,	577
6	Chris Walker,	525

7 Stuart Easton, 231; **8** James Ellison, 223; **9** Josh Waters, 192; **10** John Hopkins, 125; **11** Peter Hickman, 120; **12** Jon Kirkham, 118; **13** James Westmoreland, 96; **14** Howie Mainwaring, 82; **15** Jakub Smrz, 82.

British Supersport Championship
Final points:

1	Billy McConnell,	364
2	Alastair Seeley,	360
3	Graeme Gowland,	341
4	Glenn Irwin,	315
5	Luke Jones,	279
6	Luke Stapleford,	262

7 Luke Mossey, 244; **8** Jake Dixon, 162; **9** James Rispoli, 150; **10** Taylor Mackenzie, 148; **11** Samuel Hornsey, 124; **12** Luke Hedger, 112; **13** Alex Olsen, 85; **14** Dean Hipwell, 78; **15** Bjorn Estment, 68.

British Motostar Moto3 Championship
Final points:

1	Jordan Weaving,	225
2	Joe Irving,	222
3	Jayson Uribe,	163
4	James Hobson,	107
5	Chris Taylor,	94
6	Charlie Nesbitt,	91

7 Mike Brouwers, 80; **8** Sam Burman, 65; **9** Joe Thompson, 62; **10** Olly Simpson, 61; **11** Asher Durham, 60; **12** Ernst Dubbink, 45; **13** Brian Slooten, 43; **14** Bo Bendsneyder, 25; **15** Tom Booth-Amos, 17.

British Motostar 125GP Championship
Final points:

1	Edward Rendell,	245
2	Taz Taylor,	174
3	Bradley Ray,	141
4	Arnie Shelton,	141
5	Elliot Lodge,	92
6	Greg Greenwood,	80

7 Daniel Hermansson, 63; **8** Georgina Polden, 62; **9** Josh Owens, 61; **10** Asher Durham, 51; **11** Jake Archer, 47; **12** Alex Persson, 45; **13** Kai Johnson, 41; **14** Louis Valleley, 38; **15** Jamie Ashby, 36.

Supersport World Championship

PHILLIP ISLAND, Australia, 23 February, 2014, 2.762-mile/4.445km circuit.
Supersport World Championship, Round 1 (5 laps, 13.810 miles/22.225km)
1 Jules Cluzel, FRA (MV Agusta), 7m 57.585s, 104.098mph/167.530km/h.
2 Kev Coghlan, GBR (Yamaha); **3** Raffaele de Rosa, ITA (Honda); **4** Florian Marino, FRA (Kawasaki); **5** Roberto Tamburini, ITA (Kawasaki); **6** Kevin Wahr, GER (Yamaha); **7** Graeme Gowland, GBR (Triumph); **8** Riccardo Russo, ITA (Honda); **9** Fabio Menghi, ITA (Yamaha); **10** Christian Gamarino, ITA (Kawasaki); **11** Roberto Rolfo, ITA (Kawasaki); **12** Tony Coveña, NED (Kawasaki); **13** Nacho Calero, ESP (Honda); **14** Marco Bussolotti, ITA (Honda); **15** Fraser Rogers, GBR (Honda).
Fastest lap: Roberto Tamburini, ITA (Kawasaki), 1m 33.883s, 105.910mph/170.446km/h.
Championship points: **1** Cluzel, 25; **2** Coghlan, 20; **3** De Rosa, 16; **4** Marino, 13; **5** Tamburini, 11; **6** Wahr, 10.

ARAGON, Spain, 13 April, 2014, 3.321-mile/5.344km circuit.
Supersport World Championship, Round 2 (15 laps, 49.809 miles/80.160km)
1 Kenan Sofuoglu, TUR (Kawasaki), 30m 43.276s, 97.279mph/156.556km/h.
2 Michael van der Mark, NED (Honda); **3** Florian Marino, FRA (Kawasaki); **4** Lorenzo Zanetti, ITA (Honda); **5** Kev Coghlan, GBR (Yamaha); **6** Raffaele de Rosa, ITA (Honda); **7** Roberto Tamburini, ITA (Kawasaki); **8** Vladimir Leonov, RUS (MV Agusta); **9** Christian Gamarino, ITA (Kawasaki); **10** Ratthapark Wilairot, THA (Honda); **11** Jack Kennedy, IRL (Honda); **12** Roberto Rolfo, ITA (Kawasaki); **13** Dominic Schmitter, SUI (Yamaha); **14** Patrick Jacobsen, USA (Kawasaki); **15** Fabio Menghi, ITA (Yamaha).
Fastest lap: Jules Cluzel, FRA (MV Agusta), 2m 1.708s, 98.220mph/158.070km/h (record).
Championship points: **1** Coghlan, 31; **2** Marino, 29; **3** De Rosa, 26; **4** Sofuoglu, 25; **5** Cluzel, 25; **6** Van der Mark, 20.

ASSEN, Holland, 27 April, 2014, 2.822-mile/4.542km circuit.
Supersport World Championship, Round 3 (18 laps, 50.801 miles/81.756km)
1 Michael van der Mark, NED (Honda), 29m 47.030s, 102.339mph/164.699km/h.
2 Florian Marino, FRA (Kawasaki); **3** Jules Cluzel, FRA (MV Agusta); **4** Kev Coghlan, GBR (Yamaha); **5** Lorenzo Zanetti, ITA (Honda); **6** Roberto Rolfo, ITA (Kawasaki); **7** Roberto Tamburini, ITA (Kawasaki); **8** Raffaele de Rosa, ITA (Honda); **9** Patrick Jacobsen, USA (Kawasaki); **10** Kevin Wahr, GER (Yamaha); **11** Marco Bussolotti, ITA (Honda); **12** Vladimir Leonov, RUS (MV Agusta); **13** Ratthapark Wilairot, THA (Honda); **14** Riccardo Russo, ITA (Honda); **15** Fabio Menghi, ITA (Yamaha).
Fastest lap: Michael van der Mark, NED (Honda), 1m 38.587s, 103.058mph/165.856km/h (record).
Championship points: **1** Marino, 49; **2** Van der Mark, 45; **3** Coghlan, 44; **4** Cluzel, 41; **5** De Rosa, 34; **6** Tamburini, 29.

Imola, Italy, 11 May, 2014, 3.067-mile/4.936km circuit.
Supersport World Championship, Round 4 (17 laps, 52.140 miles/83.912km)
1 Lorenzo Zanetti, ITA (Honda), 31m 53.543s, 98.093mph/157.866km/h.
2 Michael van der Mark, NED (Honda); **3** Florian Marino, FRA (Kawasaki); **4** Patrick Jacobsen, USA (Kawasaki); **5** Roberto Rolfo, ITA (Kawasaki); **6** Fabio Menghi, ITA (Yamaha); **7** Marco Bussolotti, ITA (Honda); **8** Riccardo Russo, ITA (Honda); **9** Kevin Wahr, GER (Yamaha); **10** Alessandro Nocco, ITA (Kawasaki); **11** Jack Kennedy, IRL (Honda); **12** Raffaele de Rosa, ITA (Honda); **13** Christian Gamarino, ITA (Kawasaki); **14** Tony Coveña, NED (Kawasaki); **15** Jules Cluzel, FRA (MV Agusta),
Fastest lap: Kenan Sofuoglu, TUR (Kawasaki), 1m 51.733s, 98.820mph/159.036km/h.
Championship points: **1** Van der Mark, 65; **2** Marino, 65; **3** Zanetti, 49; **4** Coghlan, 44; **5** Cluzel, 42; **6** De Rosa, 38.

DONINGTON PARK, Great Britain, 25 May, 2014, 2.500-mile/4.023km circuit.
Supersport World Championship, Round 5 (20 laps, 49.996 miles/80.460km)
1 Michael van der Mark, NED (Honda), 30m 47.132s, 97.440mph/156.814km/h.
2 Jules Cluzel, FRA (MV Agusta); **3** Kev Coghlan, GBR (Yamaha); **4** Kenan Sofuoglu, TUR (Kawasaki); **5** Florian Marino, FRA (Kawasaki); **6** Patrick Jacobsen, USA (Kawasaki); **7** Jack Kennedy, IRL (Honda); **8** Roberto Tamburini, ITA (Kawasaki); **9** Raffaele de Rosa, ITA (Honda); **10** Roberto Rolfo, ITA (Kawasaki); **11** Marco Bussolotti, ITA (Honda); **12** Ratthapark Wilairot, THA (Honda); **13** Riccardo Russo, ITA (Honda); **14** Alessandro Nocco, ITA (Kawasaki); **15** Vladimir Leonov, RUS (MV Agusta),
Fastest lap: Michael van der Mark, NED (Honda), 1m 31.483s, 98.370mph/158.311km/h.
Championship points: **1** Van der Mark, 90; **2** Marino, 76; **3** Cluzel, 62; **4** Coghlan, 60; **5** Zanetti, 49; **6** De Rosa, 45.

SEPANG, Malaysia, 8 June, 2014, 3.447-mile/5.548km circuit.
Supersport World Championship, Round 6 (14 laps, 48.263 miles/77.672km)
1 Michael van der Mark, NED (Honda), 30m 23.854s, 95.264mph/153.312km/h.
2 Jules Cluzel, FRA (MV Agusta); **3** Kenan Sofuoglu, TUR (Kawasaki); **4** Roberto Rolfo, ITA (Kawasaki); **5** Lorenzo Zanetti, ITA (Honda); **6** Ratthapark Wilairot, THA (Honda); **7** Raffaele de Rosa, ITA (Honda); **8** Patrick Jacobsen, USA (Kawasaki); **9** Zaqhwan Zaidi, MAS (Honda); **10** Marco Bussolotti, ITA (Honda); **11** Christian Gamarino, ITA (Kawasaki); **12** Riccardo Russo, ITA (Honda); **13** Alessandro Nocco, ITA (Kawasaki); **14** Vladimir Leonov, RUS (MV Agusta); **15** Tony Coveña, NED (Kawasaki).
Fastest lap: Kev Coghlan, GBR (Yamaha), 2m 9.178s, 96.073mph/154.615km/h (record).
Championship points: **1** Van der Mark, 115; **2** Cluzel, 82; **3** Marino, 76; **4** Zanetti, 60; **5** Coghlan, 60; **6** Sofuoglu, 54.

MISANO, Italy, 22 June, 2014, 2.626mile/4.226km circuit.
Supersport World Championship, Round 7 (19 laps, 49.892 miles/80.294km)
1 Jules Cluzel, FRA (MV Agusta), 31m 40.587s, 94.504mph/152.089km/h.
2 Michael van der Mark, NED (Honda); **3** Patrick Jacobsen, USA (Kawasaki); **4** Kenan Sofuoglu, TUR (Kawasaki); **5** Roberto Tamburini, ITA (Kawasaki); **6** Lorenzo Zanetti, ITA (Honda); **7** Florian Marino, FRA (Kawasaki); **8** Kev Coghlan, GBR (Yamaha); **9** Ratthapark Wilairot, THA (Honda); **10** Roberto Rolfo, ITA (Kawasaki); **11** Alessandro Nocco, ITA (Kawasaki); **12** Jack Kennedy, IRL (Honda); **13** Kevin Wahr, GER (Yamaha); **14** Massimo Roccoli, ITA (MV Agusta); **15** Christian Gamarino, ITA (Kawasaki).
Fastest lap: Patrick Jacobsen, USA (Kawasaki), 1m 39.436s, 95.069mph/152.999km/h.
Championship points: **1** Van der Mark, 135; **2** Cluzel, 107; **3** Marino, 85; **4** Zanetti, 70; **5** Coghlan, 68; **6** Sofuoglu, 67.

PORTIMAO, Portugal, 6 July, 2014, 2.853-mile/4.592km circuit.
Supersport World Championship, Round 8 (12 laps, 34.240 miles/55.104km)
1 Michael van der Mark, NED (Honda), 21m 15.438s, 96.644mph/155.534km/h.
2 Jack Kennedy, IRL (Honda); **3** Kenan Sofuoglu, TUR (Kawasaki); **4** Raffaele de Rosa, ITA (Honda); **5** Patrick Jacobsen, USA (Kawasaki); **6** Lorenzo Zanetti, ITA (Honda); **7** Kev Coghlan, GBR (Yamaha); **8** Florian Marino, FRA (Kawasaki); **9** Roberto Rolfo, ITA (Kawasaki); **10** Massimo Roccoli, ITA (MV Agusta); **11** Ratthapark Wilairot, THA (Honda); **12** Alessandro Nocco, ITA (Kawasaki); **13** Marco Bussolotti, ITA (Honda); **14** Valentine Debise, FRA (Honda); **15** Fabio Menghi, ITA (Yamaha).
Fastest lap: Michael van der Mark, NED (Honda), 1m 45.777s, 97.110mph/156.284km/h.
Championship points: **1** Van der Mark, 160; **2** Cluzel, 107; **3** Marino, 93; **4** Sofuoglu, 83; **5** Zanetti, 80; **6** Coghlan, 77.

JEREZ, Spain, 7 September, 2014, 2.748-mile/4.423km circuit.
Supersport World Championship, Round 9 (19 laps, 52.218 miles/84.037km)
1 Michael van der Mark, NED (Honda), 33m 34.503s, 93.316mph/150.178km/h.
2 Patrick Jacobsen, USA (Kawasaki); **3** Florian Marino, FRA (Kawasaki); **4** Jack Kennedy, IRL (Honda); **5** Kev Coghlan, GBR (Yamaha); **6** Lorenzo Zanetti, ITA (Honda); **7** Roberto Rolfo, ITA (Kawasaki); **8** Ratthapark Wilairot, THA (Honda); **9** Alessandro Nocco, ITA (Kawasaki); **10** Roberto Tamburini, ITA (Kawasaki); **11** Dominic Schmitter, SUI (Yamaha); **12** Vladimir Leonov, RUS (Honda); **13** Kenan Sofuoglu, TUR (Kawasaki); **14** Valentine Debise, FRA (Honda); **15** Christian Gamarino, ITA (Kawasaki).
Fastest lap: Kenan Sofuoglu, TUR (Kawasaki), 1m 44.849s, 94.364mph/151.864km/h.
Championship points: **1** Van der Mark, 185; **2** Marino, 109; **3** Cluzel, 107; **4** Zanetti, 90; **5** Coghlan, 88; **6** Jacobsen, 87.

MAGNY-COURS, France, 5 October, 2014, 2.741-mile/4.411km circuit.
Supersport World Championship, Round 10 (12 laps, 32.890 miles/52.932km)
1 Jules Cluzel, FRA (MV Agusta), 23m 54.426s, 82.545mph/132.844km/h.
2 Michael van der Mark, NED (Honda); **3** Roberto Rolfo, ITA (Kawasaki); **4** Lorenzo Zanetti, ITA (Honda); **5** Florian Marino, FRA (Kawasaki); **6** Kev Coghlan, GBR (Yamaha); **7** Roberto Tamburini, ITA (Kawasaki); **8** Patrick Jacobsen, USA (Kawasaki); **9** Ratthapark Wilairot, THA (Honda); **10** Dominic Schmitter, SUI (Yamaha); **11** Luca Marconi, ITA (Honda); **12** Mason Law, GBR (Kawasaki); **13** Matt Davies, AUS (Honda); **14** Christian Gamarino, ITA (Kawasaki); **15** Massimo Roccoli, ITA (MV Agusta),
Fastest lap: Kenan Sofuoglu, TUR (Kawasaki), 1m 56.887s, 84.416mph/135.854km/h.
Championship points: **1** Van der Mark, 205; **2** Cluzel, 132; **3** Marino, 120; **4** Zanetti, 103; **5** Coghlan, 98; **6** Jacobsen, 95.

LOSAIL, Qatar, 2 November, 2014, 3.343-mile/5.380km circuit.
Supersport World Championship, Round 11 (15 laps, 50.145 miles/80.700km)
1 Michael van der Mark, NED (Honda), 30m 42.722s, 97.964mph/157.658km/h.
2 Ratthapark Wilairot, THA (Honda); **3** Jules Cluzel, FRA (MV Agusta); **4** Lucas Mahias, FRA (Yamaha); **5** Kev Coghlan, GBR (Yamaha); **6** Roberto Rolfo, ITA (Kawasaki); **7** Lorenzo Zanetti, ITA (Honda); **8** Kenan Sofuoglu, TUR (Kawasaki); **9** Roberto Tamburini, ITA (Kawasaki); **10** Massimo Roccoli, ITA (MV Agusta); **11** Florian Marino, FRA (Kawasaki); **12** Patrick Jacobsen, USA (Kawasaki); **13** Raffaele de Rosa, ITA (Honda); **14** Christian Gamarino, ITA (Kawasaki); **15** Mason Law, GBR (Kawasaki).
Fastest lap: Jules Cluzel, FRA (MV Agusta), 2m 1.999s, 98.646mph/158.755km/h (record).

World Supersport Championship
Final points:

1	Michael van der Mark, NED,	230
2	Jules Cluzel, FRA,	148
3	Florian Marino, FRA,	125
4	Lorenzo Zanetti, ITA,	112
5	Kev Coghlan, GBR,	109
6	Patrick Jacobsen, USA,	99

7 Roberto Rolfo, ITA, 97; **8** Kenan Sofuoglu, TUR, 94; **9** Ratthapark Wilairot, THA, 70; **10** Raffaele de Rosa, ITA, 70; **11** Roberto Tamburini, ITA, 70; **12** Jack Kennedy, IRL, 56; **13** Marco Bussolotti, ITA, 30; **14** Alessandro Nocco, ITA, 27; **15** Christian Gamarino, ITA, 27.